PROTECTING ANIMALS WITHIN AND ACROSS BORDERS

Protecting Animals Within and Across Borders

EXTRATERRITORIAL JURISDICTION AND THE CHALLENGES OF GLOBALIZATION

Charlotte E. Blattner

OXFORD
UNIVERSITY PRESS

OXFORD
UNIVERSITY PRESS

Oxford University Press is a department of the University of Oxford. It furthers the University's objective of excellence in research, scholarship, and education by publishing worldwide. Oxford is a registered trademark of Oxford University Press in the UK and certain other countries.

Published in the United States of America by Oxford University Press
198 Madison Avenue, New York, NY 10016, United States of America.

The pre-press of this publication was supported by the Swiss National Science Foundation.

Library of Congress Cataloging-in-Publication Data

Names: Blattner, Charlotte E., author.
Title: Protecting animals within and across borders: extraterritorial jurisdiction and the challenges of globalization / Charlotte E. Blattner.
Description: New York: Oxford University Press, 2019. | based on author's thesis (doctoral—Universität Basel, 2016) issued under title: The extraterritorial protection of animals: admissibility and possibilities of the application of national animal welfare standards to animals in foreign countries. | Includes bibliographical references and index.
Identifiers: LCCN 2018051660 | ISBN 9780190948313 ((hardback): alk. paper)
Subjects: LCSH: Animal welfare—Law and legislation. | Exterritoriality. | Universal jurisdiction. | International and municipal law. | Law and globalization.
Classification: LCC K3620 .B53 2019 | DDC 346.04/6954—dc23
LC record available at https://lccn.loc.gov/2018051660

9 8 7 6 5 4 3 2 1

Printed by Sheridan Books, Inc., United States of America

Cover illustration: Dana Ellyn

To Bobby and Balou

Contents

Preface and Acknowledgments

GLOBAL ENTANGLEMENTS AND challenges abound in animal law, as multinationals rise in number and power, production facilities move to other countries, and animals are shipped for use and slaughter across borders by the millions. None of these issues have preoccupied international law, which has been engaged in its own fights against poverty, corruption, the sex trade, and environmental degradation. This focus on other matters has eroded the trust and confidence of states in the regulatory powers of international law to tackle matters of animal law. At the same time, it has become increasingly difficult for states to gain legal certainty about whether or under what circumstances they themselves can protect animals in cases involving a cross-border element. Even worse, many states do not even know whether it is worth protecting animals within their border, as they have a deep and abiding fear of outsourcing and consider industries that use animals reliable and valuable taxpayers, even as they probe the limits of the law. These developments paint a dystopian future for animals, one in which corporations reign law, the free market equates to exploitation, and globalization translates as "globalization of animal cruelty."[1]

Many believe the best way for states to resolve this dilemma is to conclude a treaty. In theory, finding consensus through international agreements would be an admirable and possibly an effective accomplishment, but chances of uniting states in their quest to protect animals are slim and only marginally promising in case of success because treaties unnecessarily boil consensus down to the lowest common denominator. Others argue there is an alternative and better way to respond to these challenges by enabling states to regain

[1] Steven White & Deborah Cao, *Introduction: Animal Protection in an Interconnected World, in* ANIMAL LAW AND WELFARE: INTERNATIONAL PERSPECTIVES 1, 2 (Deborah Cao & Steven White eds., 2016).

their regulatory power and begin forming a dense and overlapping jurisdictional net across borders. There are good reasons to believe that extraterritorial jurisdiction—the authority of states to prescribe law across state borders—can do just this. It can fill gaps in transboundary governance, offer perspective-taking through legal pluralism, and encourage international treaty efforts. Extraterritorial jurisdiction is an established legal tool in human rights law, criminal law, antitrust law, securities law, and environmental law, but its boundaries remain fuzzy, its usage selective, and its potential not fully tapped. Clarifying the boundaries of extraterritorial jurisdiction, pushing it toward coherence, and harnessing its power to protect animals across borders has been the goal of this work.

In this book, I challenge the law of jurisdiction to become more definitionally precise, and I propose a sophisticated extraterritoriality framework that can be used to categorize and assess jurisdictional norms by their importance, reach, and legality. My main claim is that the law of jurisdiction cannot afford to turn a blind eye to the struggles of animal law, in particular, because it carries potential to bring to a halt and prevent races to the bottom, which we owe animals on grounds of justice. The topic invites readers to engage in broader discussions about global justice, interspecies ethics, and the ever-lingering struggle between economics and social welfare. But the book also aims to find closure and ways to resolve these controversies. It has at its heart a detailed catalogue of jurisdictional options for states to strengthen their animal laws under the *lex lata*. The core purpose and primary motivation of asserting jurisdiction over animals is to protect them, but doing so can also amount to an act of oppression by reaffirming animals' controversial status as commodities and objects of law. As Kristen Stilt eloquently put it:

> Animals did not ask us, as humans, to make laws that apply to them. Nor did we ask them if they wanted our laws. Under an alternative framework, we might relate to animals as differing self-governing societies relate to one another. Instead, we impose our jurisdiction and our laws on animals. We use law to put animals into categories of our own choosing and control them, both conceptually and physically. We use law not to recognize, embrace, cultivate and enable their own innate characteristics and abilities but rather to position them in a way that is convenient and conducive to our own wants and needs. Animals do not have the ability to challenge us on our own terms because they are not formally part of any society's lawmaking process.[2]

As Stilt implies, we must go beyond simply expanding the status quo of the law, and begin reformulating and repurposing law so that it becomes more inclusive. I believe there are reasons and ways to realize this claim in the law of jurisdiction, which I do by proposing reasonable *lex ferenda* options that respect animals as self-determining social and legal agents.

But why advocate for extraterritorial jurisdiction in an age of postcolonialism, you may ask. After all, both extraterritorial jurisdiction and animal law can be and have been used to oppress minorities and nonhegemonic ways of living and being. Once combined, their potential to feed neocolonial power structures significantly rises, and efforts to counter it must be multiplied. These dangers, though compelling and ubiquitous, do not prompt us to recoil

---

[2] Kristen Stilt, *Law*, *in* Critical Terms for Animal Studies 197, 198 (Lori Gruen ed., 2018).

from extraterritorial jurisdiction because it would mean fully succumbing law, and, with it, the regulation of social life, to the law of the market. This book takes serious these competing demands and seeks to reconcile them by providing explanations and precautions that help us avoid reinscribing existing forms of oppression and creating new wrongs through extraterritorial jurisdiction. Taken as a whole, extraterritorial jurisdiction in animal law is as much a quest for justice for animals as it is for the empowerment of human people.

As I sought to understand the role the law of jurisdiction plays in a world of complex and diverse social, legal, and political relations, I was quickly humbled by the task. I initially thought I would write a very focused work on a niche subject, but one line of inquiry opened another. The tricky questions raised by applying the law of jurisdiction to animals captured my imagination and propelled me through my research. Though the discussion about protecting animals through extraterritorial jurisdiction has not yet gained a strong foothold in political and academic discourse, we see the first traces of this practice emerge across the board. This is encouraging because the global problems it sets to tackle are more pressing than ever. It is my profound hope that this book will make a difference in our private and public thinking about global justice and animals, and, ultimately, in the policies we formulate.

This work was accepted by the Faculty of Law of the University of Basel as a doctoral thesis in November 2016 and takes into account literature, judicature, and legislation up to January 2019.I have received much encouragement and the support of many people and institutions in writing this book, for which I am deeply grateful. I would like to thank the Swiss National Science Foundation (SNSF), whose excellent funding scheme (Doc.CH) enabled me to pursue my research for this book project full-time for several years, and whose generous open access funding makes this book accessible to people from all disciplines and outside. My heartfelt thanks go to the Haldimann-Stiftung and the University of Basel for their generous impetus grant, and to the Schweizerische Universitätskonferenz (SUK) and the University of Basel for their generous financial support of the doctoral program, "Law and Animals: Ethics at Crossroads," at the Law Faculty of the University of Basel.

During my research and writing, I have greatly profited from Professor Anne Peters' guidance and expertise. She has been a source of inspiration in many ways, and I am especially thankful for her open-mindedness, academic versatility, and deep dedication to both respecting and challenging the law. Professor Christine Kaufmann did me the honor of supervising this book project and my work as an assistant for the Swiss Center of Expertise in Human Rights. Throughout this time, she offered me excellent opportunities to challenge and put to the test the strengths and promises of the law of extraterritoriality, and gain a deeper understanding of its role in international relations. I owe many thanks to Dr. Gieri Bolliger for serving as an expert member of the committee that evaluated my work, and for allowing me to benefit from his long-standing expertise in animal law.

During my research on this topic, I was offered the unique opportunity to join the renowned Center for Animal Law Studies at the Lewis & Clark Law School in Portland, Oregon, as a visiting scholar. My deepest thanks go to Professor Kathy Hessler, Professor Pamela Frasch, Natasha Dolezal, and Lindsay Kadish for welcoming me so warmly to the CALS community and giving me an insight into the academic rigor with which you advance animal law and explore its intersections. I want to thank the Antelope Career Program of the University of Basel, organized by Dr. Andrea Flora Bauer and Patricia Zweifel, who played a crucial role in empowering me, and many other women, in academia. This book has benefited from the valuable advice of my colleagues in the doctoral program and personal conversations with Dr. Janine Dumont-Rosas, for which I am very grateful. I also want to thank Ellen Campbell for kindly helping me solve the puzzles of encapsulated postscripts.

Versions of the proposals and arguments this book makes were presented at Harvard Law School in Cambridge, Massachusetts, the Center for Animal Law Studies at Lewis & Clark Law School in Portland, Oregon, the Pace University and New York University in New York, the University of Vienna in Austria, and the University of Basel in Switzerland. At these events, I was fortunate enough to profit from challenging questions from the audiences and organizers, and the intriguing conversations I had with them. I also want to thank Professor Will Kymlicka for sharing his thoughts about the book and offering advice as I began my postdoctoral work under his supervision at Queen's University, Kingston. Special thanks go to the anonymous referees at Oxford University Press, whose encouragement and recommendations have helped make this book a better version of what it was before. I'd especially like to thank my editor at Oxford University Press, Blake Ratcliff, for his sustained interest in the subject and his willingness and patience to respond to any special requests I had, as well as Meera Seth and David Lipp, who took over these tasks during Blake's much-deserved parental leave. My heartfelt thanks also go to the many people working behind the scenes at Oxford University Press, including my copy editor, project manager, typewriter, and indexer. Of all people, I am most indebted to Dr. Kali Tal for her meticulous editing, for pushing me beyond my boundaries, and for her unwavering enthusiasm for the book.

I have gained all the confidence to write this book from two people who, like no other, have shown a deep understanding for the many hours I spent poring over books, and who have expressed their unwavering trust in this project: Bobby and Balou. I hope they approve it was worth the wait. No words can convey my gratitude for the unconditional support of my family—my parents, my brothers, and my partner—and of Sarah Small and Steve Schreiner, who have become a solid part of it. Thank you.

Cambridge, February 2019

List of Cases

INTERNATIONAL CASES

International Court of Justice (ICJ)

Acquisition of Polish Nationality, Advisory Opinion, 1923 P.C.I.J. (ser. B) No. 7 (September 15).

Ahmadou Sadio Diallo (Guinea v. Dem. Rep. Congo), Judgment, 2010 I.C.J. Rep. 639 (May 24).

Application of the Convention on the Prevention and Punishment of the Crime of Genocide (Bosn. and Herz. v. Serb. and Monten.), Preliminary Objections, 1996 I.C.J. Rep. 595 (May 28).

Case Concerning Application of the Convention on the Prevention and Punishment of the Crime of Genocide (Bosn. & Herz. v. Serb. and Montenegro), Judgment, 2007 I.C.J. Rep. 43 (February 26).

Case Concerning the Arrest Warrant of 11 April 2000 (Dem. Rep. Congo v. Belg.), Judgment, 2002 I.C.J. Rep. 3 (February 14).

Case Concerning the Barcelona Traction, Light and Power Company, Limited (Belg. v. Spain), Judgment, 1970 I.C.J. Rep. 3 (February 5).

Case Concerning the Payment of Various Serbian Loans Issued in France (Fr. v. Kingdom of Serbs, Croats and Slovenes), Judgment, 1929 P.C.I.J. (ser. A) No. 20/21 (July 12).

Certain Criminal Proceedings in France (DRC v. France), Order, 2003 I.C.J. Rep. 102 (June 17).

Certain German Interests in Polish Upper Silesia (Ger. v. Pol.), Judgment, 1926 P.C.I.J. (ser. A) No. 7 (May 25).

Colombian-Peruvian Asylum Case (Colom. v. Peru), Judgment, 1950 I.C.J. Rep. 266 (November 20).

Corfu Channel Case (U.K. & N. Ir. v. Alb.), Judgment, 1949 I.C.J. Rep. 4 (April 9).

Elettronica Sicula S.p.A. (ELSI) (U.S. v. Italy), Judgment, 1989 I.C.J. Rep. 15 (July 20).

Fisheries Case (U.K. v. Nor.), Judgment, 1951 I.C.J. Rep. 116 (December 18).

Gabcikovo-Nagymaros Project (Hungary/Slovakia), Judgment, 1997 I.C.J. Rep. 7 (September 25).

Legal Consequences for States of the Continued Presence of South Africa in Namibia (South West Africa) notwithstanding Security Council Resolution 276 (1970), Advisory Opinion, 1971 I.C.J. Rep. 16 (June 21).

Legality of the Threat or Use of Nuclear Weapons, Advisory Opinion, 1996 I.C.J. Rep. 226 (July 8).

Military and Paramilitary Activities in and Against Nicaragua (Nicar. v. U.S.), Judgment, 1986 I.C.J. Rep. 14 (June 27).

Nationality Decrees issued in Tunis and Morocco (Fr. v. U.K.), Judgment, 1923 P.C.I.J. (ser. B) No. 4 (February 7).

Nottebohm Case (Liech. v. Guat.), Judgment (second phase), 1955 I.C.J. Rep. 4 (April 6).

Oil Platforms (Iran v. U.S.), Judgment, 2003 I.C.J. Rep. 161 (November 6).

Reparations for Injuries Suffered in the Service of the United Nations, Advisory Opinion, 1949 I.C.J. Rep. 174 (April 11).

Request for an Examination of the Situation in Accordance with Paragraph 63 of the Court's Judgment of 20 December 1974 in the Nuclear Tests Case (N.Z. v. France), Order, 1995 I.C.J. Rep. 288 (September 22).

Reservations to the Convention on the Prevention and Punishment of the Crime of Genocide, Advisory Opinion, 1951 I.C.J. Rep. 15 (May 28).

S.S. Lotus (Fr. v. Turk.), Judgment, 1927 P.C.I.J. (ser. A) No. 10 (September 7).

Western Sahara, Advisory Opinion, 1975 I.C.J. Rep. 12 (October 16).

Special international courts and tribunals

Aguas del Tunari v. Bolivia, ICSID Case No. ARB/02/3, Decision on Jurisdiction, Oct. 21, 2005.

Award between the United States and the United Kingdom Relating to the Rights of Jurisdiction of the United States in the Bering's Sea and the Preservation of Fur Seals (U.S. v. U.K.), R.I.A.A. 263 (Arbitral Tribunal 1893).

Flegenheimer Case (U.S. v. Italy), 182 R.I.A.A. 327 (United States–Italian Conciliation Commission 1958).

Hussein Nuaman Soufraki v. United Arab Emirates, ICSID Case No. ARB/02/7, Decision of the ad hoc Committee, June 5, 2007.

Island of Palmas Case (U.S. v. Neth.), 2 R.I.A.A. 829 (Perm. Ct. Arb. 1928).

Prosecutor v. Gojko Jankovic, Case No. IT-96-23/2-AR11*bis*2, Decision on Rule 11*bis* Referral (Nov. 15, 2005).

Rompetrol v. Romania, ICSID Case No. ARB/06/3, Decision on Respondent's Preliminary Objections on Jurisdiction and Admissibility, Apr. 18, 2008.

SOABI v. Senegal, ICSID Case No. ARB/82/1, Award, Feb. 25, 1988.

The Juno Trader (Saint Vincent and the Grenadines v. Guinea-Bissau), Case No. 13, Judgment, 2004 ITLOS Rep. 17 (Dec. 18).

Tokios Tokeles v. Ukraine, ICSID Case No. ARB/02/18, Award, July 26, 2007.

Inter-American Court of Human Rights (IACtHR)

International Responsibility for the Promulgation and Enforcement of Laws in Violation of the Convention (Arts. 1 and 2 of the American Convention on Human Rights), Advisory Opinion OC-14/94, Inter-Am. Ct. H.R. (ser. A.) No. 14 (Dec. 9, 1994).
Proposed Amendments to the Naturalisation provision of the Constitution of Costa Rica, Advisory Opinion OC-4/84, Inter-Am. Ct. H.R. (ser. A) No. 4 (Jan. 19, 1984) [IACtHR, *Naturalisation Costa Rica*].

European Court of Human Rights (ECtHR)

Cha'are Shalom Ve Tsedek v. France, 350 Eur. Ct. H.R. 233 (2000).
Fayed v. United Kingdom, 294-B Eur. Ct. H.R. (ser. A.) (1994).
Jorgic v. Germany, 2007-IX Eur. Ct. H.R. 1 (2007).
Rasmussen v. Denmark, 87 Eur. Ct. H.R. (ser. A.) (1984).

European Court of Justice (ECJ)

Case 265/87, Schräder HS Kraftführer GmbH & Co KG v. Hauptzollamt Gronau, 1989 E.C.R. 2237.
Case 36/74, Walrave and Koch v. Union Cycliste Internationale, 1974 E.C.R. 1405.
Case 48/69, Imperial Chemical Industries Ltd. v. Commission of the European Communities [ICI v. Commission], 1972 E.C.R. 619.
Case C-1/96, The Queen and Minister of Agriculture, Fisheries and Food, ex parte Compassion in World Farming Limited, 1998 E.C.R. I-1251.
Case C-27/76, United Brands v. Commission, 1978 E.C.R. 207.
Case C-286/98, Stora Kopparbergs Bergslags AB v. Commission of the European Communities, 2000 E.C.R. I-9925.
Case C-424/13, Zuchtvieh-Export GmbH v. Stadt Kempten, 2015 E.C.R. I-1251.
Case C-6/72, Continental Can v. Commission, 1973 E.C.R. 215.
Case C-97/08 P, Akzo Nobel NV et al. v. Commission of the European Communities, 2009 E.C.R. I-8237.
Case T-102/96, Gencor Limited v. EC Commission, 1999 E.C.R. II-753.
Case T-11/89, Shell v. Commission, 1992 E.C.R. II-757.
Case T-201/04, Microsoft Corp. et al. v. Commission, 2007 E.C.R. II-3601.
Case T-210/01, General Electric Company v. Commission, 2005 E.C.R. II-5575.
Joined Cases 89/85, 104/85, 114/85, 116-7/85, and 125-9/85, A. Ahlström Osakeyhtiö v. Commission, 1988 E.C.R. 5214.
Joined Cases C-6/73 and C-7/73, Commercial Solvents, 1974 E.C.R. 223.
Joined Cases T-71/03, T-74/03, T-87/03, and T-91/03, Tokai Carbon v. Commission, 2005 E.C.R. II-00010.

Commission decisions

Commission Decision of 14 December 1972, Relative to a Procedure for Application of Article 86 of the Treaty Establishing the European Economic Community (IV/26.911 – ZPJA/CSC –ICI) (72/457/EEC), 1972 O.J. (L 299) 51.

Commission Notice, Guidelines on the Effect on Trade Concept Contained in Articles 81 and 82 of the Treaty (2004/C 101/07), 2004 O.J. (C 101) 81.

World Trade Organization (WTO) reports

Appellate Body Report, Argentina—Measures Affecting Imports of Footwear, Textiles, Apparel and Other Items, WTO Doc. WT/DS56/AB/R (adopted Apr. 22, 1998).

Appellate Body Report, Australia—Measures Affecting the Importation of Salmon, WTO Doc. WT/DS18/AB/R (adopted Nov. 6, 1998) [*Australia—Salmon*, AB Report].

Appellate Body Report, Australia—Measures Affecting the Importation of Salmon—Recourse to Article 21.5 of the DSU by Canada, WTO Doc. WT/DS18/RW (adopted Mar. 20, 2000).

Appellate Body Report, Australia—Measures Affecting the Importation of Apples from New Zealand, WTO Doc. WT/DS367/AB/R (adopted Dec. 17, 2010) [*Australia—Apples*, AB Report].

Appellate Body Report, Brazil—Measures Affecting Imports of Retreaded Tyres, WTO Doc. WT/DS332/AB/R (adopted Dec. 17, 2007) [*Brazil—Retreaded Tyres*, AB Report].

Appellate Body Report, Canada—Certain Measures Concerning Periodicals, WTO Doc. WT/DS31/AB/R (adopted July 30, 1997) [*Periodicals*, AB Report].

Appellate Body Report, Canada—Continued Suspension of Obligations in the EC—Hormones Dispute, WTO Doc. WT/DS321/AB/R (adopted Nov. 14, 2008) [*Canada—Continued Suspension*, AB Report].

Appellate Body Report, EC—Conditions for the Granting of Tariff Preferences to Developing Countries, WTO Doc. WT/DS246/AB/R (adopted. Apr. 20, 2004) [*EC—Tariff Preferences*, AB Report].

Appellate Body Report, EC—Measures Affecting Asbestos and Products Containing Asbestos, WTO Doc. WT/DS135/AB/R (adopted Apr. 5, 2001) [*Asbestos*, AB Report].

Appellate Body Report, EC—Measures Affecting Meat and Meat Products, WTO Doc. WT/DS26/AB/R, WT/DS48/AB/R (adopted Feb. 13, 1998) [*EC—Hormones*, AB Report].

Appellate Body Report, EC—Measures Prohibiting the Importation and Marketing of Seal Products, WTO Doc. WT/DS400/AB/R, WT/DS4001/AB/R (adopted June 18, 2014) [*Seals*, AB Report].

Appellate Body Report, EC—Trade Description of Sardines, WTO Doc. WT/DS231/AB/R (adopted Oct. 23, 2002).

Appellate Body Report, EC and Certain Member States—Measures Affecting Trade in Large Civil Aircraft, WTO Doc. WT/DS316/AB/R (adopted June 1, 2011) [*EC—Large Civil Aircraft*, AB Report].

Appellate Body Report, Japan—Measures Affecting Agricultural Products, WTO Doc. WT/DS76/AB/R (adopted Mar. 19, 1999) [*Japan—Agricultural Products II*, AB Report].

Appellate Body Report, Japan—Taxes on Alcoholic Beverages, WTO Doc. WT/DS8/AB/R, WT/DS10/AB/, WT/DS11/AB/R (adopted Nov. 1, 1996) [*Japan—Alcoholic Beverages*, AB Report].

Appellate Body Report, Philippines—Taxes on Distilled Spirits, WTO Doc. WT/DS396/AB/R, WT/DS403/AB/R (adopted Jan. 20, 2012) [*Philippines—Distilled Spirits*, AB Report].

Appellate Body Report, US—Anti-Dumping Measures on Certain Hot-Rolled Products from Japan, WTO Doc. WT/DS184/AB/R (adopted Aug. 23, 2001).

Appellate Body Report, US—Final Anti-Dumping Measures on Stainless Steel from Mexico, WTO Doc. WT/DS344/AB/R (adopted May 20, 2008).

Appellate Body Report, US—Import Prohibition of Certain Shrimp and Shrimp Products, WTO Doc. WT/DS58/AB/R (adopted Nov. 6, 1998) [*Shrimp/Turtle I*, AB Report].

Appellate Body Report, US—Measures Affecting the Cross-Border Supply of Gambling and Betting Services, WTO Doc. WT/DS285/AB/R (adopted Apr. 20, 2005).

Appellate Body Report, US—Measures Affecting the Production and Sale of Clove Cigarettes, WTO Doc. WT/DS406/AB/R (adopted Apr. 14, 2012) [*US—Clove Cigarettes*, AB Report].

Appellate Body Report, US—Subsidies on Upland Cotton, WTO Doc. WT/DS267/AB/R (adopted Mar. 21, 2005) [*US—Subsidies on Upland Cotton*, AB Report].

Mutually Agreed Solution, Canada—Tax Exemptions and Reductions for Wine and Beer, WTO Doc. G/L/806/Add. 1, G/SCM/D72/a/Add. 1, WT/DS354/2 (adopted Dec. 23, 2008).

Panel Report, Argentina—Measures Affecting the Export of Bovine Hides and the Import of Finished Leather, WTO Doc. WT/DS155/R (adopted Feb. 16, 2001) [*Argentina—Hides and Leather*, Panel Report].

Panel Report, Belgium—Belgian Family Allowances, WTO Doc. G/32–1S/59 (adopted Nov. 7, 1952).

Panel Report, Canada—Administration of the Foreign Investment Review Act, WTO Doc. L/5504—30S/140 (not adopted, circulated Feb. 7, 1984).

Panel Report, Canada—Measures Affecting Exports of Unprocessed Herring and Salmon, WTO Doc. L/6268—35S/98 (adopted Mar. 22, 1988) [*Herring and Salmon*, Panel Report].

Panel Report, China—Measures Affecting Trading Rights and Distribution Services of Certain Publications and Audiovisual Entertainment Products, WTO Doc. WT/DS363/R (adopted Jan. 19, 2010) [*China—Audiovisuals*, Panel Report].

Panel Report, Dominican Republic—Measures Affecting the Importation and Internal Sale of Cigarettes, WTO Doc. WT/DS302/R (adopted May 19, 2005).

Panel Report, EC—Conditions for the Granting of Tariff Preferences to Developing Countries, WTO Doc. WT/DS246/R (adopted Apr. 20, 2004).

Panel Report, EC—Measures Affecting the Approval and Marketing of Biotech Products, WTO Doc. WT/DS291/R, WT/DS292/R, WT/DS293/R (adopted Nov. 21, 2006) [*EC—Biotech Products*, Panel Report].

Panel Report, EC—Measures Prohibiting the Importation and Marketing of Seal Products, WTO Doc. WT/DS400/R, WT/DS4001/R (adopted June 18, 2014) [*Seals*, Panel Report].

Panel Report, EC—Payments and Subsidies Paid to Processors and Producers of Oilseeds and Related Animal-Feed Proteins, WTO Doc. L/6627—37S/86 (adopted Jan. 25, 1990).

Panel Report, Japan—Tariff Imports on Spruce, Pine, Fir (SPF) Dimension Lumber, WTO Doc. L/6470—36S/167 (adopted July 19, 1989) [*Japan—Lumber*, Panel Report].

Panel Report, Korea—Measures Affecting Government Procurement, WTO Doc. WT/DS163/R (adopted June 19, 2000).

Panel Report, Thailand—Customs and Fiscal Measures on Cigarettes from the Philippines, WTO Doc. WT/DS371/R (adopted July 15, 2011) [*Thailand—Cigarettes (Philippines)*, Panel Report].

Panel Report, US—Imports of Certain Automotive Spring Assemblies, WTO Doc. L/5333—30S/107 (adopted May 26, 1983).

Panel Report, US—Measures Affecting the Cross-Border Supply of Gambling and Betting Services, WTO Doc. WT/DS285/R (adopted Nov. 10, 2004).

Panel Report, US—Measures Concerning the Importation, Marketing and Sale of Tuna and Tuna Products, WTO Doc. WT/DS381/R (adopted June 13, 2012) [*Tuna/Dolphin III*, Panel Report].

Panel Report, US—Prohibition of Imports of Tuna and Tuna Products from Canada, WTO Doc. L/5198—29S/91 (adopted Feb. 22, 1982) [*US—Tuna I*, Panel Report].

Panel Report, US—Restrictions on Imports of Tuna, WTO Doc. DS21/R—39S/155 (not adopted, circulated Sept. 3, 1991) [*Tuna/Dolphin I*, Panel Report].

Panel Report, US—Restrictions on Imports of Tuna, WTO Doc. DS29/R (not adopted, circulated June 16, 1994) [*Tuna/Dolphin II*, Panel Report].

Panel Report, US—Sections 301–310 of the Trade Act 1974, WTO Doc. WT/DS152/R (adopted Jan. 27, 2000).

Panel Report, US—Standards for Reformulated and Conventional Gasoline, WTO Doc. WT/DS2/R (adopted May 20, 1996) [*US—Gasoline*, Panel Report].

NATIONAL CASES

Australia

ACCC v. Australian Egg Corporation Limited [2016] FCA 69 (Feb. 10, 2016) (Austl.).

Australian Competition and Consumer Commission v. Pirovic Enterprises Pty Ltd. (No. 2) [2014] FCA 1028 (Sept. 23, 2014) (Austl.).

CSR v. Wren (1997) 44 N.S.W.L.R. 463 (C.A. NSW) (Austl.).

Belgium

Hof van Cassatie [Cass.] [Court of Cassation], May 26, 1978, Stagno v. Vanhoyland q.q., RW 846 (1978–9) (Belg.).

Brazil

ADI 1, 856-6/RJ (1998), Sept. 3, 1998 (Braz.).

RE No. 153.531-8/SC (1997), June 3, 1997 (Braz.).

Canada

Amfac v. Int'l Systems & Controls Corp., [1981] 654 P.2d 1092 (Ore Ct. App.) (Can.).
Association Canadienne Contre l'Impunité (ACCI) v. Anvil Mining Ltd., [2012] QCCA 117 (Can.).
Canadian Dredge and Dock Co. Ltd. v. The Queen, [1985] 1 SCR 662 (Can.).
R v. Hape, [2007] 2 SCR 292 (Can.).

France

Cour de cassation [Cass.] [Supreme Court for Judicial Matters], Recueil Dalloz Sirey 395, 1991, "Serre et Régnier" (Fr.).

Germany

Appellationsgericht Berlin, Dec. 21, 1965, North-Transylvania Nationality Case (Ger.).
Appellationsgericht Kassel, Oct. 5, 1990, NStZ 1991, 443–5 (Ger.).
BGHSt 5, 230, 234, NJW 510, 1954 (Ger.).
BGHZ 173, 246, NJW 2689, 2007 "Trihotel" (Ger.).
BVerfG, May 16, 1995, 1 BvR 1087/91 (Ger.).
BVerfG, Dec. 13, 2006, 1 BvR, 2084/05 (Ger.).
BVerfG, Sept. 28, 2009, 1 BvR 1702/09 (Ger.).
BVerfG, Nov. 6, 2001, 1 BvR 1783/99 (Ger.).
BVerwG, 3 C 30.05, Nov. 23, 2006 (Ger.).

India

Animal Welfare Board of India v. A. Nagaraja et al., AIR 2014 SC 547 (India).
Centre for Environment Law, WWF 1 v. Union of India et al., AIR 2013 8 SC 234 (India).
Mohd. Habib v. State of Uttar Pradesh, Civil Misc. Writ Petition No. 38469 of 1994 (HC Allahabad 1997) (India).
Mohd. Hanif Quareshi et al. v. The State of Bihar, AIR 1959 SC 629 (India).
Narayan Dutt Bhatt v. Union of India (UOI) et al., Writ Petition No. 43 of 2014 (HC Uttarakhand at Nainital 2014) (India).
N.R. Nair et al. v. Union of India (UOI) et al., AIR 2000 Ker 340 (India).
N.R. Nair et al. v. Union of India (UOI) et al., AIR 2001 SC 2337 (India).
People for Animals et al. v. State of Goa et al., Writ Petition No. 347 of 1996 (HC Bombay 1997) (India).
Shriomani Gurudwara Prabandhak Committee, Amritsar v. Shri Somnath Dass et al., AIR 2000 SC 1421 (India).
State of Gujarat v. Mirzapur Moti Kureshi Kassab Jammat et al., AIR 2006 SC 212 (India).
Vidya Varuthi Thirtha v. Balusami Ayyar, 24 BOMLR 629 (1922) (India).

Israel

HCJ 6446/96 Cat Welfare Society v. Arad Municipality IsrSC 55(1) 769 (1996) (Isr.).
HCJ 9232/01 Noah v. Att'y General 215 PD (2002–2003) (Isr.).

LCA 1684/96 Let the Animals Live v. Hamat Gader 51(3) PD 832 (1997) (Isr.).
LCA 4217/12 Mamut v. Ministry of Agriculture (2012) (Isr.).
LCA 537/08 Kagan v. Unicol (2008) (Isr.).

Netherlands

Hoge Raad der Nederlanden (HR) (Supreme Court of the Netherlands) Nov. 13, 1951, NJ 1951, 42 (Public Prosecutor v. L.) (Neth.).

Switzerland

AppGer Basel, Jan. 15, 2019, VG.2018.1 (AG.2019.40) (Switz.).
Bundesgericht [BGer] [Federal Supreme Court] Mar. 17, 1982, Entscheidungen des schweizerischen Bundesgerichts [BGE] 108 II 122 (Switz.).
BGer Aug. 27, 1991, BGE 117 II 432 (Switz.).
BGer Dec. 12, 1991, BGE 117 II 570 (Switz.).
BGer Nov. 15, 1994, BGE 120 II 331 (Switz.).
BGer Oct. 29, 2001, BGE 128 III 92 (Switz.).
BGer Oct. 7, 2009, 2C_421/2008 (Switz.).
BGer Oct. 7, 2009, 2C_422/2008 (Switz.).
BGer Feb. 8, 2010, 4A_306/2009 (Switz.).
BGer Sept. 26, 2011, BGE 137 III 550 (Switz.).
VGer Zürich, Apr. 5, 2017, VB.2016.00048 (Switz.).

United Kingdom

Adams v. Cape Industries PLC [1990] Ch. 433, [1990] 2 WLR 786 (U.K.).
Amalgamated Investment & Property Co. v. Texas Commercial Bank [1982] QB 84 (U.K.).
DHN Food Distributors Ltd. v. Tower Hamlets London Borough Council [1976] 1 WLR 852 (U.K.).
DPP v. Doot [1973] AC 807 (U.K.).
DPP v. Stoenhouse [1978] AC 55 (U.K.).
Ebbw Vale Urban District Council v. South Wales Traffic Area Licensing Authority [1951] 2 KB 366 (U.K.).
Gold Coast Ltd. v. Caja de Ahorros del Mediterraneo [2001] EWCA Civ. 1806 (U.K.).
Hodges v. Humkin, 2 Bulst. 139 [1615] 80 KB 1015 (U.K.).
In re (FG) Films [1953] 1 WLR 484 (U.K.).
Macleod v. A.G. for N.S.W. [1891] AC 455 (U.K.).
Prest v. Petrodel Resources Limited et al. [2013] 2 AC 415 (U.K.).
Provimi Ltd. v. Roche Products Ltd. et al. [2003] EWHC 961 (Comm) (U.K.).
R v. Burke, Casey and Mullady (1868) 11 Cox C.C. 138 (U.K.).
R v. Casement [1917] 1 KB 98 (U.K.).
R v. Elling [1945] AD 234 (U.K.).
R v. Jones [2007] 1 AC 36 (U.K.).
R v. Lynch [1903] 1 KB 444 (U.K.).

Re Southard and Co. Ltd. [1979] 1 WLR 1198 (U.K.).
Salomon v. A. Salomon & Co. Ltd. [1897] AC 22 (U.K.).
Smith, Stone and Knight v. Birmingham [1939] 4 All. E.R. 116 (U.K.).
Stone & Rolls v. Moore Stephens [2009] 1 AC 1391 (U.K.).
Tesco Supermarkets Ltd. v. Nattrass [1972] AC 153 (U.K.).
Compania Naviera Vascongado v. SS Cristina [1938] AC 485 (U.K.).
Viscound Simonds in Metliss v. National Bank of Greece [1958] AC 509 (U.K.).

United States

Arnold v. Phillips, 117 F.2d 497 (5th Cir. 1941) (U.S.).
Associated Vendors Inc. v. Oakland Meat Co., 210 Cal. App.2d 825 (1962) (U.S.).
Association des Éleveurs de Canards et d'Oies du Québec v. Becerra, 870 F.3d 1140 (9th Cir. 2017) (U.S.).
Bowoto v. Chevron Corp., 312 F. Supp. 2d 1299 (N.D. Cal. 2004) (U.S.).
Carte Blanche (Singapore) Pte. Ltd. v. Diners Club Int'l, 2 F.2d 24 (2d Cir. 1993) (U.S.).
Castleberry v. Branscum et al., 721 S.W.2d 270 (S. Ct. Tex. 1986) (U.S.).
DeWitt Truck Brokers v. W. Ray Fleming Fruit Co., 540 F.2d 681 (4th Cir. 1976) (U.S.).
Doe v. Unocal Corp., 395 F.3d 915 (9th Cir. 2002) (U.S.).
Doe v. Unocal Corp., 395 F.3d 978 (9th Cir. 2003) (U.S.).
Dred Scott v. Sandford, 60 U.S. 393 (1857) (U.S.).
EEOC v. Arabian Am. Oil Co., 857 F.2d 1014 (5th Circ. 1988) (U.S.).
Empagran SA v. F. Hoffmann-LaRoche Ltd., 315 F.3d 388 (D.C. Circ. 2003) (U.S.).
Erie Railroad Co. v. Tompkins, 304 U.S. 64 (1938) (U.S.).
F. Hoffmann-La Roche v. Empagran, 542 U.S. 155 (2004) (U.S.).
Friends of the Earth Inc. et al. v. Mosbacher et al. (also known as v. Watson or as v. Spinelli), 488 F. Supp. 2d 889 (N.D. Cal. 2007) (U.S.).
Hamilton v. Water Whole International Corp., 302 F. Appx. 789 (10th Cir. 2008) (U.S.).
Hartford Fire Insurance Co. v. California, 509 U.S. 764 (1993) (U.S.).
House of Koscot Dev. Corp v. Am. Line Cosmetics Inc., 468 F.2d 64 (5th Cir. 1973) (U.S.).
In re Investigation of World Arrangements, 13 FRD 280 (D.D.C. I 1952) (U.S.).
In re Oil Spill by "Amoco Cadiz," 1984 A.M.C. 2123 (D.C. Ill. 1984) (U.S.).
In re Uranium Antitrust Legislation, 473 F. Supp. 382 (N.D. Ill. 1979) (U.S.).
International Labor Rights Research and Education Fund et al. v. George Bush et al., 954 F.2d 745 (D.C. Cir. 1992) (U.S.).
International Shoe Co. v. Washington, 326 U.S. 310 (1945) (U.S.).
Jones v. Butz, 374 F. Supp. 1284 (S.D.N.Y. 1974) (U.S.).
Justice v. Vercher, Case 18CV17601, Opinion Letter by Judge Knowles, Sept. 17, 2018 (U.S.).
Kimes v. Grossnerc, 195 Cal. App. 4th 1556 (2011) (U.S.).
Kiobel v. Royal Dutch Petroleum, 133 S. Ct. 1659 (2013) (U.S.).
Laker v. Sabena, Belgian World Airlines, 731 F.2d 909 (D.C. Cir. 1984) (U.S.).
Lowendahl v. Baltimore & Ohio Railroad, 247 A.D. 144 (N.Y. App. Div. 1936) (U.S.).
Lujan v. Defenders of Wildlife, 504 U.S. 555 (1992) (U.S.).
Mannington Mills Inc. v. Congoleum Corporation, 595 F.2d 1287 (3d Cir. 1979) (U.S.).
Martinez v. Robledo, 210 Cal. App. 4th 384 (2012) (U.S.).

Matter of Nonhuman Rights Project, Inc. v Stanley, 2015 NY Slip Op 25257 [49 Misc 3d 746] (2015) (U.S.).
McDonald v. Mabee, 243 U.S. 90 (1917) (U.S.).
McElderry v. Cathay Pacific Airways, 678 F. Supp. 1071 (S.D.N.Y. 1988) (U.S.).
McGlinchy v. Shell Chemical Co., 845 F.2d 802 (9th Cir. 1988) (U.S.).
Minn-Chem, Inc. v. Agrium, Inc., 683 F.3d 845 (7th Cir. 2012) (U.S.).
New York Central & Hudson River R.R. v. United States, 212 U.S. 481 (1909) (U.S.).
New York Trust Co. v. Carpenter, 250 F. 668 (6th Cir. 1918) (U.S.).
Parker v. Bell Asbestos Mines Ltd., 607 F. Supp. 1397 (E.D. Pa. 1985) (U.S.).
Pennoyer v. Neff, 95 U.S. 714 (1878) (U.S.).
People v. Rogers, 703 N.Y.S.2d 891 (N.Y. City Ct. 2000) (U.S.).
Radaszewski v. Telecom Corp., 981 F.2d 305 (8th Cir. 1992) (U.S.).
Robertson v. Methow Valley Citizens Council, 490 U.S. 332 (1989) (U.S.).
Rocker MGMT, L.L.C. v. Lernout & Hauspie Speech Products N.V., 2005 WL 3658006 (D.N.J. 2005) (U.S.).
RRX Indust. Inc. v. Lab-Con Inc., 772 F.2d 543 (9th Cir. 1985) (U.S.).
Santa Clara County v. Southern Railroad, 118 U.S. 394 (1886) (U.S.).
Scenic Hudson Preservation Conference v. Federal Power Commission, 407 U.S. 926 (1972) (U.S.).
Slater v. Mexican Nat. R. Co., 194 U.S. 120 (1904) (U.S.).
State of Arizona v. Willoughby, 862 F.2d 1319 (Ariz. Sup. Ct. 1995) (U.S.).
State of Colorado v. Hess, Nos. 14CA1435, Nov. 3, 2016, Cert Denied Oct. 2, 2017 (U.S.).
State of Oregon v. Nix, 355 Or. 77, 334 P.3d 437 (2014) (U.S.).
Strycker's Bay Neighborhood Council v. Karlen, 444 U.S. 223 (1980) (U.S.).
Tauza v. Susquehanna Coal Co., 115 N.E. 915 (N.Y. 1917) (U.S.).
The Schooner Exchange v. McFaddon, 11 U.S. 116 (1812) (U.S.).
Tilikum v. SeaWorld Parks & Ent., Inc., 842 F. Supp. 2d 1259 (S.D. Cal. 2012) (U.S.).
Timberlane Lumber Co. v. Bank of America, NT & SA, 549 F.2d 597 (9th Cir. 1976) (U.S.).
United States v. Aluminum Company of America, 148 F.2d 416 (1945) (U.S.).
United States v. Imperial Chemical Industries, 105 F. Supp. 215 (S.D.N.Y. 1952) (U.S.).
United States v. Jon-T Chemicals Inc., 768 F.2d 686 (5th Cir. 1985) (U.S.).
United States v. LSL Biotechnologies et al., 379 F.3d 674 (9th Cir. 2004) (U.S.).
United States v. Nippon Paper Industries Co., 109 F.3d 1 (1st Cir. 1997) (U.S.).
United States v. Scophony Corp, 333 U.S. 795 (1948) (U.S.).
United States v. The Watchmakers of Switzerland Information Center, 133 F. Supp. 40 (S.D.N.Y. 1955) (U.S.).
United States v. Watchmakers of Switzerland Information Center Inc., 1963 Trade Cases CCH 70600 (U.S.).
United States v. Yousef, 327 F.3d 56 (2d Cir. 2003) (U.S.).
United States v. Yunis, 681 F. Supp. 896 (D.C. 1988) (U.S.).
Westinghouse Electric Corp. v. Rio Algom Ltd. 617 F.2d 1248 (7th Cir. 1980) (U.S.).

List of Legal Material

INTERNATIONAL CONVENTIONS, QUASI-CONVENTIONS, AND DECLARATIONS

African Charter on Human and Peoples' Rights, Oct. 21, 1986, 1520 U.N.T.S. 217 [Banjul Charter].

African Convention on the Conservation of Nature and Natural Resources, Sept. 15, 1968, 1001 U.N.T.S. 3.

Agreement between the European Communities and the Government of the United States of America on the Application of Positive Comity Principles in the Enforcement of Their Competition Laws, June 4, 1998 O.J. (L 173) 28.

Agreement between the Government of the United States of America and the Commission of the European Communities Regarding the Application of Their Competition Laws, Exchange of Interpretative Letters with the Government of the United States of America (U.S.-EC Competition Law Agreement), Sept. 23, 1991, 1995 O.J. (L 95) 47.

Agreement between the Office International des Epizooties and the World Trade Organization, July 8, 1998, WT/L/272.

Agreement Between the United States and Cuba for the Lease of Lands for Coaling and Naval Stations, Feb. 23, 1903, T.S. No. 418.

Agreement Concluded between the Delegates of the Kingdom of Italy and the Kingdom of the Serbs, Croats and Slovenes, Regarding a Draft Convention for the Regulation of Fishing in the Adriatic, Sept. 14, 1921, 19 L.N.T.S. 39.

Agreement Establishing an Association between the European Community and its Member States, of the One Part, and the Republic of Chile, of the Other Part, Nov. 18, 2002.

Agreement for the Implementation of the Provisions of the United Nations Convention on the Law of the Sea of 10 December 1982 Relating to the Conservation and Management of Straddling Fish Stocks and Highly Migratory Fish Stocks, Sept. 8, 1995, 2167 U.N.T.S. 3.

Agreement Governing the Activities of States on the Moon and Other Celestial Bodies, Dec. 18, 1979, 1363 U.N.T.S. 3 [Moon Agreement].

Agreement on Encouragement and Reciprocal Investments Between the Kingdom of the Netherlands and the Republic of Venezuela, Oct. 22, 1991.

Agreement on International Humane Trapping Standards between the European Community, Canada and the Russian Federation, Dec. 15, 1997, 1998 O.J. (L 42) 43.

Agreement on the Conservation of Polar Bears, Nov. 15, 1973, 27 U.S.T. 3918.

American Convention on Human Rights, July 18, 1978, 1144 U.N.T.S. 123.

Bamako Convention on the Ban of the Import into Africa and the Control of Transboundary Movement and Management of Hazardous Wastes within Africa, Jan. 30, 1988, 2101 U.N.T.S. 177.

Bergen Ministerial Declaration on Sustainable Development in the ECE Region, U.N. Doc. A/CONF.151/PC/10 (May 16, 1990).

Bonn Convention on the Conservation of Migratory Species of Wild Animals, June 23, 1979, 1651 U.N.T.S. 355.

Charter of the Organization of African Unity, May 25, 1963, 479 U.N.T.S. 39.

Charter of the United Nations, Oct. 24, 1945, 1 U.N.T.S. 16.

Commission for Democracy through Law (Venice Commission), Declaration on the Consequences of State Succession for the Nationality of Natural Persons, Sept. 13–4, 1996, CDL-NAT(1996)007rev-e.

Comprehensive Economic and Trade Agreement, Sept. 21, 2017 [CETA].

Consolidated Version of the Treaty European Union, 2016 O.J. (C 202) 01 [TEU].

Consolidated Version of the Treaty on the Functioning of the European Union, 2016 O.J. (C 202) 01 [TFEU].

Constitution of the International Labor Organization (Part XIII of the Treaty of Peace between the Allied and Associated Powers and Germany), June 28, 1919, 15 U.N.T.S. 40.

Convention against Torture and Other Cruel, Inhuman or Degrading Treatment or Punishment, Dec. 10, 1984, 1465 U.N.T.S. 85.

Convention Establishing the Multilateral Investment Guarantee Agency, Oct. 11, 1985, 1508 U.N.T.S. 99 [MIGA Convention].

Convention for the Conservation of Antarctic Seals, June 1, 1972, 1080 U.N.T.S. 175.

Convention for the Protection of Human Rights and Fundamental Freedoms, Nov. 4, 1950, 213 U.N.T.S. 221 [ECHR].

Convention for the Suppression of Unlawful Acts against the Safety of Civil Aviation, Sept. 23, 1971, 974 U.N.T.S. 178 [Montreal Convention].

Convention for the Suppression of Unlawful Seizure of Aircraft, Dec. 16, 1970, 860 U.N.T.S. 105 [Hijacking Convention].

Convention Implementing the Schengen Agreement, June 14, 1985, 2000 O.J. (L 239) [CISA].

Convention of 19 October 1996 on Jurisdiction, Applicable Law, Recognition, Enforcement and Co-operation in Respect of Parental Responsibility and Measures for the Protection of Children, Jan. 1, 2002, 35 I.L.M. 1391.

Convention on Access to Information, Public Participation in Decision Making and Access to Justice in Environmental Matters, June 28, 1998, 2161 U.N.T.S. 447 [Aarhus Convention].

Convention on Biological Diversity, June 5, 1992, 1760 U.N.T.S. 79 [CBD].

Convention on Environmental Impact Assessment in a Transboundary Context, Feb. 25, 1991, 1989 U.N.T.S. 309 [Espoo Convention].

Convention on International Trade in Endangered Species of Wild Fauna and Flora, Mar. 3, 1973, 993 U.N.T.S. 243 [CITES].

Convention on Offences and Certain Other Acts Committed on Board Aircraft, Sept. 14, 1963, 704 U.N.T.S. 220 [Tokyo Convention].

Convention on the Conservation of Antarctic Marine Living Resources, May 20, 1980, 1329 U.N.T.S. 48.

Convention on the Control of Transboundary Movements of Hazardous Wastes and Their Disposal, Mar. 22, 1989, 1672 U.N.T.S. 126 [Basel Convention].

Convention on the High Seas, Apr. 29, 1958, 450 U.N.T.S. 11.

Convention on the Prevention and Punishment of the Crime of Genocide, Dec. 9, 1948, 78 U.N.T.S. 277.

Convention on the Settlement of Investment Disputes between States and Nationals of Other States, Mar. 18, 1965, 575 U.N.T.S. 159 [ICSID Convention].

Convention Relative to the Preservation of Fauna and Flora in their Natural State, Nov. 8, 1933, 172 U.N.T.S. 241.

Council of Europe (CoE), Convention for the Protection of Animals during International Transport, Dec. 13, 1968, C.E.T.S. No. 065.

Council of Europe (CoE), Convention for the Protection of Animals during International Transport (revised), Nov. 6, 2003, C.E.T.S. No. 193.

Council of Europe (CoE), Convention for the Protection of Animals Kept for Farming Purposes, Mar. 10, 1976, C.E.T.S. No. 087.

Council of Europe (CoE), Convention for the Protection of Animals for Slaughter, May 10, 1979, C.E.T.S. No. 102.

Council of Europe (CoE), Convention for the Protection of Pet Animals, Nov. 13, 1987, C.E.T.S. No. 125.

Council of Europe (CoE), Convention for the Protection of Vertebrate Animals Used for Experimental and Other Scientific Purposes, Mar. 18, 1986, C.E.T.S. No. 123.

Council of Europe (CoE), Convention on Laundering of Search Seizure and Confiscation of the Proceeds from Crime, Nov. 8, 1990, C.E.T.S. No. 141.

Council of Europe (CoE), Convention on Mutual Assistance in Criminal Matters, Apr. 20, 1959, C.E.T.S. No. 30.

Council of Europe (CoE), Convention on Nationality, Nov. 6, 1997, C.E.T.S. No. 166.

Council of Europe (CoE), Convention on Preventing and Combating Violence against Women and Domestic Violence, May 11, 2011, C.E.T.S. No. 210.

Council of Europe (CoE), Convention on the Conservation of European Wildlife and Natural Habitats, Sept. 19, 1982, C.E.T.S. No. 104.

Council of Europe (CoE), Convention on the Prevention of Terrorism, May 16, 2005, C.E.T.S. No. 196.

Council of Europe (CoE), Convention on the Protection of Children against Sexual Exploitation and Sexual Abuse, Oct. 25, 2007, C.E.T.S. No. 201.

Council of Europe (CoE), Convention on the Protection of the Environment through Criminal Law, Nov. 4, 1998, C.E.T.S. No. 172.

Council of Europe (CoE), Criminal Law Convention on Corruption, Jan. 27, 1999, C.E.T.S. No. 173.

Council of Europe (CoE), European Convention for the Protection of Human Rights and Fundamental Freedoms (ECHR), Nov. 4, 1950, C.E.T.S. No. 5.

Council of Europe (CoE), Explanatory Report to the Convention on the Protection of Environment through Criminal Law, Nov. 4, 1998.

Declaration of the United Nations Conference on Environment and Development, U.N. Doc. A/CONF.151/26, 31 I.L.M. 874 (June 14, 1992) [Rio Declaration].

Declaration of the United Nations Conference on the Human Environment, U.N. Doc. A/CONF.48/14/Rev. 1, 11 I.L.M. 1416 (June 6, 1972) [Stockholm Declaration].

Ecuador-France Bilateral Investment Agreement, Paris, Sept. 7, 1994.

EU-Singapore Free Trade Agreement, Brussels, June 29, 2015.

Free Trade Agreement between the European Union and its Member States, of the One Part, and the Republic of Korea, of the Other Part, Oct. 6, 2010.

Geneva Convention (I) for the Amelioration of the Condition of the Wounded and Sick in Armed Forces in the Field, Aug. 12, 1949, 75 U.N.T.S. 31.

Geneva Convention (II) for the Amelioration of the Condition of Wounded, Sick and Shipwrecked Members of Armed Forces at Sea, Aug. 12, 1949, 75 U.N.T.S. 85.

Geneva Convention (III) Relative to the Treatment of Prisoners of War, Aug. 12, 1949, 75 U.N.T.S 135.

Geneva Convention (IV) Relative to the Protection of Civilian Persons in Time of War, Aug. 12, 1949, 75 U.N.T.S. 287.

Hague Convention (IV) Respecting the Laws and Customs of War on Land and Its Annex: Regulations Concerning the Laws and Customs of War on Land, Oct. 18, 1907, T.S. 539.

Hague Convention Concerning the Recognition of the Legal Personality of Foreign Companies, Associations and Institutions, June 1, 1956, 1 A.J.C.L. 277.

Inter-American Convention on Human Rights, Nov. 22, 1969, 1144 U.N.T.S. 123 [IACHR].

International Convention Concerning the Transit of Animals, Meat and Other Products of Animal Origin, Feb. 20, 1935, 193 L.N.T.S. 39.

International Convention for the Protection of All Persons from Enforced Disappearance, Dec. 20, 2006, 2716 U.N.T.S. 3.

International Convention for the Regulation of Whaling, Nov. 10, 1948, 161 U.N.T.S. 72 [ICRW].

International Convention for the Suppression of the Financing of Terrorism, Dec. 9, 1999, 2178 U.N.T.S. 197.

International Convention on the Harmonized System, June 14, 1983, 1503 U.N.T.S. 168 [HS Convention].

International Convention on the Suppression and Punishment of the Crime of Apartheid, Nov. 30, 1973, 1015 U.N.T.S. 243.

International Covenant on Civil and Political Rights, Dec. 16, 1966, 999 U.N.T.S. 171 [ICCPR].

International Covenant on Economic, Social and Cultural Rights, Dec. 16, 1966, 933 U.N.T.S. 3 [ICESCR].

International Dolphin Conservation Program Agreement, May 5, 1998, 1999 O.J. (L 132) 3 [AIDCP].

International Labor Organization (ILO), Tripartite Declaration of Principles Concerning Multinational Enterprises and Social Policy, ILO Official Bulletin, Series A, No. 3 (ILO, Geneva 2000).

League of Nations Convention on Certain Questions Relating to the Conflict of Nationality, Apr. 13, 1930, 179 U.N.T.S. 89.

Montevideo Convention on the Rights and Duties of States (Inter-American), Dec. 26, 1933, 165 L.N.T.S. 19.

Montreal Protocol on Substances that Deplete the Ozone Layer, Sept. 16, 1987, 1522 U.N.T.S. 3.

North American Free Trade Agreement, Dec. 17, 1992, 32 I.L.M. 289 (1993) [NAFTA].

Protocol Additional to the Geneva Conventions of 12 August 1949, and Relating to the Protection of Victims of International Armed Conflicts (Protocol I), June 8, 1977, 1125 U.N.T.S. 3.

Rome Statute of the International Criminal Court, July 17, 1998, 2187 U.N.T.S. 90 [Rome Statute].

Statute of the International Court of Justice, June 26, 1945, 33 U.N.T.S. 993 [ICJ Statute].

The Antarctic Treaty, Dec. 1, 1959, 402 U.N.T.S. 71.

The Cambridge Declaration on Consciousness in Non-Human Animals, July 7, 2012, *available at* http://fcmconference.org/img/CambridgeDeclarationOnConsciousness.pdf (last visited Jan. 10, 2019).

The Convention on the Prevention and Punishment of the Crime of Genocide, Dec. 9, 1948, 78 U.N.T.S. 277.

Trans-Pacific Partnership, Oct. 4, 2015 [TPP], *available at* https://www.tpp.mfat.govt.nz/text (last visited Jan. 10, 2019).

Treaty between the United States of America and the Oriental Republic of Uruguay Concerning the Encouragement and Reciprocal Protection of Investment, Oct. 25, 2004.

Treaty Establishing the European Economic Community, Mar. 25, 1957, 298 U.N.T.S. 11.

U.N. Convention on the Law of the Sea, Dec. 10, 1982, 1833 U.N.T.S. 3 [UNCLOS].

U.N. Economic Commission for Europe (UNECE), Convention on the Protection and Use of Transboundary Watercourses and International Lakes, Mar. 17, 1992, 1936 U.N.T.S 269.

U.N. Treaty on Principles Governing the Activities of States in the Exploration and Use of Outer Space, including the Moon and Other Celestial Bodies, Jan. 27, 1967, 610 U.N.T.S. 205 [Outer Space Treaty].

U.S.-EU Agreed Minute on Humane Trapping Standards, 1998 O.J. (L 219) 26.

Vienna Convention for the Protection of the Ozone Layer, Mar. 22, 1985, 1513 U.N.T.S. 293.

Vienna Convention on Consular Relations, Apr. 24, 1963, 596 U.N.T.S. 261 [VCCR].

Vienna Convention on the Law of Treaties, May 23, 1969, 1155 U.N.T.S. 331 [VCLT].

World Organization for Animal Health (OIE), International Agreement for the Creation of the OIE, Jan. 25, 1924.

World Trade Organization (WTO), Agreement on Agriculture, Apr. 15, 1994, 1867 U.N.T.S. 410 [AoA].

World Trade Organization (WTO), Agreement on Implementation of Article VI of the General Agreement on Tariffs and Trade 1994, Apr. 15, 1994, 1868 U.N.T.S. 201 [Anti-Dumping Agreement, ADA].

World Trade Organization (WTO), Agreement on Subsidies and Countervailing Measures, Apr. 15, 1994, 1867 U.N.T.S. 14 [SCM Agreement].

World Trade Organization (WTO), Agreement on Technical Barriers to Trade, Apr. 15, 1994, 1868 U.N.T.S. 120 [TBT].

World Trade Organization (WTO), Agreement on the Application of Sanitary and Phytosanitary Measures, Apr. 15, 1994, 1867 U.N.T.S. 493 [SPS].

World Trade Organization (WTO), General Agreement on Tariffs and Trade, Apr. 15, 1994, 1867 U.N.T.S. 187 [GATT].

World Trade Organization (WTO), General Agreement on Trade in Services, Apr. 15, 1994, 1869 U.N.T.S. 183 [GATS].

World Trade Organization (WTO), Marrakesh Agreement Establishing the World Trade Organization, Apr. 15, 1994, 1867 U.N.T.S. 154 [WTO Agreement].

World Trade Organization (WTO), Understanding on Rules and Procedures Governing the Settlement of Disputes, Apr. 15, 1994, 1869 U.N.T.S. 401 [Dispute Settlement Understanding, DSU].

UN documents

Bonn Declaration on Rio+20, Presented to the General Assembly, 64th UN DPI/NGO Conference, U.N. NGO Branch, Department of Economic and Social Affairs (Apr. 26, 2011).

G.A. Res 375, U.N. GAOR 4th Sess., Draft Declaration on the Rights and Duties of States, U.N. Doc. A/RES/375 (Dec. 6, 1949).

G.A. Res. 1514, U.N. GAOR 15th Sess., Declaration on the Granting of Independence to Colonial Countries and Peoples, U.N. Doc. A/RES/1514(XV) (Dec. 14, 1960).

G.A. Res. 20/2131, U.N. GAOR 20th Sess., Declaration on the Inadmissibility of Intervention in the Domestic Affairs of States and the Protection of their Independence and Sovereignty, U.N. Doc. A/RES/20/2131 (Dec. 21, 1965).

G.A. Res. 217 A (III), U.N. GAOR 3rd Sess., Universal Declaration of Human Rights, U.N. Doc. A/RES/810 (Dec. 10, 1948) [UDHR].

G.A. Res. 2625, U.N. GAOR 25th Sess., Declaration on Principles of International Law Concerning Friendly Relations and Cooperation among States in Accordance with the Charter of the United Nations, U.N. Doc. A/RES/25/2625 (Oct. 24, 1970) [Friendly Relations Declaration].

G.A. Res. 3281 (XXIX), U.N. GAOR 29th Sess., Charter of Economic Rights and Duties of States, U.N. Doc. A/RES/29/3281 (Dec. 12, 1974).

G.A. Res. 36/103, U.N. GAOR 36th Sess., Declaration on the Inadmissibility of Intervention and Interference in the Internal Affairs of States, U.N. Doc, A/RES/36/103 (Dec. 9, 1981).

G.A. Res. 37/7, U.N. GAOR 37th Sess., World Charter for Nature, U.N. Doc. A/RES/37/7 (Oct. 28, 1982).

G.A. Res. 55/610, U.N. GAOR 55th Sess., International Law Commission (ILC), Draft Articles on Nationality of Natural Persons in Relation to the Succession of States, U.N. Doc. A/RES/55/610 (Nov. 28, 2000).

G.A. Res. 56/10, U.N. GAOR 53rd Sess., International Law Commission (ILC), Draft Articles on Responsibility of States for Internationally Wrongful Acts, Supp. No. 10, U.N. Doc. A/RES/56/10 (Apr. 23–June 1 and June 2–Aug. 10, 2001) [ARSIWA].

G.A. Res. 66/750, U.N. GAOR 66th Sess., Letter dated 7 October 2011 from the Permanent Representative of Germany to the United Nations addressed to the President of the General Assembly, U.N. Doc. A/RES/66/750 (Mar. 20, 2012).

Human Rights Council Res. 10/13, 13th Sess., Human Rights and Arbitrary Deprivation of Nationality, U.N. Doc. A/HRC/13/34 (Dec. 14, 2009).

Human Rights Council, 17th Sess., Special Representative of the Secretary-General, Report on the Issue of Human Rights and Transnational Corporations and Other Business Enterprises, Guiding Principles on Business and Human Rights: Implementing the United Nations "Protect, Respect and Remedy" Framework, U.N. Doc. A/HRC/17/31 (Mar. 21, 2011) (by John Ruggie).

Human Rights Council, 19th Sess., Guiding Principles on Human Rights Impact Assessments of Trade and Investment Agreements, U.N. Doc. A/HRC/19/59/Add.5 (Dec. 19, 2011).

Human Rights Council, 8th Sess., Special Representative of the Secretary-General John Ruggie, Protect, Respect and Remedy: A Framework for Business and Human Rights, U.N. Doc. A/HRC/8/5 (Apr. 7, 2008).

Human Rights Council, 8th Sess., Special Representative of the Secretary-General John Ruggie, Business and Human Rights: Mapping International Standards of Responsibility and Accountability for Corporate Acts, U.N. Doc. A/HRC/4/35 (Feb. 19, 2007).

International Law Commission, 47th Sess., First Report on State Succession and its Impact on the Nationality of Natural and Legal Persons (Special Rapporteur Vaclav Mikulka), U.N. Doc. A/CN.4/467 (Apr. 17, 1995).

International Law Commission, 48th Sess., State Succession and Its Impact on the Nationality of Natural and Legal Persons, U.N. Doc. A/CN.4/472/Add. 1 (Jan. 10, 1996).

International Law Commission, 58th Sess., Report of the International Law Commission, Supp. No. 10, U.N. Doc. A/61/10 (May 1–June 9 and July 3–Aug. 11 2006), Annex E. Extraterritorial Jurisdiction.

International Law Commission, 58th Sess., Report of the Study Group of the International Law Commission, Fragmentation of International Law, Difficulties Arising from Diversification and Expansion of International Law (finalized by Martti Koskenniemi), U.N. Doc. A/CN.4/L.682 (Apr. 13, 2006).

Report of the United Nations Conference on the Human Environment, U.N. Doc. A/CONF. 48/14 (1972).

S.C. Res. 827, U.N. SCOR 48th Sess., on Establishing an International Tribunal for the Prosecution of Persons Responsible for Serious Violations of International Humanitarian Law Committed in the Territory of the Former Yugoslavia, U.N. Doc. S/RES/827 (May 25, 1993).

S.C. Res. 955, U.N. SCOR 49th Sess., On Establishment of an International Tribunal and Adoption of the Statute of the Tribunal, U.N. Doc. S/RES/955 (Nov. 8, 1994).

Special Representative of the Secretary-General Allens Arthur Robinson, 'Corporate Culture' as a Basis for the Criminal Liability of Corporations (Feb. 2008), *available at* http://198.170.85.29/Allens-Arthur-Robinson-Corporate-Culture-paper-for-Ruggie-Feb-2008.pdf (last visited Jan. 10, 2019).

U.N. Diplomatic Conference of Plenipotentiaries on the Establishment of an International Criminal Court, Draft Statute for the International Criminal Court, U.N. Doc. A/CONF.183/2/Add.1 (Apr. 14, 1998).

U.N. Environmental Program (UNEP), Goals and Principles of Environmental Impact Assessment, U.N. Doc. UNEP/WG.152/4 Annex (Jan. 16, 1987).

European Union

Commission Directive 2002/4 on the Registration of Establishments Keeping Laying Hens, 2002 O.J. (L 30) 44.

Commission Implementing Regulation 577/2013 on the Model Identification Documents for the Non-commercial Movement of Dogs, Cats and Ferrets, the Establishment of Lists of Territories and Third Countries and the Format, Layout and Language Requirements of the Declarations Attesting Compliance with Certain Conditions Provided for in Regulation (EU) No. 576/2013 of the European Parliament and of the Council, 2013 O.J. (L 178) 109.

Commission of the European Communities, Opinion of the Commission Pursuant to Article 251 (2), Third Subparagraph, Point (c) of the EC Treaty, on the European Parliament's Amendments to the Council's Common Position Regarding the Proposal for a Directive of the European Parliament and of the Council Amending for the Seventh Time Council Directive 76/768/EEC on the Approximation of the Laws of the Member States Relating to Cosmetic Products, COM(2002) 435 final (July 26, 2002).

Commission Regulation 1361/2014 Amending Regulation (EC) No. 1126/2008 Adopting Certain International Accounting Standards in Accordance with Regulation (EC) No. 1606/2002 of the European Parliament and of the Council as Regards International Financial Reporting Standards 3 and 13 and International Accounting Standard 40, 2014 O.J. (L 365) 120.

Commission Regulation 1771/94 Laying Down New Provisions on the Introduction into the Community of Pelts and Manufactured Goods of Certain Wild Animal Species, 1994 O.J. (L 184) 3.

Commission Regulation No. 589/2008 Laying Down Detailed Rules for Implementing Council Regulation No. 1234/2007 as Regards Marketing Standards for Eggs, 2008 O.J. (L 163) 6.

Commission Staff Working Paper, Impact Assessment Accompanying the Document Communication from the Commission to the European Parliament, the Council and the European Economic and Social Committee on the European Union Strategy for the Protection and Welfare of Animals 2012–2015, SEC(2012) 55 final (Jan. 19, 2012).

Committee on External Economic Relations, Report on the Communication from the Commission to the Council and the European Parliament on Trade and Environment, COM(96)0054—C4-0158/96, Rapporteur Wolfgang Kreissl-Dörfler (Oct. 14, 1996).

Council Directive 1999/22 Relating to the Keeping of Wild Animals in Zoos, 1999 O.J. (L 94) 24.

Council Directive 1999/74 Laying Down Minimum Standards for the Protection of Laying Hens, 1999 O.J. (L 203) 53.

Council Directive 2007/43 Laying Down Minimum Standards for the Protection of Chickens Kept for Meat Production, 2007 O.J. (L 182) 19.

Council Directive 2008/119 Laying Down Minimum Standards for the Protection of Calves, 2009 O.J. (L 10) 7.

Council Directive 2008/120 Laying Down Minimum Standards for the Protection of Pigs, 2009 O.J. (L 47) 5.

Council Directive 92/43/EEC on the Conservation of Natural Habitats and Wild Fauna and Flora, O.J. (L 206) 7.

Council Directive 93/119/EC on the Protection of Animals at the Time of Slaughter or Killing, 1992 O.J. (340) 21.

Council Directive 98/58/EC Concerning the Protection of Animals Kept for Farming Purposes, 1998 O.J. (L 221) 23.

Council Framework Decision on Combating Terrorism (2002/475/JHA), 2002 O.J. (L 164) 3.

Council Framework Decision on the European Arrest Warrant and the Surrender Procedures between Member States (2002/584/JHA), 2002 O.J. (L 190) 1.

Council Regulation 1/2003 on the Implementation of the Rules on Competition Laid Down in Articles 81 and 82 of the Treaty, 2003 O.J. (L 1) 1.

Council Regulation 1/2005 on the Protection of Animals During Transport and Related Operations and Amending Directives 64/432/EEC and 93/119/EC and Regulation 1255/97/EC, 2005 O.J. (L 3) 1, and corrigendum 2011 O.J. (L 336) 86.

Council Regulation 1099/2009 on the Protection of Animals at the Time of Killing, 2009 O.J. (L 303) 1.

Council Regulation 1215/2012 on Jurisdiction and the Recognition and Enforcement of Judgments in Civil and Commercial Matters (Recast), 2012 O.J. (L 351) 1 [Brussels Regulation].

Council Regulation 2271/96 Protecting Against the Effects of the Extra-Territorial Application of Legislation Adopted by a Third Country, and Actions Based Thereon or Resulting Therefrom, 1996 O.J. (L 309) 1.

Council Regulation 3254/91 Prohibiting the Use of Leghold Traps in the Community and the Introduction into the Community of Pelts and Manufactured Goods of Certain Wild Animal Species Originating in Countries Which Catch Them by Means of Leghold Traps or Trapping Methods Which Do Not Meet International Humane Trapping Standards, 1991 O.J. (L 308) 1.

Council Regulation 3626/82 on the Implementation in the Community of the Convention on International Trade in Endangered Species of Wild Fauna and Flora, 1982 O.J. (L 384) 1.

Council Regulation 44/2001 on Jurisdiction and the Recognition and Enforcement of Judgments in Civil and Commercial Matters, 2000 O.J. (L 12) 1.

Directive 2008/99/EC of the European Parliament and of the Council on the Protection of the Environment through Criminal Law, 2008 O.J. (L 328) 28.

Directive 2010/63 of the European Parliament and the Council on the Protection of Animals Used for Scientific Purposes, 2010 O.J. (L 276) 33.

Directive 2011/92 of the European Parliament and of the Council on Combating the Sexual Abuse and Sexual Exploitation of Children and Child Pornography, and Replacing Council Framework Decision 2004/68/JHA, 2011 O.J. (L 335) 1.

Directive 2014/52 of the European Parliament and of the Council Amending Directive 2011/92/EU on the Assessment of the Effects of Certain Public and Private Projects on the Environment, 2014 O.J. (L 124) 1.

Directive 2014/95 of the European Parliament and of the Council Amending Directive 2013/34/EU as Regards Disclosure of Non-financial and Diversity Information by Certain Large Undertakings and Groups, 2014 O.J. (L 330) 1.

Eleventh Council Directive Concerning Disclosure Requirements in Respect of Branches Opened in a Member State by Certain Types of Company Governed by the Law of Another State (89/666/EEC), 1989 O.J. (L 395) 36.

European Commission, Action Plan "Simplifying and Improving the Regulatory Environment," COM(2002) 278 final (June 5, 2002).

European Commission, Comments on the US Regulations Concerning Trade with the USSR, Aug. 12, 1982.

European Commission, Commission Staff Working Document, Impact Assessment on the Animal Testing Provisions in Regulation (EC) 1223/2009 on Cosmetics, Accompanying the Document Communication from the Commission to the European Parliament and the Council on Animal Testing and Marketing Ban on the State of Play in Relation to Alternative Methods in the Field of Cosmetics, SWD(2013) 66 final (Mar. 11, 2013).

European Commission, Commission Staff Working Document, Impact Assessment Report Accompanying the Report from the Commission to the European Parliament, the Council, the European Economic and Social Committee and the Committee of the Regions, Options for Animal Welfare Labelling and the Establishment of a European Network of Reference Centres for the Protection and Welfare of Animals, SEC(2009) 1432 (Oct. 28, 2009).

European Commission, Communication from the Commission to the Council and the European Parliament on Animal Welfare Legislation on Farmed Animals in Third Countries and the Implications for the EU, COM(2002) 626 final (Nov. 18, 2002).

European Commission, Communication from the Commission to the Council and the European Parliament on Trade and Environment, COM(96) 54 final (Feb. 28, 1996).

European Commission, Communication from the Commission to the European Parliament, the Council, the European Economic and Social Committee and the Committee of the Regions, A Renewed EU Strategy 2011–2014 for Corporate Social Responsibility, COM(2011) 681 final, Oct. 25, 2011.

European Commission, Communication from the Commission to the European Parliament, the Council and the European Economic and Social Committee on the European Union Strategy for the Protection and Welfare of Animals 2012–2015, COM(2012) 6 final/2 (Feb. 15, 2012).

European Commission, Health & Consumer Protection Directorate-General, Labelling: Competitiveness, Consumer Information and Better Regulation for the EU (European Communities 2006), *available at* http://ec.europa.eu/food/safety/docs/labelling-nutrition_better-reg_competitiveness-consumer-info_en.pdf (last visited Jan. 10, 2019).

European Commission, Implementation of Humane Trapping Standard in the EU (2015), *available at* http://ec.europa.eu/environment/biodiversity/animal_welfare/hts/index_en.htm (last visited Jan. 10, 2019).

European Communities, Communication from the Commission on the Precautionary Principle, COM(2000)1 (Feb. 2, 2000).

European Parliament Legislative Resolution on the Proposal for a Regulation of the European Parliament and of the Council Concerning Trade in Seals Products (COM(2008)0469—C6-0295/2008—2008/0160(COD)), 2010 O.J. (C 212 E) 169.

European Parliament, Resolution of the European Parliament on European Union Strategy for European Enterprises Operating in Developing Countries: Towards a European Code of Conduct, 1999 O.J. (C 104) 180.

Proposal for a Council Regulation Amending Council Regulation 3254/91 Prohibiting the Use of Leghold Traps in the Community and the Introduction into the Community of Pelts and Manufactured Goods of Certain Wild Animal Species Originating in Countries Which Catch them by Means of Leghold Traps or Trapping Methods Which Do Not Meet International Humane Trapping Standards, 1996 O.J. (C 58) 17.

Proposal for a Regulation of the European Parliament and of the Council Concerning Trade in Seal Products, COM(2008) 469 final (July 23, 2008).

Regulation 1007/2009 of the European Parliament and of the Council of 16 September 2009 on Trade in Seal Products, 2009 O.J. (L 286) 36.

Regulation 1221/2009 of the European Parliament and of the Council on the Voluntary Participation by Organisations in a Community Eco-management and Audit Scheme (EMAS), 2009 O.J. (L 342) 1.

Regulation 1223/2009 of the European Parliament and of the Council on Cosmetic Products, 2009 O.J. (L 342) 59.

Regulation 1523/2007 of the European Parliament and of the Council Banning the Placing on the Market and the Import to, or Export from, the Community of Cat and Dog Fur, and Products Containing such Fur, 2007 O.J. (L 343) 1.

Regulation 576/2013 of the European Parliament and of the Council on the Non-commercial Movement of Pet Animals and Repealing Regulation (EC) No. 998/2003, 2013 O.J. (L 178) 1.

Regulation 593/2008 of the European Parliament and of the Council on the Law Applicable to Contractual Obligations (Rome I), 2008 O.J. (L 177) 6.

Regulation 648/2012 of the European Parliament and of the Council on OTC Derivatives, Central Counterparties and Trade Repositories, 2012 O.J. (L 201) 1.

Report from the Commission to the European Parliament, the Council, the European Economic and Social Committee and the Committee of the Regions, Options for Animal Welfare Labelling and the Establishment of a European Network of Reference Centres for the Protection and Welfare of Animals, COM(2009) 584 final (Oct. 28, 2009).

NATIONAL LEGISLATION

Argentina

Ley Nacional 14.346 de Protección Animal, Sancionada en el Congreso Nacional el 27/9/54, Incluida en el Codigo Penal, Dec. 27, 1954 [Law No. 14.346, Animal Welfare Code] (Arg.).

Australia

Animal Care and Protection Act 2001 (Qld) (Austl.).
Animal Welfare Act 1985 (SA) (Austl.).
Animal Welfare Act 1992 (ACT) (Austl.).
Animal Welfare Act 1993, Act No. 63 (Tas) (Austl.).
Animal Welfare Act 2002 (WA) (Austl.).
Animal Welfare Act (NT) (Austl.).
Australian Citizenship Act 2007, Act No. 20 (Austl.).
Australian Meat and Live-stock Industry (Export of Live-stock to Egypt) Order 2008, Nov. 28, 2008, Annex A, Memorandum of Understanding on the Handling and Slaughter of Live Australian Animals (Austl.).
Corporations Act 2001, Act No. 50 (Austl.).
Crimes Act 1900 (NSW) (Austl.).
Criminal Code Act 1995, Act No. 12 (Austl.).
Prevention of Cruelty to Animals Act 1979, Act No. 200 (NSW) (Austl.).
Prevention of Cruelty to Animals Act 1986 (Vic) (Austl.).

Austria

Allgemeines Bürgerliches Gesetzbuch [ABGB] [Civil Code], BGBl. I No. 43/2016 (Austria).
Bundesgesetz über die Verantwortlichkeit von Verbänden für Straftaten [Verbandsverantwortlichkeitsgesetz (VbVG)] [Federal Act on the Responsibility of Entities for Criminal Offenses], BGBl. I No. 151/2005 (Austria).
Bundesgesetz über Versuche an lebenden Tieren [Tierversuchsgesetz, TVG] [Austrian Animal Experimentation Act], BGBl. I No. 114/2012 (Austria).
Bundesgesetz vom 23. Jänner 1974 über die mit gerichtlicher Strafe bedrohten Handlungen [StGB] [Criminal Code], BGBl. No. 60/1974 (Austria).
Tierschutzgesetz [TSchG] [Animal Protection Act], BGBl. I No. 118/2004 (Austria).

Belgium

Code des sociétés [Companies Code], No. 1999A09646, Moniteur Belge [M.B.] [Official Gazette of Belgium] 29440, May 7, 1999 (Belg.).
Code pénal [Criminal Code], No. 1867060850, M.B. 3133, June 8, 1867 (Belg.)
Loi relative à la protection et au bien-être des animaux [Animal Protection Act], No. 1986016195, M.B. 16382, Aug. 14, 1986 (Belg.).

Bosnia and Herzegovina

Criminal Code of Bosnia and Herzegovina, Official Gazette 3/03, *translation in* Official Gazette of Bosnia and Herzegovina 37/03 (Bosn. & Herz.).

Botswana

Cruelty to Animals Act, Cap. 37:02, May 8, 1936, consolidated version of the Proclamation 27 of 1936 as of Dec. 31, 2008 (Bots.).

Brazil

Constituição da República Federativa do Brasil [C.F.] [Constitution], Oct. 5, 1988 (Braz.).
Decreto Lei N° 24.645, de 10 de Julho de 1934 [Federal Decree on Anti-Cruelty N° 24.645], July 10, 1934 (Braz.).
Lei N° 9.605, de Fevereiro de 1998 [Environmental Crimes Law N° 9.605] Feb. 12, 1998 (Braz.).

Bulgaria

Zakon za Zashtita na Zhivotnite [Law on the Protection of Animals] of Jan. 31, 2008, Durzhaven Vestnik [D.V.] [State Gazette], Feb. 8, 2008 (Bulg.).

Canada

Animal Care Act, C.C.S.M. c. A84 , 1996 (MB, Can.).
Animal Health and Protection Act, c. A-11.1, 2005 (PEI, Can.).
Animal Protection Act, c. A-41, 2000 (AB, Can.).
Animal Protection Act, c. 33, 2008 (NS, Can.).
Animal Protection Act, c. 6, 2002 (YK, Can.).
Animal Protection Act, c. A-21.1, c. 38, 1999 (SK, Can.).
Animal Welfare and Safety Act, c. B-3.1, 2016 (QC, Can.).
Civil Code of Québec, c. 64, 1991 (QC, Can.).
Criminal Code, c. C-46, 1985 (Can.).
Ontario Society for the Prevention of Cruelty to Animals Act, c. O.36, 1990 (ON, Can.).
Prevention of Cruelty to Animals Act, c. 372, 1996 (BC, Can.).

Colombia

Ley 1774/2016, por medio de la cual se modifican el Código Civil, la Ley 84 de 1989, el Código Penal, el Código de Procedimiento Penal y se dictan otras disposiciones, enero 6, 2016, Diario Oficial [D.O.] (Colom.).

Costa Rica

Decreta Ley de Bienestar de los Animales [Decree on the Well-being of Animals], No. 7451, June 20, 2012 (Costa Rica).

Croatia

Zakon o zaštiti životinja [Animal Protection Act], No. 71-05-03/1-06-2, Dec. 7, 2006 (Croat.).

Czech Republic

Občanský Zákoník [C. Civ.] [Civil Code], No. 89/2012 Coll., Feb. 3, 2012 (Czech.).

Denmark

Act Amending the Environmental Protection Act (Green Accounts), Act No. 403, June 14, 1995 (Den.).
Animal Protection Act, Act No. 473, May 15, 2014 (Den.).
Danish Criminal Code, Order No. 909, Sept. 27, 2005 (Den.).
Financial Business Act, Consolidated Act No. 1125, Sept. 23, 2010 (Den.).
Financial Statements Act, Act No. 448, June 7, 2001 (Den.).

Egypt

Constitution of The Arab Republic of Egypt, Jan. 15, 2014 (Egypt).

Estonia

Lomakaitseseadus [Animal Protection Act], Dec. 13, 2000, Riigi Teataja [R.T.], I 2001, 3, 4 (Est.).
Karistusseadustik [Penal Code], Sept. 1, 2002, R.T. I 2001, 61, 364 (Est.).

Fiji

Animals (Control of Experiments) Act, May 13, 1957, c. 161, by Ordinance No. 11 of 1957 (Fiji).

Finland

Eläinsuojelulaki [Animal Welfare Act], 247/1996 (Fin.).

France

Code civil [C. Civ.] [Civil Code], Dec. 19, 2015 (Fr.).
Code de commerce [Business Act], Sept. 21, 2000 (Fr.).
Code pénal [C. Pén.] [Penal Code], Dec. 19, 2015 (Fr.).
Code rural et de la pêche maritime [Rural and Maritime Fisheries Code], Dec. 1, 1979 (Fr.).
Loi n°2001-420 relative aux nouvelles régulations économiques [La loi NRE] [Law on New Economic Relations], May 15, 2001 (Fr.).

Germany

Aktiengesetz [AktG] [Stock Corporation Act], Sept. 6, 1965, BGBl. I at 1089 (Ger.).
Bürgerliches Gesetzbuch [BGB] [Civil Code], Jan. 2, 2002, BGBl. I at 42, 2909; 2003 at 738 (Ger.).
Gesetz zur Änderung des Grundgesetzes (Staatsziel Tierschutz) [Law to Change the Basic Law (State Objective of Animal Protection)], July 31, 2002, BGBl. I at 2862 (Ger.).
Grundgesetz [GG] [Basic Law], May 23, 1949, BGBl. I at 2438 (Ger.).

Strafgesetzbuch [StGB] [Criminal Code], Nov. 13, 1998, BGBl. I at 3322 (Ger.).
Tierschutzgesetz [TierSchG] [Animal Welfare Act], May 18, 2006, BGBl. I at 1206 (Ger.).

Gibraltar

Animal Experiments (Scientific Procedures) Act, Principal Act, No. 1999-03, Mar. 3, 1999 (Gibr.).

Greece

Nomos (2012:4039) Gia Ta Deopozomena Kai Ta Adeopota Zōa Syntrophiaskai Tēn Zōōnapotē Ekmetalleysē ē Tē Chrēsimottoiēsē me Kerdookopikookotto [Law Concerning Domestic and Stray Companion Animals and the Protection of Animals from any Exploitation or Use for Economic Profit], Ephemeris Tes Kyverneseos Tes Hellenikes Demokratias [E.K.E.D.] 2012 (Greece).

Hong Kong

Prevention of Cruelty to Animals Ordinance (1997) Cap. 169, June 20, 1997, [L.N.] 331 of 1999 (Originally 44 of 1935 (Cap 169 1950)) (H.K.).

Iceland

Act on Animal Welfare, No. 55, Apr. 8, 2013 (Ice.).

India

Code of Criminal Procedure, Act No. 2 of 1974 (India).
Constitution of India, Jan. 26, 1950 (India).
The Prevention of Cruelty to Animals Act, Act No. 59 of 1960 (India).

Indonesia

Indonesian Penal Code, Feb. 27, 1982 (Indon.).

Israel

Cruelty to Animals Law (Animal Protection), Jan. 11, 1994, 5754-1994, Passed the Knesset 28 Tevet 5754 (Isr.).

Japan

の動物の愛護及び管理に関する法律 [Act on Welfare and Management of Animals], Law No. 105 of 1973 (Japan).
刑法 Keihō [Penal Code], Act No. 45 of 1907 (Japan).

Kenya

Prevention of Cruelty to Animals Act, Cap. 360, 1983, [L.N.] 119/1984 (Kenya).

Latvia

Dzīvnieku aizsardzības likums [Animal Protection Law], Dec. 9, 1999, Latvijas Vēstnesis [Latvian Herald], 444/445 (Lat.).

Liechtenstein

Tierschutzgesetz [TSchG] [Animal Welfare Act], Sept. 23, 2010 (Liech.).

Lithuania

Gyvūnų Gerovės ir Apsaugos Įstatymas [Law on Welfare and Protection of Animals], Oct. 3, 2012, No. XI-2271, Valstybės Žinios [Official Gazette], Oct. 20, 2012, No. 122-6216 (Lith.).

Luxemburg

Constitution du Grand-Duché du Luxembourg [The Constitution of the Grand Duchy of Luxembourg], Oct. 17, 1868 (Lux.).
Loi du 27 juin 2018 sur la protection des animaux [Animal Protection Act], July, 3, 2018 (Lux.).

Malaysia

Animals Act, Apr. 30, 1953, Laws of Malaysia, Act 647 (Malay.)

Malta

Animal Welfare Act, Feb. 8, 2002, c. 439, Act No. XXV of 2001 (Malta).

Mexico

Constitución Política de la Ciudad de México [Constitution of the City of Mexico], Gaceta Oficial de la Ciudad de México, Feb. 5, 2017 (Mex.).

Myanmar

Animal Health and Development Law, Nov. 25, 1993, No. 17/93 (Myan.).

Netherlands

Wet houdende regelen met betrekking tot het verrichten van proeven op dieren [Wet op de dierproeven] [Animal Experimentation Act], Jan. 12, 1977 (Neth.).
Wet van 19 mei 2011, houdende een integraal kader voor regels over gehouden dieren en daaraan gerelateerde onderwerpen (Wet dieren) [Act of May 19, 2011, containing an integrated framework for rules on animals kept and related subjects (Animal Law)], May 19, 2011 (Neth.).

New Zealand

Animal Welfare Act, Public Act No. 142, Oct. 14, 1999 (N.Z.).
Animal Welfare Amendment Act (No. 2) 2015, Public Act No. 49, May 9, 2015 (N.Z.).

Nigeria

Criminal Code Act, c. 77 (1990) (Nigeria).

Norway

Animal Welfare Act, 2009, LOV I 2009 hefte 7 (Nor.).

Papua New Guinea

Animals Act 1952, c. 329 (Papua N.G.).
Animals Regulation 1967, c. 329 (Papua N.G.).

Paraguay

Ley N° 4840 de Protección y Bienestar Animal El Congreso de la Nacion Paraguaya Sanciona con Fuerza de Ley [Law for the Protection and Well-being of Animals], Jan. 28, 2013, Gaceta Oficial [G.O.] [Official Gazette of Paraguay], No. 21, Jan. 30, 2013 (Para.).

Philippines

An Act to Promote Animal Welfare in the Philippines, otherwise known as "The Animal Welfare Act of 1998," Republic Act No. 8485 (Phil.).

Poland

Kodeks karny [Penal Code Act], June 6, 1997, Dziennik Ustaw Rzeczypospolitej Polskiej [Journal of Laws of the Republic of Poland], No. 88 Item 553 (Pol.).
O Ochronie Zwierzat [Act Regarding Animal Protection], Aug. 21, 1997, Dziennik Ustaw Rzeczypospolitej Polskiej [Journal of Laws of the Republic of Poland], No. 111 Item 724 (Pol.).

Portugal

Código Civil [Civil Code], Nov. 25, 1967, No. 47344/66, Diario do Governo Ser. 1, p. 1883 (Port.).
Protecção aos Animais [Protection of Animals Act], Sept. 12, 1995, No. 92/95, Diario do Governo Ser. 1, p. 5722 (Port.).

Puerto Rico

Animal Protection and Welfare Act, No. 154, Aug. 4, 2008, P.R. Laws Ann. tit. 5, ch. 58 (Puerto Rico).

Singapore

Animals and Birds Act, c. 7, Dec. 31, 2002 (Sing.).

Slovenia

Ustava Republike Slovenije [Constitution of the Republic of Slovenia] Dec. 23, 1999, URS-NPB9 (Slovn.).
Zakon o Zaščiti Živali [Animal Protection Act], Nov. 18, 1999, Uradni List No. 98/1999, p. 14645 (Slovn.).

Solomon Islands

Animals (Control of Experiments Act, c. 97, 13 of 1957, LN 46A of 1978, Sept. 11, 1957 (Solom. Is.).

South Africa

Animals Protection Act, No. 71 of 1962 (S. Afr.).
Protection of Businesses Act, No. 99 of 1978 (S. Afr.).

South Korea

Dongmulbohobeob [Animal Protection Law], Act. No. 8282, Jan. 26, 2007 (S. Kor.).

Sri Lanka

Prevention of Cruelty to Animals Ordinance, Cap. 573, July 10, 1907 (Sri Lanka).

Sudan

Sudan Constitution, July 6, 2005 (Sudan).
Transitional Constitution of the Government of South Sudan, 2011 (Sudan).

Sweden

Djurskyddslag [Animal Protection Act], Svensk författningssamling [SFS] 1988:534 (Swed.).

Switzerland

Bundesgesetz über die Landwirtschaft [Landwirtschaftsgesetz, LwG] [Federal Act on Agriculture], Apr. 29, 1988, SR 910.1 (Switz.).
Schweizerische Bundesverfassung [BV] [Federal Constitution of the Swiss Confederation], Apr. 18, 1999, SR 101 (Switz.).
Schweizerische Tierschutzverordnung [TSchV] [Animal Welfare Ordinance], Apr. 23, 2008, SR 455.1 (Switz.).
Schweizerisches Tierschutzgesetz [TSchG] [Animal Welfare Act], Dec. 16, 2005, SR 455 (Switz.).
Schweizerisches Zivilgesetzbuch [ZGB] [Civil Code], Dec. 10, 1907, SR 210 (Switz.).

Taiwan

動物保護法 (民國90年12月2日修正) Animal Protection Law, Nov. 4, 1998, Xianxing Fagui Huibian (Taiwan).

Tanzania

The Animal Welfare Act, No. 19 of 2008 (Tanz.).

Tonga

Pounds and Animals Act, 1988, c. 147 (Tonga).

Turkey

Hayvanlari Koruma Kanunu [Animal Protection Bill Law], June 24, 2004, No. 5199, Resmî Gazete, July 1, 2004, No. 25509 (Turk.).
Türk Ceza Kanunu [Criminal Code], Sept. 26, 2004, No. 5237, Resmî Gazete, Oct. 12, 2004, No. 25611 (Turk.).

Uganda

The Animals (Prevention of Cruelty) Act, Dec. 5, 1957, c. 220 (Uganda).

United Kingdom

An Act to Prevent the Cruel and Improper Treatment of Cattle 1822, c. 71 (U.K.).
Animal Welfare Act 2006, c. 45 (U.K.).
Antarctic Act 1994, c. 15 (U.K.).
Crime (International Co-operation) Act 2003, c. 32 (U.K.).
Football Spectators Act 1989, c. 37 (U.K.).
Offences Against the Person Act 1861, c. 100 (U.K.).
Official Secrets Act 1989, c. 6 (U.K.).
Protection of Animals Act 1911, c. 27 (U.K.).
Protection of Trading Interests Act 1980, c. 11 (U.K.).
Sexual Offences Act 2003, c. 42 (U.K.).
Terrorism Act 2000, c. 11 (U.K.).
The (Draft) Overseas Companies Regulations 2009, No. 1801 (U.K.).
The Horse Passports Regulations 2009, No. 1611 (U.K.).
Treason Act 1351, c. 2 (U.K.).

Ukraine

Pro Zakhyst Tvaryn Vid Zhorstokoho Povodzhennya [On the Protection of Animals from Cruelty], Feb. 21, 2006, No. 3447—IV (Ukr.).

United States

Alien Tort Claims Act (ATCA), 28 U.S.C. § 1340 (U.S.).

Animal Welfare Act (AWA), 7 U.S.C. § 2131 (U.S.).
Cuban Liberty and Democratic Solidarity (Libertad) Act of 1996 by the U.S. (Helms-Burton Act), 22 U.S.C. § 6021 (U.S.).
Dog and Cat Protection Act, 19 U.S.C. § 1308 (U.S.).
Endangered Species Act (ESA), 16 U.S.C. § 1531 (U.S.).
Export Administration Act of 1979, 50 U.S.C. § 2405 (U.S.).
Export-Import Bank Act, 12 U.S.C. § 635 (U.S.).
Federal Meat Inspection Act, 21 U.S.C. § 620(a) (U.S.).
Foreign Assistance Act of 1961, 22 U.S.C. § 2151 (U.S.).
Foreign Corrupt Practices Act (FCPA), 15 U.S.C. § 78dd-1 (U.S.).
Foreign Trade Antitrust Improvements Act (FTAIA), 15 U.S.C. § 6a (U.S.).
Generalized System of Preferences Renewal Act of 1996, 19 U.S.C. § 2461 (U.S.).
Humane Methods of Slaughter Act (HMSA), 7 U.S.C. § 1901 (U.S.).
Internal Revenue Code, 26 U.S.C. § 7701(a)(4) (U.S.).
Marine Mammal Protection Act (MMPA), 16 U.S.C. § 31 (U.S.).
National Environmental Policy Act (NEPA), 42 U.S.C. § 4321 (U.S.).
Regulations For Implementing the Procedural Provisions of the National Environmental Policy Act, 40 C.F.R. §1500 (U.S.).
Sarbanes-Oxley Act, 15 U.S.C. § 7201 (U.S.).
Sherman Antitrust Act, 15 U.S.C. § 1 (U.S.).
The Agriculture, Rural Development, Food and Drug Administration, and Related Agencies Appropriations Act, 2014, 128 U.S. 5, Public Law 113-76, H.R. 3547 (U.S.).
The Agriculture, Rural Development, Food and Drug Administration, and Related Agencies Appropriations Act, 2006, 119 U.S. 2120, Public Law 109-97, H.R. 2744-45 (U.S.).
Title VII Civil Rights Act, 42 U.S.C. § 2000 (U.S.).
Twenty-Eight Hour Law, 49 U.S.C. § 80502 (U.S.).
U.S. Public Law, 101-102, 16 U.S.C. § 1537 note, amending the Endangered Species Act (ESA), 16 U.S.C. § 1531 (Apr. 19, 1996) (U.S.).
Wild Bird Conservation Act, 16 U.S.C. § 4907 (U.S.).

Vanuatu

Prevention of Cruelty to Animals Act, Feb. 13, 1974, Laws of the Republic of Vanuatu Consolidated Edition 2006, ch. 78, JR 58 of 1973 (Vanuatu).

Venezuela

La Asamblea Nacional de la República Bolivariana de Venezula [Law for the Protection of Domesticated Animals and Wildlife in Captivity], Gaceta Oficial [G.O.] [Official Gazette of Venezuela], 39.338, Jan. 4, 2010 (Venez.)

Zambia

Prevention of Cruelty to Animals Act (1921), Cap. 245, Laws of Rep. of Zambia (1994) (Zam.).

Zimbabwe

Prevention of Cruelty to Animals Act, Cap. 19:09, Consolidated Version of Act No. 25 of 1960 (Zim.).

GOVERNMENTAL COMMUNICATIONS, STATEMENTS, INITIATIVES, BILLS, AND *AMICUS CURIAE* BRIEFS

Attorney General's Domestic Guidance for Handling Criminal Cases Affecting both England, Wales or Northern Ireland and the United States of America (2007), *available at* http://www.publications.parliament.uk/pa/ld200607/ldlwa/70125ws1.pdf (last visited Jan. 10, 2019).

Bill no. 54, An Act to Improve the Legal Situation of Animals, National Assembly, 1st Sess., 41st Legisl., introduced by Mr. Pierre Paradis, Minister of Agriculture, Fisheries and Food, Québec Official Publisher 2015, *available at* http://www.assnat.qc.ca/en/travaux-parlementaires/projets-loi/projet-loi-54-41-1.html (last visited Jan. 10, 2019).

Botschaft zur Revision des Tierschutzgesetzes [Federal message on the revision of the Animal Welfare Act], Dec. 9, 2002, SR 02.092 (Switz.).

Brief of the United Kingdom of Great Britain and Northern Ireland and the Kingdom of the Netherlands as Amici Curiae in Support of Petitioners, No. 03-724, Feb. 3, 2004, F. Hoffmann-La Roche v. Empagran, Ltd. 541 U.S. 155 (2004) (U.S.).

Comments of the European Community on the Amendments of 22 June 1982 to the U.S. Export Regulations (Aug. 12, 1982).

Daniel Hannan, Member of the European Parliament, Debates of May 5, 2009, Strasbourg, Explanations of Vote, Report by Diana Wallis (A6-0118/2009), *available at* http://www.europarl.europa.eu/sides/getDoc.do?pubRef=-//EP//TEXT+CRE+20090505+ITEM-006+DOC+XML+V0//FR (last visited Jan. 10, 2019).

Denmark, Germany, and the Netherlands, Joint Declaration on Animal Welfare, Dec. 14, 2014, *available at* http://www.bmel.de/SharedDocs/Downloads/EN/Agriculture/AnimalProtection/JointDeclarationAnimalWelfare.html (last visited Jan. 10, 2019).

Det Dyreetiske Råd Udtalelse om menneskers seksuelle omgang med dyr [Danish Ethical Council, Opinion on Human Sexual Intercourse with Animals] 21 (Nov. 2006), *available at* http://detdyreetiskeraad.dk/udtalelser/udtalelse/pub/hent-fil/publication/udtalelse-om-menneskers-seksuelle-omgang-med-dyr-2006/ (last visited Jan. 10, 2019).

Deutscher Bundestag, 18. Wahlperiode, Gesetzesentwurf des Bundesrates zur Änderung des Tierschutzgesetzes, Drucksache 18/6663, Nov. 11, 2015, Stellungnahme der Regierung (Ger.).

Directorate-General for External Policies, Policy Department, The Extraterritorial Effects of Legislation and Policies in the EU and US, requested by the European Parliament's Committee on Foreign Affairs (European Union 2012).

European Commission, Comments on the US Regulations Concerning Trade with the USSR, Aug. 12, 1982.

European Commission, Minutes of the Civil Society Dialogue, EU-China Trade and Investment Relations: State of Play, Feb. 13, 2014, Brussels, *available at* http://trade.ec.europa.eu/doclib/docs/2014/june/tradoc_152627.pdf (last visited Jan. 10, 2019).

F.W. Rogers Brambell, Report of the Technical Committee to Enquire into the Welfare of Animals Kept under Intensive Livestock Husbandry Systems (Her Majesty's Stationery Office, London 1965).

Guide to the Animal Welfare Act 1999, MAF Policy Information Paper No. 27, Jan. 1999 (N.Z.).

House of Commons, Environmental Audit Committee, The Export Credits Guarantee Department and Sustainable Development, Eleventh Report of Session 2007–8, Evidence 7 (The Stationery Office, London 2008).

Media Statement by the South African Law Reform Commission Governing its Investigation into Consolidated Legislation Pertaining to International Co-operation in Civil Matters (Project 121), Issued by the Secretary, Aug. 15, 2008, *available at* http://www.justice.gov.za/salrc/media/2008%2008%2018_Project121ReportFinalRelease.pdf (last visited Jan. 10, 2019).

Note from the British Government addressed to the U.S., Oct. 18, 1982, UKMIL (1982), 53 BY 337 (U.K.).

Parlamentarische Initiative 06.464 "Verbot von mittel- und schwerbelastenden Tierversuchen an Primaten," Maya Graf, Oct. 5, 2006, Bericht der Kommission für Wissenschaft, Bildung und Kultur, Apr. 19, 2007 (Switz.), *available at* http://www.lscv.ch/de/pages/tierschutz/curiavista/06.464_primaten.html (last visited Jan. 10, 2019).

Abbreviations

AB	Appellate Body
ACCC	Australian Competition and Consumer Commission
ACHR	American Convention on Human Rights
ADA	WTO Anti-Dumping Agreement
AECL	Australian Egg Corporation Limited
AFDA	Argentina Association of Professional Lawyers for Animal Rights
AIDCP	Agreement on the International Dolphin Conservation Program
ALDF	Animal Legal Defense Fund
AoA	WTO Agreement on Agriculture
APA	Animal Protection Act
API	Animal Protection Index
ARSIWA	Draft Articles on Responsibility of States for Internationally Wrongful Acts
art., arts.	article, articles
ATCA	US Alien Tort Claims Act
AWA	Animal Welfare Act
AWO	Animal Welfare Ordinance
BBFAW	Business Benchmark on Farm Animal Welfare
BCE	Before the Common Era
BIT	Bilateral investment treaty
BRIC states	Brazil, Russia, India, and China
c.	chapter
CAFO	Concentrated animal feeding operation
CBD	Convention on Biological Diversity
CCRF	UN Code of Conduct for Responsible Fisheries
CCTV	Closed circuit television
CEO	Chief executive officer
CETA	Comprehensive Economic and Trade Agreement
cf.	compare

CFI	Court of First Instance
CHF	Swiss francs
CISA	Convention Implementing the Schengen Agreement
CITES	Convention on International Trade in Endangered Species of Wild Fauna and Flora
CIWF	Compassion in World Farming
CMS	Conservation of Migratory Species of Wild Animals
cmt.	comment
CNMC	Spanish National Commission of Markets and Competition
CO_2	Carbon dioxide
COA	WTO Committee on Agriculture
CoE	Council of Europe
CSR	Corporate social responsibility
dBA	A-rated decibel
DEFRA	UK Department for Environment, Food and Rural Affairs
DOJ	US Department of Justice
DSB	WTO Dispute Settlement Body
ECHR	European Convention on Human Rights
ECJ	European Court of Justice
ECtHR	European Court of Human Rights
ed.	edition or editor
eds.	editors
EEC	European Economic Community
EEP	European Endangered Species Programme
EFSA	European Food Safety Authority
EFTA	European Free Trade Association
e.g.	*exempli gratia*
EIA	Environmental impact assessment
EMAS	Eco-management and Audit Scheme
ESA	US Endangered Species Act
ESG	Environmental, social, and governance
et al.	*et alii, et aliae*, or *et alia*
et seq.	*et sequens* or *et sequentia*
etc.	*et cetera*
EU	European Union
EUR	Euro
ff.	following pages
FAIRR	Farm Animal Investment Risk & Return
FAO	UN Food and Agriculture Organization
FAOSTAT	UN Food and Agriculture Organization Corporate Statistical Database
FAWC	UK Farm Animal Welfare Council
FDI	Foreign direct investment
FTA	Free trade agreement
FTAIA	US Foreign Trade Antitrust Improvements Act
FTSE	Financial Times Stock Exchange

GATS	WTO General Agreement on Trade in Services
GATT	WTO General Agreement on Tariffs and Trade
GC	UN Global Compact
GRI	Global Reporting Initiative
GSP	Generalized System of Preferences
HMSA	US Humane Methods of Slaughter Act
HRK	Croatian kuna
HS	Harmonized System
HSI	Humane Society International
HSUS	Humane Society of the US
IACHR	Inter-American Convention on Human Rights
IACtHR	Inter-American Court of Human Rights
IACUC	Institutional Animal Care and Use Committee
IAS	International Accounting Standards
IBA	International Bar Association
ICC	International Criminal Court
ICCPR	International Covenant on Civil and Political Rights
ICESCR	International Covenant on Economic, Social and Cultural Rights
ICJ	International Court of Justice
ICPA	International Convention for the Protection of Animals
ICRW	International Convention for the Regulation of Whaling
ICSID	International Center for Settlement of Investment Disputes
ICTR	International Criminal Tribunal for Rwanda
ICTY	International Criminal Tribunal for the former Yugoslavia
IDCP	International Dolphin Conservation Program
i.e.	*id est*
IFAW	International Fund for Animal Welfare
IFC	International Finance Corporation
IFRS	International Financial Reporting Standards
ILA	International Law Association
ILC	International Law Commission
ILO	International Labor Organization
IO	International organization
IOC	International Olympic Committee
ISO	International Organization for Standardization
ITLOS	International Tribunal for the Law of the Sea
IWC	International Whaling Commission
JAES	Joint Africa-EU Strategy
kg	kilogram
lit.	*litera*
m^2	square meter
MIGA	Multilateral Investment Guarantee Agency
MLAT	Mutual legal assistance treaty
MMPA	US Marine Mammal Protection Act
MNE	Multinational enterprise

MPEPIL	Max Planck Encyclopedia for Public International Law
n.	note
NAFTA	North American Free Trade Agreement
NCC	UK National Consumer Council
NEPA	US National Environmental Policy Act
NFACC	Canadian National Farm Animal Care Council
NGO	Nongovernmental organization
NhRP	Nonhuman Rights Project
NPR-PPM	Non-product-related process and production method
NY	New York
NZD	New Zealand dollar
OECD	Organization for Economic Co-operation and Development
OIE	World Organization for Animal Health
p., pp.	page, pages
para., paras.	paragraph, paragraphs
PBA	South African Protection of Business Act
PCIJ	Permanent Court of International Justice
PETA	People for the Ethical Treatment of Animals
PPM	Process and production method
SEA	Single European Act
SME	Small and medium-sized enterprise
SOX	US Sarbanes-Oxley Act
SPS	WTO Agreement on the Application of Sanitary and Phytosanitary Measures
SRSG	Special Representative of the Secretary-General to the UN
TBT	WTO Agreement on Technical Barriers to Trade
TEU	Treaty on European Union
TFEU	Treaty on the Functioning of the European Union
TPP	Trans-Pacific Partnership
TRIPS	Agreement on Trade-Related Aspects of Intellectual Property Rights
TTIP	Transatlantic Trade and Investment Partnership
UDAW	Universal Declaration on Animal Welfare
UDHR	Universal Declaration of Human Rights
UN	United Nations
UNCLOS	UN Convention on the Law of the Sea
UNCTAD	UN Conference on Trade and Development
UNECE	UN Economic Commission for Europe
UNEP	UN Environmental Program
USD	US dollar
USDA	US Department of Agriculture
USEF	US Equestrian Federation
USSR	Union of Soviet Socialist Republics, or Soviet Union
v./vs.	versus
VACI	Voiceless Animal Cruelty Index
VCCR	Vienna Convention on Consular Relations
VCLT	Vienna Convention on the Law of Treaties

vol.	volume
WAP	World Animal Protection
WHO	World Health Organization
WSPA	World Society for the Protection of Animals
WQP	Welfare Quality Project
WTO	World Trade Organization
WWF	World Wildlife Fund
ZAR	South African dollar

Introduction: Protecting Animals in an Age of Globalization

UNDER INTERNATIONAL LAW, states have a duty to protect their people and anyone within their jurisdiction from human rights violations. The state duty to protect "lies at the very core of the international human rights regime."[1] But does a home state's responsibility to protect human rights extend beyond its territory? The international community disagrees on the answer to this question. Some scholars argue extending rights beyond a state's territory opens the door to neocolonialist laws and interventions that are not only unhelpful, but even counterproductive to global justice. Others contend there is an urgent need to acknowledge the many ways human rights abroad are thwarted by home states and to hold those states responsible.[2] Regardless of which conclusion the international community reaches, these

[1] U.N. Human Rights Council, 8th Sess., Special Representative of the Secretary-General John Ruggie, Protect, Respect and Remedy: A Framework for Business and Human Rights, U.N. Doc. A/HRC/8/5, para. 9 (Apr. 7, 2008) [*Protect, Respect and Remedy Framework*].

[2] *See further* KAREN DA COSTA, THE EXTRATERRITORIAL APPLICATION OF SELECTED HUMAN RIGHTS TREATIES (2013); OLIVIER DE SCHUTTER, EXTRATERRITORIAL JURISDICTION AS A TOOL FOR IMPROVING THE HUMAN RIGHTS ACCOUNTABILITY OF TRANSNATIONAL CORPORATIONS (Business and Human Rights Resource Center 2006); MARKO MILANOVIC, EXTRATERRITORIAL APPLICATION OF HUMAN RIGHTS TREATIES: LAW, PRINCIPLES, AND POLICY (2011); MALCOLM LANGFORD ET AL. EDS., GLOBAL JUSTICE, STATE DUTIES (2013); Robert McCorquodale & Penelope Simons, *Responsibility Beyond Borders: State Responsibility for Extraterritorial Violations by Corporations of International Human Rights Law*, 70 MOD. L. REV. 598 (2007); ESCR-NET, GLOBAL ECONOMY, GLOBAL RIGHTS, A PRACTITIONER'S GUIDE FOR INTERPRETING HUMAN RIGHTS OBLIGATIONS IN THE GLOBAL ECONOMY (2014); JENNIFER A. ZERK, EXTRATERRITORIAL JURISDICTION: LESSONS FOR THE BUSINESS AND HUMAN RIGHTS SPHERE

questions, which lie at the heart of contemporary debates in international law, make it difficult to deny that many people now expect states to act responsibly toward individuals and communities situated on foreign soil.

Advocating at this day and age for the protection of animals abroad, by contrast, seems to lie outside the realm of the possible. The way we treat animals is regarded as a domestic matter, subject to each state's own judgment, and dependent on social attitudes that vary greatly across states and cultures. We also lack a clear commitment by the international community to protect animals,[3] something we cannot say about human rights, considering their proliferation after World War II and the adoption of various human rights treaties like the Universal Declaration of Human Rights (UDHR).[4] One could argue that despite the absence of a written agreement or declaration, we must take into account the fact that most states have a common conception of behavior respecting animals and of acts committed against animals they deem despicable. In the abstract, this seems to be true, but states differ greatly in their decisions about which animals are worthy of protection and which can be legitimately exploited. These different views have often not been respected or treated as equal before the law. To date, animal law has been appropriated and used to oppress minorities, whether by prohibiting kosher and halal slaughter, live animal markets, horse-tripping, cock-fighting, indigenous hunts, or other practices that do not conform to the hegemonic Western ideal of how animals are "properly used and killed."[5] These contemporary and historical circumstances suggest that protecting animals across the border risks exacerbating existing sociocultural tensions and multiplying their potential to cause conflict across the border.

Yet, declaring extraterritorial jurisdiction a dead end for animal law carries its own risks. Over the last decades, human-animal relationships have become increasingly internationalized. The volume of trade in animals and animal products has exploded, foreign direct investment has been spurring the activity of multinational corporations around the globe, and animal production chains are now dispersed over the territories of many states.[6]

FROM SIX REGULATORY AREAS (Corporate Social Responsibility Initiative Working Paper No. 59, Harvard University 2010).

[3] On the international level, there is no treaty in force that expresses a uniform commitment of states to recognize animal sentience, prohibit cruelty toward animals, prevent suffering, demand humane treatment, lay down robust rights for animals, or the like. This gap is also noted by Peggy Cunniff & Marcia Kramer, *Developments in Animal Law, in* THE GLOBAL GUIDE TO ANIMAL PROTECTION 230 (Andrew Linzey ed., 2013); David Favre, *An International Treaty for Animal Welfare, in* ANIMAL LAW AND WELFARE: INTERNATIONAL PERSPECTIVES 87, 92 (Deborah Cao & Steven White eds., 2016); Anne Peters, *Global Animal Law: What It Is and Why We Need It*, 5 TEL 9, 13 (2016).

[4] G.A. Res. 217 A (III), U.N. GAOR 3rd Sess., Universal Declaration of Human Rights, U.N. Doc. A/RES/810 (Dec. 10, 1948) [UDHR].

[5] For critical analyses, *see, e.g.*, Maneesha Deckha, *Animal Justice, Cultural Justice: A Posthumanist Response to Cultural Rights in Animals*, 2 J. ANIMAL L. & ETHICS 189 (2007); CLAIRE JEAN KIM, DANGEROUS CROSSINGS: RACE, SPECIES, AND NATURE IN A MULTICULTURAL AGE 4 (2015); Will Kymlicka & Sue Donaldson, *Animal Rights, Multiculturalism, and the Left*, 45(1) J. SOC. PHIL. 116, 126 (2014).

[6] For example, between 1986 and 2016, trade in eggs, meat, and dairy increased threefold. In this period, the increase in "fresh" products (excluding frozen, condensed, evaporated, prepared, or dried products) was astonishing: egg trade increased from 748,241 to 2,107,373 tons, meat trade increased from 17,814,372 to 71,877,429 tons, and trade in milk increased from 6,266,492 to 18,587,86 tons: FAOSTAT (search criteria

A vast complex of multibillion dollar industries uses animals in sectors including agriculture, research, breeding, and trade in companion animals, creating a dense web of cross-border economic relationships in breeding, cage systems, feed, veterinary practices, technologies, slaughter, packaging, and distribution. The global entanglement of activities that touch on animals has created a situation in which jurisdictional connections can rarely be traced to a single state. In most cases, multiple states share an interest in regulating the very same state of facts when it comes to producing and protecting animals, as evidenced by common newspaper headlines like, "U.N. Court Orders Japan to Halt Whaling,"[7] "Indian Border Guards Deployed to Stop Cattle Crossing into Bangladesh,"[8] "Europe Strengthens Ban on Seal Products after WTO Challenge,"[9] "EU Court: Animal Welfare Rules Apply to Animals Leaving EU,"[10] "After Cecil Furor, U.S. Aims to Protect Lions Through Endangered Species Act,"[11] "Death at Sea of 4,200 Australian Sheep Prompts New Call for Live Export Bans,"[12] "UK and India Call on China to Ban Tiger Farms,"[13] or "MEP Call on Bulgarian PM to Ban Stray Dog Euthanasia."[14]

These factual and economic entanglements have not made protecting animals an easier task for states, whether the animals they seek to regulate are within or outside their territory. On the contrary, the dense web of socioeconomic activity has accentuated regulatory disparities and led states to compete with each other to attract and retain manufacturers and investors by lowering rather than increasing the protection of animals.[15] In this competition, the state with the lowest standard "wins," and ends up defining the global level of animal protection that will ultimately prevail. The competition in laxity, also known as the race to the bottom, is a common phenomenon in labor law, environmental protection, and human rights law.[16] Regulatory economists have not yet weighed in on whether competition in laxity exists in animal law, but there are strong indicators for this economic downward spiral.[17] If the predictions about the trajectory of competition in animal law are true, this will have serious consequences for the regulatory authority of states within their own territory,

---

"Eggs"+"Milk"+"Meat"+"Export Quantity"+"World"+"1986, 2016"), *available at* http://faostat.fao.org/ (last visited Jan. 10, 2019).

[7] Hiroko Tabuchi & Marlise Simons, *U.N. Court Orders Japan to Halt Whaling*, N.Y. Times, Mar. 31, 2014.

[8] David Millward, *Indian Border Guards Deployed to Stop Cattle Crossing into Bangladesh*, The Telegraph, July 4, 2015.

[9] Arthur Neslen, *Europe Strengthens Ban on Seal Products after WTO Challenge*, The Guardian, Sept. 8, 2015.

[10] Charles Siebert, *EU Court: Animal Welfare Rules Apply to Animals Leaving EU*, BBC News, Apr. 23, 2015.

[11] Erica Goode, *After Cecil Furor, U.S. Aims to Protect Lions Through Endangered Species Act*, N.Y. Times, Dec. 20, 2015.

[12] Daniel Hurst, *Death at Sea of 4,200 Australian Sheep Prompts New Call for Live Export Bans*, The Guardian, Jan. 17, 2014.

[13] Gaia Vince, *UK and India Call on China to Ban Tiger Farms*, The Guardian, July 26, 2012.

[14] *MEP Call on Bulgarian PM to Ban Stray Dog Euthanasia*, Novinite, May 20, 2012.

[15] Deregulation is only one of four factors that can account for competition in laxity: Dale D. Murphy, The Structure of Regulatory Competition: Corporations and Public Policies in a Global Economy 7 (2004).

[16] Mathias Koenig-Archibugi, *Global Regulation*, *in* The Oxford Handbook of Regulation 407, 414 (Robert Baldwin et al. eds., 2010).

[17] The existence of competition in laxity in animal law is studied in detail in Chapter 2, §3.

undermining their efforts to enact or uphold laws that protect domestic animals. In response to an actual or perceived loss of regulatory power, states committed to protecting animals will be more inclined to use the tools of extraterritorial jurisdiction to undercut competition in laxity in animal law, secure their levels of animal protection, and prevent corporations from forcing them to lax their laws.[18]

States express their interests in applying animal law extraterritorially mainly in response to public sensitivities to animals, rather than from a sense of legal duty owed to animals. When agricultural businesses systematically outsource or laboratory units move their operations abroad in response to stricter animal protection laws, this has and will likely continue to provoke moral outrage among the public.[19] The 2016 Eurobarometer shows that 97 percent of EU citizens today believe that the European Union should do more to raise awareness for animals internationally.[20] Because we are witnessing the "globalization of animal cruelty,"[21] citizens and governments are now concerned with the status and well-being of animals beyond their borders.[22] It is exactly this tension between public demand for better laws for animals and governmental concerns about outsourcing that has brought jurisdictional issues to the forefront of the discussion in animal law.

International law *prima facie* seems to acknowledge and be responsive to these concerns. The *Shrimp/Turtle* case[23] litigated at the World Trade Organization (WTO) in the 1990s made clear that what one state does or permits to be done within its territory can be "of legitimate interest in another state, however distant."[24] In the 2014 *Seals* case, the WTO acknowledged that the concerns of citizens from one state for the well-being of animals located in the territory of another are worthy of legal protection.[25] In the same year, the International Court of Justice (ICJ) led by example in the *Whaling in the Antarctic* case, demonstrating that international obligations in matters of animal law are adjudged with vigor equivalent to that of any other international obligation.[26] This bloom of interest in fields that touch

---

[18] Barbara Gabor, Regulatory Competition in the Internal Market: Comparing Models of Corporate Law, Securities Law and Competition Law 3 (2013).

[19] *E.g.*, Jill Laster, *Plan to Breed Lab Monkey Splits Puerto Rican Town*, U.S. News & World Report, Nov. 30, 2009.

[20] European Commission, Special Eurobarometer 442 Report: Attitudes of Europeans towards Animal Welfare 11 (2016).

[21] Steven White & Deborah Cao, *Introduction: Animal Protection in an Interconnected World*, *in* Animal Law and Welfare: International Perspectives 1, 2 (2016).

[22] Miyun Park & Peter Singer, *The Globalization of Animal Welfare: More Food Does Not Require More Suffering*, 91 Foreign Aff. 122 (2012).

[23] Appellate Body Report, *US—Import Prohibition of Certain Shrimp and Shrimp Products*, WTO Doc. WT/DS58/AB/R (adopted Nov. 6, 1998) [*Shrimp/Turtle I*, AB Report].

[24] Philippe Sands, *Turtles and Torturers: The Transformation of International Law*, 33 N.Y.U. J. Int'l L. & Pol. 527, 537 ff. (2000).

[25] Panel Report, *EC—Measures Prohibiting the Importation and Marketing of Seal Products*, WTO Doc. WT/DS400/R, WT/DS401/R (adopted June 18, 2014) [*Seals*, Panel Report]. Affirmed in Appellate Body in Appellate Body Report, *EC—Measures Prohibiting the Importation and Marketing of Seal Products*, WTO Doc. WT/DS400/AB/R, WT/DS401/AB/R (adopted June 18, 2014) [*Seals*, AB Report].

[26] Whaling in the Antarctic (Austl. v. Japan: N.Z. Intervening), Judgment, 2014 I.C.J. Rep. 2014 (Mar. 31) [Whaling in the Antarctic, 2014 I.C.J.]. The International Whaling Commission (IWC), though originally commissioned to ensure a stable stock of whales for continuous hunting, is now considering the welfare of whales in fringe meetings and subgroup meetings: David Broom, *International Animal Welfare Perspectives, Including Whaling and Inhumane Seal Killing as a W.T.O. Public Morality Issue*, *in* Animal Law and

on the lives of animals may quickly expand to an unexpected magnitude, including, for example, the entire agricultural sector. In an era of ever-increasing international disputes over jurisdictional competence, when public concerns about animals and their intrinsic needs, desires, and interests have become an issue in world courts and tribunals, animal law solicits our attention from the broader perspective of extraterritorial jurisdiction.

Although animal law has been growing quickly as a field,[27] and has taken notice of the many cross-border issues that challenge the core of its achievements, the literature has insufficiently responded to these developments. In the fields of criminal, human rights, environmental, labor, antitrust, securities, and banking law, it is settled that states share an interest in applying national standards extraterritorially and that doing so can be legal under international law.[28] But in animal matters, scholars have not yet addressed, much less answered the question of whether cross-border concerns for animals deserve legal protection under international law, notably through extraterritorial jurisdiction. This book takes a broad and inclusive approach to close the most pressing research gaps that unfold at this juncture. I offer a novel and systematic method to define extraterritorial jurisdiction, elucidate the circumstances under which resorting to extraterritorial jurisdiction is justified, and explain how states can succeed at using their jurisdictional powers to protect animals within and across borders without endangering international relations or oppressing minority groups.

Chapter 1 responds to fact that law of jurisdiction is one of the most misunderstood areas of international law, because its rules are derived from the customary practice of states and have rarely been studied and defined *in abstracto*. The chapter illuminates and clarifies the concept of jurisdiction and its complex relation to extraterritoriality. I begin by explaining the historical and conceptual reasons that led to a recomposition of jurisdictional space on the international level. I then sketch an analytical framework and provide legal evidence that adds nuance and background, creating a comprehensive legal framework that enables us to categorize jurisdictional norms into different, objective elements: their anchor point, their regulated content, and their ancillary effects. To this, I add geographical factors, which help to determine if a matter is territorial, indirect extraterritorial, or direct extraterritorial. Territorial jurisdiction regulates domestic affairs, direct extraterritorial jurisdiction regulates a state of facts abroad, and indirect extraterritorial laws have ancillary effects on foreign territory.[29] The framework enables us to

---

WELFARE: INTERNATIONAL PERSPECTIVES 45, 55 (2016). In December 2018, Yoshihide Suga, Japan's chief cabinet secretary, announced that the country will leave the IWC, after the organization put in place a global ban on all commercial whaling: Daniel Victor, *Japan to Resume Commercial Whaling, Defying International Ban*, N.Y. TIMES, Dec. 26, 2018.

[27] Animal law is taught at nine universities in Australia, seven universities in Canada, one university in China, two universities in Israel, three universities in New Zealand, one university in Spain, six universities in the United Kingdom, and 167 law schools in the United States: Animal Legal Defense Fund, Animal Law Courses, *available at* http://aldf.org/animal-law-courses/ (last visited Jan. 10, 2019).

[28] *See* for a general overview, CEDRIC RYNGAERT, JURISDICTION IN INTERNATIONAL LAW (2d ed. 2015); Joanne Scott, *Extraterritoriality and Territorial Extension in EU Law*, 62 AJCL 87 (2014); ZERK, EXTRATERRITORIAL JURISDICTION (2010).

[29] This third type is sometimes also called intraterritorial regulation with extraterritorial effect: WERNER MENG, EXTRATERRITORIALE JURISDIKTION IM ÖFFENTLICHEN WIRTSCHAFTSRECHT 11 (1994); ANNE PETERS, VÖLKERRECHT ALLGEMEINER TEIL 148–9 (4th ed. 2016).

take a more systematic approach to extraterritorial jurisdiction because it unravels the competing jurisdictional interests of states and decelerates their reciprocal accusations of transgressing each other's sovereignty. I next apply the framework to animal law, making plain how animal law challenges the *moda operandi* of the law of jurisdiction and how states could *prima facie* devise their laws to protect animals abroad. Because the law of jurisdiction can be rather technical, I use four case groups to make the topic more approachable. The case groups represent the breadth of the issues that currently preoccupy international relations, including the exploitation of weak animal laws abroad by corporations (e.g., by outsourcing production), the question of trade liberalization and trade restrictions, animal migration, and the exploitation of weak standards abroad by individuals (e.g., through trophy hunting or bestiality).

Scholars frequently raise the concern that applying animal law across the border can be an illegitimate way to influence the organization of other states, which amounts to a paradigmatic form of neocolonialism. Chapter 2 responds to these concerns by positing the extraterritorial protection of animals as an increasingly accepted practice in international law. Extraterritorial jurisdiction traditionally prevails in fields of law that regulate economic matters, like antitrust, stock exchange, and securities law, because global entanglement of finances and assets warrant transborder regulation. Extraterritorial jurisdiction also dominates the criminal law discourse, to the extent that states share a core concern about and condemnation of the most repulsive crimes. I examine whether the rationale of economic entanglement and the rationale of a common consensus also exist in animal law and if states have a shared interest in using their laws to protect animals more effectively across borders. If both conditions are met, there is a good chance that cross-border animal laws will proliferate in the future and will increasingly be regarded as legitimate by the international community.

Chapters 3 to 7 explore the options states have under international law to apply their laws to animals in foreign countries. Chapters 3 and 4 study indirect options for protecting animals under the laws of the WTO. Academic contributions at the intersection of trade law and animal law have significantly proliferated after the Appellate Body's (AB) report in the 2014 *Seals* case,[30] but they tend to settle for examining the general conflict between trade liberalization and animal law. Chapter 3 advances the discussion and fills a gap in legal scholarship by examining whether and how states can use trade law to indirectly protect animals abroad through, for instance, import prohibitions, taxes and tariffs, or labels. I ask if trade-restrictive measures that indirectly protect foreign animals are legal under the General Agreement on Tariffs and Trade (GATT),[31] and then turn to justifications for potential violations of the agreement. In Chapter 4, I examine the extraterritorial reach of agreements typically neglected in the literature on animals in trade law, namely, of the Agreement on Technical Barriers to Trade (TBT),[32] the Agreement on the Application of Sanitary and

[30] *See supra* note 25.

[31] General Agreement on Tariffs and Trade, Apr. 15, 1994, 1867 U.N.T.S. 187 [GATT].

[32] Agreement on Technical Barriers to Trade, Apr. 15, 1994, 1868 U.N.T.S. 120 [TBT].

Phytosanitary Measures (SPS),[33] the Anti-Dumping Agreement (ADA),[34] the Agreement on Agriculture (AoA),[35] and the Special Treatment Clause.[36] As case reports show, these agreements increasingly play a role in litigation, so studying them gives us a more comprehensive picture of indirect extraterritoriality, particularly as regards labels, standards, measures aimed at eliminating food- and pest-borne risks, dumping, and special treatment for majority world countries.

Chapter 5 answers a question that scholars have not asked before: Can jurisdictional principles under general international law be used to *directly* protect animals abroad? In this *lex lata* analysis, I explore how and to what extent states can invoke the general territoriality principle, the subjective and objective territoriality principles, the personality principle, and the protective principle in the realm of animal law. These analyses grapple with several problematic issues like cross-border offenses (e.g., violation of transportation standards or cross-border duties of care), prescribing behavior of nationals abroad (including multinational enterprises), and practices of foreign agricultural industries that significantly pollute the environment across borders.

In addition to indirect and direct extraterritorial jurisdiction, states can use a broader form of extraterritorial jurisdiction to protect animals across borders, which I call "extended extraterritorial jurisdiction." These subtler forms of extraterritorial regulation are fully established in human rights law and comprise foreign policy rules, investment agreements, jurisdiction assigned to international bodies, and forms of self-regulation by private actors. Chapter 6 explores the use of these instruments for states that want to protect animals abroad, and focuses on investment rules, export credit standards, bilateral investment treaties, bilateral free trade agreements, impact assessments, reporting, corporate social responsibility, codes of conduct, and the Guidelines on Multinational Enterprises, issued by the Organization for Economic Co-operation and Development (OECD).[37]

Because extraterritorial animal law is novel and challenges the standard operability of the law of jurisdiction, Chapter 7 develops a set of *lex ferenda* options for states to protect animals more effectively across the border. Taking a critical positivist approach, I argue that animals ought to have functional nationality, like ships and corporations, that establishes a jurisdictional link to their home state. By treating animals as nationals, the home state has the power to use the passive personality principle to broadly protect them abroad. I then turn to whether the universality principle can be used to prohibit the most egregious crimes against animals, wherever they are committed and by whomever. This principle may allow states to extend their laws to, for instance, animals trafficked and exposed to organized crime that escapes the jurisdiction of all states (such as illegal wildlife trafficking). I also analyze current

---

[33] Agreement on the Application of Sanitary and Phytosanitary Measures, Apr. 15, 1994, 1867 U.N.T.S. 493 [SPS].

[34] Agreement on Implementation of Article VI of the General Agreement on Tariffs and Trade 1994, Apr. 15, 1994, 1868 U.N.T.S. 201 [Anti-Dumping Agreement, ADA].

[35] Agreement on Agriculture, Apr. 15, 1994, 1867 U.N.T.S. 410 [AoA].

[36] WTO, Differential and More Favourable Treatment, Reciprocity and Fuller Participation of Developing Countries, Decision of 28 November 1979, L/4903, Dec. 3, 1979.

[37] ORGANIZATION FOR ECONOMIC CO-OPERATION AND DEVELOPMENT (OECD), GUIDELINES FOR MULTINATIONAL ENTERPRISES, CONCEPTS AND PRINCIPLES (OECD Publishing, Paris 2011).

arguments for a noneconomic version of the effects principle that justifies the use of extraterritorial laws to prevent or penalize actions that damage a state's reputation.

Next, I offer an overarching analysis of options available to protect animals across the border within the extraterritoriality framework. Using this broader perspective, I can begin to describe trends in the law of jurisdiction, including the types of jurisdiction the international community is most likely to accept. I return to the four case groups and introduce them to the extraterritoriality framework, demonstrating how states could manifest their jurisdiction in these cases, which helps us test and adapt the results obtained earlier.

A study of extraterritorial jurisdiction in animal law may comfortably stop at this point, as do most legal inquiries after they mapped states' options under the law of jurisdiction. But in animal law, states lack guidance on how to meaningfully connect this young but growing field to their jurisdictional powers. Chapters 8 to 10 describe the contours of this connection. A central question Chapter 8 raises and answers whether states can use extraterritorial jurisdiction only to protect animals abroad, or whether they can also rely on this concept to lower animal laws, for example, as a side effect to lucrative trade deals. I analyze the moral direction of extraterritorial animal laws from three perspectives: general international law (including considerations of global justice and the precautionary principle), trade law, and animal law. All three perspectives converge on the idea that states cannot apply animal norms extraterritorially if these laws are detrimental to animals.

Since these results do not tell us how consistently states must protect animals, I turn to this question next. I establish a hierarchy of presumptions to guide public authorities and help them decide which animal laws meet the basic parameters of beneficence and consistency. The hierarchy includes presumptions in favor of transparency in animal law, recognizing animal interests, integrating animal interests, detailed standards, adequately balancing interests, prohibitions, and animal rights. I then explore whether we can look to human rights law for guidance on the content of extraterritorial animal law, in particular by drawing on the United Nations' (UN) "Protect, Respect and Remedy" framework.[38] The framework promises to shed light on the questions of whether states have a duty to protect animals across the border, and whether corporations operating abroad are bound to respect the interests of animals.

In focusing on the content of extraterritorial animal law, another set of critical questions must be answered. Chapter 9 asks if all criminal, administrative, and civil standards can be employed extraterritorially, and compares the benefits of applying each of them across the border. I illustrate the benefits of constitutional animal law, including constitutional state objectives to protect animals, constitutional rights and prohibitions, and duties of compassion. I also demonstrate the benefits we can anticipate by using criminal animal law (including advanced rules on corporate liability) and administrative animal law (including standards on keeping, transporting, and slaughtering) to protect animals across borders. I end with exemplary models and achievements that could guide the law of jurisdiction in the future.

Since the belief that it is valuable and necessary to protect animals across the border does not answer the legality of extraterritorial animal law under international law, I tackle

---

[38] *See* the *Protect, Respect and Remedy Framework*.

the issue of legality in Chapter 10. I describe the types of jurisdictional conflicts that could emerge in animal law and explain the strategies states can use to unilaterally manage, prevent, and mitigate them, by respecting the principle of the rule of law, the prohibition of double jeopardy, and the principle of reasonableness. When the jurisdictional interests of two or more states in protecting animals abroad conflict, I offer guidance to help resolve conflicts by means of the principle of comity and bilateral or multilateral negotiations. Another central task of Chapter 10 is to describe the circumstances in which states prescribing law across the border violate international law and the consequences of their breach. I approach this delicate topic by analyzing the scope of the principles of sovereign equality, nonintervention, territorial integrity, and self-determination of peoples. Gaining knowledge about these limits is essential for states to assess the legal risks involved in passing extraterritorial animal laws. But are those legal limits strong enough to ensure animal laws are not applied in an imperialist manner across the border or targeting ethnic and cultural minorities? My analysis suggests that existing limits are not sufficient to remove concerns about neocolonialism and new forms of discrimination. Given these dangers, and because there is a strong need for the law of jurisdiction to grow beyond its tainted *renomée*, I discuss useful precautions advanced by scholars who specialize in posthuman and postcolonialist studies.

The broader limits of the law of jurisdiction drawn in this chapter are picked up in more detail in Chapter 11. I here return to the structural challenges of animal law in an era of globalization and multiculturalism and take a broader, multidisciplinary approach to determine whether extraterritorial jurisdiction can help tackle them. Though many challenges exist, I here focus on three obstacles that deserve our full attention. First, I turn to whether the law of jurisdiction truly has the potential to bolster domestic efforts to protect animals, or whether it simply creates confusion and chaos. Second, I ask if there are benefits to using laws to protect animals across the border when states' laws are only marginally better than those of their neighboring states. This brings me to the third concern, namely, the social and societal risks (as opposed to legal risks) we take when adopting this strategy, in particular the risk of exacerbating power hierarchies and sweeping forms of oppression associated with them. These concerns pose a real challenge to the law of jurisdiction and demand that we do not blindly advocate the blanket use of the extraterritorial jurisdiction. At the same time, we cannot afford to ignore the need to protect animals across the border, as this would succumb them to economic laissez-faire. I end by offering ideas about complementary measures we must take to ensure extraterritorial animal law will fill regulatory gaps, and discuss how animal law must change before it can be usefully and meaningfully applied across borders. In the last section, I show how extraterritorial animal law can break away from its aversion to multiculturalism and become a conduit for cross-cultural sensibility, by raising awareness of shared histories and offering opposition to oppression.

Throughout the book, I use the international law method to identify, analyze, and interpret sources of international law, based on article 38 of the Statute of the International Court of Justice (ICJ Statute) (international conventions, customary international law, and general principles of law recognized by nations).[39] The principal source used to determine extraterritorial jurisdiction in animal matters would ideally be international treaty law, but so far,

[39] Statute of the International Court of Justice, June 26, 1945, 33 U.N.T.S. 993 [ICJ Statute].

states have neither concluded a treaty on this particular subject (jurisdiction over animals involving cross-border relations), nor have they established an international convention on prescriptive jurisdiction in general. Trade law is by and large the only realm in which treaties have been concluded, and these will inform my analysis of jurisdiction to indirectly protect animals. As my focus lies on developing direct means to protect animals more effectively at home and abroad, the main source I use throughout this book are norms of customary international law pursuant to article 38 para. I lit. b of the ICJ Statute. Determining if a norm is sufficiently practiced and accepted as law among states to constitute a binding international custom can be difficult because we must examine and interpret a whole range of administrative acts, domestic legislation (including constitutions, statutes, regulations, communications, and case law), and unilateral state acts.[40] General principles of international law serve as a complementary means to determine the applicable law (article 38 para. I lit. c ICJ Statute). These principles constitute wide-ranging, unwritten municipal norms that states can transpose to the international level.[41] Judicial decisions (including precedents, arbitral tribunal decisions, and international decisions) and scholarly works, pursuant to article 38 para. I lit. d of the ICJ Statute, are the secondary means by which I determine international norms. Among these are also authoritative statements like the Restatement of the United States,[42] guidelines of respected international organizations like the UN,[43] and representative codes of conduct by multinational enterprises. I use hermeneutic methods based on articles 31 and 32 of the Vienna Convention on the Law of Treaties (VCLT) to interpret international norms.[44] When interpreting principles, I rely on a doctrinal and systematic analysis of international law. And when I identify animal laws and analyze them in a comparative way, I use a functional comparative method that identifies relevant similarities and differences between jurisdictions.[45]

---

[40] States' stance toward the topic is expressed through physical and verbal acts of their legislative, judicial, and executive organs: INTERNATIONAL BAR ASSOCIATION (IBA), REPORT OF THE TASK FORCE ON EXTRATERRITORIAL JURISDICTION 18 (IBA, London 2009).

[41] Alain Pellet, *Art. 38, in* THE STATUTE OF THE INTERNATIONAL COURT OF JUSTICE 731, 741 ff. (Andreas Zimmermann et al. eds., 2d ed. 2012).

[42] American Law Institute, Restatement (Fourth) of the Foreign Relations Law of the United States (2018) [U.S. Restatement (Fourth) of the Foreign Relations Law].

[43] *E.g.*, U.N. Human Rights Council, 17th Sess., Special Representative of the Secretary-General John Ruggie, Guiding Principles on Business and Human Rights: Implementing the United Nations "Protect, Respect and Remedy" Framework, U.N. Doc. A/HRC/17/31 (Mar. 21, 2011) [*Guiding Principles on Business and Human Rights*]; OECD, GUIDELINES FOR MULTINATIONAL ENTERPRISES (2011).

[44] Vienna Convention on the Law of Treaties, May 23, 1969, 1155 U.N.T.S. 331, arts. 31 and 32 [VCLT].

[45] This method is primarily used and discussed in Chapter 9.

1 Mapping the Territory of Animal Law

§1 Cornerstones of Jurisdiction

The law of jurisdiction is a topic that is becoming increasingly important in international law, at a time when trade, commerce, finance, and their spillover effects are ever more entangled. Sorting out which state is competent to regulate an entangled matter brings order into chaos, it connects threads that are currently in disarray, and helps to resolve disputes that arise at this interface. But the concept of jurisdiction is not a simple one. What it is, how it can be used, and who defines it are all questions that defy succinct summation. This chapter aims to shed light on these foundational questions and bring to the fore the historical and conceptual factors that have led states to redistribute jurisdictional space. I then define and unpack the terms and concepts of territoriality and extraterritoriality. To do so, I develop a comprehensive extraterritoriality framework that categorizes jurisdictional norms by splitting them into different structural elements: anchor points, content regulation, and ancillary effects. These tools will help unravel complex cross-border relationships and determine the roles animals play in them. To demonstrate the feasibility of the framework, I develop four case groups that each highlight a key area: corporate exploitation of low animal protection standards abroad (i.e., outsourcing), trade in animals and animal products, animal migration, and exploitation of weak animal laws abroad by individuals (e.g., trophy hunting or bestiality).

Protecting Animals Within and Across Borders. Charlotte E. Blattner.

A. JURISDICTION AS A META-ORDERING DOCTRINE

In principle, states are their own regulators and have jurisdictional *Kompetenz-Kompetenz* or *originary* jurisdiction.[1] In this first, very abstract state, states gradually placed limits on their authority and began to define when and how they can use that authority. Many states decided to transfer some of their jurisdictional authority to another state, a regulatory entity, an institution, or an international court, like the UN,[2] the ICJ,[3] the International Criminal Court (ICC),[4] or special tribunals.[5] The jurisdictional authority a state confers on another such entity is called *derivative* jurisdiction. Supranational bodies may also exercise jurisdiction, but they rely on international agreements that reach beyond the nation-state and create an "autonomous and *sui generis* constitutional order."[6] Herein, however, I am primarily interested in originary jurisdiction of states and the jurisdiction of supranational organizations that perform acts *in lieu of* states, like the European Union that possesses jurisdictional competence in a quasi-originary position. In other words, this study inquires into extraterritorial jurisdiction that expands horizontally rather than vertically.

Although states enjoy inalienable and originary jurisdictional authority, they are not competent to determine the spatial limits of their jurisdictional competence individually and autonomously. Because disagreements over the reach of the jurisdictional competences of states, *ratione loci*, only arise when jurisdiction conflicts or concurs, they rarely touch matters under the exclusive purview of a single state.[7] In most cases, international law is the competent body to govern questions concerning the territorial powers of states, not least because the regulatory ideals of international law are to create order and peace, and to ensure states' sovereign equality.[8]

The jurisdictional limits determined by international law operate in an *ultima ratio* manner. The norms of international law do not provide an optimum level of regulation but require that states meet minimum standards when they exercise jurisdiction in cross-border

---

[1] MENG 4 (1994); Anne Peters, *Humanity as the A and Ω of Sovereignty*, 20 EJIL 513, 515, n. 4 (2009).

[2] Charter of the United Nations, Oct. 24, 1945, 1 U.N.T.S. 16, art. 25 [UN Charter].

[3] Statute of the International Court of Justice, June 26, 1945, 33 U.N.T.S. 993, arts. 36, 37, and 53 para. 2 [ICJ Statute].

[4] Rome Statute of the International Criminal Court, July 17, 1998, 2187 U.N.T.S. 90, art. 1 [Rome Statute].

[5] Special tribunals include, among others, those created by the United Nations Convention on the Law of the Sea, Dec. 10, 1982, 1833 U.N.T.S. 3, art. 188 ff. [UNCLOS]; S.C. Res. 827, U.N. SCOR 48th Sess., on Establishing an International Tribunal for the Prosecution of Persons Responsible for Serious Violations of International Humanitarian Law Committed in the Territory of the Former Yugoslavia, U.N. Doc. S/RES/827 (May 25, 1993); S.C. Res. 955, U.N. SCOR 49th Sess., On Establishment of an International Tribunal and Adoption of the Statute of the Tribunal, U.N. Doc. S/RES/955 (Nov. 8, 1994).

[6] Achilles Skordas, *Supranational Law, in* MAX PLANCK ENCYCLOPEDIA OF PUBLIC INTERNATIONAL LAW [MPEPIL] 2 (Rüdiger Wolfrum ed., online ed. 2014) (emphasis in original).

[7] Moreover, the reserved domain may shrink as international law incrementally expands because "[t]he question whether a certain matter is or is not solely within the jurisdiction of a State is an essentially relative question; it depends upon the development of international relations" (Nationality Decrees in Tunis and Morocco, Advisory Opinion, Judgment, 1923 P.C.I.J. (ser. B) No. 4, at 24 (Feb. 7) [Nationality Decrees, 1923 P.C.I.J.]).

[8] MITSUE INAZUMI, UNIVERSAL JURISDICTION IN MODERN INTERNATIONAL LAW: EXPANSION OF NATIONAL JURISDICTION FOR PROSECUTING SERIOUS CRIMES UNDER INTERNATIONAL LAW 17 (2005); VAUGHAN LOWE, INTERNATIONAL LAW 171 (2007).

scenarios. These minimum standards manifest as prohibitory rules like the duty not to intervene in the domestic affairs of another state. They can also take the form of positive, permissive rules on which states can base their extraterritorial jurisdiction. Conversely, international law does not require states to legislate extraterritorially.[9] A notable anomaly in this respect is human rights law, where mandatory jurisdictional rules for states to respond to governance gaps that facilitate human rights violations is widely debated.

The international doctrine of jurisdiction provides a framework of rules and principles that apply to all fields of law: criminal, administrative, constitutional, and private law.[10] In matters of public law, which encompasses criminal, administrative, and constitutional law, states usually apply domestic law to a case or dismiss it. This approach is known as the unilateral determination of the application of domestic law. In contrast, private law uses all-sided rules of conflict that mandate applying either domestic or foreign substantive law. When it applies foreign law, a state's court simply borrows another state's laws to resolve the dispute. The legal rules that address the territorial reach of private law are well established and methodologically independent. But "private international law," contrary to what the term seems to indicate, is by and large domestic law, while its reference or function is international.[11] Where private international law forms part of states' domestic law, it must stand the test of public international law, just as domestic law generally does.[12] Some states have entered harmonized jurisdictional rules in the realm of private law, like those established under the European Union's aegis.[13] In this case, the international doctrine of jurisdiction uses both customary international law and treaty law.

---

[9] IBA Report Extraterritorial Jurisdiction 17–8 (2009); Alexander Orakhelashvili, Akehurst's Modern Introduction to International Law 214 (8th ed. 2019). Jurisdiction to prescribe law is thus not mandatory, but permissive: Roger O'Keefe, *Universal Jurisdiction: Clarifying the Basic Concept*, 2 J. Int'l Crim. Just. 735, 738, n.12 (2004); Meng 458 (1994).

[10] Martin Dixon, Textbook on International Law 151 (7th ed. 2013); Alex Mills, The Confluence of Public and Private International Law 24, 125, 164, 207 (2009); U.S. Restatement (Fourth) of the Foreign Relations Law, §402, cmt. d; American Law Institute, Restatement (Second) of Conflict of Laws of the United States, §2, cmt. d (1971) [U.S. Restatement (Second) of Conflict of Laws].

[11] Case Concerning the Payment of Various Serbian Loans Issued in France (Fr. v. Kingdom of Serbs, Croats and Slovenes), 1929 P.C.I.J. (ser. A) No. 20/21, at 41 (July 12) [Serbian Loans, 1929 P.C.I.J.]; Meng 189 (1994); Clive Parry et al., Encyclopaedic Dictionary of International Law 481 (3d ed. 2009) "private international law"; Ryngaert, Jurisdiction 18 (2015).

[12] Angus Johnston & Edward Powles, *The Kings of the World and Their Dukes' Dilemma: Globalisation, Jurisdiction and the Rule of Law, in* Globalisation and Jurisdiction 13, 13 ff. (Piet Jan Slot & Mielle Bulterman eds., 2004); Elihu Lauterpacht ed., International Law: Collected Papers of Hersch Lauterpacht, vol. I, 38 (1970); Frederick A. Mann, *The Doctrine of International Jurisdiction Revisited after Twenty Years*, 186 RCADI 9, 21, 31 (1984); Meng 165 (1994); Patrick Wautelet, *What Has International Private Law Achieved in Meeting the Challenges Posed by Globalisation?, in* Globalisation and Jurisdiction 55, 57 (2004). *Contra* Michael Akehurst, *Jurisdiction in International Law*, 46 BYIL 145, 187 (1972–3). Mills argues that international norms create the structure of private international law by limiting states' regulatory authority, but gives them discretion in exercising authority, which renders private international law a set of hybrid rules: Mills 296 (2009).

[13] *E.g.*, Council Regulation 44/2001 on Jurisdiction and the Recognition and Enforcement of Judgments in Civil and Commercial Matters, 2000 O.J. (L 12) 1; Regulation 593/2008 of the European Parliament and of the Council on the Law Applicable to Contractual Obligations (Rome I), 2008 O.J. (L 177) 6.

B. *POTENTIA, POTESTAS,* AND OTHER CORE ELEMENTS OF JURISDICTION

Critics repeatedly voice their fears about extraterritorial jurisdiction, arguing that politically stronger states can use it to oppress and impose values on economically weaker or dependent states. The law of jurisdiction undoubtedly is politically charged, which can, at least in part, be explained by its close connection to the concept of power. Earlier rulings make the link clear, as when the US Supreme Court ruled in *McDonald v. Mabee* in 1917 that "[t]he foundation of jurisdiction is physical power."[14] Though jurisdiction may be intricately tied to physical power, this does not imply that power legitimates jurisdiction or, indeed, that it is equivalent to jurisdiction. The relationship between the two is vexed, and this becomes apparent in scholars' struggle to define jurisdiction. Two elements reappear in their definitions. The first cluster of definitions relates to *physical power* (i.e., the power,[15] ability,[16] or capacity[17] to act or affect), and the second relates to *legality* (i.e., the competence[18] or right[19] to decide or regulate). The definitional dichotomy of jurisdiction reflects broader debates about the legitimation of power either by one's capacity to use force (*potentia*) or by the authorization to use force (*potestas*).[20] Earlier conceptions of jurisdiction might have been correct in identifying power as their base, but jurisdiction, as understood today, does not represent a physical, forcible act as an expression of sovereign power per se, but is preoccupied with (international) law-bound state acts that prescribe and enforce law. Because the law of jurisdiction is a system of rules-based authorization of power, the relatively neutral term *authority*[21] seems to be the closest and best definitional equivalent of jurisdiction.

The law of jurisdiction operates by different sets of rules when it determines the limits of states' jurisdiction, depending on whether it deals with regulatory or enforcement authority. *Enforcement authority* is the authority of states to induce compliance and punish noncompliance with their norms.[22] Law enforcement is brought about by governmental force but may also include elements of persuasion. In exercising *regulatory authority*, in contrast, states connect a state of affairs with legal consequences. Regulatory authority refers to the authority to create and pass laws, binding rules below the level of laws by the legislature (e.g., decrees, nonadministrative regulations, etc.), regulation by administrative agencies, and judgments issued by courts (judge-made law and interpretation of other laws).

---

[14] McDonald v. Mabee, 243 U.S. 90, 91 (1917) (U.S.).

[15] *E.g.*, Case Concerning the Arrest Warrant of 11 April 2000 (Dem. Rep. Congo v. Belg.), Judgment, 2002 I.C.J. Rep. 59, 60 (Feb. 14) (Separate Opinion of Judge Koroma) [Arrest Warrant, 2002 I.C.J.].

[16] *E.g.*, Johnston & Powles, *The Kings of the World and Their Dukes' Dilemma*, *in* GLOBALISATION AND JURISDICTION 25 (2004).

[17] *E.g.*, Derek W. Bowett, *Jurisdiction: Changing Patterns of Authority over Activities and Resources*, 53 BYIL 1, 1 (1982).

[18] E.g., JAMES CRAWFORD, BROWNLIE'S PRINCIPLES OF PUBLIC INTERNATIONAL LAW 456 (8th ed. 2012).

[19] *E.g.*, Frederick A. Mann, *The Doctrine of Jurisdiction in International Law*, 111 RCADI 1, 9 (1964).

[20] The dichotomy between *potentia* and *potestas* was originally established by Spinoza: JIŘÍ PŘIBÁŇ, SOVEREIGNTY IN A POST-SOVEREIGNTY SOCIETY: A SYSTEMS THEORY OF EUROPEAN CONSTITUTIONALISM 54 (2015).

[21] CRAWFORD 448 (2012); DIXON 148 (2013); ROSALYN HIGGINS, PROBLEMS AND PROCESS, INTERNATIONAL LAW AND HOW WE USE IT 56 (1995); O'Keefe 736 (2004); ROBERT JENNINGS & ARTHUR WATTS EDS., OPPENHEIM'S INTERNATIONAL LAW, vol. I, 457 (9th ed. 1992).

[22] U.S. Restatement (Fourth) of the Foreign Relations Law, § 401(c).

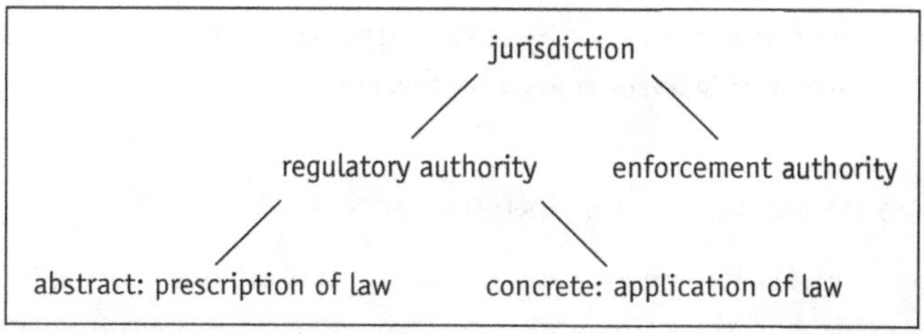

FIGURE 1.1 Elements of jurisdictional authority.

Regulatory authority operates both abstractly and concretely. Abstract regulatory authority manifests when a state prescribes law; concrete regulatory authority is exercised by applying law. The prescription of law is abstract, as it regulates a multitude of facts, and it is general, as it applies to an unknown circle of prospective addressees. Prescriptive jurisdiction is aimed at organizing state institutions, determining substantive values of the state order (basic rights and axiomatic principles of a state, such as good faith or public morality), creating obligations (actions and omissions), and creating legal relationships or statuses of persons (e.g., legal personhood or civil status) and goods (e.g., property or ownership).[23] The application of law, in contrast, is concrete, as it applies to a specific situation, and it is individual, as it applies to a specific circle of addressees.[24] The law is applied either through decisions of the court or through administrative acts. Adjudicative jurisdiction arises as a distinct legal question only in private international law, where a state court's jurisdiction over a case and the application of domestic law might not be congruent.[25] Under international law, we still speak of adjudicative jurisdiction in reference to all fields of law. Figure 1.1 illustrates the elements of jurisdictional authority and the three types of jurisdiction: prescriptive, adjudicative, and enforcement jurisdiction.

Under public international law, enforcement jurisdiction is clearly distinct from all other types of jurisdiction. The basic rule is that every state's jurisdiction to enforce law is limited to its own territory, marked by the "continued salience of territorialism."[26] Acts of enforcement include the use of physical force and other acts of *imperium*, like investigations, issuance of writs, service of documents, and approaching or hearing witnesses.[27] The prohibition of enforcement jurisdiction on foreign territory derives from the principle of territorial integrity and the principle of nonintervention as enshrined in article 2 paras. 4 and 7 of the UN Charter. Exceptions to this rule can only be created by consent, say, through mutual

---

[23] MENG 5 (1994).

[24] *Id.* at 6–8.

[25] This is because private international law includes all-sided rules of conflict that may point to the application of foreign or domestic law: JÜRGEN SCHWARZE, DIE JURISDIKTIONSABGRENZUNG IM VÖLKERRECHT 20 (1994).

[26] Hannah L. Buxbaum, *Territory, Territoriality and the Resolution of Jurisdictional Conflict*, 57 AJCL 631, 673 (2009). The principle of territorial enforcement jurisdiction was reinforced by the PCIJ in the *Lotus* case: "[T]he first and foremost restriction imposed by international law upon a State is that—failing the existence of a permissive rule to the contrary—it may not exercise its power in any form in the territory of another State" (S.S. Lotus (Fr. v. Turk.), Judgment, 1927 P.C.I.J. (ser. A) No. 10, at 18 (Sept. 7) [Lotus, 1927 P.C.I.J.]).

[27] Prosper Weil, *International Limitations on State Jurisdiction*, *in* EXTRA-TERRITORIAL APPLICATION OF LAWS AND RESPONSES THERETO 32, 33 (Cecil J. Olmstead ed., 1984).

assistance treaties in criminal law,[28] or by customary international law, like customary rules governing the issuance of passports or visas on foreign soil.[29]

C. USEFULNESS OF PRESCRIPTIVE JURISDICTION

Though extraterritorial enforcement raises interesting questions and debates in international law, I here focus solely on the admissibility of extraterritorial prescriptive jurisdiction. This analysis may appear unduly narrow and may throw into question the usefulness of extraterritorial prescriptive jurisdiction. Why should states seek to regulate certain facts, persons, or things present on foreign territory, if they lack the necessary jurisdiction to enforce their laws? States continue to regulate matters on foreign territory because they may hark back to judicial assistance treaties with foreign states to ensure their laws are enforced abroad. However, assistance agreements commonly cover only a fraction of prescriptive authority (e.g., only certain criminal laws) and do not enshrine a strict duty to assist.[30] The promise of enforcement across the border, hence, is a feeble one.

Alternatively, states may use indirect means to ensure compliance with their norms on foreign territory. By leading addressees of a norm into a conflict of compliance, states can expect adherence to their laws even where they cannot enforce them. A state prescribing laws with extraterritorial reach may threaten to sue the foreign addressee of the norm on its territory, to seize their assets, to bar them from entering its territory, or to prevent them from establishing an enterprise on its territory. Diplomatic or financial cooperation might also be ended or frozen, and indirect penalties might be imposed through international money markets.[31] These means of territorial enforcement ensure that norms are observed even across the border. The addressee of a norm performs a cost-effectiveness analysis of available options and finds that the potential negative effects of not complying with the norms are greater than the positive effects of ignoring them. Through "the appeal of persuasion,"[32] states can affect people, places, and things beyond their territories, and this gives practical relevance to their extraterritorial animal laws without raising controversial issues of extraterritorial enforcement.

---

[28] These treaties may be multilateral, *e.g.*, CoE, Convention on Mutual Assistance in Criminal Matters, Apr. 20, 1959, C.E.T.S. No. 30; CoE, Convention on Laundering of Search Seizure and Confiscation of the Proceeds from Crime, Nov. 8, 1990, C.E.T.S. No. 141, or bilateral, *see e.g.*, Agreement Between the United States and Cuba for the Lease of Lands for Coaling and Naval Stations, Feb. 23, 1903, T.S. 418.

[29] Vienna Convention on Consular Relations, Apr. 24, 1963, 596 U.N.T.S. 261, art. 5 (consular functions) [VCCR].

[30] In other words, a state follows another state's assistance request at its own discretion. When the requesting state's jurisdiction conflicts with the requested state's jurisdiction, it is unlikely the latter will follow the former's request.

[31] Directorate-General for External Policies, Policy Department, The Extraterritorial Effects of Legislation and Policies in the EU and US, requested by the European Parliament's Committee on Foreign Affairs 39 (European Union 2012).

[32] Translated from the German term "Persuasionswirkung" (MENG 113 (1994)). Himelfarb refers to the same process as a "geopsychological factor" (Allison J. Himelfarb, *The International Language of Convergence: Reviving Antitrust Dialogue between the United States and the European Union with a Uniform Understanding of "Extraterritoriality,"* 17 U. PA. J. INT'L ECON. L. 909, 918 n. 41 (1996)).

§2 The Rise of Extraterritorial Jurisdiction

A. THE HISTORICAL RISE

At the beginning of the twentieth century, the territorial ambit of states' jurisdictional authority was nearly unfettered. The Permanent Court of International Justice's (PCIJ) judgment in the 1927 *Lotus* case represents the last cornerstone of the then-predominant laissez-faire attitude. The Court determined that states are free to exercise jurisdiction beyond their territory unless international law explicitly restricts them from doing so.[33] The judgment was decided by the casting vote of the president and has been widely criticized by scholars and in subsequent court rulings for taking a stance toward states' authority that was too libertarian, and for prompting an increase in jurisdictional disputes.[34]

In the following decades, scholars moved to view the territorial connection of a state as "the strongest ground for asserting that a state has jurisdiction."[35] It was frequently maintained that states enjoy exclusive jurisdiction within and over their territory. In the *Island of Palmas* case, the sole arbitrator, Max Huber, held that the "principle of exclusive competence of the State in regard to its own territory" is the "point of departure in settling most questions that concern international relations."[36] From the alleged exclusivity of territorial jurisdiction, some inferred that other jurisdictional principles merely function as exceptions to the territoriality principle and that there is a complementary *prima facie* illegality of extraterritorial jurisdiction.[37] For instance, in India, the United Kingdom, and the United States, crime was commonly viewed as local and excluded jurisdiction over aliens abroad.[38]

After World War II, jurisdictional principles in criminal law were in upheaval, since traditional territorial interpretations stoked the public's fears of impunity for war criminals.[39] The failure of the international community to establish effective criminal tribunals and fears that foreign corporations would come to dominate national markets spurred demands for jurisdictional expansion. During the advent of the first wave of globalization in the 1970s through 1980s, the extraterritoriality dispute gained momentum in antitrust law and securities regulation. From the 1990s on, terrorist activities increased around the globe and so did the jurisdictional responses to them (including the Tokyo Convention, the Hague Hijacking Convention, and the Montreal Convention).[40] The debate on the territorial limits

---

[33] Lotus, 1927 P.C.I.J. 19. *See also* INAZUMI 30–1 (2005).

[34] Mann, for instance, views the *Lotus* principle as "a most unfortunate and retrograde theory" (Mann 35 (1964)). He finds it "difficult to believe" that an international court would deny the pervasive influence of international law (Mann 32 (1984)). *See*, for a critique of the Lotus decision, Chapter 5, §1.

[35] RICHARD K. GARDINER, INTERNATIONAL LAW 311 (2003).

[36] Island of Palmas Case (U.S. v. Neth.), 2 R.I.A.A. 829, 838 (Perm. Ct. Arb. 1928) [Island of Palmas, 1928 R.I.A.A.]. Similarly, in *The Schooner Exchange v. McFaddon*, the US Supreme Court stated: "The jurisdiction of the nation within its own territory is necessarily exclusive and absolute. It is susceptible of no limitation not imposed by itself. All exceptions, therefore, must be traced up to the consent of the nation itself." (The Schooner Exchange v, McFaddon, 11 U.S. 116, 136 (1812) (U.S.)).

[37] Akehurst 181 (1972–3); RYNGAERT, JURISDICTION 34 (2015).

[38] Ram Narain v. The Central Bank of India Ltd., (1951) High Court of India, ILR 1951 Case No. 49 (India); Macleod v. A.G. for N.S.W. [1891] AC 455 (U.K.); Slater v. Mexican Nat. R. Co., 194 U.S. 120 (1904) (U.S.).

[39] INAZUMI 33 (2005).

[40] Convention on Offences and Certain Other Acts Committed on Board Aircraft, Sept. 14, 1963, 704 U.N.T.S. 220 [Tokyo Convention]; Convention for the Suppression of Unlawful Seizure of Aircraft, Dec. 16, 1970, 860

of criminal jurisdiction peaked with the prosecutions of universal crimes in the 1990s, including the creation of the International Criminal Court (ICC), the International Criminal Tribunal for the former Yugoslavia (ICTY), and the International Criminal Tribunal for Rwanda (ICTR).[41] In the following years, spurred by these legal developments and the need to tackle some of the most sweeping onsets of globalization, states began to use extraterritorial jurisdiction in antitrust law, banking law, bribery and corruption regulation, criminal law, insolvency law, securities law, tax law, tort law, trade law, data protection, human rights law, and other areas.[42] Questions of how far, and under which conditions the laws of one state can or must reach into the territory of another are now emerging in areas like labor law, environmental law, and animal law.[43]

B. EMERGING SPHERES OF JURISDICTION

Possibly because extraterritorial jurisdiction appears to be a self-explicating term, it invites a host of *prima facie* value judgments that fail to pay sufficient regard to the different forms and types of jurisdiction. Jurisdictional spheres, as established by Meng and Rudolf, can help us unpack these confusions and begin to understand why extraterritorial jurisdiction is a popular means of persuasion for states and why and when it is considered legal.[44]

The sphere of jurisdiction (*Regelungsgebiet*) describes the spatial sphere in which a state's regulation is designed to operate. The sphere of jurisdiction has two aspects: the sphere of regulation and the sphere of validity. The sphere of validity (*Geltungsbereich*)[45] is the spatial area within which prescriptive jurisdiction can be enforced autonomously by a state. Due to the prohibition of extraterritorial enforcement, a state's sphere of validity is in principle limited to its territory. The sphere of regulation (*Regelungsbereich*)[46] is the sphere in which

U.N.T.S. 105 [Hijacking Convention]; Convention for the Suppression of Unlawful Acts against the Safety of Civil Aviation, Sept. 23, 1971, 974 U.N.T.S. 178 [Montreal Convention].

41 *See supra* note 5. *See also* INAZUMI 44 (2005).

42 IBA REPORT EXTRATERRITORIAL JURISDICTION 33 (2009).

43 *See* for an examination of extraterritorial jurisdiction in labor law: Harry W. Arthurs, *Extraterritoriality by Other Means: How Labor Law Sneaks Across Borders, Conquers Minds, and Controls Workplaces Abroad*, 21 STAN. L. & POL. REV. 527 (2010); Harry Arthurs, *Reinventing Labor Law for the Global Economy: The Benjamin Aaron Lecture*, 22 BERKELEY J. EMP. & LAB. L. 271 (2001); Yifeng Chen, *ILO, Extraterritoriality and Labor Protection in Republican Shanghai, in* FUNDAMENTAL LABOR RIGHTS IN CHINA: LEGAL IMPLEMENTATION AND CULTURAL LOGIC 83 (Ulla Liukkunen & Yifeng Chen eds., 2016). *See* for extraterritorial jurisdiction in animal law: George Cameron Coggins & John W. Head, *Beyond* Defenders: *Future Problems of Extraterritoriality and Superterritoriality for the Endangered Species Act*, 43 WASH. U. J. URB. & CONTEMP. L. 59 (1993); Asif H. Qureshi, *Extraterritorial Shrimps, NGOs and the WTO Appellate Body*, 48 ICLQ 199 (1999); Sands 529 (2001); Mitsuhiko A. Takahashi, Okinawa Dugong v. Rumsfeld: *Extraterritorial Operation of the U.S. Military and Wildlife Protection under the National Historic Preservation Act*, 28 ENVIRONS. ENVTL L. & POL'Y J. 181 (2004).

44 MENG 10–3 (1994); Walter Rudolf, *Territoriale Grenzen der staatlichen Rechtsetzung*, 11 BERDGVöR 7, 9–10 (1973).

45 The same translation is used by ERICH VRANES, TRADE AND THE ENVIRONMENT: FUNDAMENTAL ISSUES IN INTERNATIONAL LAW, WTO LAW, AND LEGAL THEORY 97 (2009).

46 Vranes calls this the "area of application" (VRANES 97 (2009)).

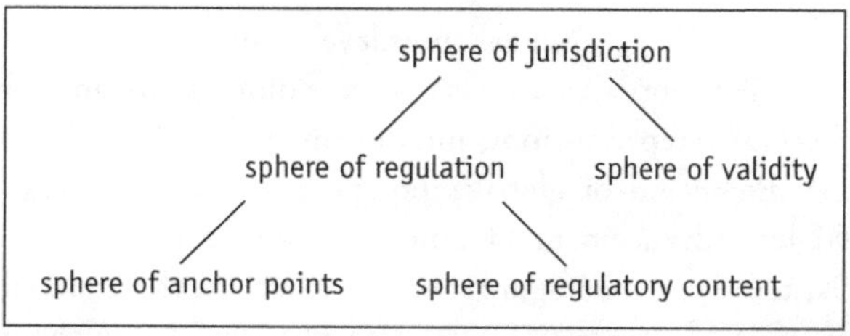

FIGURE 1.2 Jurisdictional spheres.

persons, things, and legal relationships subject to regulation are situated. The sphere of regulation can be larger or narrower than the territory of the state, and thus broader or narrower than the sphere of validity. The sphere of regulation is defined by means of local (e.g., the location of goods or legal relationships, residence, domicile, or seat), personal (e.g., nationality or domicile of persons), and material (i.e., criteria of substantive matter, e.g., security) nexuses.

The sphere of regulation can be further divided into the sphere of anchor points and the sphere of regulatory content. The sphere of anchor points (*Anknüpfungsbereich*) is the spatial area in which persons, things, and legal relationships connected to their legal consequences are located. The sphere of regulatory content (*Regelungsinhaltsbereich/Rechtsfolgebereich*) is the sphere in which the legal consequences of a regulation should manifest. Figure 1.2 illustrates these jurisdictional spheres.

Extraterritorial prescriptive jurisdiction arises when the sphere in which persons, things, or legal relationships subject to regulation are located (the sphere of regulation) exceeds the sphere within which prescriptive jurisdiction can be autonomously enforced (the sphere of validity). We should always be clear what sphere of jurisdiction we are talking about when we debate the legality of extraterritorial jurisdiction. For instance, when we speak of "exclusive territorial jurisdiction," we typically refer to a state's sphere of validity and not its sphere of regulation. Yet many infer from this principle that a state's regulatory sphere may not exceed its territory, which runs counter to the manifold regulatory interests of states and the international law of jurisdiction that has emerged in response thereto. Scholars in the seventeenth century were the first to notice discrepancies between the sphere of regulation and the sphere of validity. Grotius, in particular, used *territorium* "not only to refer to territory in the geographical sense, but also to the sphere within which state jurisdiction exists."[47]

C. GLOBALIZATION AND DETERRITORIALIZATION OF SOVEREIGN SPACE

As globalization has advanced, the discrepancy between the sphere of validity and the sphere of regulation has increased along with it and is now much larger than when Grotius first observed this development. Yet, how, exactly, did globalization trigger this shift? Before we can explain this development, we must first unpack the disputed notion of globalization.

---

[47] Walter Rudolf, *Territoriale Grenzen der staatlichen Rechtsetzung*, *in* REFERATE UND DISKUSSION DER 12. TAGUNG DER DEUTSCHEN GESELLSCHAFT FÜR VÖLKERRECHT IN BAD GODESBERG VOM 14. BIS 16. JUNI 1971 33 (Walther J. Habscheid & Walter Rudolf eds., 1973).

Globalization is an umbrella term for multileveled instances of increased global connectedness and can be conceptualized as having three dimensions: an economic dimension, the dimension of its global repercussions, and the dimension of juridico-political responses thereto.[48] The first dimension of globalization is economic and was notably triggered by rapid technological advancements. Communication technologies of the early 1950s, combined with the trend toward linguistic convergence, quickly granted countless people access to a vast amount of information served at great speed.[49] In the following decades, the means of transportation greatly improved and became accessible to vast numbers of people, which spurred cross-border business activity.[50] This activity increased as states began to adopt open border policies. The 1970s and early 1980s heralded the first meaningful rounds of trade and services liberalization at an international level. The launch of the Uruguay Round in 1985 created the WTO with its explicit goal of liberalizing trade around the globe. In 1986, EU member states agreed to adopt the Single Europe Act (SEA), which established a single European market. The SEA was followed by the Maastricht Treaty in 1992, designed to foster more economic and political cooperation among the newly created European Union and its members.[51] Around the same time, Canada and the United States concluded their first free trade agreement in 1988, and in 1992, they extended it to Mexico under the North American Free Trade Agreement (NAFTA).[52] Liberalizing trade through international conventions led to unprecedented increases of flows of goods, services, and capital between countries.

The driving factors behind globalization (enhanced transport, communication technologies, flow of goods and services) radically cut costs and saved time. New structures of production appeared, where loosely connected industries became part of a web of multinational entities, pieces of an unimaginably vast puzzle.[53] Lower costs and technological change gradually began to shift investment flows. The accelerated mobility of capital led to

---

[48] Peters, Völkerrecht 15 (2016). *See also* Anne Peters, *Privatisierung, Globalisierung und die Resistenz des Verfassungsstaates, in* Staats- und Verfassungstheorie im Spannungsfeld der Disziplinen 100, 100 ff. (Philippe Mastronardi & Denis Taubert eds., 2006).

[49] Johnston & Powles, *The Kings of the World and Their Dukes' Dilemma, in* Globalisation and Jurisdiction 14 (2004). Strange's description vividly exemplifies the rise of communication technology: "It took hundreds—in some places, thousands—of years to domesticate animals so that horses could be used for transport and oxen [. . .] could be used to replace manpower to plough and sow ground for the production of crops in agriculture. It has taken less than 100 years for the car and truck to replace the horse and for aircraft to partly take over from road and rail transport. The electric telegraph as a means of communication was invented in the 1840s and remained the dominant system in Europe until the 1920s. But in the next eighty years, the telegraph gave way to the telephone, the telephone gave way to radio, radio to television and cables to satellites and optic fibres linking computers to other computers" (Susan Strange, The Retreat of the State 7 (1996)).

[50] Wenhua Shan et al. eds., Redefining Sovereignty in International Economic Law xiii (Wenhua Shan, Penelope Simons, & Dalvinder Singh eds., 2008).

[51] The SEA was the first major amendment of the Treaty establishing the European Economic Community (EEC): European Union, Consolidated Version of Treaty on European Union, Treaty of Maastricht, 1991 O.J. (C 191) 1 [TEU].

[52] North American Free Trade Agreement, Dec. 17, 1992, 32 I.L.M. 289 (1993) [NAFTA].

[53] John H. Jackson, *Sovereignty: Outdated Concept or New Approaches, in* Redefining Sovereignty in International Economic Law 3, 6 (2008).

more interconnectedness in finance and culminated in the liberalization of foreign direct investment (FDI). The benefits of being a host or home state to multinational corporations raised investment levels and technology output in agriculture, manufacturing, and, more broadly, the mobilization of services, products, and processes.[54]

The first, economic dimension of globalization set in motion its second dimension, the problematic repercussions of economic growth, clearly noticeable on a global scale. Among its disruptive effects are environmental degradation and pollution, human migration and class segregation, transnational organized crime, terrorism, the pitfalls of the internet, as well as increased migration of animals, trade in animals, cross-border production, and spread of disease.

This gave rise to the third dimension of globalization, which encompasses the juridico-political responses to the first two dimensions. This is the realm in which challenges posed by globalization to regulatory regimes and political branches must be resolved and the role of states as regulators—whose ability to individually fulfill state duties, such as ensuring security, rights, welfare, and protection from crime and environmental pollution, is dwindling—must be determined. Globalization modified these previously centralist concerns, because solving them now requires coordination and cooperation between multiple states.[55]

The three dimensions of globalization have shifted our understanding of sovereign space. Many scholars have asked what role is left for the state to play when borders begin to dissolve, and consequently lose relevance—factually, economically, and politically. The most extreme prediction of the outcome of globalization is the decline of the sovereign state.[56] The argument that globalization will lead to a complete loss of state sovereignty, however, is primarily political in nature and defended by a minority of hyperglobalist scholars.[57] Legal scholarship, in contrast, finds that the concept of sovereignty has been "remarkably resilient both epistemically and normatively."[58] State sovereignty still plays a central role in international law;

---

[54] John Stopford & Susan Strange, Rival States, Rival Firms: Competition for World Market Shares 5 (1991); Strange 9 (1996).

[55] Peters, Völkerrecht 15 (2016). *Cf.* on the juridico-political dimension: Piet Jan Slot & Mielle Bulterman, *Introduction, in* Globalisation and Jurisdiction 1, 1 (2004).

[56] Jackson, *Sovereignty: Outdated Concept or New Approaches, in* Redefining Sovereignty in International Economic Law 24 (2008); Robert Howse, *Sovereignty, Lost and Found, in* Redefining Sovereignty in International Economic Law 61, 61 (2008); Edward Kwakwa, *Regulating the International Economy: What Role for the State?, in* The Role of Law in International Politics: Essays in International Relations and International Law 227, 229 (Michael Byers ed., 2000); Shan et al. xiii (2008); Anne-Marie Slaughter, *The Real New World Order*, 76 Foreign Aff. 189 (1997).

[57] Globalization and internationalization must be strictly distinguished. Rather than internationalizing the international legal order, globalization has shifted the focus away from state-centered issues to transnational ones: Christine Kaufmann, Globalisation and Labour Rights: The Conflict between Core Labour Rights and International Economic Law 6–7 (2007); James Turner Johnson, Sovereignty: Moral and Historical Perspectives 117 ff. (2014).

[58] Samantha Besson, *Sovereignty, in* MPEPIL 4 (Rüdiger Wolfrum ed., online ed. 2011); Jean L. Cohen, Globalization and Sovereignty: Rethinking Legality, Legitimacy, and Constitutionalism 4 (2012); Shaunnagh Dorsett & Shaun McVeigh, Jurisdiction 41 (2012) ("claims of the end of sovereignty [. . .] seem premature"); Flavio G.I. Inocencio, Reconceptualizing Sovereignty in the

it is the starting point of any inquiry into legal responsibility and the introduction of new rights and duties. Newer developments suggest that states are in fact re-emphasizing state sovereignty, such as during the rise of the BRIC states (Brazil, Russia, India, and China).[59]

Although state sovereignty remains a core pillar of the international legal order, it has changed fundamentally. The main factors that drive globalization—political, economic, social, and ecological activities—have caused seismic shifts in traditional conceptions of sovereignty. Globalization, as some say, has "unbundled" territoriality from state sovereignty, it has deterritorialized state sovereignty.[60] Three processes support this claim: the movement from state independence to interdependence, the shift from state sovereignty to sovereignty of the people, and the rise of global legal pluralism. I will briefly look at each of these in turn.

First, we are observing a movement from state independence to interdependence. Goods are often produced in the territories of several states, and diverse suppliers, producers, workers, buyers, managers, consultants, etc., contribute to their manufacture. Seemingly trivial business decisions made in one state may fundamentally shape the interests of foreign individuals, groups, or states, so government institutions cannot satisfactorily coordinate these actions without cooperating, or at least coordinating, across borders.[61] In an attempt to recover their capacity to solve problems caused and exacerbated by globalization, states resort to global, nonterritorial regulatory structures. Sovereign independence thus has given way to state interdependence.[62]

The second observation is that sovereignty of the state has shifted to sovereignty of the people. In an era of interdependence, the Westphalian model of sovereign, exclusive state power no longer matches reality: matters are no longer left as far as possible to states' discretion. State sovereignty now entails fundamental duties like protecting people from serious crimes or ensuring their human rights. When the people become the ultimate units of concern, sovereignty no longer lies with the ruler, but shifts to the people (from *imperium*

Post-National State: Statehood Attributes in the International Order: The Federal Tradition 197 (2014); Kate Seaman, UN-Tied Nations: The United Nations, Peacekeeping and Global Governence 112, 120 (2014); Margaret A. Young, *Fragmentation, Regime Interaction and Sovereignty*, *in* Sovereignty, Statehood and State Responsibility: Essays in Honour of James Crawford 71, 86, 89 (Christine Chinkin & Freya Baetens eds., 2015).

[59] Zaki Laïda, *BRICS: Sovereignty Power and Weakness*, 49 Int'l Pol. 614, 614 (2012): "The BRICS form a coalition of sovereign state defenders. [. . . T]hey are concerned with maintaining their independence of judgment and national action in a world that is increasingly economically and socially interdependent. They consider that state sovereignty trumps all, including, of course, the political nature of its underpinning regimes."

[60] Suzanne E. Gordon, Changing Concepts of Sovereignty and Jurisdiction in the Global Economy: Is There a Territorial Connection? (The Canadian Centre for German and European Studies/Le Centre canadien d'études allemandes et européennes 2 (CCGES/CCEAE), Working Paper Series Number 1, 2001). MacMillan and Linklater suggest that the new economy, which cuts across national boundaries, erodes the significance of territory and the territorial character of conceptions about sovereignty: John MacMillan & Andrew Linklater eds., Boundaries in Question: New Directions in International Relations (1995). *See also* Simon Caney, Justice Beyond Borders: A Global Political Theory 150 (2005); John G. Ruggie, *Territoriality and Beyond: Problematizing Modernity in International Relations*, 47 Int'l Org. 139 (1993).

[61] Gordon 12 (2001); Jackson, *Sovereignty: Outdated Concept or New Approaches*, *in* Redefining Sovereignty in International Economic Law 6 (2008).

[62] Peters, Völkerrecht 15, 34 (2016); Shan et al. xiii (2008).

to *populus*). In Peters' view, a new principle of humanity has thus emerged—the principle that human rights, human interests, and human needs must be respected—and this has become the first principle of sovereignty.[63] The rise of popular sovereignty can be seen in major founding documents of international law. Article 1 of the UN Charter lays down the duty to respect the principles of equal rights and self-determination of the peoples. Article 21 para. 3 of the 1948 UDHR declares that "[t]he will of the people shall be the basis of the authority of government [...]."[64] Sovereignty, previously bundled in a few powerful governments, now emphasizes collective, popular sovereignty.[65]

The third factor that weakens a strong territorial understanding of sovereignty is the shift from territorially defined regulatory structures to multilayered governance that "more closely reflect[s] the different spatial structures in which issues and problems arise."[66] The creation of adjudicatory bodies on the international level (including the ICC, ICTY, and ICTR) and the ongoing proliferation and fragmentation of international law gave rise to a new structure of regulation that is heterogeneous, multilayered, and overlapping. As a consequence, there are "many alternative competing and contending sovereignties,"[67] which lie at the heart of modern global legal pluralism.[68]

D. THE RISE OF JURISDICTION BASED ON PERSONAL AND ORGANIZATIONAL SOVEREIGNTY

Because sovereignty is the foundation on which jurisdiction is exercised,[69] its deterritorialization has begun to shift our understanding of the doctrine of jurisdiction as primarily

---

[63] From this follows that "[...] conflicts between state sovereignty and human rights should not be approached in a balancing process in which the former is played off against the latter on an equal footing, but should be tackled on the basis of a presumption in favour of humanity." (Peters, *Humanity as the A and Ω of Sovereignty* 514 (2009)). Hobe calls this "enlightened sovereignty" (Stephan Hobe, *Globalisation: A Challenge to the Nation State and to International Law, in* TRANSNATIONAL LEGAL PROCESSES: GLOBALISATION AND POWER DISPARITIES 378, 388 (Michael Likosky ed., 2002)). Dederer calls it "functional sovereignty" because the function of sovereignty is to establish state responsibility: (Hans-Georg Dederer, *"Responsibility to Protect' and 'Functional Sovereignty," in* RESPONSIBILITY TO PROTECT (R2P): A NEW PARADIGM OF INTERNATIONAL LAW?, 156, 157 (Peter Hilpold ed., 2015)). *See also* COHEN 180 ff. (2012); TURNER JOHNSON 137 ff. (2014).

[64] UDHR, art. 21 para. 3.

[65] Howse, *Sovereignty, Lost and Found, in* REDEFINING SOVEREIGNTY IN INTERNATIONAL ECONOMIC LAW 64 (2008).

[66] Alexander B. Murphy, *The Sovereign State System as Political-Territorial Ideal: Historical and Contemporary Considerations, in* STATE SOVEREIGNTY AS A SOCIAL CONSTRUCT 81, 84 (Thomas J. Biersteker & Cynthia Weber eds., 1996).

[67] Aoileann Ní Mhurchú, *Citizenship beyond State Sovereignty, in* ROUTLEDGE HANDBOOK OF GLOBAL CITIZENSHIP STUDIES 119, 120 (Engin F. Isin & Peter Nyers eds., 2014).

[68] PAUL SCHIFF BERMAN, GLOBAL LEGAL PLURALISM: A JURISPRUDENCE OF LAW BEYOND BORDERS (2012); COHEN 58 ff. (2012); MARTTI KOSKENNIEMI, THE POLITICS OF INTERNATIONAL LAW 228–9 (2011); Ralf Michaels, *Global Legal Pluralism*, 5 ANN. REV. L. & SOC. SCI. 243 (2009). The mechanism of multilayered governance is also called "Althusian" (INOCENCIO 196 (2014)).

[69] IAN BROWNLIE, PRINCIPLES OF PUBLIC INTERNATIONAL LAW 204 (7th ed. 2008). In the words of the PCIJ in *Lotus*, a state's "title to exercise jurisdiction rests in its sovereignty" (Lotus, 1927 P.C.I.J. 19). *See also*

territorial. Reliance on territorial considerations is today regarded as "static preservation of the legal order," a "jurisdictional artifact," that stems from the "obsolescent and no longer viable notion of state sovereignty."[70] The principle of territorial jurisdiction is said to suffer from the categorical shortcoming of never having been able to satisfactorily and permanently resolve conflicts. As early as 1957, Jennings pointed out: "In our present shrunken world such a strictly territorial division of jurisdiction may, it can be suggested, be unworkable [. . .]."[71]

While mere geographical boundaries might have effectively allocated state competence for earlier, simpler forms of government, business, and private activities, these boundaries are today less practicable. The traditional image of states as bodies with prescriptive authority limited to their territories cannot capture the complex realities of modern life or serve the plethora of interests that states and the international community at large have. Events that occur nowhere (cyberspace) and everywhere (global markets) have caused jurisdictional gaps and overlaps that recompose jurisdictional space. As states' territories and the regulatory scope of their laws are increasingly losing congruence, the chief function of territorial jurisdiction—the effective organization of jurisdictional space—is withering away. In a highly connected world, territorial jurisdiction can no longer serve as a reliable guide for the doctrine of jurisdiction.[72]

In an effort to find workable bases of jurisdiction that respond to these challenges, states have established solutions freed from territorial underpinnings.[73] Each of the common principles (the nationality principle, the protective principle, the universality principle, the effects principle, and the objective and subjective territoriality principles) is evidence "that in some circumstances a state is legally free to act, outside its territory to reprehend and punish activities."[74] In the *Arrest Warrant*, a landmark judgment on extraterritorial jurisdiction, former ICJ President Guillaume considered established the territoriality principle, the nationality principle (both the active and passive version), the protective principle, and the universality principle.[75] The growing acceptance that jurisdictional principles must be decoupled from territoriality is not as remarkable as it may first appear since state sovereignty is defined by more than territory. The three aspects that together constitute sovereignty are: territorial sovereignty, personal sovereignty, and organizational sovereignty.[76] And while the law of

---

Lotus, 1927 P.C.I.J. 305 (Dissenting Opinion by Altamira, M.): "Of course, every sovereign State may *by virtue of its sovereignty* legislate as it wishes within the limits of its own territory" (emphasis added).

70 Harold G. Maier, *Jurisdictional Rules in Customary International Law*, *in* EXTRATERRITORIAL JURISDICTION IN THEORY AND PRACTICE 64, Comment by Andrea Bianchi 84 (Karl M. Meessen ed., 1996).

71 Robert Jennings, *Extraterritorial Jurisdiction and the United States Antitrust Laws*, 33 BYIL 146, 149 (1957).

72 Buxbaum, *Territory, Territoriality and the Resolution of Jurisdictional Conflict* 674–5 (2009); ABDELHAMID EL OUALI, TERRITORIAL INTEGRITY IN A GLOBALIZING WORLD, INTERNATIONAL LAW AND STATES' QUEST FOR SURVIVAL 92 (2012); Kal Raustiala, *The Evolution of Territoriality: International Relations and American Law*, *in* TERRITORIALITY AND CONFLICT IN AN AGE OF GLOBALIZATION 219, 219 (Miles Kahler & Barbara Walter eds., 2006).

73 *See, e.g.*, Scott 106 (2014); Christopher Staker, *Jurisdiction*, *in* INTERNATIONAL LAW 289, 308 (Malcolm D. Evans ed., 5th ed. 2018).

74 Maier, *Jurisdictional Rules in Customary International Law*, *in* EXTRATERRITORIAL JURISDICTION IN THEORY AND PRACTICE 68 (1996).

75 Arrest Warrant, 2002 I.C.J. 35, 44 (Separate Opinion of President Guillaume).

76 *See also* Benedict Kingsbury, *Sovereignty and Inequality*, 9 EJIL 599, 615 (1998).

jurisdiction has so far been concerned, mostly, with territoriality, jurisdictional principles that have emerged from personal sovereignty (e.g., the nationality principle) or from organizational sovereignty (e.g., the protective principle) rank equally with territorial jurisdiction.[77]

Contemporary developments suggest that jurisdictional principles founded on personal and organizational sovereignty are gaining relevance in this age of globalization. Examples include the US Alien Tort Claims Act, which permits foreign citizens to seek remedies in national courts for human rights violations committed abroad,[78] or the European Union's Derivatives Regulation, which imposes obligations on nonresident entities to prevent them from evading its provisions.[79] Zerk, who assisted the Special Representative of the UN Secretary-General (SRSG) on Business and Human Rights, finds in her report on extraterritorial jurisdiction that "[i]ncreasingly, governments recognise that, in some areas, effective regulation of activities within their territories demands some degree of control over private activities beyond their borders."[80] As expressed by Judges Higgins, Koojmans, and Buergenthal in their Separate Opinion in the *Arrest Warrant*, "[t]he movement is towards bases of jurisdiction other than territoriality."[81]

§3 The Extraterritoriality Framework

A. JURISDICTIONAL NORMS AND THE EXTRATERRITORIALITY FRAMEWORK

Even though states increasingly resort to extraterritorial jurisdiction, certainty about the legal limits of their jurisdictional authority has not developed at the same rate. To date, there is no authoritative determination in international law, much less a consensus on the grasp of the term "extraterritorial jurisdiction" or "extraterritoriality," which explains the mixed views on its legality. Extraterritorial jurisdiction has often been associated with the extraordinary,[82] illegality,[83] excessive governance,[84] outrageousness,[85] aggressive unilateralism, or legal hegemony,[86] and this exacerbated existing uncertainties. The law of jurisdiction seems trapped

---

[77] Rutsel Silvestre J. Martha, *Extraterritorial Taxation in International Law, in* EXTRATERRITORIAL JURISDICTION IN THEORY AND PRACTICE 19, 23 (1996); MENG 46 (1994); RYNGAERT, JURISDICTION 39 (2015).

[78] Alien Tort Claims Act 28 U.S.C. § 1350 (U.S.) [ATCA].

[79] Regulation 648/2012 of the European Parliament and of the Council on OTC Derivatives, Central Counterparties and Trade Repositories, 2012 O.J. (L 201) 1, at 23.

[80] ZERK, EXTRATERRITORIAL JURISDICTION 5 (2010). *Also* Buxbaum, *Territory, Territoriality and the Resolution of Jurisdictional Conflict* 634 (2009).

[81] Arrest Warrant, 2002 I.C.J. 63, 76 (Joint Separate Opinion of Judges Higgins, Kooijmans, and Buergenthal).

[82] Mark Gibney, *On Terminology: Extraterritorial Obligations, in* GLOBAL JUSTICE, STATE DUTIES: THE EXTRATERRITORIAL SCOPE OF ECONOMIC, SOCIAL AND CULTURAL RIGHTS IN INTERNATIONAL LAW 32, 40 (Malcolm Langford et al. eds., 2013).

[83] Maier, *Jurisdictional Rules in Customary International Law, in* EXTRATERRITORIAL JURISDICTION IN THEORY AND PRACTICE 76 (1996).

[84] Andrew T. Guzman, *Is International Antitrust Possible?*, 73 N.Y.U. L. REV. 1501, 1506 (1998).

[85] Andreas F. Lowenfeld, *International Litigation and the Quest for Reasonableness*, 245 RCADI 9, 43–4 (1994).

[86] Gunther Handl, *Extra-territoriality and Transnational Legal Authority, in* BEYOND TERRITORIALITY: TRANSNATIONAL LEGAL AUTHORITY IN AN AGE OF GLOBALIZATION 3, 4 (Gunther

in a dichotomy between "legitimate" territorial jurisdiction and "problematic" extraterritorial jurisdiction. This pejorative connotation has caused scholars and practitioners to avoid the term,[87] but bypassing the terminological obstacles of extraterritoriality only delays what will inevitably reappear when we must determine the legality of extraterritorial jurisdiction. Unpacking this charged terminology is a necessary first step.

The starting point of extraterritorial jurisdiction is territory, because in the absence of territory, the law of jurisdiction (or of extra-*territoriality*, as it were) has no meaning. "Territory" denotes a stable, physically identified base, delimited in space by means of natural frontiers, by undisputed outward signs of delimitation, by frontier conventions, and by mutual recognition of states.[88] Extraterritoriality, which comes from the Latin *extra territorium*, must *a contrario* mean "outside a state's territory." Approaching the term in this negative sense leaves extraterritoriality with two possible meanings: it can mean "on the territory of another state" or "on state-free territory."

These definitions may appear to be relatively clear and unequivocal, but there are several problems with them. *Extra*-territoriality implies that jurisdiction is exercised without any link to sovereign territory, and hence without a link to the state exercising jurisdiction. The nationality principle, in which nationality rather than territory is the decisive criterion, would thus be extraterritorial, as would the protective and universality principles.[89] Yet, if we look closer, all of these hinge on a territorial base. Nationality can only be defined by the state that endows a person with nationality. Since states are distinguished from one another mainly by their territory, nationality is valid only because a territorially defined state has granted it, so every single jurisdictional principle is ultimately linked to the distinct territories of states. The effects principle is based on the territorial effects of an extraterritorial measure. The protective principle is based on the desire of each state to ensure its territorial security, and so on. Every jurisdictional principle is based on some territorial link, but, the crux is, that might not be the only territorial link to a state.[90] So a strictly linguistic definition of extraterritorial jurisdiction leaves unresolved the problems that plague the law of jurisdiction.

To tackle these terminological inadequacies, we must first acknowledge that all forms and types of extraterritorial jurisdiction are (intra)territorial by their provenance. Extraterritorial norms are generated through domestic legislative or adjudicative processes. Judges Higgins, Kooijmans, and Buergenthal recognized this in the *Arrest Warrant* when they argued that "territorial jurisdiction for extraterritorial events"[91] more accurately describes extraterritorial

---

Handl & Joachim Zekoll eds., 2012); Kal Raustialia, *Empire and Extraterritoriality in Twentieth Century America*, 40 Sw. L. Rev. 604 (2011).

[87] U.S. Restatement (Fourth) of the Foreign Relations Law, § 401, reporters' note 1; Inazumi 23 (2005); Ryngaert, Jurisdiction 7 (2015).

[88] Island of Palmas, 1928 R.I.A.A. 838-9. Or, as Khan says, without frontiers or natural barriers, "[l]and as such is no territory" (Daniel-Erasmus Khan, *Territory and Boundaries*, *in* The Oxford Handbook of the History of International Law 225, 231 (Bardo Fassbender & Anne Peters eds., 2012)).

[89] Higgins, Problems and Process 74 (1995); Ryngaert, Jurisdiction 7 (2015).

[90] *See also* Ryngaert, Jurisdiction 7 (2015).

[91] Arrest Warrant, 2002 I.C.J. 63, 76, ¶ 42 (Joint Separate Opinion of Judges Higgins, Kooijmans, and Buergenthal).

jurisdiction. But norms that are (intra)territorial still capture (more or less considerable) extraterritorial aspects. So far, legal scholarship has unjustifiably collapsed these aspects and failed to ask the pivotal question: What factor is decisive in rendering jurisdiction territorial or extraterritorial? This question goes to the core of jurisdiction, and to answer it, we must scrutinize in detail the structure of jurisdictional norms.

Jurisdictional norms aim to identify connecting points to establish a state's regulatory competence. From these points, links or nexuses can be made to the state's jurisdiction. For instance, the nationality of persons is the source of the prescriptive authority that the state of nationality exercises over them. The connecting point "nationality" anchors and legitimizes attaching content to it, making it an anchor point. Anchor points might seem to represent the object and ends of regulation. For example, if a state intends to assert jurisdiction over a case that involves a dog's well-being, it establishes a territorial anchor to the dog based on the dog's current location. The dog, in this case, is both the anchor point and the object of regulation because the norm's purpose is to ensure the dog's well-being. But this is not necessarily the case for all forms of jurisdiction. Imagine a state that wishes to prescribe minimum standards of parental leave for corporations. The anchor point for the jurisdictional norm will be the corporation (by way of the corporation's nationality or seat). But the regulated content pertains to social rights of third persons (in this case, parental leave for employees), so the anchor point is not necessarily the object of regulation where the consequences of a norm are intended to be felt.

The regulated content represents the centerpiece of every jurisdictional norm. Its purpose, by and large, is to fulfill the norm's *Regelungszweck*. Put differently, the regulated content is a norm's raison d'être. The anchor literally anchors, thus, legitimates and rationalizes, the sphere of regulated content to a state. Sometimes the anchor is cast exactly into the sphere of regulated content, and sometimes it is not. Moreover, dropping anchors and regulating content may cause ripple effects, so-called ancillary repercussions. A jurisdictional norm can thus be structured by its anchor point, by its regulated content, and by its ancillary repercussions.[92] Figure 1.3 illustrates the basic structure of a jurisdictional norm.

Adding spatial dimensions to the jurisdictional norm generates a new set of considerations that brings us closer to distinguishing territorial from extraterritorial jurisdiction. A norm's anchor point can lie within or outside a state's territory, as can regulated content and ancillary repercussions. The three elements of a jurisdictional norm can thus be distinguished

[92] Scholars other than Meng and Rudolf have proposed ways to define extraterritorial jurisdiction. Vranes distinguishes between unilateral or multilateral creation of norms, the regulation of domestic or foreign conduct, and the pursuance of territorial or extraterritorial concerns (VRANES 174 ff. (2009)). Vranes' distinction of norms/regulation/pursuance of concerns is almost the same as the anchor point/content regulation/ancillary repercussion distinction I apply. Scott has conceptualized extraterritorial laws, differentiating between so-called extraterritorial laws and territorial extensions. Extraterritorial laws translate into "[t]he application of a measure triggered by something other than a territorial connection with the regulating state." Territorial extensions, by contrast, occur where "[t]he application of a measure is triggered by a territorial connection but in applying the measure the regulator is required, as a matter of law, to take into account conduct or circumstances abroad." *See* Scott 90 (2014). But Scott's conceptualization fails to determine which factors should be territorial and which not, so it is not specific enough to address the prevailing problems of extraterritorial jurisdiction.

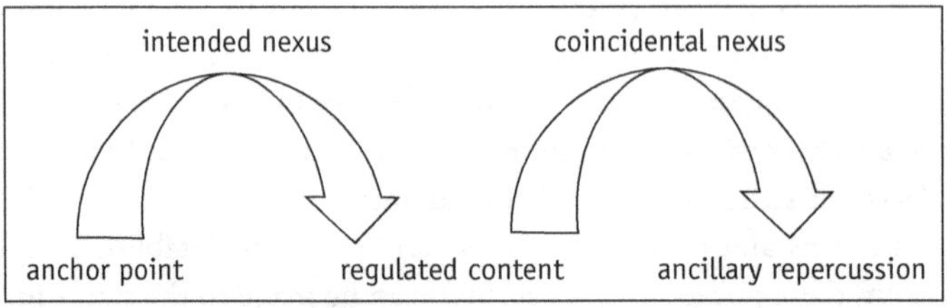

FIGURE 1.3 Basic structure of a jurisdictional norm.

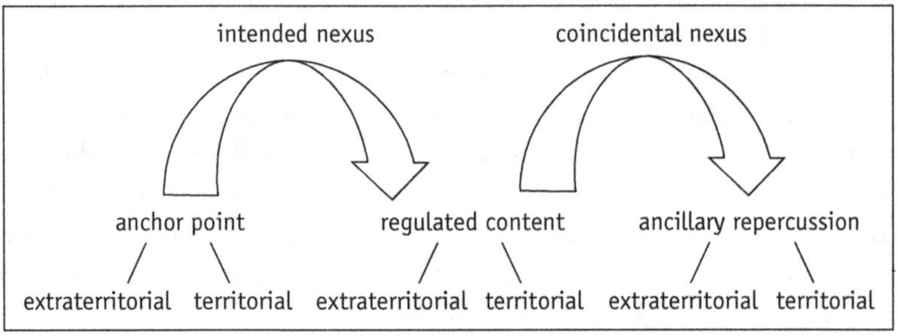

FIGURE 1.4 Basic structure and spatial dimensions of a jurisdictional norm.

by their location: territorial and extraterritorial anchor point, territorial and extraterritorial regulated content, and territorial and extraterritorial ancillary repercussions. Figure 1.4 illustrates the spatial dimensions of a jurisdictional norm, which form the backbone of the extraterritoriality framework.

B. EXTRATERRITORIAL JURISDICTION *STRICTO SENSU*, OR DIRECT EXTRATERRITORIALITY

The extraterritoriality framework distinguishes between direct and indirect extraterritorial jurisdiction. A jurisdictional norm is indirect extraterritorial if and only if ancillary repercussions occur on foreign territory, or, put differently, if there is neither an extraterritorial anchor point nor an extraterritorial content regulation. By contrast, a norm is extraterritorial *stricto sensu* (or direct extraterritorial) if its anchor point *or* the regulated content lies outside the prescribing state's territory. Figure 1.5 illustrates this limited focus of extraterritorial jurisdiction *stricto sensu*.

As we approach the many conundrums of the extraterritoriality framework, it is crucial to keep the following caveat in mind: the extraterritoriality framework is an analytical tool that seeks to impartially define jurisdictional norms as extraterritorial or territorial. The framework dissects any jurisdictional norm into subfactors ([extra]territorial anchor point, [extra] territorial regulated content, and [extra]territorial ancillary repercussions) on the basis of which it classifies the norm as extraterritorial or territorial. The extraterritoriality framework is a formidable tool for tackling definitional conundrums and for conducting empirical research on jurisdictional practices (examining, e.g., what types of jurisdiction states use and how often they do so). However, the framework does not allow us to judge the legality of a

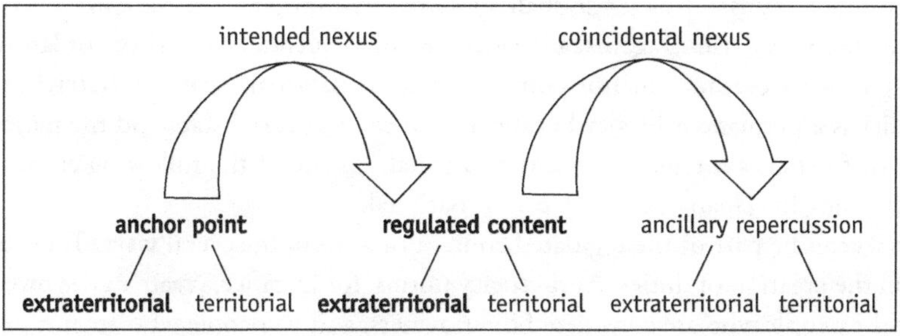

FIGURE 1.5 Extraterritorial jurisdiction *stricto sensu* (bold).

norm under international law. Only after this framework is applied to the norm under scrutiny can questions of legality or illegality be addressed.

Returning to the two forms of extraterritorial jurisdiction *stricto sensu*, I will now examine extraterritorial anchor points and extraterritorial content regulation. Extraterritorial anchor points may focus on personal, objective, or legal factors. Anchor points that relate to *persons* include the nationality of natural or legal persons, their seat, domicile, or residence.[93] For instance, pursuant to section 5 para. 8 of the German Criminal Code, German criminal law applies when German nationals commit offenses against a person's sexual self-determination abroad.[94] The offender's nationality is the anchor point to the state's jurisdiction; it is personal in character and was created by a loyalty connection from the person to the state (intraterritorial anchor point). In some states, animals might qualify as person-related anchors. Animals could operate as anchors to a state either by virtue of their "nationality" (as arguably created by, for example, pet passports),[95] or by their domicile or residence.

A state may also base its jurisdiction on anchor points related to *objects*, including the location of assets, events, or circumstances. Even if animals are considered mere property, they can constitute an independent anchor point as property, just as immovable property. Or, in the criminal realm, wrongs (e.g., cruelty or unnecessary suffering) inflicted on animals could be brought under a state's jurisdiction by linking it to the place where the crime was committed.

A state may also link its jurisdiction to anchor points that relate to *legal relations and statuses*, like the place where matrimony was entered, or where someone's legal personhood was established. So if animals are recognized as legal persons, the place that gave rise to this status would operate as an anchor point.

Since an anchor point is not necessarily the object of regulation where the intended consequences of a norm are felt, animals can also be part of a norm's regulated content. Extraterritorial content regulation determines the content of a regulation outside a state's territory by regulating, e.g., the institutions and substantive values of a state, obligations and rights, and legal relations of persons and of goods.[96] For instance, article 3-2 of the Japanese

---

[93] MENG 74–5 (1994).

[94] STRAFGESETZBUCH [STGB] [CRIMINAL CODE], Nov. 13, 1998, BGBl. I at 3322, art. 5 para. 8 (Ger.).

[95] On pet passports, *see, e.g.*, European Commission, DG Health and Consumers, Animal Health and Welfare, Movements of Pets, Pet Passports, *available at* http://ec.europa.eu/food/animal/liveanimals/pets/qanda_en.htm (last visited Jan. 10, 2019).

[96] MENG 5, 75 (1994).

Criminal Code states: "This Code shall apply to any non-Japanese national who commits one of the following crimes against a Japanese national outside the territory of Japan [...]."[97] Article 3-2 uses a personal anchor point (a Japanese national) that is intraterritorial since nationality is a permanent loyalty bond between the territorial state and the national. The content that article 3-2 regulates is extraterritorial: "None of the following crimes shall be committed outside Japan against a Japanese national."

Animals can be part of the regulated content of a norm in several ways. They can be involved in the creation of duties. Anti-cruelty norms, for instance, create duties owed to animals by the people who are considered their owners, and by people who are not part of the property relationship.[98] Animals can arguably also be rights holders. For instance, the United Kingdom's Five Freedoms of Animal Welfare confer—as the name implies—five freedoms on animals: freedom from hunger or thirst, freedom from discomfort, freedom from pain, injury, or disease, freedom to express normal behavior, and freedom from fear and distress.[99] These freedoms are sometimes regarded as freedom rights of animals.[100] If these rights are created for animals located abroad, we identify this as extraterritorial content regulation. Finally, it is possible to create legal relations or statuses that involve animals in foreign territory. This is the case when ownership or some form of usufruct is asserted over animals, or when animals are accorded legal personality.

The two types of extraterritorial jurisdiction *stricto sensu*—extraterritorial anchor point and extraterritorial content regulation—can be combined in different ways. I explore and differentiate these combinations by flagging them as types of jurisdiction (α, ß, γ, and δ). Extraterritorial anchor points can entail intraterritorial or extraterritorial content regulation. A person whose primary business is in the territory of one state may possess assets abroad (extraterritorial anchor point) subject to taxation in their home country (intraterritorial content regulation), which is type ß. Conversely, extraterritorial content regulation can be based on intraterritorial or extraterritorial anchor points. Foreigners might have a duty to pay taxes (extraterritorial content regulation) based on real property in the state's territory (intraterritorial anchor point), which is type γ. Another example of type γ is a domestic duty a state imposes on a domestic corporate parent (intraterritorial anchor point), demanding the corporation's foreign subsidiaries report on their employee policies (extraterritorial content regulation). Extraterritorial anchor points and extraterritorial content regulation may also overlap, and so may intraterritorial anchor points and intraterritorial content regulation. An intraterritorial norm may use an extraterritorial anchor point and aim to regulate content outside its territory. An example of this is the direct duty imposed on a foreign subsidiary (extraterritorial anchor point) to report on its human rights performance (extraterritorial

[97] 刑法 KEIHŌ [PENAL CODE], Act No. 45 of 1907, art. 3-2 (Japan) [KEIHŌ [PENAL CODE] (Japan)], *translation at* http://www.cas.go.jp/jp/seisaku/hourei/data/PC.pdf.

[98] Early animal protection laws protected only the interests of people owning animals, whereas contemporary anti-cruelty laws criminalize acts against animals regardless of ownership: BRUCE A. WAGMAN & MATTHEW LIEBMAN, A WORLDVIEW OF ANIMAL LAW 148–9 (2011).

[99] FARM ANIMAL WELFARE COUNCIL (FAWC), THE FIVE FREEDOMS (FAWC, Surbiton 1992).

[100] *See* Chapter 8, §3 VII, on freedoms and animal rights.

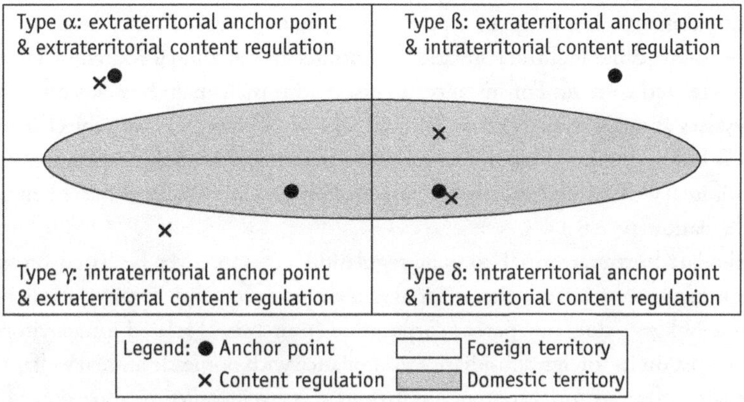

FIGURE 1.6 Types of extraterritorial jurisdiction *stricto sensu.*

content regulation), which is type α.[101] The simplest form is type δ, which is intraterritorial prescription of content based on an intraterritorial anchor point, such as prohibiting nationals from committing murder on domestic territory. Figure 1.6 illustrates the different combinations of these types of jurisdiction.

C. THE ANIMAL RELATION

Though the extraterritoriality framework is already fairly complex, it requires another set of factors. Here, I examine how the different types of jurisdiction just explained relate to animals, such as when states use them as anchors or regulate aspects of their lives. I use the term *animal-related* to determine if animals are an integral part of anchor points or regulated content in jurisdictional norms. As noted above, type α norms regulate content extraterritorially and use extraterritorial anchor points. If we add to that the *animal-related* dimension, three distinct types of jurisdiction emerge. First, type α_1 emerges when animal-related extraterritorial anchor points and animal-related extraterritorial content regulation correlate (type α_1): a state uses extraterritorial animal-related anchor points, and also aspires to regulate animal-related content outside its territory. This, likely, is the most extreme form of extraterritoriality. An example of type α_1 jurisdiction is when a state imposes duties on foreign owners of animals (extraterritorial anchor points) to ensure adherence to its animal law (extraterritorial content regulation) (type α_1). Second, animal-related extraterritorial anchor points can meet non-animal-related extraterritorial content regulation (type α_2). One can imagine a state imposing a tax on dog owners if their dog is located on domestic territory, regardless of where the owners live. Third, animal-related extraterritorial content regulation can be based on non-animal-related extraterritorial anchor points (type α_3), as, for example, when a direct duty is imposed on a foreign subsidiary to report on its compliance with domestic animal welfare standards.

---

[101] *See, e.g.*, Human Rights Council, 17th Sess., Special Representative of the Secretary-General John Ruggie, Guiding Principles on Business and Human Rights: Implementing the United Nations "Protect, Respect and Remedy" Framework, U.N. Doc. A/HRC/17/31, 7 (Mar. 21, 2011) [*Guiding Principles on Business and Human Rights*].

The same dimensions emerge in type ß jurisdictional norms. Animal-related extraterritorial anchor points can entail the regulation of intraterritorial animal-related or intraterritorial non-animal-related content. For instance, a person with their main business on domestic territory possesses animals abroad (extraterritorial anchor point); these are subject to taxation in the person's home country (non-animal-related intraterritorial content regulation, type ß$_1$), or subject to animal welfare regulation in the person's home country (animal-related intraterritorial content regulation, type ß$_2$).

Animal-related extraterritorial content regulation can moreover be based on an animal-related or non-animal-related intraterritorial anchor point (type γ). Type γ_1 jurisdiction occurs when a state obliges a domestic parent corporation (non-animal-related intraterritorial anchor point) to report on its foreign subsidiaries' compliance with domestic animal welfare standards (animal-related extraterritorial content regulation). Type γ_1 jurisdiction also exists where a state requires its nationals (non-animal-related intraterritorial anchor points) to adhere to its animal laws when operating abroad (animal-related extraterritorial content regulation). Type γ_2 jurisdiction is different. Based on the universality principle, a state may criminalize especially gruesome acts committed against animals wherever they are (animal-related extraterritorial content regulation), after the animal returns to the forum (animal-related intraterritorial anchor point) (type γ_2). Table 1.1 illustrates the animal relation of anchor points and regulated content by the types presented and exemplified, and makes clear this book's focus on the animal-relation of extraterritorial jurisdiction *stricto sensu*.

TABLE 1.1

TYPES OF JURISDICTION IN ANIMAL LAW UNDER THE EXTRATERRITORIALITY FRAMEWORK

			Anchor point			
			Intraterritorial		Extraterritorial	
			Animal-related	Non-animal-related	Animal-related	Non-animal-related
Content regulation	Intraterritorial	Animal-related	—	—	ß$_2$	—
		Non-animal-related	—	—	ß$_1$	—
	Extraterritorial	Animal-related	γ_2	γ_1	α_1	α_3
		Non-animal-related	—	—	α_2	—

D. EXTRATERRITORIAL ANCILLARY REPERCUSSIONS, OR INDIRECT EXTRATERRITORIALITY

Ancillary repercussions have no bearing on whether a norm is extraterritorial *stricto sensu* or not. In contrast to anchor points and regulated content, ancillary repercussions refer to the many implications of a norm that extend beyond the effects it was intended to have, i.e., beyond the regulated content. Lawmakers may be able to predict a norm's ancillary repercussions, but those are not the reason a norm was initially enacted for or the reason why it is still upheld. Animals may be part of or an ancillary repercussion where they are positively or negatively affected by a norm, as a side effect. If a norm has such an effect, it has an animal-related ancillary repercussion.

Extraterritorial ancillary repercussions—also known as indirect extraterritorial jurisdiction or domestic measures with extraterritorial implications—are considered another attribute of the two forms of extraterritorial jurisdiction, rather than a distinct third form.[102] Not including ancillary repercussions in the definition of extraterritoriality *stricto sensu* means we make some delineation to a potentially vast causal chain of events triggered by a norm. The purpose of this delineation, ideally, is to mirror a norm's reasonable sphere of influence.[103]

Distinguishing extraterritorial content regulation from extraterritorial ancillary repercussions can be challenging, and the most useful test to make this task easier is the *sine qua non* test. If the purpose of the jurisdictional norm is not met by the extraterritorial ancillary repercussion, then the norm does not regulate content extraterritorially. Subsidy regulations are an apt example: a regulation that grants a recipient a domestic subsidy improves its market position both on the domestic and on the global market. To judge what type of extraterritorial jurisdiction the regulation is, we must determine which effects of the norm form part of the regulated content and which are ancillary repercussions. We can distinguish between the two by examining the purpose of the jurisdictional norm. Typically, subsidy regulations seek to strengthen the recipient's economic position on the domestic market (intraterritorial content regulation). We can verify the proposition by applying the *sine qua non test*. If the global market position of the subsidized body does not improve (i.e., there are no extraterritorial ancillary repercussions), has the norm missed the mark? In most cases, the subsidy norm will retain its regulatory purpose since it is designed to improve the recipient's position on the domestic market. We are thus dealing with intraterritorial content regulation that potentially has extraterritorial ancillary repercussions, and is therefore, at best, a form of indirect extraterritorial jurisdiction.

---

[102] John G. Ruggie, UN SRSG for Business & Human Rights, Keynote Presentation at EU Presidency Conference on the "Protect, Respect and Remedy" Framework Stockholm, Nov. 10–11, 2009; ZERK, EXTRATERRITORIAL JURISDICTION 13 (2010).

[103] MENG 76 (1994).

§4 Spatial Dimensions of Animal Law

Though I have established the necessary tools for beginning an inquiry from the perspective of the law of jurisdiction, we must also determine the tools of animal law. In this section, I define the scope of this study from the perspective of animal law and show why animal law deserves a distinct and careful examination under the law of jurisdiction.

A. OF HUMANS AND OTHER ANIMALS

Questions about our treatment of animals have received broad scholarly attention only in the past two decades. New insights from neurological, biological, and psychological studies about animal behavior and cognition, like Jane Goodall's research with chimpanzees, began garnering the attention of scholars outside these disciplines. Social sciences and humanities were the site of the initial explosion of writings and teachings about animals. Philosophy quickly caught up by developing ethical imperatives that ought to govern our manifold interactions with animals. With a heightened academic focus on the study of human-animal relationships, a new research paradigm emerged in scholarship: the animal turn.[104] From a legal perspective, the animal turn eventually culminated in what is now known as animal law, namely, the study of legal norms related to animals.

In the legal discourse on the human-animal relationship, we typically identify animals as such in a generalizing and sweeping way. From a linguistic perspective, "animal" comes from the Latin word *animalis*, meaning "having breath of life."[105] The term was first used to describe any living being, as opposed to inanimate objects.[106] Natural science then produced the necessary knowledge to distinguish between distinct forms of animate life. Contemporary science recognizes animals as eukaryotic (organisms that dispose over a membranous cell nucleus), heterotroph (they ingest other organisms or their products), multicellular, and mostly freely movable organisms of the kingdom *Animalia* (also called *Metazoa*).[107] Animals differ from plants in having cells without cellulose walls, in lacking chlorophyll and the capacity for photosynthesis, in requiring more complex food materials, in being organized to a greater degree of complexity, and in having the capacity for spontaneous movement

---

[104] The phrase "animal turn" was coined by Sarah Franklin at the Cultural Studies Association of Australasia in 2003: Helena Pedersen, *Knowledge Production in the "Animal Turn": Multiplying the Image of Thought, Empathy, and Justice, in* EXPLORING THE ANIMAL TURN: HUMAN-ANIMAL RELATIONS IN SCIENCE, SOCIETY AND CULTURE 13, 13 (Erika Andersson Cederholm et al. eds., 2014). *See also* Harriet Ritvo, *On the Animal Turn*, 136 DAEDALUS 118 (2007).

[105] JULIA CRESSWELL, THE OXFORD DICTIONARY OF WORD ORIGINS 16 (2d ed. 2010).

[106] CRESSWELL 16 (2010).

[107] The term "animal" thus includes all living beings that are not part of the zoological kingdom of plants, mushrooms, blue algae, and other microorganisms. ELIZABETH MARTINA & ROBERT HINE, A DICTIONARY OF BIOLOGY (2014) ("animal"). *See also* RITA JEDELHAUSER, DAS TIER UNTER DEM SCHUTZ DES RECHTS: DIE TIERETHISCHEN GRUNDLAGEN EINES RECHTLICHEN SCHUTZMODELLS FÜR DAS TIERSCHUTZRECHTLICHE VERWALTUNGSHANDELN 13 (2011).

and rapid motor responses to stimulation.[108] Members of the kingdom *Animalia* are commonly divided into multiple subgroups called *phyla*. These include vertebrates (mammals [including humans], birds, amphibians, reptiles, and fishes), arthropods (insects, spiders, crabs, millipedes, centipedes, scorpions, lobsters, shrimp), mollusks (octopuses, snails, oysters, clams, and squid), annelids (leeches and earthworms), jellyfish, and sponges. Because the kingdom *Animalia* includes both those commonly referred to as "animals" and those commonly referred to as "humans," taxonomies of natural science are a testament the continuity of species: any proclaimed difference between humans and animals is, at most, one of degree, not kind.[109]

Because humans are—biologically speaking—animals, every single legal document that was ever passed is—strictly speaking—a document of animal law. Obviously, legislators who enacted laws on bodily liberty, property, nuisance, territory, and so forth, did not intend to imbue these laws with such a wide application. A famous example for the law's narrow reading is the *Tilikum* case, brought by People for the Ethical Treatment of Animals (PETA) on behalf of Tilikum, an orca kept in the SeaWorld Orlando park, against the SeaWorld corporation. The plaintiff asked the court to rule that the terms of the Thirteenth Amendment to the US Constitution applied to Tilikum, and thus that the orca's confinement amounted to involuntary servitude or slavery. The Court was not convinced by the plaintiff's arguments and held that the Thirteenth Amendment only applied to persons. Because Tilikum was not a person, the Court argued, he could not be accorded constitutional protection.[110] The legal definition of animals is thus often much narrower than its linguistic and natural science counterpart: animals are all animals except human animals. As we tend to forget about our own taxonomic nomenclature, anthropologists and ethicists developed the expression "nonhuman animals" as a more correct term to describe the group generally referred to as animals in common usage.[111] The term "nonhuman animal" is widely used in ethics, politics, anthropology, and natural sciences, but is less common in legal academic writing. In this

---

[108] Merriam-Webster, "Animal," *available at* http://www.merriam-webster.com/dictionary/animal (last visited Jan. 10, 2019).

[109] Seminal: CHARLES DARWIN, ON THE ORIGIN OF SPECIES BY MEANS OF NATURAL SELECTION, OR THE PRESERVATION OF FAVOURED RACES IN THE STRUGGLES FOR LIKE (1859); CHARLES DARWIN, THE DESCENT OF MAN, AND SELECTION IN RELATION TO SEX (1871).

[110] Tilikum v. SeaWorld Parks & Ent., Inc., 842 F. Supp. 2d 1259, 1261 (S.D. Cal. 2012) (U.S.). The court held: "The Amendment's language and meaning is clear, concise, and not subject to the vagaries of conceptual interpretation—'Neither slavery nor involuntary servitude [. . .] shall exist within the United States or any place subject to their jurisdiction.' As 'slavery' and 'involuntary servitude' are uniquely human activities, as those terms have been historically and contemporaneously applied, there is simply no basis to construe the Thirteenth Amendment as applying to non-humans." (*Id.* at 6). *See* for a useful discussion of the case: Jeffrey S. Kerr et al., *A Slave by Any Other Name Is still a Slave: The* Tilikum *Case and Application of the Thirteenth Amendment to Nonhuman Animals*, 19 ANIMAL L. 221 (2013).

[111] *See, e.g.*, ARRAN STRIBBE, ANIMAL ERASED: DISCOURSE, ECOLOGY, AND RECONNECTION WITH THE NATURAL WORLD (2012), stating: "Non-speciesist language guidelines are receiving a similar treatment. Lists of pseudo 'politically correct' terms related to animals have started appearing on a number of humerous websites." *See also* Michael Tooley, *Are Nonhuman Animals Persons?*, *in* THE OXFORD HANDBOOK OF ANIMAL ETHICS 332 (Tom L. Beauchamp & R.G. Frey eds., 2011).

work, I use the word "animal" for reasons of conformity and because I want to refrain from defining a group of individuals by what they are not; however, it should be clear that I mean nonhuman animal.

Animal law is typically concerned with both the protection of animals and their welfare. *Animal protection law* describes all regulatory measures designed to protect animals from negative affective states, like pain, suffering, harm, anxiety, or distress.[112] These laws negatively determine how animals should be treated by prohibiting acts of cruelty or neglect. Animal law has also evolved to regulate the *welfare of animals*. The origins of animal welfare can be traced back to the science of animal welfare, which identifies indicators for animal well-being or lack thereof from the perspectives of physiology, veterinary science, ethology, and comparative psychology.[113] The World Organization for Animal Health (OIE) defines animal welfare in article 7.1.1. of its Terrestrial Animal Health Code:

> Animal welfare means how an animal is coping with the conditions in which it lives. An animal is in a good state of welfare if (as indicated by scientific evidence) it is healthy, comfortable, well nourished, safe, able to express innate behaviour, and if it is not suffering from unpleasant states such as pain, fear, and distress.
>
> Good animal welfare requires disease prevention and appropriate veterinary treatment, shelter, management and nutrition, humane handling and humane slaughter or killing.[114]

The OIE's definition of animal welfare features two elements: the *state of the animal*, which corresponds to the scientific definition of animal welfare and refers to the physical and mental health of an animal, their well-being, and life; and the corollary *treatment of animals* by humans, which typically relates to humane treatment, or good animal husbandry. These terms are closely related and often mutually dependent. For example, where humans dominate important dimensions of animals' lives, the ability of animals to thrive and experience good physical and mental well-being largely depends on humans treating them properly. And because life is a prerequisite to any enjoyment of well-being, animal welfare also covers animal life.[115] In contrast to animal protection law, animal welfare laws *positively* regulate

---

[112] Andreas Rüttimann, *Tierschutzbewegung, in* LEXIKON DER MENSCH-TIER-BEZIEHUNGEN 371, 372 (Arianna Ferrari & Klaus Petrus eds., 2015).

[113] Animal welfare started as a formal discipline with the Brambell report on the welfare of farmed animals, issued by the British Government in 1965 (Report of the Technical Committee to Enquire into the Welfare of Animals Kept under Intensive Livestock Husbandry Systems, Her Majesty's Stationery Office, London 1965): David Fraser, *Animal Ethics and Animal Welfare Science: Bridging Two Cultures*, 65 APPL. ANIM. BEHAV. SCI. 171 (1999) (clarifying the interplay of normative and empirical elements in the assessment of animal welfare).

[114] OIE, TERRESTRIAL ANIMAL HEALTH CODE, art. 7.1.1 (OIE, Paris 2018) (emphasis omitted). *See for a discussion,* Barry Bousfield & Richard Brown, *What Is Animal Welfare?*, 1 ANIMAL WELFARE 1, 1 (2010), noting that animal welfare ensures that an animal's physical and mental state and their ability to fulfill their natural needs and desires are considered, and that animals are not treated cruelly, or subjected to unnecessary pain or suffering.

[115] GIERI BOLLIGER, MICHELLE RICHNER, & ANDREAS RÜTTIMANN, SCHWEIZER TIERSCHUTZSTRAFRECHT IN THEORIE UND PRAXIS 23 (2011).

the treatment of animals. Taken as a whole, laws on animal welfare and animal protection positively and negatively protect the same values (i.e., animal life and physical and mental well-being), so they are best seen as two sides of the same coin.[116]

Examining the territorial limits of animal protection or animal welfare laws can easily be mistaken for identifying with the welfare position in the animal welfare versus animal rights debate in animal ethics.[117] The animal welfare position (also called legal welfarism or new welfarism) recognizes animal interests are worthy of protection but regards the use of animals for human interests and benefits per se as morally justifiable. Animals are only protected from human exploitation if the pain or suffering inflicted upon them is deemed unnecessary. Because humans unilaterally determine when animal suffering is necessary, laws enacted on this basis are virtually meaningless. Animal rights theorists maintain that, instead of effectively protecting animals, animal protection or welfare standards legitimate the use and exploitation of animals.[118] For animals to enjoy meaningfully protected interests, they should have fundamental and actionable rights instead of simple protections.[119]

Prima facie, both welfarist and abolitionist norms can be examined for their territorial reach. For example, we can study the territorial limits of laws that protect whales from unnecessary suffering or of laws that respect whales' right to life. Though I defend a strong animal rights position, the inquiry into extraterritorial jurisdiction applies to both a welfarist and an abolitionist approach. Most modern legal systems are founded on the premise that animals are property and take the welfarist position, but some have introduced certain absolute prohibitions, which may be manifestations of abolitionism as negative freedom rights.[120] For example, Australia, Belgium, the Balearic Islands, the Netherlands, and New Zealand have banned invasive research on great apes, which some scholars view as negative freedom rights of great apes.[121] Because these developments are in flux, subject to social change, and

---

[116] Clare Palmer & Peter Sandøe, *Welfare, in* CRITICAL TERMS FOR ANIMAL STUDIES 424, 427–8 (Lori Gruen ed., 2018).

[117] *See* generally on this debate SUE DONALDSON & WILL KYMLICKA, ZOOPOLIS: A POLITICAL THEORY OF ANIMAL RIGHTS 73 ff. (2011); SABINE LENNKH, DIE KODIFIKATION DES TIERSCHUTZRECHTS, MODELLVORSTELLUNGEN 28 ff. (2012); BERNARD E. ROLLIN, ANIMAL RIGHTS AND HUMAN MORALITY (3d ed. 2006); PAUL WALDAU, ANIMAL RIGHTS: WHAT EVERYONE NEEDS TO KNOW (2011); STEVEN M. WISE, DRAWING THE LINE: SCIENCE AND THE CASE FOR ANIMAL RIGHTS (2013).

[118] *See* GARY FRANCIONE, ANIMALS, PROPERTY, AND THE LAW 18 (2007): "I refer to the current regulatory structure in this country as it pertains to animals as *legal welfarism*, or the notion, represented by and in various legal doctrines, that animals, which are the property of people, may be treated solely as means to ends by humans as long as this exploitation does not result in the infliction of 'unnecessary' pain, suffering or death." (Emphasis in original).

[119] *E.g.*, STEVEN M. WISE, RATTLING THE CAGE: TOWARD LEGAL RIGHTS FOR ANIMALS 53 ff. (2000).

[120] From the legal perspective of the status quo, attempts to distinguish protections and rights might be overstated: JOAN E. SCHAFFNER, AN INTRODUCTION TO ANIMALS AND THE LAW 171 (2011).

[121] BUNDESGESETZ ÜBER VERSUCHE AN LEBENDEN TIEREN [TIERVERSUCHSGESETZ, TVG] [AUSTRIAN ANIMAL EXPERIMENTATION ACT], BGBl. I No. 114/2012, § 4(5)(a) (Austria), stating that experimentation with great apes is illegal in all cases (including gibbons). Animal Welfare Act, Public Act No. 142, Oct. 14, 1999 §§ 85 ff. (N.Z.) forbids use of nonhuman hominids in research, testing, or teaching without the Director-General's approval, and only "in the interests of the species to which the non-human hominid belongs." *See also id.* § 85(5)(a). For the other states, *see* COLIN GOLDNER, LEBENSLÄNGLICH HINTER GITTERN: DIE

embedded in widely different cultural contexts, this study applies to laws that protect animals, as well as to laws that more effectively respect animals' interests by giving them rights.

B. UNCONQUERED JURISDICTIONAL TERRITORY

Though the law of jurisdiction typically operates by the same few jurisdictional principles—the objective and subjective territoriality principles, the nationality principle, the effects principle, and the universality principle—their application to animal law is anything but simple and straightforward. Animals, or animal law, deserve distinct consideration in the law of jurisdiction, based on four considerations.

First, most animal welfare acts and regulations are silent about their territorial scope.[122] Laws that fail to speak to this issue include those of Argentina,[123] the states and territories of Australia,[124] Austria,[125] Belgium,[126] Botswana,[127] Brazil,[128] Bulgaria,[129] Canada and its provinces and territories,[130] Costa Rica,[131] Croatia,[132] Estonia,[133] the European Union,[134]

WAHRHEIT ÜBER GORILLA, ORANG UTAN & CO IN DEUTSCHEN ZOOS (2014); Carl Saucier-Bouffard, *The Legal Rights for Great Apes*, *in* THE GLOBAL GUIDE TO ANIMAL PROTECTION 235, 235 (2013); WAGMAN & LIEBMAN 190 (2011).

[122] This list, though not comprehensive, is representative of a host of states that have adopted animal welfare or animal protection acts.

[123] LEY NACIONAL 14.346 DE PROTECCIÓN ANIMAL, Sancionada en el Congreso Nacional el 27/9/54, Incluida en el Codigo Penal, Dec. 27, 1954 [Law No. 14.346, ANIMAL WELFARE CODE] (Arg.) [ANIMAL WELFARE CODE (Arg.)].

[124] *Animal Welfare Act 1992* (ACT) (Austl.); *Prevention of Cruelty to Animals Act 1979*, Act No. 200 (NSW) (Austl.); *Animal Welfare Act* (NT) (Austl.); *Animal Care and Protection Act 2001* (Qld) (Austl.); *Animal Welfare Act 1985* (SA) (Austl.); *Animal Welfare Act*, Act No. 63 (Tas) (Austl.); *Prevention of Cruelty to Animals Act 1986* (Vic) (Austl.); *Animal Welfare Act 2002* (WA) (Austl.).

[125] TIERSCHUTZGESETZ [TSCHG] [ANIMAL PROTECTION ACT], BGBl. I No. 118/2004 (Austria) [ANIMAL PROTECTION ACT (Austria)].

[126] LOI RELATIVE À LA PROTECTION ET AU BIEN-ÊTRE DES ANIMAUX [ANIMAL PROTECTION ACT], No. 1986016195, MONITEUR BELGE [M.B.] [Official Gazette of Belgium] 16382, Aug. 14, 1986 (Belg.) [ANIMAL PROTECTION ACT (Belg.)].

[127] Cruelty to Animals Act, Cap. 37:02, May 8, 1936, consolidated version of the Proclamation 27 of 1936 as of Dec. 31, 2008 (Bots.) [Cruelty to Animals Act (Bots.)].

[128] Decreto Lei N° 24.645, de 10 de Julho de 1934 [Federal Decree on Anti-Cruelty N° 24.645], July 10, 1934 (Braz.) [Federal Decree on Antri-Cruelty (Braz.)].

[129] Zakon za Zashtita na Zhivotnite [Law on the Protection of Animals] of Jan. 31, 2008, DURZHAVEN VESTNIK [D.V.] [State Gazette], Feb. 8, 2008 (Bulg.) [Animal Protection Act (Bulg.)].

[130] Criminal Code, c. C-46, 1985, §§ 444 ff. (Can.) [Criminal Code (Can.)].

[131] Decreta Ley de Bienestar de los Animales [Decree on the Well-being of Animals], No. 7451, June 20, 2012, (Costa Rica) [Decree on the Well-being of Animals (Costa Rica)].

[132] Zakon o zaštiti životinja [Animal Protection Act], No. 71-05-03/1-06-2, Dec. 7, 2006 (Croat.) [Animal Protection Act (Croat.)].

[133] Lomakaitseseadus [Animal Protection Act] Dec. 13, 2000, RIIGI TEATAJA [R.T.], I 2001, 3, 4 (Est.) [Animal Protection Act (Est.)].

[134] Council Directive 93/119/EC on the Protection of Animals at the Time of Slaughter or Killing, 1993 O.J. (L 340) 21; Council Regulation 1099/2009 on the Protection of Animals at the Time of Killing, 1993 O.J. (L 303) 1; Council Directive 1999/74 Laying Down Minimum Standards for the Protection of Laying Hens,

Fiji,[135] Finland,[136] Germany,[137] Gibraltar,[138] Greece,[139] Hong Kong,[140] Iceland,[141] Israel,[142] Japan,[143] Kenya,[144] Latvia,[145] Liechtenstein[146] Lithuania,[147] Malaysia,[148] Malta,[149] Myanmar,[150] the Netherlands,[151] New Zealand,[152] Nicaragua,[153] Papua New

---

1999 O.J. (L 203) 53; Council Directive 1999/22 Relating to the Keeping of Wild Animals in Zoos, 1999 O.J. (L 94) 24; Commission Directive 2002/4 on the Registration of Establishments Keeping Laying Hens, 2002 O.J. (L 30) 44; Council Directive 98/58 Concerning the Protection of Animals Kept for Farming Purposes, 1998 O.J. (L 221) 23; Council Directive 2008/119 Laying Down Minimum Standards for the Protection of Calves, 2009 O.J. (L 10) 7; Council Directive 2008/120 Laying Down Minimum Standards for the Protection of Pigs, 2009 O.J. (L 47) 5; Regulation 1223/2009 of the European Parliament and of the Council on Cosmetic Products, 2009 O.J. (L 342) 59; Regulation 1007/2009 on Trade in Seal Products, 2009 O.J. (286) 36 [Regulation 1007/2009, 2009 O.J. (L 286) 36]; Directive 2010/63 of the European Parliament and the Council on the Protection of Animals Used for Scientific Purposes, 2010 O.J. (L 276) 33.

135 Animals (Control of Experiments) Act, May 13, 1957, c. 161, by Ordinance No. 11 of 1957 (Fiji) [Animals (Control of Experiments) Act (Fiji)].

136 Eläinsuojelulaki [Animal Welfare Act], 247/1996 (Fin.) [Animal Welfare Act (Fin.)].

137 TIERSCHUTZGESETZ [TIERSCHG] [ANIMAL WELFARE ACT], May 18, 2006, BGBl. I, at 1206 (Ger.) [ANIMAL WELFARE ACT (Ger.)].

138 Animal Experiments (Scientific Procedures) Act, Principal Act, No. 1999-03, Mar. 3, 1999 (Gibr.) [Animal Experiments Act (Gibr.)].

139 Nomos (2012:4039) Gia Ta Deopozomena Kai Ta Adeopota Zōa Syntrophiaskai Tēn Zōōnapotē Ekmetalleysē ē Tē Chrēsimottoiēsē me Kerdookopikookotto [Law Concerning Domestic and Stray Companion Animals and the Protection of Animals from any Exploitation or Use for Economic Profit], EPHEMERIS TES KYVERNESEOS TES HELLENIKES DEMOKRATIAS [E.K.E.D.] 2012 (Greece) [Law No. 4039 (Greece)].

140 Prevention of Cruelty to Animals Ordinance, (1997) Cap. 169, June 20, 1997, [L.N.] 331 of 1999 (Originally 44 of 1935 (Cap. 169 1950)) (H.K.) [Prevention of Cruelty to Animals Ordinance (H.K.)].

141 Act on Animal Welfare, No. 55, Apr. 8, 2013 (Ice.) [Act on Animal Welfare (Ice.)].

142 Cruelty to Animals Law (Animal Protection), Jan. 11, 1994, 5754-1994, Passed the Knesset 28 Tevet 5754 (Isr.) [Cruelty to Animals Law (Isr.)].

143 の動物の愛護及び管理に関する法律 [ACT ON WELFARE AND MANAGEMENT OF ANIMALS], Law No. 105 of 1973 (Japan).

144 Prevention of Cruelty to Animals Act, Cap. 360, 1983, [L.N.] 119/1984 (Kenya) [Prevention of Cruelty to Animals Act (Kenya)].

145 Dzīvnieku aizsardzības likums [Animal Protection Law], Dec. 9, 1999, LATVIJAS VĒSTNESIS [LATVIAN HERALD], 444/445 (Lat.) [Animal Protection Law (Lat.)].

146 TIERSCHUTZGESETZ [TSCHG] [ANIMAL WELFARE ACT], Sept. 23, 2010 (Liech.) [ANIMAL WELFARE ACT (Liech.)].

147 Gyvūnų Gerovės ir Apsaugos Įstatymas [Law on Welfare and Protection of Animals], Oct. 3, 2012, No. XI-2271, VALSTYBĖS ŽINIOS [OFFICIAL GAZETTE], Oct. 20, 2012, No. 122-6216 (Lith.) [Law on Welfare and Protection of Animals (Lith.)].

148 Animals Act, Apr. 30, 1953, LAWS OF MALAYSIA, Act 647, (Malay.) [Animals Act 1953 (Malay.)].

149 Animal Welfare Act, Feb. 8, 2002, c. 439, Act No. XXV of 2001 (Malta) [Animal Welfare Act (Malta)].

150 Animal Health and Development Law, Nov. 25, 1993, No. 17/93 (Myan.) [Animal Health and Development Law (Myan.)].

151 WET VAN 19 MEI 2011, HOUDENDE EEN INTEGRAAL KADER VOOR REGELS OVER GEHOUDEN DIEREN EN DAARAAN GERELATEERDE ONDERWERPEN (WET DIEREN) [Act of May 19, 2011, containing an integrated framework for rules on animals kept and related subjects (ANIMAL LAW)], May 19, 2011 (Neth.) [ANIMAL LAW (Neth.)].

152 Animal Welfare Act 1999 (N.Z.).

153 LEY PARA LA PROTECCIÓN Y EL BIENESTAR DE LOS ANIMALES DOMÉSTICOS Y ANIMALES SILVESTRES DOMESTICADOS [LAW FOR THE PROTECTION AND WELL-BEING OF PETS AND WILD ANIMALS IN

Guinea,[154] Paraguay,[155] the Philippines,[156] Poland,[157] Portugal,[158] Puerto Rico,[159] Slovenia,[160] Solomon Islands,[161] South Africa,[162] South Korea,[163] Sri Lanka,[164] Sweden,[165] Switzerland,[166] Taiwan,[167] Tonga,[168] Turkey,[169] Uganda,[170] Ukraine,[171] Vanuatu,[172] Venezuela,[173] Zimbabwe,[174]

CAPTIVITY], Ley No. 747, May 11, 2011, LA GACETA [Official Gazette of Nicaragua], No. 96, May 26, 2011 (Nicar.) [LAW FOR THE PROTECTION AND WELL-BEING OF PETS AND WILD ANIMALS IN CAPTIVITY (Nicar.)].

154 Animals Act 1952, c. 329, (Papua N.G.) [Animals Act 1952 (Papua N.G.)]; Animals Regulation 1967, c. 329 (Papua N.G.).

155 LEY N° 4840 DE PROTECCIÓN Y BIENESTAR ANIMAL EL CONGRESO DE LA NACION PARAGUAYA SANCIONA CON FUERZA DE LEY [LAW FOR THE PROTECTION AND WELL-BEING OF ANIMALS], Jan. 28, 2013, GACETA OFICIAL [G.O.] [Official Gazette of Paraguay], No. 21, Jan. 30, 2013 (Para.) [LAW FOR THE PROTECTION AND WELL-BEING OF ANIMALS (Para.)].

156 AN ACT TO PROMOTE ANIMAL WELFARE IN THE PHILIPPINES, otherwise known as "The Animal Welfare Act of 1998," Republic Act No. 8485 (Phil.) [ANIMAL WELFARE ACT (Phil.)].

157 O Ochronie Zwierzat [Act Regarding Animal Protection], Aug. 21, 1997, DZIENNIK USTAW RZECZYPOSPOLITEJ POLSKIEJ [JOURNAL OF LAWS OF THE REPUBLIC OF POLAND], No. 111 Item 724 (Pol.) [Law Regarding Animal Protection (Pol.)].

158 Protecção aos Animais [Protection of Animals Act], Sept. 12, 1995, No. 92/95, DIARIO DO GOVERNO Ser. 1, 5722 (Port.) [Protection of Animals Act (Port.)].

159 Animal Protection and Welfare Act, No. 154, Aug. 4, 2008, P.R. LAWS ANN. tit. 5, ch. 58 (Puerto Rico) [Animal Protection and Welfare Act (Puerto Rico)].

160 Zakon o Zaščiti Živali [Animal Protection Act], Nov. 18, 1999, URADNI LIST NO. 98/1999, 14645 (Slovn.) [Animal Protection Act (Slovn.)].

161 Animals (Control of Experiments) Act, Sept. 11, 1957, c. 97, 13 of 1957, LN 46A of 1978 (Solom. Is.) [Animals (Control of Experiments) Act (Solom. Is.)].

162 Animals Protection Act, No. 71 of 1962 (S. Afr.) [Animals Protection Act (S. Afr.)].

163 Dongmulbohobeob [Animal Protection Law], Act. No. 8282, Jan. 26, 2007 (S. Kor.) [Animal Protection Law (S. Kor.)].

164 Prevention of Cruelty to Animals Ordinance, Cap. 573, July 10, 1907 (Sri Lanka) [Prevention of Cruelty to Animals Ordinance (Sri Lanka)].

165 Djurskyddslag [Animal Protection Act], SVENSK FÖRFATTNINGSSAMLING [SFS] 1988:534 (Swed.) [Animal Welfare Act (Swed.)].

166 SCHWEIZERISCHES TIERSCHUTZGESETZ [TSchG] [ANIMAL WELFARE ACT], Dec. 16, 2005, SR 455 (Switz.) [ANIMAL WELFARE ACT (Switz.)].

167 動物保護法 (民國90年12月21日修正) Animal Protection Law, Nov. 4, 1998, XIANXING FAGUI HUIBIAN (Taiwan) [Animal Protection Law (Taiwan)].

168 Pounds and Animals Act, 1988, c. 147 (Tonga) [Pounds and Animals Act (Tonga)].

169 Hayvanlari Koruma Kanunu [Animal Protection Law], June 24, 2004, No. 5199, RESMÎ GAZETE, July 1, 2004 No. 25509 (Turk.) [Animal Protection Law (Turk.)].

170 The Animals (Prevention of Cruelty) Act, Dec. 5, 1957, c. 220 (Uganda) [The Animals (Prevention of Cruelty) Act (Uganda)].

171 Pro Zakhyst Tvaryn Vid Zhorstokoho Povodzhennya [On the Protection of Animals from Cruelty], Feb. 21, 2006, No. 3447—IV (Ukr.) [Law on the Protection of Animals from Cruelty (Ukr.)].

172 Prevention of Cruelty to Animals Act, Feb. 13, 1974, Laws of the Republic of Vanuatu Consolidated Edition 2006, ch. 78, JR 58 of 1973 (Vanuatu) [Prevention of Cruelty to Animals Act (Vanuatu)].

173 LA ASAMBLEA NACIONAL DE LA REPÚBLICA BOLIVARIANA DE VENEZUELA [LAW FOR THE PROTECTION OF DOMESTICATED ANIMALS AND WILDLIFE IN CAPTIVITY], GACETA OFICIAL [G.O.] [Official Gazette of Venezuela], 39.338, Jan. 4, 2010 (Venez.) [LAW FOR THE PROTECTION OF DOMESTICATED ANIMALS AND WILDLIFE IN CAPTIVITY (Venez.)].

174 Prevention of Cruelty to Animals Act, Cap. 19:09, Consolidated Version of Act No. 25 of 1960 (Zim.) [Prevention of Cruelty to Animals Act (Zim.)].

and Zambia.[175] Because these laws are silent on their territorial reach, it is *prima facie* unknown how they apply to cases involving a cross-border element. Only India, Norway, Tanzania, and the United Kingdom have placed limits on their animal protection acts.[176] The Norwegian Animal Welfare Act, for example, applies "to Norwegian land territory, territorial waters, the Norwegian economic zone, aboard Norwegian ships and aircraft, on installations located on the Norwegian continental shelf, and to Svalbard, Jan Mayen and the dependencies."[177] Borrowing Norway's model and tailoring it to the territorial specifics of another country is a possibility, but these countries would end up placing stricter limits on their jurisdictional authority than international law requires. So neither do they serve as apt role models, nor do they illuminate the limits of jurisdiction under international law.

The second argument refuting the general applicability of the principles of jurisdiction to animal issues is conceptual. The field of animal law draws its content from criminal, civil, and administrative norms. Most animal laws are administrative or criminal in nature, but they are also found in states' constitutions, civil codes, trade treaties, etc. Under the doctrine of jurisdiction, the reach and regulatory density of these provisions may *prima facie* differ depending on whether, for example, civil or criminal jurisdiction centers the debate.[178] It is unclear if, in a case of animal abuse on foreign soil, a state can use administrative orders that prohibit a person from keeping animals in the future, or only grant extraterritorial reach to criminal provisions that sanction animal abuse. Since the legality of extraterritorial jurisdiction may depend on the nature of a norm, these criminal, civil, and administrative animal laws must be carefully examined.

Third, more and more countries are changing the status of animals in civil law, and this forces us to reconsider the default jurisdictional connection to animals as objects of law. Based on the Roman law divide between objects of law and subjects of law, it was standard to deny animals subjecthood and relegate them to the category of objects along with chairs, cups, or pieces of wood. Since the advent of the Roman era, our conception and our knowledge of animals has greatly changed. Today, we recognize that animals do not fit into the category of objects because they are sentient beings who greatly influence their environment.[179]

---

[175] Prevention of Cruelty to Animals Act (1921), Cap. 245, LAWS REP. OF ZAMBIA (1994) (Zam.) [Prevention of Cruelty to Animals Act (Zam.)].

[176] The Prevention of Cruelty to Animals Act, Act No. 59 of 1960, art. 1 para. 2 (India) [The Prevention of Cruelty to Animals Act (India)]: "It extends to the whole of India except the State of Jammu and Kashmir." Animal Welfare Act (U.K.), Explanatory Note No. 8: "The Act extends to England and Wales. It extends to Scotland only in respect of (a) section 46, which enables disqualification orders made by the courts in England and Wales to have force in Scotland, (b) sections 47 to 50, which make provision about the powers of the Scottish courts to enforce in Scotland of disqualification orders under the Act, (c) repeals of certain legislation and (d) commencement orders. It extends to Northern Ireland in respect of certain consequential and minor amendments only." The Animal Welfare Act, No. 19 of 2008, art. 2 para. 1 (Tanz.): "This act shall apply to Mainland Tanzania."

[177] Animal Welfare Act, 2009, LOV I 2009 hefte 7, § 2 (Nor.) [Animal Welfare Act (Nor.)].

[178] Akehurst is a strong defender of the view that we must strictly distinguish between civil and criminal norms, and that the law of jurisdiction gives each of these a different ambit: Akehurst (1972–3).

[179] CAROLINE RASPÉ, DIE TIERLICHE PERSON 64 ff. (2013). *Contra* Richard A. Epstein, *Animals as Objects, or Subjects, of Rights*, *in* ANIMAL RIGHTS: CURRENT DEBATES AND NEW DIRECTIONS 143 (Cass R. Sunstein & Martha C. Nussbaum eds., 2004).

A conflict between the legal classification and our social conception of animals emerged in divorce proceedings because, unlike common property, companion animals cannot be split 50/50 after separation, and because paying off a partner did not make up for the emotional loss suffered by them. Over the past decades, states began to recognize that this mismatch pervades other areas of law and started to amend legal standards to fit public perception, by declaring that animals are not mere objects of the law. For instance, in 2002, a new provision was added to the Swiss Civil Code, stipulating that "[a]nimals are not objects."[180] A special report by the Legal Affairs Committee of the Council of States (*Ständerat*), which formed part of the parliamentary debates preceding the adoption of article 641*a*, revealed that its declared aim was to meet society's growing concern for animals and to ameliorate the legal status of animals. The traditional conception that animals are things, as the Federal Council explained, is now seen by society as an ancient relict.[181] Similar content to that of article 641*a* of the Swiss Civil Code is also found in the laws of Austria, Brussels, California, Canada, Colombia, the Czech Republic, France, Germany, the City of Mexico, New Zealand, Portugal, Québec, and Spain.[182]

These ongoing developments point to the dangers and inadequacies of law when it lags behind social developments and scientific insights. Yet, as we will see when we examine these provisions in detail, far from adequately responding to the growing recognition that animals are sentient beings to whom life greatly matters, many of these laws provide that animals will continue to be treated as objects for the purposes of the law. The growing dissolution of the Roman law divide between objects and subjects of the law is far from resolved and will undoubtedly continue to dominate social and political discourse. Despite, or even because of this indeterminacy, the doctrine of jurisdiction can no longer assume that animals are merely property that blindly follows the jurisdiction of its owner. That many countries no longer regard animals as objects seems to speak for their independent legal visibility as anchor points under the doctrine of jurisdiction. For instance, dogs of some countries have passports that provide information about their name, domicile, looks, fur color, and more, much as is done in human passports. Because these passports travel with the animal, regardless of ownership, this practice might be seen as giving rise to *de facto* nationality of dogs and enabling the issuing state to manifest its jurisdiction over the dogs, without regard to the owner or their whereabouts. To respond in time to these ongoing changes, the doctrine of jurisdiction must anticipate solutions now.

Fourth, though the law is shaped and co-influenced by different, often conflicting stakeholder views, the field of animal law attracts an exceptionally wide array of interested parties, including corporate actors that want to use animals, animal advocates concerned about the welfare of animals, conservationists who seek to protect animals as ambassadors of a species, social justice movements fighting intersectional oppressions, or minorities concerned about being forced to abandon their cultural practices. These stakeholders often

---

180 The exact wording is "Tiere sind keine Sachen" (Schweizerisches Zivilgesetzbuch [ZGB] [Civil Code], Dec. 10, 1907, SR 210, art. 641*a* para. 1 (Switz.) [Civil Code (Switz.)]).

181 Parlamentarische Initiative, Die Tiere in der schweizerischen Rechtsordnung, Bericht der Kommission für Rechtsfragen des Ständerates [Parliamentary Initiative, Animals in the Swiss Legal System, Report by the Commission to the Council of States for Legal Questions], Jan. 24, 2002, SR 99.467, at 4166 (Switz.).

182 These amendments are examined in detail in Chapter 7, §1 A. IV.

have diametrically opposed views about what we owe to animals and what our relationships with them must look like. Given these disparate interests, and the fact that the animals themselves are absent in the formation, application, and enforcement of law, the law of jurisdiction is faced with a particularly complex set of issues when debating the geographical reach of such norms.

These four factors—the absence of known limits to animal protection acts; the criminal, civil, and public law nature of animal law that may give rise to different jurisdictional limits; the ongoing disobjectification of animals in the law; and the multilevel and often opposed interests in animals—evidence a high degree of legal "otherness" of animal law for the purposes of studying its spatial reach under international law. We must therefore carefully scrutinize applicable, and potentially inapplicable jurisdictional axioms.

§5 Assistants along the Way: Four Case Groups

The question of how far a state's animal laws reach *ratione loci* is raised on various fronts. It needs to be answered for a natural person who crosses borders with their companion animal, for a corporation that conducts animal research and establishes new branches or subsidiaries on foreign territory, for an international marketing company that helps domestic foie gras producers reach as many foreign markets as possible, for regulatory authorities that intend to prevent hormonally produced beef from entering their territory, for tourists who import products manufactured from the skins of endangered species, and many others. This book will shed light on the legality of all conceivable cross-border cases that involve animals by expounding a panoply of regulatory possibilities and analyzing them in the extraterritoriality framework. To guarantee this rather abstract framework is feasible, I will test and evaluate the theoretical approaches I establish herein by using them on four case groups that stand for the most common challenges now faced under the law of jurisdiction: outsourcing, trade, migration, and trophy hunting. I next present each case group and explain to what extent it is representative of broader debates faced in animal law, and in what sense it may illuminate our understanding of the doctrine of jurisdiction.

The first case group includes the increasing instances of multinational enterprises outsourcing corporate branches or entire corporations to foreign territory. Today, most domesticated animals are owned by legal persons who deal with animals for commercial reasons[183]—by breeding, raising or keeping them, using them for work, research, entertainment, therapy, display, or other purposes, or slaughtering them. Corporate behavior thus has a quantitatively and qualitatively high influence on whether animals fare well or ill in this world. It is likely a corporation will outsource its activities where an industry's capital is mobile and home states introduce or announce stricter animal protection standards.[184] For

---

[183] Park & Singer 122 (2012).

[184] Bruce G. Carruthers & Naomi R. Lamoreaux, Regulatory Races: The Effects of Jurisdictional Competition on Regulatory Standards, Tobin Project Working Paper, 1, 1 (2009); Thomas G. Kelch, Globalization and Animal Law: Comparative Law, International Law and International Trade 306–7 (2011); David Kirby, Animal Factory xiv (2010); Murphy 16–8 (2004).

example, in the United States, the public and several politicians have fought for years to ban horse slaughter state- and nationwide. Instead of banning horse slaughter directly—a strategy that proved impossible[185]—the federal government in 2006 introduced the Appropriation Act that prohibited governmental funding for federal inspectors of horse meat.[186] Because institutions that slaughter horses cannot legally run their business, the funding ban on inspections effectively rendered horse slaughter illegal in the United States. From 2006 to 2007, in reaction to the ban, horse exports to Mexico increased by 312 percent.[187] The entire horse-slaughter industry of the United States was effectively outsourced to Mexico as a consequence of the ban, a development that was publicly decried both by animal advocates who feared lax slaughter standards in Mexico and the meatpacking industry fearing loss of jobs. In an effort to reverse this process, parties proposed to also ban exporting horses with the proposed Safeguard American Food Exports Act in 2015, a bill that the House and the Senate failed to enact in the 114th Congress.[188]

That outsourcing attracts the attention of stakeholders along the entire spectrum, from ethical to economic, becomes apparent when we look at a few other examples. Live exports of farmed animals from Australia to the rest of the world are a form of outsourcing hailed or criticized by different groups. Some point to the fact that Australia loses 40,000 jobs by outsourcing sheep and cow slaughter to countries with significantly lower or no protection laws; others argue it gains economically by raising and selling the animals.[189] For animals, outsourcing amounts to more suffering through dreadful, long, harsh, and taxing transportation only to end up at another location where people will kill them.

The research industry also increasingly outsources its businesses. Rice, CEO of a US pharmaceutical corporation, said in 2006: "Animal testing [. . .] does not have the political issues it has in the US or Europe or even India, where there are religious issues as well. So now big pharma is looking to move to China in a big way."[190] Few rules, few protestors, large supplies of lab primates and beagles are part of a "whole menu of advantages" that attract multinationals like Bridge Pharmaceuticals, Novartis, Pfizer, Eli Lilly, and Roche.[191]

---

[185] In 2005, the Horse Slaughter Prohibition Bill was proposed by John Sweeney, passed by the House of Representatives, but died in the Senate: Horse Slaughter Prohibition Bill, H.R. 503 (109th) 2005–6 (U.S.).

[186] The Agriculture, Rural Development, Food and Drug Administration, and Related Agencies Appropriations Act, 2006, 119 U.S. 2120, Public Law 109-97, H.R. 2744-45, § 794 (U.S.): "Effective 120 days after the date of enactment of this Act, none of the funds made available in this Act may be used to pay the salaries or expenses of personnel to inspect horses under section 3 of the Federal Meat inspection Act (21 U.S.C. 603) or under the guidelines issued under section 903 the Federal Agriculture Improvement and Reform Act of 1996 (7 U.S.C. 1901 note; Public Law 104-127)." The ban was upheld in the Agriculture, Rural Development, Food and Drug Administration, and Related Agencies Appropriations Act, 2014, 128 U.S. 5, Public Law 113-76, H.R. 3547 (U.S.).

[187] R. Scott Nolen, *U.S. Horse Slaughter Exports to Mexico Increase 312%*, AVMA NEWS, Jan. 15, 2008.

[188] Safeguard American Food Exports Act of 2015, H.R. 1942 (U.S.).

[189] For an insightful analysis of these conflicting views in Australia, *see* Katrina J. Craig, *Beefing up the Standard: The Ramifications of Australia's Regulation of Live Export and Suggestions for Reform*, 11 MACQUARIE L.J. 51 (2013).

[190] Jehangir S. Pocha, *Outsourcing Animal Testing: US Firm Setting Up Drug-Trial Facilities in China: Where Scientists Are Plentiful but Activists Aren't*, BOSTON GLOBE, Nov. 25, 2006.

[191] *Id.*

Breeding institutions that supply research facilities with new stocks of animals have also been outsourced in large numbers. Bioculture Ltd., for example, owns 19 facilities worldwide and has outsourced all primate breeding operations to Guayama, Puerto Rico. These practices are lamented by Bioculture Ltd.'s home state but have also led to protests in the countries to which they moved.[192]

The second case group concerns trade restrictions that are frequently accused of having some extraterritorial effect and of imposing values across borders. The most recent and exemplary case for this is the 2014 *Seals* case decided at the WTO.[193] Iceland and Canada, with a number of intervening third parties, challenged the legality of EU measures that prohibited importing and marketing seal products within the European Union. The AB, a standing body of seven persons that hears appeals from reports issued by panels as part of the WTO's Dispute Settlement Body (DSB), confirmed that animal welfare is an aspect of public morality and that measures that seek to protect the welfare of animals can, under narrow circumstances, justifiably restrict trade among states.[194] Because the European Union's trade measures were considered legitimate on the basis that they only indirectly protected seals found outside the European Union, scholars argue that the AB effectively acknowledged that a state can have a legitimate interest in the welfare of animals on foreign soil.[195] The legality of trade restrictions employed for animal welfare reasons formed the center of debate at the WTO prior to *Seals*,[196] and it will likely continue to do so in the future.

The third case group deals with cross-border issues that arise when animals migrate. Animal migration denotes a type of locomotory activity in which populations move seasonally to-and-fro between regions where conditions are alternately favorable or unfavorable. Migration can also be a one-way movement that leads to redistribution of an animal population.[197] Animals migrate at sea, in the air, or on land, and they do so for behavioral reasons or in order to escape habitat destruction and fragmentation, armed conflict, resource scarcity, seasonal temperature changes, or climate change.[198] Migratory animals include birds, mammals, fishes, reptiles, amphibians, insects, and crustaceans. Since I am concerned with cross-border movements, I focus on migration across state borders, which can be a quite arbitrary threshold for inquiry from the animals' point of view.

Cross-border animal migration was subject to dispute as early as 1893. The *Bering Sea Arbitration* asked if states could assert their jurisdiction over migratory Pacific seals once

---

[192] Jill Laster, *Plan to Breed Lab Monkey Splits Puerto Rican Town*, U.S. NEWS & WORLD REPORT, Nov. 30, 2009.

[193] *Seals*, AB Report.

[194] *Seals*, AB Report. *See also Seals*, Panel Report, ¶ 7.395: "For several years, many members of the public have been concerned about the animal welfare aspects of the killing and skinning of seals and about trade occurring in products possibly derived from seals that have been killed and skinned with avoidable pain, distress and other forms of suffering, which seals, as sentient mammals, are capable of experiencing. Those concerns have therefore been expressed by members of the public *out of ethical reasons*." (Emphasis in original).

[195] Analogously for the *Shrimp/Turtle* case: Sands 537 ff. (2001).

[196] *E.g.*, Appellate Body Report, *EC—Measures Affecting Meat and Meat Products*, WTO Doc. WT/DS26/AB/R, WT/DS48/AB/R (adopted Feb. 13, 1998) [*EC—Hormones*, AB Report].

[197] Ricardo M. Holdo et al., *Migration Impacts on Communities and Ecosystems: Empirical Evidence and Theoretical Insights*, *in* ANIMAL MIGRATION: A SYNTHESIS 131, 133 (E.J. Milner-Gulland et al., 2011).

[198] HUGH DINGLE, MIGRATION: THE BIOLOGY OF LIFE ON THE MOVE 11 (2d ed. 2014).

the seals had left their jurisdictional authority at sea.[199] The United States claimed a right of property and protection over the seals that sojourned in and subsequently left its territorial sea.[200] The United Kingdom claimed a right to harvest the seals, even if it meant rendering them extinct, based on the principle of the freedom of the high seas. The arbitral tribunal found no basis under international law for the United States to apply its standards outside its territory, whether formulated in property-related or protective terms, and decided in favor of the freedom on the high seas, hence in favor of the United Kingdom.[201] More than a century after the *Bering Sea Arbitration* verdict, international law gives a different answer to the very same question. In *Shrimp/Turtle*, the United States passed an import ban on shrimp caught in a manner that threatened five species of sea turtles protected under the US Endangered Species Act (ESA) of 1973.[202] Shrimp harvested with technology that adversely affected sea turtles could not be imported into the United States unless the exporting state used a fishing tool that offered a similar level of protection as the US domestic "turtle excluder device." The AB held that US claims were provisionally justified because the country had a legally valid interest in protecting shared and endangered animals outside its jurisdiction.[203] Even though the United States lost the case because of the way it implemented and applied these laws—namely, in a discriminatory and disproportional manner—an international body had recognized that a state's interest in animal welfare may rightfully reach across territorial boundaries. More than a century before, no such legal interest was recognized or protected.[204] This change of position was likely influenced by conservationist laws that emerged post-*Bering*, and which protect species of seals, whales, polar bears, birds, elephants, and others in treaties like the International Convention for the Regulation of Whaling (ICRW)[205] or the Convention on International Trade in Endangered Species of Wild Fauna and Flora (CITES).[206]

The fourth case group highlights global ramifications and cross-border interests in trophy hunting. In July 2015, the world was outraged to hear about the death of Cecil, a black-maned lion killed by an American game hunter in Zimbabwe. Cecil was resident of the Hwange National Park, where he was a star attraction to many visitors and part of a national study on lion movement across the park that had begun in 2008. Mid-2015, Cecil was lured out of the

---

199 Award between the United States and the United Kingdom Relating to the Rights of Jurisdiction of the United States in the Bering's Sea and the Preservation of Fur Seals (U.S. v. U.K.), R.I.A.A. 263, 279 (Arbitral Tribunal 1893) [Bering Sea Arbitration, 1893 R.I.A.A. 267].

200 *Id.*

201 *Id.* 269: "[T]he United States has not any right of protection or property in the fur-seals frequenting the islands of the United States in Behring Sea, when such seals are found outside the ordinary three-mile limit."

202 The import ban became effective under § 609 of the U.S. Public Law, 101-102, 16 U.S.C. § 1537 note, amending the Endangered Species Act, 16 U.S.C. § 1531 (Apr. 19, 1996) (U.S.) [ESA].

203 According to the AB, there is "a sufficient nexus between the migratory and endangered [sea turtles] involved and the United States for the purposes of [WTO law]" (*Shrimp/Turtle I*, AB Report, ¶ 133).

204 Sands 535 (2001).

205 International Convention for the Regulation of Whaling, Dec. 2, 1946, 161 U.N.T.S. 72 [ICRW]. The ICRW was signed by 110 parties as of 2019: *Membership and Contracting Governments*, INT'L WHALING COMM'N, http://iwc.int/members (last visited Jan. 10, 2019).

206 Convention on International Trade in Endangered Species of Wild Fauna and Flora, Mar. 3, 1973, 993 U.N.T.S. 243 [CITES].

park by carcasses tied to a car driven by trophy hunters, and then shot with a bow and arrow by Walter Palmer, a US citizen who paid 50,000 USD to kill the animal. Cecil was severely wounded and killed by the hunters over 40 hours after the initial shot was released.[207] After these events became public, Palmer was subject to "a global storm of internet indignation," and "an online witch-hunt," as journalists reported.[208]

Trophy hunting is a form of sports or recreational hunting, in which individuals hunt animals to take their head or other features with them for display. Typically, hunters target the rarest and biggest animals, or those that are hardest to chase and shoot. Trophy hunting is practiced in many states but has been subject to debates particularly in the United States. According to the Humane Society International's report, "Trophy Hunting by Numbers," the United States imported 1.26 million wildlife trophies between 2005 and 2014.[209] Most trophies originated in Canada and South Africa; fewer came from Argentina, Botswana, Mexico, Namibia, New Zealand, Tanzania, and Zambia. Trophy hunters are known to pay large sums to kill wildlife animals. For an African lion trophy, for instance, they pay between 13,500 USD and 49,000 USD and for an African elephant between 11,000 USD and 70,000 USD. Among the animals hunted and imported during the same period, 32,500 were members of African Big Five: 5,600 African lions, 4,600 African elephants, 4,500 African leopards, 330 Southern white rhinos, and 17,200 African buffaloes.[210] Although the United States has prohibited some of these trophy imports under the ESA,[211] people continue to practice trophy hunting, among other things because trophy hunting remains legal in over 20 African countries while illicit trade in the United States continues unabated.[212]

Trophy hunting, in contrast to corporate outsourcing, is a form of exploitation of low animal laws abroad by individuals or groups of people. An issue that is structurally similar to trophy hunting is using another state's low animal protection standards to commit acts of bestiality. Consider Denmark, a country that legally ran animal brothels for years. According to journalists, zoophilia was not only practiced among Danish nationals, but Denmark became internationally known as "a hotspot for animal sex tourists,"[213] where "foreigners visit the country specifically to go to [...] brothels that sexually exploit animals."[214] A 2006 report issued by the Danish Ethical Council revealed that 17 percent of the Danish veterinarians

---

[207] Simon Allison, *Stories of 2015: Man Who Identified Cecil the Lion's Killer Vows Death Will Not Be in Vain*, The Guardian, Dec. 25, 2015; The Editorial Board, *The Death of Cecil the Lion*, N.Y. Times, July 31, 2015.

[208] Christina Capecchi & Katie Rogers, *Killer of Cecil the Lion Finds Out That He Is a Target Now of Internet Vigilantism*, N.Y. Times, July 29, 2015.

[209] Humane Society International (HSI), Trophy Hunting by the Numbers: The United States' Role in Global Trophy Hunting (HSI, Washington D.C. 2016).

[210] Other animals subject to trophy hunting are snow geese, mallards, Canada geese, American black bears, impalas, common wildebeests, greater kudus, gemsboks, springboks, and bonteboks: *Id.* at 1.

[211] The African lion is endangered and threatened under the ESA, the African elephant is threatened under the ESA, the African leopard is endangered and threatened under the ESA, and the Southern white rhino is threatened under the ESA. If animals are endangered, the trophy import requires a permit (§ 9 ESA, Appendices to the ESA).

[212] Norimitsu Onishi, *Outcry for Cecil the Lion Could Undercut Conservation Efforts*, N.Y. Times, Aug. 10, 2015.

[213] *Denmark Passes Law to Ban Bestiality*, BBC Newsbeat, Apr. 22, 2015.

[214] *At Last! Denmark Bans Bestiality*, PETAUK, Apr. 2015.

suspected an animal they treated had been subjected to sex with a human.[215] In April 2015, Denmark finally banned sexual intercourse and other sexual relations with animals by amending its Animal Protection Act.[216] Denmark's efforts are laudable but continue to be undermined until this day because sexual interactions with animals—violent or not—are still legal in neighboring countries including Finland, Hungary, and Romania.

§6 Interim Conclusion

Mapping the territory of animal law means assembling the tools necessary to begin a careful study of extraterritorial jurisdiction in animal law. Both jurisdiction and extraterritoriality have suffered from terminological deficiencies that have hampered the legal debate on the legality of extraterritorial jurisdiction. In this chapter, I built up a definitional structure that allows us to approach these charged terms systematically and impartially. States enjoy two types of jurisdictional authority—regulatory and enforcement authority—that are tied to different consequences under international law. When the sphere in which persons, things, and legal relationships subject to regulation are situated (the sphere of regulation) began to exceed the sphere in which law can be autonomously enforced by a state (the sphere of validity), the limits of the prescriptive jurisdiction of states lost congruence with the limits of their enforcement jurisdiction. As a result, international law introduced two sets of rules that apply to prescriptive and enforcement jurisdiction, respectively. Enforcement jurisdiction is in principle limited to a state's own territory, based on the principles of territorial integrity and nonintervention. Even when enforcement in a foreign state is precluded, states opt for extraterritorial prescriptive jurisdiction because they presume compliance with their laws. A common way of ensuring cross-border compliance is to use territorial enforcement that forces addressees of a norm to determine how cost-effective the available options are, and to find, eventually, that the potential negative effects of not complying with foreign law will be worse than the positive effects of ignoring it.

Contemporary voices on sovereignty converge on the idea that states have often failed to effectively organize economic, social, and political life along territorial boundaries. Sovereignty has evolved from a concept associated with state independence to one characterized by state interdependence, from bundling sovereignty in the ruler to justifying sovereignty with reference to the people, and from accentuating territorial supremacy to celebrating global legal pluralism. These developments are part and parcel of the broader deterritorialization of state sovereignty and have had a noticeable effect on how jurisdictional space is perceived and

---

[215] Det Dyreetiske Råd Udtalelse om menneskers seksuelle omgang med dyr 21 [Danish Ethical Council, Opinion on Human Sexual Intercourse with Animals] (Nov. 2006), *available at* http://detdyreetiskeraad.dk/udtalelser/udtalelse/pub/hent-fil/publication/udtalelse-om-menneskers-seksuelle-omgang-med-dyr-2006/ (last visited Jan. 10, 2019).

[216] Animal Protection Act, Act No. 473, May 15, 2014, para. 3a) chapter 1 (Den.), *available at* https://www.retsinformation.dk/forms/R0710.aspx?id=174047, implemented by LOV Nr. 533, Apr. 29, 2015 (Forbud mod seksuel omgang eller seksuelle handlinger med dyr, forbud mod salg af hunde på markeder, avl af familie- og hobbydyr, ændret rådsstruktur m.v.): "Det er forbudt at have seksuel omgang med eller foretage seksuelle handlinger med dyr, jf. dog stk."

regulated. Deterritorializing state sovereignty has eroded the primacy of the territoriality principle, which declares the home state competent to prescribe law over all matters relating to that territory. As territorial jurisdiction dwindled, states began to invoke jurisdictional bases that derive from the two other pillars of state sovereignty: personal and organizational sovereignty. The nationality, effects, protective, and universality principles—all of which emerged from personal and organizational sovereignty—gradually supplanted territorial jurisdiction and came to be seen as bases of jurisdiction that successfully respond to transnational problems.

Despite the growing popularity of extraterritorial jurisdiction, legal scholarship has not yet managed to readily distinguish between territorial and extraterritorial jurisdiction. Customary international law and scholarly opinions on the concept of extraterritorial jurisdiction have thus far failed to provide a satisfactory definition of the terms, which exacerbated the debate about the legality of extraterritorial jurisdiction. The extraterritoriality framework established in this chapter attempts to fill this gap. It enables us to disassemble norms into discrete parts, from which we can determine their geographical *locus*. The starting point for defining extraterritorial jurisdiction is the basic structure of a jurisdictional norm. A norm uses one or more anchor points to regulate content, which can have manifold ancillary repercussions. By adding territorial considerations to the structure, it is possible to distinguish norms with (extra)territorial anchor points, (extra)territorial content regulation, and (extra)territorial ancillary repercussions. To be regarded as extraterritorial jurisdiction *stricto sensu*, jurisdictional norms must have an extraterritorial anchor point and extraterritorial content regulation (type α jurisdiction), an extraterritorial anchor point and intraterritorial content regulation (type ß jurisdiction), or an intraterritorial anchor point and extraterritorial content regulation (type γ jurisdiction). The personality, protective, effects, and objective and subjective territoriality principles are all forms of direct extraterritorial jurisdiction because they use extraterritorial anchor points or regulate content extraterritorially. The definition of extraterritorial jurisdiction *stricto sensu*, or direct extraterritoriality, uses the sphere of states' regulatory influence as a guiding tool and ignores unintended effects of norms. Adding the dimension of *animal relation*—where animals form part of jurisdictional norms as anchor points or regulated content—to the jurisdictional types in the extraterritoriality framework gives rise to a new set of considerations needed to disassemble norms (types α_1, α_2, α_3, $ß_1$, $ß_2$, γ_1, and γ_2 jurisdiction).

If a norm's only extraterritorial facet is its extraterritorial repercussions, the norm is not considered extraterritorial *stricto sensu*, but instead is a territorial norm with indirect extraterritorial effects. Trade measures are typically indirect extraterritorial because they do not claim application or validity outside the state that passed the laws. Although they do not form part of extraterritorial jurisdiction *stricto sensu*, trade restrictions are examined in later chapters because they represent a popular instrument of states and are frequently accused of unduly challenging the regulatory authority of states.

The extraterritoriality framework is first and foremost a definitional tool and a tool for conducting empirical studies on the jurisdictional practices of states. As such, the framework does not claim or even allow an assessment of the legality of a jurisdictional norm, be it direct or indirect extraterritorial. The framework does, however, force us to abandon the oversimplified, conceptually problematic, and politically charged dichotomy between legal territorial and illegal extraterritorial jurisdiction. Extraterritoriality does not denote unlawful jurisdiction and vice versa, territoriality is not synonymous with lawful jurisdiction.

From a legal standpoint, animal law evidences a high degree of otherness that mandates careful scrutiny of the jurisdictional axioms applicable and potentially inapplicable to the field. Animal law is unique in four respects. First, most animal welfare or protection acts do not determine, much less address their territorial scope. Second, different jurisdictional limits may apply depending on whether we are dealing with civil, criminal, or public norms of animal law. Third, because animals are increasingly recognized as sentient beings under the law, rather than as mere objects, this throws into question the jurisdictional parameters used to date. Finally, the complex and often conflicting interests in using or protecting animals make it difficult to settle jurisdictional disputes promptly. All of these factors call into question the law of jurisdiction in its traditional form and require us to be vigilant when using extraterritorial norms in animal law.

These points of reference of the law of jurisdiction can be very technical, and it can be hard to see their practical applications. In this chapter, I developed four case groups that add plasticity to the extraterritoriality framework, and that will help us verify its legal propositions: corporate exploitation of low animal protection standards abroad (i.e., outsourcing), trade in animals and animal products, animal migration, and exploitation of weak animal laws abroad by individuals (e.g., trophy hunting or bestiality). As we inquire into the law of jurisdiction in the coming chapters, I will use these four case groups as a speculum to examine the feasibility and adequacy of existing laws and proposals made to remedy their shortcomings.

2 Shifting Spatial Dimensions of Animal Law

A COMMON COMPLAINT about extraterritorial animal law is that it illegitimately influences the organization of other states and thereby fuels fear of imperialism and neocolonialism. This argument is premised on the idea that the treatment of animals is primarily a local, domestic matter. In this chapter, I stake out a series of arguments that justify expanding animal law across state borders and show that extraterritorial animal law is part of a larger development in international law, in which jurisdictional authority standardly reaches across borders. In the first part of the chapter, I describe the most pressing challenges of animal law in an age of globalized production and ask if concluding a treaty is the most rational approach to solving them. If treaties are not a viable solution, is extraterritorial jurisdiction a reasonable alternative?

Before we can make a judgment about the desirability of extraterritorial jurisdiction in animal law, we must uncover the reasons that prompted states to expand their prescriptive authority in the fields of law in which extraterritoriality prevails. In broadly two areas of law, applying law across borders is considered necessary and legal under international law. Extraterritorial jurisdiction is established in fields of law that regulate economic matters because economic entanglements warrant transborder regulation. Extraterritorial jurisdiction also dominates in criminal law, but for other reasons; partly because of the increased cross-border movement of nationals, and partly because most states have a common understanding of the most repulsive crimes, like war crimes, torture, or inhuman and degrading treatment. In the following, I describe these processes in detail and turn to whether the rationales that underlie these developments—namely, economic entanglement and a shared view that some practices must be condemned—are also present in animal law. If this is the case, there is a high chance that instances in which animal law is applied across the border will increase in the future and that they will increasingly be considered legitimate.

§1 Animal Law at an Impasse

Few international norms regulate animals and our manifold relationships with them, and most are concerned with relations of trade among states. In the past decades, international trade in animals and animal products has grown exponentially relative to other sectors. Between 1986 and 2016, trade in meat increased fourfold, and trade in egg and dairy increased more than threefold.[1] The research industry experienced a similar surge. Statistics reveal that since 2004, the number of animals moved across borders for research purposes has increased many times over.[2] What factors are responsible for the drastic rise of trade in animals and animal products and what regulatory reactions emerged in response thereto?

The steady rise of animal trade can be ascribed to instances of the first dimension of globalization.[3] Better means of transport have saved manufacturers, breeders, and slaughterhouse managers time, and allowed them to reach more people in a shorter period of time. By intensifying animal production (e.g., reducing space per animal, using growth hormones and superfoods, mutilating animals, automatic handling and slaughter, and shortening the lifespans of animals), business radically increased its output in meat, eggs, and milk while saving on production time. This trend was registered and promptly adopted by investment strategists. Liberalizing FDI opened up new possibilities to pour large funds into the animal industry and caused the animal-industrial complex to proliferate around the globe.[4] In 2009, *The Economist* reported that China, Qatar, South Korea, Saudi Arabia, and the United Arab Emirates were acquiring unprecedented levels of farmland in other majority world countries[5] with the goal of securing their own food demands by producing feed and "livestock"

---

[1] Between 1986 and 2016, the global trade in eggs increased from 748,241 to 2,107,373 tons, the global trade in meat increased from 17,814,372 to 71,877,429 tons, and the global trade in milk increased from 6,266,492 to 18,587,86 tons: FAOSTAT (search criteria "Eggs"+"Milk"+"Meat"+"Export Quantity"+"World"+"1986, 2016"), *available at* http://faostat.fao.org/ (last visited Jan. 10, 2019).

[2] Sarah Kite, *The Trade in Primates for Research*, *in* THE GLOBAL GUIDE TO ANIMAL PROTECTION 106, 107 (2013).

[3] The three dimensions typically associated with globalization are examined in Chapter 2, §3.

[4] The animal-industrial complex is a "partially opaque network of relations between governments, public and private science, and the corporate agricultural sector" that "naturalizes the human as a consumer of other animals." (BARBARA NOSKE, BEYOND BOUNDARIES: HUMANS AND ANIMALS 22 ff. (1997)).

[5] In international law, we typically speak of "developing states" or the "Third World" to denote countries in juxtaposition to "developed countries." These terms imply that development is a standardized and linear process, and that certain countries have finished developing while others are still striving to reach this form of development. Because there are many ways in which states evolve over time, and because nations should be recognized for their different strengths and goals, these terms seem both incorrect and inappropriate. In recognition thereof, scholarship is increasingly using the terms "majority world" and "minority world." The term "majority world" highlights the fact that the majority of the world's population lives in parts of the world previously identified as "developing." Vice versa, the term "minority world" refers to those countries traditionally identified as "developed," where a minority of the world's population resides. *See, e.g.*, Shahidul Alam, *Majority World: Challenging the West's Rhetoric of Democracy*, 34(1) AMERASIA J. 87 (2008); Samantha Punch, *Exploring Children's Agency*

on that land.[6] Investment flows show that the bulk of these acquisitions go to intensive production systems, as in Iran and Pakistan.[7] The end result is that agricultural FDI prompts the majority world to mass-adopt intensive animal production systems, which is problematic among others because these countries are, on average, massively underregulated from an animal law perspective.[8]

The economic globalization of animal industries has led to a host of ethical, social, and environmental problems, which signals the second dimension of globalization. As agribusiness intensifies, animals have less space to move around and are fed high-fat diets, as a consequence of which they suffer from abscesses, lameness, cardiovascular, skeletal, and respiratory diseases, leg deformities, pneumonia, and damage to their digestive systems.[9] To suppress animals' resistance to intensification, they are castrated and mutilated—often without anesthetics—and forcefully molted and strained to the point of psychological breakdown, giving rise to aggression, frustration, and lethal stress syndromes.[10] These animals suffer in numbers previously unimaginable. In 2016, more than 73 billion land animals were killed for meat—not including animals killed to produce milk or eggs, and sea animals killed for food.[11]

Also part of the second dimension of globalization are environmental problems caused by global agribusiness. Animal agriculture uses 70 percent of the global freshwater and 38 percent of global land in use, and produces 14 percent of the world's greenhouse gases, making it the single most disastrous industry for the environment.[12] By confining animals inside and importing feed to fatten them, animal agriculture generates enormous amounts of manure

---

Across Majority and Minority World Contexts, *in* RECONCEPTUALIZING AGENCY AND CHILDHOOD: NEW PERSPECTIVES IN CHILDHOOD STUDIES 183 ff. (Florian Esser et al. eds., 2016).

6 *Outsourcing's Third Wave*, THE ECONOMIST, May 21, 2009. On agricultural investment, *see, e.g.*, the plans of the Arab Authority for Agricultural Investment and Development, Agricultural Investment (2014), *available at* http://www.aaaid.org/english/Agricultural_investment.htm (last visited Jan. 10, 2019). For a general assessment of foreign agricultural investment, *see* UN FAO, TRENDS AND IMPACTS OF FOREIGN INVESTMENT IN DEVELOPING COUNTRY AGRICULTURE, EVIDENCE FROM CASE STUDIES (FAO, Rome 2013). This document does not consider animal welfare. *See id.* at 175: "Livestock farming i.e. pigs, cattle and poultry, needs to grow as demand for food increases [. . .]."

7 *See, e.g.*, for Pakistan and Iran: Ciaran Moran, *Behind the Scenes at One of Iran's Largest Dairy Farms*, AGRILAND, Apr. 26, 2016; Farhan Sheikh, *Overview over Pakistan Poultry Industry*, THE POULTRY GUIDE, Dec. 28, 2012.

8 WORLD ANIMAL PROTECTION, ANIMAL PROTECTION INDEX, *available at* http://api.worldanimalprotection.org (last visited Jan. 10, 2019).

9 PEW COMMISSION, REPORT ON INDUSTRIAL FARM ANIMAL PRODUCTION, PUTTING MEAT ON THE TABLE: INDUSTRIAL FARM ANIMAL PRODUCTION IN AMERICA 33 (PCIFAP, Washington D.C. 2008); Claire Suddath, *The Problem with Factory Farms*, TIME MAGAZINE, Apr. 23, 2010; Jimena Uralde, *Congress' Failure to Enact Animal Welfare Legislation for the Rearing of Farm Animals: What Is Truly at Stake?*, 9 U. MIAMI BUS. L. REV. 193, 197 (2001).

10 David N. Cassuto, *Bred Meat: The Cultural Foundation of Factory Farm*, 70 L. & CONTEMP. PROBS. 59, 64–5 (2007); Franklyn B. Garry, *Animal Well-Being in the U.S. Dairy Industry*, *in* THE WELL-BEING OF FARM ANIMALS: CHALLENGES AND SOLUTIONS 207, 219 (G. John Benson & Bernard E. Rollin eds., 2004); Gaverick Matheny & Cheryl Leahy, *Farm-Animal Welfare, Legislation and Trade*, 70 L. & CONTEMP. PROBS. 325, 328 (2007); JIM MASON & PETER SINGER, ANIMAL FACTORIES 3, 22, 52 (1980 (Revised 1990)).

11 FAOSTAT (search criteria "World"+"Meat Total"+"Producing Animals/Slaughtered"+"2016," *available at* http://faostat.fao.org/ (last visited Jan. 10, 2019).

12 Animal production has a much larger ecological footprint (or hoof print) than plant-based diets, typically by a factor of 10 or 11: *2050: A Third More Mouths to Feed*, FAO MEDIA CENTRE, Sept. 23, 2009. Oxford researchers

that pollute soil and groundwater, overwhelm ecosystems, and cause more greenhouse gas emissions than the global transport sector.[13]

The agricultural industry is also linked to a host of social problems. Ever-increasing production of animal goods devours larger and larger portions of the world's crops, reducing the amount of grain for direct consumption by humans or animals.[14] Meat, dairy, and egg production triggers anthropogenic climate change that affects food security adversely, placing a disproportionate burden on the world's poorest.[15] Animal agriculture also jeopardizes public health. The widespread use of antibiotics and antimicrobials to increase animals' performance causes antimicrobial resistance in bacteria, which often directly transfer to humans (through consumption of animal products) and pose a significant risk to public health.[16]

Despite the growing knowledge of the ethical, environmental, and social problems caused by globalized animal production, there seems to be no stopping place. According to the UN Food and Agriculture Organization (FAO), the world will need to produce 50 percent more meat by 2050 to meet the rising demand for animal protein.[17] No country is (yet) committed to divest from animal production, which suggests that the multilevel problems caused by animal agriculture that we are witnessing today will likely proliferate in the coming years. Because animal agriculture spans across the globe and produces negative effects on foreign territory, its regulation exceeds the capacity of any single state and this makes apparent the need for responses beyond the nation-state. Once we begin to theorize about possible solutions, we enter the third dimension of globalization: the juridico-political responses to globalization's first and second dimension.

Poore and Nemecek were the first to conduct a meta analysis of ~38,000 farms producing 40 different agricultural goods around the world, to assess the impacts of food production and consumption. They found, specifically, that plant-based diets reduce food's emissions by up to 73 percent depending where people live. Moreover, the impacts even of the lowest-impact animal products typically exceed those of vegetable substitutes: J. Poore & T. Nemecek, *Reducing Food's Environmental Impact through Producers and Consumers*, 360(6392) SCIENCE 987 (2018). *See also* Edgar Hertwich & Ester van der Voet, ASSESSING THE ENVIRONMENTAL IMPACTS OF CONSUMPTION AND PRODUCTION: PRIORITY PRODUCTS AND MATERIALS 51, 79 (UNEP 2010).

[13] MASON & SINGER 122 (1990); PEW COMMISSION, REPORT ON INDUSTRIAL FARM ANIMAL PRODUCTION 23 (2008); UN FAO, LIVESTOCK'S LONG SHADOW, ENVIRONMENTAL ISSUES AND OPTIONS 272 (FAO, Rome 2006).

[14] CHRISTOPHER DELGADO ET AL., LIVESTOCK TO 2020, THE NEXT FOOD REVOLUTION 3 (International Food Policy Research Institute (IFPRI) 1999); TONY WEIS, THE GLOBAL FOOD ECONOMY: THE BATTLE FOR THE FUTURE OF FARMING (2007).

[15] Because of agricultural industries, as the FAO notes, "Sub-Saharan Africa's share in the global number of hungry people could rise from 24 percent to between 40 and 50 percent" (UN FAO, HOW TO FEED THE WORLD IN 2050, HIGH LEVEL EXPERT FORUM 30 (FAO, Rome 2009)).

[16] Michael J. Martin, Sapna E. Thottathil & Thomas B. Newman, *Antibiotics Overuse in Animal Agriculture: A Call to Action for Health Care Providers*, 105(12) AM. J. PUBLIC HEALTH 2409 (2015); PEW COMMISSION, REPORT ON INDUSTRIAL FARM ANIMAL PRODUCTION, ANTIMICROBIAL RESISTANCE AND HUMAN HEALTH 11 (PCIFAP, Washington D.C. 2008). In 2017, the World Health Organization (WHO) recommended that farmers and the food industry stop using antibiotics routinely to promote growth and prevent disease in healthy animals. *See* *Stop Using Antibiotics in Healthy Animals to Prevent the Spread of Antibiotic Resistance*, WHO NEWS RELEASE, Nov. 7, 2017.

[17] UN FAO, HOW TO FEED THE WORLD IN 2050, HIGH LEVEL EXPERT FORUM 11 (FAO, Rome 2009); UN FAO, LIVESTOCK'S LONG SHADOW 275 (2006).

§2 Is Extraterritorial Jurisdiction the Panacea?

The best solution to these global problems is for states to conclude bi- or multilateral agreements that would identify the most pressing issues and point to reasonably available policy options. Unlike extraterritorial jurisdiction, an agreement concluded by states is more likely to satisfy their interests since it can take special concerns into account, is voluntary, and thus more likely to be enforced. Treaty-making offers an opportunity to arrive at a broad consensus and find a long-lasting solution to the many problems caused by globalized animal production.[18]

The difficulty of coming to a broad agreement, however, is easily underestimated, and failure to reach an agreement is the rule, rather than the exception. Even if an agreement is drafted for a specific policy issue, states often profoundly disagree over what the best regulatory measures are to address or solve it. In a seminal article on antitrust law, Guzman used an economic analysis to determine the probability states would conclude an international treaty on jurisdictional matters. He hypothesized that economic incentives are states' primary motive for seeking or rejecting a treaty, and argued that finding common ground for a treaty will be difficult, if not impossible, when consumers and producers are unevenly distributed among states.[19] Let us assume state A is a majority world country, strongly influenced by investors, and state B is a minority world country, presumably investment-exporting and, therefore, more consumer-oriented. According to Guzman, the optimal policy for state A is to have no policy, since welfare losses are borne by consumers abroad. The optimal policy for state B, by contrast, is to regulate at a level that increases efficiency gains for consumers.[20]

Guzman's probability analysis can be applied to animal law because economic considerations are central to its policymaking and because a large portion of the world's animal products is produced in the majority world. Assuming that state A is investment-driven and state B is consumer-oriented, it makes sense for state A not to regulate animal production, so it will tend to underregulate. For state B, the optimal solution is regulation that better satisfies consumer preferences, so it will tend to overregulate. Both states are biased toward protecting either producers or consumers. Based on these disparate preferences, it is unlikely these states will agree on a set of norms that allocates jurisdictional competence among them. These considerations show that treaties, designed to determine the jurisdictional parameters of animal law, are a less feasible policy option than is commonly assumed.

According to Guzman, states are only likely to agree on jurisdictional authority if the ratio of consumption share to production share is about the same in both countries, in which case their interests converge. For instance, if both states produce 30 percent of all global animal products and consume 10 percent of the global animal production output, they will weigh consumer and producer interests equally.[21] In the rare cases where the ratio is roughly equal and treaty convergence is likely, the overall gains of finding agreement, however, will

---

[18] Stephen Coughlan et al., *Global Reach, Local Grasp: Constructing Extraterritorial Jurisdiction in the Age of Globalization*, 6 CAN. J.L. & TECHN. 29, 37 (2007); Mann 96 (1984).

[19] Guzman 1548 (1998).

[20] Guzman concedes that this is the simplest analytical model, but we can draw the most inferences from it: *Id.* at 1514–5.

[21] *Id.* at 1525.

be modest.[22] If Norway and Germany concluded a treaty on jurisdiction over animal protection matters, there would be a little substantial benefit. But in the unlikely event Germany concluded a treaty with Uzbekistan, we can expect it to positively affect the level of animal welfare in Uzbekistan. But as argued above, the chances of those states reaching an agreement are low. To find common ground, states with strong animal laws would need to lower their well-established standards. Citizens and their home states might consider this unacceptable given their ethical and political views of animals, and it would raise serious concerns on grounds of justice owed to animals.[23] The same difficulties, however, are met by states with weaker animal laws. For them, improving their standards to reach a common agreement with other states might run counter to established cultural, religious, or other social values.

These considerations evidence that treaties, designed to determine the jurisdictional parameters of animal law, are not necessarily the most feasible policy option. Pursuing them may frustrate the very reason for which their conclusion is sought, by driving a wedge between different cultures and societies over the question of what the "optimal treatment" of animals is. At the same time, the multidimensional ethical, societal, environmental, and public health risks caused by globalized animal industries make waiting for an agreement a poor option. One could argue that the downsides of waiting for an agreement could be balanced by the benefits of reaching an agreement, but time is not the only issue here. Since investment typically moves to the state that tolerates the cheapest production at the lowest level of regulation (hence, to state A), state B's well-established animal laws will always be undermined.[24] So while we wait, perhaps vainly, for an agreement, competition proliferates toward laxity, from which animals suffer most.[25]

In contrast to international treaties, extraterritorial jurisdiction promises to create a dense, global jurisdictional net of overlapping and concurring laws. Schiff Berman claims this jurisdictional net offers us significant benefits.[26] Multiple jurisdictional assertions that overlap and concur decrease the likelihood of regulatory gaps in animal law: "Let both States assert jurisdiction."[27] Extraterritorial jurisdiction creates an opportunity for political deliberation and negotiation, adapts sweeping or insufficient laws to a specific problem at hand, and leaves space for innovation through competition. Since we are dealing with issues of global governance, whose complexity cannot adequately or fully be addressed by an international treaty, overlapping jurisdiction draws a more realistic picture of lived relationships. The convergence and conflicts of jurisdiction offer an opportunity to recognize and celebrate cultural diversity,[28]

---

[22] *Analogously id.* at 1505.

[23] *See generally* on the problems that emerge when countries lower their standards to conclude treaties on jurisdictional matters: IBA Report Extraterritorial Jurisdiction 12 (2009).

[24] Guzman 1523 (1998).

[25] The question of whether a race to the bottom exists in animal law is examined in Chapter 2, §3 B. II.

[26] Schiff Berman argues that "we might deliberately seek to create or preserve spaces for productive interaction among multiple, overlapping legal systems by developing procedural mechanisms, institutions, and practices that aim to manage, without eliminating, the legal pluralism we see around us." (Berman, Global Legal Pluralism 10 (2012)).

[27] Bowett 14 (1982). *See also* Oppenheim's International Law 457 (1992).

[28] Different from what many may believe, extraterritorial jurisdiction is not adverse to, but may be conducive to multiculturalism. *See further* on rooted cosmopolitanism as an alternative to internationalization: Will

and prompts gradual improvement of substantive standards, including standards of animal law.[29]

Consider the steps taken by the United States to protect dolphins during the 1990s. In response to widespread public outrage about the many dolphins killed by common tuna fishing, the United States banned imports of tuna that led to the death of a set number of dolphins. As we will see in our analysis of trade law, these efforts largely failed at the WTO.[30] Though some may see this as evidence for the ban's inadequacy, these efforts were a key driver of the International Dolphin Conservation Program (IDCP). In 1999, the United States brought together Belize, Colombia, Costa Rica, Ecuador, El Salvador, the European Union, Guatemala, Honduras, Mexico, Nicaragua, Panama, Peru, Vanuatu, and Venezuela to join the Agreement on the International Dolphin Conservation Program (AIDCP), whose declared objective is to eliminate dolphin mortality.[31] Similarly, the European Union's efforts to ban the importation of furs sourced from leghold traps caused the United States and Canada to enter into a common agreement with the European Union over trapping standards.[32] Extraterritorial jurisdiction, though opposable on various grounds, can manifestly prompt states to adopt better laws for animals.

But just because extraterritorial law is an effective alternative to hard-to-reach international agreements in some areas, does not mean it will be effective or legitimate in others. In order to understand why states pass extraterritorial laws, and the conditions under which the international community considers these laws legitimate, we must take a closer look at economic and criminal law, where these practices are most common and widely accepted.[33] From these insights, we can begin to formulate a hypothesis about the usefulness and likely acceptance of extraterritorial jurisdiction in animal law.

Kymlicka & Kathryn Walker, *Rooted Cosmopolitanism: Canada and the World*, *in* ROOTED COSMOPOLITANISM: CANADA AND THE WORLD 1-30, 3 (Will Kymlicka & Kathryn Walker eds., 2012).

[29] Overlapping and concurring jurisdiction creates competition for jurisdictional authority, and competition among substantive provisions, both of which can yield advantages: BERMAN, GLOBAL LEGAL PLURALISM 237 (2012); Robert Cover, *The Uses of Jurisdictional Redundancy: Interest, Ideology, and Innovation*, 22 WM. & MARY L. REV. 639 (1981).

[30] For details on the *Tuna/Dolphin* case, *see* Chapter 3, §2 B. III.

[31] International Dolphin Conservation Program Agreement, May 5, 1998, 1999 O.J. (L 132) 3, objective 1 [AIDCP].

[32] Whereas the agreement between the European Union and Canada is binding, the agreement between the European Union and the United States solely incorporates a pledge to promote "humane" standards of trapping: Agreement on International Humane Trapping Standards between the European Community, Canada and the Russian Federation, Dec. 15, 1997, 1998 O.J. (L 42) 43; U.S.-EU Agreed Minute on Humane Trapping Standards, 1998 O.J. (L 219) 26, at 4.

[33] Environmental law might also be considered a "hot topic" for the law of jurisdiction. In environmental law, it is recognized that extraterritorial jurisdiction is necessary to effectively counter environmental risks and eradicate poor environmental practices, based on an understanding of "shared responsibility" for the environment. Zerk, however, asserts that "[. . .] states do not, as a general rule, attempt to extend their environmental laws to other states. States do apply their environmental laws extraterritorially to 'global commons'" (ZERK, EXTRATERRITORIAL JURISDICTION 176, also at 9 (2010)). Also Abate notices the different views on extraterritorial jurisdiction in environmental law, which depend on whether global commons are concerned or not (Randall S. Abate, *Dawn of a New Era in the Extraterritorial Application of U.S. Environmental Statutes: A Proposal for an Integrated Judicial Standard Based on the Continuum of Context*, 31 COLUM. J. ENVTL. L. 87, 89

§3 The Rationale of Economic Entanglement

A. THE RATIONALE OF ECONOMIC ENTANGLEMENT IN ECONOMIC LAW

Areas of law in which extraterritorial jurisdiction is most fiercely asserted by states are those relating to economic matters. In antitrust law,[34] concurring state interests and transborder jurisdictional assertions are a common phenomenon.[35] To protect domestic markets, states sanctioned the formation of cartels in foreign countries, as in the chemical and vitamin industry, the uranium supply market, or the watch industry, which, consequently, garnered the attention of the international community.[36] Similarly, from the 1950s onward, states began to use the law of export controls to steer foreign politics, as when the United States limited exports to China and Cuba to suppress communist regimes. These actions divided the international community, especially since they were used to propagate a specific political agenda.[37] In securities and stock exchange law, cross-border movement in finance boosted international stock exchange and securities transactions, which prompted states to extend their securities law to cover a wide range of transactions.[38] Extraterritorial jurisdiction also dominates the law of mergers and acquisitions,[39] investment control,[40] and banking.[41]

(2006)). Most treaties in environmental regulation lay down duties to inform, cooperate, and consult instead of encouraging states to prescribe law extraterritorially. *See, e.g.*, the Convention on Access to Information, Public Participation in Decision Making and Access to Justice in Environmental Matters, June 28, 1998, 2161 U.N.T.S. 447 [Aaarhus Convention]; Convention on the Control of Transboundary Movements of Hazardous Wastes and Their Disposal, Mar. 22, 1989, 1672 U.N.T.S. 126, art. 2 [Basel Convention]; Convention on Environmental Impact in a Transboundary Context, Feb. 25, 1991, 1989 U.N.T.S. 309, arts. 3–5 [Espoo Convention]. An exception to limited extraterritorial jurisdiction is the CoE, Convention on the Protection of the Environment through Criminal Law, Nov. 4, 1998, C.E.T.S. No. 172 (not yet in force).

34 Antitrust law is known as competition law in Europe; sometimes it is considered a subdiscipline of competition law.

35 *E.g.*, Eleanor M. Fox, *Can We Solve the Antitrust Problems of Globalization by Extraterritoriality and Cooperation? Sufficiency and Legitimacy*, 48 ANTITRUST BULL. 355 (2003); DAVID J. GERBER, GLOBAL COMPETITION: LAW, MARKETS, AND GLOBALIZATION (2010); CEDRIC RYNGAERT, JURISDICTION OVER ANTITRUST VIOLATIONS IN INTERNATIONAL LAW (2008).

36 Empagran SA v. F. Hoffmann-LaRoche Ltd., 315 F.3d 388 (D.C. Circ. 2003) (U.S.); Westinghouse Electric Corp. v. Rio Algom Ltd, 617 F.2d 1248 (7th Cir. 1980) (U.S.); United States v. The Watchmakers of Switzerland Information Center, 133 F. Supp. 40 (S.D.N.Y. 1955) (U.S.); United States v. Imperial Chemical Industries, 105 F. Supp. 215 (S.D.N.Y. 1952) (U.S.).

37 Armand L.C. De Mestral, *The Extraterritorial Extension of Laws: How Much Has Changed?*, 31 ARIZ. J. INT'L & COMP. L. 43 (2014); MENG 310 ff. (1994). For an examination of jurisdictional aspects of export control law, *see* Cedric Ryngaert, *Extraterritorial Export Controls (Secondary Boycotts)*, 7 CHIN. J. INT'L L. 625 (2008).

38 Lea Brilmayer, *The New Extraterritoriality:* Morrison v. National Australia Bank, *Legislative Supremacy, and the Presumption Against Extraterritorial Application of American Law*, 40 SW. L. REV. 655 (2011); GUNNAR SCHUSTER, DIE INTERNATIONALE ANWENDUNG DES BÖRSENRECHTS (1996).

39 Sarah Stevens, *The Increased Aggression of the EC Commission in Extraterritorial Enforcement of the Merger Regulation and Its Impact on Transatlantic Cooperation in Antitrust*, 29 SYRACUSE J. INT'L L. & COM. 263 (2002); MENG 437 ff. (1994).

40 Ulrich Bosch, *Extraterritorial Rules on Banking and Securities*, *in* EXTRATERRITORIAL JURISDICTION IN THEORY AND PRACTICE 200 (1996).

41 Richard W. Painter, *The Dodd-Frank Extraterritorial Jurisdiction Provision: What Is Effective, Needed or Sufficient?*, 1 HARV. BUS. L. REV. 195 (2011); Thomas Schobel, *Home Country or Recipient Country? Confining the Extraterritorial Reach of Domestic Banking Law*, 41 INT'L LAW. 75 (2007).

The prevalence of extraterritorial jurisdiction in areas of law concerned with economic matters raises the question of which factors occasion this trend. A common explanation is that regulatory competition prompts extraterritorial jurisdiction: the existence or threat of a race to the bottom causes states to enact laws that transcend their territory, in an effort to reclaim their "endangered" regulatory authority over domestic matters. This claim requires closer scrutiny.

Removing the most obvious barriers to the flow of goods, services, and finances between states has caused economic markets to gradually approximate and level out. This approximation has brought states' regulatory differences more sharply into focus and accentuated remaining barriers to trade.[42] Corporations began choosing home states based on the advantages they offered, which stoked fear among states that business will move somewhere more advantageous—to places with fewer and less rigid or strict laws—and compelled them to lax their standards. Rather than autonomously exercising their authority, states began to compete with each other through their regulatory systems and learned that they gain a comparative advantage by designing their laws to the investors' and producers' liking.[43] These dynamics are commonly described as regulatory competition, and are also known as jurisdictional competition or systems competition.[44]

Regulatory competition among states is frequently encouraged by non-state actors. The *Global Competitive Reports* of the Davos World Economy Forum established a "Global Competitiveness Index" that examines states' institutions, infrastructure, macroeconomic environment, educational facilities, goods and labor market efficiency, financial market development, market size, technological readiness, and innovation performance.[45] The index ranks states based on their ability to provide high levels of prosperity to citizens and to create country-specific advantages for multinationals. In this setting, the law operates as a product, an investment-relevant factor that states put on offer to attract customers.

As states compete over jurisdictional authority, regulation tends to converge toward laxity. Corporations predictably seek to maximize their output and revenues, which is more likely when governments intervene less and corporations incur fewer costs than their competitors

---

[42] *Cf.* KAUFMANN 232 ff. (2007); Sol Picciotto, *The Regulatory Criss-Cross: Interaction between Jurisdictions and the Construction of Global Regulatory Networks*, *in* INTERNATIONAL REGULATORY COMPETITION AND COORDINATION 89 (William W. Bratton et al. eds., 1996); MARKUS REPS, RECHTSWETTBEWERB UND DEBT GOVERNANCE BEI ANLEIHEN 53 (2014).

[43] Bratton et al., *Regulatory Competition and Institutional Evolution*, *in* INTERNATIONAL REGULATORY COMPETITION AND COORDINATION 2 (1996); GABOR 3 (2013); Koenig-Archibugi, *Global Regulation*, *in* THE OXFORD HANDBOOK OF REGULATION 413 (2010); MURPHY 4 (2004).

[44] Eidenmüller argues that systems competition must be differentiated from regulatory competition. Systems competition includes competition not only of legal rules but also of states' infrastructure, while regulatory competition only refers to the competition of laws: Horst Eidenmüller, *The Transnational Law Market, Regulatory Competition, and Transnational Corporations*, 18 IND. J. GLOBAL LEGAL STUD. 707, 715 (2011).

[45] The reports make use of over 110 variables in 12 distinct pillars. *See e.g.*, WORLD ECONOMIC FORUM (WEF), GLOBAL COMPETITIVENESS REPORT 2018 (WEF, Geneva 2018), earlier version *cited in* Anne Peters, *Competition between Legal Orders*, 3 INT'L L. RES. 45, 45 (2014).

in other jurisdictions.[46] To attract corporations and gain "regulatory market share," states lax their standards and create incentives for other states to follow suit. As more and more states follow this strategy, there is a global *convergence toward a lower common denominator*, also known as competition in laxity or race to the bottom.[47]

Animal law scholars often suspect regulatory competition in animal law moves toward laxity. As the market for meat, dairy, and egg products increases exponentially and competition gets tougher, the costs of input factors like labor and animals carry more weight in the corporate calculus, as do factors like production site, speed of operation, and hygiene requirements. The more rigidly laws insist corporations perform in a specific way, such as by determining how animals ought to be bred, reared, transported, or slaughtered, the harder it is for corporations to choose the cheapest factors of production, which they need to outpace competitors on the market. Because policies designed to improve animal welfare commonly place burdens on business, they are prone to blocking market growth.[48] The reverse is also true: because there is always an economically more efficient jurisdiction where capital can move, unhampered competition frustrates establishing, keeping in force, and enforcing robust animal laws.

Economic theorists do not necessarily think competition in laxity is the default trajectory of regulatory competition. From the 1990s on, they have refuted the race to the bottom hypothesis and pointed out that regulatory competition may follow different trajectories.[49] An alternative is *convergence toward a higher common denominator*, also known as the race to the top, which describes competition between states to promote better regulation through government intervention.[50] The rationale underlying this trajectory is that corporations benefit from adhering to high legal standards, certifications, or quality standards, especially in a legal environment that rewards consumers for bearing the extra cost. The third type of competition trajectory, *regulatory heterogeneity*, occurs when preferences vary greatly across states, resulting in persistent heterogeneous regulations.[51]

---

[46] Kaufmann 15 (2007); Murphy 10–1 (2004).

[47] The race to the bottom is also frequently called the "Delaware effect" (coined by David Vogel, Trading up: Consumer and Environmental Regulation in a Global Economy (1995)) or "Zug effect" (Murphy 6 (2004)).

[48] Vernon and Nwaogu argue that some recently introduced changes to the regulatory framework of the European Union may pose barriers to innovation, including testing and marketing bans of cosmetic products: Jan Vernon & Tobe A. Nwaogu, Comparative Study on Cosmetics Legislation in the EU and Other Principal Markets, Final Report Contract No. FIF.20030624, Prepared for European Commission DG Enterprise 37 (Norfolk 2004), *available at* http://rpaltd.co.uk/uploads/report_files/j457-final-report-cosmetics.pdf (last visited Jan. 10, 2019).

[49] Vogel and Kagan argue that races to the top are more likely than races to the bottom: David Vogel & Robert A. Kagan eds., Dynamics of Regulatory Change: How Globalization Affects National Regulatory Policies (2004).

[50] The race to the top is also called the "California effect" (Carruthers & Lamoreaux 2 (2009); Murphy 5 (2004)).

[51] Murphy 5 (2004).

B. THE RATIONALE OF ECONOMIC ENTANGLEMENT IN ANIMAL LAW

I. Regulatory Competition in Animal Law

To date, economic theorists have not examined the trajectory of competition in animal law. From their writings, however, we can extrapolate factors indicating the different trajectories of regulatory competition, which helps us approximate the trajectory of competition in animal law.[52] Murphy claims three factors give rise to competition in laxity: the location of regulation (production processes and market access regulations), industrial structure, and asset specificity.[53]

Murphy's first observation is that the location of production processes and market access regulations explain regulatory upward or downward movement. Process restrictions limit or prohibit certain processes of manufacturing or service industries, but they do not visibly change a product (product standards, in contrast, alter the qualities of a product).[54] Murphy argues that if process restrictions are heterogeneous among states, they prompt movement toward the lower common denominator. To improve their competitive position, corporate actors move to territories where restrictions on manufacturing processes are absent or negligible, which allows them to avoid the costs of adapting products to a specific market.[55] The most common type of regulation in animal law is process standards that lay down in detail how animals must be treated or handled. Animal welfare acts, for example, dictate cage sizes, standards of transportation, or slaughterhouse procedures. These standards, and the labels by which they are identified, greatly differ from one state to another (i.e., there is regulatory heterogeneity) and raise costs by forcing corporations to redesign, retest, relabel, and repackage products. In animal law, there is thus a strong presumption that animal protection standards lead to competition in laxity.

Market access restrictions are more restrictive than production process regulations since they block access (sale, consumption, distribution, or disposal) of products or services to a market. Murphy's observation is that market access restrictions spawn protectionism. He analyzes market access regulation in animal law in the context of the *Tuna/Dolphin* case decided at the WTO Dispute Settlement Body (DSB)[56] and concludes that market

---

[52] Mainstream regulatory competition theories are still disputed in economics, as scholars tend to think regulatory tendencies result from more complex interactions than simple competition. These processes are influenced by a multitude of regulatory tools, multilevel regulation, and regulation beyond rigid command and control structures. Moreover, scholarly work on policy convergence is spread across numerous disciplines, making it difficult to build theories and extrapolate: ROBERT BALDWIN ET AL., UNDERSTANDING REGULATION: THEORY, STRATEGY, AND PRACTICE 365 (2d ed. 2013).

[53] MURPHY 11 ff. (2004). These indicators are supported by findings of other regulatory competition experts. Gabor argues that mobility accounts for lower common denominator movement, even when regulatees are not mobile: GABOR 15 (2013). Carruthers and Lamoreaux agree with Murphy that a race heavily depends on the industry's mobility; resource-dependent industries are less likely to move than capital-intense branches: Carruthers & Lamoreaux 9 (2009).

[54] BALDWIN ET AL. 364–5 (2013).

[55] MURPHY 12 (2004). Consider in this respect the repercussions of hormone regulation on beef production in comparisons between the United States and the European Union.

[56] *United States—Measures Concerning the Importation, Marketing and Sale of Tuna and Tuna Products*, DS381.

access restrictions for tuna products led to heterogeneous regulation and were therefore protectionist.[57]

Murphy's second observation is that concentrated markets facilitate regulatory movement.[58] The industries that produce and process animals are highly susceptible to monopolistic market tendencies. For example, in the United States, four producers control 81 percent of the beef market, and two producers dominate 56 percent of the meat chicken market; in total, 2 percent of livestock farms raise 40 percent of all animals.[59] Also outside the United States, agricultural corporations have become extremely powerful and operate almost without competition.[60] As economic power concentrates among a few firms in the animal industry, the risk of regulatory movement steeply increases.

Murphy's third observation is that asset specificity of investments and transactions affect regulatory homogeneity. When asset specificity is low (investments can easily be deployed), this facilitates lower common denominator movement, but when asset specificity is high (investments have high transaction costs), corporations push for homogeneous norms. Today, a majority of domesticated animals is owned by multinationals that use them for food, research, and other purposes.[61] These multinationals, because they do business internationally and operate with mobile assets, find it easy to move animals to countries where production is cheaper. Today, horses are moved across borders so companies can profit from cheap slaughter; fish cages are relocated across territorial seas to evade regulation; sheep are transported by the millions so producers can benefit from business-friendly regulatory environments; and monkeys are relocated to profit from lax laws.[62] Because the animal industry is marked by low asset specificity (a high degree of asset mobility and low transaction costs), animal law is highly susceptible to a movement toward a lower common denominator.

---

[57] MURPHY 192 (2004).

[58] BALDWIN ET AL. 15 ff. (2013); MURPHY 14 ff. (2004).

[59] DANIELLE NIERENBERG, HAPPIER MEALS, RETHINKING THE GLOBAL MEAT INDUSTRY 12 (Worldwatch Institute, Washington D.C. 2005); U.S. Department of Agriculture, Agricultural Research Service National Program Nr. 206, Manure and Byproduct Utilization Action Plan 2004–2008 1 (USDA, Washington D.C. 2005).

[60] According to Nierenberg, only a few companies dominate the global meat market worldwide: "Tyson Foods, which touts itself as 'the largest provider of protein products on the planet', is the world's biggest meat and poultry company, with more than $26 billion in annual sales and operations in Argentina, Brazil, China, India, Indonesia, Japan, Mexico, the Netherlands, the Philippines, Russia, Spain, the United Kingdom, and Venezuela. Smithfield Foods, the largest hog producer and pork processor in the world and the fifth-largest beef packer, boasts more than $10 billion in annual sales. More than $1 billion of this is earned internationally from operations in Canada, China, Mexico, and several European countries" (NIERENBERG 12 (2005)). In *The Global Food Economy*, Weis argues that multinational enterprises seek to expand their global playing field by restricting governments' capacity to regulate them in multilateral trade systems: WEIS, THE GLOBAL FOOD ECONOMY 6 ff., 128 ff., 158 (2007).

[61] Well-known multinationals in the food sector include Smithfield Foods, Tyson Foods, Cargill, and Swift & Co.: KELCH 306–7 (2011); KIRBY xiv (2010).

[62] *See* Chapter 1.

In addition to Murphy's theoretical model, there are further indicators that point to lower common denominator movement in animal law. Competition in laxity manifests itself in four ways: *de jure* competition in laxity, *de facto* relocation competition in laxity, *de facto* market share competition in laxity, and regulatory chill.[63] *De jure* competition in laxity occurs when states actively lower their regulatory standards in response to economic pressure. This is an extreme form of a race to the bottom and is not the most common in animal law but states sometimes use it to conform to industry demands. Starting in 2001, Japan began to lax its drug control laws for all cosmetic products under the three-year deregulatory strategy of its Pharmaceutical Affairs Law.[64] Vernon and Nwaogu explained that the deregulation process was triggered by factors of "globalisation of the cosmetics market and the need to remove non-tariff barriers, the perceived high level of safety of cosmetic products and the growing administrative burden of dealing with an increasing number of new products."[65] Similarly, in line with the United Kingdom's general deregulatory agenda, the Department for Environment, Food and Rural Affairs (DEFRA) announced in 2016 it would hand its regulatory authority over farmed animal welfare to the farming industries.[66] Privatizing animal law would, predictably, entail broad deregulation of practices involved in breeding, raising, transporting, and slaughtering animals used for food purposes.[67]

De facto relocation competition in laxity occurs when domestic firms move production facilities to states where standards are less stringent. The 312 percent increase in horse exports to Mexico in reaction to the US ban on funding horse-slaughter inspections in 2006 is a prime example of *de facto* relocation.[68] Live animal exports from Australia to the rest of the world is also a kind of industry outsourcing that relocates billions of animals for slaughter to countries with inexistent or weak animal protection laws.[69] In the coming years, we are expecting massive agricultural outsourcing from the minority world to the majority world, prompted by heavy investments in farmland.[70] This is expected to be the third wave of global industry outsourcing, following the first wave of manufacturing outsourcing in the 1980s and the second wave of information outsourcing in the 1990s. The future of farmed animal production thus undoubtedly lies in the Global South. Relocation and outsourcing are also common in the research industry, especially among biomedical and pharmaceutical institutions and their supplying facilities.[71] Kelch summarizes: "Animal abuse is being

---

[63] MURPHY 7 (2004).

[64] Deregulation occurred through the abolition of pre-market approval, establishment of a prohibited and restricted ingredient list, and abolition of the designated ingredient list: Vernon & Nwaogu 27–8 (2004).

[65] Vernon & Nwaogu 28, 37 (2004).

[66] Rowena Mason, *Government Planning to Repeal Animal Welfare Codes*, THE GUARDIAN, Mar. 25, 2016.

[67] After causing a considerable public outcry, DEFRA abandoned its plans two weeks later: Rowena Mason, *Ministers Abandon Plan to Scrap Farm Animal Welfare Codes*, THE GUARDIAN, Apr. 7, 2016.

[68] *See* for an explanation of these events, Chapter 1, §5.

[69] Craig 51 ff. (2013). On the question whether live animal exports should be banned: Radhika Chaudhri, *Animal Welfare and the WTO: The Legality and Implications of Live Export Restrictions under International Trade Law*, 42 FED. L. REV. 279 (2014); Kristen Stilt, *Trading in Sacrifice*, 111 AJIL UNBOUND 397 (2017).

[70] *Outsourcing's Third Wave*, THE ECONOMIST, May 21, 2009.

[71] For examples, *see* Chapter 1, §5.

outsourced. Meat production is going south and animal experimentation is heading east. Africa now produces meat for Europe while Brazil does the same for both Asia and Europe. We see animal experimenters abandoning places like Europe in favour of India, Singapore and China."[72]

De facto market share competition in laxity occurs when multinationals increase their market share in animal production in states with lax animal protection standards. Multinational enterprises dominate industries that produce pharmaceuticals, cosmetics, chemicals, food and beverages, clothing, and other products.[73] These enterprises have a tremendous effect on animals and are better positioned than ordinary companies to influence public policy due to competitive advantages in goods markets, readily exchangeable flows of information and assets, an ability to differentiate branded products, superior management skills, global patents and trade secrets, and access to substantial capital.[74] These advantages, and the unparalleled bargaining power they provide to multinationals, uniquely enable, even encourage them to increase their market share in countries where weak animal laws prevail. As a result, multinational enterprises disproportionately influence the quality, quantity, type, location of production, and price of products at the production stage and throughout the entire food and research system.[75]

States may experience a regulatory chill if they decline to raise animal protection standards despite societal demands and new scientific evidence of animals' interest in leading a meaningful life.[76] For example, in 2002, EU authorities debated whether the long-announced marketing ban on cosmetic products sourced from animal research must finally be implemented. The Commission expressed its reservations about the ban, arguing that the industry would move abroad or challenge the ban under WTO law.[77] Several EU measures, including import bans on fur and mandatory labeling of eggs, have been weakened after they were introduced because member states feared prices would be undercut and domestic industries ousted.[78] Member states themselves have declined to improve animal protection standards for the same reason, as when Germany refused

---

[72] Thomas Kelch, *Towards Universal Principles for Global Animal Advocacy*, 5 TEL 81, 82 (2016). According to Keyserlingk and Hötzel, there is a trend toward increasing food production in majority countries, which often is paralleled by weak animal laws: Marina A.G. von Keyserlingk & Maria José Hötzel, *The Ticking Clock: Addressing Farm Animal Welfare in Emerging Countries*, 28 J. AGRI. & ENVTL. ETHICS 179, 186 (2015).

[73] Today, the majority of all domesticated animals worldwide are owned by multinationals: Park & Singer 122 (2012).

[74] Seminal: CHARLES P. KINDLEBERGER, AMERICAN BUSINESS ABROAD: SIX LECTURES ON DIRECT INVESTMENT 14–27 (1969).

[75] According to Weis, multinationals are like an "hourglass which controls the flow of sand from the top to the bottom" (WEIS, THE GLOBAL FOOD ECONOMY 13 (2007)).

[76] MURPHY 7 (2004).

[77] Commission of the European Communities, Opinion of the Commission Pursuant to Article 251 (2), Third Subparagraph, Point (c) of the EC Treaty, on the European Parliament's Amendments to the Council's Common Position Regarding the Proposal for a Directive of the European Parliament and of the Council Amending for the Seventh Time Council Directive 76/768/EEC on the Approximation of the Laws of the Member States Relating to Cosmetic Products, COM(2002) 435 final (July 26, 2002).

[78] Kate Cook & David Bowles, *Growing Pains: The Developing Relationship of Animal Welfare Standards and the World Trade Rules*, 19 REV. EUROP. COMM. & INT'L ENVTL. L. 227, 229 (2010).

to ban shredding male chicks for egg production.[79] Overall, animal law is susceptible to a high risk of competition in laxity and suffers from *de jure* competition in laxity, *de facto* relocation competition in laxity, *de facto* market share competition in laxity, and regulatory chill.

II. Heading for Lower Common Denominator Movement

From an animal law perspective, lower common denominator movement is the worst possible scenario because it cuts back important achievements for animals and thwarts future progress. But for other stakeholders, this trend is not necessarily negative. When regulatory requirements are low, the industry flourishes, which in turn, at least theoretically, benefits the community by creating jobs and ensuring steady tax revenues. Consumers profit from this environment, as animal products can be offered for sale at lower prices and hence are more accessible. Given these advantages, why should we be concerned about a possible race to the bottom in animal law? In the following, I show that these intuitions fail to take into account the many short- and long-term effects of lower common denominator movement in animal law—a failure that frustrates even the goals of the animal industry's deregulatory agenda.[80]

Today, there is a clear worldwide trend in the agricultural industry toward factory farming where thousands of animals are housed indoors at high density. By 2005, 74 percent of all pigs and 68 percent of all eggs were "produced" in concentrated animal feeding operations (CAFOs).[81] The trend pervades the Global South/Global North divide. Factory farms are the primary production method in the West, in Latin America, and in Asia, with China being the world's leading producer.[82] CAFOs view animals as "factors of production" and increase output by breeding the most productive strains and depriving animals of space to move, turn around, exhibit natural behavior, and form meaningful relationships.[83]

Extreme confinement causes animals to suffer from chronic, production-related diseases, including liver abscesses, mastitis, ascites, lameness, and uterine prolapse.[84] Breeding methods and food enhancements are geared to accelerate the growth of animals but shorten their lifespans by causing cardiovascular, skeletal, and respiratory diseases, and leg deformities.[85]

---

[79] Deutscher Bundestag, 18. Wahlperiode, Gesetzesentwurf des Bundesrates zur Änderung des Tierschutzgesetzes, Drucksache 18/6663, Nov. 11, 2015, Stellungnahme der Regierung, at 10–11.

[80] A similar version of this argument was published in Charlotte E. Blattner, *3R for Farmed Animals: A Legal Argument for Consistency*, 1 GLOBAL J. ANIMAL L. 1 (2014).

[81] Here and throughout this book, I use the terms "factory farm," "industrial farm," "industrial agriculture," and "concentrated animal feeding operation (CAFO)" interchangeably. CAFOs typically house more than 1,000 animals in one building: Claire Suddath, *The Problem with Factory Farms*, TIME MAGAZINE, Apr. 23, 2010.

[82] Garry sees the rise of concentrated farming methods as a side effect of de-peasantization and rapid urbanization: Franklyn B. Garry, *Animal Well-Being in the U.S. Dairy Industry*, *in* THE WELL-BEING OF FARM ANIMALS: CHALLENGES AND SOLUTIONS 207, 208 (G. John Benson & Bernard E. Rollin eds., 2004); Matheny & Leahy 326 (2007). Argentina, Brazil, Chile, China, India, Indonesia, Malaysia, Mexico, Pakistan, the Philippines, South Korea, Taiwan, Thailand, and Vietnam are among the countries involved in depeasantization: WEIS, THE GLOBAL FOOD ECONOMY 20 (2007).

[83] MASON & SINGER 3 (1990).

[84] Matheny & Leahy 328 (2007). Garry lists the most common diseases incurred by cows on dairy farms: Garry, *Animal Well-Being in the U.S. Dairy Industry*, *in* THE WELL-BEING OF FARM ANIMALS 219 ff. (2004).

[85] HUMANE SOCIETY OF THE UNITED STATES (HSUS), THE WELFARE OF ANIMALS IN THE BROILER CHICKEN INDUSTRY 1–2 (HSUS, Washington D.C. 2005). The animal industry has changed the morphology

Where workers wear gas masks, animals must constantly breathe ammonia, pollutants, and the smell of urine and feces, which causes pneumonia.[86] In CAFOs, animals are widely mutilated; their tails are docked; their beaks, teeth, and toes are clipped; their ears are notched; their horns removed; and there are often castrated, mostly without anesthesia.[87] To increase production, hens are forced to molt and cows are given food they cannot process, which seriously damages their digestive systems.[88] In a production facility, where minimum input and maximum output are the only determinants, illnesses, diseases, and mortality are part of the whole package that ensures a facility's economic survival. Broiler producers, for example, build 30–40 percent mortality into their profitability calculations.[89]

The conditions of factory farming cause animals to suffer aggression, frustration, constant mourning, and lethal stress syndromes.[90] By being individually penned or cramped with others, animals are by design disabled from forming their own relevant community and nurturing their social bonds. They also live deprived of any sensory, olfactory, and intellectual stimuli.[91]

As factory farms proliferated around the globe, the number of animals who suffer from these consequences has drastically increased. Between 1965 and 2005, the worldwide pig population doubled every year, and the population of chickens quadrupled every year.[92] By 2016, 73 billion farmed animals were slaughtered annually,[93] resulting in an "ever expanding boundary of suffering and filth."[94] As later chapters will show, factory farms are run at the expense of many other concerns, by being one of the greatest contributors to environmental

---

and physiology of animals, impairing their ability to adapt. Chickens now grow to 2 kg and twice as fast as they grew 50 years ago. Dairy cows were intensively bred for more productive mammary glands. Cows used for meat production now have enormous muscle mass, which strains their internal organs: Joy M. Verrinder et al., *Science, Animal Ethics and the Law*, *in* ANIMAL LAW AND WELFARE: INTERNATIONAL PERSPECTIVES 63, 63–4 (2016).

[86] The Fund for Animals, Animal Agricultural Fact Sheet #1, Ethical Eating: Exploring Vegetarianism, *available at* http://www.fundforanimals.org/pdf/Old_Urban_Wildlife_Page/fs_ag1_vegetarianism.pdf (last visited Jan. 10, 2019).

[87] Cassuto 64–5 (2007); PEW COMMISSION, REPORT ON INDUSTRIAL FARM ANIMAL PRODUCTION 33 (2008).

[88] MASON & SINGER 52 (1990); Claire Suddath, *The Problem with Factory Farms*, TIME MAGAZINE, Apr. 23, 2010.

[89] This is called the "cull rate": MASON & SINGER 25 (1990); G. Tom Tabler & A.M. Mendenhall, *Broiler Nutrition, Feed Intake and Grower Economics*, 5 AVIAN ADVICE 8, 9 (2003); Matheny & Leahy 329 (2007). On increasing mortality of farmed animals during production, *see* European Commission, Communication from the Commission to the Council and the European Parliament on Animal Welfare Legislation on Farmed Animals in Third Countries and the Implications for the EU, COM(2002) 626 final (Nov. 18, 2002), at 9.

[90] Uralde 197 (2001); MASON & SINGER 22 (1990).

[91] MARTHA C. NUSSBAUM, FRONTIERS OF JUSTICE: DISABILITY, NATIONALITY, SPECIES MEMBERSHIP (2006); TOM REGAN, THE CASE FOR ANIMAL RIGHTS (3d ed. 2004).

[92] WEIS, THE GLOBAL FOOD ECONOMY 19–20 (2007).

[93] FAOSTAT (search criteria "World"+"Meat Total"+"Producing Animals/Slaughtered"+"2016," *available at* http://faostat.fao.org/ (last visited Jan. 10, 2019).

[94] KEN MIDKIFF, THE MEAT YOU EAT: HOW CORPORATE FARMING HAS ENDANGERED AMERICA'S FOOD SUPPLY x (2004).

pollution,[95] and by threatening human health and global food security.[96] Lower common denominator movement in animal law clearly causes negative externalities on multiple levels that far exceed the short-term benefits it promises.

III. Catalysts for Extraterritorial Jurisdiction

The bargaining power multinational enterprises exert on the formation, amendment, and abrogation of animal protection standards, and their tendency to favor lax laws, suggest that a race to the bottom is immanent in animal law. Though we have found strong indicators for the existence of a race to the bottom in animal law, lower common denominator movement in animal law is not a *sine qua non* for triggering extraterritorial jurisdiction. In the following, I demonstrate that a decisive factor prompting states to apply law across the border is their *reasonable expectations* that such a race is imminent or will eventually occur.

Fears and expectations of competition toward lax animal laws—not their actual existence—are what prevent states from keeping in place and improving their animal welfare standards. In March 2015, 1.17 million citizens signed the European Citizens' Initiative "Stop Vivisection," asking the European Commission to abrogate Directive 2010/63/EU and end the use of animals in biomedical and toxicological research. In its response, the Commission essentially ignored the concerns raised, and informed citizens that "a premature ban of research using animals in the EU would likely export the biomedical research and testing outside the EU to countries where welfare standards may be lower and more animals may be needed to achieve the same scientific result."[97] In Switzerland, Maya Graf, member of the Swiss national parliament, called for a nationwide ban on the most severe experiments done on primates. In response to her petition, the responsible commission argued that it would not adopt the ban because animal research would be outsourced to foreign countries.[98] Shortly before the Swiss Animal Welfare Ordinance (AWO) was revised in 2008, the Swiss organization of bovine producers argued that high animal welfare would be unnecessary if borders remained open and that introducing stricter standards for animals would force them to move abroad.[99] In Austria, farmers argued that the EU Pig Directive would not improve pig welfare, even if strictly implemented by Austrian authorities, because production would simply shift to foreign producers who faced no regulatory barriers.[100] In 2015,

---

[95] This is also called "ecological hoof print" (UN FAO, Livestock's Long Shadow 272 (2006)).

[96] There is a high chance epizootic diseases will be imported, so security and quality requirements for animal products need to ensure the protection of public health: Nicole Claudia Henke, Tierschutzstandards im wohlfahrtsökonomischen Kontext: Hühnereiproduktion in der EU und Brasilien 41 (2011).

[97] Commission of the European Communities, Communication from the Commission on the European Citizens' Initiative "Stop Vivisection," C(2015) 3773 final (June 3, 2015), at 3.

[98] Parlamentarische Initiative 06.464, Verbot von mittel- und schwerbelastenden Tierversuchen an Primaten, Maya Graf, Oct. 5, 2006, Bericht der Kommission für Wissenschaft, Bildung und Kultur, Apr. 19, 2007 (Switz.).

[99] Schweizer Rindviewproduzenten SRP, Totalrevision der Tierschutzverordnung, Vernehmlassungsverfahren, Nov. 6, 2006, at 3, *available at* http://www.srp-psbb.ch/site/files_de/stellungnahmen/061106_VN_SRP_TSchV.pdf (last visited Jan. 10, 2019).

[100] Barbara Gerzabek, *Experten einig: Verbot der Ferkelschutzkästen verursacht Tierleid, 643.000 Ferkel würden jährlich "zu Tode geliebt,"* APA-OTS, May 17, 2011.

in its response to an initiative calling for a ban on shredding male chicks for egg production, the German government expressed its concern that the ban might provoke companies to relocate to countries that have no such bans in place.[101] In rejecting the ban, the German *Bundestag* emphasized that its goal was to find a practical solution to end the mass slaughter of male chicks "not only in Germany."[102]

These examples show that the globalization of animal production has led states into a proper regulatory impasse. Faced with the options of strengthening or weakening laws for animals, states choose the one they consider safer. This choice, however, is strongly influenced, often even manufactured by corporations that threaten to move abroad. States believe they have broadly two options: (a) keeping corporations at home where "there are at least some laws"—as many say—or, (b) adopting stricter laws and watching corporations move abroad and begin operating in seemingly lawless territory. Both options are extremely sensitive to business preferences, which shows how powerful agribusiness and the research industry are, economically and politically. In labor or human rights law, by contrast, such arguments are nowhere to be found; they are considered misplaced and improper. In animal law, however, they dominate the political debate and make states believe they have to bow to the demands of corporations, so as not to risk losing well-established levels of animal protection. Paradoxically, this is exactly what they do because even if they persuade corporations to stay, states can only do so by lowering or refusing to pass stricter laws for animals. This strategy, in effect, makes it impossible for states to maintain or improve their standards in the long term.

The only way for states to break this impasse and ensure their laws are effective and parallel social progress, is to endow their laws with extraterritorial reach. Fear of regulatory competition in laxity—not actual regulatory competition in laxity—is thus what prompts states to adopt extraterritorial laws.[103] As Gabor states:

> Competitive law-making can also emerge from the mere threat of exit, provided there are sufficient incentives for states to retain regulatees within their jurisdiction [. . .]. Regulatory arbitrage refers to the additional benefits regulatees could derive from being subjected to the norm or set of norms of a foreign jurisdiction. If such arbitrage poses a threat of movement from one jurisdiction to another, it might trigger preventive action by the law-maker.[104]

By equipping their laws with extraterritorial reach, states strip corporations of their primary bargaining power in the domestic forum, which is their threat to move abroad. Extraterritorial jurisdiction may effectively bar corporations (and individuals) from evading

---

[101] Deutscher Bundestag, 18. Wahlperiode, Gesetzesentwurf des Bundesrates zur Änderung des Tierschutzgesetzes, Drucksache 18/6663, Nov. 11, 2015, Stellungnahme der Regierung, at 10–1.

[102] *Id.*

[103] Jackson, *Sovereignty: Outdated Concept or New Approaches*, *in* Redefining Sovereignty in International Economic Law 13 (2008).

[104] Gabor 4 (2013). Reps similarly argues regulators use extraterritorial jurisdiction to counteract races to the bottom: Reps 60 (2014).

domestic law, and thereby prevent competition in laxity.[105] Indicators of lower common denominator movement are still momentous because they prove these fears are reasonable and justified. Instances of *de jure* lower common denominator, *de facto* relocation, increases in market share and mobility, regulatory chills, and a growing awareness of the global catastrophes caused by lower common denominator movement in animal law, show what is at stake for states and help us understand why states respond (or ought to respond) to these trends with extraterritorial animal law.

§4 The Universality Rationale

A. The Universality Rationale in Criminal Law

Fears of a race to the bottom are not the only reason states give extraterritorial reach to their laws. Criminal law is the other field of law in which jurisdiction frequently reaches across the border. Extraterritorial jurisdiction in criminal law is widely used to regulate terrorism,[106] trafficking in human beings,[107] sexual exploitation of children, and child pornography.[108] Fighting international crime with extraterritorial domestic laws is legal under international treaties like the Convention on Torture,[109] the Rome Statue of ICC,[110] and key humanitarian treaties like the Geneva Conventions.[111]

In criminal law, jurisdiction over crime that exceeds a state's territory is based on the active or passive personality principles (which is justified with reference to the regulatee's nationality link to the state), or the universality principle (which is justified with reference to the universal condemnation of certain crimes). Article 7 para. 4 of the International Convention for the Suppression of the Financing of Terrorism, for example, gives states a right to sanction treaty violations on the basis of the personality and universality principles.[112] The same jurisdictional bases are enshrined in conventions that combat war crimes, torture, and forced disappearance.[113] Conventions on crimes against humanity and genocide also authorize states

[105] Put differently, the decision to resort to extraterritorial jurisdiction may be based on considerations of efficiency: Armand L.C. De Mestral & Tad Gruchalla-Wesierski, Extraterritorial Application of Export Control Legislation 6 (1990); Jackson, *Sovereignty: Outdated Concept or New Approaches*, *in* Redefining Sovereignty in International Economic Law 13 (2008); Schuster 7 (1996).

[106] *E.g.*, Council Framework Decision on Combating Terrorism (2002/475/JHA), 2002 O.J. (L 164) 3, 6, art. 9.

[107] *E.g.*, Council Framework Decision on Combating Trafficking in Human Beings (EC) No. 2002/629/JHA of 19 July 2002, 2002 O.J. (L 203) 1, 3, art. 6.

[108] *E.g.*, Directive 2011/92 of the European Parliament and of the Council on Combating the Sexual Abuse and Sexual Exploitation of Children and Child Pornography, and Replacing Council Framework Decision 2004/68/JHA, 2011 O.J. (L 335) 1, 11, art. 17.

[109] Convention against Torture and Other Cruel, Inhuman or Degrading Treatment or Punishment, Dec. 10, 1984, 1465 U.N.T.S. 85, art. 5 para. 1.

[110] Rome Statute, art. 12 para. 2 and art. 70 para. 4.

[111] *See infra* note 113.

[112] Especially art. 7 para. 4 prompts states to enact laws with extraterritorial reach: International Convention for the Suppression of the Financing of Terrorism, Dec. 9, 1999, 2178 U.N.T.S. 197.

[113] Geneva Convention (I) for the Amelioration of the Condition of the Wounded and Sick in Armed Forces in the Field, Aug. 12, 1949, 75 U.N.T.S. 31, art. 49; Geneva Convention (II) for the Amelioration of the Condition of Wounded, Sick and Shipwrecked Members of Armed Forces at Sea, Aug. 12, 1949, 75 U.N.T.S. 85, art. 50; Geneva Convention (III) Relative to the Treatment of Prisoners of War, Aug. 12, 1949, 75

to establish universal jurisdiction over the crimes in question, but they do *not require* them to do so.[114] In the *Application of the Convention on the Prevention and Punishment of the Crime of Genocide*, the ICJ clarified that—based on the *erga omnes* nature of the obligations laid down in the Convention on the Prevention and Punishment of the Crime of Genocide (Genocide Convention)—"the obligation each State [. . .] has to prevent and to punish the crime of genocide is not territorially limited by the Convention."[115]

The predominant concern of extraterritorial criminal law lies with *universal crimes* (also called international crimes), like acts of aggression, war crimes, crimes against humanity, genocide, etc. Universal crimes are not to be mistaken for peremptory norms of international law, i.e., norms from which no derogation is permitted.[116] The universal facet of universal crimes derives from the fact that they are of "concern to the world community as a whole," because they "promote fundamental interests of the world community and uphold humane values."[117] These norms are *erga omnes* in character, meaning all states have a legal interest in upholding and enforcing them.[118]

What is notable form the jurisdictional perspective is that only the universal condemnation of these crimes gave rise to customary and treaty law that authorizes states to use extraterritorial personal or universal jurisdiction to combat them.[119] The rationale for extraterritorial

---

U.N.T.S. 135, art. 129; Protocol Additional to the Geneva Conventions of 12 August 1949, and Relating to the Protection of Victims of International Armed Conflicts (Protocol I), June 8, 1977, 1125 U.N.T.S. 3, art. 85 para. 1 [Protocol Additional to the Geneva Conventions (I)]; Convention against Torture and Other Cruel, Inhuman or Degrading Treatment or Punishment, art. 5 para. 2; International Convention for the Protection of All Persons from Enforced Disappearance, Dec. 20, 2006, 2716 U.N.T.S. 3, art. 9 para. 2. *See further* DE SCHUTTER 13 (2006) on the *aut dedere aut iudicare* principle.

[114] *E.g.*, Convention on the Prevention and Punishment of the Crime of Genocide, Dec. 9, 1948, 78 U.N.T.S. 277, arts. VI and VII.

[115] Application of the Convention on the Prevention and Punishment of the Crime of Genocide (Bosn. and Herz. v. Serb. and Monten.), Preliminary Objections, 1996 I.C.J. Rep. 595, 616 ¶ 31 (May 28). The universal character of the principles that underlie the Genocide Convention was acknowledged by the ICJ in *Reservations to the Convention on the Prevention and Punishment of the Crime of Genocide*: "A second consequence is the universal character both of the condemnation of genocide and of the co-operation required 'to liberate mankind from such an odious scourge' (Preamble to the Convention)" (Reservations to the Convention on the Prevention and Punishment of the Crime of Genocide, Advisory Opinion, 1951 I.C.J. Rep. 15, 23 (May 28)).

[116] Peremptory human rights norms are similar to *erga omnes* norms as they represent "projections of the individual and collective conscience" (Andrea Bianchi, *Human Rights and the Magic of* Jus Cogens, 19 EJIL 491, 491 (2008)). Yet, they are dissimilar in respect to their operability: Unlike *erga omnes* norms, *jus cogens* derogates conflicting treaty law (art. 53 VCLT).

[117] TERJE EINARSEN, THE CONCEPT OF UNIVERSAL CRIMES IN INTERNATIONAL LAW 6, 7, 11 (2012).

[118] Case Concerning the Barcelona Traction, Light and Power Company, Limited (Belg. v. Spain), Judgment 1970 I.C.J. Rep. 3, 32 (Feb. 5) [Barcelona Traction, 1970 I.C.J.]: "An essential distinction should be drawn between the obligations of a State towards the international community as a whole, and those arising vis-à-vis another State in the field of diplomatic protection. By their very nature the former are the concern of all States. In view of the importance of the rights involved, all States can be held to have a legal interest in their protection; they are obligations *erga omnes*." (Emphasis in original).

[119] Cherif Bassiouni, *Crimes Against Humanity: The Need for a Specialized Convention*, 31 COLUM. J. OF TRANSNAT'L L. 457, 480–1 (1994); Kenneth C. Randall, *Universal Jurisdiction Under International Law*, 66 TEX. L. REV. 785, 829–30 (1988).

jurisdiction in criminal law, whether expressed through the universality or personality principles, is thus embodied in this universality dimension.

B. THE UNIVERSALITY RATIONALE IN ANIMAL LAW

I. Recognition of Animal Sentience

As in criminal law, the world community seems to share certain core concerns about animals and how we treat them. A large number of states recognize animals as sentient beings, oppose the most despised acts against animals, demand that animals be treated humanely and that animal suffering be reduced. As I will argue, these steps, taken as a whole, show that there is a universality dimension in animal law which legitimates resorting to extraterritorial jurisdiction.

Most states classify animals objects of law, as a consequence of which they can be bought and sold on the market like commodities. However, animals are manifestly different from a piece of clothing, a table, or any other commodity, notably because they are sentient beings. Animals are living beings who are deeply sensitive to their immediate environment, who have their own preferences and longer-term plans, and who enjoy spending time with their relevant communities. Most states formally recognize animal sentience as the underlying rationale or guiding principle of their animal protection acts. Alternatively, when they apply animal protection acts only to sentient animals, this demonstrates their commitment to sentience.

Article 13 of the Treaty on the Functioning of the European Union (TFEU) requires the European Union and its member states to "pay full regard to animal welfare requirements of animals," in formulating and implementing the European Union's agriculture, fisheries, transport, internal market, research, technological development, and space policies, "since animals are sentient beings."[120] The consequences of tying animal law to animal sentience are exemplified in Directive 2010/63/EU of the European Parliament and of the Council on the Protection of Animals Used for Scientific Purposes. The directive, referring to article 13 TFEU, covers vertebrate animals, cyclostomes, and cephalopods, "as there is scientific evidence of their ability to experience pain, suffering, distress and lasting harm."[121] The directive also applies to all fetal forms of mammals because they "are at an increased risk of experiencing pain, suffering and distress."[122] The preamble to the European Convention for the Protection of Vertebrate Animals Used for Experimental and Other Scientific Purposes recognizes that "man has a moral obligation to respect all animals and to have due consideration for their capacity for suffering and memory" and that it is, therefore, "[d]esirous to

---

[120] Consolidated Version of the Treaty on the Functioning of the European Union, 2016 O.J. (C 202) 01, art. 13 [TFEU]. *See further* on art. 13 TFEU, Chapter 9, §2 B.

[121] Directive 2010/63 of the European Parliament and of the Council on the Protection of Animals Used for Scientific Purposes, 2010 O.J. (L 276) 33, 34, at 8.

[122] Directive 2010/63, 2010 O.J. (L 276) 33, 34, at 9.

adopt common provisions in order to protect animals used in those procedures which may possibly cause pain, suffering, distress or lasting harm."[123]

The Finnish Animal Welfare Act (AWA) declares that it applies to all animals and lays bare its objective, which is "to protect animals from distress, pain and suffering in the best possible way."[124] In France, L. 214-1 of the *Code rural et de la pêche maritime* makes clear that "[t]out animal étant un être sensible doit être placé par son propriétaire dans des conditions compatibles avec les impératifs biologiques de son espèce,"[125] i.e., *all animals that are sentient* shall be kept by the owner under conditions compatible with their species-specific needs. Section 1 of the German AWA aims "to protect the lives and well-being of animals, based on the responsibility of human beings for their fellow creatures. No one may cause an animal pain, suffering or harm without good reason."[126] The fact that pain, suffering, and harm are relevant shows that German law protects animals capable of experiencing these negative affective states; it therefore is committed to animal sentience.

Under Greek law, "[a]n animal is every living organism that has the capacity to experience feelings (*sentient being*) that lives on the land, air and sea or in any other aquatic ecosystem or wetland."[127] The Indian Prevention of Cruelty to Animals Act defines animals as any living creatures other than human beings.[128] Its purpose is "to prevent the infliction of unnecessary pain or suffering on animals [. . .]."[129] In Lithuania, animal sentience is a guiding principle of the Law on Welfare and Protection of Animals: "This Law shall lay down the remit of state and municipal authorities in ensuring the welfare and protection of animals as sentient beings (. . .)."[130] Section 2 para. 1 lit. a of New Zealand's AWA defines an animal as "any live member of the animal kingdom that is a mammal, or a bird, or a reptile, or an amphibian, or a fish (bony or cartilaginous), or any octopus, squid, crab, lobster, or crayfish (including freshwater crayfish) [. . .]."[131] Prenatal animal life is, within certain limits, also protected under the act.[132] The official Guide to the Welfare Act elaborates on this expansion:

> The Animal Welfare Act 1999 has a much wider definition of animal than the Animals Protection Act 1960. It includes most animals capable of feeling pain and applies to all such animals whether domesticated or in a wild state. It excludes animals such as

[123] CoE, Convention for the Protection of Vertebrate Animals Used for Experimental and Other Scientific Purposes, Mar. 18, 1986, C.E.T.S. No. 123, preamble.

[124] Animal Welfare Act (Fin.), §§ 1(1), 2(1).

[125] CODE RURAL ET DE LA PÊCHE MARITIME [RURAL AND MARITIME FISHERIES CODE], Dec. 1, 1979, L 214-1 (Fr.).

[126] ANIMAL WELFARE ACT (Ger.), § 1. Also in Austria, animals may not be killed without a "reasonable cause:" ANIMAL PROTECTION ACT (Austria), § 6 (1).

[127] Law No. 4039 (Greece), art. 1(a) (emphasis added).

[128] The Prevention of Cruelty to Animals Act (India), § 2(a).

[129] *Id.* preamble.

[130] Law on Welfare and Protection of Animals (Lith.), art. 1(1).

[131] Animal Welfare Act (N.Z.), § 2(1)(a)(i)–(vii).

[132] *Id.* § 2(1)(b) defines "animal" as including any mammalian fetus, or any avian or reptilian prehatched young, that is in the last half of its period of gestation or development, and any marsupial pouch young, but does not include human beings, or, except as provided in paragraph (b) or paragraph (c), any animal in the prenatal, prehatched, larval, or other such developmental stage.

shellfish and insects as there is insufficient evidence that they are capable of feeling pain.[133]

According to section 2 of the Norwegian AWA, the act applies to mammals, birds, reptiles, amphibians, fish, decapods, squid, octopi, and honeybees.[134] The second sentence of the same section, which protects prenatal forms of animal life, is especially interesting: "The Act applies equally to the development stages of the animals referred to in cases where the sensory apparatus is equivalent to the developmental level in living animals."[135] In Poland, the Law Regarding Animal Protection protects vertebrate animals and determines that "[t]he animal as a living creature, capable of suffering, is not an object. The human being should respect, protect and provide care for it."[136] In the Slovenian Animal Protection Act (APA), animals that "have developed senses for the reception of external stimuli and developed nervous system to feel painful external influences"[137] are protected. The Slovenian APA further states that the "law is strictly implemented in vertebrates, in other animals, according to their degree of sensitivity in accordance with established experience and scientific knowledge."[138]

In Switzerland, "[n]o one may inflict pain, suffering or harm on an animal, induce anxiety in an animal or disregard its dignity in any other way without justification."[139] Article 2(1) of the Swiss AWA defines animals as vertebrates, but recognizes that animals may be sentient even if they do not have a backbone: "The Federal Council decides to which invertebrates it applies and to what extent. In doing so, it is guided by scientific knowledge on the sensitivity of invertebrate animals."[140] Animal sentience hence is the guiding criterion in determining which animals count as animals for the purposes of the AWA. The Turkish Animal Protection Law states that the law's purpose is "to ensure that animals are afforded a comfortable life and receive good and proper treatment, to protect them in the best manner possible from the infliction of pain, suffering and torture, and to prevent all types of cruel treatment."[141] It, too, explicitly commits to sentience. The UK AWA declares that an animal "means a vertebrate other than man."[142] Commentary to section 1 of the AWA shows its focus on vertebrates is justified with reference to their sentience:

The Act will apply only to vertebrate animals, as these are currently the only demonstrably sentient animals. However, section 1(3) makes provision for the appropriate

[133] Guide to the Animal Welfare Act 1999, MAF Policy Information Paper No. 27, Jan. 1999 (N.Z.).

[134] Animal Welfare Act (Nor.), § 2.

[135] *Id.*

[136] Law Regarding Animal Protection (Pol.), art. 1(1).

[137] Animal Protection Act (Slovn.), art. 1.

[138] *Id.*

[139] Animal Welfare Act (Switz.), art. 4 para. 2.

[140] *Id.* art. 2 para. 1, second and third sentence. The Federal Council has only reluctantly made use of the possibility to expand the class of sentient animals, namely, to cephalopods and *Reptantia*: Schweizerische Tierschutzverordnung [TSchV] [Animal Welfare Ordinance], Apr. 23, 2008, SR 455.1, art. 1 (Switz.) [Animal Welfare Ordinance (Switz.)].

[141] Animal Protection Law (Turk.), art. 1.

[142] Animal Welfare Act (U.K.), § 1 (1).

national authority to extend the Act to cover invertebrates in the future if they are satisfied on the basis of scientific evidence that these too are capable of experiencing pain or suffering.[143]

The Ukrainian AWA provides that its purpose is "to protect animals from suffering and death as a consequence of being cruelly treated, to protect their natural rights, and to reinforce morality and compassionate behaviour in society."[144] This act, too, protects only those animals who are capable of suffering and thereby commits to animal sentience.

These are just a few examples of the many laws that explicitly recognize animal sentience or define animals for the purposes of their AWAs by resorting to animal sentience. The centrality of animal sentience in states' AWAs is proof of an emergent universal consensus among states that animal sentience is as an entry point for material protection of animals, and the guiding rationale behind laws that regulate our manifold relationships with them. Animal sentience rightfully occupies this central stage because negative and positive affective states are of intrinsic importance to animals: their well-being matters to the law because it matters to them. The importance of animal sentience, and the moral claim it places on us—that is, *de minimis*, to protect animals—are thus universally recognized.

II. Condemnation of Animal Cruelty

Most states also condemn cruelty inflicted on animals. Anti-cruelty laws, even if adopted by states that do not explicitly recognize animal sentience, "embody the law's implicit [. . .] recognition of animal sentience by their efforts to protect animals to some degree."[145] Under common law, two types of conduct can amount to a criminal act. Conduct that is criminalized only by law, and for which there is no social condemnation, constitutes *malum prohibidum*. Conduct that is considered "naturally evil," in contrast, constitutes *malum in se*. According to Wagman and Liebman, most animal anti-cruelty laws are protections from and condemnation of *malum in se*, like torturing animals, causing physical and psychological harm to them, or depriving them of their most basic needs.[146] Australia, Brazil, Canada, the European Union, France, Germany, India, New Zealand, Norway, the People's Republic of China, Switzerland, and Taiwan are just a few of the range of countries that sanction cruelty to animals and impose obligations onto society as a whole to respect them.[147] Despite their distinct regulatory nature (i.e., the kinds of prohibited activities, a hierarchy of norms, penalties for violations, etc.), these norms prove that states have a shared understanding that animal cruelty must be condemned. Sykes argues that the widespread existence of "some

[143] Animal Welfare Act (U.K.), § 1(1), Explanatory Notes, Commentary on Sections, Introductory, § 1. Furthermore, vertebrates covered by the act include only domesticated animals, which leaves wild animals essentially unprotected by the AWA: *id.* §§ 1 (1), 2.

[144] Law on the Protection of Animals from Cruelty (Ukr.), preamble.

[145] WAGMAN & LIEBMAN 141 (2011).

[146] *Id.* at 141–3.

[147] Federal Decree on Anti-Cruelty (Braz.), art. 3(I). For the remaining countries, *see* WAGMAN & LIEBMAN 152 (2011). Animal anti-cruelty norms are examined in more detail in Chapter 9, §3.

kind of broad legal prohibition of unnecessary cruelty to animals" in domestic laws is also evidence for the general expectation that animals be treated humanely and spared suffering.[148]

III. Principles of Humane Treatment and Avoidance of Animal Suffering

The universality dimension in animal law is further reflected in the principle of humane treatment of animals and avoidance of their suffering. The exact content of this combined principle is based on the wording reiterated in the legislation of so many countries. It encompasses an obligation "to treat animals humanely, that is, not to cause them unnecessary suffering."[149] The principle of humane treatment positively provides that animals must be treated humanely. The principle of avoidance of animal suffering negatively protects the same values by determining that no animal shall endure unnecessary pain, suffering, or harm. Together, the principles represent two sides of the same coin.

The number of states that have enshrined this combined principle is remarkable. The following list of countries and supranational organizations is only indicative of the principle's broad acceptance: the European Union, the Council of Europe, Argentina, Australia, Austria, Belgium, Brazil, Bulgaria, Canada, Costa Rica, Croatia, Estonia, Fiji, Finland, France, Germany, Gibraltar, Greece, Hong Kong, Iceland, India, Indonesia, Israel, Kenya, Latvia, Liechtenstein, Lithuania, Malaysia, Malta, Myanmar, the Netherlands, New Zealand, Nicaragua, Nigeria, Norway, Papua New Guinea, Paraguay the Philippines, Poland, Portugal, Puerto Rico, Slovenia, Solomon Islands, South Africa, South Korea, Sri Lanka, Sweden, Switzerland, Taiwan, Tanzania, Tonga, Turkey, Uganda, Ukraine, the United Kingdom, the United States, Vanuatu, Venezuela, and Zambia.[150]

---

[148] Katie Sykes, *Sealing Animal Welfare into the GATT Exceptions: The International Dimension of Animal Welfare in WTO Disputes*, 13 World Trade Rev. 471, 480 (2014).

[149] Catherine Sykes, Beasts in the Jungle: Animal Welfare in International Law 4 (Master Thesis, Dalhousie University, Halifax, Nova Scotia August 2011).

[150] Council Directive 98/58, art. 3, 1998 O.J. (L 221) 23; CoE, Convention for the Protection of Animals Kept for Farming Purposes, Mar. 10, 1976, C.E.T.S. No. 087, arts. 4, 6, 7; Animal Welfare Code (Arg.), art. 1; *Animal Welfare Act* (ACT) (Austl.), § 8 para. 1; Animal Protection Act (Austria), § 6 (1); Animal Protection Act (Belg.), art. 4 § 2; Cruelty to Animals Act (Bots.), art. 3 lit. a and b; Federal Decree on Anti-Cruelty (Braz.), art. 3(IV); Animal Protection Act (Bulg.), art. 14 para. 2, art. 17 para. 1, art. 20; Criminal Code (Can.), § 445.1 (1); Decree on the Well-being of Animals (Costa Rica), art. 1 lit. a and c; Animal Protection Act (Croat.), art. 4 para. 1; Animal Protection Act (Est.), § 4 para. 1; Animals (Control of Experiments) Act (Fiji), art. 6 para. 2 lit. a; Animal Welfare Act (Fin.), § 1 para. 1 and § 33 para. 1; Code pénal [C. pén.] [Penal Code], Dec. 19, 2015, art. 227-27-1 (Fr.) [Penal Code (Fr.)]; Animal Welfare Act (Ger.), § 1; Animal Experiments Act (Gibr.), art. 7 para. 5 lit. b; Law No. 4039 (Greece), art. 1 lit. b; Prevention of Cruelty to Animals Ordinance (H.K.), § 3(1)(a); Act on Animal Welfare (Ice.), art. 1; The Prevention of Cruelty to Animals Act (India), art. 3; Indonesian Penal Code, Feb. 27, 1982, art. 302 para. 1 (Indon.); LCA 1684/96 Let the Animals Live v. Hamat Gader 51(3) PD 832 (1997) (Isr.); HCJ 9232/01 Noah v. Att'y General 215 PD (2002–2003) (Isr.); Prevention of Cruelty to Animals Act (Kenya), art. 6 para. 1 lit. a; Animal Protection Law (Lat.), preamble, §§ 2 para. 6, 26 para. 3, 46; Animal Welfare Act (Liech.), art. 3 lit. b; Law on Welfare and Protection of Animals (Lith.), art. 6; Animals Act 1953 (Malay.), art. 44 lit. d and e; Animal Welfare Act (Malt.), art. 8 para. 2; Animal Health and Development Law (Myan.), art. 18; Animal Law (Neth.), art. 1.3; Animal Welfare Act (N.Z.), art. 3 para. 2 lit. b and c, art. 9 para. 2 lit. b, art. 11, art. 12 lit. c, art. 14 para. 1; Law for the Protection and Well-being of Pets and Wild Animals in Captivity (Nicar.), preamble, art. 7 lit. d; Criminal Code Act, c. 77, art. 495 para. 1 lit. b

IV. General Principle of Animal Welfare

Together, the recognition of animal sentience, the prohibition of animal cruelty, and the principle of humane treatment and unnecessary suffering of animals are, as scholars increasingly argue, part and parcel of the overarching principle of animal welfare.[151] This principle is a general principle of international law found in domestic laws and in international law.[152] On the international level, there is to date no treaty that expresses states' uniform commitment to recognize animal sentience, prohibit cruelty against animals, prevent unnecessary suffering, or demand that they be treated humanely.[153] Several international treaties undeniably affect animal welfare, but their purpose, typically, is to facilitate trade or preserve species; neither of these motivations concerns the intrinsic interests of animals.[154] This makes it easy to argue that animals are virtually absent in international law. However, as some scholars argue,

---

(1990) (Nigeria) [Criminal Code Act (Nigeria)]; Animal Welfare Act (Nor.), § 3; Animals Act 1952 (Papua N.G.), part. VI; LAW FOR THE PROTECTION AND WELL-BEING OF ANIMALS (Para.), art. 1 lit. a; ANIMAL WELFARE ACT (Phil.), § 6; Law Regarding Animal Protection (Pol.), art. 4 para. 3, art. 6 para. 2, art. 14 para. 1; Protection of Animals Act (Port.), art. 1 para. 1; Animal Protection and Welfare Act, (Puerto Rico), § 5.a; Animal Protection Act (Slovn.), art. 3; Animals (Control of Experiments) Act (Solom. Is.), art. 6; Animals Protection Act (S. Afr.), art. 2; Animal Protection Law (S. Kor.), art. 13 para. 5; Prevention of Cruelty to Animals Ordinance (Sri Lanka), art. 2 para. 1 lit. b; Animal Welfare Act (Swed.), § 2; ANIMAL WELFARE ACT (Switz.), art. 4 para. 2; Animal Protection Law (Taiwan), art. 30 para. 1; The Animal Welfare Act, art. 11 para. 2 (Tanz.); Pounds and Animals Act (Tonga), art. 23 para. 1; Animal Protection Law (Turk.), art. 1; The Animals (Prevention of Cruelty) Act (Uganda), art. 3 para. 1; Law on the Protection of Animals from Cruelty (Ukr.), preamble and art. 17; Animal Welfare Act (U.K.), § 4; David Favre, *Living Property: A New Status for Animals within the Legal System*, 93 MARQ. L. REV. 1021, 1029 (2010) (for the US); Prevention of Cruelty to Animals Act (Vanuatu), art. 3 para. 1, art. 4; LAW FOR THE PROTECTION OF DOMESTICATED ANIMALS AND WILDLIFE IN CAPTIVITY (Venez.), art. 3; Prevention of Cruelty to Animals Act (Zam.), art. 3 para. 1 lit. a and b; Prevention of Cruelty to Animals Act (Zim.), art. 3 para. 1 lit. d.

[151] Sykes, Beasts in the Jungle 4, 134 (2011). *See also* Chad J. McGuire, *Environmental Law and International Trade: Public Morality as a Tool for Advancing Animal Welfare, in* WHAT CAN ANIMAL LAW LEARN FROM ENVIRONMENTAL LAW? 293, 309 (Randall S. Abate ed., 2015), who argues that the global consensus on animal welfare supports the evolving awareness for animal sentience. *Cf.* Peters, *Global Animal Law* 12 (2016), who points out that the question of whether animal welfare expresses a universal value or is a global norm is still an open one.

[152] It has been debated for some time whether general principles of international law refer to principles common to all nations, or only those of international law proper. Today, there is near consensus that general principles are principles shared across domestic legal systems, and transposed to the international level: Elena Carpanelli, *General Principles of International Law: Struggling with a Slippery Concept, in* GENERAL PRINCIPLES OF LAW: THE ROLE OF THE JUDICIARY 125, 126 (Laura Pineschi ed., 2015). The result of this process is "a body of international law the content of which has been influenced by domestic law but which is still its own creation." (BROWNLIE 35 (2008)).

[153] The lack of animal welfare norms in international law is also noted by Cunniff & Kramer 230 (2013); Favre, *An International Treaty for Animal Welfare, in* ANIMAL LAW AND WELFARE: INTERNATIONAL PERSPECTIVES 92 (2016).

[154] Conventions that are narrowly focused on trade include, for example, the WTO's GATT or TBT. Conventions that are geared to safeguard conservationist or preservationist values include, for example, the ICRW and the Convention on Biological Diversity, June 5, 1992, 1760 U.N.T.S. 79 [CBD]. In the context of art. XX(g)

a universal consensus about animal welfare has emerged on the international plane in another form, namely, as a general principle of international law, evidenced by the practice of international organizations, regional treaty law, and reports of the WTO DSB.

The World Organization for Animal Health (OIE, formerly known as the *Office International des Epizooties*, founded in 1924) is an intergovernmental organization designed to ensure sanitary (and phytosanitary) safety in international trade in animals and products made from their bodies. In 2001, the OIE and its 182 member countries announced their new focus on improving animal welfare, and the organization has since declared animal welfare one of its mandates.[155] Under the OIE, ad hoc groups were established to draft international standards of animal welfare (the codes) that cover, *inter alia*, transport of animals, animal slaughter for human consumption, and the killing of animals to control diseases.[156] The codes are heavily influenced by the organization's scientific take on animal welfare. For example, article 7.3.6. para. 4 of the Aquatic Animal Health Code provides:

> The following methods are known to be used for killing fish: chilling with ice in holding water, carbon dioxide (CO2) in holding water; chilling with ice and CO2 in holding water; salt or ammonia baths; asphyxiation by removal from water; exsanguination without stunning. However, they have been shown to result in poor fish welfare. Therefore, these methods should not be used [. . .].[157]

The OIE's strategy is to use scientific methods to make the case that animal welfare ought to be a concern of legislators across the world. Though other strategies relying on political or cultural arguments could be used to set international standards, the organization has so far been successful with its take on establishing animal welfare as a global concern.

The UN has not yet addressed our treatment of animals as a matter of independent concern, but it touched on the subject in some interesting ways. At the 64th Annual Conference of the Department of Public Information for Non-Governmental Organizations in Bonn, Germany, the Bonn Declaration was issued as an official document to the General Assembly Resolution (A/66/750). The Declaration provides that animal welfare is integral to sustainable development and the eradication of poverty, that the Millennium Consumption Goals should respect animal welfare, and that global agricultural production should ensure good animal health and welfare.[158] The Declaration contributes to ongoing negotiations in the

---

GATT, Chapter 3 examines in more detail conservation treaties that protect animals as groups, but not as individuals. *See* Chapter 3, §2 E.

155 OIE, Third Strategic Plan 2001–2005, 69 GS/FR (OIE, Paris 2000); OIE, Sixth Strategic Plan 2016–2020, 83 SG/17, 3 (OIE, Paris 2015).

156 These standards are enshrined in the Terrestrial and the Aquatic Health Codes: OIE, Terrestrial Animal Health Code (OIE, Paris 2018); OIE, Aquatic Animal Health Code (OIE, Paris 2018).

157 OIE, Aquatic Animal Health Code, art. 7.3.6. para. 4 (OIE, Paris 2018).

158 G.A. Res. 66/750, U.N. GAOR 66th Sess., Letter dated 7 October 2011 from the Permanent Representative of Germany to the United Nations addressed to the President of the General Assembly, U.N. Doc. A/RES/66/750 (Mar. 20, 2012), at 8, 15, and 18.

UN and serves as a continual reminder for the organization to bring issues related to animals to the table.[159]

In 2012, at the Conference on Sustainable Development in Rio, the UN addressed animal welfare as part of "sustainable consumption and production."[160] The FAO, an agency of the UN leading in international efforts to defeat hunger, created the "Gateway to Farm Animal Welfare," a multistakeholder platform to exchange national and international knowledge about the welfare of farmed animals. The platform notes that "animal welfare has become an issue of increasing concern in a number of countries, including several developing ones" and that "[t]he massive increase in animal production of the last decades has raised a wide range of ethical issues, including concern for animal welfare, which has to be considered alongside with environmental sustainability and secure access to food."[161]

Also the Council of Europe (CoE) is among the organizations that aim to respond to animal welfare on a supranational level. Since 1968, five conventions dealing with animals were established under the tenets of the CoE, including the Convention for the Protection of Animals during International Transport of 1968,[162] the Convention for the Protection of Animals Kept for Farming Purposes of 1976,[163] the Convention for the Protection of Animals for Slaughter of 1979,[164] the Convention for the Protection of Vertebrate Animals Used for Experimental and Other Scientific Purposes of 1986,[165] and the Convention for the Protection of Pet Animals of 1987.[166] The purpose of these conventions is to prevent harm done to animals by ensuring their well-being and by more strictly balancing human and animal interests. The pronounced belief of the conventions is that "respect for animals [is] a common heritage of European countries closely linked to human dignity."[167]

---

[159] 64th UN DPI/NGO Conference Bonn Declaration on Rio+20, Presented to the General Assembly, UN NGO Branch, Department of Economic and Social Affairs (Apr. 26, 2011).

[160] *WSPA and Partners Get Animal Welfare onto Earth Summit Agenda*, WORLD ANIMAL PROTECTION, Sept. 16, 2011.

[161] The gateway provides news, information about events, publications, legislation, codes of practices and recommendations, standards, policies, strategies, training resources, projects, and funding opportunities related to farmed animal welfare: UN FAO, GATEWAY TO FARM ANIMAL WELFARE, *available at* http://www.fao.org/ag/againfo/themes/animal-welfare/aw-abthegat/aw-whaistgate/en/ (last visited Jan. 10, 2019).

[162] CoE, Convention for the Protection of Animals during International Transport, Dec. 13, 1968, C.E.T.S. No. 065; CoE, Convention for the Protection of Animals during International Transport (revised), Nov. 6, 2003, C.E.T.S. No. 193. The convention lays down duties to ensure the safety of animals and determines that authorized veterinary officers be present; provisions differ depending on the means of transportation.

[163] CoE, Convention for the Protection of Animals Kept for Farming Purposes, Mar. 10, 1976, C.E.T.S. No. 087, enshrines common principles on the keeping, care, and housing of animals.

[164] CoE, Convention for the Protection of Animals for Slaughter, May 10, 1979, C.E.T.S. No. 102, focuses on transportation of animals to slaughterhouses, handling of animals within slaughterhouses, lairaging, care, and slaughter.

[165] CoE, Convention for the Protection of Vertebrate Animals Used for Experimental and Other Scientific Purposes, Mar. 18, 1986, C.E.T.S. No. 123, includes principles on the care and accommodation of animals, conduct of procedure, breeding, education and training, and statistical information.

[166] CoE, Convention for the Protection of Pet Animals, Nov. 13, 1987, C.E.T.S. No. 125, sets up principles for keeping of companion animals and provides supplementary measures necessary to protect stray animals.

[167] Isabelle Veissier et al., *European Approaches to Ensure Good Animal Welfare*, 113 APPL. ANIMAL BEHAV. SCI. 279, 280 (2008).

Trade law, in particular WTO law, is also proof of the fact that member states are increasingly concerned about how we treat animals. The *Seals* case, which gave rise to the most recent reports dealing with animal welfare, garnered a great deal of attention by the international community. When the European Union prohibited importing and placing seal products on the EU market by its seals regime, Canada initiated a complaint at the WTO, arguing that the European Union violated its obligations under the WTO law. In a seminal report, the Appellate Body found that the European Union's import and market access prohibitions of seals and seal products were necessary to protect the European Union's public morals and were therefore covered by article XX(a) GATT. Suffering inflicted on seals was declared to contravene to the European Union's public values to such an extent that setting a limit to the number of seals to be killed, or simply labeling seal products as deriving from either "good" or "cruel" hunting methods, would "not meaningfully contribute to addressing EU public moral concerns regarding seal welfare."[168] Although the European Union failed to meet the *chapeau* test of article XX(a) GATT, and thus violated the agreement, *Seals* is known as a landmark decision because it explicitly confirmed that concerns for animal welfare can override obligations established under the WTO regime. Importantly, instead of justifying its violation of trade law as part of a broader conservation effort (e.g., on the basis of the Convention for the Conservation of Antarctic Seals),[169] the European Union argued that its goal is to protect seals from suffering. According to the panel, the European Union's justification is valid from a trade law perspective, because its citizens have a shared understanding of how seals must be treated:

> For several years, many members of the public have been concerned about the animal welfare aspects of the killing and skinning of seals and about trade occurring in products possibly derived from seals that have been killed and skinned with avoidable pain, distress and other forms of suffering, which seals, as sentient mammals, are capable of experiencing. Those concerns have therefore been expressed by members of the public *out of ethical reasons*. The Commission received during the last years a massive number of letters and petitions on the issue expressing citizens' deep indignation and repulsion regarding the trade in seal products in such conditions.[170]

Animal welfare thus is a valid concern of members and allows them to invoke the public morals exception, but the DSB has also made some interesting statements on this topic, divorced from its members' attitudes. The panel in *Seals* held:

> [W]e are [...] persuaded that the evidence as a whole sufficiently demonstrates that animal welfare is an issue of ethical or moral nature in the European Union. International doctrines and measures of a similar nature in other WTO Members, *while not*

[168] *Seals*, AB Report ¶ 5.279.
[169] Convention for the Conservation of Antarctic Seals, June 1, 1972, 1080 U.N.T.S. 175.
[170] *Seals*, Panel Report ¶ 7.395 (emphasis in original).

> *necessarily relevant to identifying the European Union's chosen objective*, illustrate that *animal welfare is a matter of ethical responsibility for human beings in general*.[171]

Such developments on the international plane are momentous and combined with states' commitment to treat animals humanely and avoid their suffering, they may evidence the emergence of a shared understanding of our treatment of animals. Sykes identifies this as the "general principle of animal welfare," which is so widely shared among states and universal to such a degree that it promotes fundamental interests of the world community and upholds humane values. She claims that this "consensus on animal welfare" transcends views of the minority world and lies at the heart of traditions in Buddhism, Hinduism, and Jainism.[172] Also Bowman et al. found that "[t]here are [. . .] ample grounds for recognising concern for animal welfare both as a principle widely reflected in national legal systems and as a universal value."[173] Brels likewise considers animal welfare to be an emerging concern of the international community, arguing that "[b]eing part of the animal community and sentient animals ourselves, all humans can understand animal suffering and there is evidence that almost everybody disapproves it."[174] And Trent et al. found that many countries, especially Central and South America, Japan, India, and some African states "demonstrated interest in improving and enforcing their laws"[175] that seek to protect animals.

Around the world, the question of how we treat animals emerges as an "elementary consideration of humanity."[176] Taken as a whole, these developments, as Sykes argues, support the hypothesis that the general principle of animal welfare has a reasonable prospect of evolving into a norm of customary international law in the near future.[177]

§5 Interim Conclusion

At the dawn of each new decade, we like to think we have finally grasped the full breadth of globalization, but its repercussions on the lives of animals have so far eluded public attention and academic scrutiny. Since the 1980s, better means of transport and communication, intensification of animal production, and new modes of financial investment in the animal industry drove a threefold increase in trade in eggs and dairy and quadrupled trade in meat. The globalization of agribusiness has created a multitude of far-reaching problems that heavily compromise—even thwart—efforts to create better laws for animals, along with

---

171 *Seals*, Panel Report ¶ 7.409 (emphasis added).

172 Sykes, Beasts in the Jungle 55 (2011).

173 Michael Bowman et al., Lyster's International Wildlife Law 678 (2d ed. 2010).

174 Sabine Brels, *Animal Welfare Protection: A Universal Concern to Properly Address in International Law*, J. Animal Welfare L. 34, 37 (2012).

175 Neil Trent et al., *International Animal Law, with a Concentration on Latin America, Asia, and Africa*, *in* The State of the Animals III 65, 77 (Deborah J. Salem & Andrew N. Rowan eds., 2005).

176 The expression was used in *Corfu Channel* where the Court evaluated Albania's duties not to let its territory be used so as to violate other states' rights: Corfu Channel Case (U.K. & N. Ir. v. Alb.), Judgment, 1949 I.C.J. Rep. 4, 22 (Apr. 9) [Corfu Channel, 1949 I.C.J.].

177 Sykes, Beasts in the Jungle 128–9 (2011).

sustainable development, reducing environmental pollution, and ensuring public health and food security.

As we learn more about the negative aggregate effects of globalized industries that use animals, and states' inability to regulate them, the need for solutions freed from territorial underpinnings is ever more apparent. Unfortunately, we cannot rely on states' common desire to solve these problems through international treaty-making because agreements tend to converge to the lowest common denominator and because it is difficult for states to come to an agreement in the first place. Analyses borrowed from antitrust law suggest that because consumers and producers are unevenly distributed around the world, some states will tend to underregulate, and others will tend to overregulate—which makes finding an agreement unlikely. At the same time, the ongoing proliferation of ethical, societal, environmental, and public health risks caused by global agribusiness and other industries using animals, make waiting for an international agreement a poor option. One could argue that the downsides of waiting for an agreement will easily be outweighed by the benefits of finding an agreement. But this view fails to acknowledge that the issues at stake are not only issues of time. The time used to find an agreement is time granted to a proliferating competition in laxity, from which animals suffer most.

Extraterritorial laws offer an opportunity for states to respond in a timely fashion to the global problems created by animal industries. Granted, extraterritorial jurisdiction in animal law can easily be misused to impose views and values onto other nations and their citizens, but judging extraterritorial jurisdiction on this basis alone fails to do justice to the concept and its promises. A widely shared state practice of extraterritorial jurisdiction will weave a dense jurisdictional net of overlapping and concurring laws around the globe. This legal pluralism will open opportunities for political deliberation and negotiation, foster innovation and competition, and allow states to adapt sweeping or insufficient laws to a particular case. As such, extraterritorial jurisdiction can be used as a dynamic tool to improve social welfare in an age of globalization, including the welfare and lives of animals.

The first development that supports extraterritorial animal law is the rationale of economic entanglement. Multinational enterprises that operate in industries like pharmaceutics, cosmetics, chemicals, and food and beverages own most of the domesticated animals in the world and can easily move them across borders for economic gain. The expansion of agricultural production around the globe has accentuated the different levels of animal laws, which in turn prompted states to compete with each other through their regulatory systems by offering producers and investors the most economically efficient laws. Because producers and investors prefer absent or low government intervention, it is to be expected that the competition trajectory in animal law is toward laxity (i.e., there is a race to the bottom). Though regulatory competition experts have not yet examined the trajectory of competition in animal law, Murphy's theoretical framework allowed us to cautiously begin filling this research gap. Using his indicators, this chapter demonstrated that there is a high risk of competition in laxity in animal law due to deregulation, corporate relocation competition in laxity, market share competition in laxity, and regulatory chill.

The aggregate effects of a movement toward the bottom in animal law would be disastrous, especially, but not solely, for animals. But the existence of actual competition in laxity is negligible for studying the factors that give rise to extraterritorial jurisdiction. Instead, widespread expectation and fear that competition between states causes lower common denominator movement is the single most important factor prompting states to extend their animal laws across the border. States, in essence, adopt laws with extraterritorial reach because they are interested in preventing competition in laxity and in regaining their regulatory authority over domestic affairs.

The second development that supports extraterritorial animal law is the universality rationale. From a comparative law perspective, there is a widely shared consensus among states on the proper treatment of animals, evidenced by their recognition of animal sentience, condemnation of animal cruelty, adoption of principles of humane treatment, and commitment to avoid animal suffering. Together, these are proof of the "general principle of animal welfare," which extends to cultures of majority and minority worlds and is universal to such a degree that it "promote[s] fundamental interests of the world community and uphold[s] humane values."[178] The principle is backed at the international level by the practice of international organizations like the OIE, the UN, and the FAO, and the WTO. Because the belief that animals must be treated humanely and spared suffering is as strong and widely shared as *erga omnes* norms of criminal law, extraterritorial animal laws must, on grounds of consistency, enjoy the same legitimacy as extraterritorial criminal laws.

Together, the economic and universal rationales of extraterritorial jurisdiction in animal law are proof of the fact that states share a strong interest in protecting animals within and across borders. On this basis, it is reasonable to predict that extraterritorial animal law will not only proliferate in the future but will also increasingly be considered legitimate under international law. The next chapter responds to these predictions and shows how states can use trade law as a means to protect animals across the border.

---

[178] Einarsen 6 (2012).

3 The Unanswered: Indirect Protection through the GATT

THE FIELD OF international law in which animals figure most prominently is trade law. Trade law sees animals primarily as objects, commodities, goods, resources, and other input or output factors of production, which is not surprising given the ubiquitous exploitation of animals. Animals and products made from their labor or bodies account for a large portion of agricultural production, due to a burgeoning demand for animal protein. Though most consumers like to think that animals used for agricultural production enjoy a high standard of care and are produced "at home," these animals are readily transported, shipped, and flown across borders to save production costs. In order to meet the growing demand for animal products while saving costs of land and labor, corporations have merged into multinationals and distributed their production sites around the globe. Shrimp, for instance, are harvested in the North Sea and driven 2,000 miles south to Morocco, where producers profit from cheap labor. After being shelled and enriched with preservatives to inhibit decay, they are sent back to Northern Europe for consumption.[1] Other products, including meat, eggs, milk, and compound products derived from them, may be processed even more intensively at more production sites in yet more states. By the time an animal product reaches the final market, it has typically crossed the borders of several countries.

Territorial dispersion of production steps is encouraged by the increasing division of specialized labor and fewer barriers to trade.[2] Cross-border trade in animals and animal products

[1] Documentary Presseportal, Vorsicht Krabbe!—Das grosse Geschäft mit dem kleinen Tier (Oct. 17, 2014), *available at* http://presse.phoenix.de/dokumentationen/2014/10/20141017_Krabbe/20141017_Krabbe.phtml (last visited Jan. 10, 2019).

[2] *See* on division of labor: ADAM SMITH, AN INQUIRY INTO THE NATURE AND CAUSES OF THE WEALTH OF NATIONS (1776).

Protecting Animals Within and Across Borders. Charlotte E. Blattner.

also increases because consumer preferences vary widely by nation. For example, Europe and Northern America have a high demand for chicken breasts, while Asian consumers often prefer legs and wings. Excess demand is satisfied by imports (mainly from Brazil and Thailand) and exports of less locally desirable parts solve the problem of excess production.

As trade in animals and animal products exploded within and across states, so did the purview of trade law. Every single legal standard that protects animals and negatively affects trade (or threatens to do so) must stand the rigorous tests of trade law. Unless a state produces animal products entirely within its own territory and consumes them there as well, trade law will have a say in whether and to what extent a state can protect animals during the production process. Since very few animal products are locally produced and consumed, the extent to which trade law limits the regulatory authority of states over matters of animal law is significant. With more than 164 member states accounting for 98 percent of global trade flows, WTO law is of utmost importance for animal law theorists and practitioners.[3]

Identifying the means of trade law available to states that want to protect animals is crucial, not least because WTO law is very technical, and it is almost impossible for states to avoid violating it.[4] The lingering uncertainty about the legality of measures intended to protect animals has had a real chilling effect on legislators. Ballot initiatives and bills aimed at improving the status and treatment of animals have been postponed or annulled because of the underlying fear that they might violate international trade law. For instance, the European Union repeatedly postponed its 1991 ban on importing furs from animals caught with leghold traps because it feared the WTO would strike it down due to its extraterritorial effect.[5] Since the Appellate Body's (AB) report in the 2014 *Seals* case, which, *in abstracto*,

---

[3] The WTO also hosts 24 governments and hundreds of international and intergovernmental organizations as observers: WTO, ANNUAL REPORT 2015 20 (WTO Secretariat, Geneva 2015); WTO, Understanding the WTO, Members and Observers (WTO, Geneva 2019), *available at* https://www.wto.org/english/thewto_e/whatis_e/tif_e/org6_e.htm (last visited Jan. 10, 2019).

[4] Offer and Walter point out that although only a few measures have survived the scrutiny of article XX GATT, member states have adopted otherwise GATT-inconsistent measures that clearly fall within the terms of article XX GATT and that were not challenged: Iyan I.H. Offer & Jan Walter, *GATT Article XX(a) Permits otherwise Trade-Restrictive Animal Welfare Measures*, 12(4) GLOBAL TRADE & CUSTOMS J. 158, 159 (2017).

[5] Council Regulation 3254/91 Prohibiting the Use of Leghold Traps in the Community and the Introduction into the Community of Pelts and Manufactured Goods of Certain Wild Animal Species Originating in Countries, which Catch Them by Means of Leghold Traps or Trapping Methods Which Do Not Meet International Humane Trapping Standards, 1991 O.J. (L 308) 1. First, the ban was postponed from July 1994 until January 1996: Commission Regulation 1771/94 Laying Down New Provisions on the Introduction into the Community of Pelts and Manufactured Goods of Certain Wild Animal Species, 1994 O.J. (L 184) 3. In December 1995, it was postponed for another year: Proposal for a Council Regulation Amending Council Regulation 3254/91 Prohibiting the Use of Leghold Traps in the Community and the Introduction into the Community of Pelts and Manufactured Goods of Certain Wild Animal Species Originating in Countries Which Catch them by Means of Leghold Traps or Trapping Methods Which Do Not Meet International Humane Trapping Standards, 1996 O.J. (C 58) 17. The proposal for a ban was withdrawn by the Commission with legal effect on June 2, 2012, with a statement that "[d]espite the withdrawal, the Commission will keep its commitment to continued engagement on humane trapping standards" (European Commission, Implementation of Humane Trapping Standard in the EU (2015), *available at* http://ec.europa.eu/environment/biodiversity/animal_welfare/hts/index_en.htm (last visited Jan. 10, 2019)).

declared legal the European Union's effort to ban imports of seals and seal products based on the public's concerns about seal welfare, animal welfare has become the center of the discussion in trade law. Yet, as this chapter will show, the *Seals* case dealt in passing with a problem that looms larger. What has been insufficiently addressed in WTO jurisprudence and in academic scholarship are the broader questions of when and how states can indirectly protect animals abroad via trade law, such as through import prohibitions, taxes and tariffs, or labels.

I consider this question in detail, first by examining the role animal law plays in the context of the WTO's trade regime. I begin by unpacking the conflict of animal law and trade liberalization, and then embed the tools of trade law within the extraterritoriality framework. Next, I explain how animal law can violate the GATT, in particular the most-favored-nation obligation, the national treatment obligation, reduction of quantitative restrictions, and concessions. I then ask if these violations are justified under trade law—specifically when the laws in question have extraterritorial reach.

This chapter, unlike the ones that follow, cannot, as a rule, hark back to the law of jurisdiction to answer how far laws may reach *ratione loci*. Because WTO law is *lex specialis* for measures that affect or threaten to affect trade, the legal sources I use in this chapter are, *grosso modo*, limited to international trade law.[6] But, as I will show, according to state practice, trade law must consult the general law of jurisdiction under certain circumstances.

§1 Does the Trade Law Jungle Leave Room for Animals?

A. ANIMAL LAW VS. TRADE LIBERALIZATION

As sentient beings, animals are uniquely subjected, by law, to the power of natural and legal persons. Establishing property over animals confers on owners a powerful "bundle of rights," including the right to own animals, the right to title (which formally identifies the owner of an animal), the right to use animals, the right to profit from the use of animals, the right to exclude others from animals, the right to transfer animals, and the right to destroy animals.[7] By establishing these rights over animals, the law transforms them into commodities that can freely be acquired, owned, sold, and destroyed on the economic market. In line with this commodity paradigm, trade law classifies animals as "animals" or "animal products." The word "animal" includes living and dead, entire animals, while "animal product" refers to unprocessed, fully processed, or partially processed animal parts or liquids.[8] Trade law thus *prima facie* views animals as goods, at least in an implicit manner.[9]

---

[6] In Godt's words, trade laws substitute the verdict of jurisdiction: Christine Godt, *The So-Called "Waiver Compromise" of Doha and Hong Kong: About Contested Concepts of the Nature of the International Intellectual Property System*, *in* INTELLECTUAL PROPERTY, PUBLIC POLICY, AND INTERNATIONAL TRADE 201, 221 (Inge Govaere & Hanns Hullrich eds., 2007).

[7] IAN A. ROBERTSON, ANIMALS, WELFARE AND THE LAW: FUNDAMENTAL PRINCIPLES FOR CRITICAL ASSESSMENT 24 (2015). *Seminal* on the bundle of rights: A.M. Honoré, *Ownership*, *in* OXFORD ESSAYS IN JURISPRUDENCE 107 (A.G. Guest ed., 1961).

[8] *See* the FAO's different treatment of agricultural products depending on their stage of processing (raw vs. processed) and the type of product: UN FAO, STATISTICAL YEARBOOK 2013, WORLD FOOD AND AGRICULTURE 140–4 (FAO, Rome 2013).

[9] The GATT, the Agreement on Technical Barriers to Trade (TBT), and the Agreement on the Application of Sanitary and Phytosanitary Measures (SPS) do not define the term "good." Scholars define goods as such

Yet, not all animals are solely goods under trade law. Marine animals, for example, are seen as natural resources, because they are extracted rather than "cultivated."[10] A growing number of scholars in ethics, politics, and law now argue that some animals do provide services (e.g., mules that pull carts, or cows and chickens that produce milk and eggs), so goods extracted from their labor may in the future be classified as "services" in the meaning of the General Agreement on Trade in Services (GATS).[11]

Because animals are still chiefly seen as goods, it is crucial to gain legal certainty about the possibility and degree to which states may protect animals under these laws. According to the GATT's preamble, members are committed to "entering into reciprocal and mutually advantageous arrangements directed to the substantial reduction of tariffs and other barriers to trade and to the elimination of discriminatory treatment in international commerce."[12] Any agreement between WTO members must thus be mutually advantageous, and these advantages are uniquely defined in economic terms, including the reduction of barriers to trade through the principle of nondiscrimination, setting up market access rules, and eliminating unfair trade. Trade law's success in reducing and removing the most obvious barriers to the flow of goods, services, and finances among states has led it to focus on less obvious barriers to trade: norms that seek to advance social welfare, or, to put it in the jargon of trade law, "regulatory requirements." Trade restrictions designed to protect animals are a prime example of such regulatory requirements because they represent costs and barriers:

> [Regulatory requirements are] designed to do one of two things: either to limit market access of products, services, or service suppliers by or to the target country (e.g. import

(i) if they are listed as goods in the member's Schedules of Concessions on Goods, (ii) if they are processed to a level described in the Harmonized System Nomenclature, and (iii) if they have monetary value and are tradable: Melaku Desta, To What Extent Are WTO Rules Relevant to Trade in Natural Resources? Research and Analysis of the World Trade Organization, *available at* https://www.wto.org/english/res_e/publications_e/wtr10_forum_e/wtr10_desta_e.htm (last visited Jan. 10, 2019). According to this definition, most animals will be classified as goods, except those belonging to an endangered species, who are protected under the ICRW, the CITES, the Bonn Convention on the Conservation of Migratory Species of Wild Animals (CMS, June 23, 1979, 1651 U.N.T.S. 355), the CBD, the Convention on the Conservation of Antarctic Marine Living Resources (May 20, 1980, 1329 U.N.T.S. 48), the Convention for the Conservation of Antarctic Seals, the Agreement on the Conservation of Polar Bears (Nov. 15, 1973, 27 U.S.T. 3918), the Bern Convention on the Conservation of European Wildlife and Natural Habitats (Sept. 19, 1982, C.E.T.S. No. 104), and others.

10 WTO, World Trade Report 2010, Trade in Natural Resources, Section B, Natural Resources 46 (WTO Secretariat, Geneva 2010), *available at* https://www.wto.org/english/res_e/booksp_e/anrep_e/world_trade_report10_e.pdf (last visited Jan. 10, 2019), which argues that only marine animals that are tradable are natural resources, because producing agricultural goods requires other natural resources (mainly land and water) as input. In this view, farmed animals are cultivated rather than extracted from natural environments.

11 WTO, General Agreement on Trade in Services, Apr. 15, 1994, 1869 U.N.T.S. 183 [GATS]. *See further* on animal labor, Charlotte Blattner, Kendra Coulter & Will Kymlicka, Animal Labour: A New Frontier of Interspecies Justice? (forthcoming 2019); Alasdair Cochrane, *Labour Rights for Animals*, *in* The Political Turn in Animal Ethics 15, 15 f. (Robert Garner & Siobhan O'Sullivan eds., 2016); Kendra Coulter, Animals, Work, and the Promise of Interspecies Solidarity (2016); Jocelyne Porcher, The Ethics of Animal Labor (2017).

12 GATT, preamble.

or export restrictions), or to permit discrimination among similar products, services, or service suppliers to the detriment of the target country (e.g. administrative/regulatory restrictions).[13]

Because of their trade-restrictive effects, most ethical, social, environmental, or political norms that deal with trade (so-called nontrade concerns) are at odds with axiomatic obligations established under the tenets of the WTO. Instead of consolidating nontrade concerns with trade law on a grand scale, the WTO regime is structurally biased to give preference to solutions that liberalize or protect trade. Until recently, states could not prohibit the importation of products produced under adverse or cruel circumstances; they could only prohibit the sale of such products if they are domestically produced. Because each state has its own view about when animals are treated "properly" or "cruelly," one could say this is a fair deal and leaves states concerned about animals sufficient room to protect them. However, disabling states from determining which products enter their territory renders their domestic regulatory policies plainly ineffective, and with it, animal law. Even if domestically produced, high-welfare products access domestic markets, they get swamped with products produced under conditions that pay little regard to animals because these can be offered at low cost. As domestic products must conform to high-standard domestic regulatory policies, which foreign producers can safely ignore, it is often foreign products that are produced under worse conditions. High-welfare products are still accessible on the market, but they are effectively pushed into a niche. Because their prices are constantly undercut, they become a high-end product, not the standard type of milk, egg, or meat consumers purchase.

With the focus of trade law on commercial aspects of trade, praiseworthy goals, including the goal to improve the lives of animals, rarely find their way into WTO processes.[14] Even worse, because the WTO is designed to establish a market-friendly environment, political, social, moral, cultural, environmental, and technical achievements and aspirations are often explicitly struck down.[15] For animal advocates, the systematic biases weaved into trade law make global free trade agreements the principal obstacle to achieve large-scale progress in animal law.[16]

Though the WTO is uniquely biased to protect and promote trade, the "trade and . . ." *problématique* does not always tip in favor of unlimited trade. In the preamble to the GATT, WTO members codified a basic commitment to social welfare. Their obligations include

---

[13] KRISTA NADAKAVUKAREN SCHEFER, SOCIAL REGULATION IN THE WTO: TRADE POLICY AND INTERNATIONAL LEGAL DEVELOPMENT 101 (2010).

[14] CHRISTIANE R. CONRAD, PROCESSES AND PRODUCTION METHODS (PPMs) IN WTO LAW: INTERFACING TRADE AND SOCIAL GOALS 70 (2011); NADAKAVUKAREN SCHEFER 2 (2010); Asif H. Qureshi, *International Trade and Human Rights from the Perspective of the WTO*, *in* INTERNATIONAL ECONOMIC LAW WITH A HUMAN FACE 159, 166 (Friedl Weiss et al. eds., 1998).

[15] In other words, the free market principle and regulation are in a relationship of tension: Bratton et al., *Regulatory Competition and Institutional Evolution*, *in* INTERNATIONAL REGULATORY COMPETITION AND COORDINATION 1 (1996).

[16] *E.g.*, Edward M. Thomas, *Playing Chicken at the WTO: Defending an Animal Welfare-Based Trade Restriction under GATT's Moral Exception*, 34 B.C. ENVTL. AFF. L. REV. 605, 609 (2007).

"raising standards of living, ensuring full employment and a large and steadily growing volume of real income [. . .]."[17] For years, scholars around the world have debated whether the WTO can achieve these goals, which should make us doubt trade law can ever be used to advance the interests of animals. The fact that the GATT's commitment to social welfare does not even *ab initio* cover moral considerations about animals, is also noteworthy. The absence of these concerns from the prominent preambular spot has far-reaching consequences. When goals of trade liberalization and animal protection conflict, and when in doubt about the scope of legal obligations, adjudicative bodies are obliged to give preference to trade liberalization. Legislative efforts to protect animals are thus *prima facie* at a greater disadvantage than laws intended to protect human welfare.

Though they face a lot of resistance from the WTO, member states continue to raise their concerns about how animals are treated during production. They have adopted measures that prohibit imports of animals inhumanely transported,[18] meat from inhumanely slaughtered or transported animals,[19] inhumanely trapped animals,[20] cosmetics tested on animals,[21] killing endangered animals,[22] wild birds,[23] or seals,[24] and shrimp caught in a fashion that endangers turtles.[25] These laws, though heading upwind, are not always crushed by free trade. There are conditions under which WTO law permits states to adopt laws that help them protect animals within and outside their territory.[26] As Kaufmann points out, however, "[w]hile the need for social policies that complement economic liberties is widely acknowledged, the question of how far social policy should go is still being debated among economists and lawyers."[27] We must thus ask whether and under what conditions considerations about animal welfare can prevail over trade-oriented WTO obligations, and how member states can use these insights more systematically to ensure that animal protection does not remain an exception in trade law.

B. TRADE LAW AS INDIRECT EXTRATERRITORIALITY

Trade restrictions are often accused of unduly reaching across the border by interfering in another state's regulatory affairs. For example, if a state prohibits importing eggs from hens who

---

[17] GATT, preamble.

[18] 18 U.S.C. § 42(c) (U.S.), dealing with the limits on importation or shipment of injurious mammals, birds, fish (including mollusks and crustacea), amphibia, and reptiles.

[19] Federal Meat Inspection Act, 21 U.S.C. § 620(a) (U.S.).

[20] Council Regulation 3254/91, 1991 O.J. (L308) 1.

[21] Regulation 1223/2009 of the European Parliament and of the Council on Cosmetic Products, 2009 O.J. (L 342) 59.

[22] Council Regulation 3626/82 on the Implementation in the Community of the Convention on International Trade in Endangered Species of Wild Fauna and Flora, 1982 O.J. (L 384) 1.

[23] Wild Bird Conservation Act, 16 U.S.C. § 4907 (U.S.).

[24] Regulation 1007/2009, 2009 O.J. (L 286) 36.

[25] Endangered Species Act [ESA], 16 U.S.C. § 1531 (U.S.).

[26] *See* KELCH 239 (2011): "With proper analysis and perhaps some amendments, the GATT can be a mechanism that not only rationally regulates trade, but also permits advances in animal protection."

[27] KAUFMANN 14 (2007).

were confined in battery cages,[28] it is often accused of regulating the welfare of hens located abroad and compelling foreign producers to meet its standards. Manzini and von Lutterotti argue that import prohibitions are means to ban certain practices outside a state's territorial jurisdiction,[29] implying that one state is regulating the affairs of another. Nollkaemper seems to share this view: "*Banning leghold traps outside* Europe proved more difficult. Attempts to agree with third countries on a prohibition have failed. The Community therefore decided to seek protection of wild animals in non-member states by instituting a trade ban."[30] Yet, Nollkaemper later finds that even though import bans may to some extent influence the state of affairs abroad, they do "not legally regulate such conduct."[31] Must we therefore differentiate between successful and unsuccessful regulation of foreign conduct? The answer lies elsewhere and relates to our earlier analysis of the structure of jurisdictional norms.

The scholarly consensus is that laws restricting or prohibiting trade are not a form of extraterritorial jurisdiction because they do not claim application or validity beyond the state that passes them.[32] The purpose of trade-restrictive measures is to free the domestic market from certain products, *not* to endow laws with extraterritorial application or to regulate matters on foreign territory. These laws enable states to protect domestic consumers from the "moral

---

[28] Keeping birds in battery cages prevents them from exhibiting natural behavior (wing flapping, perching, and foraging). In the European Union, where laws are comparatively progressive, typical battery cages provide 550 cm^2 per animal—a footprint smaller than an A4 sheet of paper: Martin Hickman, *The End of Battery Farms in Britain—But Not in Europe*, THE INDEPENDENT, Dec. 27, 2011. *See for many* on the effects of battery cages for animal welfare, K. Pohle & H.-W. Cheng, *Comparative Effects of Furnished and Battery Cages on Egg Production and Physiological Parameters in White Leghorn Hens*, 88 POULTRY SCI. 2042 (2009).

[29] Pietro Manzini, *Environmental Exceptions of Article XX*, *in* INTERNATIONAL TRADE LAW ON THE 50TH ANNIVERSARY OF THE MULTILATERAL TRADE SYSTEM 811, 834 ff. (Paolo Mengozzi ed., 1999); LUKAS VON LUTTEROTTI, US EXTRATERRITORIAL ECONOMIC SANCTIONS AND THE EU BLOCKING STATUTE 152 (2003).

[30] André Nollkaemper, *The Legality of Moral Crusades Disguised in Trade Laws: An Analysis of the EC "Ban" on Furs from Animals Taken by Leghold Traps*, 8 J. ENVTL. L. 237, 240–1 (1996) (emphasis added).

[31] Nollkaemper 245 (1996).

[32] Lorand Bartels, *Article XX of GATT and the Problem of Extraterritorial Jurisdiction: The Case of Trade Measures for the Protection of Human Rights*, 36 J. WORLD TRADE 353, 358 (2002); CONRAD 65–6 (2011); Paul Demaret, *Environmental Policy and Commercial Policy: The Emergence of Trade-Related Environmental Measures (TREMS) in the External Relations of the European Community*, *in* THE EUROPEAN COMMUNITY'S COMMERCIAL POLICY AFTER 1992: THE LEGAL DIMENSION 305, 375 (Marc Maresceau ed., 1993); Robert Howse & Donald Regan, *The Product/Process Distinction: An Illusory Basis for Disciplining "Unilateralism" in Trade Policy*, 11 EJIL 249, 275, 278–9 (2000); Nollkaemper 244–5 (1996); PETERS, VÖLKERRECHT 148 (2016); MIKE RADFORD, ANIMAL WELFARE LAW IN BRITAIN: REGULATION AND RESPONSIBILITY 137 (2001); ROBERTSON 212 (2015); HANS-JÜRGEN SCHLOCHAUER, DIE EXTRATERRITORIALE WIRKUNG VON HOHEITSAKTEN 11 (1962); Peter Stevenson, *The World Trade Organisation Rules: A Legal Analysis of Their Adverse Impact on Animal Welfare*, 8 ANIMAL L. 107, 120 (2002); JÜRGEN SCHWARZE, DIE JURISDIKTIONSABGRENZUNG IM VÖLKERRECHT 14 (1994); SCHWEIZERISCHES KOMPETENZZENTRUM FÜR MENSCHENRECHTE (SKMR) [SWISS CENTER FOR COMPETENCE IN HUMAN RIGHTS], EXTRATERRITORIALITÄT IM BEREICH WIRTSCHAFT UND MENSCHENRECH TE: EXTRATERRITORIALE RECHTSANWENDUNG UND GERICHTSBARKEIT IN DER SCHWEIZ BEI MENSCHENRECHTSVERLETZUNGEN DURCH TRANSNATIONALE UNTERNEHMEN 9 (SKMR, Berne 2016); VRANES 95 ff. (2009); ZERK, EXTRATERRITORIAL JURISDICTION 16 (2010).

discredit [. . .] of causing or encouraging harm or wickedness."[33] For instance, in the Dog and Cat Protection Act, which prohibits importing dog and cat fur products to the United States, Congress stated:

> The trade of dog and cat fur products is *ethically* and aesthetically *abhorrent* to United States citizens. Consumers in the United States have a right to know if products offered for sale contain dog or cat fur and to ensure that they are *not unwitting participants in this gruesome trade*.[34]

In line with the extraterritoriality framework I defined earlier, the only extraterritorial facet of norms that restrict trade are ancillary repercussions on foreign territory, namely that foreign producers will either have to target another market or abide by the importing state's preferences. Foreigner producers, however, are not legally bound to change the practices and processes through which they produce animals and animal products, no matter how cruel they are. This is why trade-restrictive norms that aim to better protect animals at home or abroad are not a form of extraterritorial jurisdiction *stricto sensu*. Instead, they are indirect extraterritorial.

At what point, however, does an indirect extraterritorial norm become direct extraterritorial, i.e., extraterritorial *stricto sensu*? If a norm's ancillary repercussion reaches the threshold of *regulated content*, the norm is direct extraterritorial, i.e., it is a form of extraterritorial jurisdiction *stricto sensu*. We can differentiate between extraterritorial content regulation and extraterritorial ancillary repercussions norms by applying the *sine qua non* test, which determines a provision's *telos* or *Regelungszweck*. If the purpose of a norm is to alter conduct abroad, then failure to attain this purpose renders the norm redundant; it misses its *Regelungszweck*. Take, for instance, a norm that prohibits importing eggs from battery cages. If the purpose of the norm that restricts trade in eggs were to alter egg production abroad in order to improve the living conditions of hens and if it failed to change conduct abroad, then it would miss its *Regelungszweck*. But most trade restrictions retain their regulatory purpose even if they do not affect behavior or events on foreign territory. This is because their *Regelungszweck* is to prevent certain products from entering the domestic market regardless of their effects on foreign territory, in order to protect domestic consumers from partaking in the cruel treatment of animals. In other words, the norm regulates content territorially (i.e., it is intraterritorial content regulation). Creating incentives for foreign producers to improve the welfare of hens by raising production standards is solely a side effect of the norm (i.e., it is an extraterritorial ancillary repercussion).[35] The point in time at which a state links its intraterritorial content regulation to a product is when the product enters its territory (i.e., the anchor point is intraterritorial).[36] In summary, trade-restrictive norms have an intraterritorial anchor point, regulate content intraterritorially, and create extraterritorial ancillary repercussions. They

---

[33] Howse & Regan 279 (2000).

[34] Dog and Cat Protection Act, 19 U.S.C. § 1308, § 1442 (7) (U.S.) (emphasis added).

[35] MENG 77 (1994).

[36] *Id.* at 204; VRANES 95 ff., 167 (2009).

are, in essence, indirect extraterritorial. Because these norms offer only an indirect possibility to protect animals abroad, they are *not* extraterritorial *stricto sensu*.

C. LABELS, TARIFFS, TAXES, AND QUANTITATIVE RESTRICTIONS

So far, I have broadly equated trade measures with import prohibitions to bring out the underlying structural problems. There are, however, many and diverse measures of trade law available to states that wish to directly protect consumers, and indirectly protect animals. These include labels, differentiated tariffs and taxes, and quantitative restrictions. Labels inform consumers about the production method, country of origin, or place of processing when they buy animals or animal products, and are considered less intrusive than import restrictions because they do not regulate market access. Common labels include "animal-friendly," "free-range," "sustainable agriculture," and "organic farming," and they either affirm that a product meets certain requirements, or identify products that fail to meet them.[37] Labels may be the product of a private venture or of a government initiative. The European Union is known for its comprehensive, standardized animal welfare indicators. In 2009, the European Commission adopted a detailed report outlining options for animal welfare labeling to facilitate better welfare through consumer choice and incentives for producers.[38] Under WTO law, labels may violate the Agreement on TBT as technical regulations, or they may violate the national treatment obligation of article III:4 GATT, by treating imported products less favorably than like domestic products.

States consider labels a better alternative to import restrictions; they inform consumers and offer them a choice, while indirectly improving the lives of animals abroad.[39] Labels may seem to be a good policy option, but they have a number of weaknesses that render them ill-suited to meet the public's concern for animals. Corporations typically have a vested interest in revealing positive and concealing negative or undesirable qualities of their products, which causes them to design labels in a way that misleads consumers.[40] Labels use common, vague language to depict a picture that eludes reality. Consumers who read "free-range husbandry" on a label picture animals who have unrestricted access to the outdoors, where they can move about and behave naturally at all times. They are unlikely to realize that these

---

[37] Ike Sharpless, Farm Animal Welfare and WTO Law: Assessing the Legality of Policy Measures 18–9 (Master of Arts in Law and Diplomacy Thesis, The Fletcher School, Tufts University 2008).

[38] Report from the Commission to the European Parliament, the Council, the European Economic and Social Committee and the Committee of the Regions, Options for Animal Welfare Labelling and the Establishment of a European Network of Reference Centres for the Protection and Welfare of Animals, COM(2009) 584 final (Oct. 28, 2009). *See also* European Commission, Health & Consumer Protection Directorate-General, Labelling: Competitiveness, Consumer Information and Better Regulation for the EU 10 (European Communities 2006).

[39] *E.g.*, Derek J.F. Eaton et al., Product Differentiation under the WTO, An Analysis of Labelling and Tariff or Tax Measures Concerning Farm Animal Welfare 11 (Agricultural Economics Research Institute [LEI] 2005).

[40] *See generally* Lorraine Mitchell, *Impact of Consumer Demand for Animal Welfare on Global Trade*, *in* CHANGING STRUCTURE OF GLOBAL FOOD CONSUMPTION AND TRADE 80, 83–5, 88 (Anita Regmi ed., 2001); UN FAO, PRODUCT CERTIFICATION AND ECOLABELLING FOR FISHERIES SUSTAINABILITY 15 (FAO, Rome 2001).

"free-ranging" animals often walk outside only 10 minutes a day, live in 25 square feet in open air, or have access to five square feet in an enclosure twice a week. Sometimes these terms are so misleading that they amount to criminal or civil wrongs. In 2014, the Federal Court of Australia imposed a 300,000 AUD (212,000 USD) on Pirovic Enterprises Pty Ltd. for fraud in labeling because the corporation used the label "free-range" even though chickens could not range freely in the open.[41] Relying on labels thus carries the risk of exploiting consumers' goodwill and giving producers the benefit of the doubt. Rather than providing consumers with an opportunity to make an informed choice, labels help gloss over and market the exploitation of animals.

Even when labels convey an accurate picture of companies' production method, they do not change consumer behavior. Consumers like to think that information on labels alters their purchasing behavior, but empirical research shows that their self-reported preferences do not match their purchasing behavior.[42] The failure of labels to change consumer habits was acknowledged by the WTO's adjudicative bodies in the *Seals* case. The panel and the AB held that labeling standards do not represent a reasonably available alternative to import prohibitions to prevent consumers from partaking in the inhumane slaughter of seals.[43] Labels may be the politically more acceptable alternative to import restrictions, but not because they are less intrusive—as is often claimed. They are more acceptable simply because they are largely ineffective. The only way labels can achieve the level of protection society desires, is to combine them with other measures.[44]

Because prices strongly influence consumer behavior, differentiated tariffs and taxes can be a reasonable option for states that want to indirectly protect animals abroad. Under WTO law, taxes are internal taxes and other charges applied directly or indirectly to products on the domestic market. Based on the production or processing methods of animal products, differentiated taxes may compensate for higher costs associated with higher animal welfare, they may levy lower taxes for products that meet high domestic welfare standards, higher

[41] *Australian Competition and Consumer Commission v. Pirovic Enterprises Pty Ltd. (No. 2)* [2014] FCA 1028 (Sept. 23, 2014) (Austl.).

[42] Labels are especially inadequate to substitute PPMs: Howse & Regan 274 (2000). That citizens demand PPM regulation despite their contrary purchasing behavior shows the following example. In 1999, the United Kingdom banned gestation crates and tethers, increasing the cost of domestic pork. As a consequence, imports of products that used systems illegal in the United Kingdom increased by 77 percent Mick Sloyan, An Analysis of Pork and Pork Products Imported into the United Kingdom 3, 9 (British Pig Executive [BPEX], London 2006). 92 percent of British resident today demand that imported animal products at least observe domestic minimum standards (European Commission, Special Eurobarometer 442 Report: Attitudes of Europeans towards Animal Welfare 4 (2016)). Most Europeans strongly agree that imported products from outside the European Union should respect the same animal welfare standards as those in the European Union (62 percent "totally agree").

[43] *Seals*, AB Report ¶¶ 5.274–5.289; *Seals*, Panel Report ¶ 7.502: "[A]n alternative measure within this range may give rise to an increase in the number of seals hunted with the accompanying risks to seal welfare through restored market opportunities within the European Union. This may undermine the objective of the EU Seal Regime of reducing the overall number of seals killed inhumanely. We recall in this regard the Appellate Body's guidance that a responding Member cannot be reasonably expected to employ an alternative measure *that involves a continuation of the very risk that the challenged measure seeks to halt*." (Emphasis added).

[44] Matheny & Leahy 352 (2007).

taxes for products produced below minimum standards, or a combination of these measures.[45] Tariffs, on the other hand, are customs duties, which means they are a border measure. As in the case of taxes, using tariffs to nudge producers to adopt higher standards of animal welfare requires differentiating between products based on the conditions under which they are produced.[46] Tariffs are lowered for products that meet animal welfare standards and raised for products that fail to meet them.

According to the WTO, tariffs are legal under article II:1(b) GATT, but since it is the WTO's declared goal to substantially reduce tariffs, members are obliged to negotiate the common reduction of customs duties pursuant to article XXVIII*bis* GATT.[47] As part of the WTO's negotiation rounds, members have agreed not to raise their customs duties on certain products. These caps are known as tariff concessions, maximum tariff rates, or tariff bindings. Since the Uruguay Round, almost all members have bound tariffs subject to maximum levels. In the Schedule of Concessions, each member's concessions are laid out in detail, and this forms an integral part of the GATT (article II:7 GATT). Because rates are bound, this makes it difficult for members to introduce new tariffs or adapt existing ones to differentiate products based on the quality of life experienced by animals.

The final tool of trade law discussed here is import restrictions. According to the AB, import restrictions and prohibitions represent "the heaviest 'weapon' in a Member's armoury of trade measures."[48] Animal protection agencies lobby strongly for them, but they are regarded as the type of measure "most unlikely" to pass WTO scrutiny. The most recent case dealing with the legality of import restrictions is the *Seals* case. With Regulation No. 1007/2009, the European Union prohibited placing any seal products, imported or domestic, on the European market, because seals are "sentient beings that can experience pain, distress, fear and other forms of suffering."[49] Whether the European Union was able to uphold its trade measures will be subject to careful scrutiny herein. Generally speaking, import restrictions or prohibitions are likely to violate the obligation to eliminate quantitative restrictions to trade (article XI GATT), as well as the national treatment obligation (article III:4 GATT).

Having identified the role of animals in trade law, the general conflict between animal law and trade liberalization, and the tools of trade law available to states, I will now examine the obligations that WTO members have under the GATT. Since we are concerned here with tools that seek to strengthen states' ability to protect animals within their borders, and their ability to indirectly protect animals across the border, I determine which of these tools are likely to violate the GATT and the circumstances under which they are justified.

---

[45] Eaton et al. 10 (2005).

[46] *Id.* at 57.

[47] In tariff negotiations, reductions are governed by the principle of reciprocity and mutual advantage, and by the most-favored-nation obligation, except for trade between majority and minority countries, which is governed by relative reciprocity.

[48] *Shrimp/Turtle I*, AB Report ¶ 171.

[49] Regulation 1007/2009, 2009 O.J. (L 286) 36, preamble.

§2 General Agreement on Tariffs and Trade (GATT)

A. MOST-FAVORED-NATION OBLIGATION

The most-favored-nation obligation (article 1 GATT) lays down the fundamental obligation of each member to treat trading partners equally. Equal treatment requires, for instance, that where a state allows importing hormone beef from one trading partner, other members are immediately and unconditionally entitled to equal treatment. Though the most-favored-nation obligation does not play a central role in assessing the legality of import restrictions, it has been successfully invoked to annul such measures. In *Seals*, the panel held that the exceptions to the general import ban on seal products—which exempted from the ban imports from indigenous communities and imports for marine resource management—violated article I:1 GATT. The exceptions granted a *de facto* advantage to products from Greenland (specifically, those produced by its Inuit population), which was not accorded immediately and unconditionally to like products from Canada, an argument upheld by the AB.[50] For animal law, however, the practical importance of the most-favored-nation obligation is negligible compared to the national treatment obligation.

B. NATIONAL TREATMENT OBLIGATION

Measures that protect animals and simultaneously affect trade are most likely to violate the national treatment obligation (article III GATT). The national treatment obligation provides that, once goods have entered the national market, imported and domestic goods shall be treated equally, *de facto* and *de jure*.[51] The purpose of the national treatment obligation is to prevent protectionism (states that use trade measures only to protect domestic production) and to guarantee equal competition between domestic and imported goods.[52]

I. Note Ad Article III GATT

Under trade law, domestic laws that protect animals and also affect trade are nontariff barriers to trade. Nontariff barriers enter WTO scrutiny in two distinct ways. First, they may be subject to review under article XI GATT, which eliminates quantitative restrictions with the declared goal of reducing nontariff barriers to trade. Second, they may be subject to article III GATT—more specifically article III:4 GATT—which ensures equal opportunities for competition between domestic and foreign products after importation.[53] A first notable difference between the two articles is that article III GATT applies to internal measures, whereas article XI GATT applies to border measures. Another difference is that while article

---

[50] *Seals*, Panel Report ¶ 7.600; *Seals*, AB Report ¶ 5.95.

[51] Peter L. Fitzgerald, *"Morality" May Not Be Enough to Justify the EU Seals Products Ban: Animal Welfare Meets International Trade Law*, 14 J. INT'L WILDLIFE L. & POL. 85, 99 (2011).

[52] Appellate Body Report, *Japan—Taxes on Alcoholic Beverages*, at 14, WTO Doc. WT/DS8/AB/R, WT/DS10/AB/R, WT/DS11/AB/R (adopted Nov. 1, 1996) [*Japan—Alcoholic Beverages*, AB Report]; Appellate Body Report, *EC—Measures Affecting Asbestos and Products Containing Asbestos*, ¶¶ 97 ff., WTO Doc. WT/DS135/AB/R (adopted Apr. 5, 2001) [*Asbestos*, AB Report].

[53] NILS STOHNER, IMPORTRESTRIKTIONEN AUS GRÜNDEN DES TIER- UND ARTENSCHUTZES IM RECHT DER WTO 21–2 (2006).

XI GATT is a stand-alone test, article III GATT relies on comparing domestic and foreign products. Under article III GATT, the question arises whether products produced at low animal welfare and products produced at high animal welfare are "like," which is answered by determining whether process and production methods (PPMs) render them like or unlike. But if import bans are subject to article XI GATT, they will likely violate the prohibition on quantitative restrictions, even if they treat like foreign and domestic products equally. Animal advocates thus consider article III GATT more favorable, and article XI GATT more harmful to animal protection.[54]

To determine the scope of the two articles in their application to trade restrictions, Note Ad Article III GATT serves as guidance.[55] The purpose of Note Ad III GATT is to allocate internal taxes or regulations (which include import restrictions) either to article III GATT or to article XI GATT. It provides:

> Any internal tax or other internal charge, or any law, regulation or requirement of the kind referred to in paragraph 1 which applies to an imported product and to the like domestic product and is collected or enforced in the case of the imported product at the time or point of importation, is nevertheless to be regarded as an internal tax or other internal charge, or a law, regulation or requirement of the kind referred to in paragraph 1, and is accordingly subject to the provisions of Article III.[56]

Because Note Ad article III GATT only refers to *products as such*, the panel in *Tuna/Dolphin I* inferred that the Note does not allow members to make distinctions between products on the basis of PPMs (including how animals are treated during production).[57] Note Ad article III, which would widen the scope of article III GATT, thus does not apply to the PPM issue. But since the report was never adopted by the AB, this ruling is not thought to represent the opinion of member states. The question of whether article III GATT applies *in addition to* article XI GATT was also left unanswered by the panel in *Tuna/Dolphin I*.[58]

The report is widely criticized for its argument that article III does not apply to import restrictions.[59] Scholars argue that, in the case of import restrictions or prohibitions, a product is stopped at the border *at the time of importation* and thus subject to article III GATT.[60] In

---

[54] *E.g.*, Thomas 614–5 (2007).

[55] The Note is a legally binding: Robert Howse & Joanna Langille, *Permitting Pluralism: The Seals Products Dispute and Why the WTO Should Accept Trade Restrictions Justified by Noninstrumental Moral Values*, 37 Yale J. Int'l L. 367, 406 (2012).

[56] GATT, Note Ad III.

[57] Panel Report, *US—Restrictions on Imports of Tuna*, ¶ 514, WTO Doc. DS21/R—39S/155 (not adopted, circulated Sept. 3, 1991) [*Tuna/Dolphin I*, Panel Report].

[58] Peter Van den Bossche & Werner Zdouc, The Law and Policy of the World Trade Organization 346 (4th ed. 2017).

[59] Conrad 30 (2011).

[60] Axel Bree, Harmonization of the Dispute Settlement Mechanisms of the Multilateral Environmental Agreements of the World Trade Agreements 35, 252 ff. (2003); Howse & Regan 249 (2000); Van den Bossche & Zdouc 346 (2017); Sebastian Puth, WTO und Umwelt: Die Produkt-Prozess-Doktrin 234 ff., 255 (2003). *Cf.* Stohner, who argues that Note Ad art. III explicitly refers to imported products, which prohibits applying art. III:4 GATT as an internal measure to prohibitions

this view, Note Ad article III GATT expands the scope of article III GATT from internal measures to measures employed at the time of importation. This interpretation is supported by three panel reports. In *Canada—Alcoholic Beverages*, Note Ad article III GATT was interpreted to mean that if a border measure applies to both domestic and imported products, it falls under the purview of article III, even if applied at the border.[61] In *FIRA*, the panel had to demarcate articles III and XI GATT, and preferred to apply article III GATT to import restrictions for the following reasons:

> If Article XI:1 were interpreted broadly to cover also internal requirements, Article III would be partly superfluous. Moreover, the exceptions to Article XI:1, in particular those contained in Article XI:2, would also apply to internal requirements restricting imports, which would be contrary to the basic aim of Article III.[62]

In *Seals*, complainants argued that the EU seal ban represented a quantitative restriction that, among others, violated article XI GATT and the national treatment obligation of article III:4 GATT.[63] The panel found that the ban did not violate article XI GATT and proceeded to examine whether it violated article III:4 GATT.[64] The three disputes, which clearly depart from the stance defended in *Tuna/Dolphin I*, show that only article III GATT should apply to import restrictions or prohibitions, regardless of whether they are based on physical differences in products or PPMs.[65]

II. Article III GATT

If adjudicative bodies declare article III GATT applicable to nontariff barriers to trade, import restrictions must follow subparagraphs 2 and 4 against the discrimination of foreign products. Article III:2 GATT prohibits discriminating against foreign and domestic products on the basis of internal taxes, whereas article III:4 GATT prohibits discrimination through nonfiscal measures. Because most trade restrictions used to protect animals belong to the latter category (e.g., import bans of fox fur), we will deal with this subparagraph first.

Whether a state violates article III:4 GATT by restricting or prohibiting the importation of animals or animal products produced in a cruel or inhumane manner stands and falls with the likeness test—the test which evaluates the "nature and extent of a competitive relationship between and among the products in question."[66] Under WTO law, there is no precise

---

of import, because the product has not yet entered the domestic market: STOHNER 22–3 (2006). *See also* CLAUDIUS TRIEBOLD, RECHTLICHE GRUNDLAGEN DES UMWELTSCHUTZES IN GATT UND WTO: AM BEISPIEL DES INTERNATIONAL WARENVERKEHRS 363 ff., 399 (2000).

[61] Mutually Agreed Solution, *Canada—Tax Exemptions and Reductions for Wine and Beer*, WTO Doc. G/L/806/Add. 1, G/SCM/D72/a/Add.1, WT/DS354/2 (adopted Dec. 23, 2008).

[62] Panel Report, *Canada—Administration of the Foreign Investment Review Act*, ¶ 5.14, WTO Doc. L/5504—30S/140 (not adopted, circulated Feb. 7, 1984).

[63] *Seals*, Panel Report ¶¶ 7.2, 7.658.

[64] *Id.* ¶ 7.663.

[65] Others argue that PPM-related import restrictions can be reviewed either under art. XI or art. III GATT, depending on the interpretation of Note Ad art. III GATT: CONRAD 38 (2011).

[66] *Asbestos*, AB Report ¶¶ 99, 103.

and absolute definition of "likeness;" the term is concretized on a case-to-case basis. As the AB explained in *Japan—Alcoholic Beverages*:

> The accordion of "likeness" stretches and squeezes in different places as different provisions of the WTO Agreement are applied. The width of the accordion in any one of those places must be determined by the particular provision in which the term "like" is encountered as well as by the context and the circumstances that prevail in any given case to which that provision may apply.[67]

In 1970, the Working Party on *Border Tax Adjustments* issued a report that determined likeness based on state practice, and which serves as a guiding document. The report identifies four criteria whereby likeness is measured:

(i) the properties, nature, and quality of the products,
(ii) the end-uses of the products,
(iii) consumers' tastes and habits—or consumers' perceptions and behavior—in respect of the products, and
(iv) the tariff classification of the products.[68]

This list is not exhaustive; in any individual case, the four criteria might be weighed differently and it might be necessary to bring in additional criteria. Nevertheless, since the *Border Tax Adjustments* report, these criteria have been quite consistently followed by panels and the AB.[69]

In *EC—Asbestos*, the AB assessed health risks under the test of consumers' habits and tastes, stating that "[a] manufacturer cannot, for instance, ignore the preferences of the ultimate consumer of its products."[70] Consumers' tastes and habits determine the likeness of products to "the extent to which consumers perceive and treat the products as alternative means of performing particular functions in order to satisfy a particular want or demand."[71] Consumers accordingly "influence—modify or even render obsolete—traditional uses of the products."[72] For instance, while cow milk and goat milk may be alike in Tunisia, British consumers may not view them as alternative means to satisfy the demand for animal milk. The likeness test, though universally applicable, heavily differs from market to market and from state to state. The rule of thumb is that the likeness test is all about the competitive

---

[67] *Japan—Alcoholic Beverages*, AB Report, 21.

[68] Working Party Report, Border Tax Adjustments, BISD 18/S/97 (WTO Secretariat, Geneva 1970). Signposts for the product-by-product analysis are tariff classifications, notably under the uniform classification in tariff nomenclatures based on the Harmonized System. Tariff bindings or concessions, on the other hand, are not reliable indicators for determining likeness of products: *Japan—Alcoholic Beverages*, AB Report, 22.

[69] These factors were recognized and used, among others, in: *Asbestos*, AB Report ¶ 101; *Japan—Alcoholic Beverages*, AB Report, 20; Appellate Body Report, *Canada—Certain Measures Concerning Periodicals*, 21, WTO Doc. WT/DS31/AB/R (adopted July 30, 1997) [*Periodicals*, AB Report]; Panel Report, *Argentina—Measures Affecting the Export of Bovine Hides and the Import of Finished Leather*, ¶ 5.3, WTO Doc. WT/DS155/R (adopted Feb. 16, 2001) [*Argentina—Hides and Leather*, Panel Report].

[70] *Asbestos*, AB Report ¶ 122.

[71] *Id.* ¶ 101.

[72] *Id.* ¶ 102.

relationship of products:[73] Do these products compete? Do laws protecting animals distort the products' conditions of competition?

At first sight, laws and regulations that treat goods differently based on the degree of animal welfare seem compatible with the national treatment obligation, since both imported and domestic products must follow them, hence they are treated indiscriminately. Yet, even if, from the standpoint of PPMs, goods are treated equally regardless of their origin, the laws and regulations in question are only legal if PPMs are in the first place admissible to evaluate the likeness of products. For instance, if cow milk produced at high welfare and cow milk produced through high animal suffering are in a competitive relationship, they are like for the purposes of article III:4 GATT, so states cannot apply different rules to them. If PPMs render products unlike for the purposes of article III:4 GATT, however, import bans of certain animal products can be upheld if domestic products produced under the same conditions are also prohibited from accessing the domestic market.

Article III:2 GATT, in contrast to article III:4 GATT, prohibits using internal taxes to discriminate against a foreign member. Taxes may give producers positive or negative incentives to increase animal welfare during the production process. For instance, meat produced in intense confinement can, in principle, be taxed at a higher rate than meat produced from animals who have more space to move around, which in turn nudges producers to keep animals in better conditions. But does this strategy meet the test of the GATT? The first sentence of article III: 2 GATT determines that imported products shall not be taxed in excess of taxes applied to domestic products. The second sentence of article III:2 GATT provides that when imported and domestic products are directly competitive or substitutable, they should be similarly taxed. But dissimilar taxation is only subject to the purview of article III:2 GATT second sentence if it protects domestic production (because of its reference to article III:1 GATT).[74]

Discrimination against members through internal taxes also hinges on whether domestic and foreign products are alike. The likeness test of article III:2 GATT, however, differs considerably from that of article III:4 GATT, as *EC—Asbestos* highlighted. The AB held that, in contrast to article III:4 GATT, likeness in article III:2 GATT first sentence is narrowly construed, stemming from article III:2 GATT, second sentence, which provides that it applies to products "directly competitive or substitutable."[75] This addition is absent in the first sentence of article III:2 GATT. But, as the AB pointed out, "the product scope of

---

[73] Diebold argues that the starting point of this analysis should be determining the purpose of the likeness test. Hence, differential treatment is only less favorable if conditions of competition are modified: Nicolas F. Diebold, Non-Discrimination in International Trade in Services: "Likeness" in WTO/GATS 70 (2010).

[74] The question of whether domestic production has been afforded protection is not an issue of intent. It is a question of how the measure is applied: *Japan—Alcoholic Beverages*, AB Report, 27–8.

[75] In determining whether shochu and vodka are like products for the purposes of art. III:2 GATT, first sentence, the AB affirmed the panel's conclusions: *Japan—Alcoholic Beverages*, AB Report, 21: "We believe that, in Article III:2, first sentence of the GATT 1994, the accordion of 'likeness' is meant to be narrowly squeezed." The theory of "aims and effects," which was widely held to apply to the likeness test in the provision—and essentially holding that article III:2 GATT is only violated by measures contrary to the object and purpose of the whole article—was rejected in *Japan—Alcoholic Beverages*, AB Report, 18–9.

Article III:4, although broader than the *first* sentence of Article III:2, is certainly *not* broader than the combined product scope of the *two* sentences of Article III:2 of the GATT 1994."[76]

As in article III:4 GATT, the question of whether products are alike for the purposes of article III:2 GATT hinges on "a determination about the nature and extent of a competitive relationship between and among products."[77] States could *prima facie* introduce differentiated taxes based on the level of animal law observed during production. For example, lasagna that contains cow meat from CAFOs, where animals are inadequately fed and raised, where they cannot behave or interact in a normal fashion, and where they are barred from forming meaningful relationships, could be taxed differently than lasagna that contains meat from "organically raised" cows. To determine if the differentiated taxes are legal, the WTO DSB must first find out if two types of lasagna are alike. To make its determination, the DSB must, in line with the *Border Tax Adjustments* report, examine the properties, the nature and quality (i.e., their physical characteristics) of the lasagna, the end uses of the lasagna, tastes and habits (or perceptions and behavior) of consumers, and the tariff classification of the lasagna.[78]

As seen with the likeness test of other GATT articles, the likeness test of article III:2 GATT depends on whether PPMs affect the competitiveness or substitutability of products.[79] On the one hand, consumers might not treat products produced with high or low welfare interchangeably, so we might find that they are not directly competitive or substitutable.[80] On the other hand, consumer choice is highly conditional on price—i.e., consumers tend to prefer low-cost products even if they wish for better animal welfare—so the two products might represent alternative ways of satisfying consumer demand. Current consumer preferences show that the latter assumption is correct, but latent and extant demand (criteria determining how products will be treated by consumers) might change this in the future.[81]

III. Process and Production Methods (PPMs)

The previous analyses have shown that the legality of laws that protect animals and simultaneously affect or threaten to affect trade hinges to a great extent on whether GATT allows products to be differentiated depending on how animals were treated during the production process. In WTO law, this question lies at the heart of the broader PPM debate, which haunts practitioners and academics since many years.

---

[76] *Asbestos*, AB Report ¶ 99 (emphasis added).

[77] *Id.*; Appellate Body Report, *Philippines—Taxes on Distilled Spirits*, ¶ 170, WTO Doc. WT/DS396/AB/R, WT/DS403/AB/R (adopted Jan. 20, 2012) [*Philippines—Distilled Spirits*, AB Report].

[78] *Philippines—Distilled Spirits*, AB Report ¶ 118 ff.

[79] *See also* Eaton et al. 59 (2005).

[80] Howse & Regan 267 (2000).

[81] *See Korea—Alcoholic Beverages*, AB Report ¶ 114: "Competition in the marketplace is a dynamic, evolving process. Accordingly, the wording of the term 'directly competitive or substitutable' implies that the competitive relationship between products is not to be analyzed exclusively by reference to current consumer preferences. In our view, the word 'substitutable' indicates that the requisite relationship may exist between products that are not, at a given moment, considered by consumers to be substitutes but which are, nonetheless, capable of being substituted for one another." (Emphasis omitted).

Measures that relate to other than physical product characteristics are based on nonphysical (product) characteristics, including non-product-related PPMs (NPR-PPMs)—process and production methods that do not change the physical appearance of a product.[82] The NPR-PPM debate (hereafter, PPM debate) revolves around whether products are alike if they are physically identical, but were differently processed or produced.[83] For instance, eggs taken from hens kept in battery cages look physically identical to eggs taken from hens that can range freely. For many people, the two types of eggs differ because they choose products based on how chickens were treated during the production process. While it might be possible to physically distinguish PPMs on animals based on their state of health (e.g., the condition of their coat, their behavior, their digestion, their physical fitness, or their behavioral responses), it is virtually impossible to determine PPMs in animal products by visual inspection. Milk, meat, and eggs look identical, regardless of how the animals used for these products were treated: "an egg is simply an egg." According to this conventional view of PPMs, laws distinguishing between PPMs are suspected of violating WTO obligations because they create unjustifiable barriers to trade and encourage protectionism.

Since the height of the PPM debate, the opinion that there is a substantial difference between products produced "humanely" and products causing "animal suffering" has entered the mainstream, whether or not those products physically resemble each other. In reaction thereto, some member states have argued for the acceptance of PPMs in the likeness determination of the GATT. For them, the PPM debate is relevant to indirectly protect animals abroad, since indirect extraterritorial laws are concerned with how animals are treated, i.e., they hinge on the PPM dispute.[84] If treating animals differently during production is thought to render products unlike, both differentiated taxation and different regulatory treatment (e.g., labeling schemes or import restrictions) would pass the test of articles III:2 GATT and III:4 GATT.

In *Tuna/Dolphin*, a panel for the first time addressed the PPM issue. The facts giving rise to the dispute were the following: common tuna fishing methods of the 1950s—the "purse seine" net fishing for yellowfin tuna—consisted of three boats encircling schools of tuna and gathering them with nets to reel them in with cables. Since dolphins tend to swim right above yellow fin tuna, masses of dolphins were killed in the hunt for tuna, which many considered brutal and unnecessary. The Southwest Fisheries Science Center estimated that, since the 1950s, over six million dolphins had been casualties of tuna-fishing practices.[85] As these

---

[82] Product-related PPMs (so-called PR-PPMs), on the other hand, change the physical characteristics of the final product. *See* Thomas 611 (2007); Alex B. Thiermann & Sarah L. Babcock, *Animal Welfare and International Trade*, 24 REV. SCI. TECH. OFF. INT. EPIZ. 747, 748 (2005).

[83] The OECD, in its 1997 report on PPMs, describes PPMs as the way in which products or services are manufactured, produced, and/or processed, and the way in which natural resources are extracted: OECD, PROCESSES AND PRODUCTION METHODS (PPMs): CONCEPTUAL FRAMEWORK AND CONSIDERATIONS ON USE OF PPM-BASED TRADE MEASURES, OCDE/GD(97)137, 7 (OECD Publishing, Paris 1997).

[84] Stevenson 111 (2002).

[85] National Oceanic and Atmospheric Administration [NOAA] Fisheries, Southwest Fisheries Science Center, The Tuna-Dolphin Issue, *available at* https://swfsc.noaa.gov/textblock.aspx?Division=PRD&ParentMenuId=228&id=1408 (last visited Jan. 10, 2019). *Further* on the dispute, *see* Tim Gerrodette, *The Tuna-Dolphin Issue*, *in* ENCYCLOPEDIA OF MARINE MAMMALS 1192 (William F. Perrin et al. eds., 2d ed. 2009).

events were exposed, public outrage grew and the United States banned all imports of tuna harvested with purse seine nets in the eastern tropical Pacific under the Marine Mammal Protection Act of 1972 (MMPA)[86] unless foreign producers could prove that their program prevented as many annual dolphin kills as the US program did.[87]

In *Tuna/Dolphin I*, [88] the United States was charged for violating its obligations under WTO law. Mexico claimed the MMPA provision qualified as a quantitative restriction and violated article XI GATT. The United States, on the other hand, claimed that the provision allowed it to distinguish between imported and domestic products based on article III:4 GATT, as laws, regulations, and requirements that affect their internal sale, offering for sale, purchase, transportation, distribution, or use. The panel in *Tuna/Dolphin I* found that Note Ad to article III, which serves as a guide to limit the scope of the two articles, allowed no distinction between products on the basis of PPMs because the note solely referred to *products as such*.[89] The panel declined to apply Note Ad article III GATT to the case and found the measure to be inconsistent with article XI GATT.

In the later *Tuna/Dolphin II* case, the European Union and the Netherlands claimed they were prevented from selling tuna because of the primary embargo, and the panel concurred with the ruling delivered in *Tuna/Dolphin I*.[90] The two *Tuna/Dolphin* reports effectively prevent states from putting in place trade measures that differentiate products based on how animals were treated, and thus from indirectly protecting animals situated abroad. Following *Tuna/Dolphin*, all animals and animal products must freely enter the domestic market, regardless of how animals were treated during production. The reports, although never adopted by the DSB, continue to constitute the "most important and potentially damaging interpretation of the GATT"[91] for animals.

The *Shrimp/Turtle* case also touched on the PPM debate. In this case, the United States required shrimp producers to use turtle-excluder devices or certified comparable measures to reduce the incidental killing of endangered turtles under Section 609(b) of Public Law 101-102.[92] Producers that were unable to prove they sufficiently protected turtles were banned from importing tuna to the United States. The panel applied article XI GATT and determined that the US measures violated it but chose not to address whether PPMs contravened article III GATT. Thereby, it effectively sidestepped the PPM debate.[93] However, by provisionally justifying the measure under article XX(g) GATT, scholars argue that the AB

---

[86] The current version is the Marine Mammal Protection Act [MMPA], 16 U.S.C. § 31 (U.S.).

[87] The former MMPA determined that tuna fishers' average killing rate may not exceed 1.25 times the average dolphin killing rate of US catches. Killing rate of foreign producers interested in exporting to the United States is thus capped at the killing rate of the United States: Kelch 251 ff. (2011).

[88] *Tuna/Dolphin I*, Panel Report.

[89] *Tuna/Dolphin I*, Panel Report ¶ 514.

[90] Panel Report, *US—Restrictions on Imports of Tuna* ¶ 5.9 WTO Doc. DS29/R (not adopted, circulated June 16, 1994) [*Tuna/Dolphin II*, Panel Report].

[91] Kelch 253 (2011).

[92] Public Law 101-102, 16 U.S.C. § 1537 (U.S.).

[93] Panel Report, *United States—Import Prohibition of Certain Shrimp and Shrimp Products* ¶¶ 161 ff., WTO Doc. WT/DS58/R (adopted Nov. 6, 1998) [*Shrimp/Turtle I*, Panel Report].

overruled *Tuna/Dolphin* and confirmed that PPM measures are in principle justifiable.[94] Many believe that the *Seals* cases also dealt with the PPM *problématique*, but by relying on regulatory differences that affect indigenous communities and commercial hunt, the European Union was concerned with producers (and the reasons for hunting seals) rather than PPMs (the way in which seals are killed).[95]

Because the PPM dispute is still not settled in WTO law, it has attracted scholarly attention for decades. Most scholars argue that PPMs are inadmissible under articles I and III GATT,[96] and point to reports to evidence their claims, like the 1952 *Belgian Family Allowances*. In this case, goods that originated from certain family allowances were held to be like other goods that did not arise from such allowances, so the measure in question violated articles I and III GATT.[97] In line with this view, the 1992 "Trade and the Environment" study by the WTO Secretariat laid down that, in principle, it is "not possible under GATT's rules to make access to one's own market dependent on the domestic environmental policies or practices of the exporting country."[98] But by 2004, the WTO Secretariat retracted its statement and declined to side with either view.[99] Some also argue that PPMs generally fall outside the purview of the WTO, because the GATT would regulate only *trade in* goods, not the *production* of goods.[100] Were the WTO to allow members to distinguish between PPMs, it would exceed its authority. Only if core cultural values or ethical convictions are substantially affected by trade regulation, states are free to invoke the exceptions of article XX GATT to try to convince a panel that the trade violations are justified.[101] If PPMs were declared legal for the purposes of article III GATT, this would render article XX GATT redundant and unduly make room for disguised protectionism.

---

[94] Catherine Jean Archibald, *Forbidden by the WTO? Discrimination Against a Product When Its Creation Causes Harm to the Environment or Animal Welfare*, 48 NAT. RES. J. 15, 17 (2008); Frank Biermann, *The Rising Tide of Green Unilateralism in World Trade Law: Options for Reconciling the Emerging North-South Conflict*, 35 J. WORLD TRADE 421, 430 (2001); CONRAD 20, 24 (2011); Fitzgerald 122 (2011); Andrew Lurié & Maria Kalinina, *Protecting Animals in International Trade: A Study of the Recent Successes at the WTO and in Free Trade Agreements*, 30 AM. U. INT'L L. REV. 431, 443–4 (2015). Bernstein and Hannah conclude that it is unclear if PPM measures comply with art. III GATT: Steven Bernstein & Erin Hannah, *Non-State Global Standard Setting and the WTO: Legitimacy and the Need for Regulatory Space*, 11 J. INT'L EC. LAW. 575, 591 (2008).

[95] *Seals*, AB Report ¶ 5.45: "We see no basis in the text of Annex 1.1, or in prior Appellate Body reports, to suggest that the identity of the hunter, the type of hunt, or the purpose of the hunt could be viewed as product characteristics."

[96] Thomas J. Schoenbaum, *Free International Trade and Protection of the Environment: Irreconcilable Conflict?*, 86 AJIL 700, 713 (1992); Michael Reiterer, *Internationaler Handel und Umwelt: Bilanz der GATT-Arbeitsgruppe über "Environmental Measures and International Trade" (EMIT) sowie der Uruguay-Runde*, 49 AUSSENWIRTSCHAFT IV 477 (1994); European Commission, Communication from the Commission to the Council and the European Parliament on Trade and Environment, COM(96) 54 final (Feb. 28, 1996), at 14. Observing this movement only: Howse & Regan 251 (2000); STOHNER 67 (2006).

[97] Panel Report, *Belgium—Belgian Family Allowances*, WTO Doc. G/32–1S/59 (adopted Nov. 7, 1952).

[98] WTO, INTERNATIONAL TRADE 1990–1991, TRADE AND ENVIRONMENT 10 (WTO Secretariat, Geneva 1992).

[99] WTO, TRADE AND ENVIRONMENT AT THE WTO 17–8 (WTO Secretariat, Geneva 2004).

[100] Eaton et al. 9 (2005).

[101] STOHNER 68 (2006).

Other scholars argue that the GATT allows, even mandates the use of PPMs to evaluate the likeness of products. Five arguments support this conclusion. First, excluding PPMs from the likeness test is not mandated by article III or Note Ad article III GATT.[102] It defies logic that the reference in Note Ad article III GATT to "products" ought to exclude PPMs, since "products" is a term entirely neutral with regard to production methods.[103] Treaty language, rather than invalidating the PPM distinction, in fact speaks for its legality. Article III:1 GATT, which forms the general rule to articles III:2 and III:4 GATT, states that, among others, "*processing or use of products* in specified amounts or proportions, should not be applied to imported or domestic products *so as to afford protection to domestic production.*" The provision, read in the context of articles III:2 and III:4 GATT, implies that states can draw PPM distinctions if PPMs are not employed in a protectionist manner.[104] Further, the PPM distinction is found in articles III:5 and III:7 GATT. In *Tuna/Dolphin I*, the panel should therefore have concluded that the US measure violated article III because it was unduly protectionist, not because it distinguished between PPMs. The strict view on PPMs also fails to consider that the AB held in *Japan—Alcoholic Beverages* that likeness of products must be narrowly construed, especially under article III:2 GATT.[105] Hence, for products produced by different PPMs, the presumption should be that they are *not* alike. Moreover, the strict view on PPMs arose from two unadopted panel reports in *Tuna/Dolphin*, which were neither recognized by the AB, nor declared binding by the members.[106]

The second consideration speaking for the legality of PPMs is that applying the four-criteria established in *EC—Asbestos* and the *Border Tax Adjustment* report shows that animal products produced with low animal welfare are typically not like animal products produced with high animal welfare. Granted, the first three criteria do not mandate paying attention to PPMs,[107] but the fourth criterion—consumer tastes and behavior—demands that PPMs be applied. In *EC—Asbestos*, the AB held:

> [E]vidence about the extent to which products can serve the same end-uses, and the extent to which consumers are—or would be—willing to choose one product instead of another to perform those end-uses, is highly relevant evidence in assessing the "likeness" of those products under Article III:4 of the GATT 1994.[108]

---

[102] Kelch 254 (2011).

[103] Howse & Regan 254 (2000).

[104] Archibald 22–3 (2008).

[105] *Japan—Alcoholic Beverages*, AB Report, 24.

[106] Stevenson 120 (2002).

[107] The first two criteria, namely, products' properties, nature, and quality, and end uses do not pay regard to the PPM distinction. Both high-welfare meat and low welfare meat (or eggs or milk or any other animal product, for that matter) are physically identical and serve the same purposes. The third criterion, tariff classification, does not speak for the legality of PPMs either. The Harmonized System Nomenclature only differentiates between fresh meat and processed meat, or fresh and frozen meat. There is also a category of "mechanically deboned meat." *See Japan—Alcoholic Beverages*, AB Report, 22. *See also* Eaton et al. 23 (2005).

[108] *Asbestos*, AB Report ¶ 117.

Fitzgerald, Thomas, Van den Bossche, and Zdouc all share the view that PPMs were formally recognized by the WTO in *EC—Asbestos* by referring to consumer tastes and behavior.[109] Others contend that the decision lacks *stare decisis*, but concede that the criterion of consumer tastes and habits was subsequently recognized in *Japan—Alcoholic Beverages* and in *Japan—Lumber*.[110] In any case, if consumer preferences about human health risks (which underlay the *EC—Asbestos* case) do not rely on physical distinctions, but influence the likeness of products, then consumer preferences of all kinds, including preferences for products guaranteeing better animal welfare, must be critical.[111] As Sharpless states, "while hog farmers might feel that 'a pig is a pig is a pig', consumers may well view the pig raised in extensive agricultural conditions differently from the pig raised in a Concentrated Animal Feeding Operation."[112] The way in which a product was made thus has the potential of becoming a "fundamental characteristic of the product itself."[113]

The third argument is that the likeness test is much more concerned with the competitive relationship between products than with their physical appearance. In *Philippines—Distilled Spirits*, the AB noted:

> [A]s long as the differences among the products, including a difference in the raw material base, leave fundamentally unchanged the competitive relationship among the final products, the existence of these differences does not prevent a finding of "likeness," if, by considering all factors, the panel is able to come to the conclusion that the competitive relationship among the products is such as to justify a finding of "likeness."[114]

For PPMs to be valid under GATT, the competitive relationship of products whose PPMs differ must be shaped by consumer behavior. Only if moral convictions of the public translate into consumers' tastes and habits, are "humanely" and "inhumanely" produced products not in a competitive relationship. Most people's beliefs about humane treatment, however, are not reflected in their purchasing behavior—simply because price dominates consumer choice.[115] It could thus be argued that because PPMs do not form part of consumer behavior, they cannot determine the likeness of products. As the AB noted in *Philippines—Distilled Spirits*, however, price differences in products are still relevant for the determination of likeness.[116] If different levels of animal welfare during the production process lead to price differences, they affect the products' competitive relationship. So even if consumers fail to

---

[109] Fitzgerald 102 (2011); Thomas 610 (2007); Van den Bossche & Zdouc 388–9 (2017).

[110] Stohner rejects that the *EC—Asbestos* case represents a case of PPMs, without substantiation, however: Stohner 67, n. 261 (2006). The PPM distinction is also mentioned in Panel Report, *Japan—Tariff Imports on Spruce, Pine, Fir (SPF) Dimension Lumber*, ¶ 3.52, WTO Doc. L/6470—36S/167 (adopted July 19, 1989) [*Japan—Lumber*, Panel Report]; *Japan—Alcoholic Beverages*, AB Report, 22.

[111] Fitzgerald 102 (2011); Thomas 610 (2007).

[112] Sharpless 44–5 (2008).

[113] Kelch 253 (2011). *See also* Thiermann & Babcock 747 (2005).

[114] *Philippines—Distilled Spirits*, AB Report ¶ 125.

[115] *See* Chapter 2, §3 B. Nollkaemper, by contrast, argues that consumers actually treat these products differently: Nollkaemper 248 (1996).

[116] *Philippines—Distilled Spirits*, AB Report ¶ 125.

align their purchasing behavior with their moral views, different prices for PPM products may affect their competitive relationship on the market.

Fourth, in acknowledgment of consumers' inability to behave according to their preference for "high-welfare" products, more and more states want PPMs to be formally endorsed.[117] The European Union[118] and Austria[119] submitted proposals to the GATT Environmental Measures and International Trade Group asking it to declare PPMs a valid means of advancing animal welfare. The World Charter of Nature, incorporated by General Assembly Resolution 37/7, calls on governments to "[e]stablish standards for products and manufacturing processes that may have adverse effects on nature."[120] The public broadly supports these efforts. In the European Union, the Eurobarometer—which interviewed 27,000 citizens in 28 member states—showed that over 90 percent of EU citizens believe protecting the welfare of farmed animals is important.[121] Thiermann and Babcock generally note that there is an increasing global concern for animal welfare, "especially in the context of food-animal production."[122]

Fifth, rejecting PPMs would have disastrous consequences at multiple levels, including animal welfare and principles of democratic governance. If PPMs are declared inadmissible at the WTO, states cannot give preferential treatment to foreign products produced with higher concerns for animals. Consequently, laws that determine how animals must be treated can only be applied to domestic products. For example, in the European Union, domestic eggs are labeled according to the farming method (cage, free-range, organic etc.), while eggs from foreign countries are only labeled based on their origin, namely as "non-EC origin."[123] Consumers lack information about how imported eggs were produced, including whether hens were held in battery cages. Maybe European consumers will simply not buy eggs of "non-EC origin," because they fear these eggs might come from intense confinement. But as we saw earlier, even consumers who say they care deeply about hens' well-being are disproportionately influenced by pricing. Since eggs of "non-EC origin," which are mostly produced in battery cages, can be offered at a lower price in the European Union than eggs produced at high welfare, domestic producers find themselves at an economic disadvantage. Ultimately, consumers' tendency to assume that animal products are humanely

[117] Kelch 254 (2011).

[118] European Community, Submission to EMIT Group, GATT Doc. TRE/W/5 (Nov. 17, 1992); European Communities Proposal, Animal Welfare and Trade in Agriculture, June 28, 2000, Committee on Agriculture, Special Session, WTO Doc. No. G/AG/NG/W/19, at 2: "In practice, our concerns with animal welfare are most acute in relation to highly-intensive and industrialised production methods for certain species, in particular poultry and pigs. This type of production is most often found in developed rather than developing and least developed countries."

[119] Austria, Submission to EMIT Group, GATT Doc. TRE/W/19 (Oct. 1, 1993).

[120] G.A. Res. 37/7, U.N. GAOR 37th Sess., World Charter for Nature, U.N. Doc. A/RES/37/7, General Principle 21(b) (Oct. 28, 1982) [World Charter of Nature].

[121] European Commission, Special Eurobarometer 442 Report: Attitudes of Europeans towards Animal Welfare 3–4 (2016).

[122] Thiermann & Babcock 747 (2005).

[123] Commission Regulation No. 589/2008 Laying Down Detailed Rules for Implementing Council Regulation No. 1234/2007 as Regards Marketing Standards for Eggs, 2008 O.J. (L 163) 6, art. 30. *Further* Fitzgerald 103 (2011).

produced is systematically misused. This should be unsettling to those who support democratic values and the basic principles of competition law, but it also sets in motion a much larger, very damaging cycle. Because foreign products produced at low welfare are granted strategic benefits, regulating animal welfare for domestic products—through bans, labeling requirements, etc.—becomes economically and politically untenable. High-welfare products do not stand a chance at the market or occupy only a market niche, while legislators refuse to introduce stricter laws to protect animals because they fear the domestic market will be swamped by cheaper imports. By rejecting PPMs, the WTO would discourage laws that protect animals and prioritize lax laws, setting in motion a competition in laxity.[124]

The opinion of the two *Tuna/Dolphin* reports has been subject to considerable change in the last 30 years. Today, the public is deeply concerned about how animals are treated, and GATT's interpretation should evolve to ensure members can take these concerns on board.[125] To avert the risk of protectionism—a fear shared by those who reject PPMs—scholars have developed interesting and creative solutions that permit PPMs while keeping protectionism in check.[126] The insecurity that dominates the PPM debate harms both trade and animal welfare. It creates incentives for members to employ even more trade-restrictive measures to fulfill their objectives,[127] and prevents them from effectively protecting animals at home and abroad. Therefore, we must hope for a timely resolution to the conflict.

---

[124] KELCH (2011) 260. On competition in laxity in animal law, *see* Chapter 2.

[125] Even rather conservative scholars, like Van den Bossche and Zdouc, argue that determining likeness now requires a more nuanced answer than that given by the panel in *Tuna/Dolphin:* VAN DEN BOSSCHE & ZDOUC 388 (2017).

[126] Charnovitz proposed a taxonomy of PPMs, namely, how-produced standards (specifying a product's processing method), government policy standards (laying down another state's regulation of PPMs), and producer characteristics standards (specifying the identity of the producer or importer). The taxonomy, he argues, introduces less coercive, more transparent and effective PPMs (Steve Charnovitz, *The Law of Environmental "PPMs" in the WTO: Debunking the Myth of Illegality*, 27 YALE J. INT'L L. 59, 67 ff. (2002)). In response to protectionist concerns about PPMs, Stevenson (2002) proposes ensuring that PPMs are (i) transparent, nondiscriminatory, proportionate, and constitute no disguised restriction; (ii) science-based; (iii) important to a significant percentage of the population in a country; and (iv) related to a matter of substance (Stevenson 135 (2002)). Wagman and Liebman argue that where PPMs contravene WTO law, physical differences between "humanely" and "inhumanely" produced goods should be better described either on the basis of chemical differences through use of antibiotics and other medications common in high-intensity farming, or on the basis of stress hormones in animals or animal products, which are less prevalent in low-intensity farming (WAGMAN & LIEBMAN 309 (2011)).

[127] For instance, the original plan of the European Union in the *Seals* case was to ban the importation of inhumanely killed seals and seal products. When the European Food Safety Authority (EFSA) pointed out it would be difficult to distinguish between humanely produced products and products from seals who were killed cruelly, the European Union expanded the measure to a full ban on all seals and seal products: Proposal for a Regulation of the European Parliament and of the Council Concerning Trade in Seal Products, COM(2008) 469 final (July 23, 2008), at 5; European Food Safety Authority (EFSA), *Animal Welfare Aspects of the Killing and Skinning of Seals, Scientific Opinion of the Panel on Animal Health and Welfare (AHAW), adopted Dec. 6, 2007*, 610 EFSA J. 1, 88 (2007) [EFSA, SEALS WELFARE REPORT (2007)].

C. REDUCTION OF QUANTITATIVE RESTRICTIONS

In addition to nondiscrimination, it is the WTO's declared goal to eliminate all restrictions on trade other than duties and other charges in its tariffication process.[128] Quantitative restrictions are a domestic measure that limits the quantity of products exported by or imported to another state. They may target product units, weight, volume, or value.[129] For example, a state can set maximum imports of cows to 5 million cows, 10 million tons, or to a worth of 100 million USD. There are four types of quantitative restrictions: prohibitions or bans (absolute or conditional), quotas (maximum quantity), licenses, and other quantitative restrictions (state trading operations, minimum price, voluntary export restraint, and others).[130]

Article XI GATT is the central norm that eliminates quantitative restrictions. Nontariff barriers that affect opportunities of importation,[131] *de jure* or *de facto*, fall under the scope of article XI:1 GATT.[132] This includes import restrictions or bans adopted for animal welfare reasons, if article III GATT does not apply or if article XI GATT applies in addition to article III GATT.[133] Any measure falling under article XI GATT is likely to violate it. The only case in which a member could avoid violating article XI GATT would be to rely on the exceptions conclusively enumerated in paragraph 2 of article XI GATT, which apply in cases of food shortage, classification of commodities, removal of temporary surplus, and related concerns. Since measures adopted to protect animals are not covered by these exceptions, they are prone to violating article XI.[134]

D. SCHEDULES OF CONCESSIONS

Earlier, I showed that differentiated tariffs can be used as a tool to protect animals within and outside a state's territory. Although in principle states can apply PPMs to product classifications for tariff purposes, they must operate within their bound rates.[135] In the Schedules of Concessions, members agreed to maximum tariffs that may not be exceeded. In the Uruguay Round (1986–94), tariff negotiations were held, as usual, on the basis of the nomenclature of the Harmonized System established under the International Convention

---

[128] GATT, preamble.

[129] VAN DEN BOSSCHE & ZDOUC 480 (2017).

[130] A tariff quota is not a quota in the sense of quantitative restrictions; it sets a quota to products that can be imported at a certain duty: VAN DEN BOSSCHE & ZDOUC 480 (2017).

[131] Panel Report, *Dominican Republic*—Measures Affecting the Importation and Internal Sale of Cigarettes, ¶ 7.261, WTO Doc. WT/DS302/R (adopted May 19, 2005). There is no violation of art. XI:1 GATT if the quantitative import or export restriction results from duties, taxes, or other charges.

[132] On *de facto* measures, *see Argentina—Hides and Leather*, Panel Report ¶ 11.17; Panel Report, *EC—Payments and Subsidies Paid to Processors and Producers of Oilseeds and Related Animal-Feed Proteins*, ¶ 150, WTO Doc. L/6627—37S/86 (adopted Jan. 25, 1990).

[133] *See* Chapter 3, §2 B. I.

[134] *See also* Sharpless 51 (2008).

[135] CONRAD 33 (2011).

on the Harmonized Commodity Description and Coding System of the World Customs Organization (WCO) and adopted by most WTO members.[136]

Article II GATT obliges members to treat products according to the obligations set out in the Schedules based on the Harmonized System (to "accord treatment no less favorable than that provided in the Schedule"). Tariffs in the Harmonized System are classified by product name and rarely have additional descriptions. Classifying products by product names gives preference to end products over production methods,[137] which makes it very difficult for states to introduce differentiated tariffs to improve animal welfare. For example, under section I, chapter 1 of the Harmonized System, headings 01.01 and 01.02 list "live horses, asses, mules and hinnies" and "live bovine animals" by different Harmonized System codes. If members are bound by these headings, they can only differentiate between live horses and live bovines, and not between, for example, humanely or cruelly bred and raised horses. This, in essence, makes it unlikely members can uphold different tariffs for products based on PPMs.

Moreover, customs duties are introduced based on customs valuation, the value of the imported merchandise for customs purposes. Pursuant to article VII GATT, customs value should be based on the *actual value* of the product and not on the value of the good of national origin. Introducing higher VATs for products that adhere to higher animal protection standards could thus only be done if it was clear that they cost more on the market of the importing state.

At the same time, as Conrad points out, we should not assume that members can refer to physical characteristics only based on the Harmonized System nomenclature headings.[138] As the panel in *Japan—SPF Dimension Lumber* explained, the "nomenclature has been on purpose structured in such a way that it leaves room for further specifications."[139] In principle, the possibilities for differentiated (animal welfare–based) tariffs are as follows. First, bound rates could be renegotiated by modifying or withdrawing concessions (based on article XXVIII:1 GATT).[140] This is a tedious procedure because members with Initial Negotiating Rights (INRs) or with principal supplying interests must participate in the negotiation, which likely results in withdrawal of mutual benefits and compensation for negative effects (that arise, e.g., from introducing animal welfare–based tariffs).[141] Second, most members do not apply tariffs as high as those laid down in the Schedule of Concessions; the tariff binding simply represents an upper limit.[142] Since the difference between the bound

---

[136] The Harmonized System is used by more than 200 members and applies to 98 percent of the international trade: World Customs Organization, What Is the Harmonized System (HS)? (WCO, Brussels 2016), *available at* http://www.wcoomd.org/en/topics/nomenclature/overview/what-is-the-harmonized-system.aspx (last visited Jan. 10, 2019).

[137] This is because classification is based on the nomenclature's headings: International Convention on the Harmonized System, June 14, 1983, 1503 U.N.T.S. 168, Annex, The General Rules for the Interpretation of the Harmonized System, No. 1, art. 3.1(a) [HS Convention].

[138] Conrad 34 (2011).

[139] *Japan—Lumber*, Panel Report ¶ 5.8.

[140] Eaton et al. 12 (2005).

[141] Van den Bossche & Zdouc 447–9 (2017).

[142] Appellate Body Report, *Argentina—Measures Affecting Imports of Footwear, Textiles, Apparel and Other Items*, ¶ 46, WTO Doc. WT/DS56/AB/R (adopted Apr. 22, 1998).

rate and the duties applied can be large, this margin could, in principle, be used to introduce differentiated tariffs based on animal welfare levels.

E. GATT JUSTIFICATIONS

Given the many ways in which states may violate the GATT by trying to better protect animals, the likelihood that they have to justify their actions by invoking the GATT's exceptions is very high. Article XX GATT allows members to justify GATT-inconsistent measures by a limited and conditional list of exceptions. Animal welfare is not listed as an exception in the GATT, but there are three clauses states can invoke to justify import restrictions adopted for animal welfare reasons. Article XX GATT provides in the relevant part:

> Subject to the requirement that such measures are not applied in a manner which would constitute a means of arbitrary or unjustifiable discrimination between countries where the same conditions prevail, or a disguised restriction on international trade, nothing in this Agreement shall be construed to prevent the adoption or enforcement by any contracting party of measures:
> (a) necessary to protect public morals;
> (b) necessary to protect human, animal or plant life or health; [. . .]
> (g) relating to the conservation of exhaustible natural resources if such measures are made effective in conjunction with restrictions on domestic production or consumption [. . .].[143]

In the following, I will examine the scope of these exceptions in detail but will not elaborate the norm's *chapeau* clause that states have to observe in any case because the existing literature on the topic is sufficient. I will first detail the contents of articles XX(g), (b), and (a) GATT, and then ask if they allow members to protect animals across borders.

I. Article XX(g) GATT

Article XX(g) enables members to justify trade-restrictive policies that relate to the conservation of exhaustible natural resources. Animals, though chiefly seen as mere goods, sometimes qualify as exhaustible natural resources. In the *Prohibition of Imports of Tuna and Tuna Products from Canada* case, the panel determined that tuna stocks constituted exhaustible natural resources.[144] In *Herring and Salmon*, parties concurred that salmon and herring are exhaustible natural resources.[145] In *Shrimp/Turtle*, however, parties argued at length over whether sea turtles protected under US Section 609 are exhaustible natural resources. The

[143] GATT, art. XX.

[144] Panel Report, *US—Prohibition of Imports of Tuna and Tuna Products from Canada*, ¶ 4.9, WTO Doc. L/5198—29S/91 (adopted Feb. 22, 1982) [*US—Tuna I*, Panel Report].

[145] Panel Report, *Canada—Measures Affecting Exports of Unprocessed Herring and Salmon*, ¶ 4.4, WTO Doc. L/6268—35S/98 (adopted Mar. 22, 1988) [*Herring and Salmon*, Panel Report].

AB rejected the argument of India, Pakistan, and Thailand that all living natural resources, including animals, are renewable and thus inexhaustible.[146] An interpretation of the treaty in light of an informed community concerned with protecting and conserving the environment would be incompatible with a static definition of "exhaustible natural resource." Instead, the obligations of the GATT would evolve with the changing expectations of the people and new scientific insights, as the AB held.[147] Accordingly, animals—regardless of how numerous they may be—can be seen as natural resources because they can become extinct.

In *Shrimp/Turtle*, the United States required imported shrimp to be harvested by a turtle excluder device or certified comparable measures to reduce the incidental killing of endangered turtles. Uncertified products that were unable to prove special protection mechanisms for turtles were banned from entering the US market. The AB held that the ban contravened the tariffication goal of article XI GATT, but that it was provisionally justified under article XX(g) GATT. However, because the measure was applied in an arbitrary and unjustifiably discriminatory manner, it failed to pass the AB's scrutiny.[148]

Despite the fact that article XX(g) GATT applies to animals and the products made from their bodies, regulation aimed at improving animal welfare that relies on article XX(g) GATT is inherently limited by the addendum "relating to conservation."[149] In animal ethics, conservationism is often strictly distinguished from animal protection. Conservationism is primarily concerned with protecting groups of animals, not individuals.[150] As a consequence, turtles, for instance, are treated as exchangeable in terms of their survival: it does not matter that one turtle dies if they are replaced by another of their species to maintain the overall number of turtles necessary for conserving their species. Moreover, animals that belong to an endangered species might be safeguarded from death, but they may still suffer under cruel conditions.[151] For instance, conservationists are concerned about the survival of the African

---

[146] India, Pakistan, and Thailand contended that the requirement of exhaustibility referred to "finite resources such as minerals, rather than renewable resources." If all natural resources were defined in these terms, "exhaustible" would be superfluous, they argued. Moreover, in their view, the mere existence of art. XX(b) GATT precluded applying art. XX(g) GATT to animals: *Shrimp/Turtle I*, AB Report ¶ 127 ff.

[147] *Shrimp/Turtle I*, AB Report ¶ 130. Pursuant to the preamble of the WTO Agreement, WTO objectives should be pursued "while allowing for the optimal use of the world's resources in accordance with the *objective of sustainable development*, seeking both to protect and *preserve the environment* [...]." (Marrakesh Agreement Establishing the World Trade Organization, Apr. 15, 1994, 1867 U.N.T.S. 154 [WTO Agreement] (emphasis added)).

[148] *Shrimp/Turtle I*, AB Report ¶ 176.

[149] According to the panel in *Herring and Salmon*, trade measures must be primarily aimed at conservation: *Herring and Salmon*, Panel Report ¶ 4.6. In *US—Gasoline*, the measures in question had a substantial relation to the objectives pursued and were thus not merely incidentally or inadvertently aimed at conservation: Panel Report, *US—Standards for Reformulated and Conventional Gasoline*, ¶ 6.19, WTO Doc. WT/DS2/R (adopted May 20, 1996) [*US—Gasoline*, Panel Report]. Similarly, in *Shrimp/Turtle*, the AB found that the connection in question has to evidence a "close and genuine relationship of means and ends." (*Shrimp/Turtle I*, AB Report ¶ 136).

[150] In this sense, Lennkh refers to conservationism as "collective animal protection" (LENNKH 27 (2012)).

[151] *See* on this point Thomas 619 (2007), arguing that it is "a separate analysis from assessing whether regulations with the singular purpose to lessen animal suffering can survive scrutiny at the WTO." *See also* LAURA NIELSEN, THE WTO, ANIMALS AND PPMs 80 (2007).

elephant (*L. Africana*),[152] but individual elephants still suffer from and remain vulnerable to diseases, parasitism, accidents, drought, starvation, drowning, predation, and stress.[153] Article XX(g) GATT fails to take into account and remains indifferent to the question of how animals are treated or how they cope with their environment. Another concern is that most animals subject to trade are not covered by the exception, because they are not endangered or threatened by extinction. In *Seals*, the European Union invoked article XX(a) GATT, as opposed to article XX(g) GATT, because it did not intend to conserve seals as a species, but aspired to spare individual seals suffering and violent death. These points suggest that states are increasingly treating conservationism and preservationism, on the one hand, and animal protection, on the other, as two different things.

II. Article XX(b) GATT

Article XX(b) GATT concerns measures necessary to protect human, animal, or plant life or health. For many years, article XX(b) GATT was believed to be the primary exception applicable to animal welfare standards that affect trade.[154] As argued before, the literature often sharply distinguishes between "animal health" and "animal welfare."[155] Though these terms overlap significantly, scholars still debate whether article XX(b) GATT's exception for animal health applies to laws that protect animals' welfare. Kelch and Thomas argue that it is not clear if animal welfare is covered by animal health,[156] Vapnek and Chapman call it an "open question,"[157] and Sykes acknowledges the limited scope of article XX(b) GATT in the current practice of the WTO, but argues that there is a strong doctrinal basis to view mitigation of suffering as a form of protecting an animal's health.[158]

From outside animal law, this dispute seems absurd. Empirical research shows that there are strong connections between animals' mental well-being and their bodily health. For example, polar bears, pandas, chimpanzees, gorillas, and many other animals prefer having options, such as having access to the outside or an additional room to hide in, even when they do not take advantage of them.[159] When animals have fewer options, negative physiological stressors increase, causing behavioral abnormalities that quickly become a welfare issue. If we keep the focus on welfare alone, we will not be able to detect stressors in time and

---

[152] CITES, Ann. I & II.

[153] David Pearce, *A Welfare State for Elephants? A Case Study of Compassionate Stewardship*, 3(2) Relations 153, 157 (2015).

[154] U.N. FAO, Legislative and Regulatory Options for Animal Welfare 16 (FAO, Rome 2010): "[I]t is generally agreed that animal welfare issues can more easily be justified as protecting human or animal health than public morals." The report concedes, however, that because of the absence of case reports at that time, scholarly opinions are speculative (*id.* at 16). *See also* Sarah Kahn & Mariela Varas, OIE Animal Welfare Standards and the Multilateral Trade Policy Framework 5 (OIE Publishing, Paris 2013).

[155] *See* Chapter 1, §4.

[156] Kelch 257 (2011); Thomas 618 (2007).

[157] FAO, Options for Animal Welfare 15 (2010).

[158] Sykes, *Sealing Animal Welfare into the GATT Exceptions* 492 (2014).

[159] For an overview, *see* Laura M. Kurtycz, *Choice and Control for Animals in Captivity*, 28(11) The Psychologist 892 (2015).

take preventive action. We must look beyond clinical health and ask how well an animal is doing in their environment and how well they are treated. The panel's observation in *Tuna/ Dolphin III* that protecting animal health requires preventing adverse effects on individual animals—in this case, the suffering inflicted on dolphins by separating mother and calves—speaks for such a broad interpretation.[160]

Legal scholarship has not yet incorporated these insights. Most scholars believe that article XX(b) GATT does not justify policy measures designed to solely protect animal welfare.[161] They argue that instead, animal welfare regulation can be covered by the provision only to the extent that animal welfare and animal health coincide.[162] Article XX(b) GATT thus seems to be of limited value for states that aim to protect animals because it risks considering the welfare of animals only to the extent that laws are needed to protect their clinical health.

III. Article XX(a) GATT

The final exception dealt with herein is the public morals exception of article XX(a) GATT, which declares trade-restrictive measures legal if they are necessary to protect public morals. Until recently, only two cases dealt with the public morals exception: *China—AV Products* and *US—Gambling*. Since case law is scarce, states have been hesitant to invoke this exception. The outcome of the recent *Seals* dispute at the WTO, however, might encourage policy advisers to change their strategies.

In 1998, *The Mirror* published a photo shot by Kent Gavin, which depicted a man clubbing a seal to death,[163] igniting public dispute about the "proper" way to kill seals. For decades, the European Union received massive numbers of letters and petitions that expressed "citizens' deep indignation and repulsion regarding the trade in seal products in such conditions."[164] By adopting Regulation No. 1007/2009 with a majority vote of 550 to 49,[165] the European Union prohibited placing domestic and foreign seals and seal products on the European market. The Regulation was motivated by the consideration that seals are "sentient beings that can experience pain, distress, fear and other forms of suffering."[166] The European Union was particularly interested in banning "all cruel hunting methods which do not guarantee the

---

[160] Panel Report, *US—Measures Concerning the Importation, Marketing and Sale of Tuna and Tuna Products*, ¶ 4.73, WTO Doc. WT/DS381/R (adopted June 13, 2012) [*Tuna/Dolphin III*, Panel Report].

[161] For many: Laura Yavitz, *The WTO and the Environment: The Shrimp Case That Created a New World Order*, 16 J. Nat. Res. & Envtl. L. 203 (2002).

[162] *E.g.*, Kelch 257 (2011).

[163] Jeremy Armstrong, *Thirty Years Ago the Mirror's Kent Gavin Took a Horrific Picture That Shocked the World: This Week He Returned to the Killing Fields of Canada, But Had Anything Changed?*, The Mirror, Apr. 4, 1998.

[164] Proposal for a Regulation of the European Parliament and of the Council Concerning Trade in Seal Products, COM(2008) 469 final (July 23, 2008), at 2.

[165] European Parliament Legislative Resolution on the Proposal for a Regulation of the European Parliament and of the Council Concerning Trade in Seals Products (COM(2008)0469–C6-0295/2008–2008/0160(COD)), 2010 O.J. (C 212 E) 169.

[166] Regulation 1007/2009, 2009 O.J. (L 286) 36, 36, preamble (1).

instantaneous death, without suffering, of the animals, to prohibit the stunning of animals with instruments such as hakapiks, bludgeons and guns, and to promote initiatives aimed at prohibiting trade in seal products."[167] Almost instantly, seal-exporting states like Canada, Norway, and Iceland filed complaints alleging that the European Union had violated the TBT (articles 2.1 and 2.2) and the GATT (articles I and III:4). The case is particularly interesting because the DSB had to determine, for the first time, if concerns for animal welfare are part of public morals, and if they can override the WTO's foundational principle of trade liberalization.

Public morals comprise all rules, principles, and values in a certain social environment that characterize a certain action or inaction as right or wrong, or prescribe certain action or inaction, the content and scope of which is subject to change over time.[168] Can moral views about seals constitute such values? In principle, given the open-ended definition of public morals, the answer should be yes. Does this mean each state can unilaterally define what values form part of its public morals? In *US—Gambling*, the panel held that members "should be given some scope to define and apply for themselves the concepts of 'public morals' and 'public order' in their respective territories, according to their own systems and scales of values."[169] It thus seems that each state has the authority to decide for itself whether ethical views about animals and our relationships with them are an integral part of its public morals.

Pre-*Seals*, most scholars agreed that animal welfare represents a form of public morals.[170] Kelch argued that article XX(a) GATT is the most significant exception for animal welfare: "After all, are animal welfare regulations not based on a moral imperative that animals are morally entitled to humane treatment?"[171] However, shortly before the first *Seals* report was issued, scholars raised the concern that the public morals exception could lead to political tensions among WTO members. They argued that protecting animals through article XX(a) GATT could open a Pandora's box, giving way to sweeping forms of moral and cultural imperialism.[172]

---

[167] *Id.*

[168] *Seals*, AB Report ¶ 5.199; Stohner 77 (2006).

[169] Panel Report, *US—Measures Affecting the Cross-Border Supply of Gambling and Betting Services*, ¶ 6.461, WTO Doc. WT/DS285/R (adopted Nov. 10, 2004) [*US—Gambling*, Panel Report]. This was confirmed in Panel Report, *China—Measures Affecting Trading Rights and Distribution Services of Certain Publications and Audiovisual Entertainment Products*, ¶ 7.759, WTO Doc. WT/DS363/R (adopted Jan. 19, 2010) [*China—Audiovisuals*, Panel Report]; *Seals*, AB Report ¶ 5.199.

[170] Steve Charnovitz, *The Moral Exception in Trade Policy*, 38 Va. J. Int'l L. 689, 737 (1998); Anne-Marie de Brouwer, *GATT Article XX's Environmental Exceptions Explored: Is There Room for National Policies? Balancing Rights and Obligations of WTO Members under the WTO Regime*, *in* The WTO and Concerns Regarding Animals and Nature 9, 34 (Anton Vedder ed., 2003); Kelch 256 (2011); David B. Wilkins, Animal Welfare in Europe: European Legislation and Concerns (1997). Feddersen, in contrast, applied art. XX(b) GATT to animal welfare: Christoph T. Feddersen, *Focusing on Substantive Law in International Economic Relations: The Public Morals of GATT's Article XX(a) and "Conventional" Rules of Interpretation*, 7 Minn. J. Global Trade 75, 102 (1998). *See also* Eaton et al. 46 (2005); Sharpless 52 (2008); Thomas 619 (2007).

[171] Kelch 256 (2011).

[172] Observing this phenomenon: Kelch 257 (2011).

With the *Seals* case, the panel and the AB ended scholarly insecurity and ruled that the European Union can invoke the public morals exception to justify trade-restrictive laws that aim to protect animals. The DSB identified a few signposts and limits for states to successfully invoke the exception. It underlined that the objective sought by a measure, namely, to protect public morality about animal welfare, must be the measure's principal or main objective.[173] The DSB determined that the European Union, having set up an animal welfare scheme that is comprehensive and well established, was truly dedicated to improving the lives of animals. It drew attention to the fact that the European Union recognizes the sentience of animals[174] and developed laws on the slaughter of animals,[175] their transport,[176] the treatment of farmed animals,[177] of animals used in experimentation,[178] cosmetic testing,[179] animals kept in zoos,[180] fur trapping,[181] and the sale of cat and dog fur.[182] In the DSB's view, this proved that the ways in which seals were killed violated the moral conviction of EU member states and their citizens.[183] Public concerns about seal welfare were backed by scientific reports that the panel discussed at length. In 2007, the European Food Safety Authority's Panel on Animal Health and Welfare established that, from a scientific perspective, the common hunting methods clearly impair the welfare of seals.[184] With this, *Seals* made a strong *prima facie* case for any type of animal law to successfully pass article XX(a) GATT scrutiny.

The public morals exception is of special importance in animal law. Most animals subject to trade do not qualify as natural resources and are not endangered or threatened, so they do not fall under the scope of article XX(g) GATT. And if animal welfare laws are not seen as protecting animal health under article XX(b) GATT, article XX(a) GATT becomes the most relevant defense of animal law to justify trade restrictions. Recognizing this, the

[173] *Seals*, AB Report ¶¶ 5.139, 5.146, 5.166.

[174] Art. 13 TFEU recognizes that animals are sentient beings and that their welfare must be given full regard in formulating and implementing the European Union's agriculture, fisheries, transport, internal market, research and technological development, and space policies.

[175] Council Directive 93/119/EC on the Protection of Animals at the Time of Slaughter or Killing, 1992 O.J. (340) 21; Council Regulation 1099/2009 on the Protection of Animals at the Time of Killing, 2009 O.J. (L 303) 1.

[176] Council Regulation 1/2005 on the Protection of Animals During Transport and Related Operations and Amending Directives 64/432/EEC and 93/119/EC and Regulation 1255/97/EC, 2005 O.J. (L 3) 1.

[177] *See especially* Chapter 9, §4 B.

[178] Directive 2010/63 of the European Parliament and of the Council on the Protection of Animals Used for Scientific Purposes, 2010 O.J. (L 276) 33.

[179] Regulation 1223/2009 of the European Parliament and of the Council on Cosmetic Products, 2009 O.J. (L 342) 59.

[180] Council Directive 1999/22 Relating to the Keeping of Wild Animals in Zoos, 1999 O.J. (L 94) 24.

[181] Council Regulation 3254/91, 1991 O.J. (L 308) 1.

[182] Regulation 1523/2007 of the European Parliament and of the Council Banning the Placing on the Market and the Import to, or Export from, the Community of Cat and Dog Fur, and Products Containing such Fur, 2007 O.J. (L 343) 1.

[183] *See also* Regulation 1007/2009, 2009 O.J. (L 286) 36, recital 4: "The hunting of seals has led to expressions of serious concerns by members of the public and governments sensitive to animal welfare considerations due to the pain, distress, fear and other forms of suffering which the killing and skinning of seals, as they are most frequently performed, cause to those animals."

[184] EFSA, Seals Welfare Report 88 (2007).

European Parliament, in a report on trade and environment, urged the Commission and the member states of the European Union "to do everything in their power to persuade the other Member States of the WTO to agree to give genuine and serious consideration to the drawing up of a set of principles or an understanding on the application of Article XX(a) of the General Agreement, which concerns the protection of public morals, including animal protection legislation."[185] Though the *Seals* debate will continue to preoccupy scholars in the near future, panels and the AB are unlikely to overturn it. In *US—Stainless Steel*, the AB emphasized that consistency and stability in the interpretation of rights and duties are of utmost importance to the predictability of the WTO system and the prompt settlement of disputes.[186]

F. EXTRATERRITORIAL ANIMAL PROTECTION IN THE GATT

So far, we have examined whether and to what extent article XX GATT is a useful defense to justify violations of trade law motivated by concerns about animals. The question of whether the justifications enumerated in article XX GATT can be invoked when trade-restrictive laws reach across the border is conceptually different. In *Tuna/Dolphin I*, the United States was accused of exceeding its jurisdiction by restricting imports of tuna produced in a manner harmful to dolphins outside its territory. The panel warned that "[...] if the extrajurisdictional interpretation of Article XX(b) suggested by the United States were accepted, each contracting party could unilaterally determine the conservation policies from which other contracting parties could not deviate without jeopardizing their rights under the General Agreement."[187] It then used a historical interpretation to arrive at the finding that "[...] the concerns of the drafters of Article XX(b) focused on the use of sanitary measures to safeguard life or health of humans, animals or plants *within the jurisdiction* of the importing country."[188] The panel thought article XX(b) GATT could only be invoked by the United States if its measures were intended to protect animals within its territory. But in the later *Tuna/Dolphin II*, the panel held that "states are *not* in principle barred from regulating the conduct of their nationals with respect to persons, animals, plants, and natural resources outside of their territory."[189] In *Shrimp/Turtle*, the AB seems to have settled the dispute. Although turtles were found outside US territory, the measures it adopted to indirectly protect them were fully covered by article XX(g) GATT.[190] Then again, in *EC—Tariff Preferences*, the AB held that "[...] the policy reflected in the Drug Arrangements is *not* one

---

[185] Report on the Communication from the Commission to the Council and the European Parliament on Trade and Environment, COM(96)0054–C4-0158/96, Oct. 14, 1996, Rapporteur Wolfgang Kreissl-Dörfler.

[186] Appellate Body Report, *US—Final Anti-Dumping Measures on Stainless Steel from Mexico*, ¶ 161, WTO Doc. WT/DS344/AB/R (adopted May 20, 2008).

[187] Panel Report, *US—Restrictions on Imports of Tuna*, ¶ 532, WTO Doc. DS21/R–39S/155 (not adopted, circulated Sept. 3, 1991) [*Tuna/Dolphin I*, Panel Report].

[188] *Tuna/Dolphin I*, Panel Report ¶ 526 (emphasis added).

[189] Panel Report, *US—Restrictions on Imports of Tuna*, ¶¶ 5.16–5.17, 5.32, WTO Doc. DS29/R (not adopted, circulated June 16, 1994) [*Tuna/Dolphin II*, Panel Report] (emphasis added).

[190] *Shrimp/Turtle I*, AB Report ¶ 133.

designed for the purpose of protecting human life or health *in the European Communities* and, therefore, the Drug Arrangements are *not* a measure for the purpose of protecting human life or health under Article XX(b) of GATT 1994."[191]

With these conflicting judgments, members face a high degree of uncertainty about the jurisdictional limits of article XX GATT. Most scholars are reluctant to find that articles XX(a)–(j) GATT allows members to protect animals abroad, even indirectly. Schoenbaum argues that using article XX GATT to protect animals abroad would create "chaos and anarchy."[192] Feddersen finds it doubtful that a panel would view article XX GATT as the optimal tool for states to protect animals abroad because doing so would violate the principle of state equality under international law.[193] Stohner argues for a more nuanced approach. He distinguishes between "national," "foreign," and "common" goods, and believes jurisdiction over goods not "national" (so, foreign and common goods) is extraterritorial and illegal.[194] Jurisdiction exercised over goods that are "national," in contrast, is both legitimate and legal. Other scholars deem extraterritorial measures justified exactly where a measure affects common interests, and unjustified if they impinge on the internal affairs of another state.[195]

The dispute is still fraught and cannot be resolved by assembling and contrasting scholarly opinions. In the following, I adopt a more systematic approach to solve the *problématique* and import insights from the law of jurisdiction to illuminate the debate in trade law. For each subparagraph of article XX GATT, I interpret their territorial scope, first based on a general treaty analysis under GATT, and second, on an analysis of the doctrine of jurisdiction under general international law. I start by clarifying the terms and descriptions used in the debate.

I. Terminology and Means of Interpretation

In the WTO reports that deal with the extraterritorial scope of article XX GATT, the terms "territory" and "jurisdiction" are used interchangeably. In *Tuna/Dolphin I*, the panel

---

[191] Panel Report, *EC—Conditions for the Granting of Tariff Preferences to Developing Countries*, ¶ 7.210, WTO Doc. WT/DS246/R (adopted Apr. 20, 2004) (emphasis added).

[192] Schoenbaum 703 (1992): "If every country were allowed to impose its own domestic environmental standards on other countries, the result would not be greater environmental protection but chaos and anarchy." *See also* Vinod Rege, *GATT Law and Environment-Related Issues Affecting the Trade of Developing Countries*, 28 J. World Trade 95, 110 (1994): "The countries, however, have no right under the GATT law to require that the imported products must have been produced according to the PPM standards which they impose on their industries."

[193] Feddersen 117 (1998).

[194] Stohner 31–2 (2006). *See also* Andreas Diem, Freihandel und Umweltschutz in GATT und WTO 17 (1996). Compared to environmental law, international agreements for the protection of animals do not offer a viable alternative to trade-restrictive measures, as evidenced by the efforts of the United States in the *Tuna/Dolphin* cases. Therefore, Stohner's proposition is of limited value in the context of extraterritorial animal protection.

[195] John H. Jackson, The World Trading System: Law and Policy of International Economic Relations 232–5 (2d ed. 1997); Ted L. McDorman, *The GATT Consistency of US Fish Import Embargoes to Stop Driftnet Fishing and Save Whales, Dolphins and Turtles*, 24 Geo. Wash. J. Int'l L. & Econ. 477, 520 (1991); Rege 111 (1994).

repeatedly referred to animals "outside US jurisdiction," "extrajurisdictional application," and "extrajurisdictional approaches."[196] Because neither the panel nor the AB defined the term "extrajurisdictionality," we must examine if it corresponds to extraterritoriality or not.[197]

From the perspective of public international law, jurisdiction is not necessarily conterminous with territory, nor is *extra*jurisdictionality with *extra*territoriality. The Latin term *extra iurisdictio* implies that the law in question lies outside a state's *jurisdiction*; a state has exceeded its jurisdictional authority. Because extrajurisdictionality implies the absence of legality, it can be translated as illegal extraterritorial jurisdiction. The Latin term *extra territorium*, on the other hand, refers to jurisdiction asserted outside a state's *territory*, i.e., extraterritorial jurisdiction. This term does not indicate if a state's jurisdiction is legal or not. It refers to a simple question of facts, namely, whether the referential object, subject, or event in question lies outside a state's territory. The fact that a state's prescriptive authority can *legally* exceed a state's territory is one of the most important lessons from the doctrine of jurisdiction.[198] Legal extraterritorial jurisdiction is thus both extraterritorial and intrajurisdictional. Where extraterritorial jurisdiction is illegal, it is labeled extrajurisdictional, because it exceeds a state's authority. Extraterritorial extrajurisdictionality thus occurs where a state *illegally* exercises jurisdiction outside its territory.

Legal scholarship and the DSB do not clearly distinguish these terms. By stating that article XX(b) GATT allows states "to safeguard life or health of humans, animals or plants *within the jurisdiction* of the importing country,"[199] the panel in *Tuna/Dolphin I* merely asserted that jurisdiction beyond the allowed limits is illegal, which comes close to claiming that illegal measures are illegal. The decisive question, however, must be: Based on which criteria does WTO law distinguish between legal and illegal extraterritorial jurisdiction? This is what I will attempt to answer in the following.

Before proceeding, we must determine the kinds of tools that can be used to interpret the territorial scope of the GATT exceptions. The primary sources for any interpretation of WTO law are WTO treaties, including the WTO's Dispute Settlement Understanding (DSU).[200] Pursuant to article 3.2 DSU, the rights and obligations of members must be clarified in accordance with customary rules of interpretation of public international law. In *US—Gasoline*, the AB in this sense laid down that WTO treaties are "not to be read in clinical isolation from public international law."[201] Article 31 para. 1 of the VCLT, which states that treaties are to be interpreted in good faith starting with the contextualized ordinary meaning of the text forms part of these customary rules of interpretation, as the AB determined.[202] Later, *Japan—Alcoholic Beverages* confirmed the applicability of articles 31 and 32 VCLT "as a whole" for interpreting trade law.[203] This brings article 31 para. 3 lit. c VCLT

---

[196] *Tuna/Dolphin I*, Panel Report ¶¶ 530–2.

[197] This is also criticized by Charnovitz: *id.* at 719 (1998).

[198] *See* Chapter 2.

[199] *Tuna/Dolphin I*, Panel Report ¶ 526 (emphasis added).

[200] WTO, Understanding on Rules and Procedures Governing the Settlement of Disputes, Apr. 15, 1994, 1869 U.N.T.S. 401 [Dispute Settlement Understanding, DSU].

[201] *US—Gasoline*, AB Report, 17.

[202] *Id.*

[203] *Japan—Alcoholic Beverages*, AB Report, 16. *See also Asbestos*, AB Report ¶ 91 (which applied art. 33 para. 1 VCLT).

to application, according to which *any relevant rules of international law applicable in the relations between the parties* shall be taken into account in interpreting trade rules (so not only customary rules of interpretation). Because of its broad scope, article 31 para. 3 lit. c VCLT is known for bridging "WTO law and the rest of public international law."[204] The view that WTO law should be embedded in and guided by general international law is supported by the International Law Commission's Report on the Fragmentation of International Law.[205] The report determines that the two fields of law are "parts of some coherent and meaningful whole."[206] Nadakavukaren Schefer describes the interplay of trade law and general public international law as follows:

> As a multilateral public organization, the WTO's law is part of international law, and in setting out operational rules affecting Member's trade relations, its law is subject to the substantive and procedural principles of general international law to the extent that general norms are not displaced by more specialized regime-rules.[207]

This insight is based on the panel's decision in *Korea—Procurement*, which provided that customary international law as a whole applies "to the extent that the WTO treaty agreements do not 'contract out' from it."[208] Many other reports have relied on general principles of law to support their findings,[209] and the DSB's stance is broadly supported by WTO members. According to the Council of Europe's Report on Extraterritorial Criminal Jurisdiction, for example, doctrines governing legislative conflicts in international trade are, on the whole, derived from the theories of the doctrine of jurisdiction.[210]

---

[204] VRANES 90 (2009). Sykes argues that there are three main reasons why WTO law should be guided by general international law. First, because international law "resembles a dense web of overlapping and detailed prescriptions," so it is not realistic to clinically separate WTO law and public international law. Second, guidance by general international law brings democratic legitimacy of general international law to trade, which matters because WTO institutions are often accused of lacking accountability. Third, clinically separating trade and general international law would create safe heavens from obligations under general international law: Sykes, *Sealing Animal Welfare into the GATT Exceptions* 487–8 (2014). *See also* Bruno Simma & Dirk Pulkowski, *Of Planets and the Universe: Self-contained Regimes in International Law*, 17 EJIL 483, 484, 511 (2006); JOOST PAUWELYN, CONFLICT OF NORMS IN INTERNATIONAL LAW: HOW WTO LAW RELATES TO OTHER RULES OF INTERNATIONAL LAW 38 (2003).

[205] The report was cited in *EC—Large Civil Aircraft*: Appellate Body Report, *EC and Certain Member States—Measures Affecting Trade in Large Civil Aircraft*, ¶¶ 844–5, WTO Doc. WT/DS316/AB/R (adopted June 1, 2011) [*EC—Large Civil Aircraft*, AB Report].

[206] International Law Commission, 58th Sess., Report of the Study Group of the International Law Commission, Fragmentation of International Law, Difficulties Arising from Diversification and Expansion of International Law (finalized by Martti Koskenniemi), U.N. Doc. A/CN.4/L.682 (Apr. 13, 2006), at 414.

[207] NADAKAVUKAREN SCHEFER 100 (2010).

[208] Panel Report, *Korea—Measures Affecting Government Procurement*, ¶ 7.96, WTO Doc. WT/DS163/R (adopted June 19, 2000) [*Korea—Procurement*, Panel Report].

[209] In *Shrimp/Turtle*, the AB invoked the principle of good faith: *Shrimp/Turtle I*, AB Report ¶ 158. In other cases, the principles of proportionality, due process, judicial economy, nonretroactivity, effectiveness, and others were applied to trade law: VAN DEN BOSSCHE & ZDOUC 61 (2017).

[210] CoE, Committee on Crime Problems, *Extraterritorial Criminal Jurisdiction*, 3 CRIM. L.F. 441, 444 (1992).

All of these developments indicate that the law of jurisdiction, which is part of general international law, has a say in determining the scope of jurisdiction in WTO law. Only when the two conflict, does trade law, as *lex specialis*, override the law of jurisdiction. The method I adopt for the following analyses, therefore, is to interpret extraterritoriality, first, under trade law, and second, from a general international law perspective.

To begin, I explore the territorial scope of articles XX(b) and (g) GATT. Then I examine the territorial scope of article XX(a) GATT. I use two, instead of three analyses because article XX(b) "protect[s] human, animal or plant life or health" and (g) GATT protects "exhaustible natural resources." Questions about the territorial reach of these exceptions mean it is unclear whether state A may protect animal life or health or exhaustible natural resources present in state B or on stateless territory. Article XX(a) GATT, on the other hand, protects public morals of state A, not the values covered by them (which may be located in state B). These structural differences make it necessary to undertake two analyses of territorial limits.

II. General Treaty Analysis of Articles XX(b) and (g) GATT

The general treaty analysis of the GATT relies on six different tools of interpretation: grammatical, systematic, teleological, subsequent practices, public law, and historical. The *grammatical* interpretation, which is based on article 31 para. 1 VCLT, demands treaty language be interpreted "in accordance with the ordinary meaning to be given to terms." Since no explicit limits are placed on the territorial reach of articles XX(b) and (g) GATT, the grammatical interpretation is of little help: there could be a presumption the provisions cover more than territorial goods,[211] or there could be a presumption that they protect only territorial goods.

The *systematic* interpretation, also based on article 31 para. 1 VCLT, requires taking into account the provisions surrounding articles XX(b) and (g) GATT. Scholars argue that the scope of article XX(e) GATT, which justifies import embargoes for products manufactured by prisoners abroad, analogously applies to all other *literae*. All exceptions enumerated in article XX GATT must apply extraterritorially,[212] because we cannot justify giving the exceptions of article XX GATT different territorial reach.[213] But the *argumentum a contrario* suggests that because some exceptions explicitly provide for extraterritorial application, other exceptions were not intended to have the same jurisdictional reach.[214] Then again, article XX(f) GATT speaks against this interpretation, because it explicitly determines that it only applies to national cultural goods. By this logic, if members wished to restrict the reach of articles XX(b) and (g) GATT to domestic territory, they would have expressly provided for it.[215] A systematic interpretation thus leads to ambiguous results. What is clear though is that the exceptions have variable territorial reach. As the AB elaborated in *US—Gasoline*, "[i]t does not seem reasonable to suppose that the WTO Members intended to require, in

[211] STOHNER 33 (2006).

[212] Nollkaemper 248 (1996).

[213] Steve Charnovitz, *Green Roots, Bad Pruning: GATT Rules and Their Application to Environmental Trade Measures*, 7 TULANE ENVTL. L.J. 299, 341 (1994).

[214] Feddersen 107 ff. (1998). *See also* Bartels 358 (2002).

[215] STOHNER 34 (2006).

respect of each and every category, the same kind or degree of connection or relationship between the measure under appraisal and the state interest or policy sought to be promoted or realized."[216]

In accordance with article 31 para. 2 VCLT, *preambular language* must be used to interpret the rights and obligations of members. The preamble to the Marrakesh Agreement lays down that members are committed "to protect and preserve the environment" in accordance with "the objective of sustainable development." Because protecting and preserving the environment requires some degree of extraterritorial jurisdiction, national and foreign goods must be covered by the exceptions.[217] Not using tools of extraterritoriality would, in the case of environmental protection, be tantamount to undermining the very object and purpose of the GATT. Preambular language hence indicates that articles XX(b) and (g) GATT apply extraterritorially.

A *teleological* approach interprets members' rights and obligations based on the object and purpose of the treaty (article 31 para. 1 VCLT). The purpose of article XX is to allow high-ranking social goals to trump trade norms. Because endangered species—whether migratory or domestic—can only be protected by measures that reach across the border, the teleological interpretation suggests that article XX(g) GATT must be applied extraterritorially.[218] A teleological reading of article XX(b) GATT seems to point to a different conclusion. It does not seem reasonable that members should be able to protect the life or health of animals outside their territory. However, globalization makes it necessary that even if members solely focus on protecting humans, animals, and plants' life and health within their territory, they would have to rely on extraterritorial laws. For instance, to stop avian influenza from spreading across domestic territory and threatening the life and health of people and domestic birds, a state will need to pass import restrictions, as indirect extraterritorial means with extraterritorial ancillary repercussions.

Treaty language may also be interpreted by taking into account any *subsequent agreement or practices* between members, pursuant to article 31 para. 3 lit. a and b VCLT. Since the objective of article XX(g) GATT is to protect animal species, it is tempting to resort to international conservation treaties, as done in *Shrimp/Turtle*.[219] But Stohner and others argue that conservation treaties may not be used to interpret the GATT's scope, based on the VCLT.[220] In the context of article XX(b) GATT, by contrast, all agreements dealing with sanitary and phytosanitary measures can be used to interpret the norm. The SPS thus forms *lex specialis* to article XX(b) GATT. Article 1 para. D of Annex A of the SPS allows measures to protect animal life or health within the territory of members and, additionally, measures that prevent or limit sanitary or phytosanitary damage within the territory, but which potentially

---

216 *US—Gasoline*, AB Report, 18.

217 STOHNER 34 (2006).

218 As Conrad argues in this context, extraterritorial jurisdiction is necessary because protecting endangered species is a common good: CONRAD 299 (2011).

219 In *Shrimp/Turtle*, the AB referred to CITES, but it did so only to determine the level of endangerment faced by turtles: *Shrimp/Turtle I*, AB Report ¶ 132.

220 JAN NEUMANN, DIE KOORDINATION DES WTO-RECHTS MIT ANDEREN VÖLKERRECHTLICHEN ORDNUNGEN: KONFLIKTE DES MATERIELLEN RECHTS UND KONKURRENZEN DER STREITBEILEGUNG 336 (2002); PUTH 185 (2003); STOHNER 35 (2006).

arises from animals found abroad. By permitting these measures, the SPS suggests that article XX(b) GATT can be used to indirectly protect animals abroad.

A *public international law* interpretation pursuant to article 31 para. 2 lit. c VCLT demands that the GATT be interpreted by considering "[a]ny relevant rules of international law applicable in relations between the parties." In this context, international treaties on environmental protection and conservation of species can guide us in interpreting article XX(g) GATT.[221] Conservation treaties like CITES, for example, express the parties' desire to give animal protection preference over trade rules,[222] and make it unlikely that trade laws indirectly protecting animals abroad will be declared invalid.

Using a *historical* interpretation (article 32 VCLT), Stohner argues that the explicit reference to extraterritoriality in the treaty negotiations of 1947 and the fact that article XX GATT was not thereafter limited to domestic territory speak for its broad application.[223] Other scholars argue that the parties were not concerned with extraterritoriality.[224] However, the rights and obligations of members are not set in stone but must be interpreted dynamically. In *Shrimp/Turtle*, the AB determined that the treaty language of the GATT is "not 'static' in its content or reference" but is "by definition evolutionary."[225] Since members have lost their ability to effectively protect animals in today's globalized economy, a dynamic interpretation of article XX GATT speaks in favor of its extraterritorial application. As Nollkaemper argues, if a state policy was deemed important enough to pass the primary bar of the exceptions, nothing should discourage a state from pursuing its legitimate policy objective.[226]

In sum, these treaty interpretations lead to mixed results that slightly tip in favor of extraterritorial jurisdiction. Cook and Bowles found that while article XX(g) GATT has overcome territorial limitation, the geographical limits placed on article XX(b) GATT are still unclear.[227] My teleological analysis suggests a more nuanced take on article XX(b) GATT. To protect the life and health of animals found *in* their territory, states must resort to laws with extraterritorial reach. If members seek to protect the life and health of animals found *outside* their territory, however, the results are less clear.

More legal certainty about the territorial scope of article XX(b) GATT might be reached if we consider whether there is a *sufficient nexus* of a jurisdictional norm to a state. In *Shrimp/Turtle*, the AB ruled:

> The sea turtle species here at stake, i.e., covered by Section 609, are all known to occur in waters over which the United States exercises jurisdiction. Of course, it

---

[221] STOHNER 36–42 (2006).

[222] *E.g.*, Convention Relative to the Preservation of Fauna and Flora in their Natural State, Nov. 8, 1933, 172 U.N.T.S. 241, art. 9; CITES, art. III para. 3; African Convention on the Conservation of Nature and Natural Resources, Sept. 15, 1968, 1001 U.N.T.S. 3, art. IX. *See also* Nollkaemper 248 (1996); STOHNER 36–42 (2006).

[223] STOHNER 42 (2006).

[224] CONRAD 303 (2011).

[225] *Shrimp/Turtle I*, AB Report ¶ 130.

[226] Nollkaemper 249 (1996).

[227] Cook & Bowles 235–6 (2010).

is not claimed that all populations of these species migrate to, or traverse, at one time or another, waters subject to United States jurisdiction. [. . .] We do not pass upon the question of whether there is an implied jurisdictional limitation in Article XX(g), and if so, the nature or extent of that limitation. We note only that in the specific circumstances of the case before us, *there is a sufficient nexus between the migratory and endangered marine populations involved and the United States for purposes of Article XX(g).*[228]

According to the AB, the regulating state needs a connection, link, or other relationship to the animals it wants to protect,[229] but neither it nor any panel has clarified the nature of such a connection. Some scholars claim that requiring a sufficient nexus means the measure must effectively achieve the regulatory goal for which it was established. Whether a state can use articles XX(b) and (g) GATT extraterritorially thus depends on whether its measure can prevent resource exploitation or unnecessary animal suffering.[230] From a public international perspective, however, this argument is flawed. If the legality of a measure is determined by whether it reaches its regulatory goal, enforcement jurisdiction could remedy excessive prescriptive jurisdiction. An alternative proposal could be that by introducing the term "jurisdictional nexus," the AB tentatively suggested the answer to the problem lies in public international law. The AB, however, has not (yet) taken this route, or explicitly denounced it.[231] In either case, the potential requirement of a "sufficient nexus" is very vague. Below, I offer a jurisdictional analysis that helps resolve this dilemma.

III. Jurisdictional Analysis of Articles XX(b) and (g) GATT

My earlier analysis of the interplay between public international law and trade law showed that the customary doctrine of jurisdiction serves as a basis for interpreting the territorial scope of WTO law.[232] From a jurisdictional perspective, the starting point for resolving any conflict is to determine which parts of a norm are anchor points (or jurisdictional links) and which are regulated content.[233]

Article XX(g) GATT allows members to keep trade-restrictive measures in place if they are necessary to protect exhaustible natural resources. The regulatory tools members use to do so are indirect extraterritorial. For example, the United States' import ban of shrimp harvested in a manner that endangered turtles does not per se protect exhaustible natural resources

---

[228] *Shrimp/Turtle I*, AB Report ¶ 133 (emphasis altered).

[229] Conrad similarly argues that a scholarly consensus on the legality of PPMs might be limited to PPMs "applied with a jurisdictional link, such as the territorial link underlying the measures in the *Shrimp Turtle* dispute due to the nature of the turtles at issue as a migratory species." (CONRAD 30 (2011)).

[230] Aline Schuster, Trade and the Environment: The Legality of Unilateral Measures with Extraterritorial Effect to Protect the Environment under the WTO/GATT 36 (Minor Dissertation, University of Cape Town 2012).

[231] *Shrimp/Turtle I*, AB Report ¶ 133.

[232] *See* Chapter 3, §2 F. I. Bartels and Conrad also argue that customary international law should be used to clarify the extraterritoriality debate in trade law: Bartels 354 (2002); CONRAD 305 (2011).

[233] Or in Conrad's words, the exceptions of article XX GATT have different objects of protection and different behaviors they target (CONRAD 282 (2011)).

(turtles), or force persons abroad to refrain from endangering them. This is the purpose of conservation treaties. Instead, the norm allows the United States to restrict trade in shrimp if this is necessary to protect its public from unknowingly participating in endangering turtles. The norm applies at the point of importation (there is an intraterritorial anchor point) and aims to free the domestic market from products threatening endangered species (so content regulation is intraterritorial). Turtles found abroad may or may not benefit from this measure, but if they do, this is only an ancillary effect of the norm (i.e., it is an extraterritorial ancillary repercussion).

Article XX(b) GATT allows trade measures to violate the GATT if necessary to protect the life and health of humans, animals, and plants (though here I am concerned only with animals). Article XX(b) GATT also applies when the product is imported (so the anchor point is intraterritorial). The desired consequence is not to eradicate or prevent diseases (which is the purpose of international treaties like the terrestrial or aquatic codes of the World Organization for Animal Health [OIE]). Instead, it protects nationals and domestic animals from diseases imported or about to be imported (so content regulation is intraterritorial). If animals abroad are indirectly protected by this measure, the norm has extraterritorial ancillary repercussions.

In sum, the primary goal of states invoking articles XX(b) or (g) GATT is to regulate content in their territory. Because there is intraterritorial content regulation, laws issued on the basis of these articles are not extraterritorial *stricto sensu*. As Howse and Regan explain:

> To be sure, whether a particular product may be imported depends on what has previously happened to it outside the border. But nothing that has happened outside the border attracts, for itself, any criminal or civil sanction. Foreign producers can use whatever processes they want, and use them with impunity. The only thing they cannot do is bring products produced with certain processes into the country.[234]

That trade measures adopted on the basis of articles XX(b) and (g) GATT are only indirect extraterritorial suggests that they should be more readily considered legal than norms regulating actions abroad. One could object that measures ought to have no extraterritorial reach, direct or indirect. But trade-restrictive measures that have some effect abroad are not automatically illegal under trade law. In *Shrimp/Turtle*, the AB recognized the need to give articles XX(b) and (g) GATT some extraterritorial reach because exceptions constituted legitimate and important deviations from trade obligations:

> It is not necessary to assume that requiring from exporting countries compliance with, or adoption of, certain policies (although covered in principle by one or another of the exceptions) prescribed by the importing country, renders a measure *a priori* incapable of justification under Article XX. *Such an interpretation renders most, if not all, of the*

---

[234] Howse & Regan 274 (2000).

> *specific exceptions of Article XX inutile*, a result abhorrent to the principles of interpretation we are bound to apply.[235]

IV. General Treaty Analysis of Article XX(a) GATT

The interpretative instruments of articles 31 ff. VCLT also influence the question of whether article XX(a) GATT allows states to indirectly protect animals on foreign soil. Article XX(a) GATT does not expressly set a jurisdictional limit to public morals, so the *grammatical* interpretation is of little help.[236] As the analysis of articles XX(b) and (g) GATT showed, the *systematic* interpretation that takes into account a norm's surrounding suggests that the exceptions of article XX GATT apply both intra- and extraterritorially, i.e., it leads to ambiguous results. *Subsequent agreements* and agreements or instruments concluded by the parties in connection with the GATT do not exist for article XX(a) GATT.[237]

A *historical* interpretation of article XX(a) GATT mandates that we examine some of the earliest trade treaties, like the 1921 Agreement Concluded between the Delegates of the Kingdom of Italy and the Kingdom of the Serbs, Croats and Slovenes, Regarding a Draft Convention for the Regulation of Fishing in the Adriatic, and the 1935 International Convention Concerning the Transit of Animals, Meat and Other Products of Animal Origin. These treaties provided that inhumanely caught fish (particularly if they were caught by explosives) and improperly loaded or unsuitably fed animals would not be granted permission to enter any of the parties' territory.[238] Considerations of morality and rectitude have therefore already a century ago prompted states to adopt trade restrictions to indirectly protect animals abroad, which speaks in favor of their legality under current law.[239]

Interpreting the provision in *teleological* terms shows that XX(a) GATT does not protect animals but instead, it protects moral beliefs about how animals ought to be treated. From an ethical perspective, moral beliefs about the treatment of animals do not change simply because production occurs abroad.[240] Article XX(a) GATT is uniquely anchored by focusing on the prevailing sentiments of a nation, regardless of whether these beliefs have extraterritorial reach. The AB appears to have concurred on this point in the *Seals* case, by holding that the European Union's seal regime contributed to its objective of protecting seals by reducing the global demand for seal products.[241] Levy and Regan describe article XX(a) GATT's unique position in the extraterritoriality debate:

> The oddity of the claim of moral offense in *EC-Seals* is that there is very little natural limitation to its reach. It reaches across boundaries, but requires no international

---

[235] *Shrimp/Turtle I*, AB Report ¶ 121 (emphasis altered).

[236] Stevenson 138 (2002).

[237] Charnovitz 701–2 (1998).

[238] Agreement Concluded between the Delegates of the Kingdom of Italy and the Kingdom of the Serbs, Croats and Slovenes, Regarding a Draft Convention for the Regulation of Fishing in the Adriatic, Sept. 14, 1921, 19 L.N.T.S. 39, 51, art. 28; International Convention Concerning the Transit of Animals, Meat and Other Products of Animal Origin, Feb. 20, 1935, 193 L.N.T.S. 39, 45, art. 5.

[239] Charnovitz 713 (1998).

[240] STOHNER 93 (2006).

[241] *Seals*, AB Report ¶ 5.289. The European Union declared in another context: "The concern for animal welfare goes beyond the EU's borders, and the EU considers that taking account of this issue is an aspect of

consensus. The principal test for legitimacy of a "public morals" claim under GATT Article XX(a) seemed to be the sincerity of public sentiment.[242]

Au fond, the AB report speaks for the following conclusion: article XX(a) GATT protects citizens' public morals, which are territorially anchored. These morals can refer to conditions that exist outside the territory of the regulating state, and the fact that import prohibitions have repercussions in foreign states does not preclude their legality under the GATT.[243] That article XX(a) GATT has extraterritorial ancillary effects is accepted because denying it would inevitably force countries into a race to the bottom. Adopting an internal ban on cruel practices, without imposing an import ban on products derived from the same practices, would put domestic producers at a market disadvantage since ethically produced goods are known to cost more.[244] As a result, domestic markets would be swamped with less expensive products produced under lax conditions.

These dynamics have been observed worldwide. For example, in 1999, the United Kingdom banned gestation crates and tethers, which increased the cost of domestically produced pig products. As a consequence, imports of products that used systems illegal in the United Kingdom rose by 77 percent, and it became impossible, politically and economically, to uphold the domestic ban.[245] Similar events took place in Sweden around 2013,[246] and in the European Union around 2007, when it prohibited battery cages in egg production but failed to adopt an import ban for eggs produced in the same manner.[247] In these cases, "consumers are supplied with the very products they charged their government with regulating,"[248] as Thomas notes. Refusing to apply the exceptions extraterritorially produces adverse effects on domestic levels of animal welfare, because better animal welfare regulations are discouraged, and lax laws are given priority. Because of such regulatory impasses, 62 percent of EU residents now demand that imported products at least conform to domestic minimum standards.[249]

---

added value in international trade" (European Commission, The Common Agricultural Policy (CAP) and Agriculture in Europe, Press Release (Brussels, June 26, 2013)).

[242] Philipp I. Levy & Donald H. Regan, *EC—Seal Products* (TBT Aspects of the Panel and Appellate Body Reports): Seals and Sensibilities, Robert Schuman Centre for Advanced Studies Research Paper No. 2014/108, 10.

[243] Because of its focus on territorially anchored morals, article XX(a) GATT is considered less problematic in terms of its extraterritorial reach than articles XX(b) and (g) GATT: Offer & Walter 161 (2017).

[244] Kelch 260 (2011). EU policy debates show these products are likely to be replaced by imports produced at lower standards: EC Proposal, Animal Welfare and Trade in Agriculture (2000), *supra* note 118.

[245] Mick Sloyan, An Analysis of Pork and Pork Products Imported into the United Kingdom 3, 9 (British Pig Executive [BPEX], London 2006).

[246] Gerard O'Dwyer, *Swedish Pig Farmers Call for State Support*, Global Meat News, Mar. 3, 2014.

[247] Under the common free trade agreement (FTA), the European Union was forced to import battery cage eggs from Ukraine, which frustrated the objectives of its public morality: Jan Grossarth, *Käfig-Eier aus der Ukraine*, Frankfurter Allgemeine, June 13, 2013.

[248] Thomas 609 (2007).

[249] Most Europeans strongly agree that imported products from outside the European Union should respect the same levels of animal welfare as those in the European Union (62 percent "totally agree"): European

From a policy perspective, this argument makes sense. As stated in *Shrimp/Turtle*, the exceptions of article XX GATT represent a legitimate concern of states and allow them to put issues that are of high importance to them over trade liberalization.[250] Some might argue that the WTO cannot authorize one state to interfere in another state's domestic affairs, but trade restrictions almost never impinge on a state's domestic affairs. These states are free to keep in place or adopt lower standards; they will simply be restricted from exporting certain products to certain countries. By contrast, declaring extraterritorial jurisdiction illegal in trade law would ignore that states have legitimate interests in maintaining regulatory authority over affairs integral to their public morality. This, ultimately, would violate the very purpose of article XX GATT. The *teleological* interpretation hence mandates that article XX(a) GATT be used to indirectly protect animals abroad.

V. Jurisdictional Analysis of Article XX(a) GATT

From a jurisdictional perspective, article XX(a) GATT does not protect animals per se, but it protects *concerns about animals*.[251] The object to be protected (public morals) is always on domestic territory because that is the home of a state's public. The purpose of the norm is to prevent goods from being offered for purchase on domestic territory that were produced in a manner the public deems immoral (there is intraterritorial content regulation). The norm is not intended to ensure the humane treatment of animals abroad. Conrad argues: "The primary motivation for the non-physical product aspects trade measure is [. . .] not an actual change of the violating situation, but the prevention of any direct or indirect participation or contribution by the country the moral standards of which are violated and its population."[252] The norm only takes effect when goods enter a state at the point of importation (the norm has an intraterritorial anchor point). If animals located on foreign territory profit from this measures, they are only ancillary beneficiaries of these concerns. Overall, article XX(a) GATT uses intraterritorial anchor points, regulates content within territory, but has extraterritorial ancillary repercussions.

Because its content regulation is always territorial, Feddersen and Stohner argue that all measures that fall within the scope of public morals of article XX(a) GATT have the necessary connection to domestic territory.[253] If public morals are violated, "this society will disapprove of any such cruelty regardless of where it occurs and regardless of the nationality of the persons involved."[254] Foreign producers do not have a right to sell all their products on domestic markets since this would violate the state's right to prioritize public morals over

---

Commission, Special Eurobarometer 442 Report: Attitudes of Europeans towards Animal Welfare 4 (2016).

[250] Free trade, in other words, should not overrule all other policy concerns: *Shrimp/Turtle I*, AB Report ¶ 121. *See also* Paul Richli & Claudia Ruf, Wieviel Tierschutz erlaubt das GATT? 38 (1995).

[251] Robert Howse et al., *Pluralism in Practice: Moral Legislation and the Law of the WTO After* Seal Products, 48 Geo. Wash. Int'l L. Rev. 81, 125 (2015); Offer & Walter 165 (2017).

[252] Conrad 327 (2011). *See* analogously, Chapter 3, §2 F. III.

[253] Christoph T. Feddersen, Der *ordre public* in der WTO, Auslegung und Bedeutung des Art. XX lit. a) GATT im Rahmen der WTO-Streitbeilegung 266–7 (2002); Stohner 93 (2006).

[254] Conrad 325–6 (2011). In other words, for article XX(a) GATT, "the relevance of the substance of public policies outweighs questions of geographical location." (*Id.* at 309).

economic laissez-faire. The only values not protected by article XX(a) GATT are public morals located outside the territory of a regulating state, as this would amount to extraterritorial content regulation.

The reach of the public morals exceptions is admittedly broad, but there are two reasons why concern about protectionism is unjustified. First, the *chapeau* clause excludes measures that unjustifiably discriminate. Second, only fundamental values of public morality are protected by article XX(a) GATT. The more intensely a nation is dedicated to protecting animals or ensuring interspecies justice, the more its trade measures are justified under article XX(a) GATT.[255]

§3 Interim Conclusion

For decades, scholars have debated whether the WTO promotes global welfare—as it claims to do—or whether it thwarts it by perpetuating poverty and polluting the environment. Among trade law experts, there is a persistent claim that international trade law possesses "enormous potential as a tool to tackle [. . .] global problems successfully."[256] The negative effects of globalization on the interests of animals, however, are not typically seen as part of these global problems, and this explains why the question of whether animal law is rendered toothless by trade law is of little concern to most scholars in trade law. They see animal law as contradicting the WTO's declared goal of liberalizing trade, so it is *prima facie* difficult to make the case that norms geared to protect animals, but which have some effect on trade, are legal under WTO law.

This chapter has shed light on the conflicts that have emerged at the intersection of animal law and trade law, and developed strategies to tackle them. I first clarified the nature of trade-restrictive laws in the extraterritoriality framework. Animal law that limits trade is not extraterritorial jurisdiction *stricto sensu* but a means for states to protect their people from being exposed to products they deem abhorrent. Foreign producers can either respect the importing state's preference or offer their products for sale elsewhere. Even when producers change their production methods—and hence improve the welfare of animals abroad—these effects are only ancillary. Animal law that restricts trade qualifies as indirect extraterritorial jurisdiction because it aims to protect the public from being exposed to products that produce and reproduce animal cruelty. Whether foreign producers actually change their practices is beyond its reach.

The means available to indirectly protect foreign animals include labels, taxes, tariffs, and quantitative restrictions. Under the GATT, the most powerful tools are import restrictions

---

[255] For example, the Swiss Constitution protects the dignity of animals, so trade measures that aim to protect the essence of this constitutional principle will likely pass the public morals test: PETER KREPPER, ZUR WÜRDE DER KREATUR IN GENTECHNIK UND RECHT: THESEN ZUM GENTECHNISCHEN UMGANG MIT TIEREN IN DER SCHWEIZ UNTER BERÜCKSICHTIGUNG DES INTERNATIONALEN RECHTSUMFELDS 411 (1998); NEUMANN 141 (2002); STOHNER 129–30 (2006); HANS RUDOLF TRÜEB, UMWELTRECHT IN DER WTO: STAATLICHE REGULIERUNGEN IM KONTEXT DES INTERNATIONALEN HANDELSRECHTS 432 (2001).

[256] CONRAD 1 (2011).

or bans on, e.g., cruelly produced eggs, meat, or dairy. In WTO law, it is debatable if they are subject to the national treatment obligation of article III GATT (in which case the PPM debate will determine the measure's legality) or subject to the obligation to eliminate quantitative restrictions under article XI GATT (in which case the GATT is, as a rule, violated). Treaty law, Note Ads, panel reports, and scholarly opinions all suggest that import bans must be analyzed under article III GATT. Assuming this is the case, the treaty language and an evolutionary interpretation of article III GATT demonstrate that PPMs must be declared legal, or, alternatively, justifiable under WTO law. In addition to import restrictions, members can, in certain circumstances, apply differentiated tariffs to products depending on how animals were treated during the production process.

When using any of these measures, members likely violate the GATT because its provisions are very technical and broad (they tackle both *de jure* and *de facto* discrimination). States can invoke the general exception of article XX GATT as a justification. Article XX(g) GATT allows indirectly protecting animals who are viewed as natural resources, as was done in *Shrimp/Turtle*. The narrow focus of article XX(g) GATT on conservation, however, renders it insufficient for the purposes of animal law. Article XX(g) GATT leaves most animals (namely, those who are not endangered or threatened) unprotected. For many years, article XX(b) GATT, which protects animal health, was therefore thought to be the primary exception for states concerned with protecting animals. In this context, the debate has emerged whether animal health also encompasses animal welfare. Most scholars find that only to the extent animal welfare laws are conducive to an animal's clinical state of health, can article XX(b) GATT protect their welfare. This position—and in fact the entire animal health versus animal welfare debate—ignores the overwhelming scientific evidence that the well-being of animals is inextricably tied to their health. Since the *Seals* case, the public morals exception of article XX(a) GATT has therefore become the primary tool of states to declare admissible trade restrictions geared to protect animals.

Of special concern to this chapter was the territorial scope of these exceptions. Case law on this question is contradictory and scholarly opinion is divided, so a more expansive analysis was required, using treaty interpretation and the doctrine of jurisdiction. For articles XX(b) and (g) GATT, the *general treaty analysis* has produced mixed results that slightly tip in favor of extraterritoriality. Indirect extraterritorial measures are legal under article XX(g) GATT, but the geographical limits of article XX(b) GATT are still disputed. *The jurisdictional analysis* showed that both articles XX(b) and (g) GATT should not be territorially restricted. These articles use an intraterritorial anchor point (i.e., they apply at the time of importation), and regulate content intraterritorially (by ensuring that products that endanger exhaustible natural resources or threaten animal life and health do not enter domestic territory).

Article XX(a) GATT allows states to respond to concerns about animals, rather than protecting animals per se. From a *jurisdictional perspective*, animal laws relying on the exception regulate content intraterritorially by ensuring that domestic consumers are not exposed to products they deem abhorrent. These laws have an intraterritorial anchor point, by preventing products at the border from entering domestic territory. This is supported by the *general treaty analysis* of article XX(a) GATT. From a teleological perspective, public morality about production methods does not change simply because production takes place abroad. In *Seals*, the AB concurred on this point, declaring legal measures that were essentially concerned with the global reduction of seal suffering. If the public morals exception cannot be invoked to justify trade measures that have an ancillary effect on animals abroad, this has far-reaching consequences. States cannot live up to their people's ethical convictions solely by banning cruel practices without adopting an import ban on products derived from the same cruel practices. Their markets will be swamped by less costly products manufactured at low-welfare levels, making their efforts to offer high-welfare products politically and economically untenable. Ultimately, declaring indirect extraterritorial trade measures illegal would bereave states of their regulatory authority to prioritize public morality over economic laissez-faire.[257] These consequences are disproportionately harmful compared to the ancillary effects of indirect extraterritorial norms, which leave foreign producers with plenty of options to redirect or remarket their products. As the treaty and jurisdictional analyses showed, there are no legal or conceptual grounds to prevent states from indirectly protecting animals abroad by invoking article XX(a) GATT.

The findings of this chapter are comparatively detailed and the developments at the interface of animal law, trade law, and the law of jurisdiction require a final analysis and broad assessment. Following my analysis of the extraterritorial reach of the Agreement on Technical Barriers to Trade (TBT), the Agreement on the Application of Sanitary and Phytosanitary Measures (SPS), the Anti-Dumping Agreement (ADA), the Agreement on Agriculture (AoA), and the Special Treatment Clause, I will take a bird's-eye view on these developments and speculate about future trends.

---

[257] In the context of antitrust law, Pieter J. Kuyper, *European Community Law and Extraterritoriality: Some Trends and New Developments*, 33 ICLQ 1013, 1015 (1984), argues that states have to accept that their failure to regulate is used "as a hatching-ground for cartels." ANDREAS V. LOWE, EXTRATERRITORIAL JURISDICTION: AN ANNOTATED COLLECTION OF LEGAL MATERIALS 4 (1984) refers to US Attorney General Griffin Bell, who asserted that not applying domestic antitrust law across the border would mean that "values of others, alien to our own values, will be forced upon us in our territory." Radford argues that unlimited trade imposes low or nonexistent standards on importing states: RADFORD 137 (2001).

4 The Ignored: Indirect Protection through the TBT, the SPS, the ADA, the AoA, and the Special Treatment Clause

THE GENERAL AGREEMENT on Tariffs and Trade (GATT) is the default agreement to which scholars turn when they examine the animal law versus trade law debate. But the GATT is only one of several agreements a state must comply with when it passes or uses animal laws that affect trade. Case reports of the DSB make clear that trade agreements other than the GATT are increasingly relevant in litigation. Because the bulk of scholarly work is focused on GATT, little is known about whether and to what extent a state's animal laws pass the scrutiny of the Agreement on Technical Barriers to Trade (TBT), the Agreement on the Application of Sanitary and Phytosanitary Measures (SPS), the Anti-Dumping Agreement (ADA), the Agreement on Agriculture (AoA), and the Special Treatment Clause. Indirect extraterritorial jurisdiction under the TBT is relevant for animal law because both animal-welfare labels and import restrictions could qualify as technical barriers to trade and could, therefore, violate the TBT. The SPS raises the fraught dispute in animal law whether sanitary and phytosanitary measures cover animal welfare concerns. This debate has a bearing on the discretion of states to use the SPS to protect animals by indirect extraterritorial means. Under the ADA, it is necessary to examine how members can appropriately react to instances of animal welfare dumping. Because most animals and animal products qualify as agricultural products, the legality of indirect extraterritorial measures under the AoA must also be determined. Finally, we need to get a sense of when the Special Treatment Clause enables states to indirectly improve the welfare of animals situated abroad by giving preference to products from the majority world that observe high levels of animal protection.

Gaining legal certainty about the territorial limits of these agreements will enable us to assess trade law from a broader perspective, by evaluating the aggregate effects of all trade

Protecting Animals Within and Across Borders. Charlotte E. Blattner.

treaties on efforts to protect animals. This is what I do in the final part of this chapter. By answering these questions, we can make a reliable determination of how trade law can be used in an age of globalized animal production, and venture a look into the future.

§1 Agreement on Technical Barriers to Trade (TBT)

Since its inception, the WTO's foremost goal has been to liberalize trade, and the measures it adopted to achieve this have chiefly focused on eliminating and reducing the most obvious trade barriers. As negotiation rounds, new agreements, and processes of quasi-adjudication felled many of these barriers, the WTO's gaze slowly shifted toward nontariff barriers to trade. Nontariff barriers are different from tariff barriers because they are more difficult to identify and eliminate. The main agreement the WTO adopted in response to these challenges is the TBT, which deals with technical regulations, standards, and conformity assessment procedures. The TBT represents a paradigm shift in the set of competences assigned to the WTO. Rather than simply prohibiting certain measures (as previous agreements did), the TBT determines which laws states are allowed to uphold. Thereby, the powers of the WTO have expanded incrementally and transformed it from a nondiscriminatory model to a regulatory model.[1]

But different from what could be implied by that, the TBT does not aim to prohibit technical regulations. In its preamble, it recognizes that no country should be prevented from taking measures necessary to ensure the protection of human, animal, or plant life or health, the environment, or from preventing deceptive practices "at the levels it considers appropriate." States remain capable of pursuing legitimate policy objectives on to their own terms, as long as doing so does not amount to an abuse of their rights under WTO law.[2] In essence, the TBT is focused on eradicating arbitrary and unjustifiable discrimination in technical regulations.

When a state is accused of having violated the TBT, it cannot assume that it is cleared of other charges. A state may still violate the GATT because the two agreements are not mutually exclusive and there is no presumption that TBT-consistent measures are also GATT-consistent.[3] The SPS, in contrast, is considered *lex specialis* to the TBT. TBT measures that regulate or relate to diseases carried by plants or animals are subject to the SPS. The TBT covers all other cases, including most human disease controls (diseases not carried by animals or plants), labeling requirements, nutrition claims, and quality and packaging regulations.[4]

---

[1] Michael Ming Du, *Domestic Regulatory Autonomy under the TBT Agreement: From Non-discrimination to Harmonization*, 6 CHINESE J. INT'L L. 269, 274, 297 (2007).

[2] PETER L. FITZGERALD, INTERNATIONAL ISSUES IN ANIMAL LAW: THE IMPACT OF INTERNATIONAL ENVIRONMENTAL AND ECONOMIC LAW UPON ANIMAL INTERESTS AND ADVOCACY 207–8 (2012).

[3] *Asbestos*, Panel Report ¶ 8.16. The General Interpretative Note to Annex 1A of the WTO Agreement determines that the TBT will prevail over the GATT to the extent of conflict.

[4] WTO, Understanding the WTO, Agreement on Sanitary and Phytosanitary Measures (WTO, Geneva 2019), *available at* https://www.wto.org/english/tratop_e/sps_e/spsund_e.htm (last visited Jan. 10, 2019) [Understanding the WTO, SPS].

A. SCOPE OF THE TBT

There are three trade measures the TBT is concerned with: technical regulations, standards (articles 2–4 TBT), and conformity assessment procedures (articles 5–9 TBT). Article 1 Annex 1 TBT identifies four types of technical regulations: documents that mandate compliance with specified product characteristics; documents that mandate compliance with related processes and production; documents that mandate compliance with applicable administrative provisions; and documents that designate terminology, symbols, packaging, marking or labeling requirements as they apply to a product, process, or production method.

In *EC—Asbestos*, the AB established a three-tiered definition of *technical regulation* subsequently used in *EC—Sardines*. It determined that a document (i) must apply to an identifiable product or group of products, (ii) must lay down one or more characteristics of the product, and (iii) must comply with the characteristics.[5] It defined characteristics as "any objectively definable 'features', 'qualities', 'attributes', or other 'distinguishing mark' of a product."[6] Product labels that feature information about how animals are bred, raised, kept, treated, or slaughtered during the production process, are often thought to fit the three-tiered definition of *EC—Asbestos*, and, hence, to constitute a technical regulation under the TBT.[7]

Article 2 Annex 1 TBT defines *standards* subject to the agreement. Standards refer to documents "for common and repeated use, rules, guidelines or characteristics for products or related processes and production methods" with which compliance is *not* mandatory. Standards may also include or deal exclusively with terminology, symbols, packaging, marking, or labeling requirements as they apply to a product, process, or production method. Article 3 of Annex 1 TBT, finally, provides that *conformity assessment procedures* include any "procedure used, directly or indirectly, to determine that relevant requirements in technical regulations or standards are fulfilled."[8]

Labels and import restrictions are often suspected of violating the TBT, but this is only possible if they qualify as TBT measures in the first place. Labeling schemes may be binding or voluntary, depending on their regulatory environment. Labels tend to be voluntary in the North American region, whereas European states frequently declare labeling duties mandatory in order to increase consumers' access to information about production processes. Council Directive 2007/43/EC, which determines minimum standards for chickens used for meat production, called for a

> [...] report on the possible introduction of a specific harmonised *mandatory* labelling scheme at Community level for chicken meat, meat products and preparations based on compliance with animal welfare standards, including the possible socio-economic

---

[5] *Asbestos*, AB Report ¶¶ 61, 68. *See also* Appellate Body Report, *EC—Trade Description of Sardines*, ¶¶ 176 ff., WTO Doc. WT/DS231/AB/R (adopted Oct. 23, 2002).

[6] *Asbestos*, AB Report ¶ 67.

[7] Fitzgerald 98 (2011).

[8] TBT, Annex 1.3.

> implications, the effects on the Community's economic partners and compliance of such a labelling scheme with World Trade Organization rules.[9]

The labeling scheme the European Union planned at that time qualifies as a "document laying down products' related process and production methods, with which compliance is mandatory," in the meaning of article 1 Annex 1 TBT, so it is a technical regulation. Even when a state establishes a labeling scheme that is voluntary, the way it is implemented or applied can render it compulsory. In other words, standards can be mandatory *de jure* and *de facto*. For instance, the dolphin-safe labeling standards subject to review in *Tuna/Dolphin III* were classified by the panel as a technical regulation (pursuant to article 1 Annex 1 TBT). Although the United States asserted that its labels were voluntary and should thus qualify as a standard, the AB found that its labeling scheme included administrative provisions that prescribed in a broad and exhaustive manner the conditions under which an assertion of "dolphin-safety" could be made.[10] The US measures were *de facto* mandatory and thus a technical regulation. Against the background of the PPM debate discussed earlier in the context of the GATT, it is also important to note that sentence two of article 1 Annex 1 TBT explicitly covers labels whether they relate to physical product properties or PPMs.[11] The PPMs envisaged by Council Directive 2007/43/EC, therefore, qualify as a technical regulation.

Import prohibitions, by contrast, are not clearly a technical regulation, especially if they use PPMs. According to scholars, article 1 Annex 1 TBT and its reference to "their related processes and production methods," determines that a PPM must have a sufficient nexus to the characteristics of a product to be considered "related" to it.[12] The addendum "their related" limits the scope of PPMs to those that manifest as physical differences in product characteristics (i.e., PR-PPMs).[13] This view is supported by the *travaux préparatoires*. During the Uruguay Negotiation Rounds, Mexico proposed to add "their related" to article 1 Annex 1 TBT to narrow the coverage of the TBT to a subset of PPMs.[14] But scholars argue that the WTO DSB rarely relies on *travaux préparatoires* and is more likely to include all kinds of PPMs (including non-product-related PPMs [NPR-PPMs]) because the measures in question would otherwise only be subject to the GATT.[15] By broadly interpreting article 1

---

[9] Council Directive 2007/43/EC Laying Down Minimum Standards for the Protection of Chickens Kept for Meat Production, 2007 O.J. (L 182) 19, at 13 (emphasis added).

[10] *Tuna/Dolphin III*, AB Report ¶ 199.

[11] WTO, Labelling and Requirements of the Agreement on Technical Barriers to Trade (TBT): Framework for Informal Structured Discussions, Communication from Canada, WTO Doc. WT/CTEV/229, June 23, 2003, para 6.

[12] Ming Du, *What Is a "Technical Regulation" in the TBT Agreement?*, 6 Eur. J. Risk Reg. 396, 400–1 (2015).

[13] OECD Secretariat, Processes and Production Methods (PPMs): Conceptual Framework and Considerations on Use of PPM-Based Trade Measures, OECD/GD (97) 137, 11 (1997); Conrad 381 (2011).

[14] WTO Secretariat, Negotiating History of the Coverage of the Agreement on Technical Barriers to Trade with Regard to Labeling Requirements, Voluntary Standards, and Processes and Production Methods Unrelated to Product Characteristics, WTO Doc. WT/CTE/W/10, Aug. 29, 1995, para. 146.

[15] Conrad 386 (2011); Du 402 (2015).

Annex 1 TBT, the WTO will be able to cover as many measures as possible to prevent any likely restriction of trade.

This view is supported by state practice. In *Tuna/Dolphin III*, the US law that laid down how tuna must be fished in order to be sold and marketed within its territory qualified as a technical regulation.[16] The law did not alter the physical components or appearance of tuna; hence, it was an NPR-PPM. *Tuna/Dolphin III* therefore suggests that the TBT covers all kinds of PPMs. The *Seals* case is sometimes said to have dealt with NPR-PPMs, as well. The panel, however, after noting that the phrase "their related processes and production methods" of article 1 Annex 1 TBT had never before been examined by the AB, held that the EU ban laid down a product characteristic "in the negative form by requiring that all products not contain seal."[17] The AB was more critical and reversed the panel's finding:

> Although the administrative provisions under the EU Seal Regime "apply" to products containing seal, this does not, in our view, mean that the measure at issue amounts to a technical regulation for that reason alone. Rather, as we see it, the administrative provisions serve to identify the exempted products, *through the type and purpose of the relevant seal hunt, and the identity of the hunter*. [... W]hen viewed together with the exceptions under the EU Seal Regime, we consider that this aspect of the measure is ancillary, and does not render the measure a "technical regulation" within the meaning of Annex 1.1.[18]

Characterizing the measure as hunter-based instead of process-based allowed the DSB to sidestep the fraught question of whether technical regulations under the TBT include those laying down NPR-PPMs. It is to be hoped that the DSB will provide more guidance on this point in the future. Until this happens, any state anticipating litigation must assume that all types of PPMs qualify as a technical regulation.[19]

B. ARTICLE 2 TBT

Once a measure that aims to protect animals passes for a technical regulation, it is likely to violate the TBT. Article 2.1 TBT provides that when a member issues technical regulations, it must abide by the most-favored-nation obligation and the national treatment obligation. Animal laws are likely to conflict with the national treatment obligation because they are suspected of unjustifiably protecting domestic products vis-à-vis imported products. The obligation of article 2.1 TBT, namely, that a technical regulation does not accord imported products less favorable treatment than domestic products, hinges on the likeness of domestic and imported products.[20] The concept of likeness is just as important for determining a

---

[16] *Tuna/Dolphin III*, AB Report ¶ 199.

[17] *Seals*, Panel Report ¶¶ 7.103–6.

[18] *Seals*, AB Report ¶ 5.57 (emphasis added).

[19] Du 403 (2015).

[20] Appellate Body Report, *US—Measures Affecting the Production and Sale of Clove Cigarettes*, ¶ 87, WTO Doc. WT/DS406/AB/R (adopted Apr. 14, 2012) [*US—Clove Cigarettes*, AB Report]. Less favorable treatment occurs when the technical regulation in question gives rise to adverse conditions of competition and

violation of the TBT as it is for article III GATT. As a matter of fact, likeness, as defined under article III GATT, is instructive for article 2.1 TBT, even if the two are not conterminous.

In the context of article 2.1 TBT, it is debated if technical regulations may respond to how animals were treated during the production process. The debate, which is decisive for determining whether the TBT is violated, is distinct from the question I examined earlier, namely, if PPMs qualify as technical regulations (i.e., whether the TBT is applicable). In the context of article 2.1 TBT, treaty language is ambiguous. Though Annex 1 TBT mentions "processes and production methods," it is unclear whether the phrase refers to NPR-PPMs or only to PR-PPMs.[21] Some scholars maintain that because Annexes 1.1 and 1.2 of the TBT refer to "product characteristics or related process and production methods," they exclude NPR-PPMs. They argue that the phrase alludes to characteristics and methods related to the product *as such*.[22] Others point to Annex 1.2 TBT, which concerns technical regulations, standards, and conformity assessment procedures "related to products *or processes and production methods*." This phrase, they argue, suggests that NPR-PPMs can be used to determine likeness.[23]

Reports on this debate are sparse, but the few that exist point to the latter interpretation.[24] In *US—Clove Cigarettes*, the AB determined that the Border Tax Report's four-criteria likeness test, developed in the context of the GATT, also applies to the TBT.[25] Among these criteria are consumer tastes and habits, which may justify distinguishing between products based on PPMs. If consumers do not treat cruelly produced animal products identical to "humanely" produced animal products, this means NPR-PPMs may render products unlike. Even members bringing cases to the WTO seem to accept this. For example, in neither *Tuna/Dolphin III* nor *US—COOL* did the applicants argue that NPR-PPMs do not inform the TBT likeness test. In sum, the question of whether NPR-PPMs influence the likeness test of article 2.1 TBT, though disputed, will likely be answered in the positive.

Should "humanely" and "inhumanely" produced products in a given case nonetheless be considered like, one group of products may not be treated less favorably than the other. The AB in *US—Clove Cigarettes* argued article III:4 GATT must be used to clarify the meaning

---

illegitimately discriminates between like products: Gregory Shaffer & David Pabian, *The WTO EC-Seal Products Decision: Animal Welfare, Indigenous Communities and Trade*, 109 AJIL 154 (2015).

21 Negotiations on these issues have been unsuccessful thus far: Committee on Technical Barriers to Trade, Negotiating History of the Coverage of the Agreement on Technical Barriers to Trade with Regard to Labelling Requirements, Voluntary Standards and Process and Production Methods Unrelated to Product Characteristics, Note by the Secretariat, G/TBT/W/11, Aug. 29, 1995.

22 Du 287 (2007).

23 Howse & Regan 96 (2000).

24 In *Seals*, the DSB was also concerned with TBT measures, but the measure of the European Union prohibited seal products per se, rather than inhumanely produced seal products. The AB in *Seals* did not deal with the question of NPR-PPMs, because it held that hunter-based regulations do not constitute PPMs, by which it overruled the panel's prior judgment. Previously, the panel held: "[T]he type or purpose of the seal hunt does not affect in any way the final product's physical characteristics, end-use, or tariff classification. As regards the criterion of consumers' tastes and habits, the complainants presented evidence to demonstrate that, prior to the EU Seal Regime, consumers did not make any distinction between seal products based on the type or purpose of the hunt" (*Seals*, Panel Report ¶¶ 7.138–9).

25 *US—Clove Cigarettes*, AB Report ¶¶ 136 ff.

of the phrase "treatment less favorable" as found in article 2.1 TBT.[26] Treatment less favorable occurs where conditions of competition in the relevant market are modified to the detriment of imported products, which can occur *de jure* or *de facto*.[27] For example, in *Seals*, the panel held that the indigenous communities exception created a *de facto* discrimination against Canada in relation to Greenland, because Greenland produced as many seals in Inuit hunts as Canada did in commercial hunts.[28] This broad interpretation of "treatment less favorable" greatly increases the likelihood the TBT will be violated. However, "treatment less favorable" is interpreted through the sixth recital of the preamble to the TBT, which provides that no country should be prevented from taking measures necessary to protect animal life or health, or the environment. Accordingly, article 2.1 TBT is violated only if, after considering the legitimate regulatory objectives, the measure is still less favorable (similar to article XX GATT).[29]

In addition to duties of nondiscrimination, the TBT stipulates in article 2.2 that technical regulations shall not create unnecessary obstacles to trade. More specifically, technical regulations shall not be more trade restrictive than necessary to fulfill a legitimate objective and must consider the risks of nonfulfillment. Among the legitimate objectives listed in article 2.2 TBT are protecting animal life or health and protecting the environment.[30] In *Seals*, the panel noted that "animal welfare is a matter of ethical responsibility for human beings in general"[31] and accepted it as a legitimate objective of article 2.2 TBT. The panel moreover found that the objectives pursued by the ban were undermined by the indigenous communities exception, which exposed European consumers to inhumanely killed seals and seal products. The EU measure, rather than being excessively trade restrictive, was held to insufficiently protect the values of the European Union. "Fulfilling a legitimate objective," in the sense of article 2.2 TBT, thus means to fully provide what is wished for.

Determining if a measure is more trade restrictive than necessary requires undertaking both a relational and a comparative analysis. The relational analysis, as used in *Tuna/Dolphin III*, considers the contribution a measure makes to the legitimate objective, the extent to which it restricts trade, and the nature of risks created if the measure fails to fulfill the stipulated objective. The comparative analysis, which is done in the next step, considers if there is an alternative measure that makes an equivalent contribution to the objective and is reasonably available, but less trade-restrictive.[32]

---

[26] *US—Clove Cigarettes*, AB Report ¶ 179.

[27] *Korea—Various Measures on Beef*, AB Report ¶ 137.

[28] *Seals*, Panel Report ¶¶ 7.319, 7.353. *See also* Brendan McGivern, *The WTO Seal Product Panel: The "Public Morals" Defense*, 9 Global Trade & Customs J. 70, 71–2 (2014).

[29] *US—Clove Cigarettes*, AB Report ¶¶ 172 ff. *See also* Gabrielle Marceau & Joel P. Trachtman, *The Technical Barriers to Trade Agreement, the Sanitary and Phytosanitary Measures Agreement, and the General Agreement on Tariffs and Trade: A Map of the World Trade Organization Law of Domestic Regulation of Goods*, 36 J. World Trade 811, 872 (2002).

[30] The policy goals of article 2.2 TBT, unlike those of article XX GATT, are only illustrative (the article refers to "inter alia"). *See also* McGivern 72 (2014); Van den Bossche & Zdouc 914 (2017).

[31] *Seals*, Panel Report ¶ 7.409.

[32] *Tuna/Dolphin III*, AB Report ¶¶ 318, 322.

Even if a measure is justified under article 2.2 TBT, it only passes the TBT's scrutiny if the technical regulations issued by a member are based on international standards (article 2.4 TBT). International animal welfare standards, like the Terrestrial and Aquatic Animal Health Codes of the OIE, could qualify as such.[33] Though they are generally instructive for evaluating how animals must be treated, the standards might be too vague and lax for states with well-established levels of animal law. These states can invoke the exception of article 2.4 TBT, which discharges them of the duty to rely on international standards if they are an ineffective or inappropriate means to fulfill their legitimate objective.

C. EXTRATERRITORIAL ANIMAL PROTECTION IN THE TBT

Just as the GATT leaves scope for indirect extraterritorial jurisdiction, WTO members can indirectly protect animals under the TBT. The European Union's regulatory regime for the Registration, Evaluation, Authorisation and Restriction of Chemicals (REACH), which prohibits testing chemical substances on vertebrate animals,[34] is often accused of illegally reaching across the border. In several TBT Committee meetings, representatives of Canada, China, and India expressed their concern about the extraterritorial reach of REACH, arguing that its duties to register, share information, and restrict competition would raise costs for their producers.[35] It is thus necessary to determine if and possibly how the TBT enables members to use TBT measures to indirectly protect animals situated abroad.

In *Seals*, the panel examined whether import restrictions, employed for animal welfare reasons, may reach across state territory under the TBT. The AB reversed the panel's decision to apply the TBT, holding that the import ban on seals and seal products did not constitute a technical regulation, so the TBT did not apply.[36] The panel's finding on the extraterritorial reach of the TBT is nonetheless instructive for our purposes since it is the only DSB report that dealt with the matter. The panel held, first, that public morals constitute a legitimate objective of article 2.2 TBT, and that, second, concerns about seal welfare qualify as public morals, in the meaning of the same article.[37] The panel clarified that it need not determine if these morals "exhibit the existence of a global social norm."[38] In other words, a matter of public morality must not be shared by the global community; it is sufficient that

[33] Note that no organization is yet explicitly recognized as a standard setter under the TBT: Kahn & Varas 7 (2013).

[34] For a general examination of REACH under the TBT, *see* Lawrence A. Kogan, *REACH Revisited: A Framework for Evaluating Whether a Non-Tariff Measure Has Matured into an Actionable Non-Tariff Barrier to Trade*, 28 Am. U. Int'l L. Rev. 489 (2013).

[35] WTO, Committee on Technical Barriers to Trade, Note by the Secretariat: Minutes on the Meeting of 24–25 March 2011, G/TBT/M/53, May 26, 2011, para. 147; WTO, Committee on Technical Barriers to Trade, Note by the Secretariat: Minutes on the Meeting of 3–4 November 2010, G/TBT/M/52, Mar. 10, 2011, para. 89; WTO, Committee on Technical Barriers to Trade, Note by the Secretariat: Minutes on the Meeting of 1 July 2004, G/TBT/M/33, Aug. 31, 2004, para. 45.

[36] *Seals*, AB Report ¶¶ 5.58–9.

[37] *Seals*, Panel Report ¶¶ 7.415–21.

[38] *Id.* ¶ 7.420. The panel continued on this point: "Nevertheless, these various actions concerning animal welfare at the international as well as national levels suggest in our view that animal welfare is a globally recognized issue. This [. . .] supports our conclusion above that the objective of addressing the public moral concerns

the sentiment prevails in the state invoking the public morals exception. Here, it is useful to hark back to our examination of public morals under the GATT, since the exceptions of the GATT and the TBT are broadly identical.[39] Analogous to article XX(a) GATT, article 2.2 TBT protects public morals that prevail in a state (it is an intraterritorial content regulation), which can be concerned with values that rest outside its territory (there are extraterritorial ancillary repercussions). This renders the norm indirect extraterritorial. Accordingly, as under the GATT, trade-restrictive laws employed for reasons of public morality cannot be denied legality under the TBT simply because they create ancillary repercussion on foreign territory.

If, however, a technical regulation, standard, or conformity assessment procedure protects values other than public morals—for example, exhaustible natural resources or animal health—we will come to a different conclusion because these values, for the purposes of our examination, lie outside state territory. Analogous to the GATT, we might conclude that TBT measures can, in principle, protect exhaustible natural resources abroad, but that the geographical limits placed on protecting the life and health of animals on foreign soil are less clear.[40] This is the result of the general treaty analysis. An analysis based on the doctrine of jurisdiction suggests that foreign animals can be covered by technical regulations, whether they protect exhaustible natural resources or animals' life and health.

§2 Agreement on the Application of Sanitary and Phytosanitary Measures (SPS)

Because animals and animal products traded across borders might host pests and diseases or pose other risks through toxins, additives, or food contaminants, WTO members established the SPS, which is exclusively concerned with preventing and mitigating sanitary and phytosanitary risks that affect trade. The SPS focuses on two types of risks: food safety risks and pest- and disease-borne risks.[41] These risks must not only be managed to protect human health and life but also to protect the life and health of animals, as the SPS determines.[42]

The SPS is *lex specialis* in relation to the TBT (article 1.5 TBT), so all technical regulations that pose food or pest- and disease-borne risks for humans or animals must only abide by the SPS. The relationship between the SPS and the GATT is different. Measures that comply with the SPS are presumed to be consistent with article XX(b) GATT.[43]

---

on seal welfare falls within the scope of legitimate objectives within the meaning of Article 2.2 of the TBT Agreement."

[39] There is no reason why the territorial scope of the GATT should differ from that of the TBT, since the exceptions to the TBT and the GATT are almost identical.

[40] Cook & Bowles 235–6 (2010).

[41] Annex A para. 1 SPS. *See also* VAN DEN BOSSCHE & ZDOUC 938 (2017).

[42] *See* Annex A para. 1 lit. a-d SPS.

[43] This presumption is rebuttable: FITZGERALD 208 (2012).

A. SCOPE OF THE SPS

The SPS only applies to sanitary or phytosanitary measures that directly or indirectly affect trade. They are defined as any measure applied

(a) to protect animal or plant life or health within the territory of the Member from risks arising from the entry, establishment or spread of pests, diseases, disease-carrying organisms or disease-causing organisms;
(b) to protect human or animal life or health within the territory of the Member from risks arising from additives, contaminants, toxins or disease-causing organisms in foods, beverages or feedstuffs;
(c) to protect human life or health within the territory of the Member from risks arising from diseases carried by animals, plants or products thereof, or from the entry, establishment or spread of pests; or
(d) to prevent or limit other damage within the territory of the Member from the entry, establishment or spread of pests.[44]

For our purposes, it is necessary to determine if labeling and product characteristics, tariffs, taxes, import bans, and other quantitative restrictions have a sanitary or phytosanitary purpose. Rather than relying on state intent, a norm's purpose is objectively evaluated, as determined by the AB in *Australia—Apples*.[45] Furthermore, the purposes as laid out in article 1 Annex 1 SPS are narrowly interpreted, because, as the WTO states, a "sanitary or phytosanitary restriction which is not actually required for health reasons can be a very effective protectionist device, and because of its technical complexity, a particularly deceptive and difficult barrier to challenge."[46]

B. ARTICLES 2–5 SPS

Article 2 SPS lays down the basic rights and obligations of members under the SPS. Article 2.1 SPS determines that it is a basic right of any member to adopt SPS measures that protect humans and animals from food safety risks and pest- and disease-borne risks. Members have three options in determining their level of protection. They may base their measures on international standards (3.1 SPS), they may want their measures to conform to international standards (3.2 SPS), or they may lay down a higher level of protection (3.3 SPS). The last standard is particularly relevant because the WTO states that it is the "basic aim of the SPS Agreement [. . .] to maintain the sovereign right of any government to provide the level of health protection it deems appropriate."[47] The AB further clarified in *EC—Hormones* that

---

[44] Annex A para. 1 SPS.
[45] Appellate Body Report, *Australia—Measures Affecting the Importation of Apples from New Zealand*, ¶ 172, WTO Doc. WT/DS367/AB/R (adopted Dec. 17, 2010) [*Australia—Apples*, AB Report].
[46] Understanding the WTO, SPS, *supra* note 4.
[47] *Id.*

"this right of a Member to establish its own level of sanitary protection under Article 3.3 of the SPS Agreement is an *autonomous right and not an 'exception'* from a 'general obligation' under Article 3.1."[48]

A contrario, this does not mean that members are free to read risks into products or trade routes where there are none. Pursuant to article 2.2 SPS, levels of protection must be based on scientific principles and on sufficient scientific evidence, with the exception of article 5.7 SPS. Where they exceed international standards, measures must be based on a risk assessment (article 5.1 SPS). According to article 4 Annex A SPS, there are two kinds of risk assessments: risk assessments that apply to SPS measures associated with risks from pests and diseases, and risk assessments that apply to SPS measures aimed at tackling food-borne risks. Risk assessments and management include an objective decision on the "appropriate level of protection." With reference to article 5 Annex A SPS, however, members have a prerogative of choosing their level of protection, even down to a zero-risk level.[49]

Article 5.2 SPS provides that processes and production methods are relevant factors to consider in a risk assessment, but it is not clear whether they cover NPR-PPMs or are limited to PR-PPMs. To be on the safe side, Eaton et al. recommend establishing a scientific link between poor welfare conditions and the spread of diseases for the purposes of the risk assessment.[50] This recommendation is useful, but it has no bearing on whether NPR-PPMs may legitimately influence a state's level of protection and the measures taken in pursuance thereof. Because treaty interpretation leads to ambiguous results, we must approach the question from a broader perspective. Ultimately, the admissibility of NPR-PPMs hinges on whether members can use the SPS to promote *animal welfare* or only to protect *animal health*. This prominent debate is examined in detail below.[51]

The SPS also uniquely enables members to take preemptive action to avoid taking unreasonable risks. Because animal welfare is not typically considered in scientific risk assessments, states might choose to take action to prevent harm done to animals. The requirements for precautionary trade restrictions are laid out in article 5.7 SPS. Members must refrain from setting levels of protection in a manner that results in arbitrary or unjustifiable differentiation, discrimination, or disguised restrictions on trade (article 5.5 SPS). Any precautionary measure is exempted from article 2.2 SPS,[52] and serves only as a temporary safety valve.[53]

Under article 2.2 SPS, it must be determined if an SPS measure is necessary to protect human, animal, or plant life or health. Alternatives to unnecessary trade restrictions shall

---

[48] *EC—Hormones*, AB Report ¶ 172 (emphasis added).

[49] Appellate Body Report, *Australia—Measures Affecting the Importation of Salmon*, ¶ 197, WTO Doc. WT/DS18/AB/R (adopted Nov. 6, 1998) [*Australia—Salmon*, AB Report]. Members' right to choose higher levels of protection was recognized in *Canada—Continued Suspension*: Appellate Body Report, *Canada—Continued Suspension of Obligations in the EC—Hormones Dispute*, ¶ 532, WTO Doc. WT/DS321/AB/R (adopted Nov. 14, 2008) [*Canada—Continued Suspension*, AB Report].

[50] Eaton et al. 42 (2005).

[51] *See* Chapter 4, §2 C.

[52] *Japan—Agricultural Products II*, AB Report ¶ 80.

[53] *Canada—Continued Suspension*, AB Report ¶ 678.

be technically and economically feasible while providing the same level of food safety or animal and plant health.[54] Thus, a state cannot challenge another state's desired level of protection; it can only challenge the measures used to reach the objective. Panels have discretion in evaluating if there is a rational relationship between the measures adopted and the scientific evidence offered in their support. In *EC—Hormones*, for instance, the United States argued the European Union failed to base its ban on beef containing growth hormones on a risk assessment, pursuant to article 5.1 SPS. The panel and the AB affirmed this claim and found that the ban failed to create a rational and objective relationship between the measure employed and the risk assessment.[55]

Finally, article 2.3 SPS requires that all SPS measures be nondiscriminatory. It lays down a most-favored-nation and national treatment obligation and declares discrimination impermissible if it is arbitrary or unjustifiable. Moreover, measures shall not constitute a disguised restriction on international trade.[56]

C. ANIMAL WELFARE VS. ANIMAL HEALTH: THE ROLE OF THE WORLD ORGANIZATION FOR ANIMAL HEALTH (OIE)

In its quest to mitigate and prevent food safety risks and pest- and disease-borne risks that arise in international trade, the SPS prompts members to make use of international standards. The WTO does not itself set up harmonized standards, but it established the Committee on Sanitary and Phytosanitary Measures that identifies respected third-party organizations and validates their standards for the SPS (article 12.1 SPS). By virtue of article 12.3 SPS and article 3 lit. b Annex A SPS, the WTO recognizes the OIE as a standard setter in matters of animal health and zoonoses.

The OIE was established as an intergovernmental organization in 1924 to fight animal diseases by determining minimum international standards. The organization's pillars include principles of transparency, scientific information, international solidarity, sanitary safety, promotion of veterinary services, and food safety.[57] A turning point came in 2001, when the OIE declared animal welfare a mandate of the organization, which it has since expanded.[58] The OIE's ad hoc groups established international standards and guidelines for animal welfare on transporting animals by land, sea, and air (chapters 7.2–7.4), slaughtering animals for human consumption (chapter 7.5), killing animals for purposes of disease control

---

[54] Appellate Body Report, *Japan—Measures Affecting Agricultural Products*, ¶ 84, WTO Doc. WT/DS76/AB/R (adopted Mar. 19, 1999) [*Japan—Agricultural Products II*, AB Report]; *Australia—Salmon*, AB Report ¶ 194.

[55] *EC—Hormones*, AB Report.

[56] In *Australia—Salmon*, the AB held that article 2.3 SPS determines if the measure at hand discriminates between members, if discrimination is arbitrary or unjustifiable, and if conditions in the relevant countries are identical or similar. When the measures are compared, the *similarity of the risks* associated with the products must be assessed: Appellate Body Report, *Australia—Measures Affecting the Importation of Salmon—Recourse to Article 21.5 of the DSU by Canada*, ¶¶ 7.111–2, WTO Doc. WT/DS18/RW (adopted Mar. 20, 2000).

[57] *See generally* OIE, FIFTH STRATEGIC PLAN 2011–2015, 78 SG/20 (OIE, Paris 2010). *See also* OIE, SIXTH STRATEGIC PLAN 2016–2020, 83 SG/17 (OIE, Paris 2015).

[58] OIE, THIRD STRATEGIC PLAN 2001–2005, 69 GS/FR (OIE, Paris 2010). *See also* FAO, OPTIONS FOR ANIMAL WELFARE 7 (2010).

(chapter 7.6), controlling stray dog populations (chapter 7.7), using animals in research and education (chapter 7.8), animal welfare in beef cattle production systems (chapter 7.9), animal welfare in broiler chicken production systems (chapter 7.10), animal welfare in dairy cattle production systems (chapter 7.11), and the welfare of working equids (chapter 7.12).[59] When these chapters on animal welfare came into force, the question emerged whether the SPS incorporates only the OIE's standards on animal health, or also its standards on animal welfare.

Before approaching this question, we must recall our earlier definitions of animal health and animal welfare. Traditionally, *animal health* was seen as the state of an animal in absence of pests, diseases, and food-borne risks, i.e., as mere animal sanitary health.[60] This is only part of the scientific definition of animal welfare. Natural sciences define *animal welfare* as an animal's state of good health, physical and mental well-being, and the absence of pain and suffering.[61] Newer contributions suggest that animal health under the SPS refers to this broader scientific definition of animal welfare. The question thus emerges whether the SPS allows states to employ trade-restrictive measures not only to protect animals from pests, diseases, and food-borne risks but also to ensure animals' physical and mental well-being and the absence of pain and suffering.

Several arguments strongly support the claim that the WTO does *not* allow animal welfare standards to trump trade liberalization through the back door of the OIE. Article 12 para. 3 SPS, the basis of the negotiating power of the SPS Committee, provides that any collaboration between the SPS Committee and the OIE occurs in "the field of sanitary and phytosanitary protection." The document that details cooperation among the organizations, the Agreement between the *Office International Des Epizooties* and the WTO of 1998, includes a clause on cooperation and mutual consultation "concerning the sanitary aspect of international trade in animals and products of animal origin and zoonoses."[62] According to article 1 of the clause, the two organizations "act in collaboration and [...] consult each other on questions of mutual interest," "to facilitate the accomplishment of their respective missions as set out in the International Agreement for the creation of the OIE, and the texts relating to the WTO."[63] Animal welfare is manifestly a mutual interest of the OIE and the WTO if their mission statements contain such evidence. The mission the WTO envisages for the SPS is limited to sanitary and phytosanitary health, as clarified by article 12.3 SPS. The founding document of the OIE, the International Agreement for the Creation of the OIE, lacks a mission statement, but we must assume that the OIE's mission includes animal welfare, because it explicitly identifies animal welfare as its mandate.[64] Since the mission statements of the two organizations do not coincide on the

---

[59] OIE, TERRESTRIAL ANIMAL HEALTH CODE (OIE, Paris 2018).

[60] Annex A SPS, article 1; OIE, Animal Welfare at a Glance (OIE, Paris 2016), *available at* http://www.oie.int/en/animal-welfare/animal-welfare-at-a-glance/ (last visited Jan. 10, 2019).

[61] *See* Chapter 1, §4 A.

[62] Agreement between the Office International des Epizooties and the World Trade Organization, July 8, 1998, WT/L/272, art. 1.

[63] *Id.*

[64] OIE, International Agreement for the Creation of the OIE, Jan. 25, 1924.

question of animal welfare, this analysis does not support the argument that the OIE's animal welfare standards are accepted by the WTO for the purposes of the SPS.

On its public website, the WTO makes clear its position on the debate, explaining that the SPS requires "sanitary and phytosanitary measures be applied *for no other purpose than that of ensuring food safety and animal and plant health.*"[65] On the same page, the WTO explicitly makes the point: "Measures for [. . .] the *welfare of animals* are *not covered* by the SPS Agreement. These concerns [. . .] are addressed by other WTO agreements (i.e., the TBT Agreement or Article XX of GATT 1994)."[66] The FAO shares this view in its Report on Animal Welfare: "Because the SPS agreement does not include animal welfare, the animal protection standards of the OIE cannot be referenced in the case of disputes between countries over international trade."[67]

Teleologically, there is no support for the claim that standards on killing (trapping, fishing, hunting of seals, slaughtering of farmed animals, etc. as found in the OIE Terrestrial Health Code) aim to protect animal life or health. They might set up more "humane" methods of handling and killing animals, but these standards, as a matter of fact, facilitate slaughter and exploitation and are hence *not* geared to *protect* animal life or health.[68]

But it can be argued that the animal welfare provisions of the OIE, if interpreted individually, serve the goal of protecting animal life or health in the meaning of the SPS: safe and secure transport of animals by land, sea, or air is necessary to ensure animals' health (chapters 7.2–7.4); the "humane" slaughter of animals for human consumption (chapter 7.5) ensures smooth business practices and prevents injuries and, hence, diseases; killing animals for purposes of disease control (chapter 7.6) is at the forefront of the SPS's concerns; regulating stray dog populations (chapter 7.7) is necessary to prevent the spread of diseases; the proper use of animals in research and education (chapter 7.8) prevents outbreaks of uncontrolled diseases; and animal welfare in beef cattle production systems (chapter 7.9), broiler chicken production systems (chapter 7.10), dairy cattle production systems (chapter 7.11), and the welfare of working equids (chapter 7.12) are all conducive to ensuring animal health. These claims rely on the argument, that there is, factually, a close connection between animal health and animal welfare. If animals lack exercise, social interaction, or adequate food, they will likely develop a bodily or mental dysfunction or become susceptible to disease. Analogously, treating animals cruelly or inhumanely will cause tissue damage, which compromises their health.

That there is a strong connection between animal health and animal welfare is not a new claim. One of the OIE's guiding principles is that there is a critical relationship between animal health and welfare, as laid down in article 7.1.2 para. 1 of its Terrestrial Animal Health Code.[69] For the OIE, animal health refers to the state of an animal in absence of pests,

---

[65] Understanding the WTO, SPS, *supra* note 4 (emphasis added).

[66] *Id.*

[67] UN FAO, Capacity Building to Implement Good Animal Welfare Practices: Report of the FAO Expert Meeting 18 (FAO, Rome 2009).

[68] *See also* Feddersen 102–3 (1998); Richli & Ruf 56–7 (1995).

[69] OIE, Terrestrial Animal Health Code, article 7.1.2 para. 1 (OIE, Paris 2018).

diseases, and food-borne risks, and to the state of an animal in good health, good physical and mental balance, and free from pain and suffering. While protecting animal health once meant only preventing disease, Sykes contends it has "evolved to encompass a moral commitment to reducing animal suffering."[70] Accordingly, animal welfare measures should fall under the purview of the SPS.

Throughout the *acquis* of the WTO, DSBs have expressed the need to interpret treaties in an evolutionary manner, as done by the AB in *Shrimp/Turtle*.[71] Perhaps it is time to interpret article 12.3 SPS and article 3 lit. b Annex A SPS the same way. An evolutionary interpretation of the term "animal health," and rapid developments within the OIE and around the globe in matters of animal welfare suggest that states can rely on the OIE's animal welfare standards to justify trade restrictions under the SPS. Support for this interpretation is found in *EC—Biotech*, where the panel argued that subparagraph (d) of para. 1 Annex A SPS, which declares legal measures that "prevent or limit other damage" than damage to human or animal life or health, encompasses damage to the environment.[72] If the SPS covers damage to the environment, then it must *a fortiori* cover animal welfare since its explicit purpose is to protect animals' life and health.

But before we argue that the WTO should accept the OIE's animal welfare standards, we should ask ourselves whether those standards are desirable in the first place. Relying on harmonized standards instead of invoking a justification based on public morality or animal health seems to reduce the risk of litigation. WTO members, by agreeing on common standards, accept the motive and scope of protection and are not likely to challenge trade restrictions adopted on this basis. But, as Matheny and Leahy note, harmonized standards will almost certainly fall short of the level of animal protection many countries have today.[73] Instead of challenging the exploitation of animals, as Horta argues, OIE standards put a cap on animal protection. This, he continues, ultimately proves that the standards are designed to serve human health and economic goals, *not* animals.[74] The OIE standards, while useful for other purposes, are therefore unlikely to serve as a basis for a full-fledged regime on global animal welfare.[75] One way in which international standards could be established without compromising stricter animal laws is to allow states to keep their laws in place if international standards are ineffective or inadequate, so that they can reach their chosen level of protection. This, however, is a *de lege ferenda* proposal and does not reflect the current state of trade law, as evidenced by *EC—Hormones*.[76]

---

[70] Sykes, *Sealing Animal Welfare into the GATT Exceptions* 494 (2014). Sharpless similarly views the OIE as representing "the WTO-sanctioned body pertaining to animal welfare" (Sharpless 5 (2008)).

[71] *Shrimp/Turtle I*, AB Report ¶ 130. *See also* Thiermann & Babcock 750 (2005).

[72] Panel Report, *EC—Measures Affecting the Approval and Marketing of Biotech Products*, ¶¶ 7.197–7.211, WTO Doc. WT/DS291/R, WT/DS292/R, WT/DS293/R (adopted Nov. 21, 2006).

[73] Matheny & Leahy 351 (2007).

[74] Oscar Horta, *Expanding Global Justice: The Case for the International Protection of Animals*, 4 Global Pol'y 371, 372 (2013).

[75] Caley Otter et al., *Laying the Foundations for an International Animal Protection Regime*, 2 J. Animal Ethics 53, 57 (2012).

[76] In *EC—Hormones*, the United States challenged the EU ban on cow meat produced by using growth-promoting hormones. The ban was introduced in reaction to an EU-wide public outcry about the excessive use of hormones in meat production. The European Union sought to justify its measures on the basis of the SPS,

To begin to resolve the debate on animal welfare versus animal health, it is helpful to return to the treaty language of the SPS. Para. 1 Annex A SPS clearly and unequivocally lays down the scope of the agreement. The values it protects are, for the purposes of our analysis, "animal [. . .] life or health." We can debate at length whether animal welfare is conducive to the goal of animal life and health, but the question is one of measures, not objectives. Para. 1 Annex A SPS makes clear that it regulates measures that protect animal life or health from "pests, diseases, disease-carrying organisms or disease-causing organisms" (lit. a), and from "risks arising from additives, contaminants, toxins or disease-causing organisms in foods, beverages or feedstuffs" (lit. b). Rather than covering all measures that secure animal life and health, the SPS clearly limits the available measures to a handful. This is what distinguishes the scope of the SPS from that of article XX(b) GATT. If measures are designed to protect the life and health of animals from risks other than those enumerated in the SPS—for instance, from the risk of suffering due to violence or negligence—these measures are covered by the GATT or the TBT. Any other conclusion would render article XX(b) GATT redundant.

The only way the SPS can become a conduit for animal welfare is for the WTO to enlarge the scope of article 1 Annex A SPS, which defines the measures encompassed by the SPS—rather than enlarging the concept of animal health. In *Australia—Apples*, the AB determined that the list of SPS measures is only indicative,[77] so members can, in principle, expand the list to cover measures designed to protect animal health and welfare from nonsanitary risks.

Under current law, animal welfare can only be subject to the SPS if the measures designed to ensure the animals' welfare protect them from food-borne or pest- and disease-related risks.[78] For instance, if a WTO member restricts trade in chickens and cows (or products produced from them) to avoid importing avian influenza (AI) or bovine spongiform encephalopathy (BSE), this measure might also be conducive to animal welfare. Imagine farmers in Iowa, one of the regions worst-hit by avian flu,[79] are ordered to decrease the stocking density of factory farms to prevent disease mutation and spread.[80] Animals would benefit from these sanitary measures because they would have more space and access to fresh air, and suffer less physical and psychological pain. Since risks of antibiotic resistance and disease outbreak are intimately tied to CAFO operations,[81] it might be possible to prohibit the importation of

---

but the AB found that the measure violated the treaty because no international standard demanded that trade in meat containing high levels of hormones be restricted. The European Union was also unable to base its ban on a risk assessment, as required by article 5 SPS: *EC—Hormones*, AB Report ¶ 124. *See further*, Cherie O'Neal Taylor, *Impossible Cases: Lessons from the First Decade of WTO Dispute Settlement*, 28 U. Pa. J. Int'l Econ. L. 309, 357 (2007).

[77] *Australia—Apples*, AB Report ¶ 176.

[78] *See also* Kevin C. Kennedy, *Resolving International Sanitary and Phytosanitary Disputes in the WTO: Lessons and Future Direction*, 55 Food & Drug L.J. 81, 90 (2000).

[79] Maryn McKenna, *The Looming Threat of Avian Flu*, N.Y. Times. Apr. 13, 2016.

[80] Sharpless 55 (2008).

[81] Greger argues that "[i]f changes in human behavior can cause new plagues, changes in human behavior may prevent them in the future" (Michael Greger, Bird Flu: A Virus of Our Own Hatching x (2006)).

CAFO products on a broader scale with reference to sanitary risks,[82] which would help reduce the cruelest forms of factory farming.

D. EXTRATERRITORIAL ANIMAL PROTECTION IN THE SPS

Where measures are designed to protect animals from food-borne or pest- and disease-related risks, the question emerges if they can cover animals on foreign territory. The measures enumerated in Annex A para. 1 lit. a and b SPS explicitly aim to prevent damage "within the territory of the member." On this basis, scholars argue that the SPS precludes applying sanitary measures extraterritorially.[83] But this conclusion is not necessarily warranted. Para. 1 lit. d Annex A SPS declares legal measures that "prevent or limit other [pest-related] damage within the territory." The paragraph limits the geographical scope of *damages* to domestic territory, but it does not limit the geographical scope of *measures*. Considering the rapid spread of diseases, it seems necessary for states to use measures that reach across the border in order to prevent or limit damage within their territory. The more reasonable interpretation hence is that the SPS may indirectly protect animals abroad if doing so is necessary to limit or prevent food-borne or pest- or disease-related damage within a state's territory.[84] Some scholars go further and argue that if disease outbreaks pose a serious threat to the international community, states should be able to adopt sanitary measures that prevent damage outside their territories.[85]

The extraterritoriality framework does not necessarily support the latter view, but it does support the conclusion that the SPS can be used to indirectly protect animals abroad. From a jurisdictional perspective, SPS measures allow states to protect the health and life of domestic animals (intraterritorial content regulation), which compels foreign producers to either guarantee their products observe good animal health and welfare, or not export their products to these states. If foreign animals are protected in the same breath, this effect is only incidental (extraterritorial ancillary repercussion). Thus, the SPS measure is indirect extraterritorial.

§3 Anti-Dumping Agreement (ADA)

A. ADA AND ARTICLE VI GATT

My earlier analysis of regulatory developments in animal law demonstrated that competition in laxity is the most likely regulatory trajectory of animal law. Given the mobility of agricultural and research industries, well-established animal laws are susceptible to being undercut by lower standards abroad that attract investors who want to lower production costs. But

---

[82] Marceau & Trachtman 862 (2002); Sharpless 33–4 (2008).

[83] UNCTAD, DISPUTE SETTLEMENT, WORLD TRADE ORGANIZATION, 3.9 SPS MEASURES 4 (U.N. Publication, New York, Geneva 2003).

[84] Sarah H. Cleveland, *Human Rights Sanctions and the WTO*, *in* ENVIRONMENT, HUMAN RIGHTS AND INTERNATIONAL TRADE 199, 234 (Francesco Francioni ed., 2001).

[85] Gabrielle Marceau & Joel P. Trachtman, *GATT, TBT and SPS: A Map of the WTO Law of Domestic Regulation*, *in* THE WTO DISPUTE SETTLEMENT SYSTEM 1995–2003 275, 328 n. 219 (Federico Ortino & Ernst-Ulrich Petersmann eds., 2004).

cheaper production abroad only makes economic sense if products can be imported back into countries that consume them. Breeding, raising, using, and killing animals in states with lax animal laws with the intent of putting them and the products made from their bodies back on the market in states with stricter laws, at lower prices, is called dumping (also known as eco-dumping, social dumping, or animal welfare dumping).[86] While dumping is not prohibited under WTO law, it regulates how WTO members can react to dumping. Article VI GATT and the ADA[87] allow members to use anti-dumping measures to contravene, and, ultimately, to prevent importation of products manufactured in exploitive dumping environments.

Anti-dumping measures are permissible pursuant to article VI:1 GATT against products offered on the domestic market below their normal value if this threatens or injures a domestic industry. Responses to dumping include provisional measures, price undertakings, and definitive anti-dumping duties. In its determination of dumping, article VI GATT compares the product's export price and the price for like products in the country of production. Unlike article III GATT, it is advantageous if humanely produced animal products and products derived from cruel practices are in a competitive relationship because only then can dumping occur.[88]

The ADA defines dumping differently from article VI GATT. Pursuant to article 2.1 ADA, dumping occurs when products are introduced into commerce at less than their normal value, based on a fair comparison between the export value and the normal value (article 2.4 ADA).[89] According to Conrad, social dumping unfairly exploits competitive advantages and thereby qualifies as dumping in the meaning of the ADA.[90] The same, *mutatis mutandis*, must be true for animal welfare dumping. A domestic injury is incurred where domestic producers of like products are affected as a whole, or "those of them whose collective output of the products constitutes a major proportion of the total domestic production" (article 4.1 ADA). It is insufficient, for instance, for a few meat producers to be adversely affected by dumping; the whole meat industry must suffer injury for the purposes of the ADA. Footnote 9 to article 3 ADA further details that an injury is constituted by a material injury, the threat of a material injury, or material retardation of the establishment of a domestic injury. Pursuant to article 3.5 ADA, a causal link between dumped imports and the injury must be established, but it must also be ensured that there is no attribution of dumping by other factors.[91]

---

[86] *See further* on dumping and animal law, Chapter 2, §3.

[87] Agreement on Implementation of Article VI of the General Agreement on Tariffs and Trade 1994, Apr. 15, 1994, 1868 U.N.T.S. 201 [Anti-Dumping Agreement, ADA].

[88] CONRAD 47 (2011). For a discussion of likeness under the GATT, *see* Chapter 3, §2 B. III.

[89] The normal value is examined to determine if the sale is in the ordinary course of trade, products are like, the product is destined for consumption in the exporting country, and prices are comparable. The export price is based on the transaction price of the product from a producer to an importer: Appellate Body Report, *US—Anti-Dumping Measures on Certain Hot-Rolled Products from Japan*, ¶ 98, WTO Doc. WT/DS184/AB/R (adopted Aug. 23, 2001). For dumping calculations, *see* ANDREAS F. LOWENFELD, INTERNATIONAL ECONOMIC LAW 271 ff. (2d ed. 2008).

[90] CONRAD 47 (2011).

[91] Pursuant to article 3.5 ADA, these factors include: (i) the volume and prices of imports not sold at dumping prices; (ii) contraction in demand or changes in the patterns of consumption; (iii) trade-restrictive practices of

B. EXTRATERRITORIAL ANIMAL PROTECTION IN THE ADA AND ARTICLE VI GATT

The previous analysis suggests the ADA and article VI:1 GATT are mainly geared to protect domestic producers from injury but do they also allow states to indirectly protect animals situated on foreign territory? Anti-dumping duties are not primarily interested in increasing standards in "low-welfare states;" they aim to mitigate instances where high welfare is effectively impaired by dumping products on a state's domestic market. Anti-dumping duties are contingent on products entering the domestic market (intraterritorial anchor point). They regulate the circumstances under which members can link anti-dumping duties to foreign products brought into domestic commerce (intraterritorial content regulation), but invariably create repercussions for producers or even entire economies abroad (extraterritorial ancillary repercussion). The ADA and article VI GATT indirectly penalize foreign states with low animal welfare by determining the conditions under which production in exploitative environments can be countered and, ultimately, prevented by diminishing demand abroad. Anti-dumping duties thus indirectly enable states to protect animals abroad.

§4 Agreement on Agriculture (AoA)

A. APPLICABLE AOA PROVISIONS

Agriculture is a sensitive policy area, especially when it comes to financial supports that governments provide to agricultural industries, which explains the WTO's many failed negotiation rounds on trade liberalization in agriculture.[92] Since agriculture has become a quasi-taboo at the WTO, subsidies in the agricultural sector have effectively been pushed out of the domain of the Agreement on Subsidies and Countervailing Measures (SCM Agreement),[93] and into the domain of the AoA. The subsidy rules of the AoA now prevail over those of the SCM and the GATT (notably over article XVI para. 1 GATT).[94] Other measures that deal with agriculture, like import restrictions, labels, taxes, customs valuation, import licensing procedures, preshipment inspection, emergency safeguard measures, and subsidies, are still subject to review of other WTO agreements like GATT.[95] But pursuant to article 21.1 AoA, other agreements apply to agricultural products only subject to the provisions of the AoA. In *US—Upland Cotton*, the AB interpreted this article to mean that other agreements apply

---

and competition between foreign and domestic producers; (iv) developments in technology; and (v) export performance and productivity of the domestic injury.

[92] Although agriculture was never formally excluded from negotiations, the WTO has never effectively covered it: LOWENFELD 318 (2008).

[93] Agreement on Subsidies and Countervailing Measures, Apr. 15, 1994, 1867 U.N.T.S. 14 [SCM Agreement].

[94] On the relation between art. XVI GATT, the SCM Agreement, and the Code on Subsidies and Countervailing Duties, *see* LOWENFELD 216 ff. (2008).

[95] WTO, Agriculture, Introduction (WTO, Geneva 2019), *available at* https://www.wto.org/english/tratop_e/agric_e/ag_intro01_intro_e.htm (last visited Jan. 10, 2019)

"except to the extent that the Agreement on Agriculture contains specific provisions dealing specifically with the same matter."[96]

Products subject to the AoA are listed in Annex 1 to the AoA. Article 1(i) Annex 1 AoA covers all products listed in chapters 1 to 24 of the Harmonized System Nomenclature, except fishes and products made from fishes. Most animals and animal products fall under Section I of the Harmonized System. Chapter 1 covers all "live animals," chapter 2 "meat and edible meat offal," chapter 3 "fish and crustaceans, mollusks and other aquatic invertebrates," chapter 4 "dairy produce, birds' eggs, natural honey, edible products of animal origin," and chapter 5 "products of animal origin, not elsewhere specified or included."[97] The AoA accordingly applies to all of these product categories.[98]

In the AoA, laws regulating agricultural trade stretch from market access rules to laws on domestic support and export competition.[99] Most of the measures that states adopted to restrict trade in agricultural products have been subject to the WTO's tariffication process. So, like GATT, the AoA demands that quantitative restrictions be converted into tariffs with equivalent protection and that they not be raised by members (article 4.2 AoA).

Domestic agricultural support measures are subject to part IV of the GATT Schedule of Concessions that lays down maximum caps (article 6.3 AoA). Only domestic agricultural support measures that do not provide price support to domestic producers are exempted from reduction, under narrowly defined conditions. These "Blue Box" or "Green Box" measures are regulated in Annex 2 and article 6 AoA, respectively, which follow the objective agreed on by states in the Uruguay Round, namely, to assess domestic support measures associated with agriculture by their effect on trade and production. Examples of Green Box measures are direct payments to producers and government service programs that do not influence production (Annex 2 to the AoA). Green Box payments must also not, or only minimally, distort trade (para. 1(a) Annex 2 AoA). This rule is intended to curb domestic subsidy measures that could stimulate national production to excessive levels and which would eventually have a dumping effect.[100]

Governments can implement these standards in different ways. Regarding production, domestic support measures must not be tied to the requirement that certain products be produced or not produced.[101] Broadly speaking, payment must not be linked to production. In Switzerland, for example, articles 70 and 70a of the Federal Act on Agriculture provide that direct payment be made to farmers based on farmland, to ensure supply, biodiversity, quality of landscape, production systems, efficient resource use, or to bridge subsidies, but *not* to support production per se.[102] Regarding trade, distortion of trade is measured

[96] Appellate Body Report, *US—Subsidies on Upland Cotton*, ¶ 532, WTO Doc. WT/DS267/AB/R (adopted Mar. 21, 2005) [*US—Subsidies on Upland Cotton*, AB Report] (emphasis omitted).

[97] HS Convention; World Customs Organization (WCO), Harmonized System Nomenclature (WCO, Brussels 2012).

[98] Pursuant to article 1(ii) Annex 1 AoA, the agreement also covers raw fur skins, wool, and animal hair.

[99] WTO, Agriculture, Introduction, *supra* note 95.

[100] Kevin R. Gray, Right to Food Principle vis à vis Rules Governing International Trade 18 (British Institute of International and Comparative Law 2003).

[101] *US—Subsidies on Upland Cotton*, AB Report ¶ 342.

[102] Bundesgesetz über die Landwirtschaft [Landwirtschaftsgesetz, LwG] [Federal Act on Agriculture], Apr. 29, 1988, SR 910.1 (Switz.).

empirically. If direct payments minimally distort trade, they are seen as non-trade-distorting because they are not employed with the intent to stimulate production.[103]

In principle, a government could support local farmers with Green Box payments to level out competitive disadvantages associated with producing animal products at higher levels of animal welfare if these measures only minimally distort trade. But the WTO does not define "non-trade distorting support" in either relative or absolute terms.[104] Since we must assume that giving payments to high-welfare producers increases the market share of their products, there is a risk of trade-distortion. It would further be difficult to control and limit the effects of this distortion enough to ensure animal welfare payments pass as legitimate domestic payments not subject to the AoA's duty of reduction. Animal welfare–based subsidies also typically aim to stimulate the production of high-welfare products, so in the worst case, animal welfare–based payments will be seen as stimulating or intending to stimulate production and therefore drop out of the Green Box category. To make things worse, Annex 2 of the AoA, which lists potential Green Box measures, does not refer to animal welfare or animals.[105]

Many members consider the fact that the AoA is silent on animal welfare a significant weakness of the agreement. The European Union, for example, urged the WTO to include animal welfare as a Green Box measure. In its Luxembourg Common Agricultural Policy (CAP) Reform Agreement, it decoupled direct payments from domestic production and linked it to production that implements certain environmental, animal health-related, and animal protection standards.[106] The European Union's Animal Welfare Strategy shows that the European Agriculture Fund for Rural Development pays 71 percent of 70 million EUR (86 million USD) annually to farmers to support animal welfare.[107] The comprehensive information provided on the WTO's homepage does not explicitly provide that the European Union's strategy is legal under the AoA; its statement has been treated as a proposal, which indicates that animal welfare–related payments are currently excluded from the Green Box.[108]

---

[103] Jan Wouters & Dominic Coppens, An Overview of the Agreement on Subsidies and Countervailing Measures—Including a Discussion of the Agreement on Agriculture, Working Paper No. 104, 70 (Institute for International Law, K.U. Leuven 2007).

[104] *See also* UNCTAD, Training Module for Multilateral Trade Negotiations on Agriculture 45 (U.N. Publication, New York, Geneva 2007). Studies by the India UNCTAD team suggest that subsidies rarely cause minimal trade distortion: UNCTAD India Team, Green Box Subsidies: A Theoretical and Empirical Assessment, Prepared under UNCTAD—Govt. of India—DFID Project "Strategies and Preparedness for Trade and Globalization in India" (2007), *available at* http://wtocentre.iift.ac.in/DOC/Studies_GreenBoxSubsidiesATheoreticalAndEmpericalAssessmen.pdf (last visited Jan. 10, 2019).

[105] *See also* Harald Grethe, *High Animal Welfare Standards in the EU and International Trade: How to Prevent Potential "Low Animal Welfare Havens"?*, 3 Food Pol'y 315, 327 (2006).

[106] *See* European Commission, Communication from the Commission to the Council and the European Parliament on Animal Welfare Legislation on Farmed Animals in Third Countries and the Implications for the EU, COM(2002) 626 final (Nov. 18, 2002).

[107] EU Animal Welfare Strategy 2012–5, at 3.

[108] WTO, Agriculture Negotiations, Domestic Support: Amber, Blue and Green Boxes (WTO, Geneva 2019), *available at* https://www.wto.org/english/tratop_e/agric_e/negs_bkgrnd13_boxes_e.htm (last visited Jan. 10, 2019). *See also* Royal Society for the Prevention of Cruelty and Eurogroup for Animal Welfare, Getting

Because animal welfare–based subsidies are not (yet) explicitly endorsed as a Green Box measure by the WTO, they are generally subject to incremental reduction and countervailable under the SCM. Under the *lex lata*, the only way a state can use subsidies to advance animal welfare is if its Green Box measures of Annex 2 AoA cover animal welfare in the same breath. For instance, agricultural payments made to promote biodiversity or maintain farmland preclude funding CAFO production, which helps animals. Members should not rely on these possibilities *mala fide*, however. If, in the future, these measures eventually fall under the Green Box, they will be exempted from the general obligation of gradual reduction and could not be countervailed under the SCM Agreement.[109]

B. EXTRATERRITORIAL ANIMAL PROTECTION IN THE AOA

Under the doctrine of jurisdiction, domestic subsidies seem to reflect a territorially anchored concern. They make financial payments to national actors (territorial anchor point) to strengthen their position on the domestic market (territorial content regulation). Acknowledging the drastic effects of these financial contributions on foreign markets, WTO members argue that repercussions of subsidies felt abroad may concern other states and should thus be covered by the AoA. If the AoA explicitly allowed subsidies for high animal welfare, this would reduce the number of products produced abroad under low standards. Nudging foreign producers to produce to higher welfare standards is an extraterritorial ancillary repercussion, which means the norm is indirect extraterritorial.

§5 Special Treatment Clause

CAFOs are now the dominant production system for animal products, by using a minimum of human resources, exponentially increasing output, and promising the highest economic returns. These promises, coupled with increasing demand for animal products, help explain why high-intensity production systems in the animal agricultural sector are incrementally expanding from the minority world to the majority world. But not all support this development. Countries of the minority world have had long experience with high-intensity production and are aware of its many adverse effects on the environment, public health, animal health, welfare, and world food security. Many of these countries are interested in entering partnerships with the majority world to help them avoid the mistakes of the minority world, by reducing high-intensity production and preventing the problems associated with it.[110] The Africa-EU Partnership, for instance, makes preferential treatment for livestock exports from African states to the European Union

---

Animal Welfare into the Green Box, *available at* http://www.fao.org/fileadmin/user_upload/animalwelfare/Green%20Box%20briefing.pdf (last visited Jan. 10, 2019).

[109] Wouters & Coppens 74 (2007).

[110] For a review of case studies in beef, *see* David Bowles et al., *Animal Welfare and Developing Countries: Opportunities for Trade in High-Welfare Products from Developing Countries*, 24 Rev. Sci. Tech. Off. Int. Epiz. 783 (2005).

contingent on high animal welfare performance.[111] Some claim these measures unfairly prevent the majority world from achieving a state of economic wealth (and health) that the majority world enjoys since centuries. If CAFO practices of the minority world go unchecked, while those of the majority world are subject to close environmental and ethical scrutiny, this will undoubtedly be the case. Then again, absent nudges for higher animal welfare, trade relationships will devolve into full liberalization, which means that the minority world ends up prompting the majority world to "go CAFO." In sum, preferential treatment is a great tool to counter the expansion of CAFOs to the majority world but it should only be used if the same practices are challenged in the minority world.

Within the WTO, members are entitled to enact measures that give some states preferential treatment even if these measures contravene the WTO's most-favored-nation obligation. The basis for this is the Enabling Clause, also known as the 1979 Decision on Differential and More Favorable Treatment and Fuller Participation of Developing Countries.[112] By virtue of the Enabling Clause, WTO members established the Generalized System of Preferences (GSP).[113] GSP allows states to give preferential (reduced) nonreciprocal tariffs for goods imported from majority world countries; GSP+ allows full removal of tariffs. GSP-granting countries determine unilaterally which countries are included in their GSP schemes by concluding Preferential Trade Agreements. The only requirement, as set out by the Special Treatment Clause, is that all countries in a similar situation must have access to special treatment, so special treatment must be accorded in a nondiscriminatory manner.[114]

In determining the conditions and scope of special treatment, states can link preferential tariffs to high animal welfare standards. The same method has been used in labor law. The US Generalized System of Preferences Renewal Act (GSP Renewal Act), for instance, makes preferences contingent on whether beneficiary majority world countries adhere to, *inter alia*, internationally recognized worker rights and whether they abolished the worst forms of child labor.[115] If countries do not observe these rights, they are not eligible for the US GSP.[116] Merely ratifying International Labor Organization (ILO) conventions is not sufficient to fulfill these requirements; there must be proof the standards are met. GSP-receiving countries must, however, have some flexibility in implementing their obligations due to differences in climate, habits and customs, economic opportunity, and industrial

---

[111] The Africa-EU Partnership, Improving Food Safety in Africa, *available at* http://www.africa-eu-partnership.org/en/newsroom/all-news/improving-food-safety-africa-through-training (last visited Jan. 10, 2019). The political framework for cooperation between the European Union and Africa is the Joint Africa-EU Strategy (JAES), established in 2007.

[112] WTO, Differential and More Favourable Treatment, Reciprocity and Fuller Participation of Developing Countries; Decision of 28 November 1979, L/4903, Dec. 3, 1979. The Enabling Clause is an exception from the most-favored-nation obligation: Appellate Body Report, *EC—Conditions for the Granting of Tariff Preferences to Developing Countries*, WTO Doc. WT/DS246/AB/R (adopted. Apr. 20, 2004) [*EC—Tariff Preferences*, AB Report].

[113] GSP must be distinguished from the Global System of Trade Preferences (GTSP), through which majority world countries make trade concessions with each other.

[114] With reference to footnote 3 to para. 2(a) of the SCM: *EC—Tariff Preferences*, AB Report ¶¶ 153–4.

[115] Generalized System of Preferences Renewal Act of 1996, 19 U.S.C. § 2461, § 2467(4) and (6) (U.S.).

[116] *Id.* § 2462(b)(2)(G) and (H) (U.S.).

tradition.[117] A notable weakness of the scheme is that while the GSP Renewal Act binds payments to certain performances, the duties imposed on GSP-receiving countries are not always justiciable. In *International Labor Rights Research and Education Fund et al. v. George Bush et al.*, labor and human rights organizations accused the US executive of failing to enforce worker rights on the basis of the GSP Renewal Act. The D.C. Court of Appeals, however, held that these rights are nonjusticiable.[118]

Analogous to the GSP Act, states could set animal protection standards that majority countries have to adhere to if they wish to benefit from a GSP scheme. Because majority countries will produce 60 percent of all animal products by 2020, these measures could have a colossal impact on the way most animals will be treated.[119] Though linking special treatment to high animal welfare performance is a promising strategy, a crucial caveat is that the needs of majority world countries are not the only basis on which special treatment is accorded to them. The needs envisaged must be developmental, financial, or trade-related and should be based on objective and internationally shared motivations.[120] Because high-intensity animal production endangers animal and human health, the environment, and food security around the globe, these effects (and the measures that aim to remedy them) are objectively critical and internationally condemned. In the past decades, international bodies have become aware of the dangers associated with CAFO production. For instance, in 2001, the World Bank's declared action was to "[a]void funding large-scale commercial, grain-fed feedlot systems and industrial milk, pork, and poultry production."[121] The International Finance Corporation (IFC), a member of the World Bank Group, also drafted principles on animal welfare that must be observed by funding institutions.[122] Hence, giving preferential treatment to goods produced at high animal welfare levels can be a viable option to work toward higher animal laws across the globe.

---

[117] Constitution of the International Labor Organization (Part XIII of the Treaty of Peace between the Allied and Associated Powers and Germany), June 28, 1919, 15 U.N.T.S. 40, art. 19 para. 3: "In framing any Convention or Recommendation of general application the Conference shall have due regard to those countries in which climatic conditions, the imperfect development of industrial organisation, or other special circumstances make the industrial conditions substantially different and shall suggest the modifications, if any, which it considers may be required to meet the case of such countries." *See also* James M. Zimmerman, Extraterritorial Employment Standards of the United States: The Regulation of the Overseas Workplace 29 ff. (1992).

[118] International Labor Rights Research and Education Fund et al. v. George Bush et al., 954 F.2d 745 (D.C. Cir. 1992) (U.S.).

[119] Delgado et al., Livestock to 2020 22 (1999).

[120] With reference to n. 3 to para. 2(a) of the SCM: *EC—Tariff Preferences*, AB Report ¶ 163.

[121] Cornelis de Haan et al., Livestock Development, Implications for Rural Poverty, the Environment, and Global Food Security 65 (The World Bank 2001).

[122] International Finance Corporation (IFC), Creating Business Opportunity through Improved Animal Welfare (World Bank, Washington D.C. 2006). Chapter 6, §1 A studies these measures in detail.

§6 Interim Conclusion

Since treaties other than the GATT have come to play a significant role in the WTO, the question of whether and to what extent the GATT's sister treaties (the TBT, the SPS, the ADA, the AoA, and the Special Treatment Clause) place limits on members to indirectly protect animals beyond their territory, has become increasingly important.

Labels and import restrictions are particularly likely to qualify as technical regulations or standards, which would bring to application the TBT. Where labels and import restrictions are adopted to protect animals, it is questionable whether PPM-sensitive measures are technical regulations and whether technical regulations allow distinguishing between products based on PPMs. With regard to the first question, the AB in *Seals* narrowly interpreted technical regulations and declined to apply the TBT to the case. By distinguishing between hunter- and hunting-based laws, the AB essentially avoided answering the question of whether PPMs are technical regulations. Assuming that the TBT applies to the second question, the panel in *Seals* responded that animal welfare regulation can render products like or unlike, which, in effect, renders PPMs legal under the TBT. Should a panel still find that PPMs violate the TBT, they can be justified under article 2.2 TBT as a measure needed to protect animal welfare. The extraterritorial scope of the TBT differs depending on which exception a state invokes. TBT exceptions strongly resemble those of the GATT, so their scope is similarly broad. The public morals exception of article 2.2 TBT protects public morals; these morals are always territorially anchored but can concern animals abroad. Its territorial anchoring renders the public morals exception "perpetually territorial" and justifies its preoccupation with values outside a state's territory. In matters concerning exhaustible natural resources, there are good reasons to accept that this exception, too, allows indirectly protecting animals abroad. Conclusions are mixed when the goal of trade norms is to protect the lives or health of foreign animals, and depend on whether we use a general treaty analysis of the TBT or also a jurisdictional analysis of general international law.

A major point of contention in my examination of the SPS was whether sanitary measures can be interpreted to cover concerns for animal welfare. The point at issue culminated in a debate over whether the role of the OIE as a standard setter for the SPS also encompasses the OIE's mandate to deliver animal welfare standards. A treaty interpretation and several documents support the conclusion that animal welfare is not fully covered by the SPS, but many scholars argue that there is a critical link between animal health and animal welfare, to the effect that animal health has "evolved to encompass a moral commitment to reducing animal suffering."[123] Because the measures available under the SPS are limited by the treaty, the correct view seems to be a middle position: animal welfare is covered by the SPS to the extent that measures protect animals from food-borne and pest- or disease-related risks. This is not necessarily the best outcome for animals, but it is the most sound from a legal perspective, and it leaves animal advocates sufficient room to maneuver. Given the risks of antibiotic resistance and the spread of influenza

---

[123] Sykes, *Sealing Animal Welfare into the GATT Exceptions* 494 (2014).

in common concentrated farming, prohibiting products manufactured by these processes will likely go hand in hand with eliminating the cruelest forms of animal farming. But can the SPS be used to indirectly protect animals situated abroad? Article 1 para. d Annex A SPS primarily allows measures to protect human or animal life or health within the territory of members and measures that prevent or limit sanitary or phytosanitary damage within the territory. To guarantee the latter, a state will, however, have to use measures that protect animals located abroad.

The ADA and article VI GATT empower members to appropriately react to instances of animal welfare dumping. The ADA is not primarily interested in improving standards in low-welfare states but aspires to mitigate instances where high welfare is considerably impaired by products placed on the domestic market at dumping prices. But unlike the GATT and the TBT, dumping can occur only when products produced at low welfare and products produced at high welfare are considered like. Since prohibiting dumping negatively affects foreign producers who manufacture animal products with low standards, the ADA in a sense enables states to indirectly protect animals abroad.

Most animals and animal products are considered to be agricultural products in the meaning of article 1 lit. i Annex 1 AoA, an agreement that is relevant for evaluating the legality of financial support measures. Domestic contributions to production systems or producers that endorse high animal welfare are susceptible to trade distortion, even when they only level out adverse competitive effects associated with higher animal welfare production. WTO members are, however, interested in declaring animal welfare subsidies a Green Box measure, which would exempt states from having to gradually reduce their subsidies and which would make them unavailable to countervailing measures under the SCM Agreement.

Also the Special Treatment Clause for Developing Countries enables states to indirectly improve the welfare of animals situated abroad, by giving majority world countries preferential treatment for products that meet high animal welfare standards. Because 60 percent of all animals used in the agricultural sector will be produced in the majority world by 2020, the Special Treatment Clause will have a significant impact on farmed animals.

Indirect Extraterritorial Protection of Animals in Trade Law: Evaluation and Outlook

Given the diverse matters that are subject to WTO scrutiny and the many policy areas they affect, I can offer only a cautious evaluation of how trade and animal law interact, and how their interplay will continue to shape the lives of animals in the future. It is indisputable that the laws of most states view animals as mere goods that can be bought, sold, exchanged, and destroyed on a whim. As the worldwide commodity market has expanded, animals and the products made from their bodies have become a popular object of trade. If the only role ascribed to animals is as objects of trade, the issue of animal law—if it is ignored or downplayed at the WTO—will virtually disappear from the international plane. The chances of this happening are great. The WTO focuses almost exclusively on trade liberalization, for which animal laws are merely an obstacle to trade.

The developments of the past years suggest that the WTO slowly seems to be shedding its image as a mere "puppet of commercial interests."[124] In general, WTO treaties still only exceptionally declare animal laws affecting trade legal, but the DSB has become more responsive to the growing call of the public and WTO members that animal welfare should play a greater role at the WTO. Among scholars, there is a consensus that the WTO considers protecting animals a legitimate regulatory interest of states. And thanks to the WTO's openness to and expertise in globalized markets, measures that reach across borders to protect animals are tolerated.[125] Members thus have some ability to indirectly protect animals abroad in the realm of trade law.

Full compliance with the technicalities of trade law, however, is difficult. Even if the WTO permits extraterritorial animal law, this does not obviate the need for members to be attentive to the different preferences and socioeconomic conditions of other states. Members must initiate negotiations to conclude bilateral or multilateral agreements, and have transparent and predictable procedures in place when they adopt new measures or amend existing ones. Often, the extent to which efforts to protect animals are accepted by the WTO depends on whether states have comprehensive domestic programs in place that aim to improve the legal environment for animals.[126] The European Union's experience proves that animal welfare has a reasonable chance of passing WTO scrutiny if pursued with sincerity and embedded in a broad, multi-institutional, multileveled, long-term, transparent, and progressive policy agenda. Building on the *Seals* case, the public morality exception could be used more broadly in the future to indirectly protect animals abroad who are subject to systematic abuse, like calves penned for veal production, pigs withering in gestation crates, or hens rotting in battery cages.[127]

WTO law still only selectively provides a platform for members to better protect animals, and manifestly fails to offer them a comprehensive scheme to respond to the needs of animals in a globalized era. In the remainder, I give a brief overview of interpretations and amendments that could remedy this situation and strengthen the role of animals at the WTO. At a minimum, the exceptions of article XX GATT should be clarified so one or a few of them clearly cover animal welfare.[128] Few reports have followed a narrow interpretation of article XX GATT based on the widely criticized and unadopted *Tuna/Dolphin I* judgment,[129] but nothing in the VCLT allows article XX GATT to be interpreted as demanding

---

[124] Lauren Sullivan, *The Epic Struggle for Dolphin-Safe Tuna: To Be Continued—A Case for Accommodating Nonprotectionist Eco-labels in the WTO*, 47 VAND. J. TRANSNAT'L L. 861, 888 (2014). *See also* Gregory C. Shaffer, *The World Trade Organization under Challenge: Democracy and the Law and Politics of the WTO's Treatment of Trade and Environment Issues*, 25 HARV. ENVTL. L. REV. 1, 1–3 (2001).

[125] As evidenced by *Shrimp/Turtle II* and *Seals*, the AB has in principle upheld domestic measures designed to protect animals abroad: *Shrimp/Turtle II*, AB Report; *Seals*, AB Report.

[126] In *Brazil—Retreaded Tyres*, the AB clarified that measures "must be viewed in the broader context of the comprehensive strategy designed and implemented [. . .] to deal with [the problem]" (Appellate Body Report, *Brazil—Measures Affecting Imports of Retreaded Tyres*, WTO Doc. WT/DS332/AB/R, ¶ 154 (adopted Dec. 17, 2007)). *See also* Sharpless 8 (2008). On the sincerity of beliefs: Howse & Langille 373 (2012).

[127] Broom, *International Animal Welfare Perspectives, Including Whaling and Inhumane Seal Killing as a W.T.O. Public Morality Issue*, *in* ANIMAL LAW AND WELFARE: INTERNATIONAL PERSPECTIVES 59 (2016).

[128] Eaton et al. 11 (2005).

[129] Just three years later, in another unadopted panel report (*Tuna/Dolphin II*), the narrow interpretation was held to be a "long-standing practice" of the WTO: *Tuna/Dolphin II*, Panel Report ¶¶ 5.26, 5.38.

that exceptions be narrowly construed.[130] Instead, Archibald argues, ambiguous provisions should be interpreted in the manner most favorable to protecting animals and the environment. Her proposal takes up the spirit of the preamble to the Marrakesh Agreement, which provides that members are committed to protect and preserve the environment. Since the AB recognizes that ambiguities should be interpreted in a manner that fulfills the objective and purpose of the WTO Agreement (in line with article 18 VCLT),[131] trade obligations that harm these objectives should be stringently limited through article XX GATT.[132] The changing societal views about what we owe to animals further support an evolutionary interpretation of treaties—a method popularized in *Shrimp/Turtle*.[133]

A more drastic change could be achieved by concluding an understanding that clarifies the provisions of the WTO agreements and operates as a secondary source of WTO law.[134] Under current law, members might have a few options to protect animals, but the intricate duties of WTO law make it easy for them to violate the treaties, which in turn nudges them away from taking the extra effort to protect animals through trade law. An unequivocal commitment to protect animals within the WTO would significantly increase the likelihood that members will try to protect animals through trade law by default in the future.

Several of these proposed amendments are discussed at the WTO. In June 2000, the European Union submitted a proposal to the WTO Committee on Agriculture (CoA) to directly address the issue of animal welfare in the WTO. It noted that animals are more and more relevant in state politics, within and outside the European Union, and that consumers and producers increasingly care about how animals are treated. On this basis, it argued that trade should not undermine the efforts of WTO members to improve animal welfare protection and to avoid protectionism, and that "animal welfare should be globally addressed in a consistent manner within the WTO."[135] To achieve these goals, the European Union offered three options. First, multilateral agreements could be drafted to make the relationship between WTO rules and animal law clearer. Second, appropriate labeling under article 2.2 TBT should be guaranteed to empower consumers to make an informed choice. Third, members should have the right to provide financial compensation to producers that observe high animal welfare standards if trade rules produce unequal conditions of competition.[136] Though the WTO never formally responded to the proposal, it continues to form part of ongoing trade negotiations.[137] Within the European Union, members also push for a stronger role of animal welfare in trade. In their "Joint Declaration on Animal Welfare," Denmark, Germany, and the Netherlands urged EU member states and the European Commission "to acknowledge the need for better regulation, better animal welfare, and to promote awareness, EU-standards and knowledge," and to "promote in trade agreements and

---

[130] Feddersen 94 (1998). *See also for a critique* Charnovitz 720 (1998).

[131] *See* for a similar line of argument: *Japan—Alcoholic Beverages*, AB Report 18.

[132] Archibald 18–9 (2008).

[133] *Shrimp/Turtle I*, AB Report ¶ 130.

[134] Nadakavukaren Schefer 284 (2010).

[135] EC Proposal, Animal Welfare and Trade in Agriculture (2000), at 3.

[136] *Id.*

[137] FAO, Options for Animal Welfare 17 (2010).

in international forums, EU standards and knowledge as regards the protection and welfare of animals and work towards the full recognition of animal welfare as a non-trade concern in the framework of the WTO."[138]

If we take a broad view of the developments at the intersection of trade law and animal law, we see that "[t]he global community is indisputably more concerned with and aware of the potential for abusive practices that affect animals."[139] The panel in *Seals* sensed these concerns when it declared that "animal welfare is a matter of ethical responsibility for human beings in general."[140] These concerns are part and parcel of the general principle of animal welfare that has emerged in public international law.[141] In relation to this principle, "WTO law, forming part of the much larger realm of public international law, must be construed in a coherent way that does not impair the essential problem-solving capacities of global society."[142] When in doubt, the balance should thus tip toward measures intended to "reflect a genuine concern for animal welfare that is in harmony with international norms."[143] This dovetails with the argument that WTO agreements must be treated as living documents, like a constitution or an international declaration, able to adapt and respond to contemporary values.[144]

---

[138] Denmark, Germany, and the Netherlands, Joint Declaration on Animal Welfare 1, 3 (2014). Members *inter alia* demand that the European Union introduces animal welfare indicators, improves consumer information and transportation regulation for animals (including space allowance and transportation hours), phases out mutilation like tail docking and beak trimming, and establishes an EU platform to promote discussion.

[139] Wagman & Liebman 307 (2011).

[140] *Seals*, Panel Report ¶ 7.409.

[141] *See further* on the general principle of animal welfare, Chapter 2, §4 IV.

[142] Conrad 3 (2011). *See also* Wagman & Liebman 308 (2011).

[143] Sykes, *Sealing Animal Welfare into the GATT Exceptions* 498 (2014).

[144] Wagman & Liebman 307 (2011).

5 The Unexplored: Direct Extraterritoriality

§1 Jurisdictional Principles in Animal Law

Because animals are still predominantly seen as objects of law, and, hence, as commodities for trade, trade law has a tremendous impact on states' ability to protect animals within and outside their borders. But from a jurisdictional perspective, WTO law, through which states can protect animals *indirectly*, is only one area where extraterritorial jurisdiction matters. General international law addresses debates and unpacks problems of extraterritorial jurisdiction that that loom larger. At a time when institutions finance projects abroad, where multinationals directly affect animals in foreign states, where animals are moved easily across borders to evade laws, and where animal production is split among numerous countries, one of the most pressing global problems of our time is how to *directly* protect animals abroad, namely, by tying jurisdiction to an anchor point located abroad or regulating content abroad.[1]

Direct jurisdiction is more controversial than indirect jurisdiction because it is considered a more intrusive form of extraterritoriality, but it is neither illegal nor rare. In business law, competition law, mergers and acquisitions, human rights law, environmental law, and other fields, states routinely regulate matters abroad. Under international law, any state that claims direct jurisdiction across its borders must show a jurisdictional basis by any of the so-called

[1] *See* for an analysis of these elements, Chapter 1, §3.

Protecting Animals Within and Across Borders. Charlotte E. Blattner.

principles of jurisdiction, like the territoriality, personality (or nationality), protective, effects, or universality principle.[2]

Traditionally, states had jurisdiction over all persons and objects present on their territory and events that took place there (territoriality principle), as well as jurisdiction over their nationals wherever they are located (nationality principle).[3] The principles of territoriality and nationality, however, did not to satisfy the many regulatory interests of states, especially after globalization took off. As the needs of states for effective regulation deepened, the international community began to recognize more jurisdictional principles and refined, modified, and extended extraterritorial jurisdiction through state practice. Today, the most common jurisdictional principles are the territoriality, personality (or nationality), protective, effects, and universality principle. Together, these principles are believed to cover the full range of states' social, economic, and legal interests, and they essentially determine the matters in which and the extent to which states can regulate extraterritorially.[4] Thus, international law, rather than per se prohibiting states from prescribing law across the border, follows the permissive principles approach.[5]

---

[2] Arrest Warrant, 2002 I.C.J. 44 (Separate Opinion of President Guillaume); LOUIS HENKIN, INTERNATIONAL LAW: POLITICS AND VALUES 232 (1995); MENG 466 (1994); Bernard H. Oxman, *Jurisdiction of States*, *in* MPEPIL 11 (Rüdiger Wolfrum ed., online ed. 2007).

[3] Oxman, *Jurisdiction of States*, *in* MPEPIL 11 (2007).

[4] Given the dynamic state of customary international law, this list is not considered exhaustive. New principles can emerge in the future but they almost always meet strong resistance. Meng studies in detail the admissibility of and requirements for introducing new jurisdictional principles: MENG 498 ff. (1994).

[5] In the early jurisdictional era, the PCIJ held that states are free to assert jurisdiction unless there is a prohibitive rule of international law. In principle, therefore, international law "leaves [States] in this respect a wide measure of discretion which is only limited in certain cases by prohibitive rules; as regards other cases, every State remains free to adopt the principles which it regards as best and most suitable." (Lotus, 1927 P.C.I.J. 19.). Almost all scholars reject this assertion, for several reasons. *Lotus* was based on the theory of legal positivism, but international law has matured over the last 60 years (through the adoption of the UN Charter, resolutions passed by the UN General Assembly, the acknowledgment of state duties, and various international bodies established by the international community). Spheres unregulated by positive law are now subject to fundamental principles of the international legal order; this is normativist or naturalistic theory of the international legal order. The permissive principles approach was strengthened in the post–World War II era (and hence in the post-*Lotus* era) by the emergence of the principles of sovereign equality of states, noninterference, and mutual respect for territorial integrity. *See further* Martti Koskenniemi, *International Legal Theory and Doctrine*, *in* MPEPIL 19 (Rüdiger Wolfrum ed., online ed. 2007); MENG 485–6 (1994); SCHWARZE 18 (1994). Moreover, the *Lotus dictum* was explicitly overridden by the Convention on the High Seas, Apr. 29, 1958, 450 U.N.T.S. 11, art. 11, re-enacted in art. 97 para. I UNCLOS. These treaties establish jurisdiction based on the flag state and the active personality principle. The *Lotus* judgment was also reversed by the ICJ in these cases: Nationality Decrees, 1923 P.C.I.J., at 24; Barcelona Traction, 1970 I.C.J. 105, ¶ 70 (Separate Opinion of Sir Gerald Fitzmaurice); Corfu Channel, 1949 I.C.J. 35; Fisheries Case (U.K. v. Nor.), Judgment, 1951 I.C.J. Rep. 116, 152 (Dec. 18) (Individual Opinion of Alvarez, M.); Barcelona Traction, 1970 I.C.J. 64, 105, ¶ 70 (Separate Opinion of Sir Gerald Fitzmaurice); Legality of the Threat or Use of Nuclear Weapons, Advisory Opinion, 1996 I.C.J. Rep. 226, at 268, 270–1 ¶¶ 12–3 (July 8) (Declaration of President Bedjaoui) [Nuclear Weapons, 1996 I.C.J.]; Arrest Warrant, 2002 I.C.J. 63, 78, ¶ 51 (Joint Separate Opinion of Judges Higgins, Kooijmans, and Buergenthal): "[. . .] the dictum represents the high water mark of laissez-faire in international relations, and an era that has been significantly overtaken by other tendencies."

Some scholars argue the jurisdictional principles can fully determine the scope of states' prescriptive jurisdiction and that they reliably resolve jurisdictional conflicts.[6] But these principles operate less determinately. They are options within an array of possibilities. States can have multiple bases for their claims and more than one state can assert jurisdiction over the same matter.[7] The more reasonable view thus is that these principles are a starting point for allocating jurisdictional competence and mitigating jurisdictional conflicts by separating valid from arbitrary claims.

Though states use the jurisdictional principles in various fields of law, they have not done so in animal law. *That* states may rely on these principles in any area of law—including in animal law—is accepted, *tout court*, by virtue of fundamental principles of the international legal order, including the sovereign equality of states, the prohibition of intervention, and the protection of the *domaine réservé* of states.[8] But *how* states can or should apply the jurisdictional principles to animal law is still unanswered. In this chapter, I explore, under the *lex lata*, how and to what extent states can use the general territoriality principle, the subjective and objective territoriality principles, the personality principle, and the protective principle to protect animals across the border. As I proceed, I categorize each principle in the extraterritoriality framework and determine its scope under international law.

§2 Territoriality Principles

A. PROTECTING ANIMALS ABROAD THROUGH THE TERRITORIALITY PRINCIPLE

It is a fundamental rule of international law that states enjoy jurisdiction within their borders. Territorial jurisdiction, hailed as "one of the bedrock jurisdictional notions,"[9] covers sovereign territory, limited by natural frontiers recognized by international law, by apparent signs of delimitation, or by legal treaties on boundaries.[10] Territorial jurisdiction also covers the territorial sea of a state extending 12 nautical miles from its coast to its maritime zones, its waters, and airspace above its land and sea.[11] States use the territoriality principle to regulate

[6] Coughlan et al. 37 (2007).

[7] Oxman, *Jurisdiction of States*, *in* MPEPIL 10 (2007).

[8] Meng used these overarching principles to apply the jurisdictional principles to public economic law: MENG 499–500 (1994).

[9] Coughlan et al. 31 (2007). *See also* CRAWFORD 458 (2012); INAZUMI 22 (2005); Mann 33 (1964).

[10] Island of Palmas, 1928 R.I.A.A. 838–9.

[11] UNCLOS, arts. 2 and 3. *See also* UNCLOS, arts. 27 and 29 exempting, in certain cases, the criminal and civil jurisdiction of the coastal state on board a foreign ship passing the territorial sea. Beyond the territorial sea (and thus beyond state territory), states may exercise jurisdiction in another 12 nautical mile zone (the contiguous zone). Contiguous zone jurisdiction is limited to customs matters, fiscal laws, immigration issues, and sanitary regulation (art. 33 UNCLOS). Even beyond the maximum 24 nautical mile contiguous zone, jurisdiction can be asserted to explore and exploit living and nonliving resources and energy in the exclusive economic zone, stretching up to 200 nautical miles from the baseline and subject to other states' rights (UNCLOS, arts. 55 ff.).

not only territory or territorial appurtenances but also property, persons, and events that occur there. As a consequence, even foreign visitors are *prima facie* subject to a state's territorial jurisdiction.[12]

Territorial jurisdiction requires that we decide *what factor* is used to determine territorial connections. In criminal terms, the territoriality principle primarily refers to *the place where a tort, offense, or injury has been committed.* Common provisions provide that "[a]ny person who commits a felony or misdemeanor in [state A] is subject to this Code."[13] The practical advantages of territorial jurisdiction over local crimes are accessibility when gathering evidence and availability of parties and witnesses.[14] Prescribing law for locally committed crimes also respects a state's interest in positively and negatively defining its public order.

Just as states have an interest in penalizing and preventing crimes against humans, they have an interest in preventing and sanctioning animal abuse, cruelty, and animal suffering. For instance, the German Animal Welfare Act (AWA) determines that individuals can be imprisoned or subject to fines for "killing a vertebrate without good reason or causing a vertebrate considerable pain or suffering out of cruelty or persistent or repeated severe pain or suffering."[15] The Swiss AWA criminalizes maltreatment of animals (article 26), offenses in international trade (article 27), and other offenses (article 28).[16] The AWA of the United Kingdom lays down liability for inflicting on animals unnecessary suffering, mutilation, tail docking, poisoning, animal fighting, and other acts (section 32 paras. 1–5).[17] Most states criminalize certain acts (or omissions) that harm animals, but they do not define their laws' jurisdictional scope. States could add to the introductory articles of their animal welfare act wording like: "any person who commits a felony or misdemeanor in state A is subject to the code of state A." This wording would help clarify the jurisdictional scope of their laws and show that they are primarily interested in regulating the welfare of animals in their territory.

In animal law, administrative orders like prohibitions against keeping an animal, administrative fines, and orders are an important form of regulation. States typically like to burden perpetrators with administrative consequences based on *where their animal welfare act, ordinance, or the like was violated.* This approach aligns with their understanding of general administrative law.[18]

---

[12] Hélène van Lith, International Jurisdiction and Commercial Litigation: Uniform Rules for Contract Disputes 22 (2009). This does not only encompass criminal jurisdiction; arguably all domestic laws apply to visiting subjects. *See, e.g.*, Lord Macmillan's opinion in Compania Naviera Vascongado v. SS Cristina [1938] AC 485, 496–7 (U.K.)).

[13] *E.g.*, Criminal Code (Switz.), art. 3 para. 1.

[14] Brownlie 301 (2008); Crawford 458 (2012); Oppenheim's International Law 458 (1992).

[15] Animal Welfare Act (Ger.), § 17.

[16] Animal Welfare Act (Switz.), arts. 26–8.

[17] Animal Welfare Act (U.K.), § 32 (1)–(5).

[18] *See, e.g.*, Animal Welfare Act (Ger.), § 18 ff.; Animal Welfare Act (Switz.), art. 23 (ban on keeping animals), art. 24 (regulatory intervention). *See* on the jurisdictional scope of administrative laws more generally: Herwig C.H. Hofmann et al., Administrative Law and Policy of the European Union 310–1 (2011).

Property may also be used as a basis for jurisdiction under the territoriality principle. The rule that states have jurisdiction over *property where it is located* (*lex loci situs*) is firmly established in private international law.[19] The *lex situs* rule applies to immovable property, but some argue it also extends to animals. Klerman claims that the territoriality rule would uniformly allocate jurisdiction among states: "[T]he right to acquire wild animals is best determined by the law of the place where the animal is captured rather than by the residence of the hunter."[20] But the question of whether the *lex situs* rule is appropriate for animal law is redundant if the wrong done to an animal entails administrative orders or criminal penalties that are covered by the law of the state where the crime was committed or where administrative provisions were violated. The *lex situs* only matters when an animal's interest is violated, but the violation is not penalized by criminal laws or administrative orders. Even then, it is unclear if the *lex situs* covers animal welfare considerations since the rule is typically limited to disputes involving title to property and asset value.[21]

The territoriality principle also establishes jurisdiction on the basis of a person's *domicile or residence*, as in private law, tax law, migration law, and special criminal law concerns.[22] For instance, article 4 of the Brussels Regulation determines that a defendant's domicile is decisive for establishing jurisdiction over matters of private law, regardless of the defendant's nationality.[23] The UK Crime (International Co-operation) Act of 2003 introduced into the Terrorism Act jurisdiction on the basis of natural persons' residence.[24] And sections 402 and 410 of the US Restatement of Foreign Relations, which list nationality as an admissible link for jurisdiction, clarify that residence, domicile, and presence are equally accepted criteria.[25] If legislation relates to animals, a state may use the domicile or residence of the perpetrator or the animal's owner to establish jurisdiction. Imagine the owner of a herd of sheep has employed a shepherd to care for their sheep. The owner is domiciled in Germany, but the shepherd and the sheep reside in France. In case of negligence, Germany can apply its animal law based on the owner's domicile, and France can apply its animal law based on the shepherd's domicile.[26]

Analogous to the place of domicile or residence for natural persons, states can establish jurisdiction over legal persons based on their *seat*. Article 63 para. 1 of the Brussels Regulation defines domicile for legal persons as the statutory seat, the central administration, or the

---

[19] Mann 59 (1964). *E.g.*, Regulation 593/2008 of the European Parliament and of the Council on the Law Applicable to Contractual Obligations (Rome I), 2008 O.J. (L 177) 6, art. 4(c).

[20] Daniel Klerman, *Jurisdiction, Choice of Law and Property*, *in* LAW AND ECONOMICS OF POSSESSION 266, 276 (Yun-Chien Chang ed., 2015).

[21] Pennoyer v. Neff, 95 U.S. 714 (1878) (U.S.). *See also* Akehurst 171 (1972–3); GREGOR GEISSER, AUSSERVERTRAGLICHE HAFTUNG PRIVAT TÄTIGER UNTERNEHMEN FÜR "MENSCHENRECHTSVERLETZUNGEN" BEI INTERNATIONALEN SACHVERHALTEN 253–9 (2013); VAN LITH 46 (2009).

[22] MENG 474 (1994); Oxman, *Jurisdiction of States*, *in* MPEPIL 11 (2007).

[23] Council Regulation 1215/2012 on Jurisdiction and the Recognition and Enforcement of Judgments in Civil and Commercial Matters (Recast), 2012 O.J. (L 351) 1 [Brussels Regulation]. *See also* its preamble.

[24] Crime (International Co-operation) Act 2003, c. 32, §§ 63B and 63C (U.K.); Terrorism Act 2000, c. 11 (U.K.).

[25] U.S. Restatement (Fourth) of the Foreign Relations Law, § 402, cmt. g and reporters' note 7; *id.* §410, cmt. c.

[26] Negligence vis-à-vis sheep is quite common, *see, e.g.*, Stefan Borkert, *Tierhalteverbot für Schafbauer*, THURGAUER TAGBLATT, May 10, 2010.

principal place of business. Canada and the United States establish personal jurisdiction over corporations where they are "doing business," i.e., engaging in "systematic and continuous" activities, as opposed to "irregular or casual" ones.[27] Since corporate seats are also used to determine their nationality, this link is both territorial and personal. Below, I examine jurisdiction based on the seat of corporations as an aspect of the personality principle.[28] Overall, the territoriality principle seems to cover a wide range of cases and offer multiple anchor points to respond to globalized events in animal law.

Two caveats render the territoriality principle less "user friendly." First, even if an act or omission occurs on state A's territory, other states may have a link to the same events. The owner of an animal might reside in state A, the perpetrator might permanently live in state B, or state B might have a legal interest in prosecuting the perpetrator. So, a case that appears territorial may still attract regulatory interests of foreign states, because owners, perpetrators, and victims have different nationalities, because damages and other effects are felt on foreign territory, or because auxiliary acts were committed by foreigners. It is only in exceptional circumstances that a case will have no connections across borders. Second, the territoriality principle presumes that acts are commenced and completed in a single state.[29] This, however, runs counter to social and political reality. In Mann's words: "[A] test developed in wholly different economic, social and technical conditions and at a time when corporations did not yet play a predominant role in international life is unlikely to satisfy a generation which is suspicious of rigidity, and, indeed, of principles."[30] Instead of rejecting the territoriality principle altogether on these grounds, it is more reasonable to view it as one of many bases of jurisdiction.

B. PROTECTING ANIMALS ABROAD THROUGH SUBJECTIVE AND OBJECTIVE TERRITORIALITY PRINCIPLES

To respond to some of the structural inadequacies of the territoriality principle, the international community established the subjective and objective territoriality principles. If acts or omissions span more than one state's territory, the principles of subjective and objective territoriality cover the entire act or omission (also known as the ubiquity theory in criminal law). Consider the following case: person A is present in state A, while person B is present in state B. Person A shoots across the frontier of state A, and the bullet enters the territory of state B and kills person B. Based on the principles of objective and subjective territoriality, both

---

[27] International Shoe Co. v. Washington, 326 U.S. 310, 320 (1945) (U.S.). *Cf.* for Canada: Association Canadienne Contre l'Impunité (ACCI) v. Anvil Mining Ltd., [2012] QCCA 117 (Can.). Art. 3148(2) of the Civil Code of Québec (c. 64, 1991 (QC, Can.)) unequivocally determines that "[i]n personal actions of a patrimonial nature, a Québec authority has jurisdiction where [. . .] the defendant is a legal person, is not domiciled in Québec but has an establishment in Québec, and the dispute relates to its activities in Québec."

[28] *See* Chapter 5, §3.

[29] The territoriality principle is readily applied where an act or omission occurred on one state's territory only, which is rarely the case. Most times, states use fictitious locations for committed acts, fictitious presence of persons, and terminological fictions to stretch the territoriality principle so that it fits their interests in extraterritorial regulation. *See* in detail Chapter 2, §2.

[30] Mann 37 (1964). *See also* Viscound Simonds in Metliss v. National Bank of Greece [1958] AC 509, 524 (U.K.).

state A and state B have jurisdiction over the entire act. The subjective territoriality principle establishes jurisdiction over an act that commenced in the territory of state A. The complementary principle of objective territoriality gives the state in which the act was completed (state B) the right to exercise jurisdiction over the entire act.[31] The objective territoriality principle was recognized by the Permanent Court of International Justice (PCIJ) in the landmark *Lotus* case, where it confirmed—by the casting vote of the president—Turkey's jurisdiction over a collision of two vessels on the high seas on the basis of effects felt on Turkish territory. In doing so, the Court was convinced that "control over territory necessarily include[s] control over events that affect that territory."[32]

The objective or subjective territoriality principles give states not only jurisdiction over the fragmented part of a crime committed in their territory but over the entire act or omission.[33] By accepting both subjective and objective territoriality, the international community established parallel authority for both states.[34] But not all acts or omissions that occur in the territory of two or more states justify applying the subjective and objective territoriality principles. If negligible parts of a crime are committed on one state's territory, this does not entitle it to jurisdiction. Also, a state cannot unilaterally determine how substantive a contribution an act makes to a crime for it to have jurisdiction. The United States in this respect claims that the principles allow it to prescribe law over conduct that has "wholly or in substantial part" occurred within its territory.[35] In contrast, Crawford argues that the conduct must be a constituent element of the act or omission in question.[36] The two views are congruent. A crime is committed in whole on a state's territory if all constituent elements are committed on its territory; it is committed in part on a state's territory if one of the constituent elements is consummated there. In a given case, we must thus determine if one of the constituent elements of a norm occurred on domestic territory. The nature of these elements may vary greatly. The objective territoriality principle, for example, covers physical effects that amount to a constituent element of the offense, and nonphysical effects, as in the case of libel or defamation.[37]

According to the International Bar Association's (IBA) Report on Extraterritorial Jurisdiction, states increasingly use the subjective and objective territoriality principles to tackle business crime, corruption and international fraud, as well as internet and international financial crimes.[38] The principles have also been applied to violations of antitrust

[31] CRAWFORD 458 (2012); INAZUMI 22 (2005); Harvard Research in International Law, *Jurisdiction with Respect to Crime*, 29 AJIL 435, 484–94 (Supp. 1935).

[32] Lotus, 1927 P.C.I.J. 23.

[33] CRAWFORD 458 (2012); Harvard Research in International Law, *Jurisdiction with Respect to Crime* 484–7 (1935); ORAKHELASHVILI 218–20 (2019); Anna Petrig, *The Expansion of Swiss Criminal Jurisdiction in Light of International Law*, 9 UTRECHT L. REV. 34 (2013); State of Arizona v. Willoughby, 862 F.2d 1319 (Az. Sup. Ct. 1995) (U.S.).

[34] Akehurst 152 (1972–3); SCHWARZE 23–4 (1994).

[35] American Law Institute, Restatement (Third) of the Foreign Relations Law of the United States, § 403 para. 1(a) (1987) [U.S. Restatement (Third) of the Foreign Relations Law].

[36] CRAWFORD 458 (2012).

[37] MENG 177 (1994).

[38] IBA REPORT EXTRATERRITORIAL JURISDICTION 12 (2009).

law, immigration regulation, and, generally, in the field of policy.[39] This expansion directly responds to economic globalization. As early as 1935, the Harvard Draft Convention noted that "with the increasing facility of communication and transportation, the opportunities for committing crimes whose constituent elements take place in more than one State have grown apace."[40]

Just like humans, animals can be victims of cross-border crimes that allow states to invoke the subjective and objective territoriality principles. Animals may be moved across borders while a crime is committed against or related to them, or they may be in a single location but are affected by a crime initiated elsewhere, which is consummated where the animals are located.[41] In the first case, if animals are transported from state A to state B in a manner contrary to the laws of either state, the transporting business may face criminal, administrative, or civil charges that cover the entire transportation process. This is supported by state practice. In the 1940s, Hackworth commented on an inhumane transport of cows from the former Republic Formosa to the United States: "[T]he offence, assuming that it originated at the port of departure in Formosa, was a continuing one, and every element necessary to constitute it existed during the voyage across the territorial waters. The completed forbidden act was done within American waters [. . .]."[42]

If states consistently applied the two territoriality principles to cross-border crimes committed against animals, this would fill regulatory gaps and have a positive impact on animals' lives. Thousands of animals are transported across borders each day, mostly to produce food, and many states assume they have no jurisdiction over these transports. Australia, the world's biggest exporter of live animals, exported 878,190 live cows, 1,953,918 live sheep, and 13,694 live goats in 2017.[43] With the rising number of live animal transports across the globe, claims that these transports cause immense suffering for animals have become more widespread.[44] In an attempt to address the problem, Australia established bilateral agreements and memoranda of understanding with trading partners to oblige exporters to continually monitor the animals' well-being and to hold them accountable if their actions do not meet international levels of animal welfare.[45] This has satisfied neither Australia's nor its trading partners' interests. Australia, however, has not yet tried to establish its jurisdiction over these transports on the basis of the subjective territoriality principle.

---

[39] Crawford offers a comprehensive list of these cases: CRAWFORD 458–9 (2012). *E.g.*, DPP v. Doot [1973] AC 807 (U.K.); DPP v. Stoenhouse [1978] AC 55 (U.K.); Liangsiriprasert v. Government of the United States of America [1991] 1 AC 225 (U.K.).

[40] Harvard Research in International Law, *Jurisdiction with Respect to Crime* 484 (1935).

[41] Akehurst states that the objective and subjective personality principles apply in cases of cross-border crime, or to crimes that extend over a long period of time: Akehurst 192 (1972–3).

[42] GREEN HAYWOOD HACKWORTH, DIGEST OF INTERNATIONAL LAW, vol. 2, 222 (1940–4).

[43] MEAT AND LIVESTOCK AUSTRALIA, LIVE EXPORT STATISTICS 1–3 (Jan. 2019), *available at* http://www.mla.com.au/NLRSReportDownload/LiveLink-26-Feb-2016.PDF (last visited Jan. 10, 2019).

[44] *E.g.*, Oliver Milman & Nick Evershed, *Alive and Kicking: Australia's Animal Export Trade Booms Despite Persistent Claims of Cruelty*, THE GUARDIAN, Aug. 3, 2015.

[45] *Australian Meat and Live-stock Industry (Export of Live-stock to Egypt) Order 2008*, Nov. 28, 2008, Annex A, Memorandum of Understanding on the Handling and Slaughter of Live Australian Animals (Austl.). Robertson refers to this as the "farm-to-fork" continuum and argues that the strategy is effective because failing to abide by the standards would decrease sales for exporters: ROBERTSON 199–200 (2015).

A bolder jurisdictional assertion was recently made in Europe. In *Zuchtvieh-Export GmbH v. Stadt Kempten* (C-424/13), the European Court of Justice (ECJ) held that harmonized provisions on the transport of animals destined for exports outside the European Union apply beyond EU territory.[46] Zuchtvieh-Export GmbH addressed the Court in matters concerning the decision by the Stadt Kempten, which refused clearance for transporting a consignment of cows to Andijan (Uzbekistan). The Court sided with Kempten, holding that from the point of departure to the point of destination in a third country, the organizer of the journey must abide by Council Regulation (EC) No. 1/2005, by providing necessary information on watering and feeding intervals, journey times, and resting periods.[47] These duties, as the Court held, are due during all stages of the journey, whether inside the territory of the European Union or in the territory of third countries. To justify the Regulation's extraterritorial application, the Court argued that animal welfare is a legitimate objective of public interest, as established in article 13 of the TFEU and in article 14(1)(a)(ii) and (b) of Regulation No. 1/2005, which must be respected outside EU borders. The judgment suggests the Court viewed the transport as an export over which the European Union had jurisdiction *qua* its public morals.

The Uttarakhand High Court used a similar line of arguments in a judgment of July 2018.[48] The petitioner sought directions to restrict the movement of horse carts, or *tongas* between Indian and Nepal through Banbasa in Uttarakhand's Champawat district. After addressing enforcement deficits and lax laws applying to cart-pulling horses, the High Court enlarged the scope of the petition to promote the protection and welfare of animals. It ruled that no animal should carry excess weight, that sharp equipment be banned, that animals not be made to work during excess heat, that they be provided with suitable shelters, that they be vaccinated, and that their health be checked by a veterinarian before transport. In its judgment, the Court pointed to the treaty of trade between India and Nepal that allows restricting trade for animal welfare reasons, which essentially conforms to article XX GATT. Like the ECJ, the High Court used public morals and state interests in protecting animal life as a basis for applying its law extraterritorially.[49]

Though the line of argument used by the two courts is understandable, they failed to distinguish transporting rules from export control laws. Export controls allow or disallow exports based on the laws of the destination country and extend beyond the transportation process. In contrast, laws on transport do not purport to regulate animal welfare beyond the point of arrival; they are an application of the subjective and objective territoriality principles. These differences matter because the laws governing export controls are much more

---

[46] Case C-424/13, Zuchtvieh-Export GmbH v. Stadt Kempten, 2015 E.C.R. I-1251.

[47] Council Regulation 1/2005 on the Protection of Animals During Transport and Related Operations and Amending Directives 64/432/EEC and 93/119/EC and Regulation 1255/97/EC, 2005 O.J. (L 3) 1, and corrigendum 2011 O.J. (L 336) 86.

[48] Narayan Dutt Bhatt v. Union of India (UOI) et al., Writ Petition No. 43 of 2014 (HC Uttarakhand at Nainital 2014) (India).

[49] *Id.* at 22.

delicate, legally, than norms based on jurisdictional principles.[50] Rather than risking a venture into a heated political debate, the courts could have used a more coherent strategy by invoking the subjective territoriality principle, which gives them full jurisdiction over cross-border animal transports.

Improper transport is the most frequent crime committed against animals across the border, but it is not the only one. The principles establish extraterritorial jurisdiction over all continuing offenses—a series of offenses that trigger the legal interests of several states—and connected offenses.[51] Theft, for example, is a continuing offense.[52] Stealing an animal in state A and bringing them to state B gives jurisdiction to both states *qua* the subjective and objective territoriality principles, an insight which matters for illegal wildlife trade, for example.

The subjective and objective territoriality principles also apply to crime commenced in state A and consummated in state B, while the animal has remained in state B throughout. In this case, a constituent element of a crime must have been committed on the territory of each state. It is again useful to look at the case of an owner of sheep in France who hired a shepherd to look after them. This time, the owner is domiciled in and a national of the United Kingdom. Because the shepherd failed to take care of the sheep, they suffered from hunger, thirst, and adverse weather conditions before dying. According to section 9 para. 1 of the UK AWA, "[a] person commits an offence if he does not take such steps as are reasonable in all the circumstances to ensure that the needs of an animal for which he is responsible are met to the extent required by good practice."[53] If the owner has insufficiently chosen, instructed, or supervised the shepherd, the owner is liable for negligent omission committed on British territory, the legal consequences of which are felt on French territory.[54] Thus, jurisdiction over cross-border crimes against animals is highly relevant for more complex cases where people fail to fulfill special duties as caretakers.

Likewise, extraterritorial jurisdiction has been accepted when parties have attempted, aided or abetted, or incited criminal offenses.[55] By establishing jurisdiction over these acts,

---

[50] *See* the dismissive stance of the ECJ in Case C-1/96, The Queen and Minister of Agriculture, Fisheries and Food, ex parte Compassion in World Farming Limited, 1998 E.C.R. I-1251, paras. 66–69. In 1998, the ECJ was called by Compassion in World Farming (CIWF) and the International Fund for Animal Welfare (IFAW) to declare that the United Kingdom was entitled to ban exports of calves that would likely be confined outside its territory in veal crates, a method widely criticized for negatively affecting the welfare of calves. The ECJ held that member states were barred from invoking article 36 of the Treaty Establishing the European Community (TEU) to rely on public morality, public policy, or the protection of the health or life of animals to justify export restrictions.

[51] CoE, *Extraterritorial Criminal Jurisdiction* 447 (1992).

[52] Akehurst 153 (1972–3). This includes jurisdiction over persons who assist the thief: R v. Elling [1945] AD 234 (U.K.).

[53] Animal Welfare Act (U.K.), § 9(1).

[54] For this example, the presumption against extraterritoriality as provided for in Animal Welfare Act (U.K.), Explanatory Notes, para. 8 was ignored.

[55] *Cf.* CoE, *Extraterritorial Criminal Jurisdiction* 447 (1992). Meng makes the point that such a broad scope of jurisdiction exists in continental Europe (e.g., CRIMINAL CODE (Switz.), art. 8), but is less established in the US system: MENG 175 ff. (1994). Conspiracy connotes an agreement of two or more persons to commit a crime. Complicit persons who fail to intervene by means reasonably available to them are liable for the acts of others. Persons may also be accessorily liable when they assist, but do not actually commit a crime. The same is true

the subjective territoriality principle may confer on a state a wide degree of extraterritorial jurisdiction.[56] In *Serre et Régnier*, the French *Cour de cassation* ruled that because France had jurisdiction over one national involved in committing a crime in Belgium (Serre), it could also claim jurisdiction over the national's accomplices, even though they were not French nationals.[57] In *Doe v. Unocal*, a local Myanmar subsidiary of the multinational corporation Unocal was alleged to have been complicit in the rape, torture, and murder of Burmese citizens by the Myanmar military. Before the parties settled on the issue, the US Court of the 9th Circuit, which had adjudicative jurisdiction on the basis of the parent corporation's seat, was determined to bring to application the aiding and abetting standards to hold the US parent liable for human rights violations abroad.[58] The same considerations apply to crimes committed against animals, including when instructions to mistreat animals are given by people in one state to people of another, when people located in different countries conspire to commit a crime against animals, or for attempted cross-border crimes. For example, in 2014, a documentary called *Cowspiracy: The Sustainability Secret* (directed by Kip Andersen and Keegan Kuhn), documented the massive negative environmental, social, and animal welfare effects of modern animal agriculture and showed how Greenpeace, Rainforest Action Network, Sierra Club, Surfrider Foundation, and other environmental nongovernmental organizations (NGOs) are paid by the farmed-animal industry to remain silent about the fact that animal agriculture is the biggest climate killer.[59] Although neither public prosecutors nor animal NGOs have (yet) brought charges, Greenpeace et al. could conceivably be viewed as conspirators to environmental law offenses that span the globe.[60]

C. TERRITORIALITY PRINCIPLES IN THE EXTRATERRITORIALITY FRAMEWORK

In the extraterritoriality framework, if animals are moved across the border the regulation links to the transported animal (animal-related anchor point) who becomes a transient anchor point moving from domestic (intraterritorial) to foreign (extraterritorial) territory. The content regulated (rules on transport) moves with the animal from intraterritorial content

---

of incitement, which modern forms of communication facilitate: Oxman, *Jurisdiction of States*, *in* MPEPIL 16 (2007).

[56] *See* U.S. v. Yousef, 327 F.3d 56, 96–7 (2d Cir. 2003) (U.S.); U.S. Restatement (Fourth) of the Foreign Relations Law, § 408, cmt. c. Already investing into multinational enterprises that violate certain standards can qualify as complicity: Anne Peters, *Sind transnationale Unternehmen verpflichtet, (internationale) Menschenrechte zu respektieren und zu fördern?*, *in* Menschenrechte und Wirtschaft im Spannungsfeld zwischen State und Nonstate Actors 127, 127 (Peter G. Kirchschläger et al. eds., 2005); Jennifer A. Zerk, Multinationals and Corporate Social Responsibility: Limitations and Opportunities in International Law 111 (2006 (Reprint 2008)).

[57] Cour de cassation [Cass.] [Supreme Court for Judicial Matters], Recueil Dalloz Sirey 395, 1991, "Serre et Régnier" (Fr.).

[58] The Court did not issue its judgment due to prior settlement of the parties: Doe v. Unocal Corp., 395 F.3d 978 (9th Cir. 2003) (U.S.).

[59] Cowspiracy, About the Film, *available at* http://www.cowspiracy.com/about/ (last visited Jan. 10, 2019).

[60] *See* Chapter 9, §3 C. for a more detailed examination of the substantial tests of conspiracy and complicity liability.

regulation to extraterritorial content regulation. In the most extreme scenario, this form of jurisdiction has an animal-related extraterritorial anchor point and regulates animal-related content extraterritorially. In the extraterritoriality framework, it qualifies as a type α_1 regulation.

Jurisdiction over cross-border crimes committed against animals who have stayed in one state throughout is treated differently in the extraterritoriality framework. Again, there is a sheep owner in the United Kingdom who hires but fails to instruct the shepherd to take care of their sheep in France. The United Kingdom has jurisdiction based on the subjective territoriality principle. Its jurisdiction is based on an intraterritorial anchor point that is non-animal-related (the owner is present on domestic territory and responsible for maltreating animals). The goal of ensuring the well-being of animals abroad is extraterritorial animal-related content regulation, so this is a type γ_1 regulation. France, which has jurisdiction based on the objective territoriality principle, uses an anchor point that is animal-related and intraterritorial (sheep welfare infringed on national territory). The content it regulates is animal-related and intraterritorial (improving the lives of animals by holding the UK owner responsible for violating a duty that is owed in France).

The scope of jurisdiction conferred to states on the basis of the subjective and objective territoriality principles is limited to the acts in question (e.g., violation of cross-border duties of care owed to animals). Jurisdiction does not cover any other acts of the responsible person unless they relate to the first (e.g., as accessory and auxiliary offenses). The subjective and objective territoriality principles thus narrowly apply to a specific act commenced or consummated on a state's territory.

§3 Active Personality Principle

A. NATURAL PERSONS

The personality principle springs from a state's personal sovereignty over its permanent population. By virtue of the personality principle, "a State is competent to create legal consequences for its nationals in relation to other States, which can take the form of direct rights, obligations, or the acquisition or loss of claims and property."[61] The principle refers to jurisdictional links from a state to natural or legal persons who have its nationality, and it applies regardless of their whereabouts, whether they are present on its territory, on foreign territory, or on lawless territory. The interest of states in regulating the behavior of their nationals abroad is the most accepted and universally used basis of extraterritorial jurisdiction, as acknowledged by the ICJ in *Nottebohm*[62] and in *Ahmadou Sadio Diallo*.[63] The active personality principle applies to actions and omissions of nationals abroad, while the passive personality principle establishes jurisdiction over nationals who are victims of crimes abroad.[64]

---

[61] Oliver Dörr, *Nationality*, *in* MPEPIL 44 (Rüdiger Wolfrum ed., online ed. 2006).

[62] Nottebohm Case (Liech. v. Guat.), Judgment (second phase), 1955 I.C.J. Rep. 4 (Apr. 6) [Nottebohm, 1955 I.C.J.].

[63] Ahmadou Sadio Diallo (Guinea v. Dem. Rep. Congo), Judgment, 2010 I.C.J. Rep. 639 (May 24) [Ahmadou Sadio Diallo, 2010 I.C.J.].

[64] ORAKHELASHVILI 220 (2019).

The personality principle is justified by the special bond established between individuals and a state *qua* nationality, which is why it is also referred to as the nationality principle. Nationality is seen as a form of allegiance, loyalty, or solidarity between a person and a state, and denotes the sum of obligations and rights between them. Allegiance from a person's perspective translates as protection and submission; from the state's perspective, it translates as diplomatic protection and jurisdiction.[65]

Given the dwindling importance of nationality in a globalized era, states sometimes invoke the personality principle to link their jurisdiction to a person's residence or domicile, regardless of their nationality. Sexual intercourse with minors abroad, for example, is punishable under French law based on the habitual residence of the perpetrator.[66] Permanent residents of Australia, Denmark, Finland, Iceland, Liberia, Malaysia, the Netherlands, Norway, Russia, Sweden, the United Arab Emirates, the United Kingdom, and the United States are liable to the laws of their domiciliary state if they commit crimes abroad.[67] International law considers lawful states' expansion of their personality link from nationality to residence or domicile, if the connection is strong enough to meet the jurisdictional purposes in question.[68]

Under international law, the personality principle—whether it relies on nationality, residence, or domicile—can be used in all fields of law. A state that demands its nationals abide by its AWA when they are temporarily or permanently situated abroad, acts in line with international law. Where a state's connection to its residents is strong enough, this is true, too.

In India, 80 percent of the population is Hindu and believes cows are sacred. Under the laws of India, killing female cows or calves for human consumption is illegal,[69] but each year, cows worth several hundred million dollars are raised in India and smuggled to its Muslim neighbor Bangladesh, where they are slaughtered.[70] In the summer of 2015, 30,000 Indian border guards were ordered to stop all Indian cows from crossing the border.[71] Instead of penalizing persons unrelated to India for smuggling cows, and thereby raising delicate issues of multiculturalism, India could rely on the active nationality principle for egregious acts

[65] This is also called *protectio et subiectio*: Thomas Hobbes, Elementa Philosophica III: De Cive, ch. 5, 12. Some qualify the relationship of allegiance as a contract between individuals and a state: Paul Weis, Nationality and Statelessness in International Law 30 (2d ed. 1979).

[66] Penal Code (Fr.), art. 227-27-1.

[67] According to the IBA Report on Extraterritorial Jurisdiction, 8 of 25 examined states provide for resident or domicile jurisdiction in addition to nationality jurisdiction. Those countries are Denmark, Finland, Malaysia, Netherlands, Norway, Russia, Sweden, and the UAE: IBA Report Extraterritorial Jurisdiction 145 (2009). For Australia, *see Criminal Code Act 1995*, Act No. 12, Dec. 1, 2015, § 272 (Austl.) [*Criminal Code Act 1995* Austl.)]. For the United Kingdom, *see, e.g.*, Terrorism Act 2000, c. 11, s. 63B, s. 63C (U.K.). For the United States, *see* U.S. Restatement (Fourth) of the Foreign Relations Law, § 410, reporters' note 3. For the remaining countries, *see* Akehurst 156 (1972–3).

[68] Oppenheim's International Law 469 (1992).

[69] Constitution of India, Jan. 26, 1950, art. 48 (India). *See* on this matter also art. 51 A lit. g of the Indian Constitution.

[70] In India, illegal trade in cow meat is flourishing: Sudhir Kumar Mishra, *Illegal Cattle Trade Headache for Cops*, The Telegraph, June 16, 2018.

[71] Kate Pickles, *Killing a Cow Is Equal to Raping a Girl Claims Hindu Nationalist Organization as 30,000 Indian Troops Are Told to Stop the Sacred Animals Being Smuggled Across the Border into Bangladesh to Be Eaten*, Mail Online, July 2, 2015

committed by its nationals against animals abroad, such as killing a cow. The connection is based on personal allegiance owed by Indian nationals to their state and the rising societal belief in India that cows must be treated respectfully.[72]

This is just one example of the many ways in which the active personality principle could be made fruitful for cross-border issues in animal law. Under international law, a state is in principle free to hold its nationals or residents, who are present abroad, liable for violating its animal laws, including norms prohibiting animal cruelty, improper transport or slaughter of animals, or norms laying down positive duties toward animals. The principle also confers on states a wide jurisdictional scope, since it covers people acting in private and professional capacity (e.g., as members of administrative boards or associates).

B. LEGAL PERSONS

Like (though not identical to) natural persons, corporations, associations, foundations, and other legal persons may be subject to a state's personal jurisdiction.[73] International law recognizes the need to affiliate legal persons to a state in order to establish personal jurisdiction (and diplomatic protection).[74] This affiliation is usually based on legal persons' nationality. But unlike natural persons, legal persons' nationality is not established on the basis of a statutory norm. Nationality also is not formally conferred, and no passports are issued to legal persons.[75] On this basis, Meng and others argue that "nationality" for legal persons is only a shorthand that identifies the applicable *Personalstatut*, i.e., the laws of the state that has the closest personal connection to a legal person. The German term *Staatszugehörigkeit* and the French term *allégeance politique* thus more accurately capture the affiliation between a legal person and its home state.[76] The personality principle covers ships and aircraft, too. Ships are identified as quasi-nationals on the basis of the flag state principle,[77] as are vehicles in airspace.[78]

[72] Wagman and Liebman, examining the Indian constitution, its AWA provisions, and court cases, argue that India is particularly sensitive to animal cruelty: WAGMAN & LIEBMAN 154 (2011).

[73] In economic terms, an entity that is geared to maximize profits qualifies as a corporation. But to count as a legal person, a corporation must have rights and duties, thus, legal capacity, which is conferred on it through law. A corporation is an entity recognized by law for its independent legal existence from its owners, and which can be sued in its own name, as a legal person: PHILIP BLUMBERG, THE MULTINATIONAL CHALLENGE TO CORPORATION LAW: THE SEARCH FOR A NEW CORPORATE PERSONALITY 4, 24 (1993); GEISSER 12 (2013); Menno T. Kamminga & Saman Zia-Zarifi, *Introduction*, *in* LIABILITY OF MULTINATIONAL CORPORATIONS UNDER INTERNATIONAL LAW 1, 3 (Menno T. Kamminga & Saman Zia-Zarifi eds., 2000); Peter T. Muchlinski, *Corporations in International Law*, *in* MPEPIL 1 (Rüdiger Wolfrum ed., online ed. 2014).

[74] Dörr, *Nationality*, *in* MPEPIL 24 (2006). Nationality of legal persons is important for the law of jurisdiction, because it protects corporations from injuries by foreign states and because states may claim treaty rights on behalf of their nationals: U.S. Restatement (Third) of the Foreign Relations Law, § 213, cmt. b.

[75] CoE, *Extraterritorial Criminal Jurisdiction* 449 (1992).

[76] MENG 467 (1994); Andreas Kley-Struller, *Die Staatszugehörigkeit juristischer Personen*, 2 SZIER 163, 167, paras. 8–9, 174, para. 23 (1991).

[77] The flag state principle is enshrined in art. 91 UNCLOS. *See also* The Antarctic Treaty, Dec. 1, 1959, 402 U.N.T.S. 71, art. VIII(1); Antarctic Act 1994, c. 15, s. 21 (U.K.).

[78] United Nations Treaty on Principles Governing the Activities of States in the Exploration and Use of Outer Space, including the Moon and Other Celestial Bodies, Jan. 27, 1967, 610 U.N.T.S. 205, arts. XII lit. a and IX

International law leaves the question of how states determine nationality for legal persons largely unanswered. State practice on this question is mixed. Common law countries use the *theory of incorporation* to determine corporations as their nationals if they are incorporated in their territory.[79] A notable advantage of this theory is that nationality is definitely established, which fosters legal certainty and consistency. But the theory of incorporation may define corporations as nationals of a state when they factually lack a substantial connection to it. Civil law systems therefore favor the place of the seat of corporate management or its headquarters as a link to establish nationality (real seat theory, *siège social*, or headquarters theory).[80] The *real seat theory* is less predictable because personal jurisdiction can change when the company's seat is moved. States sometimes choose a combined approach, by determining nationality based on the seat and the place of incorporation, as done in the Hague Convention Concerning the Recognition of the Legal Personality of Foreign Companies, Associations and Institutions.[81]

Other factors that influence a state's personality jurisdiction over legal persons are the nationality of shareholders who own a substantial part of a corporation, the management of an office outside the declared seat of formal management, and the principal place of business. The theory that defines nationality in reference to persons who possess real control over a legal person is called *control theory*.[82] Unlike the incorporation theory and the real seat theory, the control theory is disputed in international law. States are hesitant to apply domestic law to a foreign corporation that shows no outward connection to them. For example, the former US Securities Exchange Act established personal jurisdiction over foreign corporations that neither possessed listed US securities, nor offered any in its territory, and thereby caused a fierce debate in the international community.[83]

C. PARENT CORPORATIONS, BRANCHES, AND SUBSIDIARIES

Corporations that do business across borders, because they are incorporated in one state, manage operations abroad, and are controlled by people in yet another state, do not squarely fit the incorporation, real seat, and control theories. Because these corporations can be viewed as nationals by multiple states, they qualify as multinationals. A multinational enterprise is neither a single corporation operating on multiple territories, nor a single corporate form. It is a cluster of corporations with different nationalities, which

---

[Outer Space Treaty]; Agreement Governing the Activities of States on the Moon and Other Celestial Bodies, Dec. 18, 1979, 1363 U.N.T.S. 3, art. 14 [Moon Agreement].

[79] Internal Revenue Code, 26 U.S.C. § 7701(a)(4) (U.S.); U.S. Restatement (Fourth) of the Foreign Relations Law, § 402, reporters' note 7; Kley-Struller 167, para. 10 (1991); Staker, *Jurisdiction*, *in* INTERNATIONAL LAW 299 (2018).

[80] Dörr, *Nationality*, *in* MPEPIL 26 (2006); Kley-Struller 168, para. 12 (1991); OPPENHEIM'S INTERNATIONAL LAW 859–60 (1992).

[81] Hague Convention Concerning the Recognition of the Legal Personality of Foreign Companies, Associations and Institutions, June 1, 1956, 1 A.J.C.L. 277, art. 1. Three states have adopted the convention so far.

[82] U.S. Restatement (Third) of the Foreign Relations Law, § 402, reporters' note 7.

[83] Akehurst 181 (1972–3); Barbara S. Thomas, *Extraterritorial Application of the United States Securities Laws: The Need for a Balanced Policy*, 7 J. CORP. L. 189 (1982).

makes it not a multi- but a polycorporate enterprise.[84] In contrast to corporations, an enterprise is neither created by law nor recognized by it as a legal person. To be clear, "multinational corporation" and "multinational enterprise" are economic terms.[85] Because multinationals come in various economic forms, their definition is quite broad: they are clusters of corporations that own, control, or manage income-generating assets in more than one country. This definition encompasses both direct investment abroad (financial stake in foreign venture and managerial control) and portfolio investment (financial stake in foreign venture only).[86]

Some may think that having multiple states assert their jurisdiction over multinationals is useful because it creates a dense jurisdictional net across the globe. But nationality theories are often systematically exploited by multinationals to advance their corporate agenda. For this reason, scholars increasingly question the incorporation, real seat, and control theories as adequate tests for determining the nationality of enterprises.

Asset and unit mobility, flexibility in accommodating conduct, superior knowledge about compliance, and retention of common control make multinational enterprises appear to hover above and beyond legal systems, detached from nation states, and escaping all legal accountability. In some fields of law, states have concluded bilateral and multilateral agreements to fill these gaps, which unequivocally determine the nationality of enterprises and allocate them to a specific state. These agreements include tax treaties, treaties of friendship, commerce, and navigation, dispute settlement agreements, investment treaties, and treaties of establishment.[87] In all other cases, domestic law determines the nationality of multinational enterprises, within the limits of international law.

I. Dissecting the Multinational

There are two ways to assert jurisdiction over multinational enterprises, whether through an international treaty or domestic law. The multinational can either be treated as a legal entity or as a cluster of legally separate units.

A multinational is usually dissected into its corporate units, each subject to a particular state by virtue of its separate nationality. Any state using this method respects the principle of corporate separateness (also called the principle of corporate entity or of legal personality),

---

[84] José Engrácia Antunes, *The Liability of Polycorporate Enterprises*, 13 CONN. J. INT'L L. 197, 207–8 (1999).

[85] Kamminga & Zia-Zarifi, *Introduction*, *in* LIABILITY OF MULTINATIONAL CORPORATIONS UNDER INTERNATIONAL LAW 1, 3–4 (2000); PARRY ET AL. 395 (2009) "multinational corporations."

[86] OECD GUIDELINES FOR MNES 17, para. 4 (2011); U.S. Restatement (Third) of the Foreign Relations Law, § 213, cmt. f.; PETER T. MUCHLINSKI, MULTINATIONAL ENTERPRISES AND THE LAW 5 (2d ed. 2007). Hofstetter explains that the requirement of some sort of control covers portfolio investment because constructs like joint ventures easily transition from foreign direct investment to multinational enterprises: KARL HOFSTETTER, SACHGERECHTE HAFTUNG FÜR MULTINATIONALE KONZERNE: ZUR ZIVILRECHTLICHEN VERANTWORTLICHKEIT VON MUTTERGESELLSCHAFTEN IM KONTEXT INTERNATIONALER MÄRKTE 15–6 (1995).

[87] *E.g.*, Convention on the Settlement of Investment Disputes between States and Nationals of Other States, Mar. 18, 1965, 575 U.N.T.S. 159, art. 25(2) [ICSID Convention]. *Further* Kley-Struller 165, para. 5 (1991).

which presumes a corporation formed by shareholders is legally separated from them by its distinct legal personality.[88] In *Barcelona Traction*, the ICJ held:

> Separated from the company by numerous barriers, the shareholder cannot be identified with [the company]. The concept and structure of the company are founded on and determined by a firm distinction between the separate entity of the company and that of the shareholder, each with a distinct set of rights.[89]

The rationale for separating the corporation from its shareholders is that legal persons and individual shareholders have structurally different interests. In addition to legal separateness, corporations have the prerogative of limited liability. Shareholders only risk their capital contribution when they invest in a corporation and are insulated from the corporation's debts, which encourages investment.[90] Although the principle of limited liability was initially designed to apply to shareholders who are natural persons, half a century later it was extended to businesses.[91] Limited liability for natural and legal persons today is an established pillar of company law around the world.[92]

Combining limited liability with corporate separateness is a major advantage for multinational enterprises. A parent corporation and its incorporated subsidiaries are recognized by law as separate and distinct legal entities with their own rights and duties.[93] If limited liability protects shareholders, and a parent is a shareholder of its subsidiary, then limited liability protects the parent. Despite the economic advantages this combination seems to offer, it carries a variety of social and legal risks. Blumberg remarks:

> In the multitiered group, there are [. . .] as many layers of limited liability as there are tiers in corporate structure. Limited liability for corporate groups thus opens the door

[88] Legal personality denotes the "extent to which an entity is recognized by a legal system as having rights and responsibilities" (ZERK, MULTINATIONALS AND CORPORATE SOCIAL RESPONSIBILITY 72 (2008)).

[89] Barcelona Traction, 1970 I.C.J. ¶ 41. The principle of separate legal personality was also recognized in Ahmadou Sadio Diallo, 2007 I.C.J. ¶ 61.

[90] Muchlinski, *Corporations in International Law*, *in* MPEPIL 2 (2014); KAREN VANDEKERCKHOVE, PIERCING THE CORPORATE VEIL 3–4 (2007).

[91] Phillip I. Blumberg, *Accountability of Multinational Corporations: The Barriers Presented by Concepts of Corporate Juridical Entity*, 24 HASTINGS INT'L & COMP. L. REV. 297, 302 (2001).

[92] Code des sociétés [COMPANIES CODE], No. 1999A09646, M.B. 29440, May 7, 1999, arts. 210 (pour la société privée) and 438 (pour la société anonyme) (Belg.) [COMPANIES CODE (Belg.)]; CODE DE COMMERCE [BUSINESS ACT], Sept. 21, 2000, art. 223-11 (Fr.). Under German law, the principle is called *Trennungsprinzip*: AKTIENGESETZ [AKTG] [STOCK CORPORATION ACT], Sept. 6, 1965, BGBl. I at 1089, § 1 para. 2 (Ger.) [STOCK CORPORATION ACT (Ger.)]. For the Netherlands, *see* KAREN VANDERKERCKHOVE, PIERCING THE CORPORATE VEIL 33 (2007). In the United Kingdom, the principle of limited liability is known as the Salomon principles established in Salomon v. A. Salomon & Co. Ltd. [1897] AC 22 (U.K.)).

[93] Antunes 203 (1999); BLUMBERG, THE MULTINATIONAL CHALLENGE TO CORPORATION LAW 59 (1993); CYNTHIA DAY WALLACE, THE MULTINATIONAL ENTERPRISE AND LEGAL CONTROL: HOST STATE SOVEREIGNTY IN AN ERA OF ECONOMIC GLOBALIZATION 11 (2002); VANDERKERCKHOVE 3 (2007); ZERK, MULTINATIONALS AND CORPORATE SOCIAL RESPONSIBILITY 149 (2008).

> to multiple layers of insulation, a consequence unforeseen when limited liability was adopted long before the emergence of corporate groups.[94]

If we accept these concepts of company law for multinationals, this results in peculiar forms of jurisdiction. Domestic laws end up regulating separate, small fractions of the multinational entity, and ignore their economic entanglement, while corporations exercise control over their subsidiaries abroad without incurring liability. Though many laws are advantageous for corporations, it seems unreasonable that the law of jurisdiction should give multinationals a free pass to circumvent domestic laws, including animal law.[95]

This legal wall still stands strong, but the principles of limited liability and corporate separateness are not immutable, nor are the obstacles to applying national animal law to corporate units abroad. In exceptional circumstances, a state's personal jurisdiction, including its prescriptive authority over animal welfare matters, can be applied extraterritorially to other members of a multinational group.

The degree to which international law allows states to extend their jurisdiction to multinationals differs considerably and depends on whether jurisdiction covers actions of branches or subsidiaries. A branch is an unincorporated legal entity, an operating arm of the parent with no separate legal status.[96] In cross-border cases where a domestic parent establishes a branch abroad, the parent acts through its branch on foreign territory, so the parent's home state has personal jurisdiction over acts and omissions of the parent's branch abroad. International law generally permits parent-based personality jurisdiction, exercised by the home state over branches abroad.[97]

Unlike branches, subsidiaries are entities that are legally separate from their parents. Through the act of incorporation, a subsidiary becomes "legally more distant from the state of the parent corporation than if it operates as a branch."[98] As a rule, the principles of

---

[94] Blumberg, The Multinational Challenge to Corporation Law 139 (1993). Vanderkerckhove agrees with Blumberg on this point: Vanderkerckhove 5 (2007).

[95] Jodie A. Kirshner, *Why Is the U.S. Abdicating the Policing of Multinational Corporations to Europe? Extraterritoriality, Sovereignty, and the Alien Tort Statute*, 30 Berkeley J. Int'l L. 259, 263 (2012); José Maria Lezcano Navarro, Piercing the Corporate Veil in Latin American Jurisprudence: A Comparison with the Anglo-American Method 16 (2016); Muchlinski 115 (2007). Blumberg argues that applying the principle to multinational enterprises is a "mockery of the underlying objective of the doctrine" (Blumberg, The Multinational Challenge to Corporation Law 59 (1993)).

[96] More specifically, branches are wholly or jointly owned unincorporated enterprises in the host country. They can either be (i) a permanent establishment or office of the foreign investor; (ii) an unincorporated partnership or joint venture between the foreign direct investor and one or more third parties; (iv) land, structures, and/or immovable equipment owned by a foreign resident; or (v) mobile equipment operating within a country other than that of the investor for at least a year: Grazia Ietto-Gillies, Transnational Corporations and International Production: Concepts, Theories and Effects 12, 25 (2d ed. 2012).

[97] U.S. Restatement (Third) of the Foreign Relations Law, § 413 paras. 1–2; Principles for the Supervision of Banks' Foreign Establishment [Basel Concordat], May 2, 1983, *available at* http://www.bis.org/publ/bcbsc312.pdf (last visited Jan. 10, 2019); Eleventh Council Directive Concerning Disclosure Requirements in Respect of Branches Opened in a Member State by Certain Types of Company Governed by the Law of Another State (89/666/EEC), 1989 O.J. (L 395) 36; The (Draft) Overseas Companies Regulations 2009, No. 1801, art. 43 para. 2 (U.K.); Meng 475 (1994); Zerk, Multinationals and Corporate Social Responsibility 105 (2008).

[98] U.S. Restatement (Third) of the Foreign Relations Law, § 413, cmt. b. Subsidiaries are affiliates with equity involvement in excess of 50 percent and have a right to appoint or remove a majority of the members of the administrative management or supervisory body: Ietto-Gillies 12, 25 (2012).

legal separateness and limited liability preclude applying parent-based jurisdiction to foreign subsidiaries. However, under exceptional circumstances, a parent's home state can exercise jurisdiction over subsidiaries abroad, (a.) by combining the incorporation and real seat theories, (b.) by adopting the control theory, or (c.) by piercing the corporate veil.

a. Combining the Incorporation and Real Seat Theories

There is no hierarchy among the common theories used to determine corporate nationality in international law,[99] so extraterritorial jurisdiction over subsidiaries or parents located abroad can in principle be asserted through either the incorporation or the real seat theory. States might declare a foreign subsidiary or parent a national and exercise jurisdiction over them while ignoring the fact other states have conferred their nationality on them already. In any given case, these claims must be based on accepted criteria. If a parent corporation in state A is connected to a foreign subsidiary incorporated in state B, their legal separateness should, in principle, be respected. But if the foreign subsidiary—although incorporated according to the laws of state B—simultaneously has its main management or headquarters in state A, which regards the *siège social* as the link to nationality, a conflict arises. The US Export Administration Act of 1979, for example, was widely criticized for conferring US nationality to subsidiaries abroad, even though they were already incorporated in foreign territory and thus nationals of another state.[100] A conflict also emerges in the reverse case. If a parent corporation of state A is linked to the foreign subsidiary in state B, where it is primarily managed and regarded as a national of state B, there is a conflict if state A declares the subsidiary its national based on the incorporation theory. The same considerations apply when one state determines a parent's nationality that is incorporated in and managed from another state. An optimist might regard these combinations as openings for applying animal law to subsidiaries abroad. Since international law leaves the determination of corporate nationality to the states, this strategy cannot per se be viewed as violating international law.

b. Adopting the Control Theory

A corporation deemed alien based on the incorporation and real seat theories can be subject to a state's personal jurisdiction on grounds of the control theory. According to the control theory, a corporation (parent or subsidiary) incorporated and managed abroad (thus otherwise foreign) qualifies as a national of a state, if controlling persons or interests are located in its territory or if most of a company's shares are owned by its nationals.[101] The United States has incorporated the control theory in Title VII of the Civil Rights Act and the Export Administration Act.[102] Section 402 of the US Restatement more generally expands the reach of US law to corporations organized under the laws of a foreign state, if they are controlled

---

[99] GEISSER 109 (2013).

[100] Export Administration Act of 1979, 50 U.S.C. § 2405 (U.S.). Para. 1 of § 2405 was invoked by former President Reagan in 1982 to impose commercial restrictions on non-US corporations (i.e., foreign subsidiaries of US corporations). Europe formulated one of the strongest critiques of this strategy: European Commission, Comments on the US Regulations Concerning Trade with the USSR, Aug. 12, 1982. *See* HIGGINS, PROBLEMS AND PROCESS 73 (1995).

[101] Dörr, *Nationality*, *in* MPEPIL 27 ff. (2006); Oxman, *Jurisdiction of States*, *in* MPEPIL 20 (2007).

[102] Title VII Civil Rights Act, 42 U.S.C. § 2000e-1(c)(1) (U.S.); Export Administration Act of 1979, 50 U.S.C. § 2415(2) (U.S.).

or owned by its nationals and if it was unreasonable not to exercise jurisdiction over them.[103] According to the Restatement, the link of ownership or control is established where a national corporation owns a majority of the voting shares of the foreign corporation, where it owns a substantial bloc of its voting shares, or is its principal creditor and exercises significant decision-making authority over the affairs of the foreign corporation.[104]

The control test is often argued to better reflect economic realities than the theories of incorporation or management, but its acceptance in international law is disputed. In *Barcelona Traction*, Belgian shareholders invoked their right to diplomatic protection by Belgium over a Catalonian-managed company incorporated in Canada. The ICJ ruled that Belgium was barred from exercising diplomatic protection for its nationals because the Barcelona Traction company still existed as a legal person. Only Canada (as the place of incorporation) and Spain (as the place of the real seat) were entitled to these enforceable rights.[105] Thereby, the ICJ rejected the control theory for the purposes of diplomatic protection.[106] According to the Court, two exceptions justify determining nationality on the basis of controlling interests: if a company ceases to exist or if the company's home country lacks authority to act on the company's behalf.[107] Contra the majority opinion, Judge Fitzmaurice considered the control theory permissible where there is no genuine link to the state of incorporation or seat, giving rise to what he called "a different test of nationality."[108]

In *Elettronica Sicula*, decided 19 years after *Barcelona Traction*, the ICJ allowed the United States to bring a claim against Italy based on the nationality of controlling shareholders (who were US citizens), even though the corporation was a national of Italy.[109] In the eyes of some scholars, this judgment changed position vis-à-vis *Barcelona Traction*.[110] However, the claims made in *Elettronica Sicula* were based on the 1948 Treaty of Friendship, Commerce and Navigation between Italy and the United States, so the judgment tells us little about the state of customary international law. Moreover, *Elettronica Sicula* is authoritative only for the interpretation of international rules on diplomatic protection,[111] which does not allow inferring rules from it about corporate nationality. The same, however, could be said of *Barcelona Traction*.

In the realm of investment, states are more willing to use the control theory. Several investment treaties allow using effective control to establish nationality from a corporation to a state. This is commonly done through the nationality of shareholders or a company's genuine economic activity within a state.[112] Article 1 lit. b of the Netherland-Venezuela bilateral

---

[103] U.S. Restatement (Fourth) of the Foreign Relations Law, § 402, reporters' note 7.

[104] U.S. Restatement (Third) of the Foreign Relations Law, § 413, cmt. e.

[105] Barcelona Traction, 1970 I.C.J. ¶ 70.

[106] Muchlinski, *Corporations in International Law, in* MPEPIL 19 (2014).

[107] Barcelona Traction, 1970 I.C.J. ¶¶ 64 ff.

[108] Barcelona Traction, 1970 I.C.J. ¶ 83 (Separate Opinion of Judge Sir Gerald Fitzmaurice).

[109] Elettronica Sicula S.p.A. (ELSI) (U.S. v. Italy), Judgment, 1989 I.C.J. Rep. 15 (July 20).

[110] *E.g.*, Alexander Palenzuela-Mauri, *The International Court of Justice and the Standing of Corporate Shareholders Under International Law:* Elettronica Sicula v. Raytheon (U.S. v. Italy), 1 U. MIAMI INT'L & COMP. L. REV. 292 (2015).

[111] Peter Tomka, Elettronica Sicula *Case, in* MPEPIL 19 (Rüdiger Wolfrum ed., online ed. 2007).

[112] RUDOLF DOLZER & CHRISTOPH SCHREUER, PRINCIPLES OF INTERNATIONAL INVESTMENT LAW 49 (2d ed. 2012).

investment treaty (BIT), for example, states that nationals comprise, *inter alia*, "legal persons not constituted under the law of that Contracting Party but controlled, directly or indirectly, by natural persons [. . .]."[113] Similarly, the Multilateral Investment Guarantee Agency Convention (MIGA Convention) defines eligible investors, *inter alia*, as legal persons whose capital is owned by a majority of members of the MIGA or nationals thereof.[114]

The Convention on the Settlement of Investment Disputes between States and Nationals of Other States (ICSID Convention) also allows states to treat any legal person as a national of another contracting state on the basis of control (article 25 para. 2 lit. b). This provision was subject to dispute in *Tokios Tokeles v. Ukraine*, a case that involved claims against Ukraine by Ukrainian controlling shareholders of a company incorporated in Lithuania.[115] In principle, the Ukraine-Lithuania BIT would have allowed nationals to bring claims before the ICSID against their own states, based on the control theory.[116] But invoking the control theory would have removed the case from the ICSID's jurisdiction by transforming it into a national dispute (*Ukraine v. Ukraine*). Moreover, the parties did not expressly agree on establishing nationality based on the control theory. The ICSID Tribunal upheld the validity of the claim because the nationality of the corporation (determined by the place of incorporation) conformed to article 25 of the ICSID Convention and the definition of "investor" in article 1 para. 1 of the Ukraine-Lithuania BIT. The same ruling underlies *Rompetrol*.[117] In sum, the Tribunal is reluctant to use criteria of substantive control to determine corporate nationality in the absence of an express agreement between the parties. Scholars who criticize this practice claim that disregarding substantive control amounts to sacrificing the international character of the ICSID.[118]

It seems that the control theory is not yet sufficiently established as a third option, in addition to the incorporation and real seat theories. Scholars are reluctant to endorse the control test for many reasons, including the fact that the nationality of corporations quickly changes when members of the board of directors are replaced or when new shareholders invest. Many believe that the control test should therefore be applied only when rights are abused, specifically when legal obligations are deliberately circumvented.[119] This does not

---

[113] Agreement on Encouragement and Reciprocal Investments Between the Kingdom of the Netherlands and the Republic of Venezuela, Oct. 22, 1991. *Cf.* Ecuador-France Bilateral Investment Agreement, Sept. 7, 1994, art. 1 para. 3(ii).

[114] Convention Establishing the Multilateral Investment Guarantee Agency, Oct. 11, 1985, 1508 U.N.T.S. 99, art. 13(a)(ii) [MIGA Convention].

[115] Tokios Tokeles v. Ukraine, ICSID Case No. ARB/02/18, Award, July 26, 2007.

[116] Muchlinski, *Corporations in International Law*, *in* MPEPIL 21–3 (2014).

[117] In *Rompetrol*, the corporation was incorporated in the Netherlands, but controlled by Romanian nationals. The tribunal ruled that jurisdiction must be granted, since Rompetrol was a foreign investor, regardless of shareholder control: Rompetrol v. Romania, ICSID Case No. ARB/06/3, Decision on Respondent's Preliminary Objections on Jurisdiction and Admissibility, Apr. 18, 2008.

[118] D'Agnone finds that "the control test is the key element to discover the real nature of the dispute—whether it is genuinely international or not" (Giulia D'Agnone, *Determining the Nationality of Companies in ICSID Arbitration*, *in* THE CHANGING ROLE OF NATIONALITY IN INTERNATIONAL LAW 153, 157 (Alessandra Annoni & Serena Forlati eds., 2013)).

[119] Ivo Schwander, *Die juristischen Personen im schweizerischen Recht*, *in* RAPPORTS SUISSES PRESENTÉS AUX XIIÈME CONGRES INTERNATIONAL DE DROIT COMPARE 23, 37 f (Montreal, Aug. 19–24, 1990).

mean the control test cannot in the future develop into a fully-fledged and accepted third theory for determining corporate nationality. That the ICJ's judgment in *Barcelona Traction* concerned a case of diplomatic protection suggests that it is of limited value for nationality jurisdiction. Moreover, *Elettronica Sicula* and the many investment treaties prove that the test is increasingly accepted. Whether a state will therefore act in line with international law by invoking the control theory in a general and broad manner remains to be seen.[120]

c. *Piercing the Corporate Veil*

Though the control test is not currently accepted as a third alternative to the incorporation and real seat theories, states frequently soften the rigid and limited principles of corporate separateness and limited liability. Lifting or piercing the corporate veil (*percer le voile*) is an exceptional tool of corporate law that allows states to extend shareholder liability to the parent corporation or subsidiary, so it is no longer limited to the shareholder's capital contribution.[121] The purpose of this exception is, by and large, to frustrate the principle of limited liability, where legal risks are taken in obvious misrelation to economic reality. Accordingly, lifting the corporate veil is sometimes argued to be an application of the control theory, which more accurately mirrors economic relationships.[122] If the subsidiary's shareholder is its parent, lifting also disregards their separate corporate personality.[123] From the jurisdictional perspective, piercing the veil allows the regulating state to extend its personal jurisdiction to shareholders with foreign nationality (which may be foreign parents or subsidiaries). Jurisdictional veil piercing is therefore largely congruent with piercing the corporate veil in company law.[124]

---

[120] Most scholars are silent on this topic: Oxman, *Jurisdiction of States*, *in* MPEPIL 20 (2007).

[121] Day Wallace 631 (2002). "Lifting the veil" is widely used in the United Kingdom, while "piercing the veil" is the most established term in the United States: Day Wallace 630 (2002). Other terms are "penetrating," "ignoring," "extending," or "parting" the veil: Vanderkerckhove 11 (2007).

[122] Kley-Struller 174, para. 24 (1991).

[123] Thomas K. Cheng, *The Corporate Veil Doctrine Revisited: A Comparative Study of the English and the U.S. Corporate Veil Doctrines*, 34 B.C. Int'l & Comp. L. Rev. 328, 343 (2011); Meng 475 (1994).

[124] According to a number of scholars (especially German scholars), there is a cardinal difference between piercing the corporate veil in substantive law (*Haftungsdurchgriff*) and piercing the corporate veil for jurisdictional purposes (*Zuständigkeitsdurchgriff*): Geisser 243 n. 898 (2013); Hofstetter 169, 171 (1995); Haimo Schack, *Der prozessuale Durchgriff im internationalen Konzern*, *in* Gedenkschrift für Jürgen Sonnenschein 705 (Joachim Jickeli et al. eds., 2003); Dietrich Welp, Internationale Zuständigkeit über auswärtige Gesellschaften mit Inlandstöchtern im US-amerikanischen Zivilprozess 131 (1982). State practice, however, does not support this distinction. In *Prest v. Petrodel Resources Limited et al.*, a case decided by the UK Supreme Court, Lord Sumption held: "'Piercing the corporate veil' is an expression rather indiscriminately used to describe a number of different things." (Prest v. Petrodel Resources Limited et al. [2013] 2 AC 415, Lord Sumption, para. 16 (U.K.)). That jurisdictional and substantive corporate veil piercing theories overlap makes sense in light of the more general observation that, as Justice Reed noted, "[t]he line between procedural and substantive law is hazy" (Erie Railroad Co. v. Tompkins, 304 U.S. 64, 91 (1938) (U.S.)). Schwenzer and Hosang note that if the corporate veil is lifted by extending liability in substantive law, procedural laws must extend accordingly (Ingeborg Schwenzer & Alain F. Hosang, *Menschenrechtsverletzungen: Schadenersatz vor Schweizer Gerichten*, 21 SZIER 273, 283 (2011)). Vandekerckhove, the author of one of the most comprehensive works on corporate veil piercing, observes that in most cases, jurisdictional questions were answered by examining traditional piercing doctrines under entity law (Vanderkerckhove 522 (2007)). The ILA Report on International Civil Litigation for Human Rights Violations argues that

States use various theories to pierce the corporate/jurisdictional veil, most of which are uncodified and subject to frequent change through judicial practice. These theories include:

- express agency (the subsidiary merely acts as an agent of the parent);[125]
- guarantee (the parent guarantees to be liable for the subsidiary's actions);[126]
- clear authorization or direction (the subsidiary is authorized or directed to follow the parent's instructions);[127]
- implied agency (attribution of a subsidiary's actions to its nonresident parent);[128]
- instrumentality (there is parental control over the subsidiary to such an extent that the subsidiary has no separate mind, will, or existence of its own);[129]
- *alter ego* (a parent and its subsidiary are fundamentally indistinguishable);[130]
- façade, sham, or paper corporation (the subsidiary has no assets, employees, or business of its own);[131]
- *faktische Organschaft* (a formally elected parent dominates a subsidiary's governance decisions);[132]

---

the theories of piercing the corporate veil, agency, control theory, integration, agent doctrines, and other substantive liability tools establish jurisdiction over corporations which *per se* do not have contact to the state in question (INTERNATIONAL LAW ASSOCIATION [ILA], INTERNATIONAL CIVIL LITIGATION FOR HUMAN RIGHTS VIOLATIONS, FINAL REPORT 8 (ILA, London 2012)). Also supporting the opinion defended herein: Peter Behrens, *Der Durchgriff über die Grenze*, 46 RABELSZ 308, 309 (1982); Hannah L. Buxbaum, *The Viability of Enterprise Jurisdiction: A Case Study of the Big Four Accounting Firms*, 48 U.C. DAVIS L. REV. 1769, 1769–70 (2015) (emphasis added); BLUMBERG, THE MULTINATIONAL CHALLENGE TO CORPORATION LAW 168 (1993).

[125] Adams v. Cape Industries PLC [1990] Ch. 433 [1990] 2 WLR 786 (U.K.); Kingston Dry Dock v. Lake Champlain Transportation, 31 F.2d 265 (2d Cir. 1929) (U.S.); Bundesgericht [BGer] [Federal Supreme Court] Mar. 17, 1982, Entscheidungen des schweizerischen Bundesgerichts [BGE] 108 II 122, at 4 and 5 (Switz.).

[126] English courts established that to be held liable for the subsidiary's obligations, a parent must operate as a guarantor: Amalgamated Investment & Property Co. v. Texas Commercial Bank [1982] QB 84 (CA) (U.K.); Gold Coast Ltd v. Caja de Ahorros del Mediterraneo [2001] EWCA Civ. 1806 (U.K.).

[127] Under the US Foreign Corrupt Practices Act, for instance, the parent is liable for damages caused when it authorizes or directs corrupt payments: Foreign Corrupt Practices Act, 15 U.S.C. § 78dd-1 (U.S.).

[128] MUCHLINSKI 143 (2007); Smith, Stone and Knight v. Birmingham [1939] 4 All. E.R. 116 (U.K.). *See also* In re (FG) Films [1953] 1 WLR 484, 486 (U.K.).

[129] Lowendahl v. Baltimore & Ohio Railroad, 247 A.D. 144, 157–8 (N.Y. App. Div. 1936) (U.S.); In Re Investigation of World Arrangements, 13 FRD 280, 285 (D.D.C. I 1952) (U.S.)); Parker v. Bell Asbestos Mines Ltd., 607 F. Supp. 1397 (E.D. Pa. 1985) (U.S.).

[130] Hamilton v. Water Whole International Corp., 302 F. Appx. 789, 793 (10th Cir. 2008) (U.S.); Doe v. Unocal Corp., 395 F.3d 932 (9th Cir. 2002) (U.S.), unreported "Ruling on the Defendants," Motion for Judgment, Decision of the Superior Court of California, County of Los Angeles, Sept. 14, 2004; Associated Vendors Inc. v. Oakland Meat Co., 210 Cal. App.2d 825, 838–40 (1962) (U.S.); RRX Indust. Inc. v. Lab-Con Inc., 772 F.2d 543, 545 (9th Cir. 1985) (U.S.); ILA, NEW DELHI CONFERENCE, COMMITTEE ON INTERNATIONAL CIVIL AND COMMERCIAL LITIGATION, FOURTH AND FINAL REPORT, JURISDICTION OVER CORPORATIONS 6, 8 (ILA, London 2002).

[131] Arnold v. Phillips, 117 F.2d 497, 502 (5th Cir. 1941) (U.S.). The less independent a business operation, the more likely the parent is to use the subsidiary as a façade: Cheng (2011) 385.

[132] BGer Dec. 12, 1991, BGE 117 II 570, 574 (Switz.). The *de facto* body must have had the power to cause, prevent, or considerably influence the subsidiary's business: BGer Oct. 29, 2001, BGE 128 III 92 (Switz.); BGer Aug. 27, 1991, BGE 117 II 432, at 2.b (Switz.).

- *la société fictive* (the subsidiary's only purpose is to benefit the parent);[133]
- *naamlening* (the subsidiary is the "straw man" of its parent);[134] and
- vicarious liability or instrumentality liability (the parent is involved in the managerial control of its subsidiary in the context of tort activities).[135]

In various cases, the concepts of agency, instrumentality, identification, and identity have been treated as interchangeable for the purpose of piercing the corporate veil.[136] Some courts have given up on identifying an overarching theory, and simply use a "laundry list" of factors to determine personal jurisdiction. The most frequently used factors to pierce the veil include involvement in management, investment, appointment, and daily business operations[137] that are seen as wrongful, inequitable, unfair, or morally wrong to such an extent that regulatory intervention is justified, even if these actions do not constitute fraud and are not per se illegal.[138]

Though states are far from abolishing limited liability and corporate separateness, they will look behind the veil where circumstances permit it. According to Matheson's recent empirical study, the overall pierce rate for his data set of 9,380 cases was 31.86 percent.[139] Under the law of Canada and the United States, two elements are needed to pierce the veil. First, the parent must have exerted excessive control over the subsidiary, such as by intruding into its day-to-day

---

[133] WERA KUCKERTZ, DER HAFTUNGSDURCHGRIFF AUF AUSLÄNDISCHE UNTERNEHMEN UND GESCHÄFTSLEITER NACH FRANZÖSISCHEM RECHT 41 (2002).

[134] Hof van Cassatie [Cass.] [Court of Cassation], May 26, 1978, Stagno v. Vanhoyland q.q., RW 846 (1978–9) (Belg.).

[135] CSR v. Wren (1997) 44 N.S.W.L.R. 463 (C.A. NSW) (Austl.); Tesco Supermarkets Ltd. v. Nattrass [1972] AC 153 (U.K.); Bowoto v. Chevron Corp., 312 F. Supp. 2d 1299 (N.D. Cal. 2004) (U.S.); In re Oil Spill by "Amoco Cadiz," 1984 A.M.C. 2123 (D.C. Ill. 1984) (U.S.).

[136] House of Koscot Dev. Corp v. Am. Line Cosmetics Inc., 468 F.2d 64 (5th Cir. 1973) (U.S.): "Although some commentators have distinguished between the 'agency' and 'instrumentality' or 'identity' rationales, the theories are interchangeable." *See also* New York Trust Co. v. Carpenter, 250 F. 668, 673 (6th Cir. 1918) (U.S.).

[137] The following factors are usually considered when assessing parental domination: common stock ownership; common directors or officers; common business departments; consolidated financial statements and tax returns; transfer of finances from the parent to the subsidiary; whether the parent caused subsidiary to incorporate; whether the subsidiary operates with grossly inadequate capital; whether the parent pays the salaries and other expenses of the subsidiary; whether the subsidiary receives no business except that given to it by the parent; whether the parent uses the subsidiary's property as its own; whether the daily operations of the two corporations are kept separate; and whether the subsidiary observes the basic corporate formalities, like keeping separate books and records and holding shareholder and board meetings: Carte Blanche (Singapore) Pte. Ltd. v. Diners Club Int'l, 2 F.2d 24 (2d Cir. 1993) (U.S.); United States v. Jon-T Chemicals Inc., 768 F.2d 686, 691 (5th Cir. 1985) (U.S.). Canadian courts have used similar criteria. In *Amfac*, the Oregon Court of Appeals relied on the following factors: inadequate capitalization; excessive dividends milling the subsidiary's funds; misrepresentation of facts; commingling of funds; representation of the parent and subsidiary as one entity; and violation or circumvention of a statute by relying on limited liability: Amfac v. Int'l Systems & Controls Corp., [1981] 654 P.2d 1092, 1101 (Ore Ct. App.) (Can.).

[138] BLUMBERG, THE MULTINATIONAL CHALLENGE TO CORPORATION LAW 83 (1993).

[139] Matheson built his database on a wide range of cases from the United States, stretching from 1990 to 2008: John H. Matheson, *Why Courts Pierce: An Empirical Study of Piercing the Corporate Veil*, 7 BERKELEY BUS. L.J. 1, 10, 58 (2010).

decisions. Second, the parent must have acted fraudulently, unjustly, or inequitably, which is broadly interpreted by courts.[140] This kind of conduct encompasses actual fraud, evading the law, dominance, commingling of assets, and other sorts of undue reliance on limited liability within multinational enterprise structures. Other criteria operate as indicia for excessive parental control, such as owning 100 percent of shares, undercapitalization, and hiring the same directors or managers.[141]

In Europe, states have a slightly different approach. The United Kingdom is rather resistant to piercing the corporate veil because of its *Salomon* principles established in 1897 that are still a cornerstone of contemporary UK company law.[142] The centuries-old rule, however, may have been significantly relaxed after the recent *Prest v. Petrodel Resources Limited et al.* case.[143] The rest of Europe appears willing to pierce the corporate veil based on factors similar to those adopted in US jurisprudence, including majority share ownership, actual direction, and excessive control.[144]

Piercing the corporate veil is often seen as a response to the lingering conflict between lawfully resorting to the principles of limited liability and corporate separateness, and abusing established principles of corporate law. Courts accordingly apply the principle of abuse of rights quite frequently when they lack statutory law that would allow them to peep behind the veil.[145] In *Castleberry v. Branscum*, the Supreme Court of Texas held:

> We disregard the corporate fiction, even though corporate formalities have been observed and corporate and individual property have been kept separately, when the corporate form has been used as part of a basically unfair device to achieve an inequitable result. [. . .] Specifically, we disregard the corporate fiction: [. . .] where the corporate fiction is resorted to as a means of *evading an existing legal obligation*; [. . .] where

---

[140] Tort, for these purposes, is not sufficient to trigger fraudulent behavior: Blumberg, *Accountability of Multinational Corporations* 306 (2001); Sandra K. Miller, *Piercing the Corporate Veil Among Affiliated Companies in the European Community and in the U.S.: A Comparative Analysis of U.S., German, and U.K. Veil-Piercing Approaches*, 36 Am. Bus. L.J. 73, 88 (1998).

[141] Various courts have held that 100 percent ownership is insufficient to pierce the veil: Ebbw Vale Urban District Council v. South Wales Traffic Area Licensing Authority [1951] 2 KB 366, 370 (U.K.); Amfac v. Int'l Systems & Controls Corp., [1981] 654 P.2d 1092 (Ore Ct. App.) (Can.). Other courts have held that undercapitalization is insufficient: Radaszewski v. Telecom Corp., 981 F.2d 305, 308 (8th Cir. 1992) (U.S.); Re Southard and Co. Ltd. [1979] 1 WLR 1198, 1208 (U.K.); DeWitt Truck Brokers v. W. Ray Fleming Fruit Co., 540 F.2d 681, 687–8 (4th Cir. 1976) (U.S.). Pursuant to article 646 of the Belgium Companies Code, concentrating all shares in one shareholder results in "l'actionnaire unique est réputé caution solidaire de toutes les obligations de la société nées après la réunion de toutes les actions entre ses mains." (Companies Code (Belg.), art 646.). *See also* United States v. Scophony Corp, 333 U.S. 795 (1948) (U.S.); Hofstetter 15 (1995); Jonathan Macey & Joshua Mitts, *Finding Order in the Morass: The Three Real Justifications for Piercing the Corporate Veil*, 100 Cornell L. Rev. 99, 107 (2014).

[142] Salomon v. A. Salomon & Co. Ltd. [1897] AC 22 (U.K.). The principles are considered "sacrosanct" in the United Kingdom: Lezcano Navarro 21 (2016); Vanderkerckhove 499 (2007).

[143] Prest v. Petrodel Resources Limited et al. [2013] 2 AC 415 (U.K.).

[144] Daniel Augenstein, Study of the Legal Framework on Human Rights and the Environment Applicable to European Enterprises Operating Outside the European Union, Prepared by the University of Edinburgh for the European Commission 63 (2010).

[145] Vanderkerckhove 33 (2007).

> the corporate fiction is used to *circumvent a statute*; and [. . .] where the corporate fiction is relied upon as a *protection of crime or to justify wrong*.[146]

Also UK courts are willing to pierce the veil when corporations circumvent the law. In the 2013 *Prest v. Petrodel Resources Limited et al.* case, Lord Sumption argued that piercing the corporate veil is justified where corporations abuse limited liability to evade or frustrate the law.[147] To achieve the same results, civil law courts rely on the principle of good faith and the prohibition of abuse of rights to pierce the veil.[148] But the line between abusive exploitation and legitimate use of the principles of company law is delicate. In *Aguas del Tunari v. Bolivia*, a case submitted to an ICSID Tribunal, the controlling company moved its seat to another state, and the respondent alleged this move was an abuse of the corporate form. The Tribunal rejected the argument: "[I]t is not uncommon in practice, and—absent a particular limitation—not illegal to locate one's operations in a jurisdiction perceived to provide a beneficial regulatory and legal environment in terms, for example, of taxation or the substantive law of the jurisdiction [. . .]."[149] Overall, whether a state will be able to successfully establish personal jurisdiction over animal matters related to foreign subsidiaries, branches, or parents thus depends strongly on the specific state of facts and the law that applies to the case.

II. The Multinational as a Single Legal Unit

Because states do not recognize multinationals as legal persons, they do not usually have rights or obligations toward them as a whole.[150] But there are important exceptions to this rule. Single economic unit theories, which consider the extent of economic integration between the parent and the subsidiary (i.e., actual exercises of power within a multinational enterprise), allow a state to bring a multinational as a single unit under its jurisdiction without having to pierce the corporate veil. Economic unit theories, by narrowly focusing on economic factors, are distinct from veil piercing theories that also look at elements of equity or fraudulent and otherwise wrongful behavior.[151]

The first cases that treated multinationals as legal units emerged in antitrust law. In *Dyestuffs*, the English parent Imperial Chemical Industries Ltd. (ICI) was accused of having engaged in

---

[146] Castleberry v. Branscum et al., 721 S.W.2d 270, 272 (S. Ct. Tex. 1986) (U.S.) (emphasis added).

[147] Prest v. Petrodel Resources Limited et al. [2013] 2 AC 415, Lord Sumption, paras. 33–5 (U.K.). *See also* Stone & Rolls v. Moore Stephens [2009] 1 AC 1391, 1447–8 (U.K.).

[148] For Belgium: VANDERKERCKHOVE 33 (2007). For Germany: BGHZ 173, 246, NJW 2689, 2007 "Trihotel" (Ger.). For Switzerland: BGer Sept. 26, 2011, BGE 137 III 550, at 2.3.1 (Switz.): "Toutefois, le voile social peut être levé et l'identité économique avec la société dominante être invoquée (*Durchgriff*) lorsque le fait d'opposer l'indépendance juridique des deux entités constitue un abus de droit." The prohibition of an abuse of law is laid down in art. 2 CIVIL CODE (Switz.).

[149] Aguas del Tunari v. Bolivia, ICSID Case No. ARB/02/3, Decision on Jurisdiction, Oct. 21, 2005.

[150] LEZCANO NAVARRO 15 (2016); ZERK, MULTINATIONALS AND CORPORATE SOCIAL RESPONSIBILITY 104 (2008).

[151] BLUMBERG, THE MULTINATIONAL CHALLENGE TO CORPORATION LAW 91 (1993); Buxbaum, *The Viability of Enterprise Jurisdiction* 1780–2 (2015) (arguing that the concept of enterprise law developed as a counterpoint to entity law and that enterprise theory focuses on economic reality rather than legal formalism like the traditional corporate veil piercing theories); Yitzhak Hadari, *The Structure of Private Multinational Enterprise*, 71 MICH. L. REV. 729, 773 (1973); Kirshner 267–8 (2012); Note, *Alternative Methods of Piercing the Corporate Veil in Contract and Tort Cases*, 48 B.U.L. REV. 123 (1968); MENG 330 (1994).

illegal practices in the European Union (before it became a member of the European Union) through acts of its subsidiaries. The ICI owned most of its subsidiaries' shares, exercised decisive influence over them, and ordered them to engage in anticompetitive behavior. Despite being legally distinct, the ECJ argued, the parent and the subsidiaries together formed a "unity of the group."[152] According to the Court, "[t]here is a presumption that a subsidiary will act in accordance with the wishes of its parent because according to common experience subsidiaries generally do so act; [. . .], unless that presumption is rebutted, it is proper for the parent and the subsidiary to be treated as one single undertaking [. . .]."[153] In this case, intragroup liability can be established that spans borders "without having to establish the personal involvement of the latter in the infringement."[154] The Court thereby clarified that a single undertaking is determined as such by reference to economic involvement rather than legal attribution.[155]

The ECJ's "unity of the group" theory, also known as economic entity theory, was used in several cases following *Dyestuffs*.[156] In *Akzo Nobel NV*, the ECJ held:

> Community competition law is based on the principle of the personal responsibility of the economic entity, which has committed the infringement. If the parent company is part of that economic unit, which [. . .] may consist of several legal persons, the parent company is regarded as jointly and severally liable with the other legal persons making up that unit for infringements of competition law. *Even if the parent company does not participate directly in the infringement*, it exercises, in such a case, a *decisive influence over the subsidiaries that have participated in it*.[157]

The *Dyestuffs* ruling marks a departure from the standard exceptions to the principles of corporate separateness and limited liability. The Court determined that a parent's *capacity* to control or influence its subsidiaries is sufficient to attribute the subsidiaries' acts to it,

[152] Case 48/69, Imperial Chemical Industries Ltd. v. Commission of the European Communities [ICI v. Commission], 1972 E.C.R. 619, paras. 132–5.

[153] Commission Decision of 14 December 1972, Relative to a Procedure of Application of Article 86 of the Treaty Establishing the European Economic Community (IV/26.911—ZPJA/CSC—ICI) (72/457/EEC), 1972 O.J. (L 299) 51.

[154] Case C-97/08 P, Akzo Nobel NV et al. v. Commission of the European Communities, 2009 E.C.R. I-8237, para. 55. *See also* Case T-11/89, Shell v. Commission, 1992 E.C.R. II-757, para. 311.

[155] Wouter P.J. Wils, *The Undertaking as a Subject of EC Competition Law and the Imputation of Infringements to Natural and Legal Persons*, 25 Eur. L. Rev. 99, 99 (2001). *See also* Nada Ina Pauer, The Single Economic Entity Doctrine and Corporate Group Responsibility in European Antitrust Law 5 (2014).

[156] Case C-6/72, Continental Can v. Commission, 1973 E.C.R. 215; Case C-27/76, United Brands v. Commission, 1978 E.C.R. 207; Joined Cases C-6/73 and C-7/73, Commercial Solvents, 1974 E.C.R. 223.

[157] Case C-97/08 P, Akzo Nobel NV et al. v. Commission of the European Communities, 2009 E.C.R. I-8237, para. 77 (emphasis added). *Akzo Nobel* upheld the decision in Case C-286/98, Stora Kopparbergs Bergslags AB v. Commission of the European Communities, 2000 E.C.R. I-9925, para. 29. The judgment in Joined Cases T-71/03, T-74/03, T-87/03, and T-91/03, Tokai Carbon v. Commission, 2005 E.C.R. II-00010, para. 60, supports the argument that 100 percent ownership is sufficient for the presumption established in *Stora*.

instead of using the parent's *actual exercise* of control or influence. This was heavily criticized by scholars, who argued that the existence of control is a necessary but not a sufficient factor to establish intragroup liability.[158] According to them, the economic unit theory should be concerned only with cases in which a parent *in fact* exercises control by intervening in a subsidiary's business in excess of normal management structures. Control can be exerted in matters of general corporate policies, budgeting, employee policies, ethical standards, planning, capital expenditure, etc. Additional factors are financial (adequate capital of the subsidiary, loans by the parent, etc.) and administrative interdependence (centralized administration, common legal, tax, accounting, finance, insurance, research, public relations, education and training, services, etc.), overlapping employment structures (mutual exchange of personnel, group insurance, etc.), or common group persona (use of same name, trademarks, logo, or style).[159]

The European Union's single economic unit theory, which emerged in antitrust law, inspired some of its member states to use this test more generally in company law.[160] US civil courts have also begun to apply the single economic unit theory, which they identify as the "single global enterprise" theory. In *Rocker Mgmt. v. Lernout & Hauspie Speech Prods.*, the New Jersey District Court held that the defendants (KPMG International, KPMG UK, and KPMG Belgium) formed integral parts of a single global enterprise and were subject to the jurisdiction of the United States, despite lacking a connection to the forum.[161] There is also a Swiss variant of the single economic unit theory, based on creditor protection. According to the theory of *Konzernvertrauen* (liability based on trust or good faith in multinational enterprises), a parent is liable for its subsidiary's actions if it gave third parties the impression it was liable for the subsidiary's debts.[162]

III. Synthesis

Piercing the corporate veil and the single economic unit theory are the two dominant exceptions to the principles of legal separateness and limited liability, which allow a state to hold multinationals accountable and establish personal jurisdiction over foreign subsidiaries or parents. Both theories, *grosso modo*, require that there is excessive economic integration, financial involvement, or managerial control among members of a multinational group. A state may also look to abuse of rights or reconcilability with an overall regulatory scheme

---

[158] Vanderkerckhove 528 (2007).

[159] Blumberg, The Multinational Challenge to Corporation Law 93–5 (1993).

[160] Provimi Ltd. v. Roche Products Ltd. et al. [2003] EWHC 961 (U.K.); DHN Food Distributors Ltd. v. Tower Hamlets London Borough Council [1976] 1 WLR 852 (U.K.).

[161] Rocker MGMT, L.L.C. v. Lernout & Hauspie Speech Products N.V., 2005 WL 3658006, 7 (D.N.J. 2005) (U.S.).

[162] BGer Nov. 15, 1994, BGE 120 II 331 (Switz.). Recently affirmed in BGer Feb. 8, 2010, 4A_306/2009, at 5.1 (Switz.). *See* for an in-depth analysis: Peter V. Kunz, *Konzernhaftung in der Schweiz*, 5 Der Gesellschafter 282, 282 (2012); Thomas Risch, Die Haftung aus Konzernvertrauen: Die Haftung des herrschenden Unternehmens aus Konzernvertrauen für konzernspezifische Handlungen und Erklärungen (2009).

to hold multinationals accountable.[163] Subsidiaries that run animal businesses abroad may come under the personal reach of their parent's home state if they are subject to excessive control or undue involvement or were founded and maintained to evade liability. Based on these (and other) factors, states can extend the reach of their criminal or civil (contract, corporate, or tort) animal laws to protect animals used or impacted by multinationals abroad. Animal law should use these theories, among others, to disincentivize multinational enterprises from outsourcing ethically risky business operations.

Domestic laws or acts of the judiciary that disregard the principles of limited liability and corporate separateness are subject to the limits of international law. The task of international law in this context is to ensure that a *Durchgriff* (piercing the corporate veil) does not turn into an *Übergriff* (intervention).[164] Scholars generally do not believe international law is violated when states lift the corporate veil or find that there is a single economic unit because these theories are limited to exceptional cases.[165] As the ICJ held in *Barcelona Traction*:

> The wealth of practice already accumulated on the subject in municipal law indicates that the veil is lifted, for instance, to prevent the misuse of the privileges of legal personality, as in certain cases of fraud or malfeasance, to protect third persons such as a creditor or purchaser, or to prevent the evasion of legal requirements or of obligations. [. . .] In accordance with the principle expounded above, *the process of lifting the veil, being an exceptional one admitted by municipal law in respect of an institution of its own making, is equally admissible to play a similar role in international law*.[166]

To ensure that theories of veil piercing and economic unity stand the test of international law, states should take into account the manner in which they exercise jurisdiction over foreign units. Jurisdiction over foreign subsidiaries can either be exercised directly, by holding a foreign subsidiary liable (*foreign-prescriptive* extraterritorial regulation), or indirectly, by holding the parent that controls the foreign subsidiary liable (*parent-based* extraterritorial regulation).[167] From a jurisdictional perspective, parent-based extraterritorial jurisdiction clearly is less controversial. Moreover, sweeping and general expansion of jurisdiction to foreign subsidiaries is more problematic than exceptional veil piercing. The international community thus views norms like section 414 para. 2(b) US Restatement, which gives the

---

[163] There is a big difference between financial control and managerial control. The fact that a subsidiary is wholly owned is not sufficient to establish liability; there must be proof of control over the subsidiary: DAY WALLACE 643–4 (2002). *See also* MENG 331 (1994); MUCHLINSKI 143 (2007).

[164] Behrens 327 (1982).

[165] JOACHIM BERTELE, SOUVERÄNITÄT UND VERFAHRENSRECHT: EINE UNTERSUCHUNG DER AUS DEM VÖLKERRECHT ABLEITBAREN GRENZEN STAATLICHER EXTRATERRITORIALER JURISDIKTION IM VERFAHRENSRECHT 237 (1998).

[166] Barcelona Traction, 1970 I.C.J. ¶¶ 56–8 (emphasis added).

[167] U.S. Restatement (Third) of the Foreign Relations Law, § 414; ZERK, MULTINATIONALS AND CORPORATE SOCIAL RESPONSIBILITY 107 (2008).

United States jurisdiction over foreign subsidiaries to serve "major national interests" or to help make national programs more effective, with suspicion.[168]

D. ACTIVE PERSONALITY PRINCIPLE IN THE EXTRATERRITORIALITY FRAMEWORK

In the extraterritoriality framework, jurisdiction over foreign branches and domestic corporations that operate abroad is based on the allegiance of the domestic parent to the issuing state (non-animal-related intraterritorial anchor point), and regulates facts and events that concern animals abroad (animal-related extraterritorial content), so it is a type γ_1 regulation. The same is true when a state uses the incorporation, real seat, or control theories to broadly determine corporate nationality, or when multinationals qualify as a single economic unit. In contrast, piercing the veil establishes a non-animal-related jurisdictional connection to a foreign corporation (extraterritorial anchor point) and is used to regulate the lives of animals abroad, which is a type α_3 regulation. Using indirect parent-based extraterritorial jurisdiction (intraterritorial anchor point) instead of direct foreign-prescriptive extraterritorial jurisdiction (extraterritorial anchor point) can prevent conflicts that might arise from type α_3 regulations, by turning them into a γ_1 norm.

If states have jurisdiction *qua* the active personality principle, they can in principle apply all their animal laws to nationals abroad (unlimited active personality principle). The Japanese Criminal Code, for example, adopted an unlimited active personality principle.[169] Though most states, like Japan, prefer to reserve full jurisdictional rights vis-à-vis nationals, they often only apply the personality principle to certain kinds of actions and omissions. In the United Kingdom, jurisdiction is exercised over nationals for, e.g., treason,[170] murder,[171] bigamy,[172] soccer hooliganism,[173] child sexual abuse,[174] and breaches of the Official Secrets Acts,[175] wherever they are committed. Business crimes committed abroad are also regularly punished based on the personality principle. In *R v. Hape*, for example, the Canadian Supreme Court exercised active personality jurisdiction over a national accused of money laundering in connection with an investment company on the Caicos Islands.[176] The same is true for acts of bribery and corruption.[177] Crawford accordingly argues that the personality principle is commonly applied to *serious* crimes only, especially in common law.[178]

---

[168] U.S. Restatement (Third) of the Foreign Relations Law, § 413 para. 2 (b). Since this provision still has to pass the overarching reasonableness test, there is less concern that it overreaches from the standpoint of international law.

[169] KEIHŌ [PENAL CODE] (Japan), art. 3.

[170] Treason Act 1351, c. 2, s. II (U.K.). *Further*: R v. Lynch [1903] 1 KB 444 (U.K.); R v. Casement [1917] 1 KB 98 (U.K.).

[171] Offences Against the Person Act 1861, c. 100, s. 9 (U.K.).

[172] *Id.* s. 57.

[173] Football Spectators Act 1989, c. 37, s. 22 (U.K.).

[174] Sexual Offences Act 2003, c. 42, s. 72, schedule 2 (U.K.).

[175] Official Secrets Act 1989, c. 6, s. 15 (U.K.).

[176] R v. Hape [2007] 2 SCR 292 (Can.).

[177] IBA REPORT EXTRATERRITORIAL JURISDICTION 146 (2009).

[178] The scope of the active personality principle will depend on what constitutes a "serious" crime: CRAWFORD 460 (2012). *See also* RYNGAERT, JURISDICTION 105 (2015).

Taking this narrow approach, states will very likely act in line with international law if they proceed cautiously and apply only core principles of animal law to nationals operating abroad, like the prohibition of animal cruelty.

Scholars sometimes also claim that the active personality principle ought not to apply if the conduct is not punishable where it was committed.[179] Only a few states limit their jurisdictional powers to double criminality (also called conditional active personality principle).[180] For instance, section 7 of the German Criminal Code covers acts of nationals abroad only if they are punishable where they were committed, or if no law applies to the acts.[181] For animal law, this would mean that nationals can only be convicted by their home state if their conduct is punishable where they acted. Since it is exactly the purpose of multinationals to move to states that have no or lax animal laws, this rule would considerably limit the active personality principle. But double criminality is not uniformly applied. States that demand double criminality for some crimes punish others irrespective of whether they are punishable at the place they were committed.[182] Since conditional personality jurisdiction is incongruently applied and not uniformly practiced, it is not required under international law.[183] State practice shows that most states favor the unlimited active personality jurisdiction, which justifies jurisdiction to avoid impunity for crimes that are either not qualified as criminal by foreign states, or which foreign authorities abroad fail to enforce.[184] States can, thus, as a rule, apply their animal laws to nationals operating abroad whether or not the conduct is punishable where it was committed.

Where the active personality jurisdiction is exceptionally relied upon, such as in cases of veil piercing, this rule does not apply. Lifting the corporate veil only deals with specific instances of excessive power, intrusion into decision-making processes, fraud, etc., so states may apply their animal laws only where the factors that gave rise to lifting the corporate veil also violated their animal laws. For instance, if the parent, Novartis Switzerland, unduly interferes in its subsidiary's (e.g., Novartis Singapore) daily decision-making on animal research, then lifting the corporate veil will make the parent responsible only for the consequences that resulted from this interference. So unless there is excessive involvement

---

179 Walter Gropp, *Kollision nationaler Strafgewalten*—nulla prescutio transnationalis sine lege, *in* CONFLICTS OF JURISDICTION IN CROSS-BORDER CRIME SITUATIONS 41, 47 (2012); MENG 182 (1994).

180 Iain Cameron, *International Criminal Jurisdiction, Protective Principle*, *in* MPEPIL 10 (Rüdiger Wolfrum ed., online ed. 2007). Conditionality requires broad identity of the elements of an offense (objective and subjective ones), whether or not criminal consequences are identical: Petrig 41 (2013).

181 STRAFGESETZBUCH [STGB] [CRIMINAL CODE], Nov. 13, 1998, BGBl. I at 3322, § 7 (Ger.), *translation at* http://www.gesetze-im-internet.de/englisch_stgb/ [CRIMINAL CODE (Ger.)]. Also article 7 para. I of the Swiss Criminal Code limits the personality principle to instances of double criminality: CRIMINAL CODE (Switz.), art. 7 para. 1.

182 The German crime of terminating pregnancy abroad is an example of this, *see* CRIMINAL CODE (Ger.), § 5. Also the Council of Europe Convention on the Protection of Children Against Sexual Exploitation and Sexual Abuse establishes unconditional active personality jurisdiction over national and resident perpetrators: CoE, Convention on the Protection of Children against Sexual Exploitation and Sexual Abuse, Oct. 25, 2007, C.E.T.S. No. 201, art. 25 paras. 1 and 2.

183 Akehurst 156 (1972–3); Harvard Research in International Law, *Jurisdiction with Respect to Crime* (1935).

184 Ilias Bantekas, *Criminal Jurisdiction of States under International Law*, *in* MPEPIL 13 (Rüdiger Wolfrum ed., online ed. 2011).

by the parent, it is unlikely that international law will accept jurisdiction over a foreign subsidiary that contravenes Swiss animal laws.

§4 Protective Principle

A. PROTECTING ANIMALS ABROAD THROUGH THE PROTECTIVE PRINCIPLE

The protective principle allows states to prescribe behavior beyond their borders if essential state interests are at stake. The principle is based on the idea that states need to be able to protect their most fundamental interests, without having to rely on the discretion of other states. In short, the protective principle is rooted in states' right to self-defense.[185]

According to the 1935 Harvard Draft Convention, the protective principle aims to safeguard a state's security, territorial integrity, and political independence.[186] Any act that endangers or violates these interests may be subject to extraterritorial jurisdiction *qua* the protective principle. Because the means threatening essential state interests in the 1930s were vastly different from those today—consider environmental pollution, technological hazards, and artificial intelligence—the protective principle is not limited to the above-mentioned interests. States are thus free to respond to new challenges by invoking the protective principle. The only limit placed on the principle is that it must be concerned with "vital issues," "essential state interests," and the like.[187]

The protective principle prevails in criminal law, but has been applied to counterfeiting of currency, which scholars argue bears out "the legitimacy of extending the principle to conduct with economic consequences."[188] Several states have expanded their jurisdiction in this manner. For example, the Polish Penal Code provides that essential economic interests are covered by the protective principle.[189] Experts in antitrust law also consider the protective principle legal where foreign conspiracies practically devastate a state's economy.[190] Any threat to the whole economic structure of a state is thus in principle covered by the protective principle.[191]

---

[185] Cameron, *International Criminal Jurisdiction, Protective Principle*, *in* MPEPIL 1–2 (2007); Petrig 42 (2013). The protective principle is sometimes considered a variant of the territoriality or effects principle: CRAWFORD 459 n. 16 (2012); RYNGAERT, JURISDICTION 82–3 (2015). *Cf.* Tentative Draft of the U.S. Restatement (Fourth) of the Foreign Relations Law, § 216, reporters' note 1.

[186] Harvard Research in International Law, *Jurisdiction with Respect to Crime* (1935), arts. 7 and 8.

[187] Staker, *Jurisdiction*, *in* INTERNATIONAL LAW 301 (2018).

[188] Bowett 10–1 (1982). *See* HR Nov. 13, 1951, NJ 1951, 42 (Public Prosecutor v. L.) (Neth.) (affirmed the conviction of a Belgian national for acts of counterfeiting against the Netherlands when present in Belgium).

[189] Kodeks karny [Penal Code Act], June 6, 1997, DZIENNIK USTAW RZECZYPOSPOLITEJ POLSKIEJ [JOURNAL OF LAWS OF THE REPUBLIC OF POLAND], No. 88 Item 553, art. 112 para. 3 (Pol.).

[190] Acevedo argues in the context of the *Dyestuffs* case that if the EC were to accept trade alongside security, territorial integrity, independence, and other high-ranking values, it would not have to rely on the effects principle: Antonia Acevedo, *The EEC Dyestuffs Case: Territorial Jurisdiction*, 36 MOD. L. REV. 320 (1973).

[191] Akehurst 207 (1972–3); Jan H. Verzijl, *The Controversy Regarding the So-Called Extraterritorial Effect of the American Antitrust Laws*, 8 NEDERLANDS TIJDSCHRIFT VOOR INTERNATIONAAL RECHT 3, 29–30 (1961); RYNGAERT, JURISDICTION OVER ANTITRUST VIOLATIONS 21 (2008). *Cf.* the CoE arguing that the principle ought not to apply to ordinary trade and industry interests: CoE, *Extraterritorial Criminal Jurisdiction* 468 (1992).

An increasing number of states also use the protective principle to protect important environmental values. Section 9 para. 1(3) of the Estonian Penal Code applies to acts committed abroad if they cause damage to the Estonian environment.[192] Article 13 lit. d of the Turkish Criminal Code applies the protective principle to cases of intentional environmental pollution.[193] The German Criminal Code regards offenses against the environment as offenses "against domestic legal interests," which are covered by the protective principle.[194] The sense and purpose of these norms are that, just like a state relies on a functioning economy to thrive, it depends on a functioning environment.[195] Any act that endangers this must thus be prevented or condemned through extraterritorial jurisdiction based on the protective principle.

Although states increasingly use the protective principle to prevent environmental threat and destruction, these interests do not easily extend to concerns about animals. The values covered by the protective principle are those necessary for the state's survival, and those it requires for its basic functioning. If the environment is thrown out of balance, public health and the economy will eventually degrade.[196] But the interests of animals are not standardly seen as affecting the core functions of a state, so the protective principle cannot be used to directly protect animals abroad.

In an indirect manner, however, the principle can be used to protect animals abroad, namely, where foreign animal industries considerably pollute a state's environment. This, unfortunately, is not an unlikely development.[197] Since 1960, the global population has more than doubled, from 3 billion to more than 7 billion people.[198] During the same period, meat production tripled and egg production increased fourfold.[199] The FAO announced that, by 2050, the world will need to produce 70 percent more food for an additional 2.3 billion people.[200] Meat production will have to increase by 50 percent since consumption will increase from 30 kg to 44 kg per capita in the minority world and from 41 kg to 52 kg per capita in the majority world.[201]

---

[192] Karistusseadustik [Penal Code], Sept. 1, 2002, R.T. I 2001, 61, 364, (Est.), § 9 para. 1(3) [Penal Code (Est.)]. *See also* Andres Parmas & Jaan Sootak, *Länderbericht Estland*, *in* CONFLICTS OF JURISDICTION IN CROSS-BORDER CRIME SITUATIONS 279, 286–7 (2012).

[193] Türk Ceza Kanunu [Criminal Code], Sept. 26, 2004, No. 5237, RESMÎ GAZETE, Oct. 12, 2004, No. 25611, art.13 lit. d (Turk.).

[194] CRIMINAL CODE (Ger.), § 5 para. 11. The offenses are enumerated in § 324 (water pollution), § 326 (unlawful disposal of waste), § 330 (aggravated cases of environmental offenses), and § 330a (causing a severe danger by releasing poison) of the same code. *See also* Liane Wörner & Matthias Wörner, *Länderbericht Deutschland*, *in* CONFLICTS OF JURISDICTION IN CROSS-BORDER CRIME SITUATIONS 203, 243 (2012).

[195] Arndt Sinn, *Das Strafanwendungsrecht als Schlüssel zur Lösung von Jurisdiktionskonflikten? Rechtsvergleichende Beobachtungen in Conflicts of Jurisdiction*, *in* CONFLICTS OF JURISDICTION IN CROSS-BORDER CRIME SITUATIONS 501, 524 (2012).

[196] Zerk agrees that vital state interests can be threatened by polluting activities: ZERK, EXTRATERRITORIAL JURISDICTION 185 (2010).

[197] Part of this analysis of environmental effects of farmed animal production was published in Blattner, *3R for Farmed Animals* 16–7 (2014). *See further* on the topic: Worldwatch Institute, Rising Number of Farm Animals Poses Environmental and Public Health Risks, *available at* http://www.worldwatch.org/rising-number-farm-animals-poses-environmental-and-public-health-risks-0 (last visited Jan. 10, 2019).

[198] U.S. Census Bureau, International Database, World Population 1950–2050, *available at* http://www.census.gov/population/international/data/idb/worldpopgraph.php (last visited Jan. 10, 2019).

[199] PEW COMMISSION, REPORT ON INDUSTRIAL FARM ANIMAL PRODUCTION 50 (2008).

[200] UN FAO, HOW TO FEED THE WORLD IN 2050, at 8 (2009).

[201] DELGADO ET AL., LIVESTOCK TO 2020, at 1 (1999); UN FAO, LIVESTOCK'S LONG SHADOW 275 (2006); UN FAO, HOW TO FEED THE WORLD IN 2050, at 11 (2009).

Ever-increasing consumption of animal products eats up a huge portion of the world's crops and raises cereal prices as it depletes what could be directly consumed by people.[202] The resultant food shortage disproportionately harms the poor. By 2050, "Sub-Saharan Africa's share in the global number of hungry people could rise from 24% to between 40 and 50%."[203] To meet the demand, majority world countries would have to produce 72 percent of the world's meat.[204] The current use of animals is thus not an elitist concern of privileged minority world countries; it is an issue of global concern.

Animal production industries are manifestly unsustainable and a massive contributor to environmental pollution. Animal products consume 70 percent of the global freshwater, use 38 percent of total land use, and produce 14 percent of the world's greenhouse gases.[205] Meat and dairy products use more resources, cause higher emissions, and have a disproportionately negative effect on the environment compared to plant-based alternatives.[206] They devour excessive amounts of water and protein-rich plants, which threatens agriculture and drinking water supplies.[207] Livestock production is responsible for more greenhouse gas emissions than the worldwide transport sector. Methane and carbon dioxide are produced while animals digest, and nitrous oxide is emitted when manure degrades microbially.[208] Massive amounts of manure, made more toxic by adding antibiotics to feed, overwhelm the environment and annihilate the natural cleansing cycle. Feed imports render the ground application of manure impossible, creating artificial lagoons of manure that pollute groundwater as they overflow or leak.[209]

Widespread abuse of antibiotics and antimicrobials also breeds bacterial resistance. Reservoirs of resistant bacteria are a serious public health concern and pose a global threat to food security.[210] Overuse of antimicrobials and antibiotics also increases the probability

---

[202] Delgado et al., Livestock to 2020 (1999); Felicity Carus, *UN Urges Global Move to Meat and Dairy-Free Diet*, The Guardian, June 2, 2010.

[203] UN FAO, How to Feed the World in 2050, at 30 (2009).

[204] *2050: A Third More Mouths to Feed*, FAO Media Centre, Sept. 23, 2009.

[205] UN FAO, Statistical Pocketbook World Food and Agriculture 30 (FAO, Rome 2015); Hertwich & van der Voet, Assessing the Environmental Impacts of Consumption and Production 5 (2010); Felicity Carus, *UN Urges Global Move to Meat and Dairy-free Diet*, The Guardian, June 2, 2010.

[206] Animal production has a much larger ecological footprint (or hoof print) than plant-based diets, typically by a factor of 10 or 11: *2050: A Third More Mouths to Feed*, FAO Media Centre, Sept. 23, 2009. Oxford researchers Poore and Nemecek were the first to conduct a meta analysis of ~38,000 farms producing 40 different agricultural goods around the world, to assess the impacts of food production and consumption. They found, specifically, that plant-based diets reduce food's emissions by up to 73 percent depending on where people live. Moreover, the impacts even of the lowest-impact animal products typically exceed those of vegetable substitutes: Poore & Nemecek 987 (2018). *See also* Hertwich & van der Voet, Assessing the Environmental Impacts of Consumption and Production 51, 79 (2010).

[207] UN FAO, Livestock's Long Shadow 270 (2006); Betsy Tao, *A Stitch in Time: Addressing the Environmental, Health, and Animal Welfare Effects of China's Expanding Meat Industry*, 15 Geo. Int'l Envtl. L. Rev. 321, 333 (2003).

[208] Pew Commission, Report on Industrial Farm Animal Production 27 (2008); UN FAO, Livestock's Long Shadow 272 (2006).

[209] Mason & Singer 122 (1990); Pew Commission, Report on Industrial Farm Animal Production 23 (2008).

[210] Martin, Thottathil & Newman 2409 (2015); Pew Commission, Report on Antimicrobial Resistance and Human Health 11 (2008); Commission on Genetic Resources for FAO, Global Plan of

of new treatment-resistant strains (superbugs) that can sometimes jump between species and have been declared epidemic.[211]

These large-scale effects show that animal agriculture can fundamentally endanger a state's environmental health and functioning, in response to which the state can invoke the protective principle. Any state affected by foreign CAFO emissions, pollution, or other negative effects on its environment can thus use its laws to reach across the border and prevent the continued endangerment of its environment. Some might caution that states will randomly use the principle to counter diffuse environmental effects, but states usually apply the protective principle in environmental matters to intentional pollution,[212] and other clearly defined offenses.[213] For instance, article 2 para. 1 of the Council of Europe's Convention on the Protection of the Environment through Criminal Law urges members to take appropriate measures to establish, *inter alia*, as criminal offenses:

> the discharge, emission or introduction of a quantity of substances [...] into air, soil or water which causes death or serious injury to any person, or creates a significant risk of causing death or serious injury to any person (lit. a);
>
> the unlawful discharge, emission or introduction of a quantity of substances [...] into air, soil or water which causes or is likely to cause their lasting deterioration or death or serious injury to any person or substantial damage to [...] protected objects, property, animals or plants (lit. b); and
>
> the unlawful operation of a plant in which a dangerous activity is carried out and which causes or is likely to cause death or serious injury to any person or substantial damage to the quality of air, soil, water, animals or plants (lit. d).[214]

Although jurisdiction established by the Convention is based only on the territoriality and the active personality principle (article 5 para. 1), the enumerated offenses can serve as indicia for serious environmental offenses that may trigger the protective principle.[215] So if a foreign

---

Action for Animal Genetic Resources (FAO, Rome 2007); Timothy F. Landers et al., *A Review of Antibiotic Use in Food Animals: Perspective, Policy, and Potential*, 127 Pub. Health Rep. 4 (2012). In 2017, the WHO recommended that farmers and the food industry stop using antibiotics routinely to promote growth and prevent disease in healthy animals: *Stop Using Antibiotics in Healthy Animals to Prevent the Spread of Antibiotic Resistance*, WHO News Release, Nov. 7, 2017.

[211] Pew Commission, Report on Industrial Farm Animal Production 15 (2008); World Health Organization (WHO), Report on Infectious Diseases c. 3 (WHO, Geneva 2000).

[212] *E.g.*, Criminal Code, Law No. 5237, Sept. 26, 2004, 13 lit. d (Turk.).

[213] *E.g.*, Penal Code (Est.), § 9 para. 1(3). CoE, Convention on the Protection of the Environment through Criminal Law, Nov. 4, 1998, C.E.T.S. No. 172, art. 5 para. 1 lit. a.

[214] CoE, Convention on the Protection of the Environment through Criminal Law, Nov. 4, 1998, C.E.T.S. No. 172, art. 2 para. 1 (the convention was ratified by three states). *See also* Directive 2008/99 of the European Parliament and of the Council on the Protection of the Environment through Criminal Law, 2008 O.J. (L 328) 28. The explanatory report to the convention establishes the effects test for polluting activities: CoE, Explanatory Report to the Convention on the Protection of Environment through Criminal Law, Nov. 4, 1998, at 8.

[215] That the convention did not set up the protective principle over these offenses does not mean the principle is not applicable to them. Drafters likely decided to refrain from interfering in states' affairs by telling them when they can rely on the protective principle.

CAFO causes or is likely to cause a person's death or serious injury, substantial damage to protected properties, animals, or plants, or substantial damage to the quality of air, soil, or water on domestic territory, then states have jurisdiction over these events by virtue of the protective principle. Cross-border environmental pollution caused by manure lagoon overspill, gaseous pollution in the proximate environment of CAFOs (which is common in pig and cow production facilities), loss of land fertility, groundwater pollution, fish kills, and other externalities entitles a state to extend its jurisdiction to prohibit or order the cessation of foreign CAFOs. This right of a state exists regardless of whether polluters acted intentionally or whether their actions were also illegal in their home state.[216] For this reason, the principle is considered "noncooperative,"[217] and one of the most effective means of extraterritorial jurisdiction.

B. PROTECTIVE PRINCIPLE IN THE EXTRATERRITORIALITY FRAMEWORK

According to the extraterritoriality framework, the protective principle identifies a state's domestic interests, like protecting their environment, as necessary anchor points to regulate content abroad. The anchor point must be intraterritorial (fundamental state interests), otherwise the principle cannot be invoked. The content it regulates (e.g., ordering polluting facilities to cease production) can lie outside or inside the territory, but presumably is extraterritorial, or a state would not need to rely on the protective principle. Neither the anchor point nor the content regulated is animal-related, since the principle does not use animals as anchors, nor does it purport to regulate animal welfare.

§5 Interim Conclusion

Under the *lex lata*, states have several possibilities to directly protect animals in foreign countries. For centuries, the territoriality principle was the standard principle used to settle jurisdictional disputes, but its utility is inherently limited, and even more so in this age of globalization. The principle fails to cover cross-border actions and offers no solution for the many cases that involve parties from more than one state (e.g., foreign perpetrators, owners present on foreign territory, animals from other states, etc.). Due to the considerable shortcomings of the territoriality principle, jurisdictional principles based on factors other than the territorial have become more important. Under customary international law, states claiming jurisdiction outside their territory must use a jurisdictional principle that determines matters in which and the extent to which they can prescribe law extraterritorially.

To protect animals abroad, states can use the subjective and objective territoriality principles. These allow them to cover continuing offenses (cross-border animal theft or improper transport), cross-border crimes where constituent elements of the same crime occur in

---

[216] Almir Maljevic, *Extraterritorial Jurisdiction: The Applicability of Domestic Criminal Law to Activities Committed Abroad in Bosnia and Herzegovina*, *in* NATIONAL CRIMINAL LAW IN A COMPARATIVE LEGAL CONTEXT 217 (Ulrich Sieber et al. eds., 2011). The CoE convention covers intentional and negligent offenses: CoE, Convention on the Protection of the Environment through Criminal Law, Nov. 4, 1998, C.E.T.S. No. 172, art. 3.

[217] IAIN CAMERON, THE PROTECTIVE PRINCIPLE OF INTERNATIONAL CRIMINAL JURISDICTION 47 (1994).

different states, and cases of cross-border duties of care owed to animals. These are useful to tackle business activities of multinational enterprises that are organized and managed by corporate units spread across multiple states.

The personality principle gives states jurisdiction over their nationals or residents when they deal with animals abroad. The principle covers public and private activities of nationals and their actions as associates or as members of administrative boards. The personality principle also applies to corporations that are considered nationals on the basis of their place of incorporation, seat, or management. This means that the personality principle is virtually useless when clusters of corporations, known as multinationals, establish branches, subsidiaries, or parents abroad to evade domestic animal laws. However, in certain circumstances, domestic animal law applies to actions of multinational enterprises wherever they operate. Whether this is possible depends in particular on the corporate form of the units of a multinational enterprise, namely, whether they are a branch, a subsidiary, or a parent. A state's jurisdiction extends to *branches* abroad (permanent offices located abroad and managed by domestic corporations) because the domestic corporation and the branch operating abroad form a legal entity. When *parent* corporations establish *subsidiaries* abroad (incorporated as separate legal entities), applying animal law across the border is virtually impossible. In certain circumstances, however, a domestic parent can be held liable under domestic law for the infringement of animal interests abroad by its subsidiaries. The conditions under which this can be done are exceptional: states can use different strategies to determine nationality, they can invoke the control theory, or pierce the corporate veil of a multinational. In even more exceptional circumstances, a state is also entitled to view a multinational as a single legal entity and hold it accountable on this basis.

Some states limit the active personality principle to double criminality or a narrow set of crimes, even though this is not required. Under international law, states are free to hold *all* their nationals—including natural and legal persons and, under certain circumstances, foreign subsidiaries and parents—responsible for *all* their actions against animals abroad.

Another principle states can use to protect animals abroad is the protective principle.The principle traditionally protects the interests of a state in its security and territorial integrity. In recent decades, states have expanded it to protect other interests, including economic, political, and environmental concerns, which they consider threatened by people or events abroad. In animal law, the principle is useful to tackle cross-border environmental pollution and degradation. If foreign actions cause or will likely cause a person's death or serious injury, substantial damage to protected properties, animals, or plants on domestic territory, or substantial damage to the quality of domestic air, soil, or water, then home states possess jurisdiction over these actions by virtue of the protective principle. Given the dominance and continued proliferation of CAFOs and their diverse and large-scale spill-over effects on foreign environments, this possibility is, sadly, a likely one.

The *lex lata* analysis has shown that international law offers states many different bases of jurisdiction to protect animals abroad, only by linking the law of jurisdiction to animal law. If states were to use the objective and subjective territoriality, active personality, and protective principles systematically to address, prevent, and punish actions abroad that considerably thwart the interests of animals, some of the worst legal loopholes caused by globalized business in agriculture, biomedicine, and entertainment could be filled. In the next chapter, I show how these principles can and must be complemented by more subtle forms of jurisdiction and cooperation initiatives with governmental and nongovernmental stakeholders.

6 Extended Jurisdiction through Foreign Policy, Soft Law, and Self-Regulation

THE PURPOSES OF extraterritorial jurisdiction—to ensure domestic animal law remains effective and to adequately respond to globally entangled facts—cannot only be achieved by using norms that are indirect or direct extraterritorial but also through "extended extraterritorial jurisdiction." By this, I mean jurisdiction over persons, objects, facts, or events abroad that is mutually established by states, assigned to international bodies, or determined in processes of self-regulation. Human rights law frequently makes use of foreign policy rules like trade policies, export credit regulation, or investment principles to affect the enjoyment of human rights abroad.[1] Human rights law also uses subtler modes of extraterritorial regulation, like corporate social responsibility (CSR), codes of conduct, best practices, and other, more informal measures. Because these means of extended extraterritorial jurisdiction developed alongside the jurisdictional principles, they are not easy to categorize in the same terms.[2] Extended jurisdiction is not typically considered extraterritorial jurisdiction *stricto sensu*, since affected states agreed beforehand to common jurisdictional norms or because regulatees voluntarily subjected themselves to the jurisdiction of foreign states.

At least in rudimentary form, some forms of extended extraterritorial jurisdiction exist in animal law. The way animals are treated has gained importance in negotiations about investment principles, export credits, best practices, and CSR. How these tools can be

---

[1] *See, e.g.*, Mark Gibney & Sigrun Skogly, *Introduction*, *in* UNIVERSAL HUMAN RIGHTS AND EXTRATERRITORIAL OBLIGATIONS 1, 3 (Mark Gibney & Sigrun Skogly eds., 2010).

[2] For example, impact assessments are not regulation per se, CSR does not form part of state jurisdiction, and investment rules are typically based on prior voluntary submission.

systematically used for animal law, however, is unexplored, as is the question of whether foreign policy rules can usefully complement direct and indirect extraterritorial jurisdiction in animal law. In this chapter, I explore the potential of these norms to protect animals abroad. I begin by describing options under foreign commerce, including investment law, export credit rules, bilateral investment treaties, free trade agreements, and impact assessments, and then examine corporate self- or mixed regulation, like reporting duties, CSR, codes of conduct, and best practices. Studying these forms of extended jurisdiction alongside direct and indirect extraterritoriality should give us a better picture of the options available to states that want to better protect animals within and outside their territory.[3]

§1 Extended Extraterritorial Jurisdiction

A. INVESTMENT RULES

International investment law primarily deals with protecting investments, i.e., securing foreign investments from interference by the host state.[4] These treaties are known to be asymmetrical, granting investor states far-reaching liberties while bereaving host states of regulatory power over investors. Lately, home states have acknowledged greater responsibility and increasingly use their regulatory influence over investors to encourage responsible social performance and hold investors accountable for their actions abroad. Progressive investment treaties and guidelines accordingly identify home states and investors as duty bearers.[5]

One of the most well-known and widely used investment guidelines is the International Finance Corporation's (IFC) Performance Standards. The IFC, a member of the World Bank Group, is a global development institution that provides investment for the private sector. The institution has a AAA credit rating and a portfolio of 67 billion USD from 2,011 companies.[6] Since 2012, the IFC has recommended that investment and advisory clients observe and meet its "Performance Standards" for environmental and social sustainability. As part of its strategy to ensure environmental and social sustainability, the IFC prioritizes the following areas: agribusiness, climate change, financial institutions, gender, oil, gas, mining, and infrastructure. The IFC acknowledges the pivotal contribution of agribusiness to food security, poverty reduction, and development. Between 2010 and 2016, it increased its investments from 1.9 to 5.6 billion USD to finance projects in farm production, sourcing, processing, trade and distribution, wholesale and retail, infrastructure, and logistics.[7]

---

[3] The arguments made herein were applied to a specific case and published in Charlotte E. Blattner, *Tackling Concentrated Animal Agriculture in the Middle East through Standards of Investment, Export Credits, and Trade*, 10(2) MIDDLE EAST LAW AND GOVERNANCE 141 (2018).

[4] Christoph Schreuer, *International Protection of Investments*, *in* MPEPIL 1 (Rüdiger Wolfrum ed., online ed. 2013).

[5] DAY WALLACE 1096 (2002): (ILO: "Governments of home countries should . . ."; ICC Guidelines: "The Investor's Country Should . . ."; OECD: "Enterprises should . . .").

[6] INTERNATIONAL FINANCE CORPORATION (IFC), GLOBAL AGRIBUSINESS: CREATING OPPORTUNITY IN EMERGING MARKETS 2, *available at* http://viewer.zmags.com/publication/24cf5263#/24cf5263/3 (last visited Jan. 10, 2019) [IFC, GLOBAL AGRIBUSINESS].

[7] INTERNATIONAL FINANCE CORPORATION (IFC), AGRIBUSINESS & FORESTRY, OVERVIEW, *available at* http://www.ifc.org/wps/wcm/connect/Industry_EXT_Content/IFC_External_Corporate_Site/Agribusiness (last visited Jan. 10, 2019).

IFC's recommendations identify eight performance standards. These are assessment and management of environmental and social risks and impacts (performance standard 1), labor and working conditions (performance standard 2), resource efficiency and pollution prevention (performance standard 3), community health, safety, and security (performance standard 4), land acquisition and resettlement (performance standard 5), biodiversity conservation and sustainable management of natural resources (performance standard 6), indigenous peoples (performance standard 7), and cultural heritage (performance standard 8).[8]

Performance standard 6 is the most relevant standard in matters of animal protection. Its objectives include protecting and conserving biodiversity, maintaining benefits from ecosystem services, and promoting sustainable management of living natural resources "through the adoption of practices that integrate conservation needs and development priorities."[9] Performance standard 6 applies both to projects in natural environments, and projects that "include the production of living natural resources (e.g., agriculture, animal husbandry, fisheries, forestry)."[10] This is surprising because environmental concerns rarely extend to animals that do not form an integral part of ecosystems.[11] Performance standard 6, strictly seen, precludes the IFC from funding CAFOs because they make poor use of natural resources, cause considerable environmental pollution, and are key drivers of biodiversity loss.[12] Performance standard 6 is broadly applicable, covering supply chains and primary production purchases.[13] This gives the IFC a great deal of influence over agribusiness, allowing it to apply its standards to business partners, whether or not they have explicitly agreed to them.

Less well known than its performance standards, the IFC's Draft Good Practice Note on improving animal welfare in livestock operations identifies poor animal welfare performance as an investment risk:

> Increased market awareness of environmental, social, and commercial values is driving changes in the way business is done, leading to the recognition of new risks and opportunities. In the case of animal welfare, failure to keep pace with changing consumer expectations and market opportunities could put companies and their investors at a competitive disadvantage in an increasingly global marketplace.[14]

---

[8] International Finance Corporation (IFC), Performance Standards on Environmental and Social Sustainability 1 (World Bank, Washington D.C. 2012).

[9] *Id.* performance standard 6, 1.

[10] *Id.*

[11] *See further* on the limited reach of environmental protection, Chapter 3, §2 E. I.

[12] *See* Chapter 7, §3 on environmental effects of CAFOs.

[13] IFC, Performance Standards on Environmental and Social Sustainability, performance standard 6, 7 (2012): "Purchasers face a duty to evaluate primary suppliers. In the verification process, it must be (i) identified where the supply is coming from and the habitat type of this area; (ii) provided for an ongoing review of the client's primary supply chains; (iii) provided for limited procurement to those suppliers that can demonstrate that they are not contributing to significant conversion of natural and/or critical habitats; and (iv) where possible, action is required that shifts the client's primary supply chain over time to suppliers that can demonstrate that they are not significantly impacting these areas in an adverse manner."

[14] International Finance Corporation (IFC), Draft Good Practice Note: Improving Animal Welfare in Livestock Operations 31–2 (World Bank, Washington D.C. 2014).

The final Good Practice Note, which went into effect in 2014, demands that animals used by agribusiness be given more space (e.g., by decreasing group stocking density and encouraging group housing instead of individual housing), provided with richer environments (e.g., straw for pigs to manipulate and nest boxes for hens), receive bulks feed supplements instead of high-energy feed (to minimize digestive problems), be spared unnecessary pain from invasive husbandry procedures (e.g., by avoiding them or by using low-pain methods and analgesics), be individually monitored, and that genetic selection focuses both on welfare traits and on increasing production (e.g., picking less aggressive or fearful animals).[15] The IFC's Good Practice Note is thus broadly animal welfare–oriented, and includes a couple of standards that could be considered progressive in international comparison.

If we look at the way IFC has allocated funds—even if purely focused on the periods since it put the Good Practice Note into effect—we see that the organization honors these goals more in the breach than the practice. The IFC played a key role in doubling pig and chicken production in BGK (Russia), doubling the size of a broiler-raising operation in Banvit (Turkey), building up an integrated broiler raising and pig-slaughtering operation in Ponaca (Ecuador), helping a producer in Halim (Korea) become the largest broiler production facility,[16] financing a producer of 650 million eggs and poultry worth 46 million USD per annum in Wadi (Egypt),[17] investing in one of the largest dairy processors in Karachi (Pakistan) to help it source 1.9 billion liters of cow milk,[18] financing the production of 59,000 tons of dairy products per annum in the semi-autonomous Kurdistan Regional Government (KRG) in northern Iraq,[19] and investing 23 million USD in stock feed, parent stock poultry operations, and hatcheries in the Jordan Valley.[20] The IFC does not even try to conceal its involvement in CAFOs. In 2014, it publicly acknowledged its financial support made the Myronivky Hliboproduct (MHP) facility one of "the most efficient poultry producers" and a "leader in the modernization of Ukraine's agriculture sector."[21]

The IFC's allocation of funds makes clear its interest are in increasing production, in the service of which it is ready to violate the FAO's goal of ensuring world food security, the IFC's own Performance Standards on Environmental and Social Sustainability (e.g., performance standard 6), and its Good Practice Note on animal welfare. These investments, in essence, mock the World Bank's declared goal to "[a]void funding large-scale commercial, grain-fed feedlot systems and industrial milk, pork, and poultry production."[22]

---

[15] International Finance Corporation (IFC), Good Practice Note: Improving Animal Welfare in Livestock Operations 13 (World Bank, Washington D.C. 2014).

[16] R. John Hatton, IFC Agribusiness Department, OIE Conference Cairo, Oct. 2008, at 9, *available at* http://www.oie.int/fileadmin/Home/eng/Conferences_Events/sites/A_AW2008/PDF/Session%20II/11_OIE_AWCairo_J_Hatton_EN.pdf (last visited Jan. 10, 2019).

[17] IFC Project No. 29309, Wadi Holdings SAE, approved June 21, 2010.

[18] IFC Project No. 38150, Koninklijke Friesland Campina N.V., approved June 28, 2016.

[19] IFC Project No. 34376, Al Safi Danone Iraq, approved Nov. 13, 2014.

[20] IFC Project No. 8145, Jordan Valley Co. Ltd., approved Nov. 17, 2007.

[21] IFC, Draft Good Practice Note 30 (2014).

[22] Cornelis de Haan et al., Livestock Development, Implications for Rural Poverty, the Environment, and Global Food Security 65 (World Bank, Washington D.C. 2001).

Why is the IFC comfortable allocating funds in a manner that violates the standards it devised? Ryan provides an explanation for the remarkable divergence between IFC theory and practice:

> While clients who supply [...] supermarkets fully understand the issues of animal welfare and have standards and audits imposed upon them, there are many current and future clients who have not reached that awareness. The IFC philosophy is that it is better to engage these clients and make a difference, rather than not engage at all.[23]

The IFC's stance, though incoherent, appears to be well-intentioned, as it thinks it must make investments that violate its own standards and goals in order to build bridges with investors who are not yet persuaded to make the lives of animals a little bit more bearable. This is not a strategy animal advocates can support because it amounts to claiming that supporting animal suffering and death will, in the long run, reduce animal suffering and death. On the other hand, the IFC at least brings the topic to the table, which is more than other international investment bodies have done. For example, the Multilateral Investment Guarantee Agency (MIGA), which encourages private investment by providing guarantees against political risks and which is also part of the World Bank Group, does not bind its investments to recognized standards of minimum labor, environmental protection, human rights, or animal welfare. In its commentary to the MIGA Convention, the organization explains: "Measures normally taken by governments to regulate their economic activities such as taxation, environmental and labor legislation as well as normal measures for the maintenance of public safety, are not intended to be covered by this provision unless they discriminate against the holder of the guarantee."[24]

That stakeholders find it difficult to use investment goals to protect animals is also clear on the level of domestic investment law. Pursuant to section 7 of the US Endangered Species Act (ESA), the Secretary of the Interior and the Secretary of Commerce must ensure that actions funded by the Environmental Protection Agency do not jeopardize or threaten endangered species.[25] In *Lujan v. Defenders of Wildlife*, the Supreme Court was asked to decide if this duty also applies to projects funded outside US territory.[26] A joint statement by the secretaries had initially determined that the ESA applies to animals on foreign territory, but the agencies subsequently reversed their stance, giving rise to the dispute at hand. Defenders of Wildlife sought to reinstate the initial rule, but the Court denied standing to

---

[23] Oliver Ryan, *Animal Welfare and Economic Development: A Financial Institution Perspective*, *in* ANIMALS, ETHICS AND TRADE: THE CHALLENGE OF ANIMAL SENTIENCE 238, 245 (Jacky Turner & Joyce D'Silva eds., 2006).

[24] MIGA, Commentary on the Convention Establishing the Multilateral Investment Guarantee Agency, 9, para. 14 (MIGA, Washington D.C. 2010).

[25] ESA, § 7(a)(2) (U.S.).

[26] Lujan v. Defenders of Wildlife, 504 U.S. 555 (1992) (U.S.). The ESA is not the only act that was challenged for its extraterritorial reach. In Okinawa Dugong v. Rumsfield, No. C-03-4350-MHP (N.D. Cal. Motion to dismiss, Aug. 4, 2004), plaintiffs claimed the Natural Historical Preservation Act (NHPA) applies to foreign projects. *See further* Takahashi (2004).

the plaintiffs, holding that they lacked injury in fact and redressability.[27] The Court, in essence, avoided resolving the debate about whether the ESA has extraterritorial reach. Even if the Court granted standing to Defenders of Wildlife, plaintiffs would next have had to overcome the domestic presumption against extraterritoriality. Scholars argue that this could be done by invoking principle 21 of the 1972 Stockholm Declaration, which determines that states have a responsibility to prevent domestic actions from damaging the environment of other states.[28] This strategy might be successful if it is paired with the argument that the ESA already applies to the reverse case, where foreign projects have an adverse impact on endangered species within the United States.[29]

Though investment law is rarely linked to good performance in the interest of animals, this might change if more experts in investment law recommend investors consider animal welfare in their investment decisions. The Farm Animal Investment Risk & Return (FAIRR) Initiative argues that few investors know how animals are treated in animal agricultural production, and that this ignorance increases risk for investors and wastes opportunities to improve performance. In its 2016 report, FAIRR found that factory farms were vulnerable to at least 28 ESG (environmental, social, and governance) problems, all of which could damage investors' financial performance and returns.[30] FAIRR thinks that ignoring animal welfare in investment is outdated because "[f]arm animal welfare is one of many ESG issues that responsible investors are beginning to take into account as part of mainstream investment practices."[31] To educate investors and encourage a race to the top, FAIRR produces case studies as a form of best practice that shows investors how to make sounder investments while maintaining high-quality standards needed to protect animals.

B. EXPORT CREDITS

Export credits are an important form of foreign direct investment and an opportunity for states that provide finance to encourage responsible performance by recipients. Guidelines of international organizations (IOs), which help states identify good performance in those who receive export credits, sometimes touch on animal issues.

The Organization for Economic Co-operation and Development (OECD) has led numerous international negotiations on export credits, which resulted in the Arrangement on Officially Supported Export Credits, dealing with financial terms and conditions, tied

---

27 Both injury in fact and redressability were rejected by Justice Scalia, although plaintiffs said they visited the site many times: Lujan v. Defenders of Wildlife, 504 U.S. 555 (1992) (U.S.). Coggins and Head argue that standing might more readily be granted to foreign nationals living in affected areas rather than to frequent US visitors: Coggins & Head 69 (1993).

28 Declaration of the United Nations Conference on the Human Environment, U.N. Doc. A/CONF.48/14/Rev. 1, 11 I.L.M. 1416 (June 6, 1972), principle 21 [Stockholm Declaration]. *See further* Coggins & Head 80 (1993).

29 Zerk, Extraterritorial Jurisdiction 184 (2010).

30 Farm Animal Investment Risk & Return (FAIRR), Factory Farming: Assessing Investment Risks 4–5 (FAIRR 2016).

31 Farm Animal Investment Risk & Return (FAIRR), Considering Farm Animal Welfare in Investment Decision-making: Case Studies & Guidance 1 (FAIRR 2015).

aid, and procedures of export credits.[32] The OECD also published recommendations for officially supported export credits that cover the social and environmental dimension of export credits (known as the Common Approaches).[33] The Common Approaches encourage members to prevent and mitigate adverse environmental and social impacts of future projects, to consider environmental and social risks associated with existing operations, to undertake environmental and social reviews and assessments for projects and operations as part of their due diligence, and to foster transparency, predictability, and responsibility in decision-making.[34] To prove they are observing the principles, members must screen, classify, and review environmental and social impacts, evaluate and monitor projects, exchange and disclose information, and report on their performance. Substantively, members must benchmark the issuance of export credits, at a minimum, against international standards. This brings to application the standards of the World Bank (Environmental, Health and Safety [EHS]) Guidelines), the IFC Performance Standards, and, in matters of animal welfare, the IFC Good Practice Note.[35] As argued above, this note and some of the IFC's standards can benefit animals located abroad.[36]

Domestic export credit agencies also often refer to these standards when they issue credits. The United Kingdom bases the Export Credits Guarantee Department's screening on the OECD Common Approaches, the World Bank Safeguard policies, and IFC Performance Standards.[37] Likewise, the policy of the US Ex-Im Bank's demands that beneficiaries operate by the Common Approaches, the Environmental and Social Due Diligence Procedures and Guidelines (ESPG), and follow rules on environmental reporting and impact assessment.[38] Other countries, like Denmark, require investees to comply with their own animal welfare standards or those of the European Union.[39]

Though the guidelines of export credit agencies look good on paper, they are inconsistently used in practice. In *Friends of the Earth v. Spinelli*, environmental organizations and governmental authorities sued the Overseas Private Investment Corporation and the Ex-Im Bank for failing to screen projects according to the National Environment Policy Act (NEPA) and the Administrative Procedure Act (APA). Friends of the Earth showed that some of the fossil

---

32 OECD, Arrangement on Officially Supported Export Credits, TAD/PG(2015)7 (OECD Publishing, Paris 2015).

33 OECD, Revised Recommendation of the Council on Common Approaches for Officially Supported Export Credits and Environmental and Social Due Diligence, TAD/ECG(2016)3 (OECD Publishing, Paris 2016) [OECD, Common Approaches].

34 OECD, Common Approaches, art. 4 v) (2016).

35 OECD, Common Approaches, arts. 5 and 25 (2016).

36 *See* Chapter 6, §1 A.

37 The department uses the IFC Performance Standards, including performance standard 6: UK Export Finance, Guidance to Applicants: Processes and Factors in UK Export Finance Consideration of Applications, §§ 3, 11 (Apr. 2013), *available at* https://www.gov.uk/government/uploads/system/uploads/attachment_data/file/274255/guidance-on-processes-and-factors-uk-export-finance.pdf (last visited Jan. 10, 2019).

38 Export-Import Bank of the United States, Ex-Im Bank and the Environment, *available at* http://www.exim.gov/policies/exim-bank-and-the-environment (last visited Jan. 10, 2019). *See also* Export-Import Bank Act, 12 U.S.C. § 635, 635(a)(11)(B) and (C) (U.S.); Foreign Assistance Act of 1961, 22 U.S.C. § 2151, 2191A (U.S.).

39 UN FAO, Home Country Measures that Promote Responsible Foreign Agricultural Investment: Evidence from Selected OECD Countries 13 (FAO, Rome 2012).

fuel projects funded by the agencies emit significant amounts of greenhouse gases and noticeably contribute to climate change—which should have been considered by the agencies before credits were issued.[40] Another case concerned the Sakhalin II project in Russia. In 2008, the World Wildlife Fund (WWF) presented scientific evidence to support their claim that Sakhalin II would increase global warming and threaten endangered Pacific gray whales, salmon fisheries, and migratory birds. Leaton, the WWF's Senior Policy Adviser, claimed that the Export Credits Guarantee Department, through its financial support, "gave the backing of the UK government to an environmental catastrophe."[41] The pressure created by the WWF, which partnered with the Corner House, eventually forced funders to drop the project.[42]

These occasional successes notwithstanding, most states' rules on export credits are still rudimentary; they disincentivize human rights violations and adverse environmental performance abroad, but lack rules that determine how animals be treated. In the future, export credits should only be granted if projects protect—or at least do not negatively impact—the lives and livelihoods of animals situated abroad. Instead of assuming that issuing export credit guidelines that protect the environment will benefit animals, too, funding schemes should directly and unequivocally demand that recipients respect animals abroad. Until these rules are in place, international investment standards on animal welfare, like performance standard 6 and the IFC's Good Practice Note, must be strictly observed.

C. BILATERAL INVESTMENT TREATIES (BITS)

Bilateral investment treaties (BITs) are agreements concluded between two states on private investment that moves from one state to another. BITs are the most important kind of foreign direct investment; more than 3,000 of these treaties are currently in force worldwide.[43] Like investment guidelines, early-generation BITs established asymmetrical rights and obligations. They conferred on investors a right to enter the host state but did not assign them any duties. Host states, commonly from the majority world, continue to enter these agreements to access the minority world's investment markets.[44]

Home and host states dissatisfied with lopsided BITs have called for a greater balance between the parties' rights and obligations—a move the UN Conference on Trade and Development (UNCTAD) supports.[45] Newer BITs take these demands seriously and oblige home states and investors to adhere to, e.g., established human rights.[46] The social side of

---

[40] Friends of the Earth Inc. et al. v. Mosbacher et al. (also known as v. Watson or as v. Spinelli), 488 F. Supp. 2d 889 (N.D. Cal. 2007) (U.S.).

[41] Terry Macalister, *Wildlife Group Sues Government Agency over Sakhalin-2*, THE GUARDIAN, Aug. 16, 2007.

[42] House of Commons, Environmental Audit Committee, The Export Credits Guarantee Department and Sustainable Development, Eleventh Report of Session 2007–8, Evidence 7 (The Stationery Office, London 2008).

[43] By the end of 2017, 2,946 BITs and 376 international investment agreements were concluded: UNCTAD, WORLD INVESTMENT REPORT 88 (2018).

[44] DOLZER & SCHREUER 14 (2012); Muchlinski, *Corporations in International Law*, *in* MPEPIL 26 (2014).

[45] UNCTAD, WORLD INVESTMENT REPORT 164 (2003).

[46] Human rights are typically part of the preamble, listed in a separate clause of BITs, or they are indirectly addressed by referring to state duties: MARC JACOB, INTERNATIONAL INVESTMENT AGREEMENTS AND

BITs, however, is still in development. Model BITs of Germany (2008), France (2006), the United States (2004), the United Kingdom (2005), China (2003), and India (2003), for example, are all silent on human rights.[47]

The emerging social side of BITs may also extend to animal issues. Newer BITs address animals indirectly in their preamble by referring to the parties' desire to protect the environment and contribute to the sustainable use of resources.[48] Preambular wording has limited reach, however. It allows favorably interpreting a BIT based on the object and purpose of the treaty, but it does not per se create duties for parties.[49] Concern for animals is typically seen only as an exception to obligations under the BIT. For example, US BITs include detailed rules on mutual performance, but in exceptional circumstances allow parties to violate these, if doing so is necessary to protect the environment, human, animal, or plant life and health, or to conserve exhaustible natural resources.[50] Just as article XX of the GATT is evidence for the limited role animals play in trade relations, exceptions in BITs prove that animals play only a marginal role in bilateral investment relations.

Even global actors that have a favorable view of animals do not consider the lives of animals important enough to include them in BITs. In the European Commission Minutes Meeting on EU-China Trade and Investment Relations in February 2014, the Royal Society for the Prevention of Cruelty asked about the role of animal welfare in BITs. The Commission explained that "animal welfare is not a part of the Commission's traditional approach to this kind of negotiations. This element is usually present in FTAs which have much broader scope."[51] The Commission manifestly failed to acknowledge that BITs cover an important stage that is not accounted for in FTAs. Before goods enter production, BITs at least co-determine if production is commended, so BITs could prevent infringing the interests of animals, while FTAs can only respond to violations.

That BITs largely ignore the immense influence of investment on the lives of animals is deplorable and increasingly unjustifiable in light of the steady growth of investments in animal agriculture. Since the early 2000s, acquisition of farmland in majority world countries increased radically. In November 2013, Saad Khalil, director of the Initiative for Saudi Agricultural Investment Abroad, announced that over 35 countries will be targeted for its

---

HUMAN RIGHTS, INEF RESEARCH PAPER SERIES ON HUMAN RIGHTS, CORPORATE RESPONSIBILITY AND SUSTAINABLE DEVELOPMENT 9 (2010). Bartels, in his study on a model human rights clause, addresses why human rights clauses are necessary, using the European Union as a model. He first notices that the European Union does not need a human rights clause to fulfill its human rights obligations (since it could easily suspend or terminate obligations that make it impossible for it to observe its human rights obligations), but argues that a human rights clause is needed to establish cooperation between home and host states, so that they can effectively fulfill their human rights obligations: Lorand Bartels, A Model Human Rights Clause for the EU's International Trade Agreements 26–8 (German Institute for Human Rights 2014).

[47] JACOB 9 (2010).

[48] *See, e.g.*, the Norway Model BIT, Draft version 191207 (2007), *available at* http://investmentpolicyhub.unctad.org/Download/TreatyFile/2873 (last visited Jan. 10, 2019).

[49] JACOB 10 (2010).

[50] Treaty between the United States of America and the Oriental Republic of Uruguay Concerning the Encouragement and Reciprocal Protection of Investment, Oct. 25, 2004, art. 8(3)(c).

[51] European Commission, Minutes of the Civil Society Dialogue, EU-China Trade and Investment Relations: State of Play, Feb. 13, 2014, Brussels, at 4.

agricultural investment. The Saudi Agricultural Development Fund established the Saudi Company for Agricultural Investment and Animal Production (SCAIAP), which exclusively funds the production of animals and animal feed.[52] As *The Economist* predicts, we will soon witness new forms and extents of outsourcing in agriculture across the world.[53] Given the massive investments from minority world countries in animal production facilities located in the majority world, BITs could have a tremendous impact on the lives of affected animals. As we understand more about how we fail animals, we will need to build on the growing trend of using BITs to enshrine minimum standards and use them to encompass duties toward animals.

D. FREE TRADE AGREEMENTS (FTAS)

FTAs are primarily concerned with trade relations among states and some of them aim to strengthen and deepen economic cooperation between parties more broadly. Most FTAs are concluded bilaterally or multilaterally, but there is a global trend toward megaregional FTAs like the Transatlantic Trade and Investment Partnership (TTIP), or the Trans-Pacific Partnership (TPP). Regular FTAs still outnumber megaregional FTAs and hence play an important role in international economic cooperation.[54]

Compared to BITs, FTAs more readily take the interests of animals into account. Some FTAs have an *information-sharing clause*. The EU-Canada FTA, known as the Comprehensive Economic and Trade Agreement (CETA), allows its parties to exchange information on matters touching animal welfare.[55] This exchange is not mandatory, as evidenced by article 21.4 CETA ("the parties may").[56] The language is slightly stronger in the EU-Korea FTA. According to article 5.9 titled "Cooperation on Animal Welfare," "parties shall [. . .] exchange information, expertise and experiences in the field of animal welfare and adopt a working plan for such activities."[57] Similarly, the EU-Chile FTA lays down states' mutual duty to inform each other on their progress in developing animal welfare standards.[58] And in the EU-Singapore FTA, the parties agreed to exchange information, expertise, and experiences in the field of animal welfare.[59]

Some FTAs stipulate that animal welfare is a *common objective* of the parties. Article 89 para. 1 of the FTA between Chile and the European Union identifies animal welfare standards as a common objective of the agreement.[60] Similarly, article 1 para. 1 of Annex IV to

---

[52] *Saudi Arabia to Target Agro-Investments Abroad*, ARAB NEWS, Nov. 11, 2013.

[53] *Outsourcing's Third Wave*, THE ECONOMIST, May 21, 2009.

[54] UNCTAD, WORLD INVESTMENT REPORT 101 (2016).

[55] Comprehensive Economic and Trade Agreement (CETA), art. 21.4 lit. s, Sept. 21, 2017 [CETA].

[56] CETA, art. X.4 para. 19.

[57] Council Decision of 16 September 2010 on the Signing, on Behalf of the European Union, and Provisional Application of the Free Trade Agreement between the European Union and its Member States, of the One Part, and the Republic of Korea, of the Other Part, 2011/265/EU, 2011 O.J. (L 127) 6, art. 5.9 para. 2 [EU-Korea FTA].

[58] Agreement Establishing an Association between the European Community and its Member States, of the One Part, and the Republic of Chile, of the Other Part, Nov. 18, 2002, art. 12 para. 2 lit. f [EU-Chile Agreement].

[59] EU-Singapore Free Trade Agreement, June 29, 2015, art. 5.11 para. 2 [EU-Singapore FTA].

[60] EU-Chile Agreement, art. 89 para. 1: "An additional objective of this section is to consider animal welfare standards."

the US-Uruguay FTA states: "[T]his Agreement aims at reaching a common understanding between the Parties concerning animal welfare standards."[61] The EU-CARIFORUM Agreement more broadly expresses the parties' desire to improve their capacity to protect animal health.[62] However, it is still a matter of debate whether animal health encompasses considerations about the well-being of the animal.[63]

Certain FTAs operate as a basis for states to *cooperate or collaborate*. Chapter Five of the EU-Singapore FTA determines that parties may collaborate on matters of animal welfare that are of mutual interest.[64] And South Korea and the European Union even agreed to "co-operate in the development of animal welfare standards in international fora, in particular with respect to the stunning and slaughter of animals."[65]

Some of the wording used in these clauses is quite vague, which makes it unlikely a party can be held accountable for failure to comply with them, but this does not render FTAs per se unsuitable to advance the interests of animals. The most notable promise of FTAs is that they may have a lasting influence on how parties regulate animal issues domestically. Subsequent to the adoption of the EU-Chile FTA, Chile passed laws that seek to ensure the welfare of animals before and during slaughter. Chile also started collaborating with Uruguay to establish a Center on Animal Welfare, with Argentina to improve the standards of animal transportation, and with Canada and the United States to engage in exchanges and training on animal welfare matters.[66] The Eurogroup, which studied these developments in detail, summarizes them as follows: "Even if Chile originally considered the inclusion of animal welfare as an EU demand, the bilateral agreement definitively played a role and brought several benefits."[67] Based on these and other successes, the European Commission declared that it will continue to include animal welfare in bilateral trade agreements and cooperation forums "to increase the strategic opportunities for developing more concrete cooperation with third countries."[68]

As the example of the EU-Chile FTA shows, some FTAs had a lasting effect on parties, while others changed little about the status quo. We do not yet know if this success depends solely on treaty language (e.g., the use of "shall" instead of "may"), or whether some parties are simply more dedicated to animal issues than others. We do know, however, that lax commitments in FTAs are not sufficient to bring about real change, so FTA clauses that pay regard to the interests of animals should be complemented by periodic impact assessments and joint councils empowered to take action.

---

61 Treaty between the United States of America and the Oriental Republic of Uruguay Concerning the Encouragement and Reciprocal Protection of Investment, Oct. 25, 2004, Annex IV (referred to in art. 89(2)).

62 Economic Partnership Agreement between the CARIFORUM States, of the One Part, and the European Community and its Member States, of the Other Part, 2008 O.J. (L 289) I 3, art. 53 lit. a.

63 *See* Chapter 4, §2 C.

64 EU-Singapore FTA, art. 5.2 para. 2.

65 EU-Korea FTA, art. 5.9 para. 2.

66 Chile also plans to collaborate with Costa Rica and Bolivia: EUROGROUP FOR ANIMALS, THE EU-CHILE FREE TRADE AGREEMENT: A BOOST FOR ANIMAL WELFARE 4, 9–10 (2013).

67 *Id.* at 10.

68 EU Animal Welfare Strategy 2012–5, at 10.

The International Institute for Sustainable Development's "Model International Agreement on Investment for Sustainable Development" has not yet begun to take seriously states' interest in protecting animals through BITs.[69] It is also regrettable that the efforts of bilateral or regional FTAs to work toward better laws for animals will likely be undermined by megaregional FTAs like the TTIP and the TTP. The TPP is an agreement on trade negotiated and signed on February 4, 2016, by Australia, Brunei, Canada, Chile, Japan, Malaysia, Mexico, New Zealand, Peru, Singapore, Vietnam, and the United States, covering 40 percent of the global GDP and one-third of the world trade in goods.[70] The TTIP is a draft agreement to regulate the relations of trade and investment between the European Union and the United States that would make up for 50 percent of the global GDP and another third of the world trade flows.[71] The two agreements, which are frequently seen as "companion agreements," are considered progressive because they each have a distinct chapter on environmental standards.[72] Both of them, however, lack a commitment to protect animals. The TTP, in its final version, only refers to the general exceptions of article XX GATT,[73] and the TTIP, in its draft version by the European Union, does the same.[74]

To this day, neither the TTIP nor the TTP has entered into force. The TTP failed after the Office of the US Trade Representative announced the United States' withdrawal in January 2017.[75] And the negotiation process over the TTIP was paused in 2016 with no further notice given.[76] It is easy to describe the failure of the parties to conclude megaregional FTAs as a success for animals, namely, as a step away from deregulation, but the mere fact that the most powerful players do not consider animals worth mentioning in negotiations on trade sends a powerful message to the world. Moreover, it is only a question of time until new megaregional treaties will be drafted and animal interests, once again, ignored and downplayed.

---

[69] INTERNATIONAL INSTITUTE FOR SUSTAINABLE DEVELOPMENT (IISD), MODEL INTERNATIONAL AGREEMENT ON INVESTMENT FOR SUSTAINABLE DEVELOPMENT (IISD, Manitoba 2005).

[70] Ken Granville, *The Trans-Pacific Partnership Trade Accord Explained*, N.Y. TIMES, July 26, 2016.

[71] European Commission, Trade Picture US-EU (Apr. 2018), *available at* http://ec.europa.eu/trade/policy/countries-and-regions/countries/united-states/ (last visited Jan. 10, 2019).

[72] The environmental chapter, however, is criticized for insufficiently protecting the environment: Chris Wold, Empty Promises and Missed Opportunities: *An Assessment of the Environmental Chapter of the Trans-Pacific Partnership* (2016).

[73] Trans-Pacific Partnership, Oct. 4, 2015, ch. 29, art. 29.1 para. 1. On the TPP in animal law, *see* HUMANE SOCIETY INTERNATIONAL (HSI), STATEMENT ON THE TRANS-PACIFIC PARTNERSHIP (HSI, Washington D.C. 2015). *See further* Lurié & Kalinina 476 ff. (2015).

[74] European Proposal for the TTIP Text on "National Treatment and Market Access for Goods" (Mar. 21, 2016), section E. The planned TTIP between the United States and the European Union is also expected to lower the level of animal welfare within the European Union, since the TTIP's main purpose is to reduce nontariff barriers to trade: Lurié & Kalinina 431 (2015); Florent Marcellesi, *TTIP: A Threat to Animal Welfare and Rights* (Green/EFA Group of the European Parliament, Feb. 24, 2015), *available at* http://ttip2015.eu/blog-detail/blog/animal%20rights%20TTIP.html (last visited Jan. 10, 2019).

[75] Office of the United States Trade Representative, The United States Officially Withdraws from the Trans-Pacific Partnership (Jan. 2017), *available at* https://ustr.gov/about-us/policy-offices/press-office/press-releases/2017/january/US-Withdraws-From-TPP (last visited Jan. 10, 2019).

[76] European Commission, Negotiations and Agreements (Aug. 2018), *available at* http://ec.europa.eu/trade/policy/countries-and-regions/negotiations-and-agreements/#_being-negotiated (last visited Jan. 10, 2019).

E. IMPACT ASSESSMENTS

Impact assessments are a popular regulatory tool in environmental law and human rights law that identify and evaluate the risks and benefits of projects and policy proposals. Article 7 of the Council Directive on Mandatory Assessment of the Effects of Certain Public and Private Projects on the Environment (EIA Directive) determines that if a project is likely to impair another state's environment, the parties shall share information bilaterally, inform the public, and establish a joint body to address the issue in detail.[77] The example makes plain that the primary purpose of impact assessments is to share information, whether with specific interest groups or the public. In an age of corporate governance, impact assessments can be a powerful tool to obtain knowledge about how animals are treated abroad and about whether a state carries the responsibility to regulate those actions. Apart from asking for information, impact assessments do not necessarily demand that decision-makers act in a specific manner. Because of their limited nature, they are not typically considered interventionist, even if they gather and evaluate data across the border.

Environmental law is well known for its high number and diversity of regulatory approaches to impact assessments. Environmental impact assessments have been established by treaties (the Espoo Convention), regional law (the EIA Directive,[78] or EMAS Regulation),[79] domestic law (like the US National Environmental Policy Act [NEPA]),[80] and IOs (for example, by the UN Environmental Program's [UNEP] Goals and Principles of Environmental Impact Assessment).[81] Environmental impact assessments evaluate norms and projects likely to cause pollution, erosion, loss of biodiversity, deforestation, or desertification, or which have any other significant impact on the environment.[82]

Because agricultural animal production has massive negative effects on the environment, its planned and ongoing activities must undergo environmental screening. According to article 4 para. 1 of the EIA Directive in connection with Annex I para. 17, installations for intensively rearing poultry or pigs with more than 85,000 places for broilers, more than 60,000 places for hens, more than 3,000 places for production pigs, or more than 900 places for sows are subject to mandatory impact assessments. The reports must identify, describe, and assess the direct and indirect effect of these installations on population and human health, biodiversity, the quality of land, soil, water, air, and climate, cultural heritage, and a combination of these factors (article 3 para. 1 EIA Directive). Directive 92/43/EEC, the Habitat Directive, requires assessing impacts of "[a]ny plan or project not directly connected with or necessary to the management of the site but likely to have a significant effect thereon,

---

[77] Directive 2014/52 of the European Parliament and of the Council Amending Directive 2011/92/EU on the Assessment of the Effects of Certain Public and Private Projects on the Environment, 2014 O.J. (L 124) 1.

[78] Directive 2014/52, 2014 O.J. (L 124) 1, 11.

[79] Regulation 1221/2009 of the European Parliament and of the Council on the Voluntary Participation by Organisations in a Community Eco-management and Audit Scheme (EMAS), 2009 O.J. (L 342) 1.

[80] National Environmental Policy Act (NEPA), 42 U.S.C. § 4332(C) (U.S.).

[81] United Nations Environmental Program (UNEP), Goals and Principles of Environmental Impact Assessment, Preliminary Note, U.N. Doc. UNEP/WG.152/4 Annex (Jan. 16, 1987).

[82] Coggins & Head 61 (1993).

either individually or in combination with other plans or projects."[83] It further provides that projects may only be carried out if they do not threaten the habitat of wild animals or plants (article 6 para. 3). If they are assessed negatively but member states decide to proceed "for imperative reasons of overriding public interest," then states must take compensatory measures (article 6 para. 4). Carefully designed and coherently applied rules on environmental impact assessments are likely to give rise to reports that negatively assess animal production industries because of their failure to use resources sustainably, their likelihood of reducing biological diversity, and their considerable polluting effect on air, ground, and water sources.

Some states have declared impact assessments a standard policy in the legislature and the judiciary. The European Union's Action Plan for Better Regulation provides for a mandatory two-stage impact assessment procedure for all legislative and policy initiatives.[84] Similarly, in the United Kingdom, regulatory impact assessments are now a substantial part of its standard regulatory procedure.[85] Because rules on impact assessments apply to any policy proposal and project, they also extend to animal law, as done in the European Union's Impact Assessment on the Animal Testing Provision in Regulation (EC) 1223/2009 on Cosmetics of 2013[86] and the European Union's Impact Assessment on Options for Animal Welfare Labelling and the Establishment of a European Network of Reference Centers for the Protection and Welfare of Animals of 2009.[87] Both impact assessments define problems (current regulation, societal demands, legal inconsistencies, competition issues, and stakeholder concerns) and objectives, and the options available to address or fulfill them. They must contain a feasibility assessment for the options identified, and predict the social, economic, and environmental impact these will have on stakeholders (e.g., farmers, retailers, consumers, and international parties). These impact assessments are especially valuable because they take into account the interests of animals not only in the area of animal law. Any regulatory proposal or project that compromises or has the potential to compromise the

[83] Council Directive 92/43/EEC on the Conservation of Natural Habitats and Wild Fauna and Flora, O.J. (L 206) 7, art. 6 para. 3.

[84] European Commission, Action Plan "Simplifying and Improving the Regulatory Environment," COM(2002) 278 final (June 5, 2002): "In principle, all legislative proposals and all other major policy proposals for adoption, i.e. set out in the Commission's work programme, will be subject to the impact assessment procedure." (*Id.* at 7). *See further* on regulatory impact assessments: Claudio M. Radaelli & Fabrizio De Francesco, *Regulatory Impact Assessment, in* THE OXFORD HANDBOOK OF REGULATION 279, 280 (2010).

[85] In 2014, the UK Department for Business, Innovation & Skills issued a report titled "Impact Assessments: Guidance for Government Departments" (DEFRA, London 2014). In 2015, the Better Regulation Executive (BRE) established guidelines for policymakers, including guidance on conducting impact assessments, along with an "Impact Assessment Toolkit."

[86] European Commission, Commission Staff Working Document, Impact Assessment on the Animal Testing Provisions in Regulation (EC) 1223/2009 on Cosmetics, Accompanying the Document Communication from the Commission to the European Parliament and the Council on Animal Testing and Marketing Ban on the State of Play in Relation to Alternative Methods in the Field of Cosmetics, SWD(2013) 66 final (Mar. 11, 2013).

[87] European Commission, Commission Staff Working Document, Impact Assessment Report Accompanying the Report from the Commission to the European Parliament, the Council, the European Economic and Social Committee and the Committee of the Regions, Options for Animal Welfare Labelling and the Establishment of a European Network of Reference Centres for the Protection and Welfare of Animals, SEC(2009) 1432 (Oct. 28, 2009).

interests of animals, such as a construction project for breeding facilities or plans to invest in production facilities, must be assessed for its impact on animals.

Given the diverse effects of regulatory actions, the weight given to animals in impact assessments is likely negligible vis-à-vis other concerns. At the same time, animals play an increasingly important role in public policy, so there are good reasons to argue that discrete impact assessments be conducted with the specific purpose of gathering information about activities that likely impair, thwart, or further animals' interests—so-called animal impact assessments. Animal impact assessments would produce readily available and accessible information about the many ways that current or proposed regulatory tools and projects compromise animals' interests. They would integrate multiple stakeholders in a pre-regulatory phase, create multileveled responsibilities, and increase the chances that laws will be observed after they are adopted. Animal impact assessments could further pave the way for future due diligence duties of states and stakeholders owed to animals.[88]

Animal impact assessments should be benchmarked against existing recommendations for impact assessments. De Schutter, in his mandate as a Special Rapporteur on the right to food to the UN Secretary-General, proposed Guiding Principles on Human Rights Impact Assessments of Trade and Investment Agreements, which were approved by the UN General Assembly. De Schutter emphasized that procedures that govern impact assessments should be independent, transparent, and ensure broad participation of affected parties. Impact assessments should only be conducted by experts who must receive funding to ensure thorough reporting and independence in decision-making.[89] Animal impact assessments can also look to the UNEP's Goals and Principles of Environmental Impact Assessment for guidance. Principle 4 requires that reports include, at the minimum, a description of the activity proposed, its potentially adverse effects, practical and appropriate alternatives, likely impacts of alternatives, measures available to mitigate adverse effects, remaining knowledge gaps and uncertainties, and information on whether other states' interests are likely going to be affected by the activity.[90] All of these steps can reasonably be expected to increase knowledge of decision makers and their constituency to ensure soundness and reasonableness of policies adopted, permits granted, projects funded, and of other major public or private actions that have an impact on the lives of animals.

The multitiered approach of environmental, regulatory, and animal impact assessments is a good starting point to devise decision-making rules that take into account the interests of animals, but it is far from certain that this suffices. In legal scholarship, it is debated whether impact assessments truly have an impact on policymaking or whether they are paper tigers that unnecessarily burden agencies. Even seemingly revolutionary laws that established duties for all governmental agencies to perform impact assessments, such as the United States' NEPA signed into law by former President Nixon in 1970, were gradually limited by the judiciary.[91] Lower courts had interpreted NEPA to "involve a balancing process" in which

[88] Analogously in human rights law: Human Rights Council, 19th Sess., *Guiding Principles on Human Rights Impact Assessments of Trade and Investment Agreements*, U.N. Doc. A/HRC/19/59/Add.5 (Dec. 19, 2011) [*Guiding Principles on Human Rights Impact Assessments*].

[89] *Guiding Principles on Human Rights Impact Assessments* 10.

[90] UNEP, Goals and Principles of Environmental Impact Assessment (1987).

[91] *See especially* Robertson v. Methow Valley Citizens Council, 490 U.S. 332 (1989) (U.S.).

"environmental costs may outweigh economic and technical benefits,"[92] but in a staggering 17 cases, the US Supreme Court held that NEPA merely requires agencies to amass data and "consider" various alternatives, placing them under no duty to choose the most environmentally sound option.[93] The United States is no outlier in this respect. When regulating impact assessments, most states neither lay down duties to balance competing interests, nor do they require a specific outcome, in the sense that the most reasonable option must be chosen, be it the most environmentally friendly, the one preventing human rights violations, or the one causing the least animal suffering.[94] As a result, these rules, at best, ensure decision-making processes that are informed; at worst, they declare legal activities that have tremendous negative effects on the environment or for affected human and animal communities. To merely demand that decision makers gather information, consider all relevant factors, and "take a hard look" is simply not enough to ensure reasonable decisions are taken, nor is it enough to justify the tremendous financial means required to conduct impact assessments. Regulators should set up very clear rules on how interests must be assessed, weighed, and balanced against one another, and they should place decision makers under a duty to give preference to those options that have the least negative effect or the biggest positive effect on the environment, humans, and animals. Finally, decision makers should be obliged to reject projects likely to have such negative effects.

Given today's conservative take on impact assessments, this demand may go too far in the absence of a clear commitment by the people to protect animals.[95] But even without broad and unequivocal legislative intent, there is a strong case to be made that decision makers should at least observe minimum standards. To determine minimum standards,

---

[92] *See, e.g.*, Calvert Cliffs' Coordinating Committee, Inc. v. United States Atomic Energy Commission, 449 F.2d 1109, para. 14 (D.C. Cir. 1971) (U.S.). This substantive reading is also evident in the dissent of Justice Douglas in Scenic Hudson Preservation Conference v. Federal Power Commission, 407 U.S. 926 (1972). The purpose of §102 NEPA, he argued, is "to insure that if a project is approved, an environmentally acceptable alternative will be chosen" (*Id.*).

[93] *See, e.g.*, Strycker's Bay Neighborhood Council v. Karlen, 444 U.S. 223, 227 (1980) (U.S.), ruling that an agency must not "elevate environmental concerns over other appropriate considerations." This limited approach is now enshrined, in the Council on Environmental Quality's Regulations For Implementing the Procedural Provisions of the National Environmental Policy Act, 40 C.F.R. §1502.23 (U.S.). Lazarus thinks that although "the Court's treatment of NEPA is best understood as evidencing the Court's hostility to NEPA in particular or to environmentalism more generally," there is a more nuanced and "more interesting story" that underlies NEPA and the Supreme Court. *See further* Richard Lazarus, *The National Environmental Policy Act in the U.S. Supreme Court: A Reappraisal and a Peek Behind the Curtains*, 100 Geo. L.J. 1501, 1511 (2012).

[94] Decision makers must only identify alternatives that are more environmentally acceptable and provide reasons why they decided not to choose those. *See* Directive 2014/52, 2014 O.J. (L 124) 1, Annex IV, 2. Goldberg did a comparative analysis of environmental impact assessment regimes in the United States, the European Union, Czech Republic, Slovakia, the World Bank, and the European Bank for Reconstruction and Development, and found that none demand that the most environmentally sound option be chosen: Donald M. Goldberg, A Comparison of Six Environmental Impact Assessment Regimes: The United States, The Czech Republic, Slovakia, The European Community, The World Bank, The European Bank for Reconstruction and Development (Washington D.C., Center for International Environmental Law 1995).

[95] Many countries have enshrined their commitment to protect animals in their constitutions or animal welfare acts. *See* Chapter 9 §2.

the *Guiding Principles* recommend impact assessments in human rights law draw on established human rights indicators.[96] Animal impact assessments could similarly rely on animal welfare indicators developed and applied in natural sciences that take into account physiological, behavioral, cognitive, and emotion-based factors. Those indicators can be general, species-specific, or specific to the purpose humans use animals for.[97] A useful starting point to develop animal welfare indicators is the Animal Welfare Indicators (AWIN) project that develops, integrates, and disseminates animal-based welfare indicators with an eye to pain perception and recognition.[98] Animal welfare indicators are already used to evaluate states' performance in animal law. The Royal Society for the Prevention of Cruelty, in its report "Five Years Measuring Animal Welfare in the UK 2005–2009," views the following as animal welfare indicators: the number of relevant government advisory nondepartmental public bodies that include animal welfare specialists; the proportion of schools that incorporate animal welfare into their curriculum; the number of local authorities that have an animal welfare charter; the number of relevant white papers published by the government that include a positive animal welfare component; the number of investigations and convictions under the AWA; the proportion of people interested in improving animal welfare; the number of animals transported live from the home state for slaughter or fattening; production of non-cage eggs in proportion to total eggs produced; the number and proportion of meat chickens reared to higher on-farm welfare standards; and piglet mortality levels between birth and weaning.[99] These and other factors should be used, *de minimis*, in animal impact assessments.

F. REPORTING

Reporting denotes the mandatory or voluntary act of making information about business activities publicly available. In its early form, reporting was limited to financial and operational data of businesses, but corporations are increasingly asked to also publicize data on their

---

[96] *Guiding Principles on Human Rights Impact Assessments* 11.

[97] *See* for examples of concepts for scientific indicators: Paul Koene, Welfare Indicators for Zoo and Wild Animals: Theories and Examples from Practice (Livestock Research and Wageningen Centre for Animal Welfare and Adaptation, Brussels 2013); Tine Rousing et al., *Indicators for the Assessment of Animal Welfare in a Dairy Cattle Herd with a Cubicle Housing System, in Improving Health and Welfare, in* ANIMAL PRODUCTION: PROCEEDINGS OF SESSIONS OF THE EAAP COMMISSION ON ANIMAL MANAGEMENT & HEALTH, THE HAGUE, NETHERLANDS, 21–24 AUGUST 2000 37 (Harry J. Blokhuis et al. eds., 2000); Veerasamy Sejian et al., *Assessment Methods and Indicators of Animal Welfare*, 6 ASIAN J. AN. & VET. ADVANCES 301 (2011). Behavioral studies are particularly useful to evaluate animal welfare. As Dawkins argues: "Far from being the poor relation of so-called 'hard science' measures of welfare (physiology and bio-chemistry), we need behaviour to make sense, particularly through its role in telling us what animals want. Because of the difficulty of interpreting physiological measures of welfare, and the stress they may cause when they are taken, there is an increasing need to find more reliable and less invasive methods of welfare assessment. The most obvious, least intrusive and potentially most powerful alternative of all is the animal's behavior." (Marian S. Dawkins, *Using Behavior to Assess Animal Welfare*, 13 ANIMAL WELFARE 3, 7 (2004)).

[98] Animal Welfare Indicators (AWIN), *available at* http://www.animal-welfare-indicators.net/site/ (last visited Jan. 10, 2019).

[99] ROYAL SOCIETY FOR THE PREVENTION OF CRUELTY (RSPCA), FIVE YEARS MEASURING ANIMAL WELFARE IN THE UK 2005–2009, 39 (RSPCA, West Sussex 2011).

societal, political, and environmental performance. The public is often most interested in acquiring information about the activities of multinational enterprises, partly because they are so powerful, partly because they operate internationally. Reporting consequently often crosses borders, but because it is not concerned with regulatory processes, outputs, or their allocation, it is only mildly interventionist.[100] Obliging a parent company to disclose information about the entire multinational enterprise is generally viewed as legal under international law. Only if the reporting duty violates foreign law—which happens if a foreign state protects the requested information—do conflicts under international law arise.[101]

International financial reporting standards oblige multinationals to disclose financial data about their global business activities. The International Accounting Standards Board (IASB), an independent, international accounting standard-setting body, has developed rules on comprehensive and transparent financial reporting in its International Financial Reporting Standards (IFRS). Corporations that wish to abide by the IFRS must complete a financial statement that provides information about their assets, liabilities, equity, income and expenses, gains and losses, contributions by and distributions to owners, and cash flows. Because these standards are recognized and applied in over 120 states,[102] most multinationals are interested in being accredited.

Also domestic rules on financial reporting may reach across borders. In the United States, accounting and reporting standards are governed by the Sarbanes-Oxley Act (SOX).[103] The range of companies covered by the SOX includes firms listed or registered on any US securities exchange.[104] The SOX has been criticized for its extraterritorial demands on foreign corporations because it requires remodulation that some argue is incompatible with their home state duties.[105]

Financial reporting produces important information about how corporations are linked to each other, new investment relations, and financial cooperation among corporations. Investments also indicate a firm's long-term plans, including its stance toward animal welfare. For instance, it is useful to know if a cosmetic multinational begins to invest in alternative research methods, or that meat-producers like Tyson Foods raise their financial stake in

---

[100] BALDWIN ET AL. 119 (2013).

[101] Foreign sovereign compulsion is discussed in Chapter 10, §2 B.

[102] The IFRS must be applied to the consolidated financial statements of EU companies whose securities are traded on a regulated EU market: Commission Regulation 1361/2014 Amending Regulation (EC) No. 1126/2008 Adopting Certain International Accounting Standards in Accordance with Regulation (EC) No. 1606/2002 of the European Parliament and of the Council as Regards International Financial Reporting Standards 3 and 13 and International Accounting Standard 40, 2014 O.J. (L 365) 120. In the United States, the US Securities and Exchange Commission (SEC) adopted the Generally Accepted Accounting Principles (GAAP). The SEC also declared to adopt the IFRS by 2014, which has rendered the IASB all the more powerful: Agatha E. Jeffers et al., *The Switch from US GAAP to IFRS*, 7 PROCEEDINGS OF THE NORTHEAST BUSINESS & ECONOMICS ASSOCIATION 48–52 (2010).

[103] Sarbanes-Oxley Act, 15 U.S.C. § 7241 (civil provision) (section 302), 18 U.S.C. § 1350 (criminal provision) (section 906) (U.S.).

[104] Detlev F. Vagts, *Extraterritoriality and the Corporate Governance Law*, 97 AJIL 289, 290 (2003).

[105] Hans Caspar von der Crone & Katja Roth, *Der Sarbanes-Oxley Act und seine extraterritoriale Bedeutung*, 2 AJP 131 (2003).

vegan corporations like Beyond Meat.[106] Ultimately, these investments are also an important indicator to speculate about the public perception of animals and the duties we owe them.

Over the past decades, reporting duties have expanded from the financial to the social and environmental, as part of corporations' responsibility to society. Reports on nonfinancial performance include data about employees (corporate structure, salary, working conditions, or training), value-added statements (attitude to long-term investment or employee maintenance), and environmental issues (water use, energy use, or contribution to global warming).[107] International guidelines in this area ensure consolidated reporting and reduce regulatory heterogeneity. The Global Reporting Initiative (GRI) developed a Sustainability Reporting Framework designed to establish standard reporting practices in matters that affect sustainability, by using guidelines, sector guidance, and other tools. The term sustainability is broadly interpreted by the GRI to encompass economic, environmental, and social impacts.[108] The OECD Guidelines for Multinational Enterprises also established rules on (nonfinancial) information disclosure.[109] In the European Union, Directive 2014/95/EU details when and what kind of nonfinancial and diversity information multinational enterprises and other large corporate groups with 500 employees and more need to provide.[110] The topics that shall be covered by companies' nonfiscal statement are "as a minimum, environmental, social and employee matters, respect for human rights, anti-corruption and bribery matters."[111]

Corporations can also be bound by domestic law to publicize data about their nonfinancial performance. Since 1995, Denmark's Green Accounting Law demands its 1,100 largest companies produce environmental reports on the use of resources and waste management.[112] In France, article 116 of *loi n° 2001-420* lays down that corporations listed on the French stock exchange must disclose information "sur la manière dont la société prend en compte les conséquences sociales et environnementales de son activité."[113] And section 299 para. 1 lit. f of the Australian Corporations Act 2001 demands all corporations detail their performance in meeting environmental regulation.[114]

Most reporting standards, whether issued by IOs or set up by domestic law, are significant for animals, at least indirectly. CAFOs have a duty to report on their environmental performance and must lay bare their emissions and pollutions along with plans to reduce them.

---

[106] Stephanie Storm, *Tyson Foods, a Meat Leader, Invests in Protein Alternatives*, N.Y. TIMES, Oct. 10, 2016. Only two years after making its investment in Beyond Meat, Tyson Foods launched its own plant-protein brand called "Green Street." *See* Alison Rabschnuk, *Tyson Launches 100% Plant-Based Brand*, THE GOOD FOOD INSTITUTE, Feb. 26, 2018.

[107] MUCHLINSKI 375–82 (2007).

[108] GLOBAL REPORTING INITIATIVE (GRI), G4 SUSTAINABILITY REPORTING GUIDELINES (2013).

[109] OECD GUIDELINES FOR MNEs (2011). The guidelines are examined in Chapter 6, §1 I.

[110] Directive 2014/95 of the European Parliament and of the Council Amending Directive 2013/34/EU as Regards Disclosure of Non-financial and Diversity Information by Certain Large Undertakings and Groups, 2014 O.J. (L 330) 1.

[111] *Id.* art. 19a para. I.

[112] Act Amending the Environmental Protection Act (Green Accounts), Act No. 403, June 14, 1995, art. 1 (Den.).

[113] LOI N°2001-420 RELATIVE AUX NOUVELLES RÉGULATIONS ÉCONOMIQUES [LA LOI NRE] [LAW ON NEW ECONOMIC RELATIONS], May 15, 2001, art. 116 (Fr.).

[114] *Corporations Act 2001*, Act No. 50, § 299 (Austl.).

Because animal agricultural industries are highly unsustainable, this duty may nudge them, over the long term, to stop rearing animals. But although agricultural industries are in theory covered by reporting duties, their contribution to environmental degradation and pollution regularly eludes sustainability reports. International climate conferences have consistently ignored animal agriculture and this calls into question their commitment to environmental goals.[115] Environmental reporting does therefore not, as a rule, have a measurable positive effect on the lives of animals.

Few reporting initiatives take the interests of animals into account. In its G4 Sector Disclosures on Food Processing (distinct from the GRI Reporting Guidelines), the GRI recommends food-processing companies publicize information about topics related to animals. The G4 Sector Disclosures on Food Processing demand information about the percentage and total number of animals raised and processed, divided by species and breed type, actions taken by the corporation to mitigate any negative impacts on animal welfare,[116] the effects of housing systems on animals,[117] policies and practices on the use of antibiotics and hormones,[118] the total number of incidents or significant noncompliance with laws and regulations, and adherence to voluntary standards related to transportation, handling, and slaughter.[119] In short, the GRI obliges multinational enterprises that operate in the agricultural sector to disclose how many and what kind of animals they breed, raise, or process, how confined these animals are, whether they are given antibiotics or hormones, whether they take animal welfare into account, how animal suffering is reduced, and if their practices comply with the law.

Another initiative designed to improve corporate reporting on farmed animal welfare issues is the Business Benchmark on Farm Animal Welfare (BBFAW), launched by Compassion in World Farming and World Animal Protection. The BBFAW assesses animal welfare management, policies, practices, processes, and performance of investors, companies, nongovernmental organizations (NGOs), and other stakeholders in the animal agricultural industry. A key finding of the BBFAW is that reporting on farmed animal welfare is still in its infancy:

> We believe that companies should be encouraged to treat animals in their supply chain with respect and adopt robust processes for managing and reporting on their farm animal welfare performance. We have engaged with food and retail companies over

---

[115] Although the United Nations urges a global move away from meat, the conferences it organizes show how weak its own commitment to this goal is. At the 2016 Paris Conference of the Parties (COP21), where more than 190 state officials met, meat consumption was never discussed: Laura Wellesley, *Can Eating Less Meat Help Reduce Climate Change?*, BBC NEWS, Nov. 24, 2015. Its meat-heavy menu at the UN Framework Convention on Climate Change conference COP24 in December 2018 contributed an estimated 4,000 metric tons of greenhouse gases to the climate crisis: Stephanie Feldstein, Claire Fitch, & Caroline Wimberly, *Meat-heavy Menu at UN Climate Conference Could Contribute 4,000 Metric Tons of Greenhouse Gases*, CENTER FOR BIOLOGICAL DIVERSITY, Dec. 2, 2018.

[116] GLOBAL REPORTING INITIATIVE (GRI), G4 SECTOR DISCLOSURES: FOOD PROCESSING 25, FP 9 (2014).

[117] *Id.* at 27, FP 11.

[118] *Id.* at 28, FP 12.

[119] *Id.* at 29, FP 13.

> many years on a diverse range of subjects and have long recognised farm animal welfare as a key business issue, yet our ability to engage effectively has been limited by poor company disclosure and an absence of investor-relevant tools to assess meaningfully company performance in this area.[120]

The BBFAW's rating seems to have a positive effect on companies. The percentage of companies publishing animal welfare policies has increased from 46 percent in 2012 to 79 percent in 2017.[121] After receiving a negative rating in the BBFAW's report in 2012, Nestlé committed to improving farmed animal welfare standards in its supply chain, which covers over 7,300 suppliers.[122] The next year, Nestlé collaborated with World Animal Protection to change its Responsible Sourcing Guideline and its Supplier Code, and set up a Commitment on Farm Animal Welfare.[123] The Nestlé Commitment on Farm Animal Welfare is a two-page document that recognizes the OIE standards and the Five Freedoms. In its Commitment, Nestlé pledges to ensure compliance with these standards, scale up traceability, focus on species-specific rules (including prohibiting practices like dehorning, tail docking, disbudding and castration without anesthetic and analgesia, veal crates, permanent tethering of cows, and other cruel practices on pigs, chickens, and other farmed animals), establish action plans with suppliers, work with animal welfare organizations, and track its progress through annual reporting.[124]

These examples aside, animal welfare is not usually considered in initiatives or rules on reporting, and almost never discussed as a separate point. The worldwide disregard for animals in reporting must be criticized because the topics covered by reporting duties or initiatives should not be based on corporate needs and interests; instead, they should respond to issues important to the public.[125] Even when corporations report on animal welfare by committing to the GRI or developing their own initiatives, "[t]he quality of reporting on farm animal

---

[120] Business Benchmark on Farm Animal Welfare (BBFAW), The Business Benchmark on Farm Animal Welfare 2014 Report 4 (Nicky Amos & Rory Sullivan, BBFAW 2015). Of the companies that included animal welfare issues, 84 percent acknowledge farmed animal welfare as a business issue, 69 percent formulated their commitment in overarching policies, 54 percent published farmed animal welfare-related objectives and targets, and 51 percent described their management responsibilities for farmed animal welfare: Business Benchmark on Farm Animal Welfare (BBFAW), The Business Benchmark on Farm Animal Welfare 2015 Report 8 (Nicky Amos & Rory Sullivan, BBFAW 2016).

[121] BBFAW, Farm Animal Welfare Report 8 (2015); Business Benchmark on Farm Animal Welfare (BBFAW), The Business Benchmark on Farm Animal Welfare 2017 Report 6 (Nicky Amos & Rory Sullivan, BBFAW 2017).

[122] Anand Chandrasekhar, *Nestlé Pledges Humane Treatment of Farm Animals*, Swissinfo, Aug. 22, 2014.

[123] Nestlé Responsible Sourcing Standard (Nestlé, Vevey 2018). The guide covers all stages of livestock processing and production (breeding, housing, feeding, manipulation of the animal, disease prevention and control, handling and transport, killing and slaughtering): *id.* at 20; Nestlé Supplier Code 4 (Nestlé, Vevey 2013).

[124] Nestlé Commitment on Farm Animal Welfare (Nestlé, Vevey 2014).

[125] The information is needed, because "[t]he lack of attention paid to farm animal welfare in sustainability and annual reports would be less of a problem if the information were readily obtainable elsewhere. In practice, this is not the case." (Rory Sullivan & Nicky Amos, *Farm Animal Welfare Consistently Ignored in Sustainability Reports*, The Guardian, Nov. 5, 2015).

welfare tends to be limited, with most companies favouring a qualitative approach typically describing processes or programmes, rather than reporting on tangible performance measures and outcomes."[126] Given society's growing concern about how we treat animals, these practices must change. Mandating disclosure does have the potential to positively affect the lives of animals worldwide, whether through public "naming and shaming," or by making it clear that corporations must be held accountable for how they treat animals.

G. CORPORATE SOCIAL RESPONSIBILITY (CSR)

Management, assurance, and reporting standards designed to help companies become more "socially responsible" have proliferated in the past decade. Corporate social responsibility (CSR) is now firmly entrenched in most of the leading companies' strategies.[127] CSR denotes the responsibility corporations have to society, including the responsibility to meet objectives that produce long-term benefits, use business power responsibly, integrate the demands of society, and improve society through ethically proper conduct.[128] Involving corporations in drafting certain rules, or having them create their own rules, is of special interest in the extraterritoriality debate. It pays deference to the fact that large corporations are, "amidst the many legal loopholes, free to act as they please, without responsibility towards society, yet, at the same time, quasi-social institutions."[129] Accepting this kind of "regulation" as a variant of or an addition to traditional lawmaking takes advantage of the fact that multinational enterprises are able to respond transnationally to transnational problems. CSR is thus particularly suited to addressing topics that exceed the territorial reach of states, and topics neglected under traditional "command and control" structures.

Because CSR is meant to respond to the needs of the public, companies cannot unilaterally determine in which areas they must act in a socially responsible manner. In the past years, we have been witnessing a thriving interest of the public in matters relating to animals. According to the Faunalytics' Animal Tracker, 7 in 10 US adults have a higher opinion of the animal protection movement than any other social movement except workers' rights. More

---

[126] *Id.*

[127] Bevan et al. state: "One-hundred-and-thirty-two of the leading FTSE 250 companies reported on their performance in at least one area of CSR in 2002/03—an increase of more than 26% on the previous year" (STEPHEN BEVAN ET AL., ACHIEVING HIGH PERFORMANCE: CSR AT THE HEART OF BUSINESS 2, 8 (2004)). Meyer et al. demonstrate the incredible increase in CSR initiatives that began in the early 1990s and continued until 2015. Before the 1990s such initiatives were rare: John W. Meyer et al., *Legitimating the Transnational Corporation in a Stateless World Society*, *in* CORPORATE SOCIAL RESPONSIBILITY IN A GLOBALIZING WORLD 27, 47 (Kiyoteru Tsutsui & Alwyn Lim eds., 2015). Also on the "spectacular expansion" of CSR: PAULA A. ARGENTI, CORPORATE SOCIAL RESPONSIBILITY 19 (2016); Alwyn Lim & Kiyoteru Tsutsui, *The Social Regulation of the Economy in the Global Context*, *in* CORPORATE SOCIAL RESPONSIBILITY IN A GLOBALIZING WORLD 1, 1 (2015); ZERK, MULTINATIONALS AND CORPORATE SOCIAL RESPONSIBILITY 107 (2008).

[128] Garriga and Melé group CSR theories into instrumental, political, integrative, and value theories: Elisabet Garriga & Domènec Melé, *Corporate Social Responsibility Theories: Mapping the Territory*, 53 J. BUS. ETHICS 51, 65–6 (2004).

[129] Paddy Ireland, *Corporate Social Responsibility (CSR)*, *in* THE NEW OXFORD COMPANION TO LAW (Peter Cane & Joanne Conaghan eds., online ed. 2009).

than 3 in 4 people believe that protecting animals in a variety of situations is "very" or "somewhat" important.[130] Gallup found that almost a third of Americans (32 percent) believe animals should be accorded the same rights as people; 62 percent say animals deserve some protection but can still be used to benefit humans.[131] The 2016 Eurobarometer poll shows 94 percent of EU citizens believe it is important to protect the welfare of farmed animals, and 82 percent believe that the welfare of farmed animals should be better protected than it is now.[132] Technomic and Context Marketing obtained similar results.[133] As societies come to care more about animals, corporations will have to address and respond to these demands.

There are many ways to design CSR policies. CSR can be corporate-based, IO-based, or a mix of law and CSR. Corporate-based CSR denotes companies' voluntary commitment to change how they affect animals. Corporations that produce or distribute products that contain animal parts can voluntarily label their products, engage in less cruel forms of animal exploitation, or decline to use animals for human profit altogether. Many health- and beauty-oriented corporations are giving up animal testing, and some have stopped using animal ingredients. Clothing manufacturers and designers are moving toward faux leather, faux fur, and other cruelty-free alternatives. Food suppliers and restaurants are pledging to quit confining hens in battery cages and pigs in gestation crates, to stop using calves for veal, or are no longer force-feeding geese for foie gras.[134] With a view on the food industry in the United States, Middleton observes:

> Recently, the country's largest grocery chain, Kroger, called on its suppliers to accelerate their movement away from gestation crates for pigs. McDonald's also recently announced a timetable to phase out all pork produced with gestation crates. Wendy's,

---

[130] Faunalytics, Animal Protection Ranked as Most Favorable Social Cause (Apr. 2015), *available at* https://faunalytics.org/seven-in-10-u-s-adults-have-a-favorable-impression-of-the-animal-cause-2/ (last visited Jan. 10, 2019).

[131] Rebecca Rifkin, *In U.S., More Say Animals Should Have Same Rights as People*, Gallup Poll, May 18, 2015, *available at* http://news.gallup.com/poll/183275/say-animals-rights-people.aspx (last visited Jan. 10, 2019).

[132] 44 percent of EU citizens said the welfare of farmed animals should "certainly" be better protected (compared to 35 percent in 2006), while 38 percent agreed that this should "probably" happen (compared to 42 percent in 2006). Combined, these two categories increased from 77 percent to 82 percent over 10 years: European Commission, Special Eurobarometer 442 Report: Attitudes of Europeans towards Animal Welfare 5, 12 (2016).

[133] Technomic found that consumers increasingly prefer vegetarian options for animal welfare reasons: Technomic, Consumer Trend Reports, *available at* https://www.technomic.com/Reports_and_Newsletters/Consumer_Trend_Reports/ (last visited Jan. 10, 2019). Context Marketing found that 77 percent of females and 64 percent of males believe that humane standards ought to apply to the care of farmed animals: Context Marketing, Ethical Food: A Research Report on the Ethical Claims that Matter Most to Food Shoppers and How Ethical Concerns Influence Food Purchases 7 (Mar. 2010), *available at* http://www.contextmarketing.com/ethicalfoodreport.pdf (last visited Jan. 10, 2019). *See* for a comprehensive overview of the latest studies on consumer behavior in matters of animal welfare: Animal Welfare Institute, Consumer Perceptions of Farm Animal Welfare (AWI, Washington D.C. 2015).

[134] *See* Reynard Loki, *Helping Animals Through CSR: Exclusive Interview with Animal Legal Defense Fund*, Justmeans, Feb. 25, 2011.

Denny's, Sonic, and Safeway have made similar commitments. And Burger King took its commitment one step further, pledging to also switch to exclusively cage-free eggs.[135]

Though this is a welcome development, most corporations have yet to respond to citizens' concerns about animals. The Royal Society for the Prevention of Cruelty's report, "Five Years Measuring Animal Welfare in the UK 2005–2009," examined FTSE 100's animal welfare policy performance in the United Kingdom. Only 20 of them had a corporate strategy that referenced animal welfare, and most of them were introduced in the past five years.[136]

Even if most corporations adopted a CSR strategy that references animals, CSR is unlikely to fill governance gaps because it lacks monitoring, control, and democratic legitimacy. As Bevan et al. warn, "[d]espite considerable research conducted over the past five years into the benefits of corporate social responsibility [. . .] it remains a fact that many business leaders still only pay lip service to CSR, or are merely reacting to peer pressure by introducing it into their organizations."[137]

Involving IOs may reduce the risk of unaccountable CSR. One of the largest and most prominent CSR initiatives is the UN Global Compact (GC), a pact of UN agencies, NGOs, civil society, and corporate representatives that encourages businesses worldwide to adopt sustainable and socially responsible policies and to report on their performance.[138] The GC is not a regulatory instrument, but a voluntary program that helps to catalyze actions in support of broader UN goals. Ten principles lie at the heart of the GC, covering human rights, labor standards, environmental protection, and anticorruption.[139] Animal welfare links indirectly to the environmental precautionary principle (principle 7), responsibility for the environment (principle 8), and the use of environmental-friendly technologies (principle 9). If those principles are taken seriously, GC-listed corporations should end and divest from animal agricultural production. This, however, is unlikely. The GC has been strongly criticized for bluewashing the public image of corporations because only a few of the 50,000 multinationals listed in the GC adhere to the 10 principles.[140] On a closer look, the GC seems to keep its entry rules lax to attract business and only gradually introduces stricter rules, which include annual letters of progress, raising the standard of participation, and delisting firms that do not adhere to its principles.[141]

---

[135] Kristie Middleton, *Three Reasons Farm Animal Welfare Is an Important CSR Tenet for the Food Industry*, Triple Pundit, June 21, 2012.

[136] RSPCA, Measuring Animal Welfare in the UK 2005–2009, 40.

[137] Baldwin et al. 2, 137 ff. (2013). On top of that, we lack comparative data: Bevan et al. 6 (2004).

[138] The UN Global Compact was launched in 2000 and is now headed by the Global Compact Office. The UN Global Compact is a network of over 13,000 companies and nonbusinesses: UN Global Compact, Our Participants, *available at* https://www.unglobalcompact.org/what-is-gc/participants/search?utf8=&search%5Bkeywords%5D=&search%5Bper_page%5D=10&search%5Bsort_field%5D=sector&search%5Bsort_direction%5D=asc (last visited Jan. 10, 2019).

[139] UN Global Compact, The Ten Principles of the UN Global Compact, *available at* https://www.unglobalcompact.org/what-is-gc/mission/principles (last visited Jan. 10, 2019).

[140] Khan Rahmatullah, *Global Compact*, *in* MPEPIL 22–4 (Rüdiger Wolfrum ed., online ed. 2011).

[141] By 2019, the GC had delisted 11,522 companies: UN Global Compact, Delisted Participants, *available at* https://www.unglobalcompact.org/participation/report/cop/create-and-submit/expelled (last

The International Organization for Standardization (ISO) is another IO that nudges corporations to commit to CSR and improve their performance. In 2010, the ISO introduced new guidelines, the ISO 26000, that lay down standards for CSR.[142] The guidelines prompt corporations to pay attention to animals by

> respecting the welfare of animals, when affecting their lives and existence, including by providing decent conditions for keeping, breeding, producing, transporting and using animals (4.4);
>
> providing consumers with information about products and services, including on [. . .] aspects related to animal welfare (including, where appropriate, use of animal testing) (6.7.5.2);
>
> adopt[ing] sustainable agricultural, fishing, and forestry practices including aspects related to animal welfare, for example, as defined in leading standards and certification schemes (6.5.6.2); and
>
> consider[ing] that wild animals and their habitats are part of our natural ecosystems and should therefore be valued and protected and their welfare taken into account (6.5.6.2).

Interesting to note, the ISO 26000's definition of sustainable consumption emphasizes that "[t]he concept of sustainable consumption also encompasses a concern for animal welfare, respecting the physical integrity of animals and avoiding cruelty" (6.7.5.1). Though these commitments are not particularly progressive, they are a step in the right direction by recognizing animal welfare issues as a standard CSR concern. If a corporation voluntarily abides by the standard, it can carry the ISO 26000 certification and is recognized for protecting animal welfare as part of its CSR.[143]

Another way to make sure corporations are not merely paying lip service to animal welfare through CSR is to create a "smart mix" of corporate and governmental actions.[144] Involvement of the government in CSR may include mandatory approval of CSR strategies by the parliament, parliamentary or departmental oversight, regulatory vetoes, judicial review, procedures for public enforcement, participation rights for the public, or reporting duties. In the last decade, we have observed a trend among states to supplement CSR with such measures. In 2009, Denmark passed legislation that obliges its largest companies to include information on CSR in their annual reports.[145] The United Kingdom's National

---

visited Jan. 10, 2019). *See also* Meyer et al., *Legitimating the Transnational Corporation in a Stateless World Society*, *in* Corporate Social Responsibility in a Globalizing World 49 (2015).

[142] International Standard Organisation, International Standard ISO 26000, Guidance on Social Responsibility ISO 26000:2010(E) (ISO, Geneva, 1st ed. 2010) [ISO 26000].

[143] *WSPA Hails New ISO Standard as First to Promote Animal Welfare*, UN FAO, Nov. 9, 2010. *See also* Maud H. Schmiedeknecht & Josef Wieland, *ISO 26000, 7 Grundsätze, 6 Kernthemen*, *in* Corporate Social Responsibility: Verantwortungsvolle Unternehmensführung in Theorie und Praxis 299 (2015).

[144] Michael Weiss, Hybride Regulierungssysteme: Eine Analyse rechtlicher, faktischer und extraterritorialer Wirkungen nationaler Corporate-Governance Kodizes 40 (2011).

[145] Financial Statements Act, Act No. 448, June 7, 2001, amendment introduced in 2009, art. 14 para. 1 (Den.). An amendment proposed in 2013 allows companies to issue their reports in English and rely on international

Consumer Council included a checklist of "credible self-regulatory schemes" in its 2000 report on models of self-regulation. On the list were strong external consultation and involvement, complaint mechanisms, sanctions for nonobservance, monitoring, and accountability through annual reports.[146] The European Union's CSR Strategy includes "a smart mix of voluntary policy measures and, where necessary, complementary regulation, for example, to promote transparency, create market incentives for responsible business conduct, and ensure corporate accountability."[147] And in the area of human rights, there is a growing expectation that nonadherence to CSR strategies must entail corporate liability.[148] In line with these achievements, animal advocates must campaign for more than corporate-based CSR and pressure governments to hold corporations socially responsible for their actions vis-à-vis animals.

H. CODES OF CONDUCT

Codes of conduct are a written set of rules and principles that focus on certain desirable behaviors of addressees.[149] Codes can be broad in scope, but most deal with specific challenges or operations of specific industries; these are sometimes termed "best practices." There are best practices for the use of animals in toxicological research,[150] animal transport in research,[151] use of analgesics in research animals,[152] animal welfare certification schemes,[153] good farming practices,[154] good dairy farming practice,[155] animal husbandry more

CSR standards. On environmental and social reporting, *see* Financial Business Act, Consolidated Act No. 1125, Sept. 23, 2010, art. 190 para. 1 (Den.).

[146] NATIONAL CONSUMER COUNCIL (NCC), MODELS OF SELF-REGULATION: AN OVERVIEW OF MODELS IN BUSINESS AND THE PROFESSIONS 51 (NCC, Technopark 2000).

[147] European Commission, Communication from the Commission to the European Parliament, the Council, the European Economic and Social Committee and the Committee of the Regions, A Renewed EU Strategy 2011–2014 for Corporate Social Responsibility, COM(2011) 681 final, Oct. 25, 2011, at 7.

[148] SCHWEIZERISCHES KOMPETENZZENTRUM FÜR MENSCHENRECHTE (SKMR) [SWISS CENTER FOR COMPETENCE IN HUMAN RIGHTS], UMSETZUNG DER MENSCHENRECHTE IN DER SCHWEIZ, EINE BESTANDESAUFNAHME IM BEREICH MENSCHENRECHTE UND WIRTSCHAFT, SKMR/CSDH I.6, 25 ff. (SKMR, Berne 2013).

[149] Jürgen Friedrich, *Codes of Conduct*, *in* MPEPIL 1 (Rüdiger Wolfrum ed., online ed. 2010).

[150] Stokes' definition of best practice seems to encompass the 3Rs: "Best practice approaches seek to enhance animal well-being, minimize or avoid pain and distress, and use fewer animals." (William S. Stokes, *Best Practices for the Use of Animals in Toxicological Research and Testing*, 1245 ANN. N.Y. ACAD. SCI. 17 (2011)).

[151] NATIONAL CENTER FOR THE REPLACEMENT REFINEMENT & REDUCTION OF ANIMALS IN RESEARCH, BEST PRACTICE FOR ANIMAL TRANSPORT (NC3R, London), *available at* https://www.nc3rs.org.uk/best-practice-animal-transport (last visited Jan. 10, 2019).

[152] JOHN C. SCHOFIELD, ANALGESIC BEST PRACTICE FOR THE USE OF ANIMALS IN RESEARCH AND TEACHING: AN INTERPRETATIVE INTERNATIONAL LITERATURE REVIEW (UN FAO 2002).

[153] David Main et al., *Best Practice Framework for Animal Welfare Certification Schemes*, 37 TRENDS FOOD SCI. & TECHN. 127 (2014).

[154] UN FAO AND WORLD ORGANIZATION FOR ANIMAL HEALTH (OIE), GUIDE TO GOOD FARMING PRACTICES FOR ANIMAL PRODUCTION SAFETY (FAO, Rome 2009).

[155] UN FAO AND INTERNATIONAL DAIRY FEDERATION, GUIDE TO GOOD DAIRY FARMING PRACTICE (FAO, Rome 2011).

generally,[156] the welfare of animals during transport,[157] and many more. Although not subject to procedural requirements and not legally binding, the codes can exert considerable pressure on corporations to observe certain minimum standards in states where no laws regulate their actions vis-à-vis animals.[158]

Codes of conduct and best practices are published by a variety of stakeholders. In animal law, governments frequently issue codes of conduct and best practices. Section 14 para. 1 of the UK AWA determines that national authorities issue and revise codes of practice to flesh out its AWA.[159] The UK Department for Environment, Food and Rural Affairs has made use of this competence and issued codes on the treatment of meat chickens, laying hens, pigs, sheep and goats, cows, horses, ponies, dogs, cats, and game birds.[160] Canada's National Farm Animal Care Council established scientific review procedures to issue codes of practice for dairy cows, horses, farmed deer, farmed fox, goats, mink, pigs, and sheep, and on animal transport.[161] Codes also exist on the state level. The government of South Australia published codes of practice (on pet trade, captive bird husbandry, the keeping of security dogs, and the welfare of animals in circuses) and model codes of practice (on farmed animals, transport in farmed animals, and other core themes).[162] Most codes of conduct and best practices issued by governments are recommendations and do not impose legal duties on farming industries. New Zealand is an exception; its codes on minimum standards for animal care and management are binding for people in charge of animals.[163]

Codes of conduct and best practices are also developed by IOs. The World Association of Zoos and Aquariums (WAZA) adopted the "Code of Ethics and Animal Welfare" in

---

[156] ZIMS by ISIS, Best Practices in Animal Husbandry and Inventory Records Keeping Using the ZIMS Application (2015).

[157] Farm Animal Welfare Advisory Council, Best Practice for the Welfare of Animals during Transport (Irish Department of Agriculture, Food and the Marine [DAFM], Dublin 2007).

[158] Like other CSR instruments, codes of conduct are designed to overcome global challenges to regulation: Meyer et al., *Legitimating the Transnational Corporation in a Stateless World Society*, *in* Corporate Social Responsibility in a Globalizing World 54 (2015). In 2000, Cynthia McKinney, former congresswomen in the Australian House of Representatives, proposed the Corporate Code of Conduct Bill that included substantive standards on human rights, labor, and environmental protection. The bill would have required corporations operating abroad and employing more than 20 employees to abide by the Code: Parliamentary Joint Statutory Committee on Corporations and Securities, Inquiry into Corporate Code of Conduct Bill 2000, Submission by the Centre for International and Public Law Australian National University.

[159] Animal Welfare Act (U.K.), § 14 para. 1.

[160] Department for Environment, Food and Rural Affairs (DEFRA), Keeping Farm Animals: Guidance on Animal Welfare (DEFRA Publications, London 2013).

[161] National Farm Animal Care Council (NFACC), Codes of Practice for the Care and Handling of Farm Animals (NFACC, Lacombe 2015).

[162] Government of South Australia, Department of Environment, Water and Natural Resources, Animal Welfare Codes of Practice, *available at* http://www.environment.sa.gov.au/managing-natural-resources/plants-and-animals/Animal_welfare/Codes_of_practice/Animal_welfare_codes_of_practice (last visited Jan. 10, 2019).

[163] The New Zealand AWA also underlines that these codes are minimum standards, which suggests that they are not best practices: Animal Welfare Act (N.Z.), § 68 lit. b (N.Z.). *See also* § 87 of the same act for codes of ethical conduct in animal research, testing, and teaching.

2003 to lay down minimum expectations for the keeping of animals in zoological parks and aquariums.[164] The UN FAO issued a "Guide to Good Farming Practices for Animal Production Safety" together with the OIE,[165] and a "Guide to Good Dairy Farming Practice" with the International Dairy Federation.[166] As the authorship reveals, many of these codes are issued by bodies with vested interests, so it is unrealistic to expect these codes to seriously address and respond to animals' interests.

Corporations also issue codes of conduct. The European Parliament seems sympathetic to this strategy in the context of animal law. In its resolution to establish a European code of conduct, the Parliament states it "[b]elieves that under the voluntary codes of conduct European companies should comply with EU environmental, animal welfare and health standards."[167] Codes of conduct can ensure better social performance of corporations abroad, including their performance vis-à-vis animals. Novartis, for example, uses its codes of conduct to "export" established animal protection standards. According to its general code of conduct, Novartis is committed to the 3Rs (refinement, reduction, and replacement of animals used in research) wherever it operates.[168] It also has a discrete code of conduct, the Animal Welfare Policy, which details how animals must be treated. The policy applies to all Novartis divisions, units, institutions, and any contracted third party engaged in animal studies and procedures, and must "be implemented in countries with less or equally stringent laws and industry codes as the US."[169] Although it is not difficult to comply with US animal laws since they are very weak, the core idea that uniform standards should be used for all units of a multinational is valuable. The policy also has its own minimum level rule: "In some countries, local laws and regulations may be more stringent than the principles set out in this Policy. Where this is the case, the more stringent rules apply."[170]

In sum, codes of conduct have the potential to promote higher standards on the treatment of animals in states even when there are no or weak animal laws. But if codes of conduct remain low-level and industry-friendly, they are simply another tool to market the exploitation of animals.[171]

---

[164] World Association of Zoos and Aquariums (WAZA), WAZA Code of Ethics and Animal Welfare (WAZA, Geneva 2003).

[165] UN FAO and World Organization for Animal Health (OIE), Guide to Good Farming Practices for Animal Production Safety (FAO, Rome 2009).

[166] UN FAO and International Dairy Federation, Guide to Good Dairy Farming Practice (FAO, Rome 2011). These standards only refer to the Five Freedoms (freedom from thirst, hunger, and malnutrition, freedom from discomfort, freedom from pain, injury, and disease, freedom from fear, and freedom to engage in relatively normal patterns of animal behavior) (*id.* at 8).

[167] European Parliament, Resolution of the European Parliament on European Union Strategy for European Enterprises Operating in Developing Countries: Towards a European Code of Conduct, 1999 O.J. (C 104) 180.

[168] Novartis, Code of Conduct 3 (Novartis International, Basel 2018).

[169] Novartis, Animal Welfare Policy 2 (Novartis International, Basel 2016).

[170] *Id.*

[171] Peters, *Sind transnationale Unternehmen verpflichtet, (internationale) Menschenrechte zu respektieren und zu fördern?*, *in* Menschenrechte und Wirtschaft im Spannungsfeld zwischen State und Nonstate Actors 131 (2005).

1. OECD GUIDELINES FOR MULTINATIONAL ENTERPRISES

Under the auspices of the OECD, governments meet to discuss and respond to the multiple challenges globalization creates for business, social welfare, and the environment. In 2011, the OECD felt a need to address the transnational problems created by and for multinationals and issued the Guidelines for Multinational Enterprises, a component of the 1976 Declaration on International Investment and Multinational Enterprises.[172] The guidelines are voluntary, but they indicate the extent to which governments expect corporations to adhere to certain minimum social and environmental standards when they operate abroad, and hence qualify as soft law.[173]

The guidelines apply only to those states that have accepted them, which includes members of the OECD and adhering states. They apply extraterritorially, however, because they cover all activities of these states' multinational enterprises, regardless of whether enterprises operate locally or globally. Para. 3 of the part "Concepts and Principles" declares:

> Since the operations of multinational enterprises extend throughout the world, international co-operation in this field should extend to all countries. Governments adhering to the Guidelines encourage the enterprises operating on their territories to observe the Guidelines *wherever they operate*, while taking into account the particular circumstances of each host country.[174]

The guidelines apply in particular to enterprise groups, including their foreign subsidiaries.[175] They also cover activities of financial institutes, so an institution that invests in foreign projects must introduce a risk-based system to administer its investments. As held in *POSCO*, the system must consider the investees' operational context (countries, regions, or high-risk operating environments like conflict zones), and operations, products, or services that pose particular risks (e.g., the investees' previous human rights or environmental performance).[176] These tweaks considerably extend the OECD's jurisdiction to the territory of states that are not signatories to it and give the guidelines broad extraterritorial application.[177]

---

[172] OECD GUIDELINES FOR MNEs (2011).

[173] ALEXANDRA GATTO, MULTINATIONAL ENTERPRISES AND HUMAN RIGHTS: OBLIGATIONS UNDER EU LAW AND INTERNATIONAL LAW 76 (2011); KAUFMANN 164 (2007); Muchlinski, *Corporations in International Law*, *in* MPEPIL 43 (2014); Peters, *Sind transnationale Unternehmen verpflichtet, (internationale) Menschenrechte zu respektieren und zu fördern?*, *in* MENSCHENRECHTE UND WIRTSCHAFT IM SPANNUNGSFELD ZWISCHEN STATE UND NONSTATE ACTORS 130 (2005).

[174] OECD GUIDELINES FOR MNEs, Concepts and Principles 17, para. 3 (2011) (emphasis added).

[175] OECD GUIDELINES FOR MNEs, Commentary on General Policies 22, para. 9 (2011).

[176] The Norwegian National Contact Point for the OECD Guidelines for Multinational Enterprises, Final Statement in the Complaint from Lok Shakti Abhiyan, Korean Transnational Corporations Watch, Fair and Green Global Alliance and Forum for Environment v. POSCO (South Korea), ABP/APG (Netherlands and NBIM (Norway)), May 27, 2013, at 30.

[177] DE SCHUTTER 2 (2006); Jan Huner, *The Multilateral Agreement on Investment and the Review of the OECD Guidelines for Multinational Enterprises*, *in* LIABILITY OF MULTINATIONAL CORPORATIONS UNDER INTERNATIONAL LAW 200 (2000); Steven Tully, *The 2000 Review of the OECD Guidelines for Multinational Enterprises*, 50 ICLQ 394, 401 (2001); ZERK, MULTINATIONALS AND CORPORATE SOCIAL RESPONSIBILITY 162 (2008).

The guidelines consist of eleven distinct chapters. The "General Policies" apply to all multinational enterprises, including those that operate with animals. They expect all enterprises to base their actions on corporate governance principles, either by supporting and applying existing principles or developing their own (para. II.A.6). The principles call on the board of the parent corporation to provide strategic guidance for the enterprise, effective monitoring, and to ensure the enterprise's integrity in accounting and financial reporting.[178] Enterprises shall also "develop and apply effective self-regulatory practices and management systems that foster a relationship of confidence and mutual trust between enterprises and the societies in which they operate" (para. II.A.7). Due diligence maxims shall be employed in risk management systems to identify, prevent, and mitigate actual and potential adverse impacts (para. II.A.10), whether they are caused or contributed to by the enterprise, or are linked to their operations, products, or services by a business relationship.[179] Here, adverse impacts should be interpreted to cover animal cruelty and suffering because they are an important social concern, and, hence, a corporate risk.

The third chapter of the guidelines covers disclosure of information by enterprises, including multinational enterprises that deal with or otherwise affect animals. Pursuant to para. III.1, enterprises must ensure the public is informed about their activities, structure, financial situation, performance, ownership, and governance in an accurate and timely fashion. This encompasses information about the enterprise's financial and operating results, its objectives, major share ownership and voting rights, structure of a group of enterprises and intragroup relations, control enhancing mechanisms, board members, foreseeable risk factors, content of corporate governance codes or policies, and the implementation process (para. III.2).[180]

Chapter six lays down guidelines on environmental issues, notably on environmental protection, public health and safety, and sustainable development. Where animals are an integral part of the environment or where their use leads to environmental pollution, these guidelines apply. Chapter six incorporates fundamental principles of the Rio Declaration and the Aarhus Convention on Access to Information, Public Participation in Decision-making, and Access to Justice in Environmental Matters.[181] The principles obligate corporations to establish and maintain environmental management systems that deliver transparent information, set specific goals, and are subject to periodic review (para. 1). They underline that the public needs to be informed about the topics addressed in the chapter, and that stakeholders promote public discussions (para. 2). Multinational enterprises should conduct impact assessments (paras. 3, 4, and 5), seek to improve their environmental performance, and promote customer awareness about environmental implications (para. 6). They must

---

[178] OECD Guidelines for MNEs, Commentary on General Policies 22, para. 8 (2011).

[179] Adverse impacts also include those of supply chains. *See* OECD Guidelines for MNEs, Commentary on General Policies 24, para. 17 (2011): "Relationships in the supply chain take a variety of forms including, for example, franchising, licensing or subcontracting. Entities in the supply chain are often multinational enterprises themselves and, by virtue of this fact, those operating in or from the countries adhering to the Declaration are covered by the Guidelines."

[180] OECD Guidelines for MNEs, Commentary on Disclosure 29, paras. 30 and 31 (2011).

[181] OECD Guidelines for MNEs, Commentary on the Environment 44, para. 60 (2011); Declaration of the United Nations Conference on Environment and Development, U.N. Doc. A/CONF.151/26, 31 I.L.M. 874 (June 14, 1992) [Rio Declaration]; Aarhus Convention.

provide adequate education and training to personnel in their employ (para. 7). Moreover, corporations are encouraged to participate in initiatives and partnerships to develop meaningful environmental public policies (para. 8).

The OECD guidelines are an important achievement in international governance, by tying together principles governing multinationals and core achievements in environmental and human rights law. The guidelines were not set up to bring about progress for animals and are accordingly limited in their use for them. However, the principles provide a useful basis for thinking about developing a separate chapter on the treatment of animals. A chapter dealing exclusively with animal issues might encourage multinational enterprises to develop animal welfare management systems, provide public information, and conduct animal impact assessments. It might also establish a duty of multinational enterprises to raise their level of animal protection, adequately educate and train personnel, and contribute to animal welfare policies through cooperative frameworks.

J. EXTENDED EXTRATERRITORIAL JURISDICTION IN THE EXTRATERRITORIALITY FRAMEWORK

Investment rules and export credit guidelines that promote the interests of animals abroad rely on particular projects to which they link a home state's jurisdictional authority. According to the extraterritoriality framework, they purport to regulate the lives of animals abroad (extraterritorial content regulation). If a credit or investment is issued on domestic territory, the anchor point is intraterritorial and non-animal-related (type γ_1 regulation). In contrast, *BITs and FTAs* are based on the mutual consent of states that submitted themselves to a common form of authority. They cannot be categorized in the extraterritoriality framework because no foreign law is applied. *Impact assessments* have either a territorial or an extraterritorial anchor point (investors, a funded project, national regulatory proposals, etc.), but do not per se regulate content; they only assess activities. At most, they can produce extraterritorial ancillary repercussions.

Reporting duties are linked to a specific corporation, like a parent corporation (non-animal-related intraterritorial anchor point), but they may expect entire enterprises to disclose information. The content they regulate is extraterritorial and animal-related, which makes this a type γ_1 regulation. *CSR, codes of conduct, best practices, and the OECD Guidelines for Multinationals* all link their principles to a national firm that operates abroad, or to a parent of a multinational enterprise. They have a non-animal-related intraterritorial anchor point and regulate animal-related content extraterritorially (type γ_1 regulation).

The scope of extraterritoriality varies for each tool of extended jurisdiction. Mutually agreed upon forms of jurisdiction like BITs and FTAs are not limited in jurisdictional scope because states are free to enter into agreements that limit their prescriptive jurisdiction. In contrast, investment rules and export credits are limited to a case at hand and can only demand that animal laws be observed abroad if actions and omissions are reasonably related to the invested, insured, or accredited project (by linking to investees, employees of the project, or subcontractors). Impact assessments, reporting, CSR, codes of conduct, best practices, and the OECD Guidelines are either less interventionist or constitute a voluntary submission to law, so they are not in principle limited in their jurisdictional scope.

§2 Interim Conclusion

Besides indirect extraterritorial jurisdiction (trade rules) and direct extraterritorial jurisdiction (permissive principles approach), there are other, more subtle ways for states to influence the lives of animals abroad. These include foreign policy rules, soft law, and self-regulation, which constitute forms of extended extraterritorial jurisdiction and are a subset of tools that states can use to ensure better treatment of animals at home or abroad. Drawing on achievements in human rights and environmental law, I examined if investment law, export credit rules, bilateral investment treaties, FTAs, impact assessments, reporting duties, CSR, codes of conduct, and best practices can be systematically employed to positively affect the lives of animals abroad.

Although national, international, and IO-based investment rules increasingly demand investees adhere to established social performance standards, they do not consider the treatment of animals an integral part thereof. An exception is the IFC's performance standard 6, which lays down expectations for grantees with respect to sustainability, pollution, and biological diversity. These objectives, strictly seen, compel the IFC to refuse any financial support for agricultural production systems because these systems are grossly unsustainable, a driving factor of environmental degradation, and chiefly responsible for the ongoing loss of biodiversity. Another guiding standard is the IFC's Good Practice Note, which seeks to improve the welfare of farmed animals in livestock operations. Together, the standards seem to suggest the IFC is a progressive and forward-looking IO that anticipates and responds to public concerns about animals. But its investment practices defy its goals and are evidence that the IFC considers the lives of animals only marginally important. States could fill this gap by putting in place investment rules that link funds for foreign projects to high animal welfare performance, as argued by plaintiffs in *Lujan v. Defenders*.[182] In the future, as the investment consulting initiative FAIRR argues, domestic and international investments should only go to projects that ensure animal welfare and lives are protected abroad. This would benefit animals affected by animal agricultural industries and greatly reduce ESG risks for investors.

Like investments, export credits can be linked to established animal protection standards. The OECD's Common Approaches and domestic export credit rules focus on environmental and social performance that is indirectly conducive to the welfare of animals. Efforts of NGOs to halt the Sakhalin II project in Russia, for instance, show that concerns about the loss of a species can benefit individual animals, at least certain ones. By and large, export credit rules still ignore animals and provide no opportunity to reflect progressively on the future of agricultural production.

Traditional BITs take account of animals in their preamble or in exceptions that justify violating the treaty. The just treatment of animals, however, is not considered a prerequisite to responsible bilateral investment. Even states dedicated to protecting animals consider BITs unsuited to address these concerns. If BITs obliged parties to observe progressive animal

[182] In Lujan v. Defenders of Wildlife, 504 U.S. 555 (1992) (U.S.), this argument was based on the ESA.

laws, they would be a formidable tool to prevent future violations of animal interests and could readily be tied to other social concerns like human rights or environmental protection.

In contrast to BITs, well-developed FTAs more readily take the interests of animals into account by establishing duties to exchange information, identifying animal welfare as a common objective of the parties, or creating different fora for collaboration and cooperation. The Eurogroup for Animals conducted research on the EU-Chile FTA that showed the FTA led to new, stricter laws in Chile, and to various collaboration centers and training exchanges between Chile and third countries. FTAs can thus manifestly raise the level of animal law *inter partes* and abroad. Megaregional FTAs like the TTP and the TTIP currently thwart these efforts, but they, too, would benefit from giving effect to citizens' growing concerns about the just treatment of animals.

Impact assessments help states evaluate the risks and benefits of their laws, policy proposals, and planned projects for animals at home and abroad. In some jurisdictions, like the United Kingdom and the European Union, impact assessments are mandatory in all fields of law, hence, also in animal law. Impact assessments focused on environmental performance do not have a direct positive effect on animals, but they should at least lead to negative environmental ratings for industrial animal agriculture. The European Union's EIA Directive, for example, demands all CAFOs with more than 9,000 places for sows to conduct impact assessments. To take into account the many interests of animals negatively affected by human action, states should do separate assessments of projects, so-called animal impact assessment. Doing separate animal impact assessments allows states to access readily available information, increase awareness of the impact of laws and projects on the lives of animals, prevent suffering at a pre-regulatory phase, and show proof of due diligence. For animal impact assessments to be effective, states must use established procedural and substantive rules on impact assessments as a benchmark.

Corporations operating abroad are under a duty to make information about their business activities publicly available. These financial reporting duties stretch beyond state borders and allow shareholders and the public to gain knowledge about corporate links, financial cooperation, past transactions, and planned investment, all of which help to determine a corporation's current and future stance toward animals. Given the young history of nonfinancial reporting, it is encouraging to see animals play a role in it, too. The GRI's G4 Sector Disclosures on Food Processing, for example, oblige corporations to disclose the number of animals raised and processed, the kinds of housing systems, the use of antibiotics and hormones, and incidents of noncompliance with laws and regulations. Concern for animals is still largely absent in reporting, which prompted the BBFAW to launch an initiative that evaluates corporate reporting performance. Since its inception in 2012, the BBFAW has had a demonstrable positive effect by nudging corporations to report on how their businesses impact animals abroad and to determine how they seek to reduce suffering inflicted on animals.

Extended extraterritorial jurisdiction in animal law may also be exercised through corporate, IO, or state-based CSR. In response to public pressure, more and more corporations are pledging to put an end to gestation crates, battery caging, the manufacturing of fur, foie gras, veal meat, and other cruel practices. The newly developed ISO 26000 standards help corporations prove their sincerity by certifying them for their CSR performance. To ensure that CSR is not an empty gesture, governments must oblige corporations to report on their practices, and hold them accountable for their activities, creating a "smart mix" of corporate and governmental action.[183]

Codes of conduct and best practices are also useful tools of extended extraterritorial jurisdiction. They are issued by governments, IOs, or corporations and cover diverse fields like farming, slaughter, research, and zoo management. Some governments' codes of conduct are binding (e.g., those issued by the New Zealand Farm Animal Care Council), but most are still voluntary. Codes of conduct could be an excellent means to ensure that corporations comply with animal laws when they operate abroad because these codes apply to all operations of a multinational. Their greatest weakness is that they are issued by bodies that have vested interests, which risks perpetuating the deplorable treatment of animals.

Finally, through the OECD Guidelines for Multinational Enterprises, states can positively affect the lives of animals abroad. The guidelines' chapter on general policies lays down corporate governance principles, parental monitoring and guidance, management liability, self-regulatory practices, and due diligence standards to prevent adverse impacts abroad. The guidelines offer principles on information sharing and the protection of the environment, which are binding for industries that use animals. The guidelines extend to all activities of a multinational enterprise whose home state is an OECD member or an adhering state. In response to the growing public demand for the proper treatment of animals, the OECD should consider establishing a discrete chapter setting out the obligations of multinationals toward animals.

Means of extended extraterritorial jurisdiction considerably help states strengthen and support their efforts to directly and indirectly protect animals abroad. By using various tools of foreign policy, soft law, and self-regulation, states can reach beyond traditional command-and-control structures and tap the expertise of various non-state actors, including powerful international organizations, multinational enterprises, investors, and NGOs. This, ultimately, enables states to meet the challenges of globalization with vigor and helps the global protection of animals to develop into a common, multi-stakeholder effort.

[183] European Commission, Communication from the Commission to the European Parliament, the Council, the European Economic and Social Committee and the Committee of the Regions, A Renewed EU Strategy 2011–2014 for Corporate Social Responsibility, COM(2011) 681 final, Oct. 25, 2011, at 7.

7 *Lex Ferenda*: Direct Extraterritoriality

THE DOCTRINE OF jurisdiction, which relies on established state practice and *opinio juris* of states, stretches back more than a century—at least in its modern form. When the jurisdictional principles were developed, negotiated, and refined, states never considered animals. This helps explain why the jurisdictional options I described in the previous chapters cannot fully account for all cross-border issues that arise in animal law, even if states use them to protect animals. Due to its humancentric focus, the law of jurisdiction suffers from structural shortcomings that compel us to take a more critical perspective and integrate animals into the law of jurisdiction not merely as an addendum but as the catalyst for more radical transformation.

Our *lex lata* analysis demonstrated that international law knows no direct jurisdictional link from a state to animals. Animals are still predominantly treated as objects of law, so jurisdiction is exercised over them by targeting their owner, their caretaker, or the perpetrator of acts against them. When these forms of jurisdiction are exercised, animals themselves remain invisible, which reinforces the view that they do not matter. This jurisdictional method falls short of doing justice to animals and is anachronistic in view of recent legal developments that consider animals to be sentient beings with lives of their own. If animals are entitled to robust laws that protect their interests on the substantive level, we must incorporate these claims at the jurisdictional level. In the following, I will show how the law of jurisdiction can respond to these demands by taking a critical positivist approach to developing *lex ferenda* options that protect animals directly across the border.

Critical positivism is rooted in the observation that legal scholars never operate as "value-neutral" bystanders who simply echo or explain existing legal norms. Their legal academic work is deeply wedded to their normative ideals, which comes to light when they justify, criticize, and evaluate norms. Critical positivism argues that failing to take into account the positionality of researchers risks overlooking different systems of thought and misinterpreting the law. It calls on researchers to acknowledge their positionality and, drawing on this knowledge, to present normatively desirable and reasonable proposals for reform.[1]

This chapter aims to live up to this expectation by mapping the limits of the law of jurisdiction and exploring more normatively sound solutions. I argue that we should reform the law of jurisdiction to take account of the interests of animals in interjurisdictional disputes. I use jurisdictional principles that exist *de lege lata* in international law—the personality principle, the universality principle, and a variant of the effects principle—to draw a direct jurisdictional link to animals. These novel applications cannot reasonably be said to reflect the customary practice of states or express their *opinio juris*; instead, they point to opportunities for the future development of the law of jurisdiction. Each jurisdictional principle I propose is categorized and evaluated in the extraterritoriality framework, and then assessed from a bird's-eye perspective.

§1 Passive Personality Principle

A. FUNCTIONAL ANIMAL NATIONALITY

Reading the title of this section, some readers may find it pretentious to argue that animals have nationality because they assume the right to be a national of a state is limited to humans and, at best, to corporations. Critics may consider animals to be like chairs or cups, at least from a legal perspective: animals can be owned, bought, sold, and even thrown away, but they cannot be nationals or citizens of a state. These are, as the following section argues, deeply ingrained prejudices that run counter to the argument that the doctrine of jurisdiction must respond to the growing importance of animals in our changing social and political climate.

In the following, I examine if a state's personality jurisdiction can be exercised directly over animals, and detail the requirements that must be fulfilled to ensure the endeavor's success. I first argue that we need a direct and stable basis of jurisdiction over animals through personality links. Then I explore three alternative strategies by which animals could be accorded nationality: as goods, as passport holders, or as hybrids of legal subjects and objects. Though I respond to and reject the claim that animals do not properly belong to those that have a strong link of loyalty to a state, my main argument does not go as far as to argue that animals are in fact nationals like humans. Though I personally support this line of argument, I believe

---

[1] The theory of critical positivism was developed by Antonio Cassese and Anne Peters (ANTONIO CASSESE, REALIZING UTOPIA: THE FUTURE OF INTERNATIONAL LAW (2012); Anne Peters, *Realizing Utopia as a Scholarly Endeavour*, 24 EJIL 533 (2013)). Legal scholars must make it explicit when a choice between two conflicting values stems from purely personal preferences or from more intersubjective and (weakly) objective considerations. Critical positivists must also complement legal analyses with empirical studies to better understand the conditions under which international law is formed, its effects, its theoretical dimensions, and its ethical approaches to the law: Peters, *Realizing Utopia* 550 (2013). *See also* Cassese, REALIZING UTOPIA 683 (2012)); MÓNICA GARCÍA-SALMONES ROVIRA, THE PROJECT OF POSITIVISM IN INTERNATIONAL LAW (2013); JÖRG KAMMERHOFER & JEAN D'ASPREMONT EDS., INTERNATIONAL LEGAL POSITIVISM IN A POST-MODERN WORLD (2014).

a more modest claim suffices to prompt international law to establish a direct link to animals. I make the case for functional nationality of animals and examine the extent to which international law places limits on such an approach. To add practical dimensions to this line of argument, I consider various ways by which animals could acquire functional nationality.

I. The Need for a Stable Jurisdictional Link to Animals

The extent to which states can influence how animals are treated after they have crossed borders—either of their own volition or as objects of trade—is inherently limited by circumstantial factors, like who owns an animal, who violates their interests, or the place where a crime is committed. These factors place significant limitations on governance. Because animals are considered mobile property, they can be moved anywhere by addressees of law who want to evade stricter laws. Under international law as it stands, no state has been allowed to claim "jurisdiction of origin" or the like over animals after they crossed borders, so their laws cannot reach these animals and thus cannot protect them. From the animals' perspective, such limitations are arbitrary, and leave them either accidentally or deliberately suspended in legal loopholes. This situation can only be changed by a new jurisdictional practice that directly and uncompromisingly links the animal to a state's jurisdiction.

The advantages of animal nationality as a basis for personal jurisdiction are the same as those of nationality in general: material consistency, temporal continuity, avoidance of jurisdictional conflicts, and international harmony. Material consistency means that the same law governs all issues related to the animal in question, regardless of ownership. Temporal continuity ensures that, even when an animal is moved around, the state of their nationality remains competent to regulate their lives and well-being. As this jurisdictional base is more stable than the territoriality principle, fewer types of conflict will arise, and conflicts will be less intense. And if a majority of states began to invoke animal nationality as a basis for their jurisdiction, this would lead to international harmony.[2]

To illustrate these arguments, let us consider the implications of nationality jurisdiction for Knut, a polar bear held captive by the Berlin Zoo, who enjoyed unprecedented popularity among the German population. Suppose at some point in his life, Knut is transferred from the Berlin Zoo to the Bronx Zoo in New York, as part of the European Endangered Species Programme (EEP) that aims to ensure genetic diversity and resilience of captive-held zoo animals. Let us also assume that upon his arrival, Knut learns that guards in New York use violence against animals to manage the zoo,[3] including against Knut. Alternatively, imagine Knut is sold to a Ukrainian zoo, which loses most of its government funding six months later,

---

[2] Nationality in particular contributes to this goal because it is a globally accepted base of jurisdiction: Pietro Franzina, *The Evolving Role of Nationality in Private International Law*, *in* The Changing Role of Nationality in International Law 193, 197 (2013).

[3] This is a purely fictional example but it mirrors the crude reality to which many animals in zoos are subjected. Historically, direct violence was frequently used against animals; today, most animals kept in zoos are victims of poor living conditions created by incarceration, lack of socialization, poor feeding regimes, paternalistic management, and the lack of opportunity to live a self-determined life: Helen Cowie, *Exhibiting Animals: Zoos, Menageries and Circuses*, *in* The Routledge Companion to Animal-Human History 298 (Hilda Kean & Philip Howell eds., 2018).

so all the animals there, including Knut, starve to death.[4] Let us also assume that all of these actions are legal under the laws of New York and Ukraine.

The law of jurisdiction currently gives Germany no authority to regulate how Knut must be treated abroad. Even subtle strategies to influence how Ukrainian or New York zoo guards treat Knut are without effect. Friendly relations among nations could be threatened if Germany used diplomatic means (letters, protests, etc.) to express its discomfort with Knut's treatment since Knut now is the property of another institution in another country. Citizen complaints and media coverage could influence the way New York or Ukrainian zoos deal with Knut, but the outcome of this strategy is uncertain, and hence not promising. However, if Knut were a German national, Germany could apply its animal law to the case and protect him as its national. Germany's link of nationality to Knut would overcome territorial boundaries and invalidate, or consider less important, property claims of foreign institutions. Germany is less likely to be accused of intervening in another state's affairs because it has a valid jurisdictional link to Knut. This nationality link would yield benefits for many more animals besides Knut, for example, for those used in the entertainment industry, farming, slaughter, research, or other forms of commercial exploitation. Suppose research animals used by German corporations were German nationals, then Germany could regulate the treatment of these animals, even when corporations relocated them to countries with laxer laws.

How feasible is this strategy and how likely is to succeed? The current practice of states shows that animals are already being nationalized, at least in a social, habitual sense. For example, every year, many wolves and bears cross the Italian border to northern territories including Austria, Germany, and Switzerland. Italy protects these animals (often through EU subsidies) but France, Germany, and Switzerland are more likely to think that wolves and bears pose a threat to their human or farmed animal community. In 2010, a dispute emerged when an Italian bear called "JJ1," also known as Bruno, left Italy to explore Bavarian territory where local authorities shot him. Italy strongly protested its neighbor's practices, arguing that an "Italian" bear or wolf ought not be put down after crossing a border they cannot recognize, or after preying on animals whose property status they cannot comprehend.[5] In these cases, bears and wolves are referred to as "Italian." They are seen, at least in a rudimentary sense, as nationals.[6] States nationalize animals in this habitual or social sense in other contexts, as when animals represent a state's values (e.g., pride, grandeur, or sociality). In the United States, for example, the bald eagle is a symbol of strength, courage, and freedom. Likewise, the panda bear is a national animal of China and stands for friendship and peace.

One might object that nationality ought not be the decisive criterion for protecting animals because that would create a scheme of jurisdiction that, from the animals' standpoint, is arbitrary. Animals would be divided into those with nationality who profit from

---

[4] Will Stewart, *The Animals Left to Starve to Death in Ukrainian Zoo as New Government of Debt-Ridden Country Divert Funds Elsewhere*, MailOnline, Mar. 7, 2014.

[5] *Italien schützt seine Wölfe, Schweiz und Frankreich schießen sie ab*, Der Standard, Nov. 13, 2006; *Italienischer Wolf streift durchs Puschlav*, Blick, May 16, 2013.

[6] Repeatedly, journalists expressed suspicion about the way Bruno was killed—allegedly illegally—and how it suddenly happened that he entered a museum as a stuffed artifact: Jörn Ehlers, *Bruno der "Problembär": Chronik eines angekündigten Todes*, World Wide Fund for Nature (WWF 2009).

direct extraterritoriality, and those who do not have a direct link to a state.[7] Or, some animals might have a nationality that secures them better protection abroad, while others are poorly protected as nationals of other states. For example, the Bronx Zoo guards might be able to use force against Norwegian polar bears but not against German polar bears, or Bavarian authorities could shoot French wolves but not Italian wolves. Because of these arbitrary effects, the better approach would be to rely on the universal acceptance of animal welfare and the furtherance thereof, so that all animals can and should be equally protected. Universal, global approaches to animal protection are in principle preferable to nationalistic approaches—in particular from the animals' perspective—but they are far from established in state practice. Until there is a robust, universal consensus on the treatment of animals, the personality principle must be used to respect and protect the lives of animals *ad interim*.

Some might object that animals do not have a right to nationality[8] and that the personality principle cannot be used to protect them. From an ethical standpoint, these claims must be rejected because animals have a right to nationality,[9] but the objection is irrelevant to the matter at hand. As Weis explained, "[i]t is not the freedom of the individual whose nationality is at issue but the rights of the State of which he is a national, that are the primary considerations of international law."[10]

Skeptics might object that even if the international community accepted this principle, it could not be implemented. They might argue that animals are mere property and as such lack what is needed to be conferred nationality, namely, the capacity to hold rights. Contemporary research suggests otherwise; there are strong ethical and legal arguments that animals qualify as rights holders and that they ought not be considered property.[11] But before making this claim, I first want to examine if their current, though inadequate, status as property prevents us from applying the personality principle to them.

[7] Similar effects were observed before the Civil War in the United States. When slavery was illegal in the north and legal in the south, slaves who escaped from the south sued for their freedom in northern territories. In the landmark 1857 *Dred Scott v. Sandford* case, the Supreme Court ruled that it was not in a position to grant escaped slaves freedom and thereby regulate slavery in southern territories. The ruling was vehemently criticized, especially by abolitionists, and marked a watershed moment in the civil rights movement: Dred Scott v. Sandford, 60 U.S. 393 (1857) (U.S.).

[8] A right to nationality of natural persons is enshrined in UDHR, art. 15 para. 1 and the Inter-American Convention on Human Rights, Nov. 22, 1969, 1144 U.N.T.S. 123, art. 20 [IACHR]. *See also* IACtHR, *Naturalisation Costa Rica* (1984) ¶ 32: "It is generally accepted today that nationality is an inherent right of all human beings."

[9] *See further* DONALDSON & KYMLICKA (2011).

[10] WEIS, NATIONALITY AND STATELESSNESS IN INTERNATIONAL LAW 112 (1979).

[11] Ethical arguments against the property status of animals are that property is not needed for our relations with animals, makes animals permanently accessible to human interests and intervention, has a legacy of subjugating the possessed, and positions animals as a caste group vis-à-vis humans: Jason Wyckoff, *Toward Justice for Animals*, 45(4) J. SOC. PHIL. 539 (2014). The legal argument is that property status is a barrier for animals to make use of their rights by creating confusion, inconsistency, inadequate enforcement, and obstacles for them to obtain standing to sue: Lisa Marie Morrish, *The Elephant in the Room: Detrimental Effects of Animals' Property Status on Standing in Animal Protection Cases*, 53(4) SANTA CLARA L. REV. 1127, 1151–2 (2014). For an in-depth discussion of both arguments, *see* FRANCIONE (2007).

A property right denotes "a relation not between an owner and a thing, but between the owner and other individuals in reference to things."[12] Property regulates social relationships between, mostly, humans and lets proprietors enjoy certain privileges to the exclusion of others.[13] A stable personality link from a state to animals would limit the ability of owners to fully enjoy their rights over animals—including their right to evade their local laws by bringing animals to another state. Such a view considers property rights to be absolute and unlimited, a conception that has been defended time and again. I do not dispute that nationality conferral onto animals and the application of the personality principle do not limit property rights; clearly, they do. What is more important is that such limitations are completely justifiable from a legal perspective. Today, most states accept that property rights can be limited if doing so is necessary to protect, *inter alia*, public health, safety, peace, and public morals.[14] Over the last decades, animal laws incrementally restricted property rights of people over animals to meet society's demand that animals be protected. Early animal laws narrowly determined how people must treat animal property, and how it can be acquired and abandoned. Today, it is generally accepted that protecting animals represents a strong societal interest and forms part of the public morals, which justifies limiting property rights over animals by conferring nationality on them. Ideally, these property rights would be wholly dismantled so that animals cease to be property. However, for the purposes of our inquiry, conferring nationality on animals and using the personality principle to protect them abroad does not require a change in the civil status of animals from property to rights holders. Corporations and ships, for example, are both nationals and owned property.

In sum, a stable jurisdictional link from animals to their home states is necessary to create material consistency and temporal continuity, avoid jurisdictional conflicts, and foster international harmony. The benefits of direct jurisdictional links to animals accrue for regulators (through international harmony), humans (through predictability), and animals (by preventing a race to the bottom). A stable personality link to animals would be easy to reconcile with the tendency of states to nationalize animals, and does not per se demand the abrogation of animals' property status or require major restructuring of a state's legal order.

II. Nationality of Animals as Goods

Animals could be conferred nationality on the basis of their current legal status as objects or goods. In the past, some states have tried to nationalize goods, yet not sentient ones. In 1985, the United States declared that it has nationality jurisdiction over goods in its export (and re-export) controls policy, specifically over goods stemming from its territory or produced by domestic technology.[15] This was one of many of the United States' attempts to expand its regulatory influence overnight and prohibit trade with the Soviet Union. Neighboring states

---

[12] Morris R. Cohen, *Property and Sovereignty*, 13 CORNELL L.Q. 8, 12 (1927).

[13] MARC DANIELS, GRUNDLAGEN UND BEGRIFF DES SACHENRECHTS 19 (2015). Cohen aptly stated that "dominion over things is also *imperium* over our fellow human beings." (Cohen 12 (1927)). Cohen did not have animals in mind when making this statement, but his message applies to the present case.

[14] James F. Childress, *Moral Considerations: Bases and Limits of Public Health Interventions*, *in* ESSENTIALS OF PUBLIC HEALTH ETHICS 21, 27 (Ruth Gaare Bernheim et al. eds., 2015); Cohen 22 (1927).

[15] Export Administration Amendments Act of 1985, U.S. Public Law 99-64 (July 12, 1985) (U.S.).

vehemently opposed the US proposal. In its note to the United States, the United Kingdom wrote that "[g]oods have no national identity which overrides changes of ownership of these goods."[16] The European Commission similarly stated that "[g]oods and technology do not have any nationality and there are no known rules under international law for using goods or technology situated abroad as a basis for establishing jurisdiction over the persons controlling them."[17] As Meng explains, the standard view about goods crossing borders is that they lose any connection to the territory where they had been located. Like the loss of nationality, which disables a former home state from exercising jurisdiction over an ex-citizen, loss of control over these goods through export means the former home state can no longer exercise jurisdiction over that good. Any aftereffect that resembles nationality is therefore considered inadmissible.[18]

Another proposal for establishing nationality for goods was developed in international securities law. Choi and Guzman proposed the concept of "portable reciprocity," which gives the issuer of securities the power to determine the initial regulatory system that applies to securities.[19] The applicable law then travels with the securities. Portable reciprocity, or the idea of portability, could be used in other regulatory areas. In animal law, portable jurisdiction could be established for single animals or groups of animals, so that the applicable law would remain the same. A state's laws would then travel with the animal wherever they go, producing the same effect as animal nationality. But portable reciprocity confers full control over the animal's future to the principal issuer, which creates a problem if they choose a regulatory regime with low standards of protection. At worst, this could result in a portable competition in laxity. Portable reciprocity may also create information overload, lead to unduly effortful coordination, and raise fraud and enforcement issues.[20] Due to these risks, no state has yet adopted or recognized this concept. Establishing animal nationality by recognizing animals as "national goods" is therefore currently not a viable approach to claim direct jurisdiction over them.

III. Nationality of Animals as Passport Holders

Nationality of animals could also be established on the basis of *de facto* nationality. Though no state today explicitly recognizes animals as nationals, there is an argument to be made that pet passports are evidence of *de facto* animal nationality. The prototypes of pet passports were vaccination cards that served two functions: facilitating cross-border travel of animals (note the use of the term "trade" for movement of farmed animals, and the use of the term "travel"

---

[16] Note from the British Government addressed to the U.S., Oct. 18, 1982, UKMIL (1982), 53 BY 337, 453 (U.K.).

[17] Comments of the European Community on the Amendments of 22 June 1982 to the U.S. Export Regulations (Aug. 12, 1982).

[18] Meng 522 (1994). *See also* Mark B. Feldman, *The Restructuring of National Security Controls under the 1985 Amendments to the Export Administration Act: Multilateral Diplomacy and the Extraterritorial Application of United States Law*, 21 Stan. J. Int'l L. 235, 242, 268 (1985); Mann 25 (1984).

[19] Stephen J. Choi & Andrew T. Guzman, *Portable Reciprocity: Rethinking the International Reach of Securities Regulation*, 71 S. Cal. L. Rev. 903, 921 ff. (1997).

[20] Johnston & Powles, *The Kings of the World and Their Dukes' Dilemma*, *in* Globalisation and Jurisdiction 44 (2004).

for movement of companion animals), and preventing and reducing animal health risks.[21] As people began to travel with their companion animals more frequently, more and more states began to issue pet passports, which serve a wider range of functions than vaccination cards.

Pet passports are documents individualized to an animal, which makes them a personal document. Countries typically issue passports only to animals that were marked with an implanted transponder or a tattoo, and vaccinated against rabies and other common diseases.[22] The model pet passport of the European Union requires a picture of the animal, their name, species, breed, sex, date of birth, color, and any other notable features or characteristics.[23] The format, front cover, and inside pages are matched to ordinary passport sizing and color.[24] The most remarkable feature of pet passports is that they exist independently of the owner of an animal. Wherever the animal moves (or is moved), and whoever their owner, the pet passport travels with the animal. As the European Commission states: "The EU pet passport has been designed to last for the lifetime of the animal bearing it."[25] From the perspective of the state, issuing a pet passport is a quasi-governmental act. The passport is designed and produced by governmental authorities, who then transfer it to veterinarians, who then issue the passport to the animal in question. Apart from the European Union, Switzerland issues pet passports that operate like human passports: they bear the Swiss emblem on a red ground and are issued by the Swiss Confederation.[26]

Companion animals are not the only animals with passports. Some countries, including the United Kingdom, the United States, and the European Union, demand that horses be identified and documented with horse passports. In the United States, the US Equestrian Federation (USEF) issues passports to horses that compete in International Federation for Equestrian Sports events.[27] In the United Kingdom, all equines, including horses, ponies, donkeys, and related animals (like zebras), must possess a passport under the Horse Passports Regulations 2009.[28]

---

[21] United States Department of Agriculture (USDA), Pet Passports—European Union, *available at* https://www.aphis.usda.gov/aphis/pet-travel/by-country/eu/pet_travel-european_union_pet_passports (last visited Jan. 10, 2019).

[22] *E.g.*, Regulation 576/2013 of the European Parliament and of the Council on the Non-commercial Movement of Pet Animals and Repealing Regulation (EC) No. 998/2003, 2013 O.J. (L 178) 1, 2.

[23] *Id.*; Commission Implementing Regulation 577/2013 on the Model Identification Documents for the Non-commercial Movement of Dogs, Cats and Ferrets, the Establishment of Lists of Territories and Third Countries and the Format, Layout and Language Requirements of the Declarations Attesting Compliance with Certain Conditions Provided for in Regulation (EU) No. 576/2013 of the European Parliament and of the Council, 2013 O.J. (L 178) 109, 120.

[24] The dimensions of the pet passport are 100 mm by 152 mm, the color is blue (Pantone Reflex Blue) and yellow stars (Pantone Yellow) in the upper quarter; the passport must bear the words "European Union," the name of the member state, and the ISO number. For more information on these requirements, *see* Regulation 577/2013, 2013 O.J. (L 178) 109.

[25] European Commission, Movement of Pets (Dogs, Cats and Ferrets), Questions & Answers, *available at* http://ec.europa.eu/food/animal/liveanimals/pets/qanda_en.htm (last visited Jan. 10, 2019).

[26] Schweizerische Eidgenossenschaft, Heimtierpass, *available at* http://www.blv.admin.ch/dienstleistungen/05972/index.html?lang=de (last visited Jan. 10, 2019).

[27] United States Equestrian Federation [USEF], Horse Passports 101 (2012), *available at* https://www.usef.org/documents/international/Passports101_2.pdf (last visited Jan. 10, 2019).

[28] The Horse Passports Regulations 2009, No. 1611 (U.K.).

Does the fact that animal and human passports bear remarkable resemblance indicate that animals are passport holders? A passport is defined as "a document of identification required by law to be carried by persons residing or traveling within a country," whose function is to "secure [. . .] admission, acceptance, or attainment."[29] Animal passports travel with animals wherever they move and allow officials to identify animals independent of their owner. Because they include comprehensive information on animal health, which often is the only entry requirement for traveling animals, these documents operate as an entry ticket at customs controls for admission to a state's territory. Pet passports hence serve a clear function (identification) and confer a status on animals (admission). Animals, therefore, are passport holders.

If animals are holders of passports that are issued by states, are they *de facto* nationals of these states? This question can only be answered in the affirmative if, according to existing passportization policies, a passport is sufficient evidence of nationality. The common law rule of "best evidence" provides that the terms of a document have to be proved by the document itself. More precisely, "[s]ince nationality is determined by the law of the country whose nationality is claimed, evidence—usually of a documentary nature—that the person was considered as a national by an authority qualified under municipal law to determine or to certify nationality will, as a rule, be the best evidence."[30] Based on the best evidence rule, if a passport clearly identifies an animal as a national of the issuing states, the international community is bound to accept animal nationality *qua* evidence of the passport.[31] To my knowledge, no pet passport has yet unequivocally identified animals as nationals, but it is possible some states might choose to do so in the future. As previously noted, more and more states are responding to the growing societal call to treat animals more justly, by determining that animals are not objects, but sentient beings who have their own lives to live. The emancipation of animals as subjects of civil law could operate be a precursor to their emancipation as nationals of public law.

Since pet passports and animal nationality are primarily used for cross-border travels, they can lead to conflicts of jurisdiction between states. The international dimension of these disputes will send these cases to international courts and tribunals that are not bound by domestic rules of evidence. In *Hussein Nuaman Soufraki v. United Arab Emirates*, the ICSID ad hoc Committee asserted that "international tribunals are empowered to determine whether a party has the alleged nationality in order to ascertain their own jurisdiction, and are not bound by national certificates of nationality or passports or other documentation in making

---

[29] Merriam-Webster, "Passport," *available at* http://www.merriam-webster.com/dictionary/passport (last visited Jan. 10, 2019).

[30] Weis, Nationality and Statelessness in International Law 215 (1979).

[31] *Id.* at 224. This presumption may be rebutted, especially where there is doubt as to whether the pet passport intended to confer nationality on an animal. As Sloane clarifies: "[W]ere international tribunals required to treat passports, certificates, government affidavits, and like documents as more than *prima facie* evidence of nationality, this would open the door for a state to confer nationality in order to achieve a jurisdictional advantage." (Robert D. Sloane, *Breaking the Genuine Link: The Contemporary International Legal Regulation of Nationality*, 50 Harv. Int'l L.J. 1, 23 (2009)).

that determination and ascertainment."[32] Under international law, the question of whether an animal has become a national of a state will regularly be one of fact rather than one of (domestic) law.[33] So while passports issued to animals can operate as *prima facie* evidence, as credible proof of nationality, they do not convey or conclusively prove nationality (at least on the international level), as determined in the *Flegenheimer* case.[34] Therefore, under international law, using a pet passport does not allow us to draw implications about the acceptance or renunciation of animal nationality. As Peters writes, "conferral of nationality and the issuing of a passport are two distinct legal acts."[35] So, if passports do not prove that animals are nationals, are there other strategies for establishing animal nationality?

IV. Nationality of Animals as Legal Hybrids

Most Western societies are structured around the view that humans have a moral and legal status that is distinct from that of animals. In ethics, animals are typically distinguished from humans by moral agency. The standard claim is that humans are moral agents, whereas animals are (at most) moral patients.[36] In law, it is standard practice to distinguish between subjects of law (who influence their environment) and objects of law (which are influenced by their environment).[37] Ever since the Romans first introduced the subject/object divide,

---

[32] Hussein Nuaman Soufraki v. United Arab Emirates, ICSID Case No. ARB/02/7, Decision of the ad hoc Committee, June 5, 2007, para. 64. *See also* SOABI v. Senegal, ICSID Case No. ARB/82/1, Award, Feb. 25, 1988.

[33] Certain German Interests in Polish Upper Silesia (Ger. v. Pol.), Judgment, 1926 P.C.I.J. (ser. A) No. 7 at 19 (May 25).

[34] The question of whether a passport evidences nationality was addressed in the *Flegenheimer* case. According to Italian authorities, Flegenheimer was not evidently a national of the United States because he had used his German passport while traveling. The Commission rejected the argument, "[. . .] because nationality is a legal notion which must be based on a state law in order to exist and be productive of effects in international law; a mere appearance cannot replace provisions of positive law governing the conditions under which a nationality is granted or lost, because international law admits that every State has a right, subject to treaty stipulations concluded with other States, to sovereignly decide who are its nationals." (Flegenheimer Case (U.S. v. Italy), 182 R.I.A.A. 327, 379–80 (United States–Italian Conciliation Commission 1958)). *See also* R v. Burke, Casey and Mullady, (1868) 11 Cox C.C. 138 (U.K.): "The mere production of a passport, found on a prisoner, which is proved to be granted by the authorities of a foreign State to natural-born subjects only, is not evidence of being an alien."

[35] Anne Peters, *Extraterritorial Naturalizations: Between the Human Right to Nationality, State Sovereignty and Fair Principles of Jurisdiction*, 53 GYIL 623, 634 (2010).

[36] The ethical debate is concerned with moral subjects (or agents) and moral objects (or patients). Moral agents are beings possessing capacities by virtue of which they can act morally or immorally, and can have duties and responsibilities; moral patients are all who can be treated rightly or wrongly and toward whom moral agents can have duties and responsibilities: PAUL W. TAYLOR, RESPECT FOR NATURE: A THEORY OF ENVIRONMENTAL ETHICS 14–7 (1986). *See also* Paul Shapiro, *Moral Agency in Other Animals*, 27 THEO. MED. & BIOETHICS 357, 357 (2006): "[H]uman beings do not have a monopoly on moral agency, which admits of varying degrees and does not require mastery of moral principles. The view that all and only humans possess moral agency indicates our underestimation of the mental lives of other animals. Since many other animals are moral agents (to varying degrees), they are also subject to (limited) moral obligations [. . .]." *See further* MARK ROWLANDS, CAN ANIMALS BE MORAL? (2012).

[37] RASPÉ 64 ff. (2013).

animals have been regarded as mere legal objects, often with an exaggerated naturalness, rather than by virtue of scientific principles or reasonably justifiable social norms. Most people now take offense at law for categorizing animals as objects because animals are manifestly not the same as a piece of wood, a cup of coffee, or a pair of sneakers. Unlike actual objects, animals are sentient beings who are conscious of themselves as individuals and as social actors, and who greatly influence their environment.

The growing demand that the law must respond to the shifting societal views about animals has given rise to a whole series of changes in the law that explicitly reject the classic Roman law divide. Article 641*a* of the Swiss Civil code boldly states that "[a]nimals are not objects."[38] Identical content is found in section 90a of the German Civil Code and section 285a of the Austrian Civil Code.[39] In 2012, the Czech Civil Code abandoned the definition of animals as "things," and replaced it with "living creature with senses."[40] On February 16, 2015, France passed article 515-14 in the French Civil Code, which provides that animals are living beings who are able to suffer.[41] In *Martinez v. Robledo*, the California Court of Appeals for the first time held that "animals are special, sentient beings, because unlike other forms of property, animals feel pain, suffer and die."[42] New Zealand recognized animals as sentient beings by its Animal Welfare Amendment Act (No. 2) in 2015.[43] The same year, Minister Paradis introduced a bill to modify the Civil Code of Québec to remove animals from the movable property category. Section 898.1 of the Civil Code of Québec, adopted by the Parliament by unanimous vote, determines that "[a]nimals are not things. They are sentient beings and have biological needs."[44]

In January 2016, Colombian President Santos signed a law introducing article 655 to Colombia's Civil Code, which recognizes animals as sentient beings, and penalizes crimes against animals with fines up to 11,000 USD and 36 months of imprisonment.[45] In December 2016, the Portuguese Party for Animals (*Partido Animalista Portugués*) successfully lobbied

---

38 The exact German wording is "Tiere sind keine Sachen" (Civil Code (Switz.), art. 641*a* para. 1, changes introduced by No I of the Federal Act of 4 Oct. 2002 (Article of Basic Principles: Animals) (Switz.), in force since Apr. 1, 2003).

39 Bürgerliches Gesetzbuch [BGB] [Civil Code], Jan. 2, 2002, BGBl. I at 42, 2909; 2003 at 738 (Ger.), § 90a [Civil Code (Ger.)], changes introduced by Gesetz zur Verbesserung der Rechtsstellung des Tieres im bürgerlichen Recht, Aug. 20, 1990, BGBl. I, 1762 (Ger.); Allgemeines Bürgerliches Gesetzbuch [ABGB] [Civil Code], BGBl. I No. 43/2016 (Austria), § 285a [Civil Code (Austria)], changes introduced by BGBl. 1988/179 (Austria).

40 Občanský Zákoník [C. Civ.] [Civil Code], No. 89/2012 Coll., Feb. 3, 2012, § 494 (Czech.), amendment introduced by the new civil code in 2012 (in force 2014).

41 Code civil [C. Civ.] [Civil Code], Dec. 19, 2015, art. 515–14 (Fr.), changes introduced by Loi n°2015-77, Feb. 16, 2015 (Fr.): "Les animaux sont des êtres vivants doués de sensibilité."

42 Martinez v. Robledo, 210 Cal. App. 4th 384 (2012) (U.S.). *See also* Kimes v. Grossnerc, 195 Cal. App. 4th 1556 (2011) (U.S.).

43 Animal Welfare Act (N.Z.), preamble, changes introduced by *Animal Welfare Amendment Act* (No. 2) 2015, Public Act No. 49, May 9, 2015, § 3A(i) (N.Z.).

44 Civil Code of Québec, S.Q. 1991, c. 64, art. 898.1 (QC, Can.), amendment introduced by Bill No. 54, An Act to Improve the Legal Situation of Animals, National Assembly, 1st Sess., 41st Legisl., introduced by Mr. Pierre Paradis, Minister of Agriculture, Fisheries and Food, Québec O.P. 2015 (Can.).

45 Ley 1774/2016, por medio de la cual se modifican el Código Civil, la Ley 84 de 1989, el Código Penal, el Código de Procedimiento Penal y se dictan otras disposiciones, enero 6, 2016, Diario Oficial [D.O.] (Colom.).

to modify the Civil Code, which lays down that animals are not legal objects and recognizes them as sentient beings.[46] In February 2017, the Parliament of the City of Mexico unanimously voted to include article 13-B in their new constitution, which recognizes animals as sentient beings whose welfare must be protected. Animals are accorded moral consideration and their care is considered a common responsibility of citizens and local authorities.[47] Less than two weeks later, on February 14, 2017, the Spanish Congress unanimously voted to reform the Spanish Civil Code so as to recognize animals as "sentient beings."[48] And on November 23, 2018, the Brussels Parliament unanimously adopted a draft ordinance that recognizes animals as living beings with dignity. As a consequence, the Federal Senate is now discussing an amendment of the constitution according to which "the Federal State and federated bodies shall ensure the well-being of animals as sentient beings."[49]

Without a doubt, these developments represent fundamental achievements that will boost future advocacy for animals, and they promise to shift societal attitudes about animals for many years to come. A final assessment of these developments seems premature since these laws are relatively new and their effects are ongoing. However, it is already clear today that designating animals as "sentient beings" has not promoted them to the category of subjects. Many of these laws are unnecessarily couched in language that compromises its potential for creating change by stating that, for reasons of convenience, animals will be treated *as if they were property*.[50] A charitable interpretation would grant that the subject/object divide has played a crucial role in defining law as we know it today, so it is no surprise that states have a hard time imagining an alternative structure. But it is not the sole function of law to anchor the status quo. As in other areas of law, legal rules on human-animal relationships must find a balance between echoing current sentiments about animals and promoting change that is socially desirable. To do one without the other means we risk letting law degenerate into a tool to sugarcoat injustices.[51]

The subject/object divide is intimately tied to the legal person/object divide that lies at the heart of most legal systems, and which was historically transported from Roman law. Although Roman law conferred the status of legal persons only to some human beings (notably to Roman citizens), today, the UDHR recognizes all humans as persons before the law.[52] And because legal personhood is integral to an agent's ability to fully

---

[46] Código Civil [Civil Code], Nov. 25, 1967, No. 47344/66, DIARIO DO GOVERNO Ser. 1, p. 1883, art. 333 and 333bis (Port.). *See further Los Animales ya no Son Cosas en Portugal*, PARTIDO ANIMALISTA PACMA, Dec. 22, 2016.

[47] CONSTITUCIÓN POLÍTICA DE LA CIUDAD DE MÉXICO [Constitution of the City of Mexico], Gaceta Oficial de la Ciudad de México, Feb. 5, 2017 (Mex.).

[48] The bill was proposed by Avelino de Barrionuevo, of the ruling Popular Party (PP): Iñigo Domínguez, *Animals to Stop Being "Objects" under Spanish Law*, EL PAÍS, Dec. 14, 2017.

[49] Christopher Vincent, *Brussels Parliament Adopts Crucial Animal Rights Bill*, THE BRUSSELS TIMES, Nov. 23, 2018.

[50] *See, e.g.*, CIVIL CODE (Switz.), art. 641*a* para. 2: "Where no special provisions exist for animals, they are subject to the provisions governing objects."

[51] For a discussion of these legal changes, *see* Will Kymlicka, *Social Membership: Animal Law beyond the Property/Personhood Impasse*, 40(1) DALHOUSIE L.J. 123 (2017).

[52] Art. 6 UDHR: "Everyone has the right to recognition everywhere as a person before the law."

function in law, legal personhood was expanded to corporations, ships, and religious idols.[53]

But despite the gradual expansion of legal personhood, animals are not considered legal persons. This gap has prompted various lawyers and legal theorists to argue that since hypothetical legal constructs are recognized as persons before the law, sentient and conscious beings should be recognized as such *a fortiori*. In 2014, Argentina's Association of Professional Lawyers for Animal Rights (AFADA) sought to free orangutan Sandra from her 20-years imprisonment in the zoo of Buenos Aires by using the writ of *habeas corpus*. Sandra was granted the writ by the local criminal court, which acknowledged that she is a nonhuman person who deserves the basic rights to life, liberty, and freedom from torture.[54] The *habeas corpus* writ was also used to move Cecilia, a female chimpanzee held captive at the Mendoza Zoo in Argentina, to a sanctuary. In his ruling of November 3, 2016, Judge Maurico recognized that Cecilia is a "nonhuman person [. . .] with inherent rights."[55] Using the same legal strategy, the Nonhuman Rights Project (NhRP) brings cases across US courts to establish legal personhood for great apes, whales, elephants, and grey parrots.[56]

---

[53] International Shoe Co. v. Washington, 326 U.S. 310, 316 (1945) (U.S.): "[T]he corporate personality is a fiction, although a fiction intended to be acted upon as though it were a fact." Tauza v. Susquehanna Coal Co., 115 N.E. 915, 917 (N.Y. 1917) (U.S.): "If the persons named are true agents, and if their positions are such as to lead to a just presumption that notice to them will be notice to the principal, the corporation must submit. The corporation is here; it is here in the person of an agent of its own selection; and service upon him is service upon his principal." Vidya Varuthi Thirtha v. Balusami Ayyar, July 5, 1921, 24 BOMLR 629 (1922) (India): "Under the Hindu law the image of a deity of the Hindu pantheon is, as has been aptly called, a 'juristic entity,' vested with the capacity of receiving gifts and holding property." In a more recent case, the Indian Supreme Court determined that "[a]n idol becomes a juristic person only when it is consecrated and installed at a public place for public at large." (Shriomani Gurudwara Prabandhak Committee, Amritsar v. Shri Somnath Dass et al., AIR 2000 SC 1421 (India)).

[54] Camara Federal de Casacion Penal, Causa No. CCC 68831/2014/CFCI, Orangutana Sandra s/ recurso de casacion s/ habeas corpus, Dec. 18, 2014, *available at* http://www.nonhumanrightsproject.org/wp-content/uploads/2014/12/Argentina-Habeas-Corpus-Decision.pdf (last visited Jan. 10, 2019). *See also* Patrick Barkham, *Sandra the "Nonhuman Person" Is Sadly Not the Face of a Welfare Revolution*, The Guardian, Dec. 22, 2014. The Nonhuman Rights Project disputes that the news of Sandra's recognized status as a legal person is true, arguing that the documents of the Court are ambiguous: Steven M. Wise, Update on the Sandra Orangutan Case in Argentina, Nonhuman Rights Project (Mar. 6, 2015), *available at* http://www.nonhumanrightsproject.org/2015/03/06/update-on-the-sandra-orangutan-case-in-argentina/ (last visited Jan. 10, 2019).

[55] Tercer Juzgado de Garantías, Juidicial Power Mendoza, File No. P.72.254/15, "Presented by A.F.A.D.A. about the Chimpanzee 'Cecilia'—Non Human Individual," Nov. 3, 2016, *available at* http://www.nonhumanrightsproject.org/2016/12/05/nonhuman-rights-project-praises-argentine-courts-recognition-of-captive-chimpanzees-legal-personhood-and-rights/ (last visited Jan. 10, 2019).

[56] The NhRP has had notable successes in court. *See e.g.*, Matter of Nonhuman Rights Project, Inc. v Stanley, 2015 NY Slip Op 25257 [49 Misc 3d 746] (2015) (U.S.), where Judge Jaffe held: "Efforts to extend legal rights to chimpanzees are [. . .] understandable; some day they may even succeed. Courts, however, are slow to embrace change, and occasionally seem reluctant to engage in broader, more inclusive interpretations of the law [. . .]. As Justice Kennedy observed in Lawrence v Texas, 'times can blind us to certain truths and later generations can see that laws once thought necessary and proper in fact serve only to oppress.' For now, however, given the precedent to which I am bound, it is hereby ordered that the petition for a writ of habeas corpus is denied." For an overview of the NhRP's substantive arguments, *see* Steven M. Wise, *Legal Personhood and the Nonhuman Rights Project*, 17 Animal L. 1 (2010). *See also* Rebekah Lam & Daniel Cung, *Animal*

These strategies are still developing and make apparent the long road ahead, but they point clearly to the fact that animals are gaining visibility in the law and that once-rigid subject/object or legal person/object dichotomies are gradually dissolving and becoming increasingly untenable. Looking into the future, it is not unreasonable to argue that animal nationality has a realistic chance of emerging from these efforts and eventually being accepted by the international community.

V. Functional Nationality

When we think of nationality, we typically see it as a strong link of allegiance and loyalty between a person and a state, established by birth or naturalization. Skeptics will argue animals cannot build up a link of loyalty to a state, but this ignores the realities underlying nationality conferral. Instead of conferring nationality on the basis of loyalty, most states use their power to assert or deny personal jurisdiction over individuals in a rather instrumental manner, namely, to advance their political interests. For example, mid-2015, Australia's Prime Minister Abbott made public his plans to remove nationality from people who hold dual nationality, from people who are Australia-born but descend from immigrants, and from immigrants who fight for the Islamic state.[57] Section 33AA of the Australian Citizenship Act now assumes that persons of dual nationality who engage in terrorist activities renounced their Australian citizenship immediately "upon [. . .] engaging in the conduct."[58] Revoking nationality from terrorists, immigrants, and other people makes it easier for the Australian government to deny them access to its territory and for other states to exercise their jurisdiction over them. That states make instrumental use of nationality also shows the lengths to which they will go to attract professional sportspeople, stars, or wealthy businesspeople. Scholars around the world have observed the growing tendency of states to increase the influx of qualified people by lowering the threshold of nationality conferral or granting other privileges.[59] States also like to attract unskilled migrant workers but do not offer them membership through nationality.[60]

In light of these developments, scholars argue states have a *functional approach to nationality*, which is based on the assumption that nationality can be recognized or denied for different ends. *Nottebohm* was one of the first decisions on the international level to recognize

---

Law: Rethinking Boundaries of Legal Personhood, 7 LSJ 90 (2015). *Contra* rights for animals: Richard L. Cupp, *Human Responsibility, Not Legal Personhood, For Animals*, 16 J. Fed. Soc. 34 (2015).

[57] Phil Mercer, *Unease Grows over New Australian Dual Citizenship Rules*, BBC News, June 1, 2015.

[58] *Australian Citizenship Act 2007*, Act No. 20 (Austl.), amendment introduced by the Australian Citizenship Amendment (Allegiance to Australia) Bill 2015, introduced June 24, 2015. The law applies to all persons aged 14 and older, and it applies retrospectively.

[59] Pohlmann studied the "brain-drain/brain-gain" pattern of migration in OECD-countries: Markus Pohlmann, *The Migration of Elites in a Borderless World: Citizenship as an Incentive for Professionals and Managers?*, *in* Citizenship and Migration in the Era of Globalization: The Flow of Migrants and the Perception of Citizenship in Asia and Europe 59 (Markus Pohlmann et al. eds., 2013).

[60] Lee compared the citizenship policies of Korea and Germany and found that neither country conferred citizenship on unskilled workers: Jong-Hee Lee, *A Comparative Analysis of Foreign Workers and Citizenship in Korea and Germany*, *in* Citizenship and Migration in the Era of Globalization 71, 86 (2013).

that nationality can be atomized by function—in this case, to accord diplomatic protection.[61] Nationality, in short, is not an end in itself, but a means to an end.

Because nationality presents itself as a tool to be used functionally, there is an argument to be made that we can confer nationality on animals, for no other reason than to establish a state's personal jurisdiction over them. This limited form of nationality strongly resembles corporate nationality. In *Barcelona Traction*, the ICJ shed light on how it compares to nationality as traditionally understood: "In allocating corporate entities to States [. . .], international law is based, but only to a limited extent, on an analogy with the rules governing the nationality of individuals."[62] Corporate nationality is only an analogy to ordinary nationality because it is not established by a governmental act of nationalization. States implicitly determine corporate nationality to establish personal jurisdiction, so it is more accurately termed *Staatszugehörigkeit, allégeance politique*, or simply "personal affiliation" to a state.[63] Like corporations, ships fly a state's national flag that links them to their home state. In this context, "[t]he term 'nationality' when used in connection with ships, is merely a shorthand for the jurisdictional connection between a ship and a State."[64] So even without conferring nationality in the fullest sense, a state could endow animals with nationality for the sole purpose of affiliating them to its jurisdiction, giving rise to what we could call *functional animal nationality*.

The functional approach of nationality does not (and is not meant to) address other questions of nationality, like diplomatic protection, the right to residence, or loyalty duties. In cases of corporate nationality or flag state jurisdiction, we do not typically ask if corporations or ships have what it takes to be a person, morally or legally, or if they can claim additional rights once they are recognized as nationals. For the sake of the present argument, I here take a similarly limited approach to functional nationality of animals.

VI. International Legal Limits

Under the current state of international law, domestic law is competent to determine to whom it grants nationality, as the PCIJ determined in *Nationality Decrees*.[65] The holding was confirmed in *Acquisition of Polish Nationality*, in *Ahmadou Sadio Diallo*, and later enshrined in the Convention on Certain Questions Relating to the Conflict of Nationality.[66] Because

---

[61] Nottebohm, 1955 I.C.J. 16–7: "[W]hat is involved is not recognition for all purposes but merely for the purposes of the admissibility of the Application [. . .]." *See also* BROWNLIE 406 (2008); HARO F. VAN PANHUYS, THE ROLE OF NATIONALITY IN INTERNATIONAL LAW: AN OUTLINE 165 (1959); Sloane 16 (2009).

[62] Barcelona Traction, 1970 I.C.J. 42, ¶ 70.

[63] Dörr, *Nationality*, *in* MPEPIL 24 (2006); Kley-Struller 163, 174, para. 23 (1991); MENG 467 (1994). The CoE stated: "One of the most surprising findings was that none of the member states has taken any statutory measures regarding the applicability of the nationality principle to legal persons, not even those states which recognise the criminal liability of corporate bodies." (CoE, *Extraterritorial Criminal Jurisdiction* 449 (1992)).

[64] The Juno Trader (Saint Vincent and the Grenadines v. Guinea-Bissau), Case No. 13, Judgment, 2004 ITLOS Rep. 17, 57, 60–61, ¶ 9 (Dec. 18) (Joint Separate Opinion of Judges Mensah and Wolfrum).

[65] Nationality Decrees, 1923 P.C.I.J. 24.

[66] Acquisition of Polish Nationality, Advisory Opinion, 1923 P.C.I.J. (ser. B) No. 7, at 16 (Sept. 15); Ahmadou Sadio Diallo, 2010 I.C.J. ¶ 104; League of Nations Convention on Certain Questions Relating to the Conflict of Nationality, Apr. 13, 1930, 179 U.N.T.S. 89, art. 1.

nationality is still regarded as a matter of the *domaine réservé* of states, they possess considerable discretion in regulating the terms and conditions of nationality.[67] This competence, albeit broad, "does not amount to omnipotence."[68] The conferral of nationality remains subject to the requirements and limits placed upon states by international law,[69] resulting in an "antithesis between autonomy in [national] legislation and the limited duty of recognition [under international law]."[70]

So what limits would a state need to observe for its conferral of functional animal nationality to be recognized under international law? International law notably reserves the right not to recognize nationality in cases of double nationality and extraterritorial naturalization.[71] Germany, Hungary, Romania, and the Russian Federation are often criticized for naturalizing persons who reside outside their territory and who lack substantial connection to them. These states are accused of systematically expanding the group of people they consider nationals to gain influence over, and even "absorb" a foreign state. Extraterritorial naturalization is seen as violating, *inter alia,* other states' sovereignty, friendly relations between states, and the prohibition of abuse of rights.[72] Analogously, if a state systematically conferred nationality on animals situated abroad, this would be a red flag for exorbitant extraterritorial naturalizations.

International law also sanctions arbitrary conferral of nationality. The UN Secretary-General noted that unlike abuse of rights, which is narrowly focused on acts that are against the law, arbitrariness refers "more broadly, [to] elements of inappropriateness, injustice and

[67] Johannes M. Chen, *The Right to Nationality as a Human Right*, 12 HRLJ 1 (1991); Oxman, *Jurisdiction of States, in* MPEPIL 19 (2007); Peters, *Extraterritorial Naturalizations* 629 (2010); Seline Trevisanut, *Nationality Cases before International Courts and Tribunals, in* MPEPIL 4 (Rüdiger Wolfrum ed., online ed. 2011).

[68] Weis, Nationality and Statelessness in International Law 241 (1979); Laura van Waas, Nationality Matters: Statelessness under International Law 39 (2008). *Cf.* The Inter-American Court of Human Rights (IACtHR) held that "[. . .] the manners in which states regulate matters bearing on nationality cannot today be deemed within their sole jurisdiction." (Proposed Amendments to the Naturalisation provision of the Constitution of Costa Rica, Advisory Opinion OC-4/84, Inter-Am. Ct. H.R. (ser. A) No. 4, ¶ 32 (Jan. 19, 1984) [IACtHR, *Naturalisation Costa Rica* (1984)]).

[69] European Commission for Democracy through Law (Venice Commission), Declaration on the Consequences of State Succession for the Nationality of Natural Persons, Sept. 13–4, 1996, CDL-NAT(1996)007rev-e, art. I.2; G.A. Res. 55/610, U.N. GAOR 55th Sess., International Law Commission (ILC), Draft Articles on Nationality of Natural Persons in Relation to the Succession of States, U.N. Doc. A/RES/55/610, preamble (Nov. 28, 2000); League of Nations Convention on Certain Questions Relating to the Conflict of Nationality, art. 1.

[70] Brownlie 387 (2008).

[71] Trevisanut, *Nationality Cases before International Courts and Tribunals, in* MPEPIL 9–10 (2011), referring to Permanent Court of Arbitration, Affaire Canevaro, the ICJ's Reparation for Injuries Suffered in the Service of the United Nations (Advisory Opinion), and the *Flegenheimer* case (*supra* note 34). *See also* Alice Sironi, *Nationality of Individuals in Public International Law, in* The Changing Role of Nationality in International Law 54, 54–5 (Alessandra Annoni & Serena Forlati eds., 2013).

[72] International Law Commission, 48th Sess., State Succession and Its Impact on the Nationality of Natural and Legal Persons, U.N. Doc. A/CN.4/472/Add. 1, para. 10 (Jan. 10, 1996). Additionally, these policies violate the human right to change nationality, good neighborliness, and stable repartition of jurisdiction: Peters, *Extraterritorial Naturalizations* 623 (2010).

lack of predictability [. . .]."[73] Persons are arbitrarily granted nationality by a state in absence of a valid link—no close and actual relationship—between them.[74] Put positively, a factual connection is required, which refers to territorial or personal links between the state and the subject on whom nationality is conferred,[75] and which warrants faithful mirroring of social reality.[76] If nationality is the "juridical expression of the fact that the individual upon whom it is conferred [. . .] is in fact more closely connected with the population of the State conferring nationality than with that of any other State,"[77] then animals may in some cases be conferred nationality, because they are connected more closely to the population of a particular state. Also animals born on a state's territory or animals situated on a state's territory for a long enough period of time may have an effective link to the state.[78] If, based on territorial or personal links, a state can evidence an effective connection to an animal, its conferral of nationality to them would neither be arbitrary nor abusive. And because nationality "create[s] [. . .] a very strong presumption both that the individual possesses that nationality and that it must be recognised or acknowledged for international purposes,"[79] there should be a presumption that functional animal nationality is legal under international law.

VII. Acquisition of Nationality

In order to make functional animal nationality operational, it is important to understand how nationality could be conferred on animals. Functional animal nationality can be established through ordinary modes of nationality acquisition. Animals could acquire nationality based on their birthplace (*jus soli*), which is the rule most frequently used to grant persons

---

[73] Human Rights Council Res. 10/13, 13th Sess., Human Rights and Arbitrary Deprivation of Nationality, U.N. Doc. A/HRC/13/34, 7, para. 25 (Dec. 14, 2009).

[74] *Id.* para. 24; BGHSt 5, 230, 234, NJW 510, 1954 (Ger.); Appellationsgericht Berlin, Dec. 21, 1965, North-Transylvania Nationality Case, 191, 194 (Ger.). For effective nationality links to ships, *see* Convention on the High Seas, Apr. 29, 1958, 450 U.N.T.S. 11, art. 5 para. I. *See further* Crawford 516 (2012). As Peters argues, requiring a factual connection and prohibiting arbitrariness are "two different ways of expressing the same idea" (Peters, *Extraterritorial Naturalizations* 681 (2010)).

[75] Nottebohm, 1955 I.C.J. 23; Weis, Nationality and Statelessness in International Law 100 (1979). Based on the *Nottebohm* judgment, some argue that a genuine link should exist between the person and state in question, namely, "a legal bond having as its basis a social fact of attachment, a genuine connection of existence, interests and sentiments, together with the existence of reciprocal rights and duties" (Nottebohm, 1955 I.C.J. 23). The judgment, however, applies only in the restricted area of diplomatic protection, and does not bear on the question of nationality for jurisdictional purposes (Nottebohm, 1955 I.C.J. 17). The genuine link unduly restricts states' right to confer nationality, and eradicates double nationality (International Law Commission, 58th Sess., Report of the International Law Commission, Supp. No. 10, U.N. Doc. A/61/10 (May 1–June 9 and July 3–Aug. 11, 2006), Annex E. Extraterritorial Jurisdiction, paras. 32–3 [ILC Report on Extraterritorial Jurisdiction (2006)]).

[76] IACtHR, *Naturalisation Costa Rica* (1984) ¶ 36; League of Nations Convention on Certain Questions Relating to the Conflict of Nationality, art. 19; ILC Draft Articles on Nationality of Natural Persons in Relation to the Succession of States; Venice Commission, Declaration on the Consequences of State Succession for the Nationality of Natural Persons, all cited in Peters, *Extraterritorial Naturalizations* 682 (2010).

[77] Nottebohm, 1955 I.C.J. 23.

[78] *Supra* note 76.

[79] Oppenheim's International Law 856 (1992). This presumption derives from the demand that statelessness must be avoided by all means: Brownlie 399 (2008).

nationality, and has been readily extended before. In territorial terms, it was stretched to apply to birth onboard ships and aircraft.[80] Accordingly, the rule could also be stretched in its personal terms to cover animal nationality.

Animals could also become nationals of a state based on the *jus sanguinis* rule if any of their parents possessed nationality at the time of their birth.[81] This rule has the merit of prolonging a state's personal jurisdiction over animals, by considering national those born on foreign territory. Though the rule is readily applicable to companion animals, it might be difficult to ascertain the nationality of farmed animals because many of them were forcefully impregnated by artificial insemination. These animals could acquire nationality by adoption. Under most domestic laws, it is accepted that minors receive the nationality of adoptive parents.[82] Based on functional nationality, the same rule could be applied to animals. This approach would be consistent with the current passportization policy vis-à-vis animals: the person who adopts a cow, dog, goat, or other companion animal registers them at the local registry office, whereupon the animal receives a pet passport from the home state; the pet passport would then serve as evidence of nationality.

Animals could also acquire nationality through voluntary naturalization (*animus manendi*) as a derivative mode of acquiring nationality. Naturalization refers to the domestic grant of nationality to an alien by means of a formal act (usually after birth),[83] and depends on factors like long residence or domicile with the intent of permanent residence.[84] Nationality could, for example, be conferred on animals *ex necessitate juris*. Children whose descent and family background are unknown are presumed by the law of many states to possess the nationality of the state where they were found. Article 14 of the Convention on Certain Questions relating to the Conflict of Nationality Laws, for example, determines that "[a] foundling is, until the contrary is proved, presumed to have been born on the territory of the State in which it was found."[85] Analogously, an animal without nationality (such as wild animals) could be viewed as a foundling if their descent and family background are unknown and if they otherwise lack a substantial connection to another state.

To acquire nationality from the state, the animal in question must consent to the act of naturalization. Usually, consent is given expressly, but it can also implicit, by showing

---

[80] BROWNLIE 389–90 (2008).

[81] *E.g.*, CoE, Convention on Nationality, Nov. 6, 1997, C.E.T.S. No. 166, art. 6(1) and (2). For the prevalence of those rules in national law, *see* CRAWFORD 511 (2012); WEIS, NATIONALITY AND STATELESSNESS IN INTERNATIONAL LAW 98 (1979).

[82] BROWNLIE 392 (2008).

[83] *Id.* at 393; Harvard Research in International Law, *The Law of Nationality* 13 (1929).

[84] *E.g.*, European Convention on Nationality, art. 6(3); Dörr, *Nationality, in* MPEPIL 14 (2006). Naturalization is "the process by which a state confers its nationality upon a natural person after birth." (Harvard Research in International Law, *The Law of Nationality*, 23 AJIL 11, 13 (Supp. 1929)). Residence and domicile are accepted as an effective link to a state, because residents shape a state's economy and social life. Jurisdiction over such persons is often determined by residence of 5 to 10 years, and additional factors such as cultural knowledge and language: VAN WAAS 33 (2008).

[85] League of Nations Convention on Certain Questions Relating to the Conflict of Nationality, art. 14. Similarly, the proposed art. 7 of the Harvard Research on Nationality states that a foundling found in the territory of a state is presumed to have been born there, but this article is without effect in some *ius soli* countries: Harvard Research in International Law, *The Law of Nationality* 34 (1929).

"unquestionably the desire and intention of a person to take the nationality of that state."[86] Because most animals do not use human language, logical preference assumption and behavioral studies could serve as a proxy for consent, possibly based on animal welfare indicators.[87] It follows that an animal's consent to the nationality of a state in which they face grave suffering or deliberate killing cannot be assumed since it is not supported by the animal's behavior or welfare indicators. Requiring consent would broadly ensure that functional animal nationality is not misused to apply oppressive and deficient laws to the animals.

B. PROTECTING ANIMALS ABROAD THROUGH THE PASSIVE PERSONALITY PRINCIPLE

Once animals are recognized as functional nationals, the state can use this link to establish personal jurisdiction over them.[88] A state generally has prescriptive jurisdiction over a national animal by virtue of the active and passive personality principles. Since I am here primarily concerned with protecting animals abroad, I focus on the passive personality principle. Passive personality jurisdiction allows states to try aliens for crimes committed abroad, if those crimes were committed against their nationals. The principle is designed to give effect to the interests states have in protecting their nationals abroad—interests considered legitimate because they are part of a state's personal sovereignty.[89] Given the above arguments for functional animal nationality, states could use the passive personality principle to exercise jurisdiction over their national animals wherever they are and regardless of whether foreign laws protect them.

In the past, the passive personality principle was opposed on the grounds that offenders often do not know the victims' nationality and are unaware of the law that applies to the crime they commit. They may even think their actions are legal. Despite these objections, the passive personality has gained greater acceptance among the international community in recent years. According to President Guillaume and the International Law Commission's 2006 report to the General Assembly, the passive personality principle belongs to the law classically formulated by states.[90] Judges Higgins, Kooijmans, and Buergenthal, in their Joint Separate Opinion in the *Arrest Warrant*, held: "Passive personality jurisdiction, for so long regarded as controversial, is now reflected [. . .] in the legislation of various countries [. . .],

---

[86] *Id.* at 53.

[87] For a discussion of whether animals need a right to self-determination and how it can be best secured through either dissent, assent, or consent, *see* Charlotte E. Blattner, *Animal Labour: Toward a Prohibition of Forced Labour and A Right to Freely Choose One's Work, in* ANIMAL LABOUR: A NEW FRONTIER OF INTERSPECIES JUSTICE? (Charlotte E. Blattner, Kendra Coulter & Will Kymlicka eds., forthcoming 2019).

[88] The allegiance must exist at the time the act or omission over which jurisdiction is asserted took place. According to the *nullum crimen sine lege* rule, retrospective personal connections used to justify jurisdiction violate international law: CRAWFORD 460 (2012); Harvard Research in International Law, *Jurisdiction with Respect to Crime* 440 (1935).

[89] According to *U.S. v. Yunis*, the principle "recognizes that each state has a legitimate interest in protecting the safety of its citizens when they journey outside national boundaries." (United States v. Yunis, 681 F. Supp. 896, 901 (D.C. 1988) (U.S.)).

[90] Arrest Warrant, 2002 I.C.J. 37 (Separate Opinion of President Guillaume); ILC Report on Extraterritorial Jurisdiction, para. 15 (2006).

and today meets with relatively little opposition [. . .]."[91] Austria, Brazil, China, Denmark, Estonia, Finland, France, Germany, Italy, Japan, the Republic of Korea, Malaysia, Mexico, the Netherlands, Poland, Russia, Sweden, Switzerland, Taiwan, Turkey, the United Arab Emirates, the United Kingdom, the United States, and Venezuela all accept the principle and exercise jurisdiction on its basis.[92]

Some states apply the passive personality principle to all crimes. The French Penal Code provides in article 113-7: "La loi pénale française est applicable à tout crime, ainsi qu'à tout délit puni d'emprisonnement, commis par un Français ou par un étranger hors du territoire de la République lorsque la victime est de nationalité française au moment de l'infraction."[93] Similarly, the Canadian Criminal Code establishes a territorial fiction for crimes committed against Canadians abroad.[94] If the principle is broadly applied, it covers all crimes and administrative offenses committed against national animals, whether or not these offenses are punishable where they were committed. From the animals' perspective, this is the preferred standard because high standards of animal protection would travel with them wherever they go or are moved. If horses are outsourced from the United States to Mexico to circumvent the domestic horse slaughter ban, the United States could exercise passive personality jurisdiction over horses who are its functional nationals. In essence, the passive personality principle would render most threats of outsourcing the production or use of animals toothless.

Other states have applied the principle in a limited manner. Some make their jurisdiction contingent on double criminality, requiring that the act or omission is penalized under the law where it was committed.[95] But this requirement removes the benefits of the passive personality principle. Another group of states applies the principle only to a specific category of crimes. For instance, section 64(1)4a.a) of the Austrian Criminal Code establishes jurisdiction over Austrian nationals if they are made victims of genital mutilation, slavery, slave trade, various forms of sexual abuse, prostitution, and other grave crimes committed abroad.[96] If we apply this rule to Knut, Germany might prescribe rules for Knut's treatment

---

[91] Arrest Warrant, 2002 I.C.J. 76 (Joint Separate Opinion of Judges Higgins, Kooijmans, and Buergenthal).

[92] For Brazil, China, Denmark, Finland, France, Germany, the Republic of Korea, Malaysia, Mexico, the Netherlands, Poland, Sweden, the United Arab Emirates, the United States, and Venezuela, *see* IBA REPORT EXTRATERRITORIAL JURISDICTION 147 (2009). For Austria, Brazil, Denmark, Estonia, France, Germany, Italy, Japan, Poland, Russia, Switzerland, Taiwan, Turkey, the United Kingdom, and the United States, *see* Sinn, *Das Strafanwendungsrecht als Schlüssel zur Lösung von Jurisdiktionskonflikten?*, *in* CONFLICTS OF JURISDICTION IN CROSS-BORDER CRIME SITUATIONS 522 (2012).

[93] PENAL CODE (Fr.), art. 113–7.

[94] Criminal Code, c. C-46, 1985, art. 3.7(d) (Can.).

[95] Estonia, Poland, Taiwan, and Brazil are among the countries that make jurisdiction conditional on double criminality: Sinn, *Das Strafanwendungsrecht als Schlüssel zur Lösung von Jurisdiktionskonflikten?*, *in* CONFLICTS OF JURISDICTION IN CROSS-BORDER CRIME SITUATIONS 522 (2012).

[96] BUNDESGESETZ VOM 23. JÄNNER 1974 ÜBER DIE MIT GERICHTLICHER STRAFE BEDROHTEN HANDLUNGEN [STGB] [CRIMINAL CODE], BGBl. No. 60/1974, § 64(1) 4a.a) (Austria). The countries that apply the principle in a limited manner are Brazil, China, Denmark, Finland, France, Germany, the Republic of Korea, Malaysia, Mexico, the Netherlands, Poland, Sweden, the United Arab Emirates, the United States, and Venezuela: IBA REPORT EXTRATERRITORIAL JURISDICTION 147 (2009). Japan also provides for limited passive personality over crimes of forcible indecency, rape, attempts, homicide, capture, confinement, kidnapping of minors, kidnapping, and robbery: KEIHŌ [PENAL CODE] (Japan), art. 3-2.

abroad only with respect to the most repugnant crimes (e.g., bestiality, willful starving, or in vivo experimentation without anesthetics), or acts that are especially painful for him (e.g., skinning, slaughter in conscious state, and other forms of torture).

The passive personality principle would not only be used to protect popular zoo animals or beloved companions but also to extend protection to the many nameless animals used and exported for food production and research. Because animals like chickens, pigs, and calves used for food purposes are usually killed when they are less than a year old,[97] one might think that the passive personality principle has little to offer them. But because their offspring can acquire their nationality (based on the *jus sanguinis* rule), functional nationality granted by the home state is prolonged and, from a jurisdictional perspective, perpetuated abroad. This, in essence, brings to the fore the strengths and benefits of the nationality principle. On a final note, if a single offense causes several animals of different nationalities to suffer, a passive nationality link to one animal's home state could be sufficient to claim jurisdiction over all aspects of the offense.[98]

C. PASSIVE PERSONALITY PRINCIPLE IN THE EXTRATERRITORIALITY FRAMEWORK

The extraterritoriality framework treats passive personality jurisdiction just like the active personality principle. The animals have a permanent link to their home state via nationality that operates as an anchor point and is hence intraterritorial. The home state has jurisdiction to protect its national animals wherever they are, so content regulation may be intra- or extraterritorial. In the most extreme case, content is regulated abroad, making this a type γ_2 regulation.

§2 Universality Principle

A. PROTECTING ANIMALS ABROAD THROUGH THE UNIVERSALITY PRINCIPLE

Extraterritorial jurisdiction is often premised on the idea that some states have a special interest in regulating a particular matter because of, for example, effects on their territory, the nationality of parties, or other factors. But there are certain acts that are considered crimes against all and for which the international community has created universal jurisdiction. The principle of universality establishes jurisdiction over an accused person wherever the alleged crime was committed, and regardless of the accused's whereabouts, nationality, residence, or other connection to the prosecuting entity.

---

[97] Broiler chickens are killed at 35–49 days (whose natural life span is 7 years), egg-laying chickens at 18 months (natural life span 7 years), pigs at 4–6 months (natural life span 10–12 years), lambs at 3–10 months (natural life span 15 years), calves at 4–6 months (natural life span 20–25 years), bobby calves at 1–2 weeks (natural life span 20–25 years), and meat cows at 12–18 months (natural life span 20–25 years): Sustainable Table, Meet Your Meat, *available at* https://sustainabletable.org.au/Hungryforinfo/Factoryfarming/tabid/106/Default.aspx (last visited Jan. 10, 2019).

[98] CoE, *Extraterritorial Criminal Jurisdiction* 450 (1992).

There are broadly two views on what crimes the universality principle covers. The conservative view is that universal jurisdiction may only be exercised over crimes as substantiated by treaty law, and concretized by state practice.[99] What makes this view conservative is that the list of crimes it considers universal is short, and it is doubtful if any state will prosecute a universal crime. The fact that a crime is universally repressed does not mean that states are obliged to use the principle to assert their jurisdiction. In this sense, the ICJ determined that article VI of the Genocide Convention[100]—which *inter alia* provides that persons charged with genocide shall be tried by the state in whose territory genocide was committed—does not impose an obligation on states to exercise universal jurisdiction even if genocide is universally condemned. However, article VI "certainly does not prohibit States, with respect to genocide, from conferring jurisdiction on their criminal courts based on criteria other than where the crime was committed which are compatible with international law."[101]

In contrast, the expansionist school, prominently defended by the Princeton Principles of Universal Jurisdiction, argues that universal jurisdiction is established for a broader category of crimes, for which customary international law operates as a basis.[102] There are good reasons to believe that universal jurisdiction exists under customary international law, since Argentina, Australia, Bahrain, Belgium, Brazil, Canada, China, Denmark, Finland, France, Germany, India, Malaysia, Mexico, the Netherlands, New Zealand, Norway, Poland, Russia, South Africa, Spain, Sweden, Tajikistan, the United Arab Emirates, the United Kingdom, the United States, and Venezuela all lay down that their courts have the power to exercise universal jurisdiction.[103] There is another notable difference between the universality principle of the conservative school and that defended by the expansionist school. Under treaty law (following the conservative position), universal jurisdiction typically punishes a breach of international law. Under customary international law (following the expansionist position), however, acts that breach national law are punished, for which international law gives states the liberty to punish, but does not itself declare criminal.[104] Here, I accept the

---

[99] These treaties include the International Convention on the Suppression and Punishment of the Crime of Apartheid (Nov. 30, 1973, 1015 U.N.T.S. 243); Convention against Torture and other Cruel, Inhuman and Degrading Treatment or Punishment (Dec. 10, 1984, 1465 U.N.T.S. 85, adopted by G.A. Res. 39/46, U.N. GAOR, Meeting No. 93, U.N. Doc. A/Res/39/46 (Dec. 10, 1984); the Hague Convention (Hague Convention (IV) Respecting the Laws and Customs of War on Land and Its Annex (Regulations Concerning the Laws and Customs of War on Land, Oct. 18, 1907, T.S. 539)); and the Geneva Conventions (especially Geneva Convention (IV)). The conservative view is also endorsed by the AU-EU Export Report on the Principle of Universal Jurisdiction, 8672/1/09 REV 1, Apr. 16, 2009, R1.

[100] The Convention on the Prevention and Punishment of the Crime of Genocide, Dec. 9, 1948, 78 U.N.T.S. 277.

[101] Case Concerning Application of the Convention on the Prevention and Punishment of the Crime of Genocide (Bosn. & Herz. v. Serb. and Montenegro), Judgment, 2007 I.C.J. Rep. 43, para. 442 (Feb. 26).

[102] Princeton Project on Universal Jurisdiction, *The Princeton Principles on Universal Jurisdiction* (Princeton University, Princeton 2001). *See also* U.S. Restatement (Fourth) of the Foreign Relations Law, § 413, reporters' note 2; Bantekas, *Criminal Jurisdiction of States under International Law*, *in* MPEPIL 22 (2011); ORAKHELASHVILI 221 (2019).

[103] IBA REPORT EXTRATERRITORIAL JURISDICTION 153 (2009); A. Hays Butler, *The Growing Support for Universal Jurisdiction in National Legislation*, *in* UNIVERSAL JURISDICTION 67, 67 (2004).

[104] BROWNLIE 306 (2008).

arguments of the expansionists and use them to examine the scope of universal jurisdiction under customary international law.

The universality principle is first and foremost concerned with universal crimes, which should not be mistaken for peremptory norms of international law.[105] Crimes are universal when they are so serious and threatening that all states have an interest in preventing or ending them.[106] Among those are acts of aggression,[107] war crimes,[108] crimes against humanity,[109] genocide,[110] international terrorism,[111] torture,[112] slave trade, and slavery.[113] These are "offenses widely recognized by states as being of universal concern,"[114] that "promote fundamental interests of the world community and uphold humane values,"[115] and are "exercised in the name of universal morality."[116]

The international community has not at this point negotiated or concluded a treaty that either defines international crimes against animals or establishes universal jurisdiction over such matters. But if we take the expansionist position, universal jurisdiction could emerge in animal law if there was a shared condemnation of certain acts committed against animals, grounded in customary international law.

I have already described and discussed various developments in international and comparative law that indicate that the international community has a common, fundamental understanding of how we must treat animals. The recognition of animal sentience and the moral duties we owe animals on this basis are now universally shared. Anti-cruelty laws of

---

[105] *Ius cogens*, according to the International Law Commission in the 2001 Draft Articles on State Responsibility, is a "serious breach of an obligation arising under a peremptory norm of general international law." (G.A. Res. 56/10, U.N. GAOR 53rd Sess., International Law Commission [ILC], Draft Articles on Responsibility of States for Internationally Wrongful Acts, Supp. No. 10, U.N. Doc. A/RES/56/10, arts. 40, 27 cmt. 3 (Apr. 23–June 1 and June 2–Aug. 10, 2001 [ARSIWA]). Peremptory norms are like universal crimes as they represent "projections of the individual and collective conscience" (Andrea Bianchi, *Human Rights and the Magic of* Jus Cogens, 19 EJIL 491 (2008)). But they differ in that only peremptory norms derogate conflicting treaty law, as laid down in article 53 VCLT.

[106] Arrest Warrant, 2002 I.C.J. 81 (Joint Separate Opinion of Judges Higgins, Kooijmans, and Buergenthal).

[107] R v. Jones [2007] 1 AC 36 (U.K.).

[108] U.S. Restatement (Fourth) of the Foreign Relations Law, § 413; *The Princeton Principles on Universal Jurisdiction* (2001), principle 2(1); ORAKHELASHVILI 223 (2019); Staker, *Jurisdiction, in* INTERNATIONAL LAW 302 (2018).

[109] U.S. Restatement (Fourth) of the Foreign Relations Law, § 413; *The Princeton Principles on Universal Jurisdiction* (2001), principle 2(1); Staker, *Jurisdiction, in* INTERNATIONAL LAW 302 (2018).

[110] The Prosecutor's Office of Salzburg v. Duško Cvjetković, 15Os99/94, July 13, 1994 (Oberster Gerichtshof) (Austria); The Prosecutor v. Nikola Jorgić, 2 BvR 1290/99, Dec. 12, 2000 (Bundesverfassungsgericht) (Ger.); U.S. Restatement (Fourth) of the Foreign Relations Law, § 413; *The Princeton Principles on Universal Jurisdiction* (2001), principle 2(1).

[111] U.S. Restatement (Fourth) of the Foreign Relations Law, § 413; ORAKHELASHVILI 223 (2019).

[112] U.S. Restatement (Fourth) of the Foreign Relations Law, § 413; *The Princeton Principles on Universal Jurisdiction* (2001), principle 2(1); Oxman, *Jurisdiction of States, in* MPEPIL 39 (2007).

[113] *Id.*

[114] U.S. Restatement (Fourth) of the Foreign Relations Law, § 413.

[115] TERJE EINARSEN, THE CONCEPT OF UNIVERSAL CRIMES IN INTERNATIONAL LAW 6, 7 (2012).

[116] Anne-Marie Slaughter, *Defining the Limits: Universal Jurisdiction and National Courts, in* UNIVERSAL JURISDICTION 168, 175 (2004).

a slew of states are based on the idea that causing physical and psychological harm to animals and depriving them of the ability to pursue their basic needs is wrong. The great majority of states has enshrined in law the obligation to treat animals humanely and to not let them suffer unnecessarily. Together, the recognition of animal sentience, the condemnation of animal cruelty, and the duties of humane treatment and avoidance of animal suffering constitute the general principle of animal welfare.[117] The principle indicates that there is, albeit diffuse, a universal conception, a consensus, if you will, of what is owed to animals. The principle of animal welfare qualifies as a general principle of international law, but given the fact that concerns for animals are rising globally, experts predict it is likely that the principle will become a norm of customary international law.[118] Let us assume, for the sake of the *lex ferenda* analysis, that this will soon be the case. If crimes condemned by the world community that undermine fundamental values are then committed against animals, every state has the right to try the perpetrator for those crimes on the basis of the universality principle.[119] Because states have generally tended to extend the universality principle to a wider range of crimes,[120] this approach would seamlessly fit into the broader, growing scheme of the law of jurisdiction.

But if we recall the fact that humans kill more than 69 billion land animals per year for food,[121] which acts done to animals could possibly be of concern for the world community? Would the universality principle not simply serve Western views of how animals must be treated? Would it then be used to oppress minorities on the basis of how they treat animals? This is a danger we must take seriously, and it relates to objections to extraterritorial jurisdiction as a whole, which is why I deal with these questions in more detail in the final chapter.[122] Here, I will just note that crimes are only considered universal if they are universally condemned, which leaves us with a very narrow application of the universality principle, such as to obvious cases of cruelty, torture, and deliberate infliction of suffering.

The universality principle also covers crimes that are not necessarily the most heinous. Among these are crimes removed from any state's jurisdiction, which might go unpunished if it were not for the universality principle.[123] For example, piracy (an act of violence by a private vessel on the high seas against another vessel) is neither particularly abhorrent nor does it usually endanger the security of the international community. What makes piracy amenable to the universality principle is the fact that it evades the jurisdictional remit of all

---

117 *See* Chapter 2, §4.

118 Sykes, Beast in the Jungle 156 ff. (2011).

119 In 1994, Schwarze proposed that the universality principle be applied to animal law to effectively protect animals effectively across the globe: SCHWARZE 88 (1994). *Cf.* In contrast, Schuster argued that only some universal interests are eligible to be covered by universal jurisdiction, notably if the interests are indispensable to ensure peace among states: SCHUSTER 63 (1996).

120 Petrig (2013), for example, shows that the Swiss criminal code introduced three new crimes amenable to universal jurisdiction: genital mutilation, offenses committed against minors abroad, and other offenses.

121 FAOSTAT (search criteria "World"+"Meat Total"+"Producing Animals/Slaughtered"+"2017," *available at* http://faostat.fao.org/ (last visited Jan. 10, 2019).

122 *See* Chapter 11.

123 Article 101(a) UNCLOS; U.S. Restatement (Fourth) of the Foreign Relations Law, § 413; *The Princeton Principles on Universal Jurisdiction* (2001), principle 2(1).

states. To fill this gap, states are increasingly applying the universality principle to serious crimes that evade territorial jurisdiction, including piracy, kidnapping, trafficking in women and children, hijacking, money laundering, drug trafficking, organized crime, and damaging oil platforms.[124]

Likewise, states could prosecute crimes against animals that are presumably not among the most atrocious, but that manifestly escape all states' jurisdictional powers. For instance, states should be able to sanction illegal wildlife trade that is part of (and often goes hand in hand with) organized crime. Interpol's Wildlife Crime Working Group estimates that illegal wildlife trade generates between 50 billion and 150 billion USD per year.[125] Wildlife trade covers the trade in exotic pets, whose survival rate is extremely low (illegally trafficked Madagascar chameleons, for example, have a 1 percent survival rate).[126] It also covers trade in live or dead wild animals associated with illegal hunting and poaching, which threaten international efforts to protect endangered species.

But even if customary international law evidences a universal condemnation of these and other crimes, "simply because certain offences are universally condemned does not mean that a state may exercise universal jurisdiction over them."[127] Customary law must show that a crime is universally condemned *and* that it can be adjudged virtually everywhere. Put differently, only if states have universal jurisdiction over universal crimes can we truly say a crime is covered by the universality principle. Animal law thus has a long way to go before it can use universal jurisdiction to address, punish, and prevent universal crimes committed against animals.

There is also contention over how broadly or narrowly states can practice universal jurisdiction. In the *Arrest Warrant*, Judges Higgins, Kooijmans, and Buergenthal underlined that even though states endorse the universality principle, they rarely provide for or exercise pure forms of universal jurisdiction. In most cases, states require some link to the forum state, such as through the nationality of the offender or victim, or actions threatening the domestic security. Only where there is no other, less disputed basis of jurisdiction, is universality an accepted basis of jurisdiction.[128] Sometimes double criminality is also required, so the act must be considered criminal where it was committed.[129] Double criminality responds to instances where there is no enforcement abroad, which, according to the Council of Europe, would already be "a major step forward in the protection of victims."[130] Likewise, double criminality would yield considerable benefits for animal victims. However, the usefulness of extraterritorial jurisdiction is comparatively low if double criminality (or subsidiary universality) is

---

124 Hijacking Convention; Montreal Convention. *See also* IBA REPORT EXTRATERRITORIAL JURISDICTION 153 (2009).

125 U.N. Environmental Program (UNEP), UNEP Yearbook 2014, Illegal Trade in Wildlife 25 (2014).

126 *See more generally* Angus I. Carpenter et al., *The Dynamics of Global Trade in Chameleons*, 120 BIOLOGICAL CONSERVATION 291 (2004).

127 *The Princeton Principles on Universal Jurisdiction* 43 (2001).

128 Arrest Warrant, 2002 I.C.J. 44 (Separate Opinion of President Guillaume).

129 *E.g.*, CRIMINAL CODE (Switz.), art. 7 para. 2.

130 CoE, Convention on Preventing and Combating Violence against Women and Domestic Violence, May 11, 2011, C.E.T.S. No. 210, explanatory report, para. 227.

required for every single crime. As Judges Higgins, Kooijmans, and Buergenthal point out, state practice is neutral on the question of limited or subsidiary universality,[131] and, perhaps more importantly, recent trends show that states increasingly opt for unlimited universal jurisdiction.[132]

States sometimes also make universal jurisdiction conditional on the accused's presence on domestic territory (forum *deprehensionis*).[133] Many scholars, however, argue that neither residence, nor domicile, nor nationality, are mandatory preconditions. They argue that *in personam/in absentia* jurisdiction is simply a rule of enforcement jurisdiction that does not indicate if the prescriptive universality principle is accepted or rejected. To speak of *in absentia* universal jurisdiction would, on grounds of consistency, require that we also speak of nationality jurisdiction *in absentia*, the protective principle *in absentia*, etc.[134] There is thus a reasonable possibility that if universal jurisdiction emerged in animal law, it would not be limited to those states that have a manifest link to the case at hand, but could be exercised by virtually any state.

B. UNIVERSALITY PRINCIPLE IN THE EXTRATERRITORIALITY FRAMEWORK

In the extraterritoriality framework, the unlimited universality principle has no anchor point, because this is the very essence and raison d'être of the principle: to prosecute universal crimes regardless of where, by whom, or against whom they were committed. Anchor points (like the animals against whom a crime was committed) can still be located in a specific case. So, depending on the whereabouts of the animal, there might be an animal-related intraterritorial or extraterritorial anchor point. The content the principle regulates are crimes committed against animals abroad, making this is a γ_2 or α_1 regulation. The limited or conditional universality principle, in contrast, covers crimes committed abroad and links them to the perpetrator's presence, their nationality, or the victim's nationality. This variant uses a non-animal-related intraterritorial anchor point to regulate animal-related content on foreign territory (type γ_1 regulation). If double criminality is required, the norm uses a non-animal-related extraterritorial anchor point to regulate animal-related content extraterritorially (type α_3 regulation).

[131] Arrest Warrant, 2002 I.C.J. 76, ¶45 (Joint Separate Opinion of Judges Higgins, Kooijmans, and Buergenthal): "[W]hile none of the national case law to which we have referred happens to be based on the exercise of a universal jurisdiction properly so called, there is equally nothing in this case law which evidences an *opinio juris* on the illegality of such a jurisdiction. In short, national legislation and case law—that is, State practice—is neutral as to exercise of universal jurisdiction."

[132] U.S. Restatement (Fourth) of the Foreign Relations Law, § 402, reporters' note 10.

[133] IBA Report Extraterritorial Jurisdiction 188 (2009); *The Princeton Principles on Universal Jurisdiction* (2001), principle 1(2) and (3).

[134] Arrest Warrant, 2002 I.C.J. 78, ¶ 56 (Joint Separate Opinion of Judges Higgins, Kooijmans, and Buergenthal); O'Keefe 749–51 (2004); Crawford 469 (2012).

§3 Effects Principle

A. PROTECTING ANIMALS ABROAD THROUGH THE EFFECTS PRINCIPLE

On the basis of the effects principle, a state can exercise jurisdiction over foreign activities that create or intend to create substantial effects on its territory. The effects principle has historically emerged in the landmark antitrust cases *Alcoa*,[135] *Hartford Fire*,[136] *Dyestuffs*,[137] *Wood Pulp*,[138] and *Gencor/Lonrho*,[139] where it faced considerable opposition by the international community. Because most states now accept and use the effects principle, including Argentina, Austria, Belgium, Brazil, Canada, China, Czech Republic, Denmark, the European Union, Finland, France, Germany, Italy, Japan, Norway, Portugal, Russia, South Africa, South Korea, Spain, Switzerland, and the United States,[140] it has become an established basis of jurisdiction in international law.

Anticompetitive behavior is a common practice in the animal production industry. In 2014, the German Federal Cartel Office imposed fines as high as 338 million EUR (394 million USD) on 21 meat producers and 33 individuals within and outside Germany for forming a cartel.[141] The fines were calculated at around 2 percent of the annual turnover of small and medium-sized businesses. For companies that belonged to a multinational enterprise, such as Herta GmbH (a subsidiary of Nestlé), the fines were calculated at the enterprise's annual turnover. Accordingly, 85 percent of the 338 million EUR total fines were shouldered

---

[135] United States v. Aluminum Company of America, 148 F.2d 416 (1945) (U.S.). Judge Learned Hand held that the agreements "were unlawful, though made abroad, if they were intended to affect imports and did affect them" (*id.*).

[136] Hartford Fire Insurance Co v. California, 509 U.S. 764, 796 (1993) (U.S.). Where extraterritorial conduct affects import commerce, it is evaluated on the basis of the *Hartford Fire* test, which requires "foreign conduct that was meant to produce and did in fact produce some substantial effect in the United States." (*Id.*).

[137] Case 48/69, Imperial Chemical Industries Ltd. v. Commission of the European Communities [ICI v. Commission], 1972 E.C.R. 619, paras. 126–8, 132–5. In this case, the actions of ICI's subsidiary were attributed to the foreign parent on the basis of the so-called "unity of the group," since the parent was held to be able to control its subsidiaries (economic entity theory). *See further* on the economic entity theory, Chapter 5, §3 C III.

[138] Joined Cases 89/85, 104/85, 114/85, 116-7/85, and 125-9/85, A. Ahlström Osakeyhtiö v. Commission, 1988 E.C.R. 5214 [*Wood Pulp*]. In *Wood Pulp*, the Commission initiated proceedings against 43 corporations (41 non-EC producers and two non-EC trade associations) that used bleached pulp to produce high-quality paper and together formed a cartel. The court based its jurisdiction on the place where the agreements were implemented.

[139] Case T-102/96, Gencor Limited v. EC Commission, 1999 E.C.R. II-753, para. 90. Muchlinski maintains that the test established by the CFI cannot be identified as a pure effects principle because it requires "substantial [domestic] business practice" by sales: MUCHLINSKI 147 (2007).

[140] IBA REPORT EXTRATERRITORIAL JURISDICTION 49 ff., 68 (2009). For the European Union, *see* Commission Notice, Guidelines on the Effect on Trade Concept Contained in Articles 81 and 82 of the Treaty (2004/C 101/07), 2004 O.J. (C 101) 81, para. 100.

[141] *Bundeskartellamt verhängt Bußgelder gegen Wursthersteller*, BUNDESKARTELLAMT, July 15, 2014; Natalia Drozdiak, *German Cartel Office Fines Wurst Makers: Authority Accused Meat Producers of Fixing Prices*, WALL ST. J., July 15, 2014.

by companies that formed an economic unit with other corporations.[142] In early 2015, the Spanish National Commission of Markets and Competition (CNMC) fined 11 dairy producers (including Danone, Nestlé Spain, and Lactalis) 88.2 million EUR (103 million USD) for forming a cartel that fixed prices of raw milk supplies for over 13 years.[143] As the CNMC stated, in matters of antitrust violations, "the livestock industry [is] the hardest hit sector."[144] Another large milk cartel was fined by China's National Development & Reform Commission in 2013 (six companies for 82 million USD).[145] And in February 2016, the Australian Competition and Consumer Commission (ACCC) initiated proceedings against Australian Egg Corporation Limited (AECL) and others for attempting to pressure their members "to enter into an arrangement to cull hens or otherwise dispose of eggs, for the purpose of reducing the amount of eggs available for supply to consumers and businesses in Australia."[146]

Although cartels are common in animal agricultural and research industries, they and the jurisdiction exercised over them cannot fruitfully be linked to concerns for animals. Let us assume poultry producers in China and Japan form a cartel agreement that targets the Saudi Arabian market. Producers and contracting importers agree not to sell poultry cuts for less than 2,500 USD per ton (reference value being 2,100 USD per ton).[147] By selling the products at fixed prices, they avoid competing with other products and distort the Saudi poultry market. The adverse effect on the market will vary, depending on the number of imports and their relative weight in the targeted market. If foreign producers violate Saudi's antitrust law, Saudi Arabia will order them to drop the price and will impose fines for price fixing. But cutting the profit of producers may cause them to lower the welfare of animals under their control by increasing production rate, reducing space, using more antibiotics, and speeding up slaughter. Should Saudi Arabia be aware of these negative repercussions, it is unlikely to allow cartels to continue engaging in anticompetitive behavior, to ensure animals do not suffer as a consequence. In essence, authorities punish anticompetitive behavior, whether that behavior is detrimental or beneficial to animals. Even under the assumption that antitrust law could coincidentally help protect animals abroad, there is no way to control or ensure this effect. So even though the effects principle applies to animals and animal products, states cannot use it to protect animals abroad.

---

[142] According to the European Commission, the limits to imposing fines are reached at 10 percent of the overall annual turnover of the company. If the company charged is part of a multinational enterprise, the 10 percent limit may be based on the turnover of the group "if the parent of that group exercised decisive influence over the operations of the subsidiary during the infringement period." (Article 23 para. 2 of Council Regulation 1/2003 on the Implementation of the Rules on Competition Laid Down in Articles 81 and 82 of the Treaty, 2003 O.J. (L 1) 1)).

[143] Of the total, Danone was fined 23.2 million EUR, Nestlé 10.6 million EUR, and Lactalis 11.6 million EUR: Emily Kokoll, *Spain Fines Danone, Nestle, Others $98M for Dairy Cartel*, Law360, Mar. 4, 2015.

[144] Translation by Emily Kokoll, *Spain Fines Danone, Nestle, Others $98M for Dairy Cartel*, Law360, Mar. 4, 2015.

[145] Kazunori Takada & Michael Martina, *China Fines Milk Powder Makers $110 for Price Fixing*, Reuters, Aug. 7, 2013.

[146] *ACCC v. Australian Egg Corporation Limited* [2016] FCA 69 (Feb. 10, 2016) (Austl.).

[147] *Cf.* Felix Osike, *Uganda Losing Billions in Poultry Imports*, New Vision (Daily Uganda), Mar. 10, 2012.

The effects principle can only be used to protect animals abroad if it is based on a radically different concept of "effects." Some consider the effects principle to be a variant of the objective territoriality principle, which means that effects felt on a state's territory will have to qualify as a constituent element of a crime.[148] But according to a more widely accepted theory, the effects principle is an independent principle of international law that does not demand the effects felt on foreign territory to be constitutive elements of a crime.[149] For example, under section 10C para. 2 of the Crimes Act of New South Wales, criminal jurisdiction extends to offenses when a constituent element was fulfilled on its territory or if "the offence is committed wholly outside the State, but the offence has an effect in the State."[150] The effects necessary to trigger the effects principle need not even be legal in nature but can be economic, environmental, or social.[151] According to "The Extraterritorial Effects of Legislation and Policies in the EU and US," a 2012 study of the EU Directorate-General for External Policies, the effects principle applies to environmental law on the basis of environmental effects (environmental pollution, loss of biodiversity, etc.).[152] The effects principle is also used in labor law, where the effects are reputational: states resent being identified with corporations that thwart their reputation by running on cheap labor, forced labor, and human rights violations abroad.[153] Zerk argues that anticorruptive acts and sex tourism also threaten a state's international reputation and that domestic law must be applied to these actions.[154] Similarly, in *Kiobel*, a minority opinion argued that foreign human rights violations should

---

[148] Akehurst 153 (1972–3); Bantekas, *Criminal Jurisdiction of States under International Law*, *in* MPEPIL 5 (2011); CRAWFORD 459 (2012); ORAKHELASHVILI 223–4 (2019); SCHWARZE 24 (1994).

[149] ILC Report on Extraterritorial Jurisdiction, para. 12 (2006). *See also* Bowett 7 (1982); O'Keefe 739, n. 16 (2004); ORAKHELASHVILI 223–4 (2019). Further on this distinction: Mika N. Hayashi, *Objective Territorial Principle or Effects Doctrine? Jurisdiction and Cyberspace*, *in* LE NUOVE FRONTIERE DEL DIRITTO INTERNAZIONALE 97 (Carlo Focarelli ed., 2008).

[150] *Crimes Act 1900*, § 10C para. 2 (NSW) (Austl.). The same is provided in art. 23 para. 1 of the Criminal Code of Bosnia and Herzegovina, Official Gazette 3/03, *translation in* Official Gazette of Bosnia and Herzegovina 37/03 (Bosn. & Herz.). The Indian Code of Criminal Procedure speaks in this context of consequences, not effects: Indian Code of Criminal Procedure, Act No. 2 of 1974, § 179 (India).

[151] Danielle Ireland-Piper, *Prosecutions of Extraterritorial Criminal Conduct and the Abuse of Rights Doctrine*, 9 UTRECHT L. REV. 68, 78 (2013); Ryngaert, JURISDICTION OVER ANTITRUST VIOLATIONS 17 (2008).

[152] Directorate-General for External Policies, Policy Department, The Extraterritorial Effects of Legislation and Policies in the EU and US, requested by the European Parliament's Committee on Foreign Affairs 5 (European Union 2012).

[153] Hazel Fox, *Jurisdiction and Immunity*, *in* FIFTY YEARS OF THE INTERNATIONAL COURT OF JUSTICE: ESSAYS IN HONOUR OF SIR ROBERT JENNINGS 210, 212 (Vaughan Lowe & Malgosia Fitzmaurice eds., 1996); SCHUSTER 6 (1996); JAMES M. ZIMMERMAN, EXTRATERRITORIAL EMPLOYMENT STANDARDS OF THE UNITED STATES: THE REGULATION OF THE OVERSEAS 164–7 (1992). In *EEOC v. Aramco*, the Court refrained from extending the Civil Rights Act of 1964 to foreign employment practices, even though the citizen employed was an American: EEOC v. Arabian Am. Oil Co., 857 F.2d 1014 (5th Cir. 1988) (U.S.). In *Walrave and Koch v. Union Cycliste Internationale*, the ECJ applied the rule of nondiscrimination to the subject matter either where the contract was entered or where it took effect: Case 36/74, Walrave and Koch v. Union Cycliste Internationale, 1974 E.C.R. 1405. The Court ordered: "The rule on non-discrimination applies in judging all legal relationships in so far as these relationships, by reason either of the place where they are entered into or of the place where they take effect, can be located within the territory of the Community."

[154] ZERK, EXTRATERRITORIAL JURISDICTION 207–8 (2010).

be remedied domestically, because they "substantially and adversely affect [. . .] an important American national interest."[155]

As these examples show, this variant of the effects principle is rather fragmentary, as it applies to environmental law, labor law, anticorruption, and sex tourism, as well as human rights issues. But what these examples have in common are reputational effects. Ryngaert refers to states that allow anticompetitive behavior and argues that "in effect, these territorial States, rather than foreign States, exercise extraterritorial jurisdiction, and abuse their sovereign rights."[156] Regulating the behavior of foreigners abroad is therefore considered necessary to protect a state from being adversely affected in its reputation.

In animal law, adverse reputational effects might arise from cruel acts committed against animals abroad. If states relied on reputational effects in animal law to protect animals across the border, this would imply that foreign behavior adversely affects animals located there *and* that another state's reputation is damaged by this behavior. The paradox is that accepting these reputational effects as a basis of jurisdiction requires some sort identifiable link to the state in question, to show that it is more affected than any other state. Reputational damage might occur where animals abused abroad were transported there from the regulating state, or where a formerly national corporation now conducts abhorrent animal experiments abroad, or in any other case with significant proximity to the state exercising jurisdiction. The New Zealand Animal Welfare Act (AWA), which obliges exporters to ensure the welfare of animals shipped abroad,[157] states, to this effect, "[t]he purpose of this Part is to *protect the welfare of animals being exported* from New Zealand and to *protect New Zealand's reputation* as a responsible exporter of animals and products made from animals."[158] New Zealand is thus in some sense already using the reputational effects principle as a basis for extending animal laws beyond its territory, at least until the animals arrive on foreign territory.

Extending jurisdiction based on reputational effects is subject to a host of caveats. There is an almost unlimited range of foreign behavior that could affect a state's reputation, so jurisdiction based on reputational effects could easily take on a universal-like dimension. This variant of the effects principle also harbors the potential for abuse. Reputations, values, and sensitivities vary widely across states. What one state perceives as offending, another does not. Extending the effects principle to reputational damages could easily lead states to impose their public morals disproportionately and unlawfully on other cultures or nations. According to Zerk, this variant of the effects principle would therefore not stand a chance under international law.[159]

The only way the international community might accept the reputational variant of the effects principle is if its scope of application is restricted. Domestic legislators, courts, and administrative bodies limit the (classic) effects principle to substantial, direct, and foreseeable effects.[160] An effect is substantial if it represents an injury to a state's entire market or

---

[155] Kiobel v. Royal Dutch Petroleum, 133 S. Ct. 1659, 1671 (2013) (Breyer, J., concurring) (U.S.).

[156] Ryngaert, Jurisdiction over Antitrust Violations 19 (2008).

[157] Animal Welfare Act (N.Z.), § 45.

[158] *Id.* § 38 (emphasis added).

[159] Zerk, Multinationals and Corporate Social Responsibility 110–1 (2008).

[160] *See* Hartford Fire Insurance Co. v. California, 509 U.S. 764 (1993) (U.S.); U.S. Department of Justice, Antitrust Enforcement Guidelines, paras. 3.1, 3.12 (Apr. 1995) [DOJ, Antitrust Enforcement Guidelines (1995)]; Commission Notice, Guidelines on the Effect on Trade Concept Contained in Articles 81 and 82 of

to its competition more generally, but not to individual parties.[161] The effect must also be "sufficiently large to present a cognizable injury,"[162] as the US Supreme Court asserted in *Timberlane*. Next, the effect must be direct; there must be a close causal connection between foreign activities and the effects felt on domestic territory.[163] Finally, the effect must have been reasonably foreseeable to those who caused it. Persons who cause damaging effects on foreign territory are seen as having submitted themselves to the jurisdiction of that state, at least to the extent that they could foresee the consequences of their conduct.[164]

Even if it is narrowed down by reasonable limits, whether states will accept this variant of the effects principle largely depends on whether they can find a consensus on *the need* to cover reputational effects and *the extent* to which behavior is condemned on this basis.[165] The more vehemently the international community rejects acts committed against animals, the more likely it is that effects-based jurisdiction over animals abroad will be considered legal.

B. EFFECTS PRINCIPLE IN THE EXTRATERRITORIALITY FRAMEWORK

In the extraterritoriality framework, the *lex ferenda* effects principle relies on reputational effects felt on domestic territory, so the anchor point is intraterritorial. The content it regulates lies abroad and relates to animals, so the norm is a type γ_2 regulation.

§4 Interim Conclusion

The law of jurisdiction as we know it today has been developed without concern for animals. Jurisdiction is exercised over them by targeting their owner, their caretaker, or their perpetrator, but animals themselves are not subject to jurisdiction. By relying only on indirect jurisdictional links to animals, animals remain invisible to the law of jurisdiction, which reinforces the view that they do not matter. This is at odds with the broader societal consensus that animals are different from ordinary objects, and that they are sentient, conscious, and relational beings who have their own lives to live. In order to align these insights with the

---

the Treaty (2004/C 101/07), 2004 O.J. (C 101) 81, para. 92 (substantial), para. 24 (direct or indirect), para. 23 (foreseeable). Ryngaert considers the test of direct, substantial, and reasonably foreseeable effects to be a norm of customary international law: Ryngaert, JURISDICTION OVER ANTITRUST VIOLATIONS 58 (2008).

[161] McGlinchy v. Shell Chemical Co., 845 F.2d 802, 812–3 (9th Cir. 1988) (U.S.), confirmed in McElderry v. Cathay Pacific Airways, 678 F. Supp. 1071, 1078 (S.D.N.Y. 1988) (U.S.).

[162] Timberlane Lumber Co. v. Bank of America, 549 F.2d 597, 613 (9th Cir. 1976) (U.S.).

[163] Minn-Chem, Inc. v. Agrium, Inc., 683 F.3d 845, 857 (7th Cir. 2012) (U.S.); United States v. LSL Biotechnologies et al., 379 F.3d 674, 680 (9th Cir. 2004) (U.S.); DOJ, Antitrust Enforcement Guidelines, para. 3.12 (1995); Florian Wagner-von Papp, *Competition Law, Extraterritoriality & Bilateral Agreements*, *in* RESEARCH HANDBOOK ON INTERNATIONAL COMPETITION LAW 29 (2012).

[164] Foreign Trade Antitrust Improvements Act [FTAIA], 15 U.S.C. § 6a para. 1 (U.S.); Commission Notice, Guidelines on the Effect on Trade Concept Contained in Articles 81 and 82 of the Treaty (2004/C 101/07), 2004 O.J. (C 101) 81, para. 23. Meng argues that requiring actors to consciously participate in another state's organization is evidence of a territorial connection: MENG 538, 540 (1994).

[165] Zerk argues that "states have exhibited greater consistency and cooperation regarding conduct that they can agree is pernicious or immoral [. . .]." (ZERK, EXTRATERRITORIAL JURISDICTION 8 (2010)).

law of jurisdiction, I took a critical positivist approach and proposed more robust and direct jurisdictional links to animals that could be used *de lege ferenda*.

I first proposed a variant of the passive personality principle. If animals are viewed as nationals of a state, their home state has the power to try foreigners for offenses committed against national animals abroad. Philosophers have convincingly argued that animals should be recognized as citizens of a state; I argued herein that a more modest claim suffices to apply the passive personality principle to animals. States can endow animals with functional nationality, whose sole purpose is to establish a steady and lasting jurisdictional link to them. Functional nationality is regularly conferred on ships and corporations for the same purpose, without raising delicate questions about diplomatic protection, personhood, or duties of citizenship. When a state confers functional nationality on an animal, it must ensure there is an effective link from it to the animal (e.g., domicile and strong social contacts). Once functional animal nationality is established, a state can assert its jurisdiction directly over the national animal. Based on the passive personality principle, the state can try anyone committing a crime against the national animal abroad. Under international law, states have the discretion to formulate the principle in broad terms (covering all acts done against national animals) or in narrow terms (covering particularly despised acts, like torture or extreme confinement). If applied to animal law, this principle can reduce jurisdictional conflicts, bring about international harmony, and make extraterritorial jurisdiction predictable through material consistency and temporal continuity.

Next, I proposed using the universality principle to prosecute the most severe violations of animal interests, regardless of where or by whom they are committed. Though opinions on how animals should be treated vary across nations and cultures, there is a growing consensus that certain acts committed against animals are so despicable and abhorrent that they are of concern to the world community. This consensus is embodied in the general principle of international law, which is expected to develop into a norm of customary international law. If it does, states have the power to prosecute universal crimes committed against any animal anywhere in the world. Even less egregious crimes could be tried, if they escape every state's jurisdiction, including trafficking of animals as part of organized crime (e.g., illegal wildlife trade). Though useful in theory for ensuring that crimes against animals do not go unpunished, the principle faces several hurdles. When universal crimes are committed against animals, states must agree on the fact that they can be prosecuted without regard to territorial ties. Even with this constraint, some states consider the universality principle too sweeping, so they limit it to double criminality. In this limited form, the scope of the universality principle is extremely narrow but would still help close legal loopholes in animal law.

My third proposal is that the effects principle could be repurposed to protect animals abroad. The effects principle emerged from antitrust law and allows states to assert jurisdiction over actions that have substantial effects within their territory. Meat cartels in animal agriculture and research industries are frequently exposed and punished on the basis of this principle, but this does not guarantee better treatment of animals. State practice shows that the effects principle is increasingly used to cover more-than-economic effects. States are using it when their reputation is adversely affected by multinationals operating at low labor and environmental standards, or when human rights standards are disregarded abroad. Similarly, the effects principle could be invoked if acts committed against animals cause another state to suffer reputational loss. New Zealand already recognizes this variant of the effects principle by applying its AWA to actions committed against animals abroad if those affect its reputation. The question of when a state's reputation is tarnished, however, is a value judgment and can, in the worst case, lead to extreme forms of extraterritoriality. To prevent this, the principle of reputational effects must be limited to substantial, direct, and reasonably foreseeable effects.

With these three jurisdictional options in place, states would be in a much better position to effectively protect animals abroad. Direct jurisdiction results in animals acting as independent anchor points and thereby shifts the focus from relations between the state and human individuals to relations between the state and individual animals. This allows states to protect animals directly, regardless of property rights, freedom of research, or other rights to use animals. This direct connection and the jurisdictional powers exercised on its basis promise to be one of the most effective ways to reconcile legal parameters with the growing social perception that animals deserve special consideration.

Synthesis of Direct Possibilities and Case Groups in the Extraterritoriality Framework

Before proceeding to examine the ways in which the law of jurisdiction can and must be connected to substantive law, I want to pause for a moment and reflect on the results from the previous chapters (Chapters 3–7), which mapped and analyzed the jurisdictional options to protect animals across the border. In the final section of this chapter, I will summarize these findings and embed them in the extraterritoriality framework. I then apply the same four case groups I developed in Chapter 1 to the framework and contrast and compare these results. This analysis enables us to extract current trends in the law of jurisdiction and make reliable predictions about how it will develop at the interface with animal law.

When I examined jurisdictional options to protect animals abroad, I classified them on the basis of the extraterritoriality framework (developed in Chapter 1). This analysis was almost exclusively descriptive; I showed which parts of a jurisdictional norm qualify as anchor points, regulated content, or ancillary effects. I then determined if those elements are present on domestic or foreign territory and if they are primarily concerned with animals. Here, I want to assemble and illustrate these findings and use them to speculate on the likely acceptability of the measures I proposed.

Eight of the principles I examined are type γ_1 regulations, three are type γ_2 regulations, two are type α_1 regulations, and two are type α_3 regulations.[166] Table 7.1 illustrates the types of extraterritorial jurisdiction and their position within the framework.

---

[166] Because I focus on extraterritorial animal-welfare-related content regulation, I do not include instances of β_1 (animal-related extraterritorial anchor points and non-animal-related intraterritorial content regulation) and β_2 (animal-related extraterritorial anchor points and animal-related territorial content regulation) in this scheme. These types regulate content solely on domestic territory. I also do not assess the territoriality principle (to which the *extra*territoriality framework does not apply), BITs and FTAs (because they are created by consensus and do not regulate content abroad), and impact assessments (because they provide information without regulating content). BITs, FTAs, and impact assessments can still be classified in the extraterritoriality framework as norms with extraterritorial ancillary repercussions. But because the scheme focuses on extraterritorial jurisdiction *stricto sensu*, it does not consider extraterritorial ancillary repercussions either, including trade measures.

TABLE 7.1

POSSIBILITIES OF PROTECTING ANIMALS UNDER THE EXTRATERRITORIALITY FRAMEWORK, ORGANIZED BY JURISDICTIONAL PRINCIPLES AND JURISDICTIONAL TYPES

			Anchor point			
			Intraterritorial		Extraterritorial	
			Animal-related	Non-animal-related	Animal-related	Non-animal-related
Content regulation	Intraterritorial	Animal-related	—	—	$ß_2$	—
		Non-animal-related	—	—	$ß_1$	—
	Extraterritorial	Animal-related	γ_2 – *lex ferenda* effects principle – *lex ferenda* passive personality principle – *lex ferenda* universality principle (strict)	γ_1 – subjective & objective territoriality principles – *lex lata* active personality principle – investment rules – reporting duties – CSR – codes of conduct, best practices, etc. – limited *lex ferenda* universality principle	α_1 – subjective & objective territoriality principles – *lex ferenda* universality principle (strict)	α_3 – *lex lata* active personality principle (piercing) – *lex ferenda* universality principle (double criminality)
		Non-animal-related	—	– protective principle	α_2	—

Before discussing these results, I want to show what happens when we submit the four case groups to the extraterritoriality framework. The four case groups I developed in Chapter 1 are outsourcing of production facilities, restrictions of trade in animals and animal products, migration, and trophy hunting. For each case group, I identify the jurisdictional options available to protect animals abroad and classify them on the basis of the extraterritoriality framework.

The first example refers to the mounting instances of multinational enterprises outsourcing animal agricultural production and animal research.

- A state may protect animals abroad affected by outsourcing, if the parent corporation directly acts abroad, or if it has affiliates or branches under its supervision that operate abroad. In this case, we are dealing with an intraterritorial and non-animal-related anchor point and regulate content extraterritorially that is animal-related (γ_1 regulation).
- The same structures are at play where the home state views an otherwise foreign parent or subsidiary as a national corporation (by combining the incorporation or real seat theories, if the relevant corporation has connections to both states).
- If a state subjects a foreign subsidiary or parent to its jurisdiction by lifting the corporate veil, there is a non-animal-related extraterritorial anchor point that allows it to regulate conduct that is animal-related and extraterritorial (α_3 regulation).
- An alternative strategy for the home state would be to base its jurisdiction over animals affected by a foreign subsidiary abroad on the nationality of the subsidiary's board members (if any board member is one of its nationals). Here, the anchor point is non-animal-related and intraterritorial, and animal-related content is regulated abroad (γ_1 regulation).
- If the multinational enterprise outsources animals and simultaneously violates the animal laws of the state in which it took up its journey, the home state can protect these animals by invoking the subjective territoriality principle. Its anchor is the affected animal (animal-related intra- or extraterritorial anchor point), and the addressee of the norm is the multinational abroad (animal-related extraterritorial content regulation; γ_1 or α_1 regulation).
- If exploiting animals abroad in factory farms, slaughterhouses, research institutions, or other facilities is domestically funded (through bilateral investments or export credits), the multinational enterprise may be obliged to observe higher standards of the investor's home state. For instance, under the IFC's Good Practice Note on Animal Welfare, investees are obliged to abide by minimal space allowance, maximum stocking density, environmental enrichment of cages, dietary prescriptions, duties to minimize pain, use of genetic selection based on welfare traits, and increase in monitoring.[167] This is animal-related extraterritorial content regulation that is based on a non-animal-related intraterritorial anchor point (type γ_1 regulation).

[167] IFC, Good Practice Note (2014).

- If a multinational that runs a factory farm abroad is polluting another state's environment (e.g., its water, soil, or air), the affected state may regulate these activities, to the extent that they affect its environment, by virtue of the protective principle. This is a non-animal-related intraterritorial anchor point, and the content regulated is non-animal-related and extraterritorial.
- If a state maintains jurisdiction over an outsourced animal based on the fact that the animal is its national, there is an animal-related intraterritorial anchor point and animal-related extraterritorial content regulation (type γ_1 regulation).
- The multinational enterprise can be subject to domestic impact assessments or reporting duties as regards its activities involving animals abroad. This is a non-animal-related intraterritorial anchor point and animal-related extraterritorial content regulation (type γ_1 regulation).
- Finally, multinational enterprises can be bound to observe higher standards abroad by virtue of their CSR policies, codes of conduct, or best practices. For instance, Marks & Spencer pledge in their Animal Welfare Mission Statement to have "prohibited specific production systems and confinement systems which can never fulfil an animals welfare needs i.e. battery cages, the forced feeding of geese and ducks for foie gras, the rearing of calves for white veal, the use of the sow stall and tether system for pork production."[168] The mission statement reflects "global commitments" that apply to any of Marks & Spencer's activities, wherever they occur. This type of regulation has a non-animal-related intraterritorial anchor point and regulates animal-related content extraterritorially (type γ_1 regulation).

The second case group concerns trade restrictions a state adopts to indirectly protect animals, in the form of labels, taxes, quantitative restrictions, or the like. From the jurisdictional perspective, import restrictions apply when animals or animal products are about to enter domestic territory, which means they make use of an animal-related intraterritorial anchor point. Through import restrictions, states aim to protect their public from being exposed to or becoming complicit in the wrongful treatment of animals abroad, so these norms regulate content intraterritorially and related to animals. Import restrictions do not claim application or validity outside the state that passed the laws. Because they leave foreign producers the choice of either conforming to the importing state's laws or not placing the products on its market, their only extraterritorial element is ancillary repercussions. Since norms that do not regulate content abroad do not qualify as extraterritorial *stricto sensu*, they are not classified in the extraterritoriality framework.

The third case group deals with animals who migrate across state borders. A state cannot assert its jurisdiction over migratory animals based on transporting standards or based on the subjective and objective territoriality principles (because, in our example, the crime is neither commenced nor completed in the relevant state's territory).

---

[168] Marks & Spencer, Animal Welfare Mission Statement (Marks & Spencer), *available at* http://corporate.marksandspencer.com/documents/policy-documents/food-animal-welfare-policy.pdf (last visited Jan. 10, 2019).

- This could be resolved if states use a temporally extended form of the territoriality principle. Migratory animals reside on domestic territory for certain, recurring periods of time each year, so the state of residency has a connection to these animals (animal-related intraterritorial anchor point). Depending on where the migratory animals are when the state of residency exercises jurisdiction over them, this form of jurisdiction can in the most extreme form regulate animal-related extraterritorial content (α_1 regulation). Admittedly, this link is rather tenuous, since jurisdictional extensions based on temporary territorial presence are not fully recognized under international law. To mitigate this deficiency, the regulation could be strengthened by appealing to common values, for example, if the migratory animals are members of an endangered species.[169] If migratory animals are not endangered or threatened, however, extraterritorial jurisdiction will likely not be accepted by international law, because the relevant state lacks an effective connection to the animals.
- But if it is true that migratory animals spend most of their seasonal stay on domestic territory, and if this is their main habitat, the state is able to show an effective link to the animal and argue that they are its "functional nationals." In this case, we are dealing with an animal-related intraterritorial anchor point and animal-related extraterritorial content regulation (type γ_1 regulation).
- If the acts committed against migratory animals are carried out by multinational enterprises, then a state can assert its jurisdiction over these activities if domestic investment rules, export credits, codes of conduct, best practices, reporting duties, or impact assessments oblige the multinational to treat animals humanely. Most of these are type γ_1 regulation.
- If the acts committed against migratory animals are particularly heinous crimes condemned by the international community, a state can invoke the universality principle to protect them or penalize perpetrators. This principle uses an animal-related extraterritorial anchor point and regulates actions affecting animals abroad (α_1 regulation).

The fourth case group centers on the issue of trophy hunting.

- A state can use extraterritorial jurisdiction to prevent its nationals from hunting trophies abroad, using the active personality principle. Here, the state links its jurisdiction via nationality (non-animal-related intraterritorial anchor point) to the animal abroad (animal-related extraterritorial content regulation). This is a γ_1 regulation.
- The state can use the objective territoriality principle by arguing that the act of trophy hunting is completed by the act of importation (since trophy hunters feel a strong need to show off trophies). In this case, the anchor point is territorial (completion of

[169] For instance, in *Shrimp/Turtle*, the AB held that US claims to protect turtles outside its territory were provisionally justified because the United States possessed a valid interest in protecting shared but endangered animals. According to the AB, there is "a sufficient nexus between the migratory and endangered [sea turtles] involved and the United States for the purposes of [WTO law]" (*Shrimp/Turtle I*, AB Report ¶ 133).

the act by an attempt to import it), and the objective of the norm is to prohibit game hunting abroad; this is extraterritorial content regulation, which makes the norm a γ_1 regulation.

- Trophy hunting is such a controversial topic because states resent being associated with trophy hunters and claim that it jeopardizes their reputation. As a result, trophy hunters are often under pressure from their home states not to cause them reputational damage. A hunter's home state might in the future use a variant of the effects principle to protect animals abroad if it suffers a reputational loss that is substantial (shared not by a minority, but by a majority of inhabitants), direct, and reasonably foreseeable (to the violator). In this case, the anchor point is the effect (animal-related intraterritorial anchor point), and the content regulated is trophy hunts carried out on foreign territory (animal-related extraterritorial content regulation), which make this a type γ_2 regulation.
- If the crime committed against the animal during the trophy hunt amounts to a universal crime under customary international law, which may at some point become the case for canned hunting or zoophilic acts,[170] the home state can extend its jurisdiction on the basis of the *lex ferenda* universality principle. This would be a type α_1 regulation because there is an animal-related extraterritorial anchor point and animal-related extraterritorial content regulation.
- Finally, the state may indirectly protect animals abroad by prohibiting the importation of trophies, which can create extraterritorial ancillary repercussions.

The case groups show increased use of type γ_1 regulation (12 instances), type α_1 regulation (4 instances), type γ_2 regulation (1 instance), and type α_3 regulation (1 instance). There are two instances of extraterritorial ancillary repercussions and one application of the protective principle. These findings are in line with those from our theoretical analysis, where type γ_1 regulations (8 instances), type γ_2 regulations (3 instances), type α_1 regulations (2 instances), and type α_3 regulations (2 instances) prevailed.

The fact that most case groups and principles tend to rely on an intraterritorial anchor point to regulate content extraterritorially demonstrates that state practice expects a state that wishes to protect animals abroad to prove a close enough connection to the state of facts. A state does so by anchoring persons, events, or properties to its territory. By far the most commonly used type of extraterritorial jurisdiction is type γ_1 (non-animal-related intraterritorial anchor point and animal-related extraterritorial content regulation). This shows that states seem to strongly prefer laws that use seemingly value-neutral anchors to which they can link their animal laws. They prefer not to use anchors when they are found abroad or if animals are the anchors. Together, these trends indicate that state practice is still relatively conservative and that states are cautious about using their jurisdictional powers under international law to the fullest extent. Alternatively, we can read this in more progressive terms, arguing that states consider it legitimate to use a territorial, non-animal-related

---

[170] For instance, in the United States, 74 percent of the population opposes canned hunting (the method used to Cecil): *New Poll Reveals Majority of Americans Oppose Trophy Hunting Following Death of Cecil the Lion*, Humane Society of the United States (HSUS), Oct. 7, 2015.

anchor point (nationality of a corporation, an owner, the initiation of a crime, etc.) to which they link their laws so that they can regulate content abroad that affects animals. States thus do not hesitate to use the principles in an instrumental manner to pursue their interests in protecting animals abroad.

The less frequent use of type γ_2 regulation is explained by the fact that it is hardly possible for a norm to have an animal-related territorial anchor point and simultaneously regulate animal-related content abroad. Either the animal-related anchor must shift territorially—which it can do in the case of passive personality or strict universality, or if an animal retuns to domestic territory after the wrong was committed—or regulation needs to be effects-based, with the animal remaining in the home country where reputational damages occur, too. Type α_1 regulation and type α_3 regulation are also less common than type γ_1. Rules on transport that was initiated on domestic territory are type α_1 regulation. Another type α_1 regulation is the unlimited universality principle that establishes jurisdiction over universal crimes committed against animals. Type α_3 regulation only exists where conditions for piercing the veil doctrine exist, or where double criminality is required to exercise universal jurisdiction.

Analyzing the possibilities to directly protect animals abroad also revealed the scope of jurisdiction for every principle. Principles that narrow the scope of a state's jurisdiction to specific acts are the subjective and objective territoriality principles, the active personality principle when the corporate veil is pierced, the protective principle, investment rules and export credits, the *lex ferenda* universality principle, the *lex ferenda* reputational effects principle, and potentially the *lex ferenda* passive personality principle. In contrast, jurisdiction conferred by the active personality principle, BITs, FTAs, impact assessments, reporting, CSR, codes of conduct, the OECD Guidelines for Multinational Enterprises, and potentially the *lex ferenda* passive personality principle are not limited in scope. Table 7.2 integrates these results into the scheme.

The updated scheme makes it clear why states tend to favor type γ_1 regulation. More than any other type of regulation, γ_1 regulation allows for the broadest scope of jurisdiction. Although this is a relatively cautious approach because it relies on a non-animal-related and intraterritorial anchor point, γ_1 regulation enables a state to cover many more issues (more subjects, longer periods of time, and more persons) than other types of jurisdiction that seem more progressive (because they rely on, e.g., an animal-related extraterritorial anchor point to regulate content extraterritorially).

The next chapter uses these insights to dig deeper and to examine how the various jurisdictional options can be put to concrete use by merging the law of jurisdiction with the underlying animal laws.

TABLE 7.2

SCOPE OF JURISDICTION UNDER THE EXTRATERRITORIALITY FRAMEWORK, ORGANIZED BY JURISDICTIONAL PRINCIPLES AND JURISDICTIONAL TYPES

<table>
<tr><th colspan="3" rowspan="3"></th><th colspan="4">Anchor point</th></tr>
<tr><th colspan="2">Intraterritorial</th><th colspan="2">Extraterritorial</th></tr>
<tr><th>Animal-related</th><th>Non-animal-related</th><th>Animal-related</th><th>Non-animal-related</th></tr>
<tr><td rowspan="4">Content regulation</td><td rowspan="2">Intraterritorial</td><td>Animal-related</td><td>—</td><td>—</td><td>$ß_2$</td><td>—</td></tr>
<tr><td>Non-animal-related</td><td>—</td><td>—</td><td>$ß_1$</td><td>—</td></tr>
<tr><td>Extraterritorial</td><td>Animal-related</td><td>γ_2
– lex ferenda effects principle: limited to act
– lex ferenda passive personality principle: not limited or limited to act
– lex ferenda universality principle (strict): limited to act</td><td>γ_1
– subjective and objective territoriality principles: limited to act
– lex lata active personality principle: not limited
– investment rules: limited to act
– reporting duties: not limited
– CSR: not limited
– codes of conduct, best practices, etc.: not limited
– limited lex ferenda universality principle: limited to act</td><td>α_1
– subjective and objective territoriality principles: limited to act
– lex ferenda universality principle (strict): limited to act</td><td>α_3
– lex lata active personality principle (piercing): limited to act
– lex ferenda universality principle (double criminality): limited to act</td></tr>
<tr><td></td><td>Non-animal-related</td><td>—</td><td>– protective principle</td><td>α_2</td><td>—</td></tr>
</table>

8 Parameters of Substantive Law

CONTEMPORARY STUDIES IN the doctrine of jurisdiction focus at length on jurisdictional options but they often do not describe how these options can be meaningfully linked to substantive law, or answer if substantive law places constraints on how jurisdiction can be exercised. These linkages are needed because they provide guidance to states for the still young and largely unexplored field of animal law, they help make extraterritorial jurisdiction operational, and ensure it is not misused for other purposes. This chapter examines these parameters of substantive law and focuses on four questions that seem most important and urgent to answer: Can states use extraterritorial jurisdiction to harm animals? Do animal laws need to be coherent for states to apply them across their borders? If so, how coherent? Can and should we ensure, by regulatory design, that extraterritorial jurisdiction in animal law converges toward a higher common denominator? Finally, do states have a duty to protect animals abroad, and do their corporations have a duty to respect animals' lives and interests when they do their business on foreign soil? I begin by examining the moral trajectory of extraterritorial animal law and turn to the question of moral consistency. Then I offer a guide to a hierarchy of extraterritorial animal laws and finally explore duties to protect and respect animals abroad.

§1 Moral Trajectory of Extraterritorial Animal Law

One of the most pressing questions for extraterritorial animal law is whether states can make use of extraterritorial jurisdiction not only to protect animals abroad but also if they want to bereave them of protection or weaken their existing rights and protections. For example, could a state oblige its citizens operating abroad to withhold anesthetics in invasive research

Protecting Animals Within and Across Borders. Charlotte E. Blattner.

on animals, even though the country in which their nationals operate mandates the use of anesthetics? Would an Indian national be punished for eating cow meat in India, but a European who travels to India could eat cows with impunity because the European's home laws authorize their nationals to eat cow meat abroad?

At first glance, applying law extraterritorially to strip animals of protection would amount to wanton cruelty, which the international community strongly condemns. But creating negative effects for animals abroad by applying norms extraterritorially might just be an unpleasant but acceptable side effect of, say, a lucrative trade deal. Moreover, laws that create net negative effects for animals abroad may be caused by mistakes in an *ex ante* analysis of the potential gains of extraterritorial jurisdiction, incorrect assessments of the level of foreign animal welfare, inexperienced handling of certain regulatory tools that affect the lives of animals, etc. We must therefore examine whether and to what extent there are substantive limits to extraterritorial animal law—an inquiry that can be summed up as "the moral trajectory of extraterritorial animal law." But rather than using philosophical arguments, I use legal arguments from general international law, international trade law, and comparative animal law to answer if *the law* places a constraint on the trajectory of extraterritorial jurisdiction to protect animals.

A. MORAL TRAJECTORY IN GENERAL INTERNATIONAL LAW

I. Global Justice

Almost none of the many books and articles written about extraterritorial jurisdiction analyze the moral trajectory of these laws, possibly because jurisdictional principles are considered inherently procedural. The law of jurisdiction might be value-based when it gives rise to collectively shared jurisdictional principles, and it might be value-based when it adjudicates concurring claims of jurisdiction.[1] But when a state invokes jurisdictional principles, international law appears mostly value-free. It determines how closely connected the state's laws are to a state of facts, but does not judge the motive or effects of that law, which makes it seem neutral on the question of whether a state can use a jurisdictional principle in a manner that creates or is conducive to producing negative repercussions abroad.

In the past, extraterritorial laws were used to improve a deficient situation, and in this sense, international law has taken a stand on the moral direction of substantive laws that will be applied extraterritorially. For example, extraterritorial antitrust laws have been deemed legal when they seek to prohibit actions abroad that harm the national market. The detrimental effects of extraterritorial jurisdiction on individuals who wanted to profit from the antitrust agreement are outweighed by the benefits created for the community by applying law extraterritorially. Similarly, extraterritorial human rights establish liability to fill accountability gaps and create legal burdens for individuals who would otherwise profit from underenforced laws abroad. And extraterritorial criminal and tort law criminalizes and remedies behavior adverse to common values that would elsewise go unpunished. Given its record, it seems that the law of extraterritoriality has preeminently served the greater common good at the expense of a few individuals, suggesting that extraterritorial animal law should do the same.

[1] The common motives of states to use extraterritorial jurisdiction are examined in Chapter 2. The international legal limits of jurisdiction are studied in Chapter 10.

Scholars seem to support this argument. Guzmann and Ryngaert argue that the only jurisdictional norms that should be applied to a case are those that maximize the overall well-being of all global players.[2] Ryngaert calls this the "substantivist approach,"[3] Buxbaum calls it "the better law approach,"[4] and Addis speaks of "maximizing aggregate social welfare."[5] Instead of viewing the law with the strongest link as the better law, these opinions converge on the idea that the law with the best welfare outcomes ought to prevail. Accordingly, jurisdictional assertions that decrease global welfare and justice must scale back, and those that increase these values must expand.[6]

In animal law, this rule suggests that norms that decrease global animal welfare cannot be applied extraterritorially. But when considering the factors on the basis of which global welfare is measured, international law might not be willing to accept that the interests of animals are of importance. After all, accounts of global welfare essentially focus on human welfare. Similarly, the prevailing ethical and political debates in the law of extraterritoriality take a humancentric perspective on whether or not the exercise of extraterritorial jurisdiction is just, say, for individual humans, groups of humans, or sovereign states.[7] So when it evaluates the net effects of jurisdiction on global welfare, the law of jurisdiction does not normally recognize animals as recipients of justice.

Scholarly contributions of the past decade, however, suggest that animals are worthy of moral consideration and that they should be included in the calculus of justice, both on the national and international level. Horta argues a cosmopolitan conception of justice must include all sentient beings. Humans have fundamental rights because they are sentient and vulnerable beings, and because they possess basic interests; since many animals are also sentient and vulnerable beings with basic interests, they must also possess fundamental rights.[8] Global justice must thus be open to claims of animals. As Nussbaum asserts: "Truly global justice requires not simply that we look across the world for other fellow species members who are entitled to a decent life. It also requires looking around the world at the other sentient beings with whose lives our own are inextricably and complexly intertwined."[9] And Peters finds that we must "push beyond pragmatic and conventional research boundaries, and consider the global improvement of animal welfare as a matter of global justice."[10]

---

[2] Guzman 1510–1 (1998). *Cf.* Ryngaert, who argues that "[*à*] *la limite*, a jurisdictional assertion could even be considered reasonable on the mere ground that it protects a global interest or a universally shared value." (Cedric Ryngaert, Unilateral Jurisdiction and Global Values 120 (2015)).

[3] Ryngaert, Jurisdiction 199 (2015).

[4] Hannah L. Buxbaum, *Conflict of Economic Laws: From Sovereignty to Substance*, 42 Va. J. Int'l L. 931, 957 (2002).

[5] Adeno Addis, *Community and Jurisdictional Authority*, *in* Beyond Territoriality 13, 16–7 (2012).

[6] Ryngaert, Jurisdiction 186 (2015). *See further id.* at 199 ff.

[7] *E.g.*, Alejandro Chehtman, The Philosophical Foundations of Extraterritorial Punishment 1 (2010); Larry May, Crimes Against Humanity: A Normative Account (2005).

[8] Horta 372 (2013). *See also* Regan, The Case for Animal Rights 269–80 (2004), who argues for animal rights based on the duty of justice.

[9] Martha C. Nussbaum, *Beyond "Compassion and Humanity," in* Animal Rights: Current Debates and New Directions 299, 319 (2004).

[10] Peters, *Global Animal Law* 22–3 (2016).

Premised on a global concept of justice that includes animal interests, we might argue that international law cannot turn a blind eye to extraterritorial laws that have adverse effects on animals abroad. Even under the assumption that a global justice calculus that includes animal interests will limit certain rights of humans (say, the right to economic freedom, or freedom of research), protecting animals still forms part of the greater common good. Protecting animals underlines core ideas of humanity, reinforces the collective will to be altruistic, and prevents us from exploiting one another.[11] Maximizing animal welfare abroad thus yields considerable benefits for animals and is conducive to the common long-term good of humans. Applying this basic rule to the doctrine of jurisdiction would moreover be consistent with the aspiration of international law to be just and fair, or, in this case, coherent. If other fields of law declare inadmissible extraterritorial laws that are detrimental to global welfare, animal law must also prevent laws from reaching across the border if they satisfy less praiseworthy interests of a few to the detriment of important values shared and cultivated by the community.

II. The Precautionary Principle

Legal duties stemming from the precautionary principle might also dictate the moral direction of extraterritorial animal law. The precautionary principle is a recognized principle of international law that guides decision-making processes in environmental law. According to Principle 15 of the Rio Declaration, the precautionary principle demands that "[w]here there are threats of serious or irreversible damage, lack of full scientific certainty shall not be used as a reason for postponing cost-effective measures to prevent environmental degradation."[12] The principle originated in the German *Vorsorgeprinzip*, which developed in the 1970s as an axiomatic principle of Germany's environmental law.[13] The principle quickly became recognized internationally and is now enshrined in the World Charter for Nature,[14] the 1987 Montreal Protocol,[15] the 1990 Bergen Ministerial Declaration on Sustainable Development,[16] the 1991 Bamako Convention on Transboundary Movement of Hazardous Wastes,[17] the 1992 Convention on the Protection and Use of Transboundary Watercourses and International Lakes,[18] the 1992 Convention on Biological Diversity,[19] the SPS Agreement,[20] and the 1995

---

[11] *See, e.g.*, note 69 on the close link between animal violence and human violence.

[12] Rio Declaration, principle 15.

[13] The principle was used in Germany to combat acid rain, global warming, and marine pollution: Meinhard Schröder, *Precautionary Approach/Principle, in* MPEPIL 6 (Rüdiger Wolfrum ed., online ed. 2014).

[14] World Charter for Nature, art. 12 lit. b.

[15] Montreal Protocol on Substances that Deplete the Ozone Layer, Sept. 16, 1987, 1522 U.N.T.S. 3, preamble.

[16] Bergen Ministerial Declaration on Sustainable Development in the ECE Region, U.N. Doc. A/CONF.151/PC/10 (May 16, 1990).

[17] Bamako Convention on the Ban of the Import into Africa and the Control of Transboundary Movement and Management of Hazardous Wastes within Africa, Jan. 30, 1991, 30 I.L.M. 773, art. 4.

[18] U.N. Economic Commission for Europe (UNECE), Convention on the Protection and Use of Transboundary Watercourses and International Lakes, Mar. 17, 1992, 1936 U.N.T.S. 269, art. 2 para. 5 lit. a.

[19] CBD, preamble, art. 8 lit. h, and art. 14 para. 1 lit. d.

[20] Article 5.7 SPS. *See* for an application of the principle in practice: *EC—Hormones*, AB Report ¶ 124.

UN Fish Stocks Agreement.[21] Due to its widespread acceptance, the precautionary principle is regarded as a guiding principle of international law.[22]

Some scholars caution against the principle, arguing that it easily exploits popular fears and anxieties. Succumbing to those would result in overly restrictive regulation that hampers economic and technical development.[23] But the principle helps us avoid taking existential risks for short-term benefits that result in long-term, often irreversible catastrophes that were not foreseeable at the time of decision-making. Since even expert decision makers make mistakes and frequently revise their hypotheses, especially in complex matters, we should use the precautionary principle to eliminate risks and err on the safe side, especially when these risks are critical for affected individuals and communities.

The prime application of the principle is in environmental law, which includes animals, who form an integral part of ecosystems. The principle is also increasingly applied to decisions that directly concern animals. In its communication on the precautionary principle, the European Commission states:

> The precautionary principle is not defined in the Treaty, which prescribes it only once—to protect the environment. But in practice, *its scope is much wider*, and specifically where preliminary objective scientific evaluation, indicates that there are reasonable grounds for concern that the *potentially dangerous effects on the environment, human, animal or plant health* may be inconsistent with the high level of protection chosen for the Community.
>
> The Commission considers that the Community, like other WTO members, has the right to establish the level of protection—particularly of the environment, human, animal and plant health—that it deems appropriate. Applying the precautionary principle is a *key tenet of its policy, and the choices it makes to this end will continue to affect the views it defends internationally, on how this principle should be applied*.[24]

The European Union accordingly applies the precautionary principle not only where an animal species is endangered but also where intrinsic interests of animals are on the line.[25] In

---

[21] Agreement for the Implementation of the Provisions of the United Nations Convention on the Law of the Sea of 10 December 1982 Relating to the Conservation and Management of Straddling Fish Stocks and Highly Migratory Fish Stocks, Sept. 8, 1995, 2167 U.N.T.S. 3, art. 6 para. 1.

[22] *See* Request for an Examination of the Situation in Accordance with Paragraph 63 of the Court's Judgment of 20 December 1974 in the Nuclear Tests Case (N.Z. v. France), Order, 1995 I.C.J. Rep. 288, 320, 342 (Sept. 22) (Dissenting Opinion Judge Weeramantry): "The law cannot function in protection of the environment unless a legal principle is evolved to meet this evidentiary difficulty, and environmental law has responded with what has come to be described as the precautionary principle—a principle which is gaining increasing support as part of the international law of the environment."

[23] Better Regulation Task Force, More Imaginative Thinking about Regulation (London 2003); Baldwin et al. 95 (2013); Schröder, *Precautionary Approach/Principle*, *in* MPEPIL 5 (2014).

[24] Commission of the European Communities, Communication from the Commission on the Precautionary Principle, COM(2000)1 (Feb. 2, 2000) (emphasis added).

[25] Scholars have already applied the precautionary principle to individual animals regardless of their endangerment as a species: Michael C. Calver et al., *Applying the Precautionary Principle to the Issue of Impacts by Pet Cats on Urban Wildlife*, 144 Bio. Cons. 6 1895 (2011); Frida Kuhlau et al., *A Precautionary Principle for Dual Use Research in the Life Sciences*, 25 Bioethics 1 (2011).

sum, states consider animal interests important enough to opt for precaution when in doubt about the risks, harms, and utility of a decision.

Since animal law is so closely linked to ethics, it must constantly draw a line between acceptable violations of animals' interests and unacceptable or "unnecessary" animal suffering. The question of whether animals suffer unnecessarily, however, is not only answered from their perspective. It is the result of a compromise made between the interests of animals, their owners, societal expectations, moral standards, scientific knowledge, and economic concerns.[26] The most severe shortcoming of animal law is that decisions on the legality of using and exploiting animals are often taken to the detriment of animals. For example, for years humans have acted on the assumption that fish do not feel pain, but today we know that most fish react strongly to negative stimuli and experience pain and suffering.[27] This prompts Gerick to argue that, even in light of considerable technical advances and the many conclusions they allow us to draw about our treatment of animals, the odds are high that the lives of animals and their cognition will remain inaccessible to us. Our conclusions are thus based on indices, rather than vigorous evidence. Since we remain insecure about the accuracy of the conclusions we draw from these indices, it is incumbent upon us decide in favor of animals wherever and whenever actions impair or are likely to impair their physical and psychological integrity: *in dubio pro animali*.[28] Applying the precautionary principle to the law of jurisdiction demands, at the very least, that extraterritorial jurisdiction refrains from creating net negative effects for animals situated abroad.

B. MORAL TRAJECTORY IN TRADE LAW

Trade law might also limit states in their application of extraterritorial laws that harm animals. History shows that unrestricted trade easily destroys ecosystems, brings resources to exhaustion, eradicates species, endangers food security, and sacrifices minority interests to benefit the majority.[29] In the scheme of trade law, any law intended to counter these effects and protect environmental and social values is classified as a *nontrade concern*, since it does not primarily focus on liberalizing trade.[30] Because nontrade concerns are not a core issue of international trade law, the WTO treats them as "exceptions." For the purposes of the present inquiry, namely, whether trade law places limits on extraterritorial jurisdiction, the

---

[26] *See* for details on the principle of unnecessary animal suffering and the balance of interests test, Chapter 8, §3 B. V.

[27] For an overview, *see* Lynn U. Sneddon & Matthew C. Leach, *Anthropomorphic Denial of Fish Pain*, 3(28) ANIMAL SENTIENCE (2016).

[28] If we denied certain animals protection on the grounds that they are not sentient and subsequently find evidence proving they are sentient, we face a tremendous moral dilemma. To prevent such worst-case scenarios, we should precautionarily consider these animals to be sentient: NICOLE GERICK, RECHT, MENSCH UND TIER 213 (2005); ROBERTSON 67, 156 ff. (2015).

[29] NADAKAVUKAREN SCHEFER 7–8 (2010).

[30] Qureshi, *International Trade and Human Rights from the Perspective of the WTO*, *in* INTERNATIONAL ECONOMIC LAW WITH A HUMAN FACE 166 (1998). *See also* Gabrielle Marceau, *The Future of International Trade Law: How Best for Trade to Deal with (New) Non-trade Concerns?*, *in* THE LAW OF THE FUTURE AND THE FUTURE OF LAW, vol. II, 279 (Sam Muller et al. eds., 2012).

crucial question is whether the WTO distinguishes between nontrade concerns based on their positive or negative effect on environmental and social values.

According to Nadakavukaren Schefer, we can classify nontrade concerns by the extent to which members support them and based on the moral direction they pursue. She classifies nontrade concerns by three categories: law-disabling, law-supporting, and law-creating norms.[31] Law-disabling nontrade concerns pursue less commendable policy goals. These goals are regulator-only oriented and have an adverse effect on the international legal system by imposing assumed benefits on nonconsenting parties. Law-supporting nontrade concerns encourage law-abiding behavior of other members by convincing or coercing them to adhere to international obligations, which benefits the international community without creating new obligations. Law-creating nontrade concerns facilitate the emergence of legal norms that further ideas and goals beneficial to the international community. The community might find these norms attractive, but they might be too progressive, novel, or costly to implement now.

For decades, animal law was considered illiberal and trade-disabling. For example, bans on eating dog meat imposed by Western countries on others were widely perceived as a form of cultural parochialism.[32] To this day, the question of who may use which animals and in what manner divides the international community. As such, proposing an international treaty in animal law can easily be seen as a manifestation of neocolonialism, by demanding that some countries adapt their laws to those of the dominant group. But there is also reason to believe that states have come to a truly common understanding of how we must treat animals. Any trade standards adopted on the basis of such an understanding will qualify as law-supporting. Nadakavukaren Schefer thinks that the laws underlying the *Shrimp/Turtle* dispute, by which the United States sought to protect five species of endangered turtles abroad, are law-supporting in this sense. These laws aim to ensure that other states abide by international obligations they entered to protect endangered turtles. In *Tuna/Dolphin*, the United States prohibited tuna imports in response to a startling increase in dolphin mortality. This norm is law-creating because it prompts the international community to develop guidelines for sustainable fishing. The European Union import ban on furs inhumanely caught by leghold traps was also law-creating, because it set up the "rights of animals to humane treatment."[33] Overall, Nadakavukaren Schefer broadly considers animal laws to be law-supporting and law-creating.

The WTO seems to prefer law-creating and law-supporting trade regulations over law-disabling ones, which we can tell from its exceptions. Article XX of the GATT allows safeguarding positively connoted values like public morals (article XX(a) GATT), animals' life and health (article XX(b) GATT), artistic, historic, or archaeological treasures (article XX(f) GATT), and endangered species (article XX(g) GATT). These exceptions do not allow member states to pursue less commendable goals, and no report suggests that states may adopt laws that are per se harmful in nature and purpose. The ethical direction of nontrade

---

[31] Nadakavukaren Schefer 3–4 (2010).

[32] During the 2002 Olympic games held in South Korea, protesters around the world demanded the country cease killing dogs for food purposes: Minjoo Oh & Jeffrey Jackson, *Animal Rights vs. Cultural Rights: Exploring the Dog Meat Debate in South Korea from a World Polity Perspective*, 32 J. Intercultural Stud. 31, 33 (2011): "Koreans—both government officials and citizens—accused protestors of cultural imperialism for their attempt to impose Western values on Koreans."

[33] Nadakavukaren Schefer 5 (2010).

regulation in trade law is made explicit in the preamble to the Marrakesh Agreement, which states that trade law should be developed while "seeking *both to protect and preserve* the environment and to enhance the means for doing so."[34] Overall, WTO law suggests that a state can only pursue equivalent or higher levels of animal protection when it indirectly protects animals abroad. The rule is supported by the general principle of animal welfare, which embodies "legitimate concerns or internationally recognized ethical positions"[35] that require systemic integration in the WTO framework.[36] As a general rule, WTO law thus demands members to channel the better protection of animals.

C. MORAL TRAJECTORY IN ANIMAL LAW

As a third source, animal law may answer whether states can rely on jurisdictional principles to harm animals. In order to find out more about the moral and legal demands of animal law, it is necessary to briefly examine its history and the development of public attitudes toward animals, since these inform our current understanding of the *Regelungszweck* of animal law.

I. From Property Protection to Animal Protection

Early animal laws reflect the social valuation of animals as a means to human ends. Animals that had exchange value on the market and gave their owners an economic advantage (primarily farmed animals) were protected from excessive use. The Babylonian Code of Hammurabi, the most important digest of the law of its time (1754 BCE), did not directly prohibit cruelty and abuse of farmed animals but declared such actions to be subject to restitution by the owner.[37] By 273 BCE, similar laws requiring *ahimsa* or nonviolence toward all living beings emerged in India.[38] In the West, one of the first acts prohibiting animal cruelty was Ireland's Thomas Wentworth Act of 1635.[39] As in the Code of Hammurabi, relationships with animals were couched in property relations and contractual obligations, which emphasized the worthiness of animals as capital. This is why farmed animals, including cows, draft horses,

---

[34] WTO Agreement, preamble (emphasis added).

[35] Simma & Pulkowski 511 (2006).

[36] To interpret trade norms that affect animals, we must consider the overarching framework of international law. General principles of international law (including the general principle of animal welfare) must consequently be taken into account when interpreting norms of WTO law: MARK E. VILLIGER, COMMENTARY ON THE 1969 VIENNA CONVENTION ON THE LAW OF TREATIES 433, para. 25 (2009).

[37] Code of Hammurabi, § 224: "If a veterinary surgeon has treated an ox, or an ass, for a severe injury, and cured it, the owner of the ox, or the ass, shall pay the surgeon one-sixth of a shekel of silver, as his fee." *Id.* § 225: "If he has treated an ox, or an ass, for a severe injury, and caused it to die, he shall pay one-quarter of its value to the owner of the ox, or the ass." *Id.* § 246: "If a man hire an ox, and he break its leg or cut the ligament of its neck, he shall compensate the owner with ox for ox." *Id.* § 248: "If any one hire an ox, and break off a horn, or cut off its tail, or hurt its muzzle, he shall pay one-fourth of its value in money." The Code of Hammurabi was put in force under the regime of King Hammurabi (1792–1686 BCE), the sixth Babylonian king. The code is one of the most comprehensive and successfully deciphered of its time. It includes norms on contractual obligations, property protections, household and family relationships, and military duties: LEONARD WILLIAM KING, THE CODE OF HAMMURABI (2014).

[38] GERICK 73 (2005).

[39] Ireland Parliament, Thomas Wenthworth, *An Act Against Plowing by the Tyle, and Pulling the Wool off Living Sheep, 1635, in* THE STATUTES AT LARGE, vol. 2, 168–9 (2d ed. 1786).

and pigs, were historically subject to these laws.[40] Companion animals, by contrast, were excluded from legal protection against abuse at the time, because they had no economic value. But even those animals visible to early animal laws were protected only insofar as they had market value, and their owners could not be held liable for animal cruelty.[41] Many may have regarded cruelty committed against owned animals as morally wrong, but law gave priority to the property rights over the interests of animals in their physical and psychological integrity. These first-generation animal laws hence emerged from and expressed the sole desire to protect human interests in property.

Around 1820, one of the early humane movements started in England, driven by mounting concerns about the suffering of farmed animals. These efforts culminated in the Martin's Act of 1822, also known as the "Ill Treatment of Horses and Cattle Bill," which is often identified as the first animal law to criminalize wanton and cruel animal abuse.[42] But it was not until the Protection of Animals Act of 1911 superseded the Martin's Act that a law finally provided that animals are protected from such actions even if committed by their owners: "For the purposes of this section, an owner shall be deemed to have permitted cruelty within the meaning of this Act if he shall have failed to exercise reasonable care and supervision in respect of the protection of the animal therefrom [...]."[43] With these norms, animal law began emancipating itself from the property paradigm, giving way to second-generation animal laws that provided for full cruelty protection.

By the late twentieth century, most states had adopted similar anti-cruelty laws that acknowledged animals are aware, can suffer and feel pain, and have an interest in leading a meaningful life. Eventually, laws went beyond prohibiting the most outrageous forms of animal cruelty and began prescribing species-specific standards of care that determine whether animals must be kept in groups, how often they must be fed, what they must be fed, whether they can go outside, duties to provide veterinary care, etc.[44] These third-generation animal laws are no longer limited to (negatively) laying down how animals must *not* be treated; they determine (positively) how animals must be treated. The titles of the acts illustrate this shift away from "anti-cruelty act(s)" to "animal protection act(s)" and "animal welfare act(s)."

Although praiseworthy, this development comes late. For centuries, the law has lagged behind scientific evidence and social beliefs about animals, which have long grappled with and recognized animal sentience. As early as the Renaissance, philosophers like Vinci, Erasmus,

[40] The Martin's Act, for example, protected horses, mares, geldings, mules, asses, oxen, cows, heifers, steers, sheep, and others: An Act to Prevent the Cruel and Improper Treatment of Cattle 1822, c. 71, preamble (U.K.).

[41] Wagman & Liebman 148 (2011).

[42] The act is sometimes also called "The Cruel Treatment of Cattle Act 1822." *See* An Act to Prevent the Cruel and Improper Treatment of Cattle 1822, c. 71, § 1 (U.K.). Cited as the first animal law: Jordan Curnutt, Animals and the Law: Contemporary Legal Issues 71 (2001); Wagman & Liebman 13 (2011). *See* for a historical analysis of the law: David Favre & Vivien Tsang, *The Development of Anti-Cruelty Laws During the 1800's*, 1 Det. C. L. Rev. 1, 4 (1993)).

[43] Protection of Animals Act 1911, c. 27, § 1(2) (U.K.).

[44] Whitfort notices that "[a]round the world, recent reforms to animal welfare legislation have demonstrated that without including negligence as a basis for criminal liability, the vast majority of animal abuse cases cannot be prosecuted. In most instances of animal suffering, the owner is not deliberately cruel, but causes suffering through negligence or ignorance. It is only where the law imposes a duty on owners to provide a reasonable minimum standard of care towards their animals that animal welfare is effectively safeguarded." (Amanda Whitfort, *Evaluating China's Draft Animal Protection Law*, 34 Sydney L. Rev. 347, 357 (2012)).

Montaigne, Shakespeare, and Bacon had accepted that animals are sentient.[45] Animal sentience was firmly recognized within the scientific community of the early nineteenth century, which should have had an influence on animal law at that time.[46] But scientists quickly began to avoid studying animal feelings thereafter.[47] Only since Harrison's *Animal Machines* of 1964—which culminated in the publication of the Brambell Report and changed animal welfare legislation in the UK and beyond—a renewed scientific focus on animal sentience emerged.[48] In the United States, it was Griffin's *The Question of Animal Awareness* of 1976 that had renewed the awareness of the scientific community about the lives and experiences of animals.[49]

II. Toward Pathocentrism

Today, 60 years after animal sentience gained momentum in social and political movements, animal sentience is virtually undisputed. Sentience includes far more than one's ability to experience nociception, which is a simple response to sensations. In reaction to noxious stimuli, sentient animals begin to adapt physically and emotionally. For example, they try to avoid negative stimuli and, if they cannot avoid them, develop anxiety or learned helplessness. Animals' reactions make clear that they feel pain, suffering, and pleasure (i.e., they experience affective states), and that they have an intrinsic interest in having or not having these feelings.[50] Some scholars clearly distinguish sentience from consciousness. Sentience, they argue, is one's ability to experience affective states, whereas consciousness is one's ability to

---

[45] Ian J.H. Duncan, *The Changing Concept of Animal Sentience*, 100 APPL. AN. BEHAV. SCI. 11, 11 (2006).

[46] Duncan argues that English veterinarians had accepted that "animals have senses, emotions and consciousness; they demonstrate sagacity, docility, memory, association of ideas and reason; they also have imagination and the moral qualities of courage, friendship and loyalty" (Duncan 12 (2006)).

[47] Duncan also argues that even though animal scientists endorsed animal sentience 120 years ago, they did not pay enough attention to the study of animal feelings, i.e., behavioral science. He argues that behaviorism had a huge effect on how we perceive animals' minds, needs, consciousness, and feelings: Duncan 12 (2006).

[48] RUTH HARRISON, ANIMAL MACHINES (1964). Harrison was motivated by more than "the fact that these animals were stressed (. . .); it was the fact that they were sentient and could *feel* stressed." (Duncan 13 (2006), emphasis added). While drafting the Brambell Report, the responsible committee said assessing animal welfare depended on acknowledging sentience: "Welfare is a wide term that embraces both the physical and mental well-being of the animal. Any attempt to evaluate welfare, therefore, must take into account the scientific evidence available concerning the feelings of animals that can be derived from their structure and functions and also from their behaviour." (F.W. Rogers Brambell, Report of the Technical Committee to Enquire into the Welfare of Animals Kept under Intensive Livestock Husbandry Systems (Her Majesty's Stationery Office, 1965), command paper 2836). The Brambell Report spurred the Agriculture (Miscellaneous Provisions) Act 1968 (U.K.) and the UK Farm Animal Welfare Advisory Body, which established the Five Freedoms: freedom from hunger and thirst (animals shall have ready access to fresh water and adequate food); freedom from discomfort (animals shall be given appropriate shelter and comfortable resting area); freedom from pain, injury, and disease (which requires acting preventively, rapidly, and with adequate treatment); freedom to express normal behavior (animals shall have sufficient space, proper facilities, and be able to maintain social relations); and freedom from fear and distress.

[49] DONALD GRIFFIN, THE QUESTION OF ANIMAL AWARENESS (1976).

[50] John Webster, *Sentience and Animal Protection*, *in* ENCYCLOPEDIA OF ANIMAL RIGHTS AND ANIMAL WELFARE 507, 508 (2010).

recognize the intrinsic importance of affective states. In this view, sentience is a minimal definition or nuance of consciousness.[51] Most legislators, however, group these concepts when they define sentience.

Because sentient animals consciously experience affective states, they must be protected from pain and suffering. Earlier, we have found that virtually all states today recognize animals as living and sentient beings, and determine that this recognition forms the guiding rationale of their animal protection acts.[52] Although sentience is a bedrock principle of animal law, many legislators refrain from deciding which animals are sentient. Instead, they determine that this decision is informed by findings from the natural sciences like animal welfare, cognitive ethology, or animal behavior.[53] Leaving such an important decision in the hands of another discipline may appear risky, but it ensures that unbiased criteria will be applied. For example, for years it was thought that only vertebrate animals are capable of feeling pain. More recent research, by contrast, revealed that many animals lacking a spinal cord have the ability to feel pain and are thus sentient. This view is prominently defended by an international group of cognitive neuroscientists, neuropharmacologists, neurophysiologists, neuroanatomists, and computational neuroscientists that together formulated the 2002 Cambridge Declaration on Consciousness:

> The neural substrates of emotions do not appear to be confined to cortical structures. [...] Artificial arousal of the same brain regions generates corresponding behavior and feeling states in both humans and non-human animals. Wherever in the brain one evokes instinctual emotional behaviors in non-human animals, many of the ensuing behaviors are consistent with experienced feeling states, including those internal states that are rewarding and punishing.
>
> [...]
>
> [N]on-human animals have the neuroanatomical, neurochemical, and neurophysiological substrates of conscious states along with the capacity to exhibit intentional behaviors. Consequently, the weight of evidence indicates that humans are not unique in possessing the neurological substrates that generate consciousness. Non-human animals, including mammals and birds, and many other creatures, including octopuses, also possess these neurological substrates.[54]

Animals that lack cortical structures, but have a subcortical neural network, are thus capable of experiencing positive and negative emotions in a conscious state, which means that most nonhuman animals (including, mammals, birds, fishes, octopi, and many other creatures) meet the scholarly definition of sentience (they are able to experience pleasure, pain, suffering, etc.) and consciousness (they are aware of themselves as experiencing pleasure, pain,

---

[51] Duncan 11 (2006); RASPÉ 183 ff. (2013). *See also* CHARLES DARWIN, THE EXPRESSION OF THE EMOTIONS IN MAN AND ANIMALS (1872): "A Sentient Animal is one for whom Feelings Matter." Other forms of consciousness are consciousness about vigilance, cognitive consciousness, awareness-consciousness, consciousness about actions, phenomenal consciousness, and self-consciousness: Markus Wild, *Bewusstsein*, *in* LEXIKON DER MENSCH-TIER-BEZIEHUNGEN 57, 57 (2015).

[52] *See* Chapter 2, §4 B I.

[53] *Id.*

[54] CAMBRIDGE DECLARATION ON CONSCIOUSNESS IN NON-HUMAN ANIMALS (2012).

suffering, etc.). These findings, if taken seriously, must lead to changes in the law in particular by granting legal protection to a vast majority of animals, many of which are still unprotected today.[55] The fact that scientific findings directly inform animal law, rather being made contingent on social sentiment, suggests that we are in much better position to detect and avoid biases against animals. Needless to say, also scientists are prone to biases, and our scientific understanding of animals' lives is still in a nascent state, so it is crucial for the law to remain critical and alert about anthropocentrically informed assumptions.

In the discipline of animal ethics, the law's recognition that animals are sentient is an expression of pathocentrism or sentientism—the belief that those who can experience pain have inherent value.[56] Sentient animals should be included in the circle of our morality because they have an interest in "living a good life" free from suffering, which has to be respected by humans. Pathocentrism is typically associated with contemporary utilitarian writings like Singer's *Animal Liberation* and *Practical Ethics*.[57] Singer argues that there are no morally justifiable grounds for excluding nonhuman animals from our moral consideration since they are able to experience positive and negative emotions just like we do. Bereaving them of protection because they are "just animals," so, by pointing to their species membership, is an unjustified form of discrimination like racism and sexism, but called *speciesism*. An unbiased view of ethics therefore mandates that the interests of animals codetermine a judgment on utility maximization. Aside from the utilitarian school, deontologists like Regan[58] and egalitarians like Krebs[59] support the theory of pathocentrism, which today is the most widely accepted basis for the moral status of animals.

In pathocentric ethics, animals deserve protection for their own sake. Their well-being matters, because it matters to them.[60] Most states implicitly acknowledge that animals have inherent value by recognizing their sentience. A number of states, however, have made this

[55] 95 percent of all animals are invertebrates, so law, by excluding them, leaves most animals unprotected: JEDELHAUSER 34 (2011).

[56] Andrew Linzey, *Sentientism*, *in* ENCYCLOPEDIA OF ANIMAL RIGHTS AND ANIMAL WELFARE 331 (Marc Bekoff & Carron A. Meaney eds., 2010); Tom Regan, *The Radical Egalitarian Case for Animal Rights*, *in* ENVIRONMENTAL ETHICS: READINGS IN THEORY AND APPLICATION 81–9 (Louis P. Pojman ed., 6th ed. 2012); Richard Ryder, *Sentientism*, *in* THE GREAT APE PROJECT 220 (Paola Cavalieri & Peter Singer eds., 1993). A footnote from Jeremy Bentham is probably the most quoted argument for sentientism: "It may one day come to be recognised that the number of the legs, the villosity of the skin, or the termination of the os sacrum are reasons equally insufficient for abandoning a sensitive being to the same fate. What else is it that should trace the insuperable line? Is it the faculty of reason or perhaps the faculty of discourse? But a full-grown horse or dog is beyond comparison a more rational, as well as more conversable animal, than an infant of a day or a week or even a month old. But suppose they were otherwise, what would it avail? The question is not, Can they reason?, nor Can they talk? but, *Can they suffer*?" (JEREMY BENTHAM, AN INTRODUCTION TO THE PRINCIPLES OF MORALS AND LEGISLATION n. 1 at 310–1 (1781) emphasis in original).

[57] PETER SINGER, ANIMAL LIBERATION (2d ed. 1990); PETER SINGER, PRACTICAL ETHICS (1993).

[58] TOM REGAN, EMPTY CAGES: FACING THE CHALLENGE OF ANIMAL RIGHTS (2005); REGAN, THE CASE FOR ANIMAL RIGHTS (2004).

[59] ANGELICA KREBS, ETHICS OF NATURE, PERSPECTIVES IN ANALYTICAL PHILOSOPHY 354 (1999).

[60] KONSTANTIN LEONDARAKIS, MENSCHENRECHT "TIERSCHUTZ": DIE VERLETZUNG VON MENSCHENRECHTEN DURCH DIE VERLETZUNG VON BELANGEN AN TIEREN 29 (2001). This postulate, as Bolliger et al. argue, also derives from the concept of human dignity, based on which humans bear a responsibility toward animals: BOLLIGER, RICHNER, & RÜTTIMANN 24–5 n. 14 (2011).

link explicit. The preamble to the Dutch Animal Welfare Act recognizes the "intrinsic value of the animal."[61] Article 3 lit. a of the Swiss Animal Welfare Act speaks of the "[i]nherent worth of the animal that has to be respected [. . .]."[62] And the preamble to the Latvian Animal Protection Law states that "[t]he ethical obligation of humankind is to ensure the welfare and protection of all species of animals, because every unique being is in itself of value."[63]

But pathocentrism is not the only theory that informs animal law. Some states still only protect animals based on their appearance, utility, and emotional value for humans. In the United States, most state anti-cruelty acts exempt farm practices, which has made farmed animals literally disappear from the law.[64] As a consequence, virtually nothing done to them is legally relevant, which is even worse than what the Code of Hammurabi required in 1754 BCE. According to these laws, animals do not have intrinsic value but are a means to satisfy human ends like property interests, economic gains, culinary pleasure, or aesthetic values. Laws that are motivated and benchmarked by human interests are mainly a product of the anthropocentric theory of animal law.[65] Etymologically, anthropocentrism (from the Greek *anthropoi*) places human beings at the center of all moral concerns. The idea of human centrality, primacy, or superiority in the "scheme of things" dates back to Aristotle's *Politics* and Kant's moral philosophy.[66] In their view, only humans have intrinsic value, so obligations that determine how animals ought to be treated are only owed to humans.[67] Whether and to what extent animals will be protected will depend on the benevolence and charity of humans, because animals themselves do not have a solid claim to protection, well-being, or rights rooted in a concept of interspecies justice.[68] Clearly, for those who seek to protect animals and recognize their rights, anthropocentrism is not the preferred theory. It bears mention, however, that even this limited approach centers around sentience. For example, because people who are cruel to humans often have a history of animal cruelty, policymakers treat animal abuse as a red flag for the abuse of another family member.[69] Anthropocentrically informed animal

---

[61] Animal Law (Neth.), preamble states "onder erkenning van de intrinsieke waarde van het dier."

[62] Animal Welfare Act (Switz.), art. 3 lit. a.

[63] Animal Protection Law (Lat.), preamble.

[64] Pamela D. Frasch, Katherine M. Hessler, & Sonia S. Waisman, Animal Law in a Nutshell 335 (2016); David J. Wolfson & Mariann Sullivan, *Foxes in the Hen House: Animals, Agribusiness, and the Law: A Modern American Fable*, *in* Animal Rights: Current Debates and New Directions 205, 212–6 (2004).

[65] Michael Allen Fox, *Anthropocentrism*, *in* Encyclopedia of Animal Rights and Animal Welfare 66, 66 (2010); Krebs 21 (1999); Gary Steiner, *Anthropozentrismus*, *in* Lexikon der Mensch-Tier-Beziehungen 28, 29 (2015).

[66] Aristotle, Politics, 350 BCE: Benjamin Jowett, *The Complete Works of Aristotle 2*, *in* Politics (Jonathan Barnes ed., 1984). *See* further on Kant's view about animals, Shelly Kagan, *Kantianism for Consequentialists*, *in* Immanuel Kant, Groundwork for Metaphysics of Morals 111, 114 (Allen W. Wood ed., 2002).

[67] Deutsches Referenzzentrum für Ethik in den Biowissenschaften (DRZE), Ethical Aspects (Bonn, June 2016).

[68] Robert Garner & Siobhan O'Sullivan, *Introduction*, *in* The Political Turn in Animal Ethics 1–14, 2 (Robert Garner & Siobhan O'Sullivan eds., 2016).

[69] Rebecca L. Bucchieri, *Bridging the Gap: The Connection between Violence Against Animals and Violence Against Humans*, 11 J. Animal & Nat. Res. L. 115 (2015); Frasch, Hessler, & Waisman 107 ff. (2016); Kathy Hessler et al., Animal Law: New Perspectives on Teaching Traditional Law 217 ff. (2017); Humane Society of the United States (HSUS), First Strike: The Violence Connection

laws recognize this link, and animal sentience with it, since this link only exists *because animals are sentient*. Property damage, which is also criminalized, is not considered a precursor to child abuse, whereas the "damage" of animals is. Quite obviously, there is thus a difference between damaging a chair and "damaging" an animal.

III. Pathocentrism and the Moral Trajectory of Animal Law

This short overview of the history of animal law shows that animals have played an ever-increasing role in animal law and that an overwhelming majority of states today protect animals for pathocentric reasons. Our commitment to pathocentrism precludes employing laws extraterritorially that inflict pain, suffering, harm, anxiety, or distress on animals. Instead, it demands that laws be extraterritorially applied only if they benefit animals. Even anthropocentrism tacitly endorses this view and thereby contributes to the universally shared commitment to animal welfare that builds on the recognition of animal sentience, criminal animal law, the principle of humane treatment, and avoidance of animal suffering.[70] Together, public international law, trade law, and animal law all determine that states cannot invoke jurisdictional principles to bereave animals of protection or otherwise harm them.

§2 Moral Consistency

The trajectory that impels us to use extraterritorial jurisdiction to the benefit, or at least not to the harm of animals is clear. But ambiguities persist, particularly if incoherent, biased, or fragmentary laws are applied extraterritorially. People belonging to Western societies, for example, frequently consume pigs but condemn those who eat dogs. Some Asiatic cultures condemn those who eat cows, yet they may consume dogs. Strictly speaking, cows, dogs, and pigs should all be protected under the law because they are sentient. And the law of jurisdiction should help us achieve this goal. But instead of addressing and resolving these inconsistent practices for the benefit of animals, the law often merely mirrors them. Ribbons explains with a view on the United States:

> In every state, the legislation that prohibits cruelty to animals exempts animals destined for human consumption. In every single one of the 50 states, if you are raising an animal for meat, for milk, or for eggs, you can without restriction subject that animal to conditions, which, if you did that to a dog or cat, would land you in jail.[71]

These and many other laws reflect an incoherent morality: "We love dogs and eat cows not because dogs and cows are fundamentally different—cows, like dogs, have feelings, preferences, and consciousness—but because our *perception* of them is different. And consequently, our

---

(HSUS, Washington D.C. 2008); ANDREW LINZEY ED., THE LINK BETWEEN ANIMAL ABUSE AND HUMAN VIOLENCE (2009); SCHAFFNER 28 ff. (2011).

[70] On the general principle of animal welfare, *see* Chapter 2, §4.

[71] MELANIE JOY, WHY WE LOVE DOGS, EAT PIGS, AND WEAR COWS: AN INTRODUCTION TO CARNISM, Foreword by John Ribbons 7–8 (2011).

perception of their meat is different as well."[72] Law simply mirrors and reproduces the many cognitive biases that inform our subjective social reality. Although law cannot force humans to abandon their psychological biases, it is reasonable to ask whether the law should legitimate and replicate such prejudices and misconceptions. How morally pure, rational, and objective can and should the law be? And what happens when we apply our biased laws in another state's territory where people have different views about animal suffering and protection? We may have good reasons to protect animals abroad, but different cultural traditions have different priorities and perceptions about animal protection, making this a charged and ethically delicate undertaking. Addressing these questions is essential for animals who suffer from biased views, but also because people may suffer if animal protection laws are instrumentally used to oppress them. In the following, I examine what international law has to offer in response to inconsistent and biased laws applied across the border. I focus specifically on WTO law because the WTO has had to deal with most of the disputes involving cross-border issues of animal protection.

Efforts to address animal welfare at the WTO have often have brought states' attitudes toward animals more sharply into contrast. Most states only want to extend protections to species they deem worthy of protection. In disputes over cross-border trade, this creates a paradox situation where members devote considerable effort to ensuring WTO law protects certain species, while readily disregarding the lives of others or even facilitating trade in them. Nollkaemper describes this inconsistency in his analysis of the European Union's effort to ban the importation of fur from leghold traps:

> The EC policy to outlaw leghold traps is an eclectic and somewhat opportunistic response to public concern that has little to do with a reasoned policy to protect animal welfare. One must doubt, for instance, whether animals living in the wild and finding themselves killed in a leghold trap are worse off than animals spending their entire life in a cramped European cage, even if those animals are more "humanely" killed.[73]

Similarly, in the *Seals* dispute, Canada contended that the EU Seal Regime "does not address genuine risks to public morals on animal welfare on the ground that the European Union 'tolerates' a similar degree of animal suffering in slaughterhouses and terrestrial wildlife hunts."[74] The Canadian press was less cautious in its judgment:

> The celebrity-studded campaign against the seal hunt has persisted for decades, but it has never demonstrated that the slaughter of a seal is systematically worse than that of a cow or a chicken. On the contrary, the Canadian government insists the highly regulated seal hunt is humane, a claim supported by veterinarians who have studied it. As well, seals are never confined as livestock; they are, to borrow a popular term, the ultimate free-range animal.[75]

---

[72] JOY 18 (2011) (emphasis in original). The social norms implicated in rendering the consumption of sentient animals legitimate is what Joy calls "carnism." Carnism is an invisible belief system, or ideology, that conditions people to eat certain animals (*id.*).

[73] Nollkaemper 241 (1996).

[74] *Seals*, AB Report ¶ 2.142.

[75] Globe Editorial, *Hunting for Logic in the WTO's Seal-Hunt Ruling*, THE GLOBE AND MAIL, Dec. 1, 2013.

Most states that have tried to establish or maintain some sort of protection for animals at the WTO were accused of operating selectively and arbitrarily.[76] Although these inconsistencies are ethically problematic, they are not necessarily condemned by law. Under WTO law, when a member state relies on an exception to protect animals, its policy must be even-handed, nonarbitrary, justifiable and reasonable, and form part of its public concerns.[77] WTO case law shows it takes laws that violate these demands seriously, perhaps even too seriously. When the European Union prohibited the importation and marketing of seals and seal products, it put in place two exceptions for what it considered valid claims to use and trade seals, exempting indigenous communities and those involved in managing marine resources. These exceptions, though well-intentioned by paying regard for minority and special interest groups, ultimately cost the European Union the AB's approval, on grounds of moral inconsistency. The exceptions allowed inhumanely killed seals and seal products to enter the European market, permitting the same cruelty from which the European Union sought to protect its consumers. The AB underlined that if members want the DSB to rule that specific trade restrictions are justified, they must be sufficiently consistent in meeting the member's policy objective.[78] So, although the WTO leaves it to states to define their own policy objectives, if their actions do not match their predefined objective, there is a claim to inconsistency.

In the absence of a specifically formulated policy objective, scholars contend we should not confuse public morals with moral purity.[79] According seals special treatment certainly is inconsistent when states deliberately subject (many) other species to extreme forms of suffering. But WTO law and general international law do not have the power to call these policies into question, mainly because they are not covered by an international treaty. Asking the WTO to intervene in these cases is tantamount to demanding that international law police domestic policies, which would encroach upon the sovereign authority of states to make their own laws. Hannan, a member of the European Parliament, noted this in the context of the seals ban:

> There is something not strictly rational about singling out seals for special treatment. They are not an endangered species—even the WWF says so. We do not get anything like the clamour about hunting seals on behalf of wasps or woodlice or wolverines or worms. Then again, democracy is not strictly rational.[80]

International law—unless it attempts to establish a totalitarian regime—is bound to accept that inconsistencies structure domestic law and that those impinge on the law of jurisdiction,

---

[76] Sykes, *Sealing Animal Welfare into the GATT Exceptions* 493 (2014).

[77] As provided in article XX GATT, for example.

[78] *Seals*, Panel Report ¶ 7.638. *See also* Broom, *International Animal Welfare Perspectives, Including Whaling and Inhumane Seal Killing as a W.T.O. Public Morality Issue*, *in* ANIMAL LAW AND WELFARE: INTERNATIONAL PERSPECTIVES 55 (2016); Fitzgerald 128 (2011).

[79] Raj Bhala et al., *WTO Case Review 2014*, 32 ARIZ. J. INT'L & COMP. L. 497 (2015); Howse & Langille 418 (2012); Offer & Walter 160 (2017).

[80] Daniel Hannan, Member of the European Parliament, Debates of May 5, 2009, Strasbourg, Explanations of Vote, Report by Diana Wallis (A6-0118/2009).

though there are exceptions for human rights violations and other breaches of international law. This suggests that, in principle, the moral inconsistency of policies does not affect their legality under trade law.[81] *US—Gambling* to this effect noted that members "should be given some scope to define and apply for themselves the concepts of 'public morals' and 'public order' in their respective territories, according to their own systems and scales of values."[82]

On grounds of consistency, the same parameters should apply to the law of jurisdiction. The rationale behind applying animal protection standards extraterritorially should align with a state's policy objective. Outside that sphere, a state's laws can, in principle, give effect to the cognitive biases of its people, as long as these laws reflect matters of public concern and are applied in an even-handed, nonarbitrary, and nondiscriminatory manner. In international law, such a postulate for relative or minimal consistency may also arise from the principle of reasonableness, or the rule of law.[83]

Even if the law of jurisdiction accepts and permits a certain degree of moral inconsistency, states should consider policies that protect animals more coherently and comprehensively. Extraterritorial jurisdiction casts a wide jurisdictional net of overlapping laws that stimulate political debate and encourage states to critically reflect on their social and legal norms. Extraterritorial jurisdiction invites us to ask why we should protect seals and rely on scientific findings that demonstrate their suffering, while ignoring research that shows farmed animals suffer equally. As long as states are vigilant and respond to such claims in intraterritorial or extraterritorial contexts, there is a reason for optimism. But many states fail to live up to these demands, and often, the very states that push to improve the legal environment for animals within the WTO are the very same states that fail animals within their borders. For instance, in 2004, the European Food Safety Authority (EFSA) published a report finding that the most common slaughter methods used in the European Union—like carbon dioxide used to kill pigs or electric current used to kill birds—are incredibly painful for these animals.[84] The EFSA recommended that Directive 93/119/EC phase out these slaughter methods, but the European Union decided not to implement its recommendations because they are "not

---

[81] Nollkaemper 241 (1996).

[82] *US—Gambling*, Panel Report ¶ 6.461. *See also China—Audiovisuals*, Panel Report ¶ 7.759.

[83] According to Corten, the functions of the principle of reasonableness are limited to providing flexibility for rules, filling *lacunae* in existing law, bringing about systematization and legitimacy for the international legal order, and providing room for different interpretations: Olivier Corten, *Reasonableness in International Law*, *in* MPEPIL 6–10 (Rüdiger Wolfrum ed., online ed. 2013). From this does not follow that the principle of reasonableness plays only a limited role in law. Particularly in legal reasoning, the principle requires consistency on grounds of syllogistic argumentation: PETER CANE, RESPONSIBILITY IN LAW AND MORALITY 17 (2002); Giacinto della Cananea, *Reasonableness in Administrative Law*, *in* REASONABLENESS AND LAW 295, 298 (Giorgio Bongiovanni et al. eds., 2009). *See* on consistency as a subprinciple of the rule of law: Esther Herlin-Karnell & Theodore Konstadinides, *The Rise and Expressions of Consistency in EU Law: Legal and Strategic Implications of European Integration*, *in* THE CAMBRIDGE YEARBOOK OF EUROPEAN LEGAL STUDIES, vol. 15, 2012–3, 139, 142 (Catherine Barnard et al., 2013).

[84] *E.g.*, OPINION OF THE SCIENTIFIC PANEL ON ANIMAL HEALTH AND WELFARE (AHAW) ON A REQUEST FROM THE COMMISSION RELATED TO WELFARE ASPECTS OF THE MAIN SYSTEMS OF STUNNING AND KILLING THE MAIN COMMERCIAL SPECIES OF ANIMALS (EFSA, Parma 2004) [AHAW/EFSA REPORT ON ANIMAL SLAUGHTER AND KILLING (2004)].

economically viable at present in the EU."[85] But what would the reaction of the European Union have been if Canada said the same about seal hunts?

In the last decade, the European Union has expressed interest in creating a more coherent scheme for protecting animals. In its Impact Assessment on the European Strategy for the Protection and Welfare of Animals 2012–2015, the European Commission states that it seeks "to improve the coherence of animal welfare across animal species."[86] In the WTO realm, trade restrictions should accordingly *a fortiori* apply to products derived from farmed animals, who are forced to endure intolerable levels of suffering.[87] More broadly, claims of inconsistency should not be used to reverse achievements of animal law, but must be interpreted positively to ensure more coherent and comprehensive protection of animals. Special attention should therefore be given to the many animals ignored or neglected by a specific legal regime.

§3 Guide to a Hierarchy of Extraterritorial Animal Laws

Extraterritorial animal law, as argued earlier, cannot be used to produce negative effects for animals abroad, but must ensure that it raises the level of protection or justice for animals abroad. Since animal law is a relatively new field of law, states may lack the knowledge needed to decide which laws benefit animals and which ones do not. In the following, I propose a hierarchy to help authorities decide which laws they should reasonably endow with extraterritorial application to ensure the required moral directionality.

A. MINIMUM STANDARDS

It would seem that minimum standards are the most useful and accepted method of evaluating if extraterritorial law is used to benefit or thwart the interests of animals. Minimum standards would determine that states apply norms extraterritorially only if those provide a certain minimum level of protection. Laws that fall below that level could not be applied across the border because they risk having a net negative effect on foreign animals. For farmed animals, the Five Freedoms, developed by the British government in 1965, are often regarded as useful minimum standards. In its initial proposal to the British government, the drafting committee determined that animals should be free to stand up, lie down, turn around, groom themselves, and stretch their limbs.[88] The UK Farm Animal Welfare Council (FAWC) used these determinations as a starting basis and developed them into the Five Freedoms. According to this scheme, animals have a right to:

(1) Freedom from hunger and thirst, by ready access to water and a diet to maintain health and vigour;

[85] Council Regulation 1099/2009, 2009 O.J. (303) 1, 2.

[86] Commission Staff Working Paper, Impact Assessment Accompanying the Document Communication from the Commission to the European Parliament, the Council and the European Economic and Social Committee on the European Union Strategy for the Protection and Welfare of Animals 2012–2015, SEC(2012) 55 final (Jan. 19, 2012), objective 4, at 4.

[87] *See also* STOHNER 193 ff. (2006).

[88] BRAMBELL REPORT (1965); FAO, OPTIONS FOR ANIMAL WELFARE 6 (2010).

(2) freedom from discomfort, by providing an appropriate environment;
(3) freedom from pain, injury and disease, by prevention or rapid diagnosis and treatment;
(4) freedom to express normal behaviour, by providing sufficient space, proper facilities and appropriate company of the animal's own kind;
(5) freedom from fear and distress, by ensuring conditions and treatment, which avoid mental suffering.[89]

The Five Freedoms are a legal standard in the AWAs of Costa Rica, Nicaragua, and other states.[90] The Welfare Quality Project (WQP), a research partnership of scientists from Europe and Latin America funded by the European Commission, embraced the Five Freedoms and complemented them with additional and more detailed criteria.[91] The OIE, an internationally recognized standard setter in matters of animal welfare, also endorses the Five Freedoms for farmed animals.[92] And for animals used in research, the OIE recognizes and recommends the 3Rs, which mandate the number of animals be reduced, experimental methods be refined, and animal use be replaced by alternatives.[93] The 3Rs, like the Five Freedoms, are a globally recognized minimum standard that determines how animals must be treated in research.[94]

Minimum standards seem to be a formidable method to gauge if extraterritorial animal laws protect, rather than harm, animals. They are supported by a representative number of people (and states), they have been used for years and are sufficiently established, and they are not overly demanding. But this is also their weakness. Minimum standards risk being an overly careful compromise and often end up codifying the lowest common denominator at the expense of robust protections of animals.[95] The 3Rs, for example, are widely accused of

---

[89] FARM ANIMAL WELFARE COUNCIL (FAWC), FARM ANIMAL WELFARE IN GREAT BRITAIN: PAST, PRESENT AND FUTURE 2 (FAWC, London 2009).

[90] Decree on the Well-being of Animals (Costa Rica), art. 3; LAW FOR THE PROTECTION AND WELL-BEING OF PETS AND WILD ANIMALS IN CAPTIVITY (Nicar.), art. 7.

[91] The 12 points are: (1) animals should not suffer from prolonged hunger; (2) animals should not suffer from prolonged thirst; (3) animals should have comfort around resting; (4) animals should have thermal comfort; (5) animals should have enough space to be able to move around freely; (6) animals should be free of physical injuries; (7) animals should be free of disease; (8) animals should not suffer pain induced by inappropriate management, handling, slaughter, or surgical procedures (e.g., castration, dehorning); (9) animals should be able to express normal, nonharmful, social behavior, such as grooming; (10) animals should be able to express other normal behavior, such as foraging; (11) animals should be handled well in all situations; (12) negative emotions such as fear, distress, frustration, or apathy should be avoided, whereas positive emotions such as security or contentment should be promoted: Welfare Quality Project, Fact Sheets, *available at* http://www.welfarequality.net/en-us/home/ (last visited Jan. 10, 2019).

[92] OIE, TERRESTRIAL ANIMAL HEALTH CODE, art. 7.1.2, para. 2 (OIE, Paris 2018).

[93] *Id.* art. 7.1.2, para. 3 and art. 7.8.3. The 3Rs were developed by psychologist Russel and biologist Burch in the late 1950s: WILLIAM M.S. RUSSELL & REX BURCH, THE PRINCIPLES OF HUMANE EXPERIMENTAL TECHNIQUE (1959).

[94] Charlotte E. Blattner, *Rethinking the 3Rs: From Whitewashing to Rights*, *in* THE ETHICS OF ANIMAL EXPERIMENTATION: WORKING TOWARDS A PARADIGM CHANGE 168, 168 (Kathrin Herrmann & Kimberley Jayne eds., 2019).

[95] *Id.*; Ray Greek, *The Extreme Consequences of Naivety, Ignorance of Current Science, and Lack of Critical Thinking Skills in the Animal Protection Community, Part 1*, AMERICANS FOR MEDICAL ADVANCEMENT, Nov. 30, 2015.

rubber-stamping the exploitation of animals, and the Five Freedoms, rather than providing any form of freedom to animals, gloss over injustices against animals held in extreme confinement and killed by the millions.[96] The argument that these standards lack detail and foresight is accepted by the OIE, when it states that "the use of animals carries with it an ethical responsibility to ensure the welfare of such animals *to the greatest extent practicable*."[97] If we used minimum standards as a yardstick, they would cap animal law by anchoring it to the bare minimum and prevent states from establishing meaningful rights for animals.[98]

This is neither acceptable nor justifiable given the moral and legal duties we owe animals. It would mean that we lag far behind achievements in science and ethics, and that we fail to respond to the growing concerns of the public. It is also not acceptable for states with well-established levels of animal law, who would be forced to considerably lower their standards in cross-border application. States should not have to compromise their high levels of animal protection to conform to bare minimum standards, especially when international law gives them the freedom to apply their laws across the border to protect animals.

B. HIERARCHY OF PRESUMPTIONS

Therefore, a more nuanced approach is needed, which consistently ensures better treatment of animals and empowers states at every level of animal law to make meaningful use of the law of jurisdiction. This is a challenging task but can be mastered by what I call "a hierarchy of presumptions." When we reflect on human rights law and its progressive development, we can identify certain signpost achievements that are considered necessary worldwide to create just legal systems: transparency, recognizing interests, integrating interests into decision-making processes, establishing concrete and specific standards, adequately balancing interests, prohibiting certain behavior, and establishing rights. These steps form a series of interrelated achievements and are the foundation on which robust rights are built. Similar developments can be observed in animal law: transparency in matters crucial to the lives of animals, recognizing animal interests, integrating animal interests, concretizing animal protections, adequately balancing interests, and establishing prohibitions and rights. This trajectory is an oversimplified model of a more complex socio-legal development that often is not linear, and which encompasses many other dimensions. Nonetheless, the model is a useful starting point for assessing the moral trajectory of extraterritorial animal laws and helps states to converge toward a higher common denominator in animal law.[99]

In the following, I propose that we operate with presumptions that rely on this gradual, progressive hierarchy. The way these presumptions work is that, for instance, norms that

[96] Stilt, for example, criticizes that rather than applying Australian standards to live animal transports from Australia to the Middle East, Australia makes use of the much weaker OIE standards: Kristen Stilt, *Trading in Sacrifice*, 111 AJIL UNBOUND 397, 400 (2017).

[97] OIE, TERRESTRIAL ANIMAL HEALTH CODE art. 7.1.2 para. 6 (OIE, Paris 2018) (emphasis added).

[98] Also, minimum standards risk legitimating practices that cannot be justified from an ethical perspective, including many of the current methods of factory farming: GERICK 93 (2005).

[99] Convergence toward a higher common denominator, also known as the race to the top, describes competition between state jurisdictions to promote better regulation through government intervention. *See* further on this, Chapter 2, §2.

recognize animal interests should be presumed to extend extraterritorially and be given preference in extraterritorial application, as opposed to norms that do not acknowledge that animals have intrinsic interests. Or, when it can, a state that applies norms to animals abroad should choose those that set up detailed animal protection standards over those that are limited to recognizing animal interests. These presumptions are designed to help states decide on the type of norms they want to apply extraterritorially (given they have jurisdiction by virtue of one or more jurisdictional principles). Because the presumptions build on each other and are ranked in a hierarchy, they ensure that extraterritorial jurisdiction will maintain or gradually increase the level of protection of the animals concerned. This helps states achieve the earlier defined objective of using extraterritorial jurisdiction only to improve the lives of animals. The presumptions are also preferable to minimum standards because they are nuanced enough to account for the interests of states with higher and lower levels of animal law.

I. Presumption in Favor of Transparency

When they are informed about the extent of suffering animals endure in research, agriculture, or the entertainment industry, most people are in shock. They have difficulty believing these cases are not an exception but that they are part and parcel of industries that use animals, and whose financial support through consumption makes us all its unwitting sponsors. The European Union's Animal Welfare Strategy 2012–2015 made clear how little information about animal welfare is provided to consumers, noting that "consumers in general are not empowered to respond to higher animal welfare standards."[100] Most people make decisions on a daily basis that strongly impact animals (and that also affect the environment, social security, and human rights), without having the necessary information about these matters readily available. At the same time, most businesses conceal information about their practices, knowing that the public would broadly oppose them if they were truly informed.[101] Laws have often helped businesses keep consumers in the dark. Procedures for animal experimentation are protected by intellectual property rights and the right to freedom of research; facts and figures in farmed animal production are concealed by ag-gag laws that prohibit filming or photographing animal cruelty; and property rights over animals permanently subjugate the interests of animals to those of humans.[102]

[100] EU Animal Welfare Strategy 2012–2015, at 11. *See also id.* at 5.

[101] Joy argues: "The industry knows that people love animals, and so makes every effort to keep the public from finding out what goes on in the windowless warehouses where hens are kept by the tens of thousands, living in cages that are so cramped they can never, in their entire lives, lift a single wing, their beaks cut off so they don't mutilate and kill each other in their fury at how they are forced to live. The industry doesn't want you to know how the animals live as they are prepared for slaughter. It doesn't want you to know that dairy cows are kept in massive concentrations on crowded dry feed-lots, hardly able to move, devoid of a single blade of grass. So the industry gives you ad campaigns telling you that 'great cheese comes from happy cows,' and showing images of cows grazing contentedly in beautiful pasture land." (Joy 8 (2011)).

[102] Maneesha Deckha, *Critical Animal Studies and the Property Debate in Animal Law*, *in* Animal Subjects 2.0 45 (Jodey Castricano & Lauren Corman eds., 2016); Doris Lin, *Ag-gag Laws and Farming Crimes Against*

But the notion that the public is only a victim of corporate manipulation to hide animal suffering is an incomplete one. Kelch asserts:

> [T]he perceptual distance between humans and the treatment of animals in a global civilization is not built just by corporate interests trying to protect their business; we consciously take advantage of that distance by erecting our own perceptual curtains as a defense to experiencing all the unpleasantness visited on animals in the world.[103]

In other words, the public is quite comfortable being left in the dark about the reality of animal use and abuse. Public calls for greater transparency and more information are usually only made after shocking and abhorrent revelations about animal suffering.[104] In 2008, the US Department of Agriculture gave a dairy farm the "Supplier of the Year" award even though the cruelty its workers inflicted on downer cows (cows that could no longer stand up) had been documented.[105] When this was publicized, the public expressed strong disapproval of the way producers trifle with the lives of sentient animals and demanded more immediate and accessible information about the industries' treatment of animals.[106]

In the past few years, animal law has been hampered by a real information crisis that makes it difficult for activists to do their work and keeps millions of people in the dark about what we do to animals.[107] But making an informed decision about actions that are of ethical, environmental, and social paramountcy requires the public to have knowledge about production numbers, the number of imports, subsidization policies, repercussions of production methods, and other facts. Accurate and sufficient information is also a prerequisite for revisiting and revising animal law because information and education shape public attitudes and can change societal expectations about the role of animal law. If we take animal suffering

---

Animals, *in* The Routledge International Handbook of Crimes of the Powerful 466 (Gregg Barak ed., 2015); Kelch 295 (2011).

[103] Kelch 296 (2011). Or, as Robertson points out: "Interestingly, while all people have an established attitude regarding animals (even having no attitude is arguably a way of thinking and feeling about animals), few have actually questioned 'why' they think/feel about animals the way they do or 'who has informed them'." (Robertson 10 (2015)).

[104] Robertson 10 (2015).

[105] *Rampant Animal Cruelty at California Slaughter Plant: Undercover Investigation Finds Abuses at Major Beef Supplier to America's School Lunch Program*, Humane Society of the United States (HSUS), Jan. 30, 2008: "In the video, workers are seen kicking cows, ramming them with the blades of a forklift, jabbing them in the eyes, applying painful electrical shocks and even torturing them with a hose and water in attempts to force sick or injured animals to walk to slaughter."

[106] For further details on these kinds of scandals, *see* Erin E. Williams, *Factory Farms*, *in* Encyclopedia of Animal Rights and Animal Welfare 245, 246 (2010).

[107] Siobhan O'Sullivan, *"Ag Gag" Laws: The Battle for Animal Welfare Is a Battle over Information*, The Guardian, May 5, 2014. Early 2017 saw a dramatic rollback of information, when the US Department of Agriculture clawed back tens of thousands of documents including reports, warning letters, records of settlement agreements, administrative complaints, and annual reports. The USDA claimed it did this to protect privacy, but the records were redacted and contained little, if any, personal information: Jessica Eisen, *Beyond Rights and Welfare: Democracy, Dialogue, and the Animal Welfare Act*, 51(3) U. Mich. J.L. Reform 469, 483–4 (2018).

seriously, at the very least, we need to produce publicly accessible and freely available information about how and where they are held, and under what conditions, and to which end.

The fact that corporations, aided by the law, can conceal such elementary information should be a serious concern even to people who approve of using animals and have no intention to protect them. Withholding information that people need to make informed decisions threatens the core values of democratically organized states.[108] Unless these states are comfortable being put on par with authoritative regimes, they must guarantee the public access to information by collecting and sharing qualitative and quantitative data about how animals are treated.[109] Austria has led the way in this effort. Its APA obliges the federal, provincial, and municipal authorities "to create and deepen understanding for animal protection on the part of the public and in particular on the part of youth and, to the extent possible within their budgets, to promote and support animal-friendly keeping systems, scientific animal protection research as well as any matters of animal protection."[110]

The duty to inform the public encompasses the actions of governments and of nonstate actors, including natural persons and corporations. The government has a duty to gather information about who is violating its animal law and to make it publicly available.[111] It also has a duty to ensure that there is symmetry of information between corporations and the people, which it discharges by issuing comprehensive rules on labeling, reporting, and public access to information. Where governments impact the lives of animals by their direct actions, funding, insurances, or other means, they may discharge their duties to inform the public by conducting comprehensive impact assessments, by ensuring the legal environment is responsive and by issuing critical *ex post* reports.[112]

From a jurisdictional perspective, provisions that provide for a duty to inform the public about animal matters should be preferred in extraterritorial application over norms that do not guarantee access to information. For example, where Austrian authorities issue export credits for animal feeding operations abroad, Austria should require operators to make public their production numbers, the number of imports, issued credits, and anticipated repercussions, especially if host countries lack duties to share information.

---

108 *See especially* Siobhan O'Sullivan, Animals, Equality and Democracy 61 (2011).

109 In human rights law, the duty to provide information is derived from the people's right to information. For instance, environmental disclosure established by national laws is derived from the human right to receive information. If the same standard is applied to animal law, the claim that information should be provided is less convincing. As Knox explains: "Basing environmental interests on human rights has limits, however. Human rights are inherently anthropogenic; they are humans' rights. Human rights law is ill-suited to protecting values not easily expressed in terms of human interests, including the conservation of biological diversity when such conservation does not directly benefit humans." (John H. Knox, *Diagonal Environmental Rights*, *in* Universal Human Rights and Extraterritorial Obligations 82, 85 (2010)).

110 Animal Protection Act (Austria), § 2.

111 Robertson 86–7 (2015). *See also* Peters, *Global Animal Law* 17 (2016), who argues that "the first stage of regulation should aim for transparency, consumer information, certification, and labelling." In the case of animal law, this duty also includes humane education in public schools: Schaffner 186 (2011).

112 *See* on impact assessments, Chapter 6, §1 E.

II. Presumption in Favor of Recognizing Animal Interests

Once duties for transparency in matters concerning animals are in place, it is important to give this information the moral weight it deserves. Producing and sharing information does not guarantee animals will be deemed worthy of consideration in the law. The next step is to ensure that the law fully recognizes the interests of animals. Only if laws acknowledge that animals possess interests, can they see, understand, and, ultimately, consider important the fact that the lives of animals matter to animals. As we saw in Chapter 3, more and more laws center around the idea of "animals as ends in themselves," and declare that it is the intrinsic value of animals that underlies and justifies these laws, not human interests in using them.[113]

If we incorporate these insights into the law of jurisdiction, provisions that recognize animal interests should be given preference in being applied extraterritorially, over norms that do not acknowledge that animals possess intrinsic desires. For instance, if Polish nationals act as directors on the board of a company incorporated in Belarus, Poland should oblige them to recognize animal interests when they make decisions that affect animals. This presumption is based on the active personality principle and article 1 para. 1 of the Polish APA, which states that "[t]he animal as a living creature, capable of suffering, is not an object. The human being should respect, protect and provide care for it."[114]

III. Presumption in Favor of Integrating Animal Interests

Informing the public about animal matters and recognizing animals' interests are indispensable for any well-developed body of animal law and states interested in applying it across the border. But just because laws recognize the intrinsic interests of animals does not mean that they are designed or empowered to give effect to these interests. We should further be guided by the presumption in favor of integrating animal interests, which means we must factor in and incorporate animals' interests into the decision-making process. Integration should primarily be understood in a procedural manner; it introduces considerations of animal welfare into policy discourse and legal decision-making.[115]

Procedural integration can mean either that relevant stakeholders *take account of* animals' interests or that they appoint persons to *represent* the interests of animals. Animal research committees, for instance, decide whether researchers may use animals for certain purposes, like the development of drugs or the treatment of human diseases, and to what extent animal use or suffering is necessary to achieve this goal.[116] Committees that assess the need for animal suffering have also been set up in agriculture. New Zealand's AWA established the National Animal Welfare Advisory Committee to make decisions about actions that impinge on the interests of farmed animals.[117] In India, the Animal Welfare Board evaluates

[113] *See* Chapter 2, §4.

[114] Law Regarding Animal Protection (Pol.), art. 1(1).

[115] The same argument is used in environmental law: Elizabeth Keysar, *Procedural Integration in Support of Environmental Policy Objectives: Implementing Sustainability*, 48 J. Envtl. Plan. & Mgmt. 549 (2005).

[116] Kelch 130 (2011). In the United States, these committees are called Institutional Animal Care and Use Committees (IACUCs): Marjorie Bekoff, *Institutional Animal Care and Use Committees: Nonaffiliated Members*, *in* Encyclopedia of Animal Rights and Animal Welfare 338, 338 (2010).

[117] Animal Welfare Act (N.Z.), preamble.

farmed animal welfare issues.[118] And in Austria, the Animal Protection Council operates as a special body to critically evaluate the application and enforcement of the APA.[119]

If animal interests are represented in committees, we must consider whether their representation is carefully designed and effective. Most committees that decide on animal research have no dedicated member that represents animals,[120] and if there is such a person, she or he is a minority member on the committee.[121] Thanks to this poor institutional fit, committees on average wave through 90 percent of applications from researchers who want to perform experiments on animals.[122] Because they are so few and have little or no power, animal representatives have a purely formal role. They give the committee the appearance of taking animal interests into account while merely sugarcoating the exploitation of animals. In essence, underrepresentation makes the presence of animal representatives—and the idea that there ought to be a committee that takes into account animal interests—pointless. In recognition of the importance of optimal representation, in extraterritorial application, norms that properly integrate animal interests in decision-making processes should be preferred over norms that do not allow animal interests to be considered in decision-making processes or that do so insufficiently.

IV. Presumption in Favor of Extensive and Detailed Laws

Once animal interests are diligently integrated into decision-making, the next step is determining the extent to which these decisions effectively protect the interests of animals. The degree of animal protection that laws provide can be determined, very roughly, on the basis of the different "generations of animal law." The first-generation animal laws only protected the monetary interests of owners. Second-generation animal laws penalized cruelty and abuse of animals, even if committed by an animal's owner. And third-generation animal laws additionally lay down binding rules on the proper care and treatment of animals.[123] The basic

---

[118] The committee comprises representatives of the government, specialized governmental animal agencies, veterinary practitioners, corporate representatives, parliament members, and one animal cruelty specialist: The Prevention of Cruelty to Animals Act (India), § 5.

[119] ANIMAL PROTECTION ACT (Austria), § 42.

[120] In the United States, no member of IACUCs represents the interests of animals: National Institutes of Health and Office of Laboratory Animal Welfare, Public Health Service Policy (PHS) on Humane Care and Use of Laboratory Animals, art. IV.3.b. (National Institutes of Health and Office of Laboratory Animal Welfare, Bethesda 2015).

[121] For example, in Chile, the seven-member committee only has one representative from an animal protection organization: Law N°20.380/2009 on the Protection of Animals, 2009, art. 9(f) (Chile).

[122] Arianna Ferrari & Vanessa Gerritsen, *Güterabwägung*, *in* LEXIKON DER MENSCH-TIER-BEZIEHUNGEN 139, 142 (2015). Gerritsen, speaking as a then-member of the committee for animal experimentation in Zurich, Switzerland, argued: "[H]ealth benefits outweigh and even overbalance the harm done to animals even if their suffering is considered to be within severity degree 3 [most severe experiments]. In fact, the committees perceive themselves as 3R boards, trying to disburden the animals in use without questioning their disposability regarding the actual project. Only in rare cases of poorly described experimental designs, project applications are challenged with respect to the harm-benefit analysis and rejected, giving the researcher ample opportunity to revise his application." (Vanessa Gerritsen, *Evaluation Process for Animal Experiment Applications in Switzerland*, 4(1) ALTEX PROCEEDINGS 37, 38 (2015)).

[123] *See* Chapter 2, §4. Robertson established a similar model by using key performance indicators that indicate states' strongest commitment to animal interests. At the lowest position are states with no animal laws. Second

structure of first-, second-, and third-generation animal laws is indicative of the progress of animal law, so it could be used to assess laws in extraterritorial application. But this basic structure uses general terms and leaves ample room for interpretation that is easily used to the detriment of animals. In this sense, the European Union, in its Animal Welfare Strategy 2012–2015, conceded that many of its existing laws, including Directive 98/58/EC, are "too general to have practical effects."[124]

Schmid and Kilchsperger proposed a more detailed scheme that is designed to better protect animals. They analyzed different regulatory standards on farmed animals (excluding breeding, slaughter, and transportation) in Australia, Brazil, Canada, China, Germany, Italy, Macedonia, the Netherlands, New Zealand, Poland, Spain, Sweden, Switzerland, the United Kingdom, and the United States. Schmid and Kilchsperger noted widespread underregulation in laws detailing our interactions with cows, calves, pigs, and chickens. The most pressing points concerned tethering, space requirements, castration practices, group accommodation, bedding, and access to adequate food and water. The researchers also categorized the countries' levels of animal protection. Group A countries (like Switzerland) set animal welfare standards higher than the European Union (more than four main aspects clearly exceed EU rules). Group B countries (like Argentina and New Zealand) have animal welfare standards comparable to EU legislation (deviations exist only on minor points). Group C countries (like Australia, Canada, and Brazil) have lower animal welfare standards than the European Union (deviations exist in more than four main aspects). Group D countries (like China and the United States) have animal welfare standards well below EU legislation (several main aspects are not regulated by national legislation).[125]

Schmid and Kilchsperger's research suggests that the broader and more detailed a state's laws, the more protection it accords to animals, at least *in abstracto*. So in matters of extraterritorial jurisdiction, extensive and detailed animal laws should be preferred when applied across the border, over norms that make general and sweeping claims. It bears mention that the presumption in favor of extensive and detailed animal laws also demands that we apply secondary sources of animal law, like decrees, regulations, codes, etc., across the border.[126] For instance, if a Swiss parent corporation has a branch in France where it rears and slaughters pigs for meat, Switzerland can oblige the branch to operate in line with the Swiss AWA and adhere to its detailed rules on spacing, feed, social interaction, roughage, and outdoor exercise, as laid down in the Swiss AWO.

---

are states with anti-cruelty legislation. Third are states that have animal welfare legislation: ROBERTSON 150 ff. (2015).

[124] EU Animal Welfare Strategy 2012–2015, at 5.

[125] OTTO SCHMID & RAHEL KILCHSPERGER, OVERVIEW OF ANIMAL WELFARE STANDARDS AND INITIATIVES IN SELECTED EU AND THIRD COUNTRIES: FINAL REPORT 10–11 (EconWelfare, Research Institute of Organic Agriculture (FiBL) 2010)).

[126] Because, as the FAWC highlights, "[t]he welfare codes are valuable additions to animal welfare legislation and are widely incorporated into farm assurance schemes and food retailer product specifications." (FAWC, POLICY INSTRUMENTS FARM ANIMAL WELFARE § 73 (2008)).

V. Presumption in Favor of Adequate Interest Balancing

In animal law, the issue of relativity is omnipresent. While *prima facie* demanding that certain ends be achieved (like ensuring the well-being of animals) or declaring certain conduct mandatory (like not treating animals cruelly), animal laws often conflict with human interests against which they are balanced. Article 26 of the Swiss AWA makes this plain: even if certain conduct violates an animal's dignity, human and animal interests will be balanced against each other; only if courts find that the interests of animals are more important than those of humans, will article 26 of the Swiss AWA be violated. This is not a *faux pas* of Swiss legislators. Across the world, states only condemn suffering inflicted on animals if it is "unnecessary." Strictly defined, animal suffering is unnecessary if it could have been averted, i.e., if there are alternatives available that do not entail animal suffering.[127] Because animals commonly desire to be free from pain, suffering, anxiety, harm, other impairments to their well-being, and death, no common use of animals (for food, entertainment, or research) is necessary for their sake.[128] But necessity is not only evaluated from the animals' perspective. Courts weigh animals' needs against human, corporate, and governmental "needs" to exploit animals to determine if animals do in fact suffer "unnecessarily."

Different stakeholders take different positions on whether and what kind of animal suffering is necessary. An animal agricultural production facility for which animals are a source of economic income, will favor using them in ways that decrease economic input and increase economic output, usually at the expense of animals' interest in not suffering. For example, an egg-producing corporation may argue that battery cages are necessary to reduce space and personnel (which reduces input) because they allow it to cram more chickens into the same space (reducing input and increasing output). Average citizens, however, may not deem necessary the suffering of chickens in battery cages, or feel that it is unjustified to keep them in spaces too small to turn around or move, preventing them from interacting with friends and family, or making them severely ill. Other factors considered when judging necessity are public health concerns, environmental pollution and degradation, and food security. Assessing necessity and balancing interest thus requires recognizing, factoring in, and assessing the interests of all relevant stakeholders.[129]

Even though animals' voice carries some weight in the balance of interests, decision-making bodies frequently use the vagueness of the necessity test to the detriment of animals. In *People v. Rogers*, the New York City Court was called to prosecute a person responsible for docking a puppy's tail with a rubber band, as a consequence of which the puppy died. The Court held that if the legislature wanted to prohibit tail docking, it should do so explicitly. Consequently, plaintiffs were barred from invoking the unnecessary animal suffering claim.[130] This is not an isolated case. As just seen, in evaluating the necessity of animal suffering in research, research committees standardly approve 90 percent of all experiments.[131]

---

127 Klaus Petrus, *Leben*, *in* LEXIKON DER MENSCH-TIER-BEZIEHUNGEN 217, 218 (2015).

128 Ferrari & Gerritsen, *Güterabwägung*, *in* LEXIKON DER MENSCH-TIER-BEZIEHUNGEN 141 (2015).

129 The goal of balancing interests is to ensure that all interests, values, and goals are adequately addressed and considered: BOLLIGER, RICHNER, & RÜTTIMANN 81 (2011); Ferrari & Gerritsen, *Güterabwägung*, *in* LEXIKON DER MENSCH-TIER-BEZIEHUNGEN 139 (2015).

130 People v. Rogers, 703 N.Y.S.2d 891 (N.Y. City Ct. 2000) (U.S.).

131 Ferrari & Gerritsen, *Güterabwägung*, *in* LEXIKON DER MENSCH-TIER-BEZIEHUNGEN 142 (2015).

And the laws governing agriculture exempt the biggest producers of meat, egg, and dairy from claims that they are inflicting unnecessary suffering on farmed animals, by declaring that "common farm practices" overrule any and all anti-cruelty norms.[132]

This deficiency could be partially remedied by stringently applying the balance of interests test to all animals and laying down more detailed requirements for balancing interests. A few states have used this strategy, including the United Kingdom. Section 4 para. 3 of the United Kingdom's AWA demands that decision makers balance interests by using the following factors:

(a) whether the suffering could reasonably have been avoided or reduced;
(b) whether the conduct which caused the suffering was in compliance with any relevant enactment or any relevant provisions of a license or code of practice issued under an enactment;
(c) whether the conduct which caused the suffering was for a legitimate purpose, such as—
  (i) the purpose of benefiting the animal, or
  (ii) the purpose of protecting a person, property or another animal;
(d) whether the suffering was proportionate to the purpose of the conduct concerned;
(e) whether the conduct concerned was in all the circumstances that of a reasonably competent and humane person.[133]

The claim that animal suffering be proportionate to the purpose for which an animal is used—a point highlighted by the UK AWA (section 4 para. 3 lit. d)—lies at the heart of animal law and needs to be examined in more detail. European countries widely use the principle of proportionality, among others to evaluate the necessity of animal suffering by requiring that anything done to animals must be proportional to the desired ends.[134] Common law countries, too, use the principle of proportionality across their legal systems.[135] On the international level, the principle is regularly applied by the European Court of Human Rights (ECtHR),

---

132 *See* Chapter 9, §4 B.

133 Animal Welfare Act (U.K.), § 4 para. 3 (emphasis added). This list is not exhaustive: ROBERTSON 100 (2015).

134 Alec Stone Sweet & Jud Mathews, *Proportionality Balancing and Global Constitutionalism*, 47 COLUM. J. TRANSNAT'L L. 72, 96 (2008): "From German origins, proportionality analysis spread across Europe into Commonwealth systems (Canada, New Zealand, South Africa) and Israel, and has also migrated to treaty-based regimes, including the European Union, the European Convention on Human Rights, and the World Trade Organization." In Europe, the principle is firmly established in all EU member states' jurisdictions and also in Switzerland. *See* SCHWEIZERISCHE BUNDESVERFASSUNG [BV] [FEDERAL CONSTITUTION OF THE SWISS CONFEDERATION], Apr. 18, 1999, SR 101, arts. 36 and 5 para. 2 (Switz.). In Israel, as Justice Strasberg-Cohen recognized, "[b]alance between interests is part and parcel of our legal system," which also applies if animal interests oppose human interests: HCJ 9232/01 Noah v. Att'y General 215 PD 254 (2002–2003) (Isr.), Justice Strasberg-Cohen.

135 The Magna Charta encompasses the principle of proportionality in British (Hodges v. Humkin, 2 Bulst. 139 [1615] 80 KB 1015 (U.K.)) and US common law (Harmelin v. Michigan. 501 U.S. 957 (1991) (U.S.)). *See further* Note, *The Eighth Amendment, Proportionality and the Changing Meaning of Punishments*, 122 HARV L. REV. 960, 960 (2009).

the ECJ, the ICJ, and the WTO DSB.[136] The principle of proportionality is therefore, as Crawford and Engle argue, an established axiom of contemporary legal thought.[137]

For a measure to be proportional, it must be suitable, necessary, and proportional *stricto sensu. Suitability* requires a measure be appropriate to achieve the desired ends. *Necessity* calls for the mildest means, so methods used to reach those ends should not be excessive.[138] To help decision makers determine when a burden is too excessive or demanding for animals, some states use a scheme that classifies pain and suffering as mild, moderate, severe, or nonrecoverable.[139] When deciding if there are reasonable alternatives, necessity is strictly interpreted. It is not sufficient to claim that there are no readily available alternatives to encroaching upon animals' interests. Alternatives must be explored and adopted even if they are more burdensome or costlier, or require more time and labor.[140] Finally, *proportionality stricto sensu* demands that interests affected by the act at hand be diligently balanced.[141] The purpose for which animals are used must also be legal, ethically sound, reasonable, and equitable. Bolliger et al. specify that using animals for pleasure, affection, luxury, sports, or entertainment, or out of boredom, wanton, revenge, need for attention, annoyance, rage, etc. would not be legitimate under this test.[142] For a measure to be proportional *stricto sensu*, the benefits of using animals must *decidedly outweigh* the suffering inflicted on animals.[143]

Because humans decide on the necessity of animal suffering, the balance of interests test is almost always biased in favor of humans. But given the firm and widespread commitment of states to animal sentience, it is reasonable to argue that they should use a qualitative approach to balancing interests. A qualitative balance of interests is based on the recognition that sentient beings have identical interests, whether they are human beings or animals.[144] If we qualitatively balance interests, then economic, culinary, or aesthetic interests cannot

---

[136] For the Eur. Ct. H.R., *see*: Rasmussen v. Denmark, 87 Eur. Ct. H.R. 84 (ser. A) (1984); Fayed v. United Kingdom, 294-B Eur. Ct. H.R. 71 (ser. A) (1994); for the ECJ, *see*: Case 265/87, Schräder HS Kraftführer GmbH & Co KG v. Hauptzollamt Gronau, 1989 E.C.R. 2237, 2269; for the ICJ, *see*: Nuclear Weapons, 1996 I.C.J. ¶ 41; Military and Paramilitary Activities in and Against Nicaragua (Nicar. v. U.S.), Judgment, 1986 I.C.J. Rep. 14, 237 (June 27); Gabčikovo-Nagymaros Project (Hungary/Slovakia), Judgment, 1997 I.C.J. Rep. 7, 56, 87 (Sept. 25); Oil Platforms (Iran v. U.S.), Judgment, 2003 I.C.J. Rep. 161, ¶ 74 (Nov. 6); art. 51 ARSIWA; for the WTO, *see: Korea—Various Measures on Beef*, AB Report ¶ 25; *US—Gambling*, AB Report ¶¶ 300 ff.

[137] Emily Crawford, *Proportionality*, *in* MPEPIL 26 (Rüdiger Wolfrum ed., online ed. 2011); Eric Engle, *The History of the General Principle of Proportionality: An Overview*, 10 DARTMOUTH L.J. 1, 1 (2012); Sweet & Mathews 96 (2008).

[138] Crawford, *Proportionality*, *in* MPEPIL 1 (2011).

[139] *E.g.*, Directive 2010/63/EU, art. 16. Categorizing pain of animals based on this scheme still leaves sufficient room for sweeping generalizations: Ferrari & Gerritsen, *Güterabwägung*, *in* LEXIKON DER MENSCH-TIER-BEZIEHUNGEN 142 (2015).

[140] BOLLIGER, RICHNER, & RÜTTIMANN 84–5 (2011).

[141] Crawford, *Proportionality*, *in* MPEPIL 1 (2011).

[142] BOLLIGER, RICHNER, & RÜTTIMANN 87 (2011).

[143] Ferrari & Gerritsen, *Güterabwägung*, *in* LEXIKON DER MENSCH-TIER-BEZIEHUNGEN 141 (2015).

[144] Ach, *Interesse*, *in* LEXIKON DER MENSCH-TIER-BEZIEHUNGEN 175 (2015); Ferrari & Gerritsen, *Güterabwägung*, *in* LEXIKON DER MENSCH-TIER-BEZIEHUNGEN 139 (2015); ROBERTSON 102 (2015). *See* on speciesism Oscar Horta, Matthias Rude, & Leonardo Caffo, *Speziesismus*, *in* LEXIKON DER MENSCH-TIER-BEZIEHUNGEN 318 (2015).

outweigh interests in bodily integrity, which would invalidate most of our current uses of animals.[145] This is the same test we accept in the human case, where interests in obtaining scientific results do not trump interests in bodily integrity; or where interests in buying cheap products are considered inferior to the bodily harms suffered by people who produce these products.

In practice, it is extremely rare to find a court using the proportionality principle in this unbiased manner. In a couple of exemplary cases, the Israeli Supreme Court has qualitatively balanced interests to evaluate the necessity of animal suffering. In *Let the Animals Live*, the Court was called to adjudge if an entertainment show that featured a battle between a man and an alligator led to unnecessary animal suffering. The show usually lasted for thirty minutes, climaxing with the interspecies battle, which the alligator always lost. When it assessed the legality of the practice, the Court addressed the following questions: Does the suffering inflicted on the animal qualify as torture, cruelty, or abuse? For what purpose was the suffering inflicted? Are the means employed proper means? Is the amount of suffering proportional to the purpose for which it was inflicted?[146] After considering these factors, the Court held that interests in profit-making and entertainment do not justify the alligator's suffering and that the show was anti-educational and sadistic.[147]

In *Cat Welfare Society*, a local animal protection organization claimed that the measures taken by veterinary services to "thin" the stray cat population were too drastic. Justice Dorner emphasized:

> [W]hen the authority decides to thin the population of cats by killing them, it must consider before making the decision the possibility of achieving the same goals using less drastic measures, and must bear this consideration in mind, because in any case it is necessary to examine the relation between the purpose and the means used to achieve it. This is the principle of proportionality that stipulates that government measures must suit the accomplishment of the goal, and not exceed what is needed to accomplish the goal.[148]

Justice Dorner's approach of resorting to milder means is, in essence, the necessity test of the principle of proportionality.

In another case, *Noah v. Attorney*, the Israeli Supreme Court had to decide whether the production of foie gras and the suffering it entails for geese are permissible. Justice Grunis used the necessity test of the proportionality principle to see whether milder means are available.[149]

---

[145] Bolliger, Richner, & Rüttimann 90 (2011).

[146] LCA 1684/96 Let the Animals Live v. Hamat Gader 51(3) PD 832 (1997), at 22 (Isr.).

[147] *Id.* at 41: "One who treats helpless animals cruelly shall become hard of heart and is one step away from hurling the same treatment upon his fellow man; those who watch someone abuse animals will also stand idly by as humans are being abused." *See further* Yossi Wolfson, *Animal Protection under Israeli Law*, *in* Animal Law and Welfare: International Perspectives 157, 160 (2016).

[148] HCJ 6446/96 Cat Welfare Society v. Arad Municipality IsrSC 55(1) 769, para. 2 (1996) (Isr.). *See* for an analysis of this case, Ariel L. Bendor & Hadar Dancig-Rosenberg, *Animals Rights in the Shadow of the Constitution*, 24 Animal L. 99 (2018).

[149] HCJ 9232/01 Noah v. Att'y General 215 PD 233–4, 247 (2002–2003) (Isr.) (Justice Grunis). *See* for an analysis of the case, Mariann Sullivan & David J. Wolfson, *What's Good for the Goose . . . The Israeli Supreme Court, Foie Gras, and the Future of Farmed Animals in the United States*, 70 L. & Contemp. Probs. 139 (2007).

Justice Strasberg-Cohen put emphasis on proportionality *stricto sensu*, and explained that "[t]he 'production of food' will have greater weight the more the food item is necessary for human existence."[150] Also with proportionality *stricto sensu* in mind, Justice Eliezer Rivlin argued that gastronomic pleasure cannot justify the "pain inflicted upon [the geese] by physical injury or by violent intrusion into their bodies."[151] On the basis of these arguments, the Court declared the laws on force-feeding geese invalid and banned foie gras production in Israel. The Court understood the effects of the ban on local farmers and granted them a transitioning period by postponing the regulation's annulment by 18 months and by offering compensation for losses.[152]

A qualitative balance of interests is useful for more than evaluating foie gras production, the use of wild animals for entertainment, or the fate of stray animals. The public increasingly rejects other uses of animals, including veal crates, sow stalls, hen cages, and other forms of extreme confinement. There is growing disapproval of debeaking chickens, docking pigs' tails, dehorning cows, and performing other mutilations.[153] In these cases, the proportionality principle should be applied with the same vigor as in *Noah v. Attorney*, to reveal if using these animals for the short-lived pleasure of humans is truly justified.

Norms that establish qualitative balances of interests in assessing the use of animals should be given preference when applied extraterritorially. Norms that do not provide for this content should not benefit from this presumption. Let us assume an Israeli domestic parent unduly interferes in its foreign subsidiary's business. When claiming jurisdiction over the subsidiaries' operations by virtue of piercing the veil theories, the law of jurisdiction expects Israel to evaluate the necessity of animal suffering by its detailed rules on interests balancing, rather than just demand it respect animal welfare.

VI. Presumption in Favor of Prohibitions

Some states prohibit certain actions done to animals because they consider them so abhorrent that human interests can never outweigh them. Prohibitions effectively preempt a balance of interests. The law determines that animals cannot at all be used or cannot be used in a certain way, and precludes adjudicative and executive bodies from evaluating whether animal suffering is or was necessary.[154] Prohibitions may cover entire species (the Swiss prohibition

---

150 HCJ 9232/01 Noah v. Att'y General 215 PD 268–9 (2002–2003) (Isr.) (Justice Strasberg-Cohen).

151 HCJ 9232/01 Noah v. Att'y General 215 PD 272 (2002–2003) (Isr.) (Justice Eliezer Rivlin).

152 Unless, of course, they kept violating the ban, which would have subjected them to the sanctions of the APA. This judgment is even more remarkable because the court is only allowed to declare parliamentary regulations illegal if the parliament acted *ultra vires*, or if the regulation suffered from a substantial legal error: Bendor & Dancig-Rosenberg 109 (2018). Bans on foie gras are mounting worldwide. On January 7, 2019, the US Supreme Court denied *certiorari* in a lawsuit challenging California's foie gras ban. Hence, the 9th Circuit ruling upholding the ban stays in place. *See* Association des Éleveurs de Canards et d'Oies du Québec v. Becerra, 870 F.3d 1140 (9th Cir. 2017) (U.S.) and SCOTUSblog, Association des Éleveurs de Canards et d'Oies du Québec v. Becerra, *available at* http://www.scotusblog.com/case-files/cases/association-des-eleveurs-de-canards-et-doies-du-quebec-v-becerra/ (last visited. Jan. 10, 2019).

153 *See* Amelia Cornish, David Raubenheimer, & Paul McGreevy, *What We Know about the Public's Level of Concern for Farm Animal Welfare in Food Production in Developed Countries*, 6(11) ANIMALS 74 (2016).

154 BOLLIGER, RICHNER, & RÜTTIMANN 82 (2011).

on owning dolphins, for instance)[155] or they may prohibit certain practices on animals (for example, force-feeding geese).

Prohibitions often reflect a society's strongest moral sentiments about the treatment of animals. For the European Union, for example, clubbing baby seals to sell their fur is not justifiable under any circumstances. Prohibitions are an extremely important regulatory tool in animal law, because they, in essence, posit that animals have a certain sphere of bodily or mental integrity that is inaccessible to humans. Due to their ethical and social paramountcy, laws that prohibit certain actions, uses, or entire species from being used, shall be presumed to apply extraterritorially and given preference over laws that legitimize the use of animals.

VII. Presumption in Favor of Animal Rights

Section 85 para. 1 of New Zealand's AWA provides that "[n]o person may carry out any research, testing, or teaching involving the use of a non-human hominid unless such use has first been approved by the Director-General and the research, testing, or teaching is carried out in accordance with any conditions imposed by the Director-General."[156] This norm can be regarded as prohibiting the use of hominids for research, testing, or teaching. But some scholars consider it a right of hominids to life and bodily and mental integrity. Wagman and Liebman argue that "the ban on certain conduct seems to grant the affected animals the 'right' to be free of such conduct."[157] If we do consider freedom rights the flip side of prohibitions, then many more states have granted rights to animals. Section 27 para. 1 of the Austrian AWA, for instance, lays down that "[s]pecies of wild habitat animals are not allowed to be kept in circuses, variety show institutions and similar facilities."[158] Accordingly, wild animals have a negative freedom right not to be held captive. Or, if animal caretakers must provide animals with care, food, and water, then these animals have a right to care, food, and water.[159]

The idea that the duties of some can be translated into rights of others (to whom the duty is owed) is disputed in animal law and animal ethics.[160] A stricter view is that these norms

---

[155] After several dolphins died in an entertainment park in Switzerland, public prosecutors started investigating their deaths. One dolphin died after a techno party was hosted in the park, and others died from an overdose of antibiotics. The same year, the parliament banned the importation of dolphins and thereby effectively ended the suffering (and existence) of dolphins in Switzerland. The veterinarians accused of misconduct were exculpated by courts. *See Nationalrat zementiert "Lex Conny Land,"* NZZ, May 29, 2012.

[156] Animal Welfare Act (N.Z.), § 85 para. 1.

[157] WAGMAN & LIEBMAN 261 (2011).

[158] ANIMAL PROTECTION ACT (Austria), § 27 para. 1.

[159] McCausland takes a deontological approach, using the structural features of rights, to argue that the Five Freedoms are liberties or claims rights of animals: Clare McCausland, *The Five Freedoms of Animal Welfare Are Rights*, 27 J. AGRIC. & ENVTL. ETHICS 649 (2014). Robertson argues that animals have "welfare rights": ROBERTSON 27 and n. 51 (2015). *See also* LENNKH 175 (2012); Cass R. Sunstein, *Introduction: What Are Animal Rights?*, *in* ANIMAL RIGHTS: CURRENT DEBATES AND NEW DIRECTIONS 3, 5 (2004); WALDAU 99 (2011).

[160] Raspé argues that the existence of duties does not mean that the objects of protection are accorded rights, and illustrates this by using the example of cultural goods: RASPÉ 284 (2013). The same argument is made by CURNUTT 19 ff., 26 ff. (2001); and Anne Peters, *Liberté, Egalité, Animalité*, 5 TEL 25, 44 (2016).

are simply prohibitions. Rights would therefore only exist if they were clearly designated and identified as such by declaring, "hominids have a right to life and a right to bodily and mental integrity." Seen from this perspective, very few states have conferred rights on animals. For example, article 4 lit. a of the Turkish Animal Protection Law provides: "All animals are born equal and have a right to life within the framework of the provisions of this Law."[161] But Turkey's overall level of animal protection may make us wonder if we can take these rights at face value. The Israeli Supreme Court seems more committed to the idea of animal rights. In confirming the permanent revocation of a veterinarian's license for gross negligence in performing surgery on animals, the Court noted that "the freedom of occupation and income of the appellant are rights and interests deserving protection, but they are not absolute rights and must be balanced against conflicting interests and rights, including the rights of animals to receive professional, appropriate, and dedicated medical treatment."[162] In another case, the Court held that limitations on the destruction of stray cats express "the emphasis placed on the animals' right to live."[163] More recently, the Court explained in detail what it understands by animal rights:

> [I]n discussing the prerogatives of the local authorities regarding the destruction of animals, we must bear in mind the right of animals to live. Even if this right is not directly enshrined in Israeli legislation, it is part of our culture and of an inner sense, ethical and utilitarian alike, regarding the obligation and the need to protect all creation that has a living spirit. The starting point of the legislation that touches upon the right of animals to live is that this right exists and is protected in our legal system.[164]

In India, the judiciary is even more outspoken about animal rights. Indian courts frequently invoke animal rights, as prominently done in *N.R. Nair et al. v. Union of India*. In this case, the High Court of Kerala found:

> [I]t is not only our fundamental duty to show compassion to our animal friends, but also to recognise and protect their rights. [. . .] In our considered opinion; legal rights shall not be the exclusive preserve of the humans which has to be extended beyond people thereby dismantling the thick legal wall with humans all on one side and all non-human animals on the other side. While the law currently protects wild life and endangered species from extinction, animals are denied rights, an anachronism which must necessarily change.[165]

Minority countries have yet to catch up with these legal developments, according to which animals have interests in living and enjoying bodily and mental integrity that deserve more

---

[161] Animal Protection Law (Turk.), art. 4 lit. a.

[162] LCA 4217/12 Mamut v. Ministry of Agriculture, para. 8 (2012) (Isr.).

[163] LCA 537/08 Kagan v. Unicol, para. 5 (2008) (Isr.).

[164] HCJ 6446/96 Cat Welfare Society v. Arad Municipality IsrSC 55(1) 769, para. 5 (1996) (Isr.). *See further* Bendor & Dancig-Rosenberg 103, fn. 18 (2018).

[165] N.R. Nair et al. v. Union of India (UOI) et al., AIR 2000 Ker 340 (India). *But see also* People for Animals et al. v. State of Goa et al., Writ Petition No. 347 of 1996 (HC Bombay 1997) (India).

than perfunctory consideration and must be respected as robust rights. Scholars around the world have demonstrated the risks of legislation that endow humans with rights (e.g., the right to research, right to art, the right to property, etc.), while providing only protections to animals (e.g., protection from abuse or unnecessary suffering). This imbalance is not just about semantics. When confronted with rights in a balance of interests, protections are effectively undermined because they are a weaker legal tool. Instead of balancing interests, the balance is performed by reference to the legal tools that encapsulate the interests. When rights and protections clash this way, protections never win. As a consequence, balancing animal interests against human interests, within the current parameter, is effectively superfluous because the bias is structural.[166]

Establishing rights for animals could remedy the balance of interests test and thereby fundamentally transform animal law. Animal rights are those rare tools that could ensure human and animal interests enter the balance of interests test without bias, giving rise to a qualitative balance of interests. As Peters explains, "animal rights would allow a fair balancing in which the proper value of fundamental animal interests (such as the interest to live) could be integrated. Animal rights would therefore preclude the current routine sacrifice of fundamental animal interests in favour of trite human interests."[167]

Like human rights, the rights of animals may be violated in exceptional and clearly defined circumstances. In the European tradition, rights can justifiably be violated if there is a legal basis for the infringement, if public interests or the protection of fundamental rights of third parties justify the violation, and if the violation is proportional to the ends desired.[168] Despite their violability (albeit limited), rights set much higher standards than protections for violations of the interests they encapsulate. Rights also respect that rights holders possess certain core interests that may not be impaired under any circumstances. This core essence grants animals a sphere of immunity and underlines the much-needed ethos that animals are not "there for us."

Unlike prohibitions that are specific and context-dependent, rights operate more broadly and are less determinate, granting advantages to rights holders because rights are applicable in myriad situations.[169] And unlike mere protections, rights render the infringement of animals' interests actionable. As rights holders, animals have the right to sue perpetrators, or the right to have humans sue on their behalf. This considerably adds to the effectiveness of animal law, because only the enforced duty of others to respect the right in question renders its worthiness palpable. This is the "reaction-constraining" function of rights as liberty rights.[170]

---

[166] Peters, *Liberté, Egalité, Animalité* 49 (2016).

[167] *Id.*

[168] Raffael Fasel et al., Fundamental Rights for Primates, Policy Paper 6 (Sentience Politics, Apr. 2016), *available at* https://ea-foundation.org/files/Fundamental-Rights-for-Primates.pdf (last visited Jan. 10, 2019).

[169] This is what Peters calls the "tendency to overshoot": Peters, *Liberté, Egalité, Animalité* 51 (2016).

[170] Applied to Hohfeld's table of rights, the rights enjoyed by animals would not be limited to liberty rights (right holders enjoy the liberty to do what they please without having a corollary duty). Rather, animals shall have claim rights that entail certain duties to respect and protect their life, bodily liberty, and integrity. These rights have to be actionable and enforceable or they would be of as little use as current protections. *See* William A. Edmundson, *Do Animals Need Rights?*, 22 J. POL. PHIL. 15 (2014). *See* on the Hohfeldian analysis of legal

Ethicists have long made the case for legal rights of animals on the basis of moral rights, arguing that animals have a moral claim to be recognized as rights holders and be granted rights. In Regan's view, animals' right to just treatment derives from the duty of justice, which is an unacquired and basic right.[171] For Wise and Francione, the principles of liberty and equality demand we consider the moral value of beings other than human. While equality demands that like be treated alike, liberty entitles individuals to be treated commensurate with their abilities.[172] Whatever basis we use to establish animal rights, the challenge is to bring justice into legal processes "by establishing a default position that animals are innately entitled to the protection of their bodily and mental integrity."[173]

In sum, rights confer more power on rights holders than protections confer on their recipients. Rights require special justification, give effective weight to animal interests in balancing tests, operate broadly, and have an inviolable core content. Rights habituate us to new ethical boundaries, but, as Donaldson and Kymlicka point out, "achieving legal rights on paper is just one stage, not the end, of the political struggle."[174] Until this is the case, jurisdictions that have introduced animal rights should give these rights preference in being applied extraterritorially. For example, if Argentina introduces basic rights to life and bodily and mental integrity for whales, it should protect these rights extraterritorially wherever its whales travel. From the perspective of international law, Argentina's claims can be based on the functional nationality it confers on whales and the passive personality principle that enables it to protect its national whales across borders.

§4 Duty to Protect and Respect Animals Across the Border

So far, the guiding parameters for extraterritorial animal law were all based on the premise that a state has the *authority* to make use of jurisdictional options to protect animals. When we look to other fields of law that practice extraterritoriality, like human rights law, an increasingly common claim is that states are under a *duty* to apply laws across the border. Does this duty also exist in animal law?

---

rights, Wesley Newcomb Hohfeld, Fundamental Legal Conceptions as Applied in Judicial Reasoning 64 (1919);

171 Regan, The Case for Animal Rights 269–80 (2004).

172 Steven M. Wise, *An Argument for the Basic Legal Rights of Farmed Animals*, 106 Mich. L. Rev. 133, 134 (2008); Gary L. Francione, *Abolitionismus*, *in* Lexikon der Mensch-Tier-Beziehungen 13 (2015).

173 Cunniff & Kramer, *Developments in Animal Law*, *in* The Global Guide to Animal Protection 231 (2013). Some states may be more inclined to choose prohibitions over rights, because formalized rights do not work well in some cultures: Paul Waldau, *Second Wave Animal Law and the Arrival of Animal Studies*, *in* Animal Law and Welfare: International Perspectives 11, 18 (2016).

174 Sue Donaldson & Will Kymlicka, *Rights*, *in* Critical Terms for Animal Studies 340–336, 333 (Lori Gruen ed., 2018).

A. LEARNING FROM THE "PROTECT, RESPECT AND REMEDY" FRAMEWORK

Extraterritorial jurisdiction is a hotly debated issue in human rights law. Although human rights are universal, efforts to implement and enforce human rights meet with the same global obstacles that animal law currently struggles to overcome:

> [. . .] States, particularly some developing countries, may lack the institutional capacity to enforce national laws and regulations against transnational firms doing business in their territory even when the will is there, or they may feel constrained from doing so by having to compete internationally for investment. Home States of transnational firms may be reluctant to regulate against overseas harm by these firms because the permissible scope of national regulation with extraterritorial effect remains poorly understood, or out of concern that those firms might lose investment opportunities or relocate their headquarters.[175]

As in animal law, the extraterritoriality debate in human rights law tries to tackle these trans-border issues by ascertaining whether and when states can prescribe law extraterritorially. But unlike animal law that is solely dealing with the question of whether states are *entitled* to exercise jurisdiction across the border, human rights law also deals with the more specific question of whether states are *obliged* to protect people against human rights violations abroad.[176]

The UN has been at the forefront of refining, promoting, and implementing extraterritorial human rights obligations. In June 2008, UN Special Representative of the Secretary-General (SRSG) John Ruggie proposed the "Protect, Respect and Remedy" framework to the UN Human Rights Council, which rests on the state duty to protect against human rights abuses, the corporate responsibility to respect human rights, and effective access to remedies.[177] The framework is grounded in the preamble to the third recital of the UDHR, which reminds peoples, nations, individuals, and organs of society to constantly keep the promotion of human rights in mind.[178] Although the UN framework does not create binding duties, it was widely hailed as making great progress toward filling cross-border governance gaps that account for human rights violations.[179] As a continuation of this success, the SRSG issued the "Guiding Principles on Business and Human Rights" under his extended mandate in 2011, which are accepted as soft law.[180] A detailed examination of the framework should reveal if and, possibly, how it can be made fruitful for animal law.

---

[175] *Protect, Respect and Remedy Framework* ¶ 14–5.

[176] *E.g.*, DA COSTA (2013); DE SCHUTTER (2006); MILANOVIC (2011); LANGFORD ET AL. EDS. (2013); McCorquodale & Simons (2007); ESCR-NET (2014); ZERK, EXTRATERRITORIAL JURISDICTION (2010).

[177] *Protect, Respect and Remedy Framework*.

[178] G.A. Res. 217 A (III), U.N. GAOR 3rd Sess., Universal Declaration of Human Rights (UDHR), U.N. Doc. A/RES/810 (Dec. 10, 1948), preamble.

[179] *Protect, Respect and Remedy Framework* ¶ 33. For an impact analysis of the framework, *see* Astrid Sanders, *The Impact of the "Ruggie Framework" and the "United Nations Guiding Principles on Business and Human Rights" on Transnational Human Rights Litigation*, *in* THE BUSINESS AND HUMAN RIGHTS LANDSCAPE: MOVING FORWARD, LOOKING BACK 288 (Jena Martin & Karen E. Bravo eds., 2016).

[180] *Guiding Principles on Business and Human Rights. See also* Christine Kaufmann, *Konzernverantwortungsinitiative: Grenzenlose Verantwortlichkeit?*, 1 SZW/RSDA 45, 46 (2016).

The framework's first pillar, the *state duty to protect*, is based on the rule of international law that states have a duty to protect against human rights abuses by nonstate actors, be they natural or legal persons.[181] For many years, states were considered competent to protect against human rights abuses committed by nonstate actors abroad, but there was no consensus among the international community as to whether they were also obliged to do so.[182] With the introduction of the framework, states have been encouraged to take action to prevent companies based on their territory from committing human rights abuses abroad.[183] The later issued *Guiding Principles* emphasized that "[t]here are strong policy reasons for home States to set out clearly the expectation that businesses respect human rights abroad."[184] On this basis, scholars and international organizations now argue that home states do have an obligation to protect against human rights violations done by nonstate actors abroad.[185] To meet their duty, the framework recommends that states prevent, investigate, punish, and provide for redress by virtue of their prescriptive, adjudicative, and enforcement jurisdiction.[186] The *Guiding Principles* more specifically demand that states

> (a) [e]nforce laws that are aimed at, or have the effect of, requiring business enterprises to respect human rights, and periodically to assess the adequacy of such laws and address any gaps;
> (b) [e]nsure that other laws and policies governing the creation and ongoing operation of business enterprises, such as corporate law, do not constrain but enable business respect for human rights;

---

[181] *Protect, Respect and Remedy Framework* ¶ 18.

[182] *See, e.g.*, Special Representative of the Secretary-General John Ruggie, *Business and Human Rights: Towards Operationalizing the "Protect, Respect and Remedy" Framework*, ¶ 15, U.N. Doc. A/HRC/11/13 (Apr. 22, 2009): "The extraterritorial dimension of the duty to protect remains unsettled in international law. Current guidance from international human rights bodies suggests that States are not required to regulate the extraterritorial activities of businesses incorporated in their jurisdiction, nor are they generally prohibited from doing so provided there is a recognized jurisdictional basis, and that an overall test of reasonableness is met. Within those parameters, some treaty bodies encourage home States to take steps to prevent abuse abroad by corporations within their jurisdiction."

[183] *Protect, Respect and Remedy Framework* ¶ 19.

[184] *Guiding Principles on Business and Human Rights* 4.

[185] Augenstein 15 (2010); Maastricht Principles on Extraterritorial Obligations of States in the Area of Economic, Social and Cultural Rights (Extraterritorial Obligations Consortium for Human Rights Beyond Borders, FIAN International, Heidelberg, Jan. 2013), general principle 3 (speaking of the state duties to respect, protect, and fulfill); Fons Coomans & Rolf Künnemann, Cases and Concepts on Extraterritorial Obligations in the Area of Economic, Social and Cultural Rights 2, 227 ff. (2012); Gibney & Skogly, *Introduction*, *in* Universal Human Rights and Extraterritorial Obligations 6 (2010); Malcolm Langford et al., *Extraterritorial Duties in International Law*, *in* Global Justice, State Duties 51, 112–3 (2013). *See however* Zerk, Extraterritorial Jurisdiction 18 (2010); and Steven R. Ratner, The Thin Justice of International Law: A Moral Reckoning of the Law of Nations 269–70, 277–8 (2015) (arguing for permissive but not mandatory extraterritorial jurisdiction in human rights law).

[186] *Protect, Respect and Remedy Framework* ¶ 18; *Guiding Principles on Business and Human Rights*, principle 1. *See also* Human Rights Council, 8th Sess., Special Representative of the Secretary-General John Ruggie, Business and Human Rights: Mapping International Standards of Responsibility and Accountability for Corporate Acts, U.N. Doc. A/HRC/4/35 (Feb. 19, 2007).

(c) [p]rovide effective guidance to business enterprises on how to respect human rights throughout their operations; [and]
(d) [e]ncourage, and where appropriate require, business enterprises to communicate how they address their human rights impacts.[187]

The second pillar of the framework, the *corporate duty to respect human rights*, is based on international soft law instruments, namely the International Labor Organization's (ILO) Tripartite Declaration of Principles Concerning Multinational Enterprises and Social Policy, and the OECD Guidelines for Multinational Enterprises.[188] This duty has also been debated for years, with one camp arguing that corporations should not get a free pass on human rights violations when they operate abroad, and the other arguing that corporations cannot be addressees of duties under international law since international law is, first and foremost, a set of rules, agreements, and treaties that are binding between states. Although this is still somewhat controversial in international law, most scholars today argue that corporations are bound to human rights law and must observe at least fundamental human rights standards when operating abroad.[189]

The corporate duty to respect human rights is discharged by corporations that act with due diligence. Due diligence describes the steps companies must take to become aware of, prevent, and address adverse effects on human rights with which they are involved.[190] Companies should pay regard to three sets of factors:

> The first is the country contexts in which their business activities take place, to highlight any specific human rights challenges they may pose. The second is what human rights impacts their own activities may have within that context—for example, in their capacity as producers, service providers, employers, and neighbors. The third is whether they might contribute to abuse through the relationships connected to their activities, such as with business partners, suppliers, State agencies, and other non-State actors. How far or how deep this process must go will depend on circumstances.[191]

The due diligence duty falls on small- and medium-sized enterprises, members of supply chains, primary investors, banks, lender financiers, and other parties closely involved in a corporation's business activities. By covering all enterprises, regardless of size, sector, operational context,

---

[187] *Guiding Principles on Business and Human Rights*, principle 3. An important point is that the state duty to protect is a standard of conduct, not a standard of result: Special Representative of the Secretary-General John Ruggie, *Business and Human Rights: Towards Operationalizing the "Protect, Respect and Remedy" Framework*, ¶¶ 13–4, U.N. Doc. A/HRC/11/13 (Apr. 22, 2009).

[188] International Labour Organization (ILO), Tripartite Declaration of Principles Concerning Multinational Enterprises and Social Policy, ILO Official Bulletin, Series A, No. 3 (ILO, Geneva 2000); OECD GUIDELINES FOR MNEs (2011).

[189] Andrew Clapham, *The Question of Jurisdiction under International Criminal Law over Legal Persons: Lessons from the Rome Conference on an International Criminal Court, in* LIABILITY OF MULTINATIONAL CORPORATIONS UNDER INTERNATIONAL LAW 139 (2000); Muchlinski, *Corporations in International Law, in* MPEPIL 30 (2014).

[190] *Guiding Principles on Business and Human Rights*, principle 11. *See also Protect, Respect and Remedy Framework* ¶¶ 24–5; Muchlinski, *Corporations in International Law, in* MPEPIL 56 (2014); RATNER 278 (2015).

[191] *Protect, Respect and Remedy Framework* ¶ 57.

ownership, or structure, and all of these actors' business partners, the corporate duty to respect human rights tackles "the entire life cycle of a project or business activity."[192]

To render these two pillars actionable, victims of human rights violations need access to mechanisms that investigate, punish, and redress abuses. *Access to remedy* is the third pillar of the framework and obliges states to put in place appropriate judicial, administrative, legislative, and other enforcement mechanisms in civil and criminal law.[193] Access to remedy may be provided by formal adjudicative or by nonjudicial mechanisms if they operate alongside formal bodies. Nonjudicial mechanisms, like the OECD national contact points, are sometimes argued to bring about more immediate, accessible, affordable, and responsive enforcement.[194] According to the SRSG, it is important that these bodies provide for redress that includes compensation, restitution, guarantees of nonrepetition, changes in the relevant law, and public apologies.[195]

Together, the three pillars of the framework are designed to close governance gaps by setting up a multilevel scheme that prevents, deters, adjudicates, and offers retribution for human rights violations abroad and at home. The framework was assessed critically by NGOs who claim that it does not create actual obligations, is ignorant about law enforcement, places too little emphasis on state cooperation, insufficiently captures corporate complexities in attributing responsibility, and fails to surmount practical barriers of cost and legal representation.[196] Though imperfect and suffering from notable weaknesses, the framework has done a tremendous job of centering cross-border governance gaps for public debate, and of reviving and revolutionizing the human rights discourse in international law, giving rise to new obligations at the national and international level. Given this success, we must determine if the framework holds the same promise for animal law: Is it, or could it be used as a basis for introducing duties to protect and respect animals abroad, and remedy violations of animal interests across the border?

B. THE "PROTECT, RESPECT AND REMEDY" FRAMEWORK IN ANIMAL LAW

In human rights law, international treaties and declarations like the UDHR operate as a basis for the "Protect, Respect and Remedy" framework. But in animal law, there is no equivalent agreement or declaration that would express the common motive of states to promote the interests of animals. NGOs have repeatedly urged states to sign and ratify the proposed International Convention for the Protection of Animals (ICAP) or the Universal Declaration on Animal Welfare (UDAW), but this has not yet happened.[197] Because animal law lacks such a basis, states are *de lege lata* under no obligation to protect animals against

---

[192] Muchlinski, *Corporations in International Law*, *in* MPEPIL 31 (2014). *See also Guiding Principles on Business and Human Rights*, principle 14.

[193] *Protect, Respect and Remedy Framework* ¶ 83; *Guiding Principles on Business and Human Rights*, principle 25.

[194] *Protect, Respect and Remedy Framework* ¶ 84.

[195] *Id.* ¶ 83.

[196] *E.g.*, Amnesty International, Comments in Response to the U.N. Special Representative of the Secretary General on Transnational Corporations and other Business Enterprises' Guiding Principles—Proposed Outline 19 (Amnesty International, London 2010).

[197] Committee for the Convention for the Protection of Animals, International Convention for the Protection of Animals (ICAP), Proposal (1988), *available at* https://www.animallaw.info/treaty/international-convention-protection-animals (last visited Jan. 10, 2019). World Society for the Protection of Animals (WSPA), Universal

infringements abroad—at least according to international law. International law solely grants states the discretion to apply animal law across the border. In other words, rather than dealing with a *duty* to protect animals extraterritorially, international law answers whether and when states are *allowed* to regulate and remedy the infringement of animal interests abroad.

Even though there is no international basis for the framework and there are no traces of its pillars in animal law, states could profit from the framework's conceptual and policy proposals that tackle "the governance gap created by globalization,"[198] to start developing analogous duties in animal law. Below, I consider the framework's state duty to protect animals, the corporate duty to respect animals, and international cooperation.[199]

A state duty to protect animals abroad can be established in domestic law by virtue of state constitutions or AWAs. When a state's constitution provides that it is under a duty to protect animals, then this duty typically binds the state in all its actions, including its authority to prescribe, adjudicate, and enforce law.[200] Considering that customary international law allows states to prescribe animal law extraterritorially, their constitutional mandate to protect animals obliges them to make use of this option. As Faller argues, a constitutionalized state objective in matters of animal protection, if it is as broad as article 20a of the German Basic Law, demands that the state protect animals beyond its borders within the limits of international law.[201]

There may be delicate cases where states lack jurisdictional authority over animals abroad but considerably control the financial, logistical, and institutional parameters that structure their exploitation. Is a state in this situation bound by its animal laws? In human rights law, scholars argue that even if a state's factual power exceeds its jurisdictional authority, it should be under a duty to protect against human rights violations simply because it has factual control.[202] This is called *control theory*. Outside the sphere of human rights law, international law also tends to expect states with factual power (*potentia*) to assume higher responsibility. Muchlinski calls this the *dependency theory*:

> [The dependency theory] predicts that less developed host states are in a permanently weaker bargaining position in relation to MNEs [multinational enterprises] as a result of

---

Declaration on Animal Welfare (UDAW), Proposal (2011), *available at* https://www.globalanimallaw.org/database/universal.html (last visited Jan. 10, 2019).

[198] *Protect, Respect and Remedy Framework* ¶ 3.

[199] Extrapolating concepts from the human rights domain to animal law must be done cautiously, since "the transposition of a concept aimed at limiting jurisdiction to a field where jurisdiction may be obligatory is not without dangers." (Cedric Ryngaert, *Jurisdiction: Towards a Reasonableness Test*, *in* GLOBAL JUSTICE, STATE DUTIES 192, 194 (2013)).

[200] However, states remain free to do this by means of their criminal, civil, or administrative laws: GEISSER 361 (2013).

[201] RICO FALLER, STAATSZIEL "TIERSCHUTZ": VOM PARLAMENTARISCHEN GESETZGEBUNGSSTAAT ZUM VERFASSUNGSGERICHTLICHEN JURISDIKTIONSSTAAT? 110 ff., 148–9 (2005).

[202] Scholars anchor the potential to affect human rights abroad in the control relationship (borrowed from diplomatic rights under BITs): Oona A. Hathaway et al., *Human Rights Abroad: When Do Human Rights Treaty Obligations Apply Extraterritorially?*, 43 ARIZ. ST. L.J. 389 (2011); Smita Narula, *International Financial Institutions, Transnational Corporations and Duties of States*, *in* GLOBAL JUSTICE, STATE DUTIES 114, 118 (2013); RATNER 278 (2015); Muthucumaraswamy Sornarajah, *Linking State Responsibility for Certain Harms Caused by Corporate Nationals Abroad to Civil Recourse in the Legal Systems of Home States*, *in* TORTURE AS TORT: COMPARATIVE PERSPECTIVES ON THE DEVELOPMENT OF TRANSNATIONAL HUMAN RIGHTS LITIGATION 491 (Craig Scott ed., 2001).

> the unequal conditions of trade and investment in the international economy, and because of the willingness of local ruling elites to submit to the interests of foreign capital. Thus, dependency theory posits a picture of exploitation of less developed host states by MNEs which cannot easily be remedied.[203]

The dependence of majority states on foreign capital is a constant challenge for international law that accepts states are equal sovereigns. Economic dependency does not call into question the principle of state sovereignty, for good reasons.[204] But it does prompt us to ask if there is a moral and legal case to be made that its detrimental effects must be eased. Joseph argues:

> [T]he developed home state is more likely to possess the requisite technical expertise to impose adequate safety standards, and to have a legal system able to cope with the proper attribution of responsibility within the complex corporate arrangements [...]. Indeed it is common for developed nations to demand higher standards of behaviour from multinational enterprises within their jurisdictions than do developing nations.[205]

Since home states provide the financial, political, and logistical support necessary for corporate actions to succeed abroad, they have "a role to play in 'encouraging' and 'promoting' "[206] positive standards abroad. For animal law, this means that states, whether they act in line with or in excess of international law, should be under a duty to protect animals abroad to the extent that they have factual control over them. Whenever they have the power to negatively affect animals abroad, states should thus be bound to protect them.

In sum, a proposed state duty to protect animals extraterritorially could be based on the control theory or on a constitutional mandate. This duty has two dimensions, following the Human Rights Council's *Guiding Principles*. A state shall *refrain from violating* the interests of foreign animals and it shall *ensure the enjoyment* of standards, by protecting animals from social actors who impede or negate those claims.[207]

As part of the second pillar of the "Protect, Respect and Remedy" framework, we must determine if there is a corporate duty to respect animals abroad. International law does not provide that corporations have a duty to respect animals abroad, but this may be expected from corporations by virtue of domestic law. In human rights law, the rationale behind the corporate duty to respect lies in the fact that corporations have the *capacity* to (especially negatively) affect human rights abroad. Analogously, if corporations affect or could affect

---

[203] MUCHLINSKI 105–7 (2007).

[204] That international law recognizes states as equal before it is not the same thing as international law offering assurance that states are equal in power, wealth, territory, and the like. The principle of sovereign equality only ensures that states hold the same position in the international legal order and have identical rights and duties: Juliane Kokott, *Sovereign Equality of States, in* MPEPIL 2, 23 (Rüdiger Wolfrum ed., online ed. 2011).

[205] Sarah Joseph, *Taming the Leviathans: Multinational Enterprises and Human Rights*, 46 NETHERLANDS INT'L L. REV. 171 (1999).

[206] ZERK, MULTINATIONALS AND CORPORATE SOCIAL RESPONSIBILITY 151 (2008).

[207] *Guiding Principles on Business and Human Rights*, principle 3.

the lives of animals abroad, they should observe certain standards, because they are, in a sense, ambassadors of their home states.[208]

In human rights law, the standard of conduct expected from corporations when they operate abroad is due diligence. Due diligence denotes the duty to detect, examine, and evaluate risks of any nature (legal, social, financial, etc.) before taking relevant decisions or actions, and is an established standard in investment law, environmental law, criminal law, and general managerial decision-making.[209] Due diligence centers on corporations' capacity to influence, manage, and avert risks, so it could be a useful parameter to adjudge the liability of corporations for infringing the interests of animals abroad.[210] Using this standard is consistent with the growing body of CSR policies, codes of conduct, and impact assessments in animal law that all suggest that corporations accept they have a responsibility toward animals abroad.[211]

Along with three pillars of the "Protect, Respect and Remedy" framework, the SRSG highlights that international cooperation and coordination are indispensable to the effective development, adjudication, and enforcement of human rights law. International bodies and special mandate holders are in a strong position to provide states with assistance, coordinate information sharing, and establish best practices.[212] The same is true for animal law. Global interspecies justice cannot be achieved by relying only on extraterritorial jurisdiction. These steps must be adequately complemented by joint international efforts to acknowledge, integrate, and properly regulate duties owed to animals. In animal law, there are plenty of options available for states to cooperate and coordinate. States can enter bilateral or multilateral agreements in criminal or civil proceedings. They can draw up or join treaties or declarations, like the UDAW proposed by the World Society for the Protection of Animals. They can actively contribute to the development of soft law by supporting recommendations by IOs, such as the Terrestrial and Aquatic Animal Health Codes by the OIE,[213] the IFC performance standards for investment,[214] or the BBFAW.[215]

The updated UDAW shows that its drafters might have taken note of the SRSG's work. Article IV UDAW reads:

> All appropriate steps shall be taken by Member States to prevent cruelty to animals and to reduce their suffering. This Declaration provides a basis for states and peoples to:
>
> work to improve their national animal welfare legislation

---

[208] ZERK, MULTINATIONALS AND CORPORATE SOCIAL RESPONSIBILITY 153 (2008). *Cf.* Kaufmann, *Konzernverantwortungsinitiative* 54 (2016), who argues in the context of human rights that a due diligence test that relies solely on the factual possibility to influence and affect human rights may be an insufficient standard for liability in domestic law.

[209] G.A. Res 375, U.N. GAOR 4th Sess., Draft Declaration on the Rights and Duties of States, U.N. Doc. A/RES/375 (Dec. 6, 1949), art. 2 cmt. 3; INTERNATIONAL COMMISSION OF JURISTS, REPORT OF THE EXPERT LEGAL PANEL ON CORPORATE COMPLICITY IN INTERNATIONAL CRIMES: CORPORATE COMPLICITY & LEGAL ACCOUNTABILITY, VOL. 1, 8 ff. (ICJ, Geneva 2008).

[210] Langford et al., *Introduction: An Emerging Field*, *in* GLOBAL JUSTICE, STATE DUTIES 3, 22 (2013).

[211] *See* Chapter 6, §1 G. and H.

[212] *Protect, Respect and Remedy Framework* ¶¶ 43 ff.

[213] OIE, TERRESTRIAL ANIMAL HEALTH CODE (OIE, Paris 2018); OIE, AQUATIC ANIMAL HEALTH CODE (OIE, Paris 2018).

[214] IFC, PERFORMANCE STANDARDS ON ENVIRONMENTAL AND SOCIAL SUSTAINABILITY (2012).

[215] BBFAW, FARM ANIMAL WELFARE REPORT (2017).

introduce animal welfare legislation in countries where it does not currently exist
encourage those businesses which use animals to keep welfare at the forefront of their policies
link humanitarian, development and animal welfare agendas nationally and internationally
inspire positive change in public attitudes towards animal welfare.

And article VI states:

> The policies, legislation and standards attained by each state on animal welfare shall be observed, recognized and promoted by improved practices and capacity-building, nationally and internationally. Whilst there are significant social, economic and cultural differences between societies, each should care for and treat animals in a humane and sustainable manner in accordance with the principles of the Declaration.[216]

The "Protect, Respect and Remedy" framework fits the UDAW, whether the drafters had it in mind or not. It lays down state responsibilities owed to animals intraterritorially (article IV: "work to improve their national animal welfare legislation") and encourages states to introduce animal laws with extraterritorial reach (article IV: "introduce animal welfare legislation in countries where it does not currently exist"). These recommendations seem inspired by the SRSG's state duty to protect. In line with the corporate duty to respect, the UDAW urges businesses to adhere to the highest standards of animal law (article IV: "encourage those businesses which use animals to keep welfare at the forefront of their policies"). The UDAW also calls for policy alignment (article IV: "link humanitarian, development and animal welfare agendas nationally and internationally"), international capacity building, and public outreach (article IV: "inspire positive change in public attitudes towards animal welfare"). Finally, the UDAW emphasizes that differences in animal law shall not prevent countries from caring for animals and treating them humanely.

HereI have outlined the most obvious commonalities between animal law and human rights law and offered suggestions on how they could be made fruitful for the extraterritoriality debate. Debates over state and corporate duties owed to animals are far from reaching the momentum of the debates in human rights law, and a lot more legal and empirical research is still required before animal law can fully profit from the debates in human rights law.[217] But it is clear that this research has great potential to link the issue of extraterritorial animal law to existing achievements in human rights law and to give it the impetus needed to design and implement political and legal initiatives.

---

216 UDAW, arts. IV and VI.

217 Future research should examine what state rights and duties exist to protect animals abroad, what duties corporations must observe in respect to animals abroad, and finally, what remedies are available to animals or representatives of their interests. This research should also uncover why and how such duties should be designed and implemented.

§5 Interim Conclusion

The aim of this chapter was to establish for animal law what is often neglected in jurisdictional studies—a meaningful connection between jurisdictional options available to states and their substantive laws, and clarity about the constraints of substantive law on the law of jurisdiction. The parameters of substantive law I devised focus on limits to harm, demands for coherence, factors needed to ensure a convergence toward a higher common denominator in animal law, and duties to protect animals abroad.

I found that general international law gives us two answers to the question of whether states can apply animal law extraterritorially for the benefit of animals, or whether they can also use this scheme to export laws that adversely affect animals living abroad. First, states typically rely on the doctrine of jurisdiction to pursue praiseworthy goals for the collective good and to the detriment of a few, based on claims of global justice. Because animals must be included in the global justice calculus in accordance with a nonspeciesist ethic, the law of jurisdiction must set limits on laws that adversely affect animals abroad. Doing so enables international law to live up to its claim to be fair and consistent. If, in most fields of law, international law implicitly demands that extraterritorial norms ensure the common good to the disfavor of a few, the same must hold for animal law. Efforts to secure just relationships with animals constitute a collective good that reinforces humanity and that must be protected from adverse actions of a few. The precautionary principle makes the same demand: states are obliged to act precautionarily toward animals, which precludes using laws that cause animals abroad to suffer.

Trade law also offers guidance for the moral trajectory of extraterritorial animal law. Because states increasingly share a common view on the proper treatment of animals, norms that restrict trade on the basis of this consensus are considered law-supporting and law-creating. The customary practice of states shows that only law-supporting and law-creating norms are accepted as exceptions to trade law. In contrast, laws that aim to deprive animals of protection are law-disabling and precluded from being used to indirectly protect animals abroad.

Animal law also provides answers to these questions. Animal law has evolved historically from protecting property interests of owners at all costs (first-generation animal laws), to protecting animals from the most heinous forms of cruelty (second-generation animal laws), and, finally, to ensuring their well-being (third-generation animal laws). For most states, this development was influenced by the recognition that animals are sentient beings who are fully conscious of their (negative and positive) affective states. From an ethical standpoint, these motivations evidence that legislators are committed to the theory of pathocentrism. From a legal standpoint, their enshrinement in law proves that the moral duty to protect animals has become a legal imperative.[218] And because the majority of states explicitly commit to ensuring animals' well-being and the absence of pain and suffering, states must be barred from prescribing laws extraterritorially that have negative effects on animals.

---

[218] JEDELHAUSER 53 (2011).

This chapter also asked whether and to what degree animal laws must be morally coherent to be applied extraterritorially. I used WTO law, which has given rise to the highest number of cross-border disputes over animal welfare, to show that many states' laws merely mirror the biased moral views of their people about the proper treatment of animals. Since moral inconsistency is a democratic reality, the measures a state uses to protect animals extraterritorially must conform only to its predefined policy objective. Outside this sphere, states have some discretion to give effect to the biases of their people, though they are advised to and seem more and more interested in making their laws and policies more coherent. Coherency in this sense does not allow states to revoke and reverse achievements in animal law. First and foremost, states are called upon to establish coherence by extending their laws to those animals that are commonly ignored. In other words, the demand for coherence must be used in favor of animals and not to their detriment.

To guide states in deciding when to apply their laws extraterritorially, I established a hierarchy of presumptions: a presumption in favor of transparency in matters crucial to animals; a presumption in favor of recognizing animal interests; a presumption in favor of integrating animal interests; a presumption in favor of extensive and concretized animal laws; a presumption in favor of adequately balancing interests; a presumption in favor of prohibitions; and a presumption in favor of animal rights. These tools, by being designed hierarchically, ensure that in cases of extraterritorial jurisdiction, the level of protection offered to animals either remains constant or increases. This precludes a race to the bottom *and* takes into account the interests of states operating at any level of animal law.

Human rights law can also guide us in assessing the demands of substantive law when protecting animals abroad. The revolutionary UN "Protect, Respect and Remedy" framework stipulates a state duty to protect, a corporate duty to respect human rights abroad, and effective access to remedies. This framework does not apply to issues of animal law *de lege lata*, but can inspire its future development. The state duty to protect animals abroad may either derive from domestic law or from the control theory. If states have a constitutional mandate to protect animals, this mandate stretches across borders, assuming international law gives the state discretion to prescribe law extraterritorially. In the rare cases where a state's factual power exceeds its jurisdiction in territorial terms, it should still be under a duty to protect animals, because it has the capacity to negatively affect the lives of animals abroad (based on the control theory). The corporate duty to respect animals relies on due diligence, traces of which we see in various domestic animal laws, CSR, codes of conduct, and best practices. The framework also points to the necessity of engaging in joint efforts in the international arena to acknowledge, integrate, and properly regulate animal interests internationally. The "Protect, Respect and Remedy" framework gave rise to spin-off principles in animal law, as set out in the recently updated UDAW, which can be further refined and strengthened. With these guiding parameters for extraterritorial animal law in place, there is a good chance it can keep its promise to meaningfully fill governance gaps in animal law, overcome the challenges of globalization, and help us work toward a more just world for animals.

9 Comparative Vantage Points of Extraterritorial Animal Law

CHAPTER 8 LAID DOWN parameters for connecting the law of jurisdiction with substantive animal law and gave us a solid idea of the direction extraterritorial animal law must take in the future. But those who specialize in international law might find these parameters too abstract to make clear the precise advantages of applying animal law across the border. Likewise, scholars who specialize in animal studies might wonder if this framework can bring about a paradigm shift since ultimately all states use and exploit animals, albeit in different ways and to different extents. This chapter offers both disciplines more background, each from its own angle. First, I ask if we are limited to applying criminal animal law across the border, or if all laws, including standards of administrative and civil law, can be used to protect animals across the border. I then carve out the relative benefits of applying each of these standards across the border, which enables us to more reliably assess the usefulness and desirability of extraterritorial jurisdiction in animal law.

Given the diversity of animal laws across the world, each jurisdiction holds its own promise for animals, which varies across time and depends on the political and sociocultural background of the states that exercise jurisdiction. The multitude of local variation does not prevent us from extracting best practices but rather enables us to point to exemplary approaches and concepts that could help guide the law of jurisdiction in the future. To determine which achievements of which states are illuminating, I use a functional comparative method that identifies commonalities and distinct traits of states' laws. The goal of this analysis is "not to compare specific legal institutions or legal rules, but to connect to the function

Protecting Animals Within and Across Borders. Charlotte E. Blattner.

that an institution or rule fulfills in a legal system and to analyze which institution or rule in other systems fulfills the same function."[1] The functional comparative method does not offer or purport to offer a full comparative analysis. Instead, it is issue-oriented, which means it helps identify relevant similarities and disparities of jurisdictions in reference to the above research questions.

§1 Equivalence of Criminal, Administrative, and Civil Animal Law

In the early history of the law of jurisdiction, criminal law in particular was granted extraterritorial reach in order to try individuals who seemed to escape the laws of all states (as in piracy) or to protect nationals from overzealous convictions in foreign states. The growth of extraterritorial norms in other fields of law with civil, criminal, and administrative character (like antitrust law, securities law, and other economically oriented fields of law) challenged the tacit assumption that jurisdiction related only to the criminal side of the law. In their early contributions to the doctrine of jurisdiction, Akehurst, Jennings, and Mann argued that the geographical scope of laws does indeed differ, namely, depending on how norms are classified. Assessing the scope of jurisdiction in this compartmentalized fashion, however, sometimes led to contradictory results. Some scholars claimed that extraterritoriality is more readily accepted in criminal law, while others argued that civil law norms have unlimited territorial reach.[2]

In animal law, it matters whether or not criminal norms are the only ones that can be used to protect animals across the border. As in antitrust, the nature of animal laws can be criminal, civil, or administrative. Criminal law penalizes violations of animal law with criminal sanctions like fines or imprisonment. Administrative law sets standards for the treatment of animals and determines the administrative actions when these standards are violated, including commands, prohibitions, authorizations, and administrative sanctions. Civil law determines the legal status of animals in civil law (notably whether animals are property or legal persons), whether the interests of animals are to be considered in cases of divorce or separation, death, sale, injury to third parties, etc. and how these issues are dealt with financially.[3] If extraterritorial jurisdiction is limited to criminal law, this considerably limits states'

---

[1] Functional comparative method originated in civil law but is now a firmly accepted method of public law: VANDERKERCKHOVE 97 (2007). In the words of Sandrock, one of the earliest scholars to have described the method and its functioning: "[M]an nimmt auf einen konkreten Lebenssachverhalt oder auf ein konkretes Rechtsproblem Bezug und fragt, welche materiale Lösung für diesen Sachverhalt oder für dieses Rechtsproblem in den verschiedenen Rechtsordnungen vorgesehen ist." (OTTO SANDROCK, ÜBER SINN UND METHODE DER ZIVILISTISCHEN RECHTSVERGLEICHUNG 67 (1966)). *See further* on the functional comparative method: HARALD KOCH ET AL., IPR UND RECHTSVERGLEICHUNG: EIN STUDIEN- UND ÜBUNGSBUCH ZUM INTERNATIONALEN PRIVAT- UND ZIVILVERFAHRENSRECHT UND ZUR RECHTSVERGLEICHUNG 280 ff. (2010); Susanne Augenhofer, *Rechtsvergleichung*, *in* GRUNDLAGEN DES RECHTS 193, 198, 212 (Julian Krüper ed., 2d ed. 2013).

[2] Akehurst 171 (1972–3); Robert Jennings, *General Course of Principles of International Law*, 121 RCADI 323, 517–8 (1967); Mann 149–50 (1964).

[3] TANJA GEHRIG, STRUKTUR UND INSTRUMENTE DES TIERSCHUTZRECHTS 219 (1999); JEDELHAUSER 120, 127 (2011).

ability to protect animals abroad. For instance, if the law of jurisdiction is limited to criminal law, Botswana could only prohibit its nationals from killing elephants abroad, but not to enter private sales contracts over elephant products. But if the law of jurisdiction extends beyond criminal law, it is likely to be much more effective, not least because most norms in animal law are administrative in nature.

Recently, the literature on the law of jurisdiction has given up its narrow focus on criminal law. Scholars either state no preference or advocate for applying identical rules to all fields of law.[4] Brownlie claims that "there is in principle no great difference between the problems created by assertion of civil and criminal jurisdiction over aliens."[5] Ryngaert supports this view in the context of antitrust law, "as it is illogical to subject non-criminal antitrust proceedings to a stricter jurisdiction regime than criminal antitrust proceedings, when criminal proceedings are generally deemed more intrusive, in particular in terms of their sanctions, than civil proceedings are."[6] State practice indicates that though most states apply norms extraterritorially in criminal matters, they have not taken a narrow view on it. As early as 1927, the PCIJ held in *Lotus*: "[T]he principles of international law are to determine questions of jurisdiction—*not only criminal but also civil*—between the contracting Parties [. . .]."[7] Since this rule applies to the law of jurisdiction at large, it must also apply to animal law. It follows that all criminal, administrative, and civil norms of animal law are, in principle, eligible to be applied extraterritorially.

§2 Applying Constitutional Animal Law Extraterritorially

Most people imagine animal law to be a single legislative act that describes in detail all duties owed to animals, such as, for example, the animal welfare act, animal protection act, or anti-cruelty act. But norms that regulate our manifold relationships with animals are enshrined in different acts and regulations, and they can be found at multiple regulatory levels. Some of the strongest tools are constitutional norms. A few states have decided to constitutionalize their perceptions about, goals regarding, or legal duties owed to animals, and thereby bring "them into the very structure of the body politic."[8] Constitutional animal law is of fundamental importance for the legal order of a state. It frames animal law at a high level of abstraction, endows it with broad application, and is likely to point to desirable future developments. Constitutional goals or duties may exist on a state level (e.g., the *Bundesverfassung* in Switzerland, or the *Grundgesetz* in Germany) or on a substate level (e.g., the state constitutions in the United States, the *Kantonsverfassungen* in Switzerland,

---

[4] U.S. Restatement (Fourth) of the Foreign Relations Law, § 402, cmt. d; Bowett 2 (1982); BROWNLIE 300 (2008); LOWE, INTERNATIONAL LAW 171–2 (2007); OPPENHEIM'S INTERNATIONAL LAW 458 (1992); ORAKHELASHVILI 213–6 (2019); RYNGAERT, JURISDICTION OVER ANTITRUST VIOLATIONS 16 (2008); SCHWARZE 21 (1994).

[5] BROWNLIE 300 (2008).

[6] RYNGAERT, JURISDICTION OVER ANTITRUST VIOLATIONS 16 (2008).

[7] Lotus, 1927 P.C.I.J. 17 (emphasis added). *See also* United States v. Nippon Paper Industries Co., 109 F.3d 1, 4 (1st Cir. 1997) (U.S.).

[8] WAGMAN & LIEBMAN 260 (2011).

or the *Landesverfassungen* in Germany). Some states identify animal protection as one of their "state objectives." Others protect the dignity of animals in their constitution. Some established a constitutional duty of compassion owed to animals that courts have reframed as rights of animals. And others have expanded their constitutional mandate to protect the environment to also protect animals from cruelty. Animals may also enter the constitutional arena when states allocate competences to institutions (or to the federal, state, or community level), as done in Austria and Slovenia.[9] I will not examine these norms here because they grapple with questions germane to constitutional law and are not directly concerned with animals. It bears mention that even in the absence of an explicit constitutional norm on animals, we cannot infer that animals are not constitutionally protected.[10] As Eisen notes, interests and experiences of animals now emerge in constitutional jurisprudence as legitimate state objectives that justify limitations on human rights, "even in jurisdictions whose constitutional texts do not expressly posit animal protection as a constitutional value."[11]

A. Brazil and Egypt: From Conservationism to Pathocentrism

Some state constitutions, like those of Portugal, Spain, Greece, Sudan, and Ecuador, determine that the state or its citizens have a responsibility to care for the environment.[12] If animals form an integral part of these environments, they are protected by the constitution.

---

[9] For example, the Austrian Constitution lays down in article 11 (1) no. 8: "In the following matters legislation is the business of the Federation, execution that of the *Länder*: [. . .] Animal protection, to the extent not being in the competence of Federal legislation according to other regulations, with the exception of the exercise of hunting or fishing." (Bundes-Verfassungsgesetz [B-VG] [Constitution] BGBl No. 1/1930, art. 11(1) no. 8 (Austria), *translation at* https://www.constituteproject.org/constitution/Austria_2009.pdf). In Austria, a popular initiative was initiated in 1996 to declare the protection of animals a constitutionally protected legal good (*Rechtsgut*). The initiative did not manage to pass parliamentary scrutiny. Today, animals are only a concern of the Austrian Constitution insofar as they form part of the protection of the environment (say, as natural resources, or as part of biological diversity). Only the constitution of the *Land* Salzburg declares that animal welfare is a constitutional concern: Lennkh 82 (2012). Notable is also that in Slovenia, article 72 of the Constitution titled "Healthy Living Environment" provides among others that "[t]he protection of animals from cruelty shall be regulated by law" (Ustava Republike Slovenije [Constitution of the Republic of Slovenia], Dec. 23, 1999, URS-NPB9 (Slovn.)).

[10] David Bilchitz, *Does Transformative Constitutionalism Require the Recognition of Animal Rights?*, *in* Is This Seat Taken? Conversations at the Bar, the Bench and the Academy about the South African Constitution 173 (Stu Woolman & David Bilchitz eds., 2012).

[11] In Austria, for example, the Constitutional Court upheld a ban on displaying dogs in pet shops even though the prohibition infringed on pet shop owners' property rights. Similarly, in the United States, the Supreme Court grappled with whether protecting animals justifies limitations on First Amendment rights: Jessica Eisen, *Animals in the Constitutional State*, 15(4) Int'l J. Const. L. 909, 926 (2017).

[12] *E.g.*, Constitution (2005), art. 11 para. 2 (Sudan): "The State shall not pursue any policy, or take or permit any action, which may adversely affect the existence of any species of animal or vegetative life, their natural or adopted habitat." *Cf.*, however, the Transitional Constitution Sudan (2011). Today, more than 100 constitutions guarantee a right to a clean and healthy environment: Dinah Shelton, *Human Rights and the Environment: Substantive Rights*, *in* Research Handbook on International Environmental Law 264, 267 (Malgosia Fitzmaurice et al. eds., 2010).

But because environmental protection primarily means conserving or preserving environmental processes,[13] these provisions may not be strong enough to effectively protect animals. Core principles of environmental law commonly ignore the moral and legal duties animal sentience places on us. For example, ensuring biological diversity is typically interpreted as warranting the killing of "invasive animals" *en masse*. In 2004, the NGO Nature Conservancy acquired some 60,000 acres of Santa Cruz Island off the coast of California and killed over 37,000 sheep in its effort to conserve and restore indigenous plants.[14] Even when environmental principles consider animals worthy of protection, individual animals are seen as exchangeable units of a larger group that needs to be protected, and no attention is paid to the persistent hardship animals suffer in nature. For instance, conservationists are anxious to ensure the survival of the African elephant (*L. Africana*),[15] but many of them consider it acceptable that individual elephants suffer from and remain vulnerable to diseases, parasitism, accidents, drought, starvation, drowning, predation, and stress.[16] Environmentalists often tacitly overlook the pain of wild animals and rationalize it as an evolutionary advantage that ensures the survival of the fittest.[17] Finally, most animals, namely, those who are not endangered or threatened, fall through the cracks of conservationism and preservationism.

Brazil has been at the forefront of uniting rather than separating environmental concerns and concerns for animals without eroding their core values. Article 225 para. 1 VII of the Brazilian Constitution, which was introduced in 1998, states:

> Everyone has the right to an ecologically balanced environment, which is a public good for the people's use and is essential for a healthy life. The Government and the community have a duty to defend and to preserve the environment for present and future generations. To assure the effectiveness of this right, it is the responsibility of the Government to [. . .] protect the fauna and the flora, prohibiting, as provided by law, all practices that jeopardize their ecological functions, cause extinction of species *or subject animals to cruelty*.[18]

---

[13] Preserving species means protecting (certain) animals from *any* use, whereas conservation seeks the *proper* use of animals while still ensuring their continued existence as a species. *Cf.* Ulrich Beyerlin & Vanessa Holzer, *Conservation of Natural Resources*, *in* MPEPIL 9 (Rüdiger Wolfrum ed., online ed. 2013): "Conservation constitutes one of three general approaches to the protection of natural resources in international law, the two other being preservation and sustainable use. The dividing lines between these concepts are blurry since they may overlap to a certain extent. Preservation is often linked to a threat of extinction faced by certain species and seems to exclude their economic utilization." *See also* Nat'l Park Serv., U.S. Dep't of Interior, Conservation vs. Preservation and the National Park Service, *available at* http://www.nps.gov/klgo/learn/education/classrooms/conservation-vs-preservation.htm (last visited Jan. 10, 2019) (providing educational tools to differentiate between conservation and preservation).

[14] Jo-Ann Shelton, *Killing Animals That Don't Fit In: Moral Dimensions of Habitat Restoration*, 13(4) Between Species 1, 5 (2004).

[15] CITES, Ann. I & II.

[16] Pearce 157 (2015).

[17] It is an anthropocentric rationalization because the same logic is not applied to human individuals: Marian S. Dawkins, *Evolution and Animal Welfare*, 73(3) Q. Rev. Biol. 305, 308 (1998).

[18] Constituição da República Federativa do Brasil [C.F.] [Constitution], Oct. 5, 1988, art. 225 (Braz.) (emphasis added).

The phrase "or subject animals to cruelty" was added to the previously established provision that protected wild and domesticated animals per environmental standards.[19] A notable difference between the two is that, while protecting and preserving the environment is a duty of both the government and the community, ensuring that animals are not treated cruelly is the sole responsibility of the government. Shortly after it amended article 225 para. 1 VII, Brazil enacted the "Environmental Crimes Law," which allows the penalty of environmental crime to be increased if an agent committed it "by using cruel methods to kill or capture animals."[20] Case law shows that the Brazilian constitutional norm was used as a basis for prohibiting cock-fighting and cultural festivals where oxen were whipped and beaten to death (*farra do boi*), even if legislative bases for this prohibition were not yet in place.[21] These examples illustrate the ubiquitous risk of animal law to be used to oppress minorities.[22] Overall, the constitutional prohibition of animal cruelty is still considered momentous for the development of Brazil's animal law. To scholars, it creates a "rupture with the environmental perspective of animals as natural resources and provides the opportunity to develop and create new paradigms to protect all animals."[23]

In 2014, Egypt passed a new constitution, in which it included a constitutional norm for animals. Like Brazilian article 225, the Egyptian Constitution is primarily dedicated to conservationism, but it also protects animals. Article 45 of the Egyptian Constitution, titled "Seas, Beaches, lakes, waterways, mineral water and natural reserves," provides:

> The state commits to protecting its seas, beaches, lakes, waterways, mineral water, and natural reserves. It is prohibited to encroach upon, pollute, or use them in a manner that contradicts their nature. Every citizen has the right to enjoy them as regulated by law. The state also commits to the protection and development of green space in urban areas; *the protection of plants, livestock and fisheries*; *the protection of endangered species*; and *the prevention of cruelty to animals*.[24]

Stilt argues that it was very unlikely from an *ex ante* point of view that Egyptians would adopt a constitutional norm to protect animals. This unusual turn of events, as she argues, can be traced back to the efforts of Amina Abaza, a local activist who worked relentlessly to remind Egyptian people that human and animal oppression are intimately related and that, in the interest of both, they should strive to ensure better laws for animals.[25] Although the

---

[19] ADI 1, 856-6/RJ (1998), Sept. 3, 1998 (Braz.).

[20] Lei N° 9.605, de Fevereiro de 1998 [Environmental Crimes Law N° 9.605], Feb. 12, 1998, art. 15 para. 2 (Braz.).

[21] RE No. 153.531-8/SC (1997), June 3, 1997 (Braz.). *See further* Jessica Eisen & Kristen Stilt, *Protection and Status of Animals*, *in* MAX PLANCK INSTITUTE FOR COMPARATIVE CONSTITUTIONAL LAW 39 (Rainer Grote, Frauke Lachenmann, & Rüdiger Wolfrum, online ed. 2017).

[22] Chapter 11 deals with these issues in detail.

[23] Tagore Trajano de Almeida Silva, *The Constitutional Defense of Animals in Brazil*, *in* ANIMAL LAW AND WELFARE: INTERNATIONAL PERSPECTIVES 181, 190 (2016).

[24] CONSTITUTION OF THE ARAB REPUBLIC OF EGYPT, Jan. 15, 2014 (Egypt), *translation at* https://www.constituteproject.org/constitution/Egypt_2014.pdf (emphasis added).

[25] Kristen Stilt, *Constitutional Innovation and Animal Protection in Egypt*, 42(3) LAW & SOC. INQUIRY 1, 2 (2017).

provision is often translated as preventing cruelty to animals, *al-rifq bil-hayawan* should be read as "the kind treatment of animals," because it connotes both kindness to (or humane treatment of) animals and the prevention of harm done to them.[26] Given the short period of time that passed since the constitution took effect, the scope of the norm is still unsettled. Scholars agree, however, that the next major step should be to establish a comprehensive animal protection act.[27]

B. GERMANY, LUXEMBOURG, AND THE EUROPEAN UNION: ANIMAL PROTECTION AS A STATE OBJECTIVE

Article 20a of the German Basic Law determines that protecting animals is an objective of the German state. The norm, which previously protected "natural foundations of life," was amended in 2002 to read: "Mindful also of its responsibility toward future generations, the state shall protect the natural foundations of life *and animals* by legislation and, in accordance with law and justice, by executive and judicial action, all within the framework of the constitutional order."[28]

Unlike constitutional rights, state objectives do not create subjective rights for either humans or animals.[29] Instead, article 20a of the German Basic Law has an objective, legally binding character and, as such, is binding for all governmental branches.[30] At the legislative and regulatory level, officials must strive to fulfill the state's objective by regulating fundamental aspects of animals' lives, setting up minimum levels of animal welfare, updating legislation based on new scientific insights and ongoing international developments, protecting animals from third parties, determining when duties owed to animals are violated, and promoting the protection of animals. Adjudicative and enforcement authorities must abide by the objective when they apply the law, concretize vague legal terms, adjudge claims, and enforce the law. The state objective also binds the government in its external affairs.[31] Before entering an agreement with another state, the German government must ensure that the prospective agreement is compatible with its constitutional mandate.

Article 20a of the German Basic Law brought with it the hope that balances of interests between humans and animals would be fundamentally altered. Prior to the amendment of

---

[26] *Id.* at 2, 37.

[27] Rana Khaled, *Animal Rights Advocates in Egypt Call for Laws to Be Activated*, DAILY NEWS EGYPT, July 25, 2016. This momentum can and should be used, as Stilt argues, because the constitutional provision has given the animal protection movement renewed legitimation in Egypt: Stilt, *Constitutional Innovation and Animal Protection in Egypt* 42, 43 (2017).

[28] GRUNDGESETZ [GG] [BASIC LAW], May 23, 1949, BGBl. I at 2438, art. 20a (Ger.) (emphasis added), amendments introduced by Gesetz zur Änderung des Grundgesetzes (Staatsziel Tierschutz) [LAW TO CHANGE THE BASIC LAW (STATE OBJECTIVE OF ANIMAL PROTECTION)], July 31, 2002, BGBl. I at 2862 (Ger.).

[29] RASPÉ 220–1 (2013). Conversely, the norm is not binding for nonstate actors: FALLER 134 ff. (2005).

[30] GERICK 103–4 (2005); ALBERT LORZ & ERNST METZGER, TIERSCHUTZGESETZ: KOMMENTAR, EINFÜHRUNG 70 69–70 n. 10, 12, 13 (6th ed. 2008).

[31] FALLER 206 (2005); JANA GLOCK, DAS DEUTSCHE TIERSCHUTZRECHT UND DAS STAATSZIEL "TIERSCHUTZ" IM LICHTE DES VÖLKERRECHTS UND DES EUROPARECHTS 46–7 (2004); LENNKH 79–80 (2012).

the norm, any provision of the German AWA that conflicted with human interests was subordinate to them. This was often justified by emphasizing the elevated constitutional status of humans. Human interests are constitutionally protected, while animal interests are "only" protected by statutes; when they conflict, constitutional norms must take precedence. The law thus created a structural bias in favor of humans and to the disadvantage of animals, which is clearly reflected in case law. In 2002, for example, the German Constitutional Court adjudicated a case where a butcher argued that his freedom of profession (a constitutional right enshrined in article 12 German Basic Law) was infringed by a national ban on kosher and halal slaughter. The Court held that the appellant's claims were important enough to let him continue kosher and halal slaughter, despite the statewide duty to stun animals before slaughter, enshrined in section 4a para. 2 of the German AWA.[32] Scholars argued that if article 20a of the German Basic Law had existed when the judgment was made, the Court would have had a much harder time justifying its decision, and it probably would have had to decide the case differently.[33] In essence, the German Basic Law was considered a "constant obstacle"[34] to effectively protect animals, which initiators of the amendment to article 20 hoped to remedy with a constitutional state objective to protect animals.

To expect that the constitutionalization of duties owed to animals will result in a less biased balance of interests is not unreasonable. Animal protection, by virtue of being a state objective, represents a high public interest and gives rise to state responsibility.[35] Declaring animal protection a public interest on a constitutional level means it has as much value as other state objectives and as constitutional guarantees and rights, like economic freedom, freedom of research, academic freedom, freedom of arts, or freedom of religion.[36] According to Germany's

---

[32] BVerfG, Nov. 6, 2001, 1 BvR 1783/99 (Ger.); ANIMAL WELFARE ACT (Ger.), § 4a para. 2. Conflicts between religious freedom and efforts to protect animals are among the most disputed. Countries that exempt religious slaughter from their animal welfare or protection acts are the United States and the European Union. Among the countries that banned religious slaughter are Denmark, New Zealand (only halal but not kosher meat), and Switzerland. Landmark cases that weigh religious freedom against animal protection are Cha'are Shalom Ve Tsedek v. France, 350 Eur. Ct. H.R. 233 (2000) (holding that France did not violate art. 9 ECHR by its slaughter ban, because the Jewish community in France is able to obtain *glatt* meat from Belgium); Jones v. Butz, 374 F. Supp. 1284 (S.D.N.Y. 1974) (U.S) (holding that there is no violation of Establishment Clause because no excessive governmental entanglement and by making it possible for those who wish to eat ritually acceptable meat to slaughter the animal in accordance with the tenets of their faith, Congress neither established the tenets of that faith nor interfered with the exercise of any other).

[33] GERICK 102 (2005). The same is true of the judgment by the Appellationsgericht Kassel, Oct. 5, 1990, NStZ 1991, 443–5 (444) (Ger.). In this case, an artist made use of a sticky pulp to render a budgie incapable of flying and justified her actions by relying on freedom of arts. The court favored the accused's position and argued that if animal welfare were enshrined in the constitution, the case would have been decided differently.

[34] Erin Evans, *Constitutional Inclusion of Animal Rights in Germany and Switzerland: How Did Animal Protection Become an Issue of National Importance?*, 18 SOC. & ANI. 231, 236 (2010).

[35] By enshrining responsibilities toward animals in the constitution, these duties become an interest of the public: JEDELHAUSER 115 (2011). The reverse is not necessarily true: not every public interest represents a state duty.

[36] GLOCK 43 (2004); Kate M. Nattrass, *". . . Und die Tiere" Constitutional Protection for Germany's Animals*, 10 ANIMAL L. 283, 303, 312 (2004). Lennkh argues that these provisions are "absolutely equal ranking," because the state objective of animal welfare allows restricting constitutionally guaranteed basic rights: LENNKH 80 (2012). Faller agrees that there is no difference in rank between basic rights and the constitutional protection of art. 20a, unless a basic right's very essence is violated: FALLER 106–7 (2005).

long-standing rules on constitutional interpretation, conflicting values are weighed and balanced through the principle of practical concordance, which strongly resembles the proportionality principle.[37] The principle demands that, instead of categorically prioritizing human interests, courts must consider factors including intensity of effect, benefits and pitfalls of the impairment, duration of impairment, and long-term ramifications.[38]

Hopes for a less biased balance of interests were quickly crushed in 2006, when the Federal Administrative Court found that, despite the constitutional amendment, the preexisting statutory exemption will be upheld unless and until the legislature explicitly revokes it.[39] Though the judgment received wide criticism, it was confirmed by the Constitutional Court in 2009, when it held that an administrative order restricting the claimant from slaughtering animals without stunning violated his constitutional rights.[40] Also in 2006, and without making reference to article 20a German Basic Law, the Constitutional Court declared legal and even encouraged state laws on hunting, which demonstrates its unwillingness to take seriously its constitutional mandate to protect animals.[41]

Another country that has a constitutional mandate to protect animals is Luxembourg. In 2007, Luxembourg amended its constitution to provide in the newly created article 11bis: "The State guarantees the protection of the human and natural environment, by working for the establishment of a sustainable balance between the conservation of nature, especially its capacity for regeneration, and the satisfaction of the needs of present and future generations. It promotes the protection and well-being of animals."[42] Like article 20 of the German Basic Law, article 11bis of the Luxembourg Constitution is a state objective that operates as a guiding principle to interpret existing law but does not give rise to justiciable rights for animals. To date, the provision has not been used as a basis to introduce new or interpret existing laws,[43] but a new AWA was passed in June 2018 that now recognizes animals as sentient and living beings.[44]

---

[37] *E.g.*, BVerfG, May 16, 1995, 1 BvR 1087/91 (Ger.).

[38] Raspé 230 (2013).

[39] BVerwG, 3 C 30.05, Nov. 23, 2006, 12 (Ger.): "Auch wenn die Einfügung des Tierschutzes als Staatsziel eine verfassungsrechtliche Aufwertung gebracht hat, genießt dieser Belang keineswegs Vorrang gegenüber anderen Verfassungsgewährleistungen [. . .]. Vielmehr ist es vorrangig Aufgabe des Gesetzgebers, dieses Anliegen zu einem gerechten Ausgleich mit etwa widerstreitenden Grundrechten zu bringen. Dementsprechend muss die an enge Voraussetzungen zum Schutz der Religionsfreiheit geknüpfte Vorschrift im Tierschutzgesetz nach wie vor als Richtschnur des Gesetzgebers betrachtet werden, diesen Ausgleich zwischen Tierschutz und Religionsfreiheit so herzustellen, dass beide Wirkung entfalten können."

[40] BVerfG, Sept. 28, 2009, 1 BvR 1702/09 (Ger.).

[41] BVerfG, Dec. 13, 2006, 1 BvR, 2084/05 (Ger.). *See further* Eisen & Stilt, *Protection and Status of Animals*, *in* Max Planck Institute for Comparative Constitutional Law 25 (2017).

[42] Constitution du Grand-Duché du Luxembourg [The Constitution of the Grand Duchy of Luxembourg], Oct. 17, 1868, art. 11bis (Lux.).

[43] Eisen & Stilt, *Protection and Status of Animals*, *in* Max Planck Institute for Comparative Constitutional Law 55–6 (2017).

[44] The "Law to ensure the dignity, protection of life, safety and welfare of animals," which supersedes the 30-year-old Animal Welfare Act, was passed unanimously on June 27 by the Luxembourg Chamber of Deputies: Loi du 27 juin 2018 sur la protection des animaux [Animal Protection Act], July, 3, 2018 (Lux.). The norm that recognizes animals as sentient beings is *id.* art. 3 para. 2. *See further* John Dyer, *Luxembourg Is Set to Become the Most Animal-Friendly Country in the World*, Vice News, May 13, 2016.

Article 13 of the TFEU can also be seen as establishing a state objective of quasi-constitutional character. Article 13 TFEU obliges the European Union and its member states to "pay full regard to animal welfare requirements of animals" in formulating and implementing the European Union's agriculture, fisheries, transport, internal market, research, technological development, and space policies. The article is celebrated as a momentous achievement, since it "puts animal welfare on equal footing with other key principles mentioned in the same title,"[45] including the promotion of gender equality, the guarantee of social protection, protection of human health, the combat of discrimination, the promotion of sustainable development, consumer protection, and personal data protection. This renders article 13 TFEU and, with it, the protection of animals, an "issue of very high importance"[46] to the European Union. The requirement to pay regard to animal welfare applies to the fields of agriculture, fisheries, transport, internal market, research, technological development, and space policies, but those are only exemplary of a broader catalogue of issues in which animal welfare must play a role.[47] The European Union's commitment to pathocentric animal ethics is notable when it provides that animal sentience was the prime reason for adopting the norm.[48] The article does not, however, allow enacting legislation specifically designed to improve animal welfare, based on the principles of conferred competences and subsidiarity.[49] Such legislation requires another legal basis, like the European Union's competence in environmental matters, common agricultural policy, or the internal market.

C. INDIA: FROM THE DUTY OF COMPASSION TO ANIMAL RIGHTS

In 1976, India added article 51 A lit. g to its constitution, which determines: "It shall be the duty of every citizen of India [. . .] to protect and improve the natural environment including forests, lakes, rivers and wild life, and to have compassion for living creatures."[50] The norm belongs to India's fundamental duties chapter, which is binding for the state and all its citizens. Fundamental duties are not per se enforceable, but they must be taken into account when statutes are interpreted and rights balanced against duties.[51] Like the German norm, India's duty to have compassion for animals has been used to promote the interests of animals when creating new laws and when applying or interpreting existing laws.

In *People for Animals v. State of Goa*, an animal protection group sued the state for its failure to prohibit bullfighting, arguing that bullfighting violates article 51 A lit. g of the

---

[45] European Commission, Health and Consumers, The EU and Animal Welfare: Policy Objectives, *available at* http://ec.europa.eu/food/animal/welfare/policy/index_en.htm (last visited Jan. 10, 2019).

[46] Markos Kyprianou, Member of the European Commission Responsible for Health and Consumer Protection, "Speech to the Animal Welfare Intergroup of the European Parliament," Brussels, June 8, 2005.

[47] Markus Kotzur, *Article 13 TFEU, in* EUROPEAN UNION TREATIES: A COMMENTARY 226 (Rudolf Geiger et al. eds., 2015).

[48] *See* TFEU, art. 13. *See generally* RASPÉ 222 (2013).

[49] *See* TEU, arts. 1, 4, and 5. Competences which have not been conferred on the European Union shall remain with the member states. In areas that fall outside the exclusive competence of the European Union, it shall act only insofar as the objectives cannot be sufficiently achieved by the member states.

[50] Constitution of India, Jan. 26, 1950, art. 51 A(g) (India).

[51] Eisen & Stilt, *Protection and Status of Animals, in* MAX PLANCK INSTITUTE FOR COMPARATIVE CONSTITUTIONAL LAW 14 (2017).

Constitution. The High Court of Bombay agreed with the plaintiffs, holding that all citizens have a duty not to partake in bullfighting and that government officials (in that case, police officers) are required to prevent cruelty against animals based on the Code of Criminal Procedure. The duty of compassion is not merely declaratory, the Court clarified, and should not be performed in a perfunctory manner. The duty of humans to treat animals compassionately, the Court continued, corresponds to a claim right of animals to life and freedom from cruelty: "It cannot be disputed that all animals are born with *an equal claim for life without any cruelty* to them. Perhaps if this *right* was given proper recognition by the human-beings, there would have been no necessity to bring on the statute book the said Act."[52]

The same development (from duties to rights) can be observed in *N.R. Nair et al. v. Union of India*. In this case, the High Court of Kerala examined the scope of the constitutional duty of compassion in the context of a complaint against the prohibition on training and exhibiting animals, especially bears, primates, tigers, panthers, and lions. The Court underlined:

> Neither the owners nor the employees of circus have a fundamental right to carry on trade or business in training and exhibiting endangered animals as the said trade is of such an obnoxious and pernicious activity geared towards mere entertainment which cannot be taken in the interest of general public to be a trade or business [. . .].[53]

The Court proceeded:

> [I]t is not only our fundamental duty to show compassion to our animal friends, but also *to recognise and protect their rights*. [. . .] In our considered opinion; legal rights shall not be the exclusive preserve of the humans which has to be extended beyond people thereby dismantling the thick legal wall with humans all on one side and all non-human animals on the other side. While the law currently protects wild life and endangered species from extinction, animals are denied rights, an anachronism which must necessarily change.[54]

With these considerations in mind, the Court used article 51 A lit. g of the Constitution to uphold the ban on use and exhibition of wild animals in Indian circuses.[55] These cases paved the way for a strong judicial practice across India that solidified the view that animals, like humans, have rights—in particular the right to life and bodily and mental integrity. For example, the *Centre for Environment Law, WWF 1 v. Union of India et al.*, the Supreme Court ruled that the constitutional right to life enshrined in article 21 applies to nonhuman species

---

[52] People for Animals et al. v. State of Goa et al., Writ Petition No. 347 of 1996 (HC Bombay 1997) (India) (emphasis added).

[53] N.R. Nair et al. v. Union of India (UOI) et al., AIR 2000 Ker 340 (India).

[54] *Id.* (emphasis added).

[55] The judgment was appealed and ultimately brought to the Indian Supreme Court. Appellants argued that the High Court of Kerala wrongfully gave effect to a notification lacking legal basis: N.R. Nair et al. v. Union of India (UOI) et al., AIR 2001 SC 2337 (India).

(in this case, Asiatic lions)[56] and in *Animal Welfare Board of India v. A. Nagaraja et al.*, the Court held that the Indian Constitution represents the "magna charta of animal rights."[57]

The Indian judiciary has developed a rich practice on how to interpret conflicting rights of humans and animals. Unlike German law, which readily accepts that humans have rights to use animals (such as by hunting or slaughtering), Indian courts have used a stricter balance of interests (perhaps because they accept that animals have rights). For example, in *Mohd. Habib v. State of Uttar Pradesh*, parties disputed whether the petitioner's wish to kill buffaloes and sell them for a living would stand in conflict with the duty of compassion for animals. The Allahabad High Court held that "the Constitution of India does not permit any citizen to claim that it is his fundamental right to take life and kill animals."[58] However, case law also shows that the Indian Supreme Court is inclined to use the constitutional norm to uphold the legality of bans on female cow and calf slaughter[59] and of bans on the slaughter of buffaloes and bullocks,[60] which suggests that India's animal rights developed alongside efforts to oppress people who belong to minority religions, and may even have been intended to achieve that goal.[61] In Chapter 11, I explain why such developments are deplorable and must be strongly repudiated. It bears mention that there are many ways in which animals can be accorded rights without oppressing others, and the fact that the provision was applied in other contexts (e.g., the ban on the use of animals in circuses) shows that Indian constitutional law is, from a comparative animal law perspective, still at the forefront of legal developments in animal law.

D. SWITZERLAND: ANIMAL DIGNITY

Article 120 para. 2 of the Swiss Constitution declares under the title "non-human gene technology":

> The Confederation shall legislate on the use of reproductive and genetic material from animals, plants and other organisms. In doing so, it shall take account of the *dignity of living beings* as well as the safety of human beings, animals and the environment, and shall protect the genetic diversity of animal and plant species.[62]

---

[56] Centre for Environment Law, WWF 1 v. Union of India et al., AIR 2013 8 SC 234, paras. 46–7 (India).

[57] Animal Welfare Board of India v. A. Nagaraja et al., AIR 2014 SC 547, para. 66 (India). *See also* Eisen & Stilt, *Protection and Status of Animals*, *in* MAX PLANCK INSTITUTE FOR COMPARATIVE CONSTITUTIONAL LAW 18 (2017).

[58] Mohd. Habib v. State of Uttar Pradesh, Civil Misc. Writ Petition No. 38469 of 1994 (HC Allahabad 1997) (India).

[59] Mohd. Hanif Quareshi et al. v. The State of Bihar, AIR 1959 SC 629 (India). In this case, the Court held that a total ban on cow slaughter was "constitutionally valid in so far as it prohibits the slaughter of cows of all ages and calves of cows, male and female, but that it is void in so far as it totally prohibits the slaughter of breeding bulls and working bullocks without prescribing any test or requirement as to their age or usefulness." (*Id.*).

[60] State of Gujarat v. Mirzapur Moti Kureshi Kassab Jammat et al., AIR 2006 SC 212 (India).

[61] *See, e.g.*, Mathilde Cohen, *Regulating Milk: Women and Cows in France and the United States*, 65 AJCL 469 (2017).

[62] FEDERAL CONSTITUTION OF THE SWISS CONFEDERATION (Switz.), art. 120 para. 2 (emphasis added).

When the "dignity of living beings" was enshrined in the Swiss Constitution in 1992 by popular vote, only a few knew what they had voted on. The norm had emerged in the context of gene technology, but by 2005 "animal dignity" had become a bedrock principle of Swiss animal law, was identified as the main purpose of the Swiss AWA (article 1 AWA), and further defined therein (article 3 lit. a AWA). Today, the "dignity of living beings" is broadly recognized to apply in the whole legal system of Switzerland.[63] The duty to take animal dignity into account is incumbent on the state and private actors and covers all animal species, regardless of their biological categorization or use for humans.[64]

At its base, the concept of animal dignity closely resembles human dignity. Both human dignity and animal dignity postulate that individuals must be respected and protected for their own sake. Animal dignity is also like human dignity in that it sets limits to whether and how others may use, dispose over, or interact with them.[65] In an influential statement of 2008, the Federal Committee on Animal Experiments and the Federal Ethics Committee on Non-Human Biotechnology jointly declared:

> Against the concept that humans alone are entitled to dignity and protection, the discussion concerning the dignity of creation stands as a corrective to the immoderate and arbitrary way in which humans treat the rest of Nature. Humans are required to show respect and restraint in the face of nature, due to their own interest in sustainable resources as well as by dint of the inherent value ascribed to a fellow living creature. Living creatures should be respected and protected for their own sake.[66]

The postulate of inherent value, while useful for interpreting existing norms and duties, has, however, only been applied to a few case groups. Animal dignity was codified and defined in article 3 lit. a AWA, which identifies three case groups that point to dignity violations: humiliation (degrading treatment, e.g., in circuses); excessive instrumentalization (e.g., extreme forms of animal research and agricultural animal production); and interference in an animal's appearance or their abilities (e.g., excessive breeding).[67] The case groups make clear that dignity violations go far beyond preventing unnecessary pain, suffering, or harm, and other damages to animals.[68] On the other hand, they focus only on protecting animals

---

[63] BGer Oct. 7, 2009, BGE 135 II 384, at 3.1 (Switz.).

[64] Bolliger, Richner, & Rüttimann 45 (2011). Private parties are bound by the Animal Welfare Act (Switz.) to respect animal dignity.

[65] Arianna Ferrari, *Eigenwert, in* Lexikon der Mensch-Tier-Beziehungen 89, 89 (2015); Philippe Mastronardi, *Kommentar zu Art. 7 BV, in* Die schweizerische Bundesverfassung 187 ff. (Bernhard Ehrenzeller et al. eds., 3d ed. 2014).

[66] The Dignity of Animals, A Joint Statement by the Federal Ethics Committee on Non-Human Biotechnology (ECNH) and the Federal Committee on Animal Experiments (FCAE) 11 (ECNH & FCAE, Berne 2008).

[67] Gieri Bolliger & Andreas Rüttimann, *Rechtlicher Schutz der Tierwürde: Status quo und Zukunftsperspektiven, in* Würde der Kreatur 65, 70 ff. (Christoph Ammann et al. eds., 2015).

[68] Botschaft zur Revision des Tierschutzgesetzes [Federal Message on the Revision of the Animal Welfare Act], Dec. 9, 2002, SR 02.092, 674 (Switz.): "[D]er Würdebegriff [umfasst] die Abwesenheit von Schmerzen, Leiden, Schäden und Angst; die Würde greift aber weiter und schliesst neben diesen biologischen auch ethische Aspekte ein."

from degrading treatment, excessive use by others, or drastic change in their aesthetic appearance, and fail to take into account systematic and more severe forms of exploitation.

Though animal dignity goes beyond traditional pillars of animal law, human dignity and animal dignity are not seen as carrying the same weight or entailing the same legal duties. While human dignity is absolutely protected, meaning that individual humans have fundamental interests that cannot be outweighed by any benefit for the community, animal dignity can be violated to safeguard "higher values" or "overriding interests" (art. 3 lit. a Swiss AWA). This structural difference between human dignity and animal dignity first emerged in parliamentary debates and is widely reiterated in early writings about animal dignity, but it is not immediately clear what puts human and animal dignity on such disparate footing. Before criticizing this approach, however, we must examine why and when human interests are thought to override the interests of animals in their dignity and integrity.

The Swiss AWA provides that when human interests violate animal dignity, a balance of interests (or of legally protected goods, *Rechtsgüter*) must be carried out.[69] As in German law, this balance is done by using the proportionality principle. Only if the balancing test fails and, thus, human interests do *not* override the animals' interests, will the violation of their dignity be subject to criminal sanctions as an act of cruelty (article 26 para. 1 lit. a of the Swiss AWA). There are few cases where human interests in using animals failed to override animals' core interests in life and bodily and mental integrity. In two cases in 2009, the Federal Court was asked to decide an appeal by the Institute for Neuroinformatics (INI) in Zurich, which was denied permission to experiment on macaques for basic neurological research.[70] The Court refused to let the experiments proceed because they promised no concrete benefits and because the net benefits of the experiments were much smaller than the harms that would be inflicted on the primates.[71] One might have expected these cases to inaugurate a new wave of case law that would finally take animal dignity seriously and balance interests diligently and qualitatively, but this did not happen. Eight years after these landmark cases, the INI submitted essentially the same proposal to carry out research on four macaques and was granted permission to do so.[72]

---

[69] *See* art. 4 para. 2 AWA. Only a few actions and behaviors are exempted from the balance of interests. Art. 16 of the Animal Welfare Ordinance (AWO) lists prohibited actions in all species, and arts. 17 *et seq*. AWO list prohibited actions in cows, pigs, sheep, goats, chickens, horses, dogs, fishes, and decapods (crustaceans with a carapace): ANIMAL WELFARE ORDINANCE (Switz.), arts. 16 ff. These norms are examined in detail in Chapter 9, §4 B.

[70] BGer Oct. 7, 2009, BGE 2C_421/2008 and 2C_422/2008 (Switz.). The two experiments the INI planned to do were designed to track changes in the macaques' cortex. An issue in the first experiment was that researchers would deny macaques water for up to twelve hours to raise the value of the reward (which would make the macaques work harder). The issue with the second experiment was that the animals would be killed so the researchers could use a microscope to follow the microcircuitry in their cortexes: *See* Alison Abbott, *Swiss Court Bans Work on Macaque Brains*, 453 NATURE 833 (2008).

[71] BGer Oct. 7, 2009, BGE 2C_421/2008 and 2C_422/2008, at 4.6.1 (Switz.).

[72] The veterinary agency of the canton of Zurich first granted its permission upon request by the research ethics committee. Three of the committee's members then filed an appeal at the Administrative Court of Zurich, which rejected their argument that the planned project would violate the dignity of the macaques: VGer Zürich, Apr. 5, 2017, VB.2016.00048 (Switz.).

This case is symptomatic of the larger failure of the Swiss legislature and judiciary to take seriously the people's commitment to animal dignity. Scholars in Switzerland find it disconcerting that article 120 para. 2 of the Swiss Constitution should permit human interests to fully override animal interests in virtually all cases. Switzerland continues to slaughter animals in the millions, permitting negligible gastronomic pleasures to routinely override basic interests in life.[73] But creating animal life for the sole purpose of extinguishing it (a common practice in food production and research), they argue, seems incompatible, in every sense, with respecting the dignity of animals, because it disregards their intrinsic value. Since the Swiss concept of animal dignity does not respect the core interests of animals, it must be a misnomer.[74]

Despite these glaring discrepancies between law and lived reality, most animal protection organizations in Switzerland are reluctant to push the concept forward because they fear that the constitutional norm will be abolished as a result. Only a few NGOs have dared to invoke animal dignity to argue for a fundamental legal change in Switzerland. In 2016, Sentience Politics launched the first citizens' initiative to establish basic rights for primates on the basis of the dignity provision.[75] The organization wants to amend the constitution of the Canton of Basel-Stadt with the aim of granting nonhuman primates constitutional rights to life and bodily and mental integrity. In a short period of time, it collected all necessary signatures but its success quickly came to a halt when the Cantonal Parliament declared the initiative invalid, arguing that it violates federal civil law and the federal AWA. In January 2019, in a highly-anticipated decision, the Cantonal Constitutional Court ruled that the primate rights initiative is valid—because cantons are free to "expand the circle of rights holders beyond the anthropological barrier" in the realm of public law—and must be submitted to the people of Basel-Stadt for a vote.[76] These and other initiatives make apparent the need for a broad societal discourse about whether the concept of animal dignity must be expanded so that it effectively protects animal life, about whether it must lead to a stricter handling of cases where animals are excessively instrumentalized, and about whether it should operate as a reliable basis for introducing basic rights for animals.

Switzerland is not the only state that has established animal dignity as a guiding legal concept. Liechtenstein enshrined its own version of animal dignity (on a legislative level), and the Netherlands recognizes the intrinsic value of animals in its Animal Experimentation

---

[73] In 2017, over 62 million animals were slaughtered in Switzerland. The country therefore kills 5 million animals a month, 169,000 a day, 7,000 an hour, 118 a minute, and 2 every second: Swissveg, Schlachtzahlen Schweiz (2017), *available at* https://www.swissveg.ch/node/26 (last visited Jan. 10, 2019).

[74] Bolliger & Rüttimann, *Rechtlicher Schutz der Tierwürde, in* WÜRDE DER KREATUR 68 (2015); JEDELHAUSER 73 (2011). Because animal dignity is considered "relative," it is also called "second class dignity": Klaus Petrus, *Würde, in* LEXIKON DER MENSCH-TIER-BEZIEHUNGEN 424, 425 (2015).

[75] In the canton of Basel, Sentience Politics has initiated a popular initiative to establish basic primate rights to life and bodily and mental integrity in the constitution of Basel: Raffael Fasel et al., Fundamental Rights for Primates, Policy Paper (Sentience Politics, Apr. 2016), *available at* https://ea-foundation.org/files/Fundamental-Rights-for-Primates.pdf (last visited Jan. 10, 2019).

[76] AppGer Basel, Jan. 15, 2019, VG.2018.1 (AG.2019.40) (Switz.). At the time of writing, the Court's decision was appealed by some members of the parliament. *See further* Raffael Fasel, *The Swiss Citizens' Initiative for Primate Rights Goes to Court*, NONHUMAN RIGHTS BLOG, Apr. 2, 2018, *available at* https://www.nonhumanrights.org/blog/swiss-citizens-primate-rights/ (last visited Jan. 10, 2019).

Act.[77] Other nations that make reference to the inherent value of animals include Germany, Latvia, Norway, and South Korea.[78]

E. CONSTITUTIONAL ANIMAL LAW IN THE EXTRATERRITORIALITY DEBATE

States have taken different approaches to give effect to animal interests in their constitutions, including through state objectives to protect animals, animal dignity, a duty of compassion that is interpreted as giving rise to animals rights, prohibiting animal cruelty, and postulating the kind treatment of animals. Each approach operates differently by addressing specific actors (the government as a whole, particular agencies or authorities of the government, substates, or individuals), and by being absolute or relative in scope of protection. Constitutional norms that protect animals are of high symbolical relevance because they serve as catalysts for future social and legal developments. As state practice shows, many of the norms examined herein have also been successfully applied in court.

A danger of applying constitutional law extraterritorially is that its provisions tend to be programmatic. The more open-ended a constitutional provision, the more difficult it is to establish beyond doubt that certain conduct violated it. The true value of constitutional norms for extraterritorial animal law is that they operate as a reliable indicator to assess a state's sincerity about protecting animals, including those located abroad.[79] For example, they make states' claims to public morality under article XX(a) of the GATT more credible.[80] Since constitutional guarantees are part of a state's *ordre public*, they serve as a viable basis to use the law of jurisdiction in a manner that helps to protect animals more effectively in the future. As such, they could help establish, *de lege ferenda*, passive personality jurisdiction over animals, and may give rise to the reputational effects principle.

§3 Applying Criminal Animal Law Extraterritorially

A. BASICS OF CRIMINAL ANIMAL LAW

Criminal animal law is a subset of criminal law that places sanctions on breaches of animal law. When an animal is abused, injured, or killed, we typically view them as a victim, so it is easy to assume that criminal animal laws protect the interests of animals in their well-being, life, integrity, or liberty. But criminal animal law differs from general criminal law in crucial respects. Animals are not typically considered to be victims in legal terms, nor do they have a right to assert a claim for their injury—a problem rooted in law's classification of animals as property.[81] But according to criminal animal law, being someone else's property—or,

---

[77] ANIMAL WELFARE ACT (Liech.), art. 1; WET HOUDENDE REGELEN MET BETREKKING TOT HET VERRICHTEN VAN PROEVEN OP DIEREN [WET OP DE DIERPROEVEN] [ANIMAL EXPERIMENTATION ACT], Jan. 12, 1977 (Neth.).

[78] Animal Protection Law (Lat.), preamble; Animal Welfare Act (Nor.), § 3. For the other jurisdictions, *see* ROBERTSON 80 (2015).

[79] *See* FALLER 148–9 (2005) on the state duty to protect animals extraterritorially.

[80] STOHNER 93 (2006). *See* on this presumption in WTO law, Chapter 4, §7.

[81] There are a few exceptions to the rule that animals are not victims. The claim that animals deserve independent standing in criminal law and must be recognized as the proper victims of crime was recognized by the Oregon Supreme Court in 2014 in *State v. Nix*. Drawing on writings of John Stuart Mill, Rachel Carson, contemporary

put differently, not being considered a legal person—does not prevent animals from being beneficiaries of criminal law.[82] As Wagman and Liebman note with astonishment, there is no parallel situation in modern law in which a living being can suffer harm and also be a piece of property.[83]

B. ADVANCED CRIMINAL ANIMAL LAWS

The actions and omissions that states criminalize through their animal welfare or protection acts vary widely. Anti-cruelty laws are among the most common and well-known laws to deal with the treatment of animals by humans, by sanctioning cruelty inflicted on animals. Animal cruelty is an umbrella term that covers particularly despicable human behavior toward animals, which causes animals to experience pain and suffering.[84] The prohibition of animal cruelty is usually formulated in an open-ended manner and rarely concretized by law, secondary legislation, or precedents. This allows it to capture a wide range of abuses, but it also leaves considerable room for interpretation. If criminal animal laws are formulated too loosely, the principle *nulla poena sine lege certa*—according to which law must be formulated in sufficient detail to allow citizens to foresee when their actions will be punishable[85]—combined with the presumption *in dubio pro reo*, gives perpetrators ample room to escape conviction. For example, in *People v. Rogers*, the New York City Court was called to prosecute a person who had docked a puppy's tail with a rubber band, as a consequence of which the puppy died. Instead of exploring whether the pain and suffering done to the animal was justified, the Court held that if the legislature wanted to prohibit tail docking, it should do so explicitly.[86]

---

newspaper articles, and state bar bulletins, the Court held that the common, ordinary meaning of the term "victim" includes animals and that the criminal statute "protects individual animals from suffering from neglect. In adopting that statute, the legislature regarded those animals as the 'victims' of the offense." (State of Oregon v. Nix, 355 Or. 77, 334 P.3d 437 (2014) (U.S.)). Two years later, in *State v. Hess*, the Colorado Court of Appeals grappled with the same question to determine if the accused's hoarding practices constituted one or many offenses. The Court held that animals qualify as victims and that each of the charged offenses had a different, identifiable animal victim (State of Colorado v. Hess, Nos. 14CA1435, Nov. 3, 2016, Cert Denied Oct. 2, 2017, § 56 (U.S.)). The US Animal Legal Defense Fund (ALDF) has taken notice of these events and filed a lawsuit in 2018 on behalf of horse Justice against his former owner to recover the costs of Justice's ongoing medical care and to compensate him for his pain and suffering. The Washington County Court dismissed the lawsuit in September 2018, holding that animals cannot sue on their own behalf (Justice v. Vercher, Case 18CV17601, Opinion Letter by Judge Knowles, Sept. 17, 2018 (U.S.). On January 22, 2019, ALDF appealed the decision. If successful, this lawsuit would be the first to establish that animals have a legal right to sue their abusers in court.

[82] BOLLIGER, RICHNER, & RÜTTIMANN 102 (2011).

[83] WAGMAN & LIEBMAN 144 (2011).

[84] Gieri Bolliger, *Tierquälerei*, *in* LEXIKON DER MENSCH-TIER-BEZIEHUNGEN 357, 357 (2015).

[85] In the European Union, for example, the principle *nullum crimen nulla poena sine lege certa* is a "general principle of Union law," which binds the Union and all its members: Christina Peristeridou, *The Principle of* Lex Certa *in National Law and European Perspectives*, *in* SUBSTANTIVE CRIMINAL LAW OF THE EUROPEAN UNION 69 (André Klip ed., 2011).

[86] People v. Rogers, 703 N.Y.S.2d 891 (N.Y. City Ct. 2000) (U.S.). *See further* on how courts have grappled with vague terms in criminal animal law: HESSLER ET AL. 111 ff. (2017).

Many states are aware of these obstacles and have chosen to identify and define in detail those acts that lead to penal sanctions. The Indian Prevention of Cruelty to Animals Act, for instance, defines cruel treatment of animals as: beating, kicking, overriding, overdriving, overloading, torturing, or otherwise causing an animal pain; allowing these acts to be committed; administering drugs that cause animals suffering; wrongly conveying or carrying an animal; keeping or confining an animal in a cage or other area that is too short or narrow; keeping an animal on too short a chain; failing to provide sufficient food, drink, or shelter; abandoning an animal; selling an animal to a person that mutilates, starves, dehydrates, overcrowds, or ill-treats them; using an animal for entertainment; or confining an animal to use as prey.[87] Similarly detailed descriptions of acts causing suffering to animals can be found, among others, in Croatian[88] and Austrian law.[89]

These anti-cruelty laws describe criminal offenses against animals in detail, but they suggest that only a handful of actions can compromise the well-being of animals. However, just like basic human interests are affected by and must be protected from a much broader range of actions and omissions, so, too, are animals' basic interests. In recent years, a few states have begun to explore what it would mean to move closer to this goal. They have begun to condemn passive and negligent behavior (in addition to intentional animal abuse and cruelty).[90] Some have adopted a broader definition of animal maltreatment to encompass inflicting psychological hardship on them. Ontario did this in its Prevention of Cruelty to Animals Act.[91] Notable in this respect is also the Zambian law, which states that "[a]ny person who shall kill an animal in the sight of any other animal awaiting slaughter shall be guilty of cruelty and of an offence under this Act [. . .]."[92] These examples show that animal law is becoming more nuanced and the line of what is acceptable and what is cruel has shifted progressively towards stricter and more detailed regulation.[93]

But, in addition to becoming more detailed, can criminal animal law become more encompassing? After all, detailed anti-cruelty laws punish only the most "nonstandard" ways in which animals are currently maltreated. Industrial use and abuse of animals, including extreme confinement, mutilation, inability to move around and socialize, and slaughter, all fall through the cracks of criminal animal law. We thus need a more nuanced *and* a more encompassing approach to criminal animal law. I will next look closely at some of the most well-developed animal laws, notably those of Switzerland, to offer a useful example of how to achieve these goals.[94]

---

87 The Prevention of Cruelty to Animals Act (India), art. 11.

88 Animal Protection Act (Croat.), art. 4.

89 ANIMAL PROTECTION ACT (Austria), §§ 5 ff.

90 Bolliger, *Tierquälerei*, *in* LEXIKON DER MENSCH-TIER-BEZIEHUNGEN 357 (2015).

91 Ontario Society for the Prevention of Cruelty to Animals Act, R.S.O. 1990, c.O.36, §§ 11(2)(1) and 11(2)(2) (Can.) (covering distress).

92 Prevention of Cruelty to Animals Act (Zam.), art. 3 para. 1 lit. f.

93 WAGMAN & LIEBMAN 154 (2011).

94 Schmid and Kilchsperger compared AWAs around the world and showed that, from the animals' perspective, Switzerland might have one of the best: SCHMID & KILCHSPERGER 10–1 (2010). This finding is confirmed by the World Animal Protection, *see* World Animal Protection, Animal Protection Index, *available at* https://api.worldanimalprotection.org/ (last visited Jan. 10, 2019).

In Switzerland, animal abuse is a generic term that encompasses more specific actions and omissions, including: mistreatment of animals; neglect (like leaving an animal in a car on a hot day or hoarding animals and failing to take care of them); unnecessarily overworking animals (in a physical, physiological, and psychological sense);[95] disregarding their dignity; killing an animal in a way that causes them to suffer unnecessarily or wantonly killing them; organizing animal fights that cause animal suffering or lead to the death of animals; inflicting pain, suffering, or harm on an animal for research purposes, if the suffering was avoidable and unnecessary from a scientific perspective; and abandoning an animal (article 26 para. 1 lit. a–e AWA). Some of these offenses are committed if the animal is injured, while others are fulfilled if an animal is put in danger (abstract imperilment includes, e.g., neglect and abandonment). Failing to protect or take care of an animal is penalized when a person is a so-called "guarantor" that has a special duty created by law, a contract, or risks, to ensure the animal's physical and psychological integrity.[96] Owners and caretakers of animals, for instance, are especially liable for omissions, but so are people who put animals in jeopardy. It also bears mention that neglect is not only caused by failing to provide sufficient care, food, or shelter, but also by failing to provide animals adequate opportunities for exercise and mental occupation.[97]

Under Swiss law, willful abuse (by action or omission) is a misdemeanor that gives rise to higher penalties. A perpetrator who willfully abuses an animal will be subject to a custodial sentence not exceeding three years or a monetary penalty not exceeding 30,000 CHF (30,000 USD). If the perpetrator acts negligently (which amounts to a contravention of law), they face detention and fines up to 20,000 CHF (20,000 USD).[98]

Animal abuse, as codified in article 26 AWA, is further specified in an implementation regulation, the Animal Welfare Ordinance (AWO). Articles 16 *et seq.* AWO list acts which are absolutely prohibited and which qualify as a failure to respect the dignity of animals (and hence violate article 26 para. 1 lit. a AWA, giving rise to criminal sanctions). Article 16 para. 2 of the Swiss AWO prohibits the following acts:

a) killing animals in a manner that involves agonizing pain;
b) striking animals on their eyes or genitalia and breaking or squeezing their tail;
c) wantonly killing animals, in particular shooting tame animals or animals in captivity;
d) organizing fights between or with animals, in which the animals are tormented or killed;

---

[95] Physical overworking means an animal is put under more strain than they can cope with (e.g., when pulling weight or accelerating). Physiological overworking strains farmed animals when they generate "output" (milk, eggs, etc.). Psychological overworking places a strain on animals' ability to concentrate or learn: BOLLIGER, RICHNER, & RÜTTIMANN 120–1 (2011).

[96] ANIMAL WELFARE ACT (Switz.), art. 26 para. 1 lit. a., in connection with CRIMINAL CODE (Switz.), art. 11 para. 2.

[97] BOLLIGER, RICHNER, & RÜTTIMANN 114 (2011).

[98] ANIMAL WELFARE ACT (Switz.), art. 26 para. 1, in conjunction with CRIMINAL CODE (Switz.), art. 333 para. 2 lit. b & art. 10 para. 3 (misdemeanor); ANIMAL WELFARE ACT (Switz.), art. 26 para. 2 and CRIMINAL CODE (Switz.), art. 103 (contravention). In Switzerland, animal abuse does not qualify as a felony.

e) using animals for exhibition, promotion, films or similar purposes if such use is obviously associated with pain, suffering or harm for the animal;
f) abandoning an animal with the intention of disposing of them;
g) administering substances and products for the purpose of influencing the performance or modifying the outward appearance of animals if this compromises their health or well-being;
h) participating in competitions and sporting events with animals, in which banned substances or products as defined in the lists issued for the sports associations are used;
i) performing actions or failing to perform actions on an animal for exhibition purposes if this results in the infliction of pain or harm on the animal or compromises their well-being in some other way;
j) sexually motivated activities with animals;
k) the shipment of animals in packaging;
l) the temporary export of animals for the performance of prohibited activities and the reimportation of these animals;
m) using electric fencing that electrifies an animal through a receiving device.[99]

Some of these prohibitions are quite progressive in a comparative perspective. Take, for example, the prohibition of zoophilia (lit. j). According to Swiss law, an animal can be a victim of zoophilia even if the perpetrator has not inflicted pain, suffering, or harm on them. In other words, zoosadism is not a defining element of the offense.[100] States like Germany, by contrast, only prohibit zoophilia if the animal is caused considerable pain or suffering and if this is done "out of cruelty."[101] In Switzerland, activities with animals need not even be sexual in nature (e.g., touching genitals, penetration etc.) to qualify as acts of zoophilia; if a person interacts with an animal in an objectively asexual manner but is motivated by sexual fantasies, the dignity of the animal is violated.[102]

Drafters of the Swiss AWA realized that though relatively broad, these prohibitions fail to take into account the many forms of animal abuse and the different contexts in which they occur. Articles 17 *et seq.* AWO fill this gap, by prohibiting conduct vis-à-vis specific species. For example, the AWO forbids docking a cow's tail, using elastic rings or caustic pastes to

---

[99] Animal Welfare Ordinance (Switz.), art. 16 para. 2. Bolliger et al. explain that many of the offenses listed in arts. 16 ff. of the AWO are not sufficiently recognized by executive authorities as amounting to violations of animals' dignity that must be penalized. The authorities incorrectly subsume these offenses under any of the elements of art. 26 para. 1 lit. a Animal Welfare Act (Switz.): Bolliger, Richner, & Rüttimann 137 n. 741 (2011).

[100] For instance, a perpetrator is convicted on the basis of art. 16 para. 2 j AWO when he rubs his penis on dogs from an animal shelter, whom he was supposed to take for a walk: Strafbefehl des Bezirksstatthalteramts Arlesheim vom 16.8.2010 (TIR-Datenbank BL10/008). More violent sexual acts done to animals are also covered by the *litera*, including penetrating an animal with body parts or objects that cause internal bleeding and death: Strafmandat des Bezirkstatthalteramts Arlesheim vom 26.9.2008 (TIR-Datenbank BL09/008).

[101] Animal Welfare Act (Ger.), § 17 para. 2 lit. b.

[102] Bolliger, Richner, & Rüttimann 129, 138–9 (2011). *See further* Gieri Bolliger, Sexualität mit Tieren (Zoophilie): Eine Rechtliche Betrachtung (2011); Andrea M. Beetz & Anthony L. Podberscek eds., Bestiality and Zoophilia: Sexual Relations with Animals (2009).

remove horns, tethering steers by a nose ring, dehorning water buffaloes or yaks, or using hot and cold branding (article 17 Swiss AWO). It is prohibited to dock pigs' tails, clip their teeth (if they are piglets), or use nose rings (article 18 Swiss AWO). Sheep and goats may not be dehorned by elastic rings or caustic pastes, and procedures may not be performed on the penis of teaser rams (article 19 Swiss AWO). Chickens may not be debeaked, trimmed off their comb, wattles, or wings, have their water withheld to induce molting, be forcibly fed, or plucked while still alive (article 20 Swiss AWO). It is prohibited to dock a horse's tail, cause them to have an unnatural hoof position, drive them with electrified devices, desensitize their limb nerves, remove their tactile hair, or tie their tongue (article 21 Swiss AWO). The AWO also prohibits docking the tail or ears of a dog, destroying their vocal organs, or preventing them from vocally expressing themselves (article 22 Swiss AWO). Fishes and decapods may, among others, not be fished with the intention of releasing them again, be used as live bait, angled with barbed hooks, or transported on ice or icy water (article 23 Swiss AWO). In comparative perspective, these are strong commitments that declare criminal many routine practices of factory farming, such as mutilations, which are still legal in most other states.

Another provision that deserves our attention in comparative perspective is article 27 Swiss AWA. The norm penalizes all actions that violate the CITES, which includes importing, exporting, transporting, and possessing animals or animal products the CITES parties have declared illegal. Switzerland has also issued its own bans on trade in animals, including import bans on cat and dog fur,[103] on dogs with docked ears or tails,[104] and on dolphins.[105] Willful contravention of any of these acts results in a custodial sentence not exceeding three years or monetary penalty. Negligent contravention may result in detention or fines up to 20,000 CHF (20,000 USD).

Other offenses listed in article 28 of the Swiss AWA are non-compliance with regulations on keeping animals, regulations on breeding or producing animals, regulations on animal trade and transport, regulations on animal experiments or surgical procedures on animals, and regulations on animal slaughter. Article 28 AWA is essential to make criminal animal law more effective because it penalizes all violations of the more detailed administrative standards and thereby gives them greater regulatory weight. Together with the general prohibitions of the AWO, these weave a dense regulatory net that catches the many actions that might otherwise slip through, so that we ultimately have a more nuanced and more encompassing approach to criminal animal law.

Although Swiss criminal law is at the forefront of many legal developments, it is also very conservative, by aligning with the "use paradigm" that prevails in animal law. By focusing on the peripheries of animal abuse and declaring the institutional confinement and killing of animals legal, regardless of whether this can in any remote sense be regarded as "humane," Switzerland misses the forest for the trees. Ultimately, it considers the interests of animals worth protecting only when they do not clash with 99 percent of human interests. The 1 percent that anti-cruelty norms tackle shows that "cruelty is acknowledged only when profitability ceases."[106] Ani Satz calls this the "interest-convergence problem," which is a sort of

---

[103] ANIMAL WELFARE ACT (Switz.), art. 14 para. 2.

[104] ANIMAL WELFARE ORDINANCE (Switz.), art. 22 para. 1 lit. a.

[105] ANIMAL WELFARE ACT (Switz.), art. 7 para. 3.

[106] HARRISON (1964).

"legal gerrymandering for human interest;"[107] a systematic pattern that makes clear the precariousness of efforts to protect animals when human and animal interests diverge. So for a country to claim that it actually has anti-cruelty laws in place, it must first begin to focus on the most widespread and accepted forms of cruelty.[108]

C. ADVANCED LIABILITIES

Most animal laws hold people responsible for primary liability or liability for participation.[109] Well-established AWAs also provide for derivative liability, which extends the liability of the principal actor responsible for ill-treatment of an animal to persons whose decisions affected the perpetrator's actions and resulted in the ill-treatment.[110] Derivative liability demands we hold superiors responsible for their instructions (based on, for instance, the *respondeat superior* theory), which is particularly useful for tackling large-scale, systematic animal abuse, as done by multinational enterprises.[111] Derivative liability in corporate structures may extend to employers, directors, officers, inspectors, or the corporation itself, but will depend on how responsibility is assigned to these actors. The higher the chain of command, the more incumbent it is on the prosecutor to prove that superiors expressed their "authority, permission, or consent" to harmful actions or omissions, or to show that they failed to take all reasonable steps to prevent harm.[112] For instance, section 165 of New Zealand's AWA, titled "liability of directors and officers of bodies corporate," states:

> Where any body corporate is convicted of an offence against this Act, every director and every person concerned in the management of the body corporate is guilty of the like offence if it is proved—(a) that the act that constituted the offence took place with his or her authority, permission, or consent; or (b) that he or she knew or should have known that the offence was to be or was being committed and failed to take all reasonable steps to prevent or stop it.[113]

---

[107] Ani Satz, *Animals as Vulnerable Subjects: Beyond Interest-Convergence, Hierarchy, and Property*, 16 ANIMAL L. 65, 70 (2009).

[108] *See further* FRANCIONE (2007); Kymlicka, *Social Membership* 126 ff. (2017).

[109] Complicity liability is not only fulfilled by physically aiding in animal abuse, but also comprises acts of planning, practical assistance, public or private investment, campaigning organizations, etc. § 29 lit. h of New Zealand's AWA determines that "[a] person commits an offence who (h) counsels, procures, aids, or abets any other person to do an act or refrain from doing an act as a result of which an animal suffers unreasonable or unnecessary pain or distress." Norway, Switzerland, and the United Kingdom also expressly sanction complicity in animal law (Animal Welfare Act (Nor.), § 37; ANIMAL WELFARE ACT (Switz.), art. 27 para. 2 and art. 28 para. 2; Animal Welfare Act (U.K.), §§ 33–4).

[110] ROBERTSON 159 (2015).

[111] INTERNATIONAL COMMISSION OF JURISTS, REPORT OF THE EXPERT LEGAL PANEL ON CORPORATE COMPLICITY IN INTERNATIONAL CRIMES: CORPORATE COMPLICITY & LEGAL ACCOUNTABILITY, vol. 2, 32 ff (ICJ, Geneva 2008).

[112] *See* Animal Welfare Act (N.Z.), §§ 164 and 165.

[113] Animal Welfare Act (N.Z.), § 165. *See also* Animal Welfare Act (U.K.), § 57: "(1) Where an offence under this Act is committed by a body corporate and is proved to have been committed with the consent or connivance of or to be attributable to any neglect on the part of (a) any director, manager, secretary or other similar officer

In addition to directors and managers, some animal laws establish liability for employers and principals. India's Prevention of Cruelty to Animals Act provides for a limited form of derivative liability for employers.[114] So does New Zealand in section 164 of its AWA, by holding that if an employee commits animal abuse, both employee and employer will be held responsible, whether or not the employer knew about or approved the employee's conduct. Under the same section, the principal and the agent are liable if the agent commits an offense against animals, and if it was done under the principal's express or implied authority.[115]

These advanced forms of liability are essential to effectively combat animal abuse. In many industries, animal cruelty is deeply embedded in industrial processes to save time and increase profits. Once cruelty is uncovered, employers tend to "name and shame" individual employees who are in precarious employment relationships. These strategies achieve short-term goals by allowing immediate retribution, but they, as a matter of fact, end up failing to combat animal cruelty because they do not get to the root of what is the real cause of animal cruelty. Many employees are coerced, by their employer, into using force against animals; when one is fired, the next is hired to do the same job.[116] And while individuals are being held responsible—through fines, incarceration, or therapy[117]—for actions they never wanted to commit in the first place, the industries that instigate these actions by instructing or forcing employees to abuse animals evade any and all legal scrutiny.

D. CORPORATE CRIMINAL LIABILITY

Up until the past decade, the laws of most states provided that corporations were only subject to civil law, which binds them contractually or by tort obligations. When it came to actions that resulted in criminal harm, it was accepted that *societas delinquere non potest*: "a

of the body corporate, or (b) any person who was purporting to act in any such capacity, he (as well as the body corporate) commits the offence and shall be liable to be proceeded against and punished accordingly [. . .]."

[114] The Prevention of Cruelty to Animals Act (India), art. 11 para. 1 lit. b.

[115] Animal Welfare Act (N.Z.), § 164 paras. 1 and 2.

[116] *See, e.g.*, David Castellon, *USDA Threatens Action on Cargill Slaughter Operation*, THE BUSINESS JOURNAL, Nov. 28, 2018. Consider Timothy Pachirat's experience as a slaughterhouse worker. After being transferred to the main area where animals are forced to enter the slaughterhouse, Pachirat quickly learned that mistreating animals is structural in the slaughterhouse. Together with three other workers, he was commissioned to "get the line moving." Unlike the other workers, Pachirat refused to use the electric prod, because "they're all moving through the line anyway" (TIMOTHY PACHIRAT, EVERY TWELVE SECONDS: INDUSTRIALIZED SLAUGHTER THE POLITICS OF SIGHT 148 (2011)). When his co-worker saw that Pachirat used a plastic paddle instead of the electric prod, he became furious, sprinted over, took away the paddle, and forced Pachirat to use the electric prod instead, saying: "Okay, [. . .] you wanna know why I use this? [. . .] I use this because I like to have my work. And if we don't keep these cows moving through, they're gonna call us up to the office and we're going to get fired. That's why." (*Id.* at 148). Even though the workers despise using force against animals, they see it as a necessary part of getting their job done as quickly and efficiently as possible. They readily accept the downside of this, including remorse, feelings of guilt, sleeplessness, and a lack of appreciation for work, because no other jobs are available for them to earn a living.

[117] *See* on the need for animal law to move away from the paradigm of incarceration: JUSTIN MARCEAU, BEYOND CAGES: ANIMAL LAW AND CRIMINAL PUNISHMENT (2019).

legal entity cannot be blameworthy."[118] New developments in national and international law suggest that states are increasingly prepared to hold corporations liable as criminal actors. This change of opinion was fueled by the gradual realization that punishing individual officers, directors, or managers is not a sufficient deterrent, particularly in corporate cultures that institutionally tolerate or even encourage misconduct to increase economic returns.[119] In (multinational) corporations, "it becomes more and more difficult to identify a natural person who may be held responsible (in a criminal law sense) for the offence. [I]f an agent of management is sentenced, the sanction can easily be compensated by the legal person."[120] Holding a corporation criminally liable is seen as an effective means to break these patterns, by threatening to cause reputational loss and stigma for corporations.[121]

To date, the laws of Austria, Belgium, Cyprus, Denmark, Estonia, Finland, France, Hungary, Ireland, Latvia, Lithuania, Luxembourg, the Netherlands, Portugal, Romania, Slovenia, Spain, Switzerland, the United Kingdom, and the United States have established that corporations can and must be held liable for engaging in criminal behavior.[122] On the international level, the OECD Anti-Bribery Convention,[123] the International Convention on the Suppression and Punishment of the Crime of Apartheid,[124] the European Convention on the Prevention of Terrorism,[125] the European Criminal Convention on Corruption,[126] and the European Convention on the Protection of the Environment through Criminal Law[127] all determine that corporations are subject to criminal law. Based on these national and

[118] Edward B. Diskant, *Comparative Corporate Criminal Liability: Exploring the Uniquely American Doctrine Through Comparative Criminal Procedure*, 118 YALE L.J. 126, 129 (2008).

[119] Although corporate criminal liability alone cannot prevent such acts, it should be considered *in addition to* individual criminal liability, not as a substitute for it: IBA REPORT EXTRATERRITORIAL JURISDICTION 234 (2009); Dominik Brodowski et al., *Regulating Corporate Criminal Liability: An Introduction*, *in* REGULATING CORPORATE CRIMINAL LIABILITY 1, 3 (Dominik Brodowski et al. eds., 2014).

[120] CoE, Explanatory Report to the Convention on the Protection of Environment through Criminal Law, Nov. 4, 1998, at 14.

[121] JAMES GOBERT & MAURICE PUNCH, RETHINKING CORPORATE CRIME 52 (2003).

[122] For Cyprus, Estonia, Finland, France, Hungary, Ireland, Latvia, Lithuania, Luxembourg, the Netherlands, Portugal, Romania, Slovenia, Spain, and the United Kingdom, *see* Guy Stessens, *Corporate Criminal Liability: A Comparative Perspective*, 43 ICLQ 493, 499 (1994). For Austria, *see* BUNDESGESETZ ÜBER DIE VERANTWORTLICHKEIT VON VERBÄNDEN FÜR STRAFTATEN [VERBANDSVERANTWORTLICHKEITSGES ETZ (VBVG)] [FEDERAL ACT ON THE RESPONSIBILITY OF ENTITIES FOR CRIMINAL OFFENSES], BGBl. I No. 151/2005, Dec. 23, 2005 (Austria). For Belgium, *see* Code pénal [CRIMINAL CODE], No. 1867060850, M.B. 3133, June 8, 1867, art. 5 (Belg.). For Denmark, *see* Danish Criminal Code, Order No. 909, Sept. 27, 2005, § 306 (Den.). For Switzerland, *see* CRIMINAL CODE (Switz.), art. 102. For the United States, *see* Santa Clara County v. Southern Railroad, 118 U.S. 394 (1886) (U.S.); New York Central v. Hudson River R.R. Co., 212 U.S. 481 (1909) (U.S.).

[123] OECD, CONVENTION ON COMBATING BRIBERY OF FOREIGN PUBLIC OFFICIALS IN INTERNATIONAL BUSINESS TRANSACTIONS, art. 2 (OECD Publishing, Paris 2011).

[124] International Convention on the Suppression and Punishment of the Crime of Apartheid, Nov. 30, 1973, 1015 U.N.T.S. 243, art. 1(2).

[125] CoE, Convention on the Prevention of Terrorism, May 16, 2005, C.E.T.S. No. 196, art. 10 para. 2.

[126] CoE, Criminal Law Convention on Corruption, Jan. 27, 1999, C.E.T.S. No. 173, art. 18.

[127] CoE, Convention on the Protection of the Environment through Criminal Law, Nov. 4, 1998, C.E.T.S. No. 172, art. 9 and preamble. To date, the convention has been ratified by three states.

international developments, the principle *societas delinquere non potest* was ousted by a more adequate understanding of the role of corporations in the modern criminal justice system.[128]

Because multinational enterprises own almost all domesticated animals,[129] corporate criminal liability is crucial to combat and prevent animal abuse. Criminal animal law can be applied to corporations in three ways. First, general criminal law can establish corporate criminal liability for all or a selected group of crimes. Article 102 para. 1 of the Swiss Criminal Code does this. If a felony or misdemeanor that harms animals and which is not attributable to a natural person was committed "in an undertaking in the exercise of commercial activities in accordance with the objects of the undertaking,"[130] then the corporation is punishable for the wrong done to the animal.

Second, animal welfare or protection acts may determine that their penal sanctions apply to acts done by corporations. The Croatian APA states its objective is to "govern [. . .] the responsibilities, obligations and duties of natural and legal persons in relation to the protection of animals." [131] Similarly, article 30 of the Swiss AWA determines that it applies to legal persons in all respects.[132] In these cases, corporations are not held liable in a subsidiary manner; they can be directly charged with a crime, they are directly liable for participatory acts (such as instigation), and they can be held jointly liable together with natural persons.

Third, corporations can be held responsible through theories of general criminal law that attribute blame to corporations. In the United States, the standard test to impute conduct to a corporation is the *respondeat superior* doctrine (also known as the agency principle).[133] The doctrine requires a corporate agent commit an illegal act (*actus reus*) in the requisite state of mind (*mens rea*), which is then attributed to the legal person. The fiction or nominalist theory, by contrast, denies the existence of corporate personality and holds that a corporation is only a group of individuals who act through a corporation at a certain time. This theory demands we identify human actions that serve as the corporation's "directing mind and will" (which is also done by the identification or alter ego theories).[134] Some states use a more encompassing theory of attribution. Company culture theory, well-known in Australia, holds corporations accountable for procedures, systems, or cultures within a company.[135] In

[128] Brodowski et al., *Regulating Corporate Criminal Liability*, *in* REGULATING CORPORATE CRIMINAL LIABILITY 1–2 (2014).

[129] Park & Singer 122 (2012).

[130] CRIMINAL CODE (Switz.), art. 102 para. 1.

[131] Animal Protection Act (Croat.), art. 1.

[132] ANIMAL WELFARE ACT (Switz.), art. 30.

[133] CELIA WELLS, CORPORATIONS AND CRIMINAL RESPONSIBILITY 130 (2d ed. 2001). *E.g.*, New York Central & Hudson River R.R. v. United States, 212 U.S. 481, 494 (1909) (U.S.). Other jurisdictions call this vicarious liability, which usually draws on the liability a master (or employer) has for their servant (or employee). *See* on employer/employee liability for corporations: Irina Kotchach Bleustein et al., *Corporate Criminal Liability*, 52 AM. CRIM. L. REV. 851 (2015).

[134] Mark Pieth & Radha Ivory, *Emergence and Convergence: Corporate Criminal Liability Principles in Overview*, *in* CORPORATE CRIMINAL LIABILITY: EMERGENCE, CONVERGENCE, AND RISK 3, 6 (Mark Pieth & Radha Ivory eds., 2011); WELLS 130 (2001). *E.g.*, Canadian Dredge and Dock Co. Ltd. v. The Queen, [1985] 1 SCR 662, verdict (Can.); Tesco Supermarkets Ltd. v. Nattrass [1972] AC 153, 170–2 (U.K.).

[135] *Criminal Code Act 1995*, Act No. 12, § 12.3 para. 2 lit. c and d (Austl.). For extensive research on criminal corporate culture, *see* Special Representative of the Secretary-General Allens Arthur Robinson, *"Corporate Culture" as a Basis for the Criminal Liability of Corporations* (2008).

international comparison, lawmakers seem increasingly willing to hold corporations liable on grounds of devious corporate culture rather than on the basis of individual misconduct. Company culture theory could accordingly become more prominent and more accepted in the future and help close accountability gaps in animal law.[136]

In comparative perspective, the New Zealand AWA provides for some of the highest fines for corporations (up to 500,000 NZD or 335,000 USD), which are five times the fines for individuals (100,000 NZD or 67,000 USD).[137] Croatia's APA fines legal persons from 50,000 HRK (7,700 USD) up to 100,000 HRK (15,000 USD), while it fines natural persons from 10,000 HRK (1,500 USD) up to 15,000 HRK (2,300 USD).[138] Due to the young history of criminal animal law, these are good starting points to capture the attention of corporations, but the immense turnover and profits of industries that exploit animals give us good reason to demand lawmakers and judges impose higher fines. For example, the US meat market, which is dominated by Tyson, Cargill, and JBS, turns over 150 billion USD each year,[139] which means that a fine of 335,000 USD is unlikely to dissuade them from engaging in practices that harm animals but are profitable for them.

§4 Applying Administrative Animal Law Extraterritorially

A. BASICS OF ADMINISTRATIVE ANIMAL LAW

There are many tools of administrative animal law, and most of them are orders. Orders oblige addressees to act, tolerate, or omit. *Orders to act* prescribe how animals must be treated, fed, cared for, how much exercise and social interaction they require, etc.[140] Orders to act lay down expectations on institutional design, like minimum measurements of stalls and boxes, floor design, room and water temperature, or daylight intake. They may also set up a duty to disclose information, either addressed to owners of animals or the public when it witnesses the wrongful treatment of an animal.[141] *Orders to tolerate* oblige addressees to grant authorities access to an animal presumed to have been neglected or abused. *Orders to omit* complement orders to act and include, for instance, providing working animals an opportunity for rest and recovery.[142]

The second set of administrative law tools are prohibitions, which prohibit certain actions or omissions. They complement orders to omit, by negatively defining how animals must be treated. Prohibitions may be directed at particular persons (such as owners or caretakers), or they can apply to all persons within a state's jurisdiction.[143] For instance, keeping whales

---

[136] Pieth & Ivory, *Emergence and Convergence: Corporate Criminal Liability Principles in Overview*, *in* CORPORATE CRIMINAL LIABILITY 5 (2011).

[137] Animal Welfare Act (N.Z.), § 28 para. 3.

[138] Animal Protection Act (Croat.), art. 66 para. 1.

[139] Marcel Sebastian, *Deadly Efficiency: The Impact of Capitalist Production on the "Meat" Industry, Slaughterhouse Workers, and Nonhuman Animals*, *in* ANIMAL OPPRESSION AND CAPITALISM VOL. I, 167, 169 (David Nibert ed., 2017).

[140] Sometimes, these orders are identified as "positive duties of care": ROBERTSON 83 (2015).

[141] LORZ & METZGER 52 n. 112 (2008).

[142] JEDELHAUSER 129 ff. (2011).

[143] LORZ & METZGER 52 n. 111 (2008).

in confinement can be prohibited for institutions unable or unwilling to properly care for whales, or it can be prohibited *in toto* because whales cannot experience well-being while being confined.[144] In the common law system, the prohibition against keeping an animal takes place in two steps: forfeiture and disqualification. The act of forfeiture transfers legal title over the animal to another owner or, temporarily, to a guardian. If the court thinks the offender is likely to continue to commit crimes against animals, they must be disqualified from purchasing or owning animals in the future.[145] Any of these prohibitions may be temporary or unlimited.[146]

Prohibitions absolutely prohibit acts, but they sometimes provide for exemptions. This is done by special permits, which operate preventively and are issued when a petitioner fulfills all previously defined requirements. Special permits are common in research, for kosher and halal slaughter, and breeding.[147] They also give authorities an opportunity to impose additional requirements onto the petitioner, in order to adequately respond to a specific problem. Like criminal law, administrative law makes use of coercive elements (forfeiture, disqualification, and other prohibitions), but they differ from criminal coercion because verdicts are pronounced by administrative agencies. Criminal and administrative coercion also differ in their degree of punishment.[148]

The expansion of animal law to the administrative realm is an important achievement because it yields benefits for animals that criminal animal law does not provide. The first is that administrative standards hold people to a higher standard than criminal norms. Criminal animal law focuses on minimally acceptable behavior, below which no one may fall. Administrative law takes a different stance by detailing how animals must be treated.[149] The second is that, while criminal animal law is sometimes formulated too loosely, creating considerable leeway for perpetrators to escape conviction, administrative standards are more specific and they elaborate in detail the legal expectations for the "proper treatment" of animals. Third, criminal animal law applies only after an animal's interests are violated (except for criminal attempts). Though penalties might have a deterring effect, criminal law does not actually protect from harm the animal affected by the criminal act. In contrast, administrative law operates more preventively, by removing animals from the offender's sphere of influence, or by disbarring the offender from keeping animals in the future.[150] The fourth benefit relates to the standard of proof. In criminal law, standards of proof to show wrongful behavior are comparatively high, since a person must have committed offenses "beyond reasonable doubt."[151] Standards of proof in administrative law, in contrast, are less stringent and hence less burdensome for victims.

---

[144] *See, e.g.*, ANIMAL WELFARE ACT (Switz.), art. 23 para. 1. *See* on whale welfare in confinement: Harvey Neo & J.Z. Ngiam, *Contesting Captive Cetaceans: (Il)Legal Spaces and the Nature of Dolphins in Urban Singapore*, 15 SOC. & CULT. GEO. 235 (2014).

[145] ROBERTSON 125–6 (2015). Forfeiture necessitates ruling on the costs of care beforehand: FRASCH, HESSLER, & WAISMAN 51 (2016).

[146] For details on prohibitions to keep animals, *see* JEDELHAUSER 200 ff. (2011).

[147] LORZ & METZGER 52 n. 113 (2008).

[148] JEDELHAUSER 137–8 (2011).

[149] *Id.* at 121; ROBERTSON 115 (2015).

[150] *E.g.*, Animal Welfare Act (U.K.), §§ 22 ff.

[151] ROBERTSON 113 ff. (2015).

Any system of law aiming to establish effective rules to protect animals should therefore lay down standards of criminal and administrative law that usefully complement each other. In the next section, I will detail the promises administrative standards hold for the law of jurisdiction, focusing, in particular, on standards of farming, transportation, and slaughter.

B. PROTECTION OF FARMED ANIMALS

The population of farmed animals is bigger than ever before. In 2017, the world was home to

- 22,847,062,000 chickens (compared to 14,117,511,000 in 1997 and 6,258,969,000 in 1977);[152]
- 1,491,687,240 cows (compared to 1,204,693,621 in 1997 and 1,308,043,508 in 1977);[153]
- 1,202,430,935 sheep (compared to 1,037,904,497 in 1997 and 1,042,188,814 in 1977);[154]
- 967,385,101 pigs (compared to 711,244,438 in 1997 and 834,867,247 in 1977);[155]
- 1,034,406,504 goats (compared to 422,399,870 in 1997 and 693,592,671 in 1977);[156]
- 200,967,747 buffaloes (compared to 114,840,922 in 1997 and 157,095,298 in 1977).[157]

These numbers, though "mind-numbing,"[158] do not begin to account for the vast numbers of animals currently confined indoors and killed in slaughterhouses every second. They do not include camels, ducks, geese and guinea fowls, horses, mules, pigeons, rabbits, rodents, turkeys, fish, and many other animals raised for human consumption.[159] Counts of live animals also exclude all animals killed before they are even a year old.[160] In 2017, the number of land animals killed for food exceeded 69 billion, including 66 billion chickens, 1.5 billion pigs, 1 billion sheep and goats, and 300 million cows.[161] If we divide the 69 billion animals

---

[152] FAOSTAT (search criteria "Chickens"+"Stocks"+"World total"+"1977, 1997, 2017," *available at* http://faostat.fao.org/ (last visited Jan. 10, 2019).

[153] FAOSTAT (search criteria "Cows"+"Stocks"+"World total"+"1977, 1997, 2017," *available at* http://faostat.fao.org/ (last visited Jan. 10, 2019).

[154] FAOSTAT (search criteria "Sheep"+"Stocks"+"World total"+"1977, 1997, 2017," *available at* http://faostat.fao.org/ (last visited Jan. 10, 2019).

[155] FAOSTAT (search criteria "Pigs"+"Stocks"+"World total"+"1977, 1997, 2017," *available at* http://faostat.fao.org/ (last visited Jan. 10, 2019).

[156] FAOSTAT (search criteria "Goats"+"Stocks"+"World total"+"1977, 1997, 2017," *available at* http://faostat.fao.org/ (last visited Jan. 10, 2019).

[157] FAOSTAT (search criteria "Buffaloes"+"Stocks"+"World total"+"1977, 1997, 2017," *available at* http://faostat.fao.org/ (last visited Jan. 10, 2019).

[158] KELCH 5 (2011).

[159] These numbers can be retrieved *at* http://faostat.fao.org/ (last visited Jan. 10, 2019).

[160] *See* Chapter 7, fn. 101 on the life spans of farmed animals.

[161] The total number is 69,389,445,483, encompassing 66,566,725,000 chickens, 1,485,986,756 pigs, 567,720,570 sheep, 464,598,299 goats, and 304,414,858 cows: FAOSTAT (search criteria "World"+"Meat total"+"Producing Animals/Slaughtered"+"2017," *available at* http://faostat.fao.org/ (last visited Jan. 10, 2019). In addition, millions of ducks, geese, guinea fowls, rabbits, turkeys, camels, horses, mules, rodents, and other animals are slaughtered (*id.*). Moreover, determining the number of animals slaughtered is only a rough estimate, because many killings are not included in the national database, as when animals are not killed for commercial purposes.

killed in 2017 into the hours in a day, we can see that almost *8 million* farmed animals were killed every single hour that year.[162] In contrast, the research industry uses an estimated 115 to 127 million animals annually.[163] These animals, although they make up a vast number of individuals, represent only 0.15 percent of the number of animals killed each year for food.[164] And due to human population growth, wealth increase, and dietary shifts, it is likely that the total number of animals suffering for food production will continue to rise sharply.

Though most people are told and taught to accept that farmed animals must be kept, killed, and consumed, this is neither morally justifiable nor necessary in itself. Section 13 para. 1 of the Austrian APA determines that "[n]o animal shall be kept unless it can reasonably be expected, on the basis of its genotype or phenotype, that it can be kept according to the recognized state of scientific knowledge without detrimental effect on its well-being."[165] Like the Austrian provision, Finland's section 22 grants the legislator the power to prohibit farming animals for the purposes of food production, "[f]or animal protection reasons."[166] Taking these norms seriously would urge us to stop farming all animals, because factory farming has vast detrimental effects on animals' well-being, be it during their short lives, or at the point of slaughter. Before being slaughtered for food production, most farmed animals live a life of misery and pain in the "live supply" chain. Between 70 percent and 80 percent of chickens are held in battery cages, and the percentage of other farmed animals reared in CAFOs is estimated to be just as high.[167] The many repercussions CAFO production has on the well-being of farmed animals were examined in detail in Chapter 2. Animals suffer constantly in all imaginable ways, from pain, diseases, anxiety, psychological disorders, lack of opportunities to socialize and interact with others, malnutrition, lack of exercise, and institutionalized violence.[168] The question of how we can create a more just world for (and with) farmed animals hence is one of the most pressing moral and legal issues of our time.

The first and most notable challenge of animal law is that several AWAs exclude farmed animals from protection. The federal US AWA, the Twenty-Eight Hour Law, and the Humane Methods of Slaughter Act (HMSA) all exempt farmed animals. The AWA bluntly declares it does not apply to farmed animals.[169] The Twenty-Eight Hour Law excludes transportation

---

[162] 69,389,445,483 is the total number of animals (counting only sheep, chickens, pigs, goats, and cows) killed in 2017. This number divided by 8,760 as the number of hours per year equals 7,921,169 animals killed per hour.

[163] Humane Society International (HSI), Animal Use Statistics (HSI, Washington D.C. 2012); Waldau 28 (2011). Knight estimates that the number of vertebrate animals used for research worldwide each year is close to 126.9 million: Andrew Knight, *Tierversuche*, *in* Lexikon der Mensch-Tier-Beziehungen 382, 383 (2015).

[164] 115 or 127 million of 69 billion are 0.15 percent.

[165] Animal Protection Act (Austria), § 13 para. 1.

[166] Animal Welfare Act (Fin.), § 22.

[167] Kelch 5 (2011).

[168] Chapter 2, §3 B.

[169] 7 U.S.C. §§ 2131, 2132(g)(3) (U.S.). The AWA thus does not apply to 95 percent of all animals raised for food in the United States: Matheny & Leahy 334 (2007); Wolfson & Sullivan, *Foxes in the Hen House*, *in* Animal Rights: Current Debates and New Directions 206 (2004). *See* for a discussion of the limits set by the US AWA for research animals, F. Barbara Orlans, *The Injustice of Excluding Laboratory Rats, Mice, and Birds from the Animal Welfare Act*, 10 Kennedy Inst. of Ethics J. 229 (2000). And for a discussion of the AWA's exclusion of farmed animals, *see* Wolfson & Sullivan, *supra*; Matheny & Leahy, *supra*.

by truck, by air, or on water, so virtually all transportation of farmed animals.[170] And the HMSA, which requires animals to be rendered insensible to pain before being hoisted, shackled, or cut, does not apply to chickens and fish, even though they are killed in the highest numbers.[171] On the state level, anti-cruelty laws have exempted all actions done to farmed animals from application, on the grounds that they are "common farm practices."[172] As Schaffner explains, this creates a paradox in which "criminal laws, designed to protect animals from the intentional infliction of pain and suffering, perpetuate and in fact endorse institutionalized cruelty to animals."[173] As a consequence, only wrongs committed against animals that do not impede farmers' common economic interests constitute animal cruelty.[174] The United States is not the only country that has in place such sweeping exemptions. Animals used for agricultural purposes are exempt under the laws of most Canadian provinces and territories, including Alberta,[175] British Columbia,[176] Manitoba,[177] Nova Scotia,[178] Ontario,[179] Prince Edward Island,[180] Québec,[181] Saskatchewan,[182] and Yukon.[183] In Australia, too, legislators are unwilling to view cruelty inflicted on farmed animals as animal cruelty.[184]

These exemptions cannot possibly be justified. Animals used for farming purposes, like cows, pigs, and chickens, suffer just as much as companion animals do, and the public has a clear and broad interest in protecting them.[185] But while it is evident *that* we need laws that detail our obligations owed to farmed animals, it might not be immediately apparent *what* those laws should prescribe. In the following section, I begin to develop answers to the latter

---

[170] 49 U.S.C. § 80502(a) (U.S.).

[171] 7 U.S.C. §§ 1901, 1902(a) (U.S.); 9 CFR § 301.2 (U.S.).

[172] FRASCH, HESSLER, & WAISMAN 335 (2016); Wolfson & Sullivan 212–6 (2004).

[173] SCHAFFNER 28 (2011). And Waldau finds: "There is some irony here, given that the original targets of anti-cruelty legislation were farm and work animals" (Waldau, *Second Wave Animal Law and the Arrival of Animal Studies, in* ANIMAL LAW AND WELFARE: INTERNATIONAL PERSPECTIVES 37 (2016)).

[174] *E.g.*, Westfall v. State, 10 S.W.3d 85 (Tex. Ct. App. 1999) (U.S.).

[175] Animal Protection Act, c. A-41, 2000, § 2(2) (AB, Can.): "This section does not apply if the distress results from an activity carried on in accordance with the regulations or in accordance with reasonable and generally accepted practices of animal care, management, husbandry, hunting, fishing, trapping, pest control or slaughter."

[176] Prevention of Cruelty to Animals Act, c. 372, 1996, § 24.02 (BC, Can.): "A person must not be convicted of an offence under this Act in relation to an animal in distress if the distress results from an activity that is carried out in accordance with reasonable and generally accepted practices of animal management that apply to the activity in which the person is engaged, unless the person is an operator and those practices are inconsistent with prescribed standards."

[177] Animal Care Act, C.C.S.M. c. A84, 1996, § 2(2) (MB, Can.).

[178] Animal Protection Act, c. 33, 2008, § 21(4) (NS, Can.).

[179] Ontario Society for the Prevention of Cruelty to Animals Act, c. O.36, 1990, § 2(a) (ON, Can.).

[180] Animal Health and Protection Act, c. A-11.1, 2005, § 4(1) (PEI, Can.).

[181] Animal Welfare and Safety Act, c. B-3.1, 2016, § 7 (QC, Can.).

[182] Animal Protection Act, c. A-21.1, c. 38, 1999, § 2(3)(b) (SK, Can.).

[183] Animal Protection Act, c. 6, 2002, § 5(3) (YK, Can.).

[184] Steven White, *Regulation of Animal Welfare in Australia and the Emergent Commonwealth: Entrenching the Traditional Approach of the States and Territories or Laying the Ground for Reform?*, 35 FED. L. REV. 347, 355 (2007).

[185] *See* the polls listed and discussed in Chapter 6, §1 G.

question, by first analyzing general norms that protect farmed animals and then proceeding to more detailed regulations. I focus on the European experience, in particular the laws of the Council of Europe, the European Union, and Switzerland, because these laws do not exempt farmed animals and because Europe has a long and comparatively well-established tradition of animal protection laws.

The 1976 Council of Europe Convention for the Protection of Animals Kept for Farming Purposes was adopted to protect animals used in intensive stock-farming systems.[186] Article 3 requires housing, food, water, and care appropriate to animals' "physiological and ethological needs in accordance with established experience and scientific knowledge." Freedom of movement shall not be restricted if it causes "unnecessary suffering or injury" (article 4). Such general wording is also used to detail the requirements for lighting, temperature, humidity, air circulation, and ventilation (article 5). Because the Convention uses general and sweeping terms, it may in the worst case be used to uphold the deficient status quo for farmed animals.[187]

Council Directive 98/58/EC Concerning the Protection of Animals Kept for Farming Purposes offers general rules that aim to reduce and prevent unnecessary pain, suffering, or injury in all vertebrate species kept for the production of food, wool, skin, fur, and other farming purposes.[188] The Directive calls on member states to ensure that the requirements on keeping and breeding, as set out in its annex, are observed and that facilities are regularly inspected (articles 4 and 6). The annex lays down several requirements in an open-ended manner. It stipulates, for example, that animals be cared for by a "sufficient number of staff" (section 1), that ill animals be cared for "appropriately" (section 4), that animals' freedom of movement be not restricted in a way that makes them "unnecessarily suffer" (section 7), that materials used in buildings do not harm animals (section 8), that air, dust, temperature, humidity, and gas concentrations not be harmful to animals (section 10), that facilities be "appropriately lit" (section 11), and that animals receive species-specific feed (section 14). The Directive does not address the mutilation of animals in factory farms, leaving this issue to the discretion of member states.

Duties owed to calves (bovine animals up to six months) are laid down in Council Directive 2008/119/EC.[189] Calves over eight weeks old shall not be confined individually unless necessary for health reasons. Isolated calves under that age shall have visual and tactile contact to their conspecifics (article 3 para. 1 lit. a). For groups of calves, the minimum spacing is laid down (article 3 para. 1 lit. a). Annex I requires animals not to be kept in permanent darkness (section 5, though keeping them inside with permanent artificial lighting is legal), to be fed twice a day (section 12), to have access to water if they are over two weeks old (section 13), and not to be permanently tethered (section 8, unless for one hour in groups

---

[186] CoE, Convention for the Protection of Animals Kept for Farming Purposes, Mar. 10, 1976, C.E.T.S. No. 087, preamble, art. 1.

[187] *See* KELCH 84–5 (2011): "[T]he CoE Farming Convention is an animal welfare convention that requires signatory countries to comply with a number of fairly vague and, one could cogently argue, lax standards in their regulation of factory farming."

[188] Council Directive 98/58, 1988 O.J. (L 221) 23, art. 3.

[189] Council Directive 2008/119 Laying Down Minimum Standards for the Protection of Calves, Annex I, 2009 O.J. (L 10) 7.

during feeding). Calf feed must contain enough iron to ensure an average blood hemoglobin level of at least 4,5 mmol/liter, and each calf over two weeks old must receive a minimum daily ration of fibrous food, namely 50g to 250g per day for calves from 8 to 20 weeks old (section 11 of the annex). Although the Directive declares legal the solitary confinement of calves under eight weeks of age (to produce white calf meat), it is claimed to be progressive because it prohibits most solitary confinement of older calves and because it improves their diet. But as scholars point out, banning the keeping of calves for veal production would be the more promising strategy to protect them, since these animals live "short, crowded and uncomfortable lives punctuated by eventual terror, followed by slaughter."[190]

The lives of animals used for food production are governed by Council Directive 2008/120/EC, which lays down minimum standards for housing, care, space, feeding, treatments, stock-handling, and inspection.[191] Notable achievements of the Directive are its prohibition on keeping sows in continuous close confinement, limits on tail docking, tooth-clipping, tooth-grinding, and castration, and its emphasis on keeping the public informed about pig welfare.[192] The annex of the Directive lays down a maximum noise level of 85 dBA (section 1), and a minimum lux level of 40 for at least eight hours a day (section 2). Lying areas shall be physically and thermally comfortable, adequately drained and clean, allowing all animals to lie at the same time, and to rest and get up normally (section 3). Pigs must have permanent access to enough material like straw, hay, wood, sawdust, mushroom compost, peat, or a mixture of these to properly investigate and manipulate their environment (section 4). They must be fed at least once a day, on which occasion all pigs must have access to food (section 6). Access to water shall be guaranteed at all times for all pigs older than two weeks (section 7). Tooth-clipping or -grinding is permitted in the first seven days of a pig's life, docking part of the tail is also legal, as is castration of male pigs unless tissue is torn (section 8). A laudable achievement of the Directive on pigs is that it seems to be slowly moving away from gestation crates for sows, permanent tethering, and certain forms of mutilation.[193] However, the Directive emphasizes that it is necessary to balance considerations for animals against social and economic gains, which means its standards can readily be compromised, and producers can avoid compliance.[194] This renders the Directive practically useless because it declares it legal to prioritize negligible economic interests over fundamental interests of animals.

Duties owed to broilers (chickens raised for meat production) are laid down in Council Directive 2007/43/EC.[195] In this Directive, the European Union states at the outset that economic considerations must be taken into account when the welfare of chickens is assessed.[196] As in the pig directive, this reminder is jarring in a legal document intended to

---

[190] KELCH 93 (2011).

[191] Council Directive 2008/120 Laying Down Minimum Standards for the Protection of Pigs, 2009 O.J. (L 47) 5.

[192] *Id.* at 5.

[193] KELCH 96 (2011).

[194] Council Directive 2008/120, 2009 O.J. (L 47) 5, 5 at 12: "A balance should be kept between the various aspects to be taken into consideration, as regarding welfare including health, economic and social considerations, and also environmental impact."

[195] Council Directive 2007/43/EC of 28 June 2007 Laying Down Minimum Rules for the Protection of Chickens Kept for Meat Production, 2007 O.J. (L 182) 19.

[196] *Id.* at 20.

protect animals. The Directive applies only to holdings with 500 or more chickens, breeding holdings, hatcheries, and extensive indoor and free-range chickens (article 1). Stocking density shall be no more than 33 kg/m^2, but derogations are possible (article 3). Annex 1 states that chickens shall have continuous access to food, and dry, friable litter (sections 2 and 3). Sound levels "shall be minimized," although no maximum sound level is defined (section 5). Ventilation shall be "sufficient" (section 4), a term too loose to hold parties liable for contravention, or even ascertain a violation. Periods of darkness shall last at least six hours of 24 (section 7). Injured and ill chickens must be "appropriately" treated or culled (section 9), meaning that if treating them is economically unreasonable, they will be killed. Furthermore, records must be kept on the number of chickens introduced, and the number of dead animals found before "depopulation" (section 11). Section 12 para. 1 of the annex lays down that "[a]ll surgical interventions carried out for reasons other than therapeutic or diagnostic purposes which result in damage to or the loss of a sensitive part of the body or the alteration of bone structure shall be prohibited." Then again, section 12 para. 2 provides for exemptions for beak trimming "if necessary to prevent injury," which undermines the entire paragraph.

Council Directive 1999/74/EC is the main legal instrument that deals with noncage systems, minimum space, cage enrichment, and other measures ensure the well-being of laying hens.[197] The Directive shares the Council's opinion that

> [. . . t]he welfare conditions of hens kept in current battery cages and in other systems of rearing are inadequate and that certain of their needs cannot be met in such cages; the highest possible standards should therefore be introduced [. . .].[198]

In this Directive, the European Union effectively abolished battery cages by introducing alternative systems (article 4: no cages, no free range, littered area of 250 cm^2 per hen), enriched cages (article 6: 750 cm^2 of cage area per hen of which 600 cm^2 shall be usable, with nests and litter), and ordinary unenriched cages (article 5: 550 cm^2 per hen of cage area, minimum height of 40 cm, with continuous access to drinking channels). Except for the laudable ban on battery cages, the Directive is as inadequate as the broiler directive: economics must be taken into account when animal welfare is assessed;[199] restrictions do not apply to holdings with less than 350 individuals (article 1); sound levels must be "minimized" and there must be "sufficient" light "about one-third" of the day (sections 2 and 3 of the annex); holding areas are cleaned only after "depopulation" (section 4 of the annex); and mutilation is generally prohibited, unless "necessary" to prevent pecking and cannibalism (section 8 of the annex). The Directive shows that the European Union has a strong interest in avoiding overcrowding and responding to the animals' needs to move about and socialize. Overall, however, hens continue to suffer under the Directive, which has cleaned up the edges of factory farming "to make the prisoners' short lives somewhat more bearable."[200]

---

197 Council Directive 1999/74 Laying Down Minimum Standards for the Protection of Laying Hens, 1999 O.J. (L 203) 53.

198 *Id.* at recital 7.

199 *Id.* at recital 9.

200 KELCH 99 (2011).

In Switzerland, standards on the welfare of farmed animals are laid down in articles 6 *et seq.* of the Swiss AWA, which states in paragraph 1: "Anyone who keeps or looks after animals must feed and care for them properly and provide them with the activities and freedom of movement needed for their well-being, as well as shelter where necessary."[201] This general statement is concretized in articles 3 *et seq.* of the AWO. Article 3 AWO, titled "proper animal husbandry," sets out the basic requirements. Animals shall be kept in a manner that does not interfere with their bodily functions or behavior and does not overstrain their adaptive capacities (para. 1); accommodation and enclosures shall be fitted with suitable feeding, drinking and dunging areas, places to rest and withdraw, and they shall give animals opportunities to investigate, socialize, and show comfort behavior (para. 2); feeding and care shall be administered based on existing experience and knowledge about animals' physiology, behavior, and need for hygiene (para. 3); and animals shall not be permanently tethered (para. 4). "Permanent tethering" is a fuzzy term that is easily circumvented (as is "free range," for example), but the AWO clarifies this in more detail. Article 40 para. 1 AWO determines that cows who are typically tethered should run free for at least 60 days during the vegetation period, and for at least 30 days during winter; the maximum tethering period during the entire year is two weeks (though there can be blocks of two weeks one after the other). Moreover, farmers are bound to keep a record of cows' exercise. Access to the outside must also be granted to animals of other species. Article 55 para. 1 AWO determines that goats should have a period during which they can run free, which is at least 120 days during the vegetation period and at least 50 days during the winter; maximum tethering period is two weeks. Daily records of their access to the outside are also mandatory. For pigs (article 48 para. 2 AWO), sheep (article 52 para. 1 AWO), lamas and alpacas (article 57 para. 2 AWO), and horses (article 59 para. 1 AWO), tethering is forbidden.

Article 4 AWO determines that animals shall be regularly and adequately fed, provided with water, and, when animals are kept in groups, keepers must ensure that every animal has access to sufficient food and water (para. 1). Moreover, animals "shall be provided with opportunities that meet their need for species-specific activity associated with feeding" (para. 2). Article 5 AWO, dealing with the care of animals, determines how often animals must be checked and how often sick or injured animals must be taken care of so that they can fully recover. All animals must be protected from adverse weather conditions, especially if they have limited ability to adapt (article 6 AWO). Article 7 AWO deals with housing, which shall not place animals at risk for injury, impair their health, or give them an opportunity to escape, and which shall "be sufficiently spacious to allow the animals to express their species-specific behavior."[202] Article 10 AWO lays down minimum spacing for each species; these are further specified in annexes 1–3 (including details on width and length for housing, box housing, dimensions of the lying area in group housing, cubicles, the width of feeding place per animal, etc.). These rules on spacing have effectively, though only implicitly, banned battery cages in Switzerland.[203]

---

[201] ANIMAL WELFARE ACT (Switz.), art. 6 para. 1.

[202] ANIMAL WELFARE ORDINANCE (Switz.), art. 7 para. 2.

[203] Even though the provision has *de facto* led to a ban on battery cages, the Directive does not conform to the needs of animals. The cages it declares lawful have a length of 14 cm to sit, a width of 16 cm to eat in

Articles 8 *et seq.* of the Swiss AWO regulate the design of standing stalls, boxes, and tethering devices, group housing, indoor climate, noise, and special needs of gregarious species (which most domesticated animals are) for social contact.[204] Social contact is detailed in the AWO for

- Calves (article 38 para. 3 AWO): group housing;
- Yaks (article 43 para. 1 AWO): group housing;
- Pigs (article 48 para. 1 AWO): group housing, except for suckling and mating periods and for boars from sexual maturity onward;
- Goats and sheep (articles 52 para. 4 and 55 para. 4 AWO): visual contact for individually housed animals, group housing for kids;
- Lamas (article 57 para. 1 AWO): group housing, except for males from sexual maturity onward; then visual contact;
- Horses (article 59 para. 3 and 4 AWO): visual, auditory, and olfactory contact if individually housed; group housing for young horses;
- Young rabbits (article 64 para. 2 AWO): group housing during the first eight weeks;
- Dogs housed in boxes or kennels (article 70 para. 2 AWO): in pairs or groups, except when they do not get along; and
- Laboratory animals (article 119 para. 2 AWO): group housing.[205]

Though farmed animals are all individuals who have their own wants and needs, species-specific laws at least bring us closer to ensuring an environment for animals that enables them to flourish. Overall, Swiss animal laws lay down detailed rules that are largely absent in other jurisdictions (need for places to rest and withdraw, unequivocal requirements on spacing, clear prohibitions of tail docking and nose rings, the perforation of floors, foraging material, and opportunity to socialize). The advantage of such detailed regulation is that it makes it harder for farmers to evade the law by interpreting it to their advantage or referring to "common farm practices."[206] Detailed laws also make it easier for judges and inspectors to ascertain if farmers are operating in line with the law. When these details are shared with the public, it, too, is empowered to recognize and report violations of the law.

If we take the perspective of the animals used for farming, it is clear that Swiss animal law must be stricter, concerning, for example, requirements for environmental enrichment, access to the outside, maximum group housing, spacing, adequate feed, and the frequency of controls. What is much more important to recognize, however, is that even if Swiss animal law is among the most progressive in the world, it still falls short as an "animal protection law." Instead of providing for conditions under which animals can thrive and experience

---

manual feeding, and 8 cm in automatic feeding, which is not enough space for an animal to live a fulfilled life: Animal Welfare Ordinance (Switz.), annex 2.

[204] Bolliger, Richner, & Rüttimann 163 (2011).

[205] Annex 3 additionally requires that laboratory animals be given enough material to investigate, such as feed (hay or straw), objects to gnaw on, shelter with two access points, nesting material, climbing facilities, litter for burrowing, opportunity to withdraw and hide, social interaction, etc.

[206] *See supra* Chapter 9, §4 B.

well-being, these laws generally determine that animals can be routinely confined and used for marginal human interests, and they lay down the conditions under which this can be done.

C. TRANSPORTATION STANDARDS

Animal transport is the process of moving live animals from one place to another by foot, train, car, truck, ship, plane, or any other means of transportation.[207] The frequency of transports of farmed animals and the distances they cover have increased enormously over the last decades, as has the number of animals transported. In 2015, an estimated 50 billion farmed animals (excluding aquatic animals) were transported alive for slaughter, many of them as far as 3,000 kilometers (on land).[208] Australia, the world's biggest exporter of live animals, is frequently faced with cross-border conflicts of animal welfare. In 2006, the Australian NGO Animals Australia released video footage of extreme cases of cruelty done to animals who were shipped over 13,000 kilometers from Australia to Egyptian slaughterhouses. In response to the widespread public outrage, shipments were halted until 2010 and resumed only after the Australian and Egyptian ministers of agriculture signed a memorandum of understanding. Upon Egypt's continued violation of the memorandum of understanding, Australia again halted live exports in 2013.[209] The issue is still unsettled, though ministers of both countries have agreed to implement the Exporter Supply Chain Assurance System (ESCAS) that recommends adherence to the OIE standards and which will make Australian exporters responsible for the welfare of farmed animals from the point of departure to the point of slaughter.[210]

Humans are usually more interested in safely transporting companion, zoo, and sports animals, while farmed animals are "about to be slaughtered anyway" and therefore especially likely to be improperly transported. These transports severely stress the animals.[211] They are

---

[207] Andreas Rüttimann, *Tiertransport*, *in* LEXIKON DER MENSCH-TIER-BEZIEHUNGEN 379, 379 (2015). *Cf.* Council Regulation 1/2005 on the Protection of Animals During Transport and Related Operations and Amending Directives 64/432/EEC and 93/119/EC and Regulation 1255/97/EC, 2005 O.J. (L 3) 1, art. 2 lit. w.

[208] Rüttimann, *Tiertransport*, *in* LEXIKON DER MENSCH-TIER-BEZIEHUNGEN 380 (2015). In the United States, the 2016 National Beef Quality Audit revealed that in its small sample of the mean values for time and distance traveled, the maximum time traveled was 39.6 hours over a distance of 1412.9 miles: Animal Welfare Institute, Legal Protections for Farmed Animals During Transport 4 (2018), *available at* https://awionline.org/sites/default/files/uploads/documents/fa-legalprotectionsduringtransport-12262013.pdf (last visited Jan. 10, 2019). The massive increase in animal transports can be traced back to the ongoing specialization in farm animal production and the division of labor. Animals are bred in one place, raised in another, and slaughtered somewhere else. Centralized slaughter facilities also require more frequent transport of animals: Rüttimann, *Tiertransport*, *in* LEXIKON DER MENSCH-TIER-BEZIEHUNGEN 380 (2015).

[209] *Shocking Abuse Uncovered in Egypt*, ANIMALS AUSTRALIA, *available at* http://www.banliveexport.com/egypt (last visited Jan. 10, 2019).

[210] Australian Government, Exporter Supply Chain Assurance System (ESCAS), Overview (Nov. 2, 2016), *available at* http://www.agriculture.gov.au/export/controlled-goods/live-animals/livestock/information-exporters-industry/escas (last visited Jan. 10, 2019). *See also* Jared Owens, *Australia to Restart Live Sheep and Cattle Exports to Egypt*, The Australian, Mar. 20, 2014.

[211] MICHAEL C. APPLEBY ET AL., LONG DISTANCE TRANSPORT AND WELFARE OF FARM ANIMALS (2008); GIERI BOLLIGER, EUROPÄISCHES TIERSCHUTZRECHT: TIERSCHUTZBESTIMMUNGEN DES

torn out of their habitual environment and randomly packed together with animals unfamiliar to them, and so close they cannot move. During transport, animals cannot relax or engage in normal behavior. They lack access to fresh air, food, and water; they must cope with temperature fluctuations and changing noise levels; and they are scared of being on a moving vehicle, often for the first time in their lives. Animals in transport experience high levels of fear and panic; they may suffer flesh wounds, internal and external bruising, skin abrasions, hematoma, bone fractures, and other injuries serious enough to kill them. Case law shows that many drivers pack together as many animals as possible to keep costs for transportation down. Drivers and shippers also repeatedly fail to adequately secure animals, and they may keep animals in the transporter too long, or load and unload them improperly.[212]

In response to ongoing welfare problems in animal transportation, the Council of Europe established the Convention for the Protection of Animals during International Transport.[213] The Convention demands animal health inspection before transport and prior veterinary supervision (article 10 para. 1), adequate space and room for animals to lie down (article 17 para. 1), protection against inclement weather conditions including air conditioning (article 6 para. 6), segregation by species (article 15 para. 1), adequate equipment for nonslip loading and unloading (article 6 para. 7) and it has special provisions for carrying animals (article 9 para. 3) and for ill or injured animals (article 9 para. 2), for transport by railway (article 26), transport on the road (article 27), transport by water (article 28), and transport by air (articles 30 et seq.). The major shortcomings of the Convention are that it allows transporters to tie up animals during transport (article 6 para. 6), to withhold food and water from them for up to 24 hours (article 6 para. 4), and that it does not specify the maximum duration of transport. The limited focus of the Convention on improving transportation for farmed animals is not surprising considering that its drafters and signatories are "[c]onvinced that the requirements of the international transport of animals are ***not incompatible*** with the welfare of the animals."[214]

In contrast, Council Regulation 1/2005 finds that "[f]or reasons of animal welfare the transport of animals over long journeys, including animals for slaughter, should be limited as far as possible."[215] Long journeys, according to the regulation, exceed eight hours; these require special authorization.[216] In matters of transport, the European Union recommends establishing detailed provisions specific to different types of transport.[217] The regulation

---

Europarats und der Europäischen Union (mit einer ergänzenden Darstellung des schweizerischen Rechts) 214 ff. (Schriften zum Europarecht 2000); Karl Fikuart et al., Hygiene der Tiertransporte 28, 497 (1995); Rüttimann, *Tiertransport, in* Lexikon der Mensch-Tier-Beziehungen 380 (2015).

[212] Bolliger, Richner, & Rüttimann 175–6 (2011); Christine Hafner & Julia Havenstein, Animal Suffering is Inherent in Long Distance Transports: Lisbon Treaty Necessitates Ban of Long Distance Transports (2012).

[213] CoE, Convention for the Protection of Animals during International Transport (revised), Nov. 6, 2003, C.E.T.S. No. 193.

[214] *Id.* preamble (emphasis added).

[215] Council Regulation 1/2005 on the Protection of Animals During Transport and Related Operations and Amending Directives 64/432/EEC and 93/119/EC and Regulation 1255/97/EC, 2005 O.J. (L 3) 1, 1.

[216] *Id.* arts. 2 lit. m and 11.

[217] *Id.* at 2.

stresses the importance of personnel training and education and the need for prior authorization by government agencies. It also calls on transporters and operators (farmers, traders, assembly centers, and slaughterhouses) to take on greater liability.[218] However, the regulation uses lax and vague language, by using terms like "sufficient floor area," "at suitable intervals," or "adequately designed" (article 3). Even so, most member states of the European Union have had serious difficulty implementing the regulation.[219]

In Switzerland, article 15 AWA lays down the general duties owed to animals who are transported for slaughter. It determines that animals must be carefully transported, for a maximum period of six hours, and without unnecessary delays. These duties are further specified in articles 150 *et seq.* AWO:

- Articles 150 *et seq.* AWO deal with personnel training: training and continuing education of livestock trade and transporting personnel, responsibility of owners, responsibilities of drivers, responsibilities of the recipient, designation of other persons responsible for carefully transporting farmed animals;
- Articles 155 *et seq.* AWO regulate the handling of animals: selection of animals "fit for transport," preparing animals for transport, handling and care of animals, keeping animals separate who do not like each other, loading and unloading animals, handling of certain animal species, the manner of driving, exceptions to maximum driving time;
- Articles 163 *et seq.* AWO concretize means of transport and containers: cleaning and disinfection, litter material, means of transport, goods carried with animals, transport containers, exceptions;
- Articles 169 *et seq.* AWO deal with international animal transport: checking animal consignments, permits, reporting violations, transport plan and travel log, special equipment, special precautions for international transport, the transit of animals, and transport by air.

These regulations are comparatively well-developed, but they have significant weaknesses. It is especially regrettable that the maximum duration of transport of six hours, as laid down in article 15 AWA, does not apply to international transports (article 162 AWO). In addition to the above rules that apply to all animals, the AWO sets out detailed rules for the transport of certain species. For pigs, for instance, article 165 para. 1 lit. g AWO requires all means of transport to have appropriately placed openings to ensure the pigs have sufficient access to fresh air. If transporting vehicles have three or more levels, there must be a ventilation system. During transport, pigs must be protected from harmful weather conditions and

---

[218] According to the regulation, transporters are natural or legal persons transporting animals on their own account, or on the account of a third party: Council Regulation 1/2005, 2005 O.J. (L 3) 1, art. 2 lit. x. An organizer is a transporter who has subcontracted to at least one other transporter for a part of a journey, or a natural or legal person who has contracted to more than one transporter for a journey, or a person who has signed § 1 of the journey log as set out in Annex II: *id.* art. 2 lit. q.

[219] This is a point criticized by the regulation: Council Regulation 1/2005, 2005 O.J. (L 3) 1, 2.

vehicle emissions. Pursuant to annex 4 AWO, minimum space requirements must be met for each pig, which vary depending on the pigs' weight.[220]

Like Australia, the European Union, and Switzerland, New Zealand is concerned about the welfare of animals during transport, especially during long-distance exports. Section 38 of the New Zealand AWA declares that its purpose is "to protect the welfare of animals being exported from New Zealand and to protect New Zealand's reputation as a responsible exporter of animals and products made from animals."[221] To export animals from New Zealand, exporters must obtain an animal welfare export certificate, which is issued after they have provided the following information:

(a) [T]he manner in which the welfare of any animals previously exported by the applicant was attended to on the journey between New Zealand and the country to which they were exported;
(b) the capability, skills, and experience of the applicant in relation to the export of animals;
(c) the species or type of animal and the number of animals proposed to be exported;
(d) the ages, and the physiological state, of the animals proposed to be exported;
(e) the mode of transport proposed and the facilities provided;
(f) the length and nature of the journey proposed;
(g) the susceptibility of the animal to harm and distress under the conditions of transport proposed;
(h) any New Zealand requirements in relation to the export of the animal;
(i) any requirements of the country into which the animal is being exported;
(j) any relevant international standard;
(k) the date on which it is intended that the animal leave New Zealand;
(ka) any regulations made under section 183C relating to the export of animals;
(kb) New Zealand's reputation as a responsible exporter of animals and products made from animals;
(l) any other matters that the Director-General considers relevant to the welfare of the animal.[222]

The Director-General, who issues the certificates, has the discretion to ask for more information (section 45 AWA) and may consider "post-arrival conditions for the management of the animals in the importing country" (section 43 lit. a AWA). People who contravene the certificate regulations may be fined up to 125,000 NZD (84,000 USD). Since animal transport is known to be subject to enforcement gaps, strict export requirements and disclosure may improve this unsatisfactory situation. Yet, one cannot help but question why it is necessary to put animals through this much pain and suffering in the first place.[223] Article 11 of the Croatian Animal Welfare Act is remarkable in this context since it allows farmers to

[220] A pig who weighs up to 15 kg requires 0.09 m^2 and 75 cm in height; a pig between 15 to 25 kg requires 0.12 m^2 and 75 cm in height; a pig between 25 to 50 kg requires 0.18 m^2 and 75 cm in height, and so on.

[221] Animal Welfare Act (N.Z.), § 38.

[222] *Id.* § 43.

[223] As Stilt argues: "The typical rules of international trade in goods cannot be sufficient, because animals are simply not like the containers of toasters in inter-national shipping channels. Exporters of toasters do not

transport animals no more than 50 km from their holding.[224] Moreover, before transporting any animal, transporters must obtain authorization by the competent authority.[225]

D. SLAUGHTER STANDARDS

Slaughter—the routine and systematic killing of domesticated animals carried out by humans for the production of their food—is one of the most pressing issues faced by the present generation.[226] Jones explains: "By virtue of numbers alone, the slaughter of animals for food represents the most compelling animal welfare concern worldwide."[227] Animal law, rather than questioning *if* we should slaughter animals, concerns itself only with *how* we slaughter them. Animal law considers problems associated with animal slaughter, including rough handling in loading and unloading, lack of food and water, stress caused by exposure to noise and wind, inability to escape stress, extreme temperatures during transport and at the slaughter facility, exhaustion, abuse at the slaughterhouse, excessive prodding, beating, dragging animals by extremities, inadequate stunning, and conscious bleeding.[228] The mounting pressure on slaughter personnel to speed up production exacerbates these problems, causing sloppy stunning and slaughtering. As a consequence, the number of animals who are conscious when they die is higher than expected. Cows are unsuccessfully bolted and electrocuted; pigs anesthetized by carbon dioxide suffocate and others regain consciousness after they are electrocuted; and chickens are only rendered immobile but not insensible before being killed.[229] Scholars accordingly argue that many animals are killed while fully conscious,[230] and workers at slaughter facilities affirm this: "Happens all the time."[231]

At the slaughterhouse, animals are frequently tormented. In 2008, the Humane Society of the United States documented acts of cruelty done to downer dairy cows (animals too sick or injured to walk) in a Californian slaughterhouse that had never been documented before. The cows were dragged with forklifts, jabbed in the eyes, tortured with electrical shock, and

---

have expectations for how their products will be treated by purchasers, and when shipments are destroyed in transit, the loss is merely one for insurers to assess" (Stilt, *Trading in Sacrifice* 397 (2017)).

[224] Animal Protection Act (Croat.), art. 11.

[225] *Id.* art. 13 para. 1.

[226] Killing domesticated animals is called slaughter. Killing wild animals is not classified as slaughter, but as hunting or fishing. Killing sick domesticated or wild animals is called disease control. Research animals are not slaughtered, they are killed (Jörg Luy, *Schlachtung, in* LEXIKON DER MENSCH-TIER-BEZIEHUNGEN 310, 310 (2015)). *See also* Council Regulation 1099/2009 on the Protection of Animals at the Time of Killing, 2009 O.J. (L 303) 1, art. 2 lit. j. *See* Chapter 9, §4 B. on the number of land animals killed for food in 2017.

[227] Dena M. Jones, *Slaughter, in* THE GLOBAL GUIDE TO ANIMAL PROTECTION 172, 172 (2013).

[228] *Id.*

[229] Jeff Welty, *Humane Slaughter Laws*, 70 L. & CONTEMP. PROBS. 175, 177 (2007); FARM ANIMAL WELFARE COUNCIL (FAWC), REPORT ON THE WELFARE OF FARMED ANIMALS AT SLAUGHTER OR KILLING, PART 1: RED MEAT ANIMALS 29 (FAWC, London 2003).

[230] REGAN, EMPTY CAGES 100 (2005).

[231] GAIL EISNITZ, SLAUGHTERHOUSE: THE SHOCKING GREED, NEGLECT, AND INHUMANE TREATMENT INSIDE THE U.S. MEAT INDUSTRY (1997).

simulated drowning. The same year, the US Department of Agriculture (USDA) awarded the facility the "Supplier of the Year" distinction.[232] Below, I show how animal law has been attempting to remedy these deficiencies, examining the applicable laws of the Council of Europe, the European Union, and Switzerland for this purpose.

The Council of Europe Convention for the Protection of Animals for Slaughter covers all processes of movement, lairaging, restraint, stunning, and slaughter of domestic solipeds, ruminants, pigs, rabbits, and birds (article 1 para. 1).[233] Animals shall be moved with care and shall not be frightened or excited; their tails shall not be crushed, twisted, or broken; their eyes should not be grasped; no blows and kicks are allowed; and animals in cages, baskets, or crates shall not be thrown to the ground or knocked over (articles 4 and 5). Animals must not be taken to the place of slaughter unless immediately slaughtered there (article 6 para. 1). There must be suitable equipment and slaughterhouse design (article 4 para. 2), including nonslip flooring (article 7). If animals spend over 12 hours at the slaughter facility, they must have access to water and food (article 8). Animals shall be rendered insensible until they are slaughtered; use of puntilla, hammer, and poleaxe is prohibited (article 16). Signatories are generally bound by these duties but can choose to set up an exemption for ritual slaughter, emergency slaughter, the slaughter of chickens and rabbits, and animal disease control (article 17).

In the European Union, Council Regulation 1099/2009 recognizes and stresses that "[k]illing animals may induce pain, distress, fear or other forms of suffering to the animals even under the best available technical conditions."[234] The regulation, which only applies to vertebrates (article 2 lit. c), demands that they be protected from injury, and prevents withholding feed or water for long periods (article 3 para. 2). Article 4 obliges operators to stun animals before killing them. Annex 1 specifies the stunning methods per species, which is necessary because:

> Depending on how [animals] are used during the slaughtering or killing process, some stunning methods can lead to death while avoiding pain and minimizing distress or suffering for the animals. Other stunning methods may not lead to death and the *animals may recover their consciousness or sensibility* during subsequent painful procedures. Such methods should, therefore, be completed by other techniques that lead to certain death before the recovery of the animals. It is, therefore, essential to specify which stunning methods need to be completed by a killing method.[235]

The regulation further requires regular inspection to determine if animals are properly stunned (article 5) and if animals are handled by competent slaughter personnel (article 7).

---

[232] *Rampant Animal Cruelty at California Slaughter Plant: Undercover Investigation Finds Abuses at Major Beef Supplier to America's School Lunch Program*, HUMANE SOCIETY OF THE UNITED STATES (HSUS), Jan. 30, 2008. *See also more generally* Erin E. Williams, *Factory Farms*, *in* ENCYCLOPEDIA OF ANIMAL RIGHTS AND ANIMAL WELFARE 245, 246 (2010).

[233] CoE, Convention for the Protection of Animals for Slaughter, May 10, 1979, C.E.T.S. No. 102, art. 1.

[234] Council Regulation 1099/2009 on the Protection of Animals at the Time of Killing, 2009 O.J. (303) 1, preamble.

[235] *Id.* at 4 (emphasis added). Note that derogations are permissible, in line with Directive 93/119/EC and the Council of Europe Convention on Slaughter.

Annex II describes in detail the design and construction of slaughterhouses, and the equipment used by workers. According to article 16, each slaughterhouse shall designate an animal welfare officer to ensure compliance with the regulation. The regulation also obliges member states to introduce penalties for contraventions (article 23).

These laws may appear progressive compared to others, and the European Union is quick to claim that its laws are among the best laws for animals, but it often fails to integrate new scientific knowledge about animal suffering that would mandate more radical change. In 2004 and 2006, the EFSA issued reports that drew attention to the most flagrant weaknesses of Directive 93/119/EC.[236] It recommended that, in order to ensure proper stunning and the least painful methods of slaughter, the European Union phase out the use of carbon dioxide in pig slaughter[237] and use of water electric current in chicken slaughter.[238] These insights are critically important since they affect most land animals slaughtered for food, but the Commission decided not to implement the EFSA's recommendations because it considered them "not economically viable at present in the EU."[239] This, ultimately, calls into question the European Union's declared objective to protect animals on the grounds that they are sentient beings (article 13 TFEU).

Under Swiss law, articles 177 *et seq.* AWO regulate welfare aspects of animal slaughter. A core duty is that animals must be rendered unconscious before slaughter (article 178 para. 1 AWO), except for chickens slaughtered by ritual or religious methods (article 184 para. 4 AWO). Animals shall be "gently herded" (article 182 para. 1 AWO) but the use of electric prods is permissible in certain situations (para. 2). Article 184 lays down permissible methods of stunning for each species, similar to article 4 of the Council Regulation 1099/2009. Article 184 demands cows be stunned by captive bolt or bullet into the brain, pneumatic guns, or electric current. Pigs shall be stunned by captive bolt, bullet, electric current, or carbon dioxide. Chickens shall be stunned by electric current, percussive blow to the head, captive bolt, or "suitable" gas mixtures. And fish shall be stunned by a blunt, vigorous blow to the head, cervical dislocation, electric current, or mechanical destruction of the brain. Methods of stunning are also specified for horses, sheep and goats, rabbits, and decapods.

---

236 *E.g.*, AHAW/EFSA Report on Animal Slaughter and Killing (2004).

237 *Id.* at 13: "In CO_2 stunning, loss of sensibility and consciousness is not immediate but immersion of pigs into 80 to 90% CO_2 usually leads to the induction of unconsciousness within 30 seconds. At a given high concentration of CO_2 (80% by volume in air) and using increasing exposure times, the duration of unconsciousness increases and the stun-stick interval can be increased proportionally without animals recovering consciousness. However, at concentrations above 30% CO_2, the gas is known to be aversive and cause hyperventilation and irritation of the mucous membranes that can be painful, and elicits hyperventilation and gasping before loss of consciousness. Hypoxic stunning induced with 90% argon in air is less aversive than hypercapnic hypoxia induced with 30% CO_2 in argon or nitrogen or stunning with 80–90% CO_2 in air."

238 *Id.* at 16: "Electrical stunning and electrical stun/killing using water baths require extremely stressful handling and shackling of live poultry. The pain and distress associated with inversion (hanging upside down) and shackling (compression of metatarsal bones) induces wing flapping in the majority of birds, and there is a potential in a significant number of animals for dislocations and fractures to occur."

239 Council Regulation 1099/2009, 2009 O.J. (303) 1, 2: "Recommendations to phase out the use of carbon dioxide for pigs and the use of waterbath stunners for poultry are not included in this Regulation because the impact assessment revealed that such recommendations were not economically viable at present in the EU."

Disregarding any of these slaughter regulations is penalized under Swiss law by article 28 para. 1 lit. f AWA.

Some say that the Swiss legislator makes a laudable effort to spare animals as much suffering as possible before and during slaughter. Some also say that states that grapple with animal slaughter are progressive because many others have not laid down any laws that deal with the topic. But these laws fall short of protecting animals. They lay down duties to use antiquated methods to stun and kill animals, methods we would never consider "humane" for companion animals. No responsible person would agree to end the life of their companion cat or dog by captive bolt, electric shock, or painful gas mixture. Though these methods are designed to "avoid[...] pain and distress and lead[...] to an immediate loss of consciousness and insensibility that lasts until death,"[240] it is difficult to see how laws that require using a captive bolt to crush the head of a healthy animal, or that require an animal to be gassed or electrocuted, actually "avoid" pain and distress. In essence, it is these laws that make it legal to put animals in severe pain and to violently end their lives.

Most laws designed to "protect animals during slaughter" use euphemisms to package institutionalized violence against animals. Consider article 3 of the EU Directive in this respect, which requires animals to be handled so that they can exhibit their "normal behavior" while being led to the slaughterhouse. As Kelch rightly notes: "How is the natural behavior of an animal ever going to be connected in a meaningful way to being led to death?"[241] Slaughter regulations demand that "[a]nimals shall be spared any *avoidable* pain, distress or suffering during their killing and relating operations."[242] But they manifestly fail to inquire if slaughter, per se, and the pain and distress it causes for animals, should be avoided. We need to ask if ending the lives of healthy sentient beings is morally justified, especially when we do this for our own gastronomic pleasure and profit, and when many alternative methods for meeting those needs are available to us.[243]

When information about the slaughter of animals leaks to the public, it often is followed by a chorus of outrage. At these times, governments and corporations are quick to join the public in declaring such acts despicable and immoral, but they typically respond by naming and shaming individual workers for misconduct and presenting these events as exceptions.[244] When footage is released that makes institutional violence impossible to deny, then the blame cannot be foisted off on individuals anymore and new responses are needed to "solve" the problem. In December 2015, after ongoing investigations in Israeli slaughterhouses showed extreme forms of animal suffering and cruelty, the Israeli Minister of Agriculture installed 400 cameras in over 50 slaughterhouses throughout the country to monitor violations of the Prevention of Cruelty to Animals Act and ensure its enforcement.[245] Likewise, the

---

[240] ANIMAL WELFARE ORDINANCE (Switz.), art. 185 para. 1.

[241] KELCH 106 (2011).

[242] Council Regulation 1099/2009, 2009 O.J. (303) 1, art. 3 para. 1 (emphasis added).

[243] *See* for an overview of some ethical and legal arguments on whether killing animals for food is justified: Blattner, *3R for Farmed Animals* 18 ff. (2014); Petrus, *Leben*, *in* LEXIKON DER MENSCH-TIER-BEZIEHUNGEN 217 (2015); Klaus Petrus, *Schaden*, *in* LEXIKON DER MENSCH-TIER-BEZIEHUNGEN 305, 305 (2015).

[244] *See generally* PACHIRAT (2011).

[245] The slaughterhouses will be monitored for 24 hours per day by the Veterinary Services of the Ministry of Agriculture's back office: *Agriculture Ministry Orders Installation of Cameras in All Slaughterhouses*, THE JERUSALEM POST, Dec. 28, 2015.

UK government confirmed in November 2017 that it will make Closed Circuit Television (CCTV) mandatory for all slaughterhouses, regardless of their size. According to the proposed regulations, the footage must be kept for 90 days, and authorities should have unhindered access to the material.[246] These efforts aim to respond to the public's growing unease about animal slaughter, but it is not at all clear whether this is an adequate response. Increasing government surveillance often misleads the public into thinking that "everything is all right at the slaughterhouse." This strategy may work well for a couple of years, but time will show that increasing transparency alone is insufficient to counter institutional violence.[247] What the public outrage really shows is that it is difficult for the people to continue to believe in the myth of "humane slaughter" when they realize that we are slaughtering millions of animals—animals who fight for survival and against slaughter. Footage shot and controlled by intransparent government agencies thus merely prolong the time it takes for the public to become fully aware of these processes.

Part of the problem is that most animal laws do not in fact protect the lives of animals; they only protect their well-being. Few states are committed to protecting the lives of animals, including Austria and Germany. Section 6 para. 1 of the Austrian AWA states that "[i]t is prohibited to kill animals without proper reason."[248] Section 1 sentence 2 of the German AWA lays down that "[n]o one may cause an animal pain, suffering or harm without good reason."[249] Any violation of this section is penalized with up to three years imprisonment or a fine (section 17 para. 1 German AWA). Scholars argue that these norms respect the intrinsic interest of animals in their lives, and that this is why states like Austria and Germany declared illegal and criminalized the termination of animal life.[250]

However, as the legislative texts make clear, too, animals may legally be killed for "good reasons." A good reason for killing an animal is one that creates "more use than damage."[251] If we took this literally, we would expect these governments to meticulously effect a balance of interest every time an animal is forced to enter the slaughterhouse. They would have to consider who the animal is, what their life has looked like, which humans crave them as food, why humans eat them, and if the human need can be met without mandating that this particular animal be killed. But the brutal reality for farmed animals in Germany and Austria (as in the rest of the world) is that norms that "protect the lives of animals" are as perfunctory as slaughterhouse regulations. Raspé's characterization of these laws is apt: "It is the objective of this act to protect animal life. This is why it regulates in detail how animals ought to be killed."[252]

---

[246] Department of Environment, Food and Rural Affairs (DEFRA), Mandatory Closed Circuit Television (CCTV) Recording in Slaughterhouses: Summary of Responses and Government Response (November 2017).

[247] Similarly, police body cams have failed to prevent violence against subjugated people and in holding the police accountable for such actions: Amanda Ripley, *A Big Test of Police Body Cameras Defies Expectations*, N.Y. Times, Oct. 20, 2017.

[248] Animal Protection Act (Austria), § 6 para. 1.

[249] Animal Welfare Act (Ger.), § 1.

[250] Raspé 194–5 (2013).

[251] Lennkh 179 (2012).

[252] Translation by the author. In German: "Ziel dieses Gesetzes ist es, das Leben der Tiere zu schützen, daher regelt dieses Gesetz ausführlich wie Tiere zu töten sind." (Raspé 195 (2013)).

§5 Interim Conclusion

This chapter examined substantive standards of animal law to demonstrate the advantages of applying animal law across the border. While early scholarly opinions distinguished between civil, criminal, and administrative law, developments of the past decades (especially in antitrust law) have led scholars to conclude that these laws are subject to the same jurisdictional scope. Because this rule applies to the law of jurisdiction at large, all norms of animal law—the criminal, administrative, and civil provisions—can in principle be applied extraterritorially.

Each of these laws contains certain promises for protecting animals across the border. Constitutional duties owed to animals, which currently exist, among others, in Brazil, Egypt, the European Union, Germany, India, Luxembourg, and Switzerland, can guide states' animal laws with foresight. Constitutions enshrine the most central concerns of states and express their unequivocal commitment to protect these in the future. They demand action and implementation by the legislative, the judiciary, and the executive and demonstrate that animal interests are, at the least, important and, at best, as important as human interests. Constitutional norms that protect animals can also serve as a basis for the protective, the passive personality, and the effects principle.

Criminal norms sanctioning infringements of the interests of animals are also a powerful tool that can be applied extraterritorially. Comparative analyses suggest that criminal law is crucial to discourage people from harming animals, and works best if duties owed to animals are broadly formulated, comprehensive, and complemented by detailed rules at the regulatory level. Strict liability tests and corporate criminal liability also contribute to making extraterritorial jurisdiction an effective tool to protect animals by tackling corporate cultures that live off the systematic abuse of animals.

Administrative standards are an important achievement of modern animal law and offer considerable advantages in extraterritorial application. They lay down "optimal behavior" instead of minimum expectations; they stipulate positive duties owed to animals; they operate preventively by making use of permits and authorizations; and they are less rigid and less costly to adjudicate, which encourages NGOs to take action on behalf of animals. Comparative analyses of the most progressive laws on the keeping, transport, and slaughter of animals made apparent the difference very detailed, specific, and unequivocal language makes for affected animals.

Many states today compare their levels of animal protection with those of other states to determine if their laws are "off standard," and, accordingly, if they must strengthen them. The World Animal Protection Index (API) is a handy system for states that want to see how their animal laws rank in comparison to other states. The API assesses laws based on the following variables: formal recognition of animal sentience; support for the Universal Declaration on Animal Welfare; the existence of laws prohibiting animal suffering; laws protecting animals in farming, captivity, companionship, draught and recreation, scientific research, or the wild; government accountability; engagement with the OIE; providing humane education; and promoting communication and awareness.[253] The Australia-based

[253] World Animal Protection (WAP), Indicators (2019), *available at* https://api.worldanimalprotection.org/indicators (last visited Jan. 10, 2019).

NGO Voiceless introduced another ranking system called Voiceless Animal Cruelty Index (VACI) that focuses exclusively on the welfare of land-farmed animals and not only ranks laws but also the harms that countries inflict on these animals. A country is ranked by three modules: producing cruelty (the number of farmed animals slaughtered for food every year); consuming cruelty (the consumption of farmed animals); and sanctioning cruelty (their regulatory framework that protects, or fails to protect, farmed animals).[254]

Based on this chapter's analysis and the ranking systems just described, is there reason to believe that any of the laws we examined herein are exemplary models and achievements that could be used to guide the law of jurisdiction? The short answer is no. The long answer is: comparative analyses have made apparent the fact that even the best laws in place to protect animals simply clean up around the edges and do not in fact protect animals from being ill-treated or killed. Most of these laws simply enshrine and make legal the routine and systematic exploitation of animals. It is easy to see why ranking systems, which hail small deviations from this norm as a success, have become popular among states and corporations that do business on their territory. But being ranked based on a limited set of factors anchored in a descriptive model neither helps animals nor does it ultimately benefit states. These ranking systems tell us nothing about the overall deficits of a system that kills animals by the millions, or the changes we need to make if we are to live up to our commitment to protect animals as sentient and conscious co-inhabitants of this world. If we were to set up a global ranking system that assesses countries based on factors that indicate where we as a global multispecies society want and must go to (i.e., a society that takes seriously the claims of animals), this system and the ranks occupied by countries would look radically different. Countries would not get a percentage of their current ranking; they would find themselves occupying the lowest ranks and would be forced to realize that their current levels of protection are much closer to one another than they thought they were—and much further away from where they ought to be.

---

[254] Voiceless, The Voiceless Animal Protection Index (2019), *available at* https://vaci.voiceless.org.au/about-the-vaci/ (last visited Jan. 10, 2019). Also ALDF offers rankings of animal protection laws, focused on US states: Animal Legal Defense Fund, 2018 U.S. Animal Protection Laws State Rankings, *available at* https://aldf.org/project/2018-us-state-rankings/ (last visited Jan. 10, 2019). To assess the performance of states, ALDF uses elements like the definition of "animal," courtroom animal advocate programs, civil nuisance abatement, and possession bans (*id.*).

10 Legality of Extraterritorial Jurisdiction under International Law

THE CASE FOR extraterritorial jurisdiction in animal law is strong, and I have outlined reasonable and desirable ways for this tool to revolutionize animal law in an age of globalization. But no matter how valuable, plausible, or necessary the jurisdictional means to protect animals across and within the border, extraterritorial animal law can still violate international law. We must next ask when a state's jurisdiction will prevail if claims to jurisdiction overlap and—regardless of concurring jurisdiction—when extraterritorial jurisdiction breaches international law and what consequences this breach would entail. Answering these questions will help states determine the political and legal risks associated with extraterritorial jurisdiction and assess whether these are worth taking. In the first part of this chapter, I turn to common objections to extraterritorial animal law before examining how jurisdictional conflicts are formed in animal law, and how they can be prevented through unilateral and bilateral action. Following this, I examine what the limits of extraterritorial animal law are under international law, and the legal consequences of a breach.

§1 Countering Extraterritorial Animal Law

A. OBJECTIONS

States might object or actively oppose other states' extraterritorial animal laws for a variety of reasons. A state may feel that such efforts undermine its authority as the sole regulator within its borders or that foreign animal law interferes in its domestic affairs.[1] A state might also

---

[1] Staker, *Jurisdiction*, *in* INTERNATIONAL LAW 309 (2018). Judge Weiss argues that not objecting to foreign

Protecting Animals Within and Across Borders. Charlotte E. Blattner.

object to extraterritoriality because it believes the principle of sovereign equality precludes foreign states from asserting their authority over it.[2] It may argue that accepting that one state's laws apply in another state's territory risks shifting the character of international law from egalitarian to hegemonic.

States may also feel that using extraterritorial jurisdiction unduly improves the socioeconomic position of some states, by offering benefits to them that would have to be negotiated in bi- or multilateral treaty processes.[3] During negotiations, states are expected to make reciprocal concessions, but if states instead resort to unilateral extraterritorial animal law, they simply cherry-pick their policies across the border without regard to the preferences and priorities of other states and their people. For example, if the United Kingdom prohibited exports of calves to spare them conditions of extreme confinement abroad,[4] it might invoke the subjective territoriality principle to impose a duty on all transporters not to export calves under a certain age. In reaction thereto, affected countries might accuse the United Kingdom of evading its international obligations, arguing that it should have negotiated export bans with them, and, in turn, adapted its tariffs concessions for other products.

A pragmatic view suggests that extraterritorial jurisdiction creates a lot of legal uncertainty, which stirs up unnecessary conflict, creates diplomatic impasses, and increases costs. Extraterritorial jurisdiction also reduces transnational efficiency by requiring more cooperation and information exchange and by raising costs that no state is willing to bear. The effects on individuals are equally disruptive. People will no longer know which laws apply to them, not even when they operate in their home state. Corporations exposed to these risks will try to avoid these pitfalls by objecting to extraterritorial jurisdiction and lobbying against its adoption. Should they fail, corporations are likely to redirect streams of investment and commerce as a reaction to uneven playing fields.[5]

States will most likely object to extraterritorial jurisdiction on the grounds that it is a form of ethical, social, or cultural value imposition, imperialism, hegemony, parochialism, neocolonialism, and the like.[6] Some argue that resistance to foreign extraterritorial animal

---

extraterritorial jursdiction in matters that intrude in a state's own territory would amount to the affected state not assuming its duties as a state: Lotus, 1927 P.C.I.J. 44 (Dissenting Opinion by Weiss, M.).

[2] Anne Peters, *The Growth of International Law between Globalization and Great Power*, 8 AUSTRIAN REV. INT'L & EUR. L. 109, 131 (2003): "If sovereignty means independence from other states, it precludes legal authority of one state over the other and implies the legal equality of states."

[3] RYNGAERT, JURISDICTION 195 (2015).

[4] *See* in this context Case C-1/96, The Queen and Minister of Agriculture, Fisheries and Food, ex parte Compassion in World Farming Limited, 1998 E.C.R. I-1251.

[5] Johnston & Powles, *The Kings of the World and Their Dukes' Dilemma*, *in* GLOBALISATION AND JURISDICTION 41 (2004); MENG 114 (1994); ZERK, EXTRATERRITORIAL JURISDICTION 210 (2010).

[6] *See* for these arguments in the context of extraterritorial human rights: Ralph Wilde, *Compliance with Human Rights Norms Extraterritorially: "Human Rights Imperialism"?*, *in* INTERNATIONAL LAW AND THE QUEST FOR ITS IMPLEMENTATION, *LIBER AMICORUM* VERA GOWLLAND-DEBBAS 319 (Laurence Boisson de Chazournes & Marcelo Kohen eds., 2010). *See* for these arguments in the context of extraterritorial antitrust law: Susan E. Burnett, U.S. *Judicial Imperialism post* Empagran v. F. Hoffmann-Laroche? *Conflicts of Jurisdiction and International Law in Extraterritorial Antitrust*, 18 EMORY INT'L L. REV. 555 (2004). And in extraterritorial criminal law: Christopher J. Duncan, *The 1998 Foreign Corrupt Practices Act Amendments: Moral Empiricism or Moral Imperialism*, 1 APLPJ 1 (2000).

law springs from a "vague sense of superiority or exceptionality"[7] that states have about their own laws. This claim, however, goes beyond what can be reasonably demanded of a democratic society in our age of globalization. Since we continue to rely on nation-states to organize international affairs, people cannot be expected to fully succumb to foreign laws even if they are, rationally speaking, the "better" laws. What is more, objections to extraterritorial jurisdiction on grounds of value imposition are often justified. After all, the West has continually used animal welfare (the ways in which animals are raised, killed, or eaten) as a tool to discriminate against others. Mexican immigrants in the United States are targeted for horse-tripping and cock-fighting, Asian immigrants are accused of engaging in "barbaric" practices by eating dogs, and native peoples are condemned for hunting whales.[8] In these cases, practices predominantly associated with non-whites are portrayed as "culturally backward" and "uncivilized," while mainstream practices of dominant cultures, such as factory farming or animal research, are considered "normal" or "neutral" even though they inflict as much or more harm on animals.[9] These forms of ethnocentrism are exacerbated by extraterritorial jurisdiction in animal law, which cannot be separated from the long history of white aggression against people of "other" cultures in an ongoing process of cultural imperialism.[10]

Minority practices can and certainly do cause great suffering for animals, but it can reinforce existing inequities if we focus exclusively on abridging rights of minorities while failing to criticize majority practices that are just as cruel and may even harm many more animals.[11] Simply expanding the "European" way of using and killing animals across the world will not improve the lot of animals or challenge their exploitation. It simply leaves unchecked and accepts as legitimate the way majorities subjugate animals by the millions, and thereby glosses over their exploitation.[12] It also shows that we fail to understand that many of the practices of minorities are a form of cultural resistance to the dominant culture that usurped its standards onto them in the first place.[13] So by targeting marginalized groups, these laws risk producing and reproducing forms of oppression including racism, sexism, ableism, and speciesism.

The case of Michael Vick is a good illustration of this problem. Michael Vick is a former American football quarterback whose stellar career in the National Football League quickly came to a halt in 2007 after the media revealed his involvement in the dog-fighting ring

---

[7] RYNGAERT, JURISDICTION 192 (2015).

[8] *See further* CLAIRE JEAN KIM, DANGEROUS CROSSINGS: RACE, SPECIES, AND NATURE IN A MULTICULTURAL AGE 4 (2015); Claire Jean Kim, *Multiculturalism Goes Imperial: Immigrants, Animals and the Suppression of Moral Dialogue*, 4(1) DUBOIS REV. 233 (2007); Kymlicka & Donaldson 126 (2014).

[9] Deckha 192–3 (2007); Oh & Jackson 31 (2011).

[10] Kim 234 (2007).

[11] Jacqueline Dalziell & Dinesh J. Wadiwel, *Live Exports, Animal Advocacy, Race and "Animal Nationalism," in* MEAT CULTURE 73 (Annie Potts ed., 2017).

[12] Oh & Jackson 45 (2011).

[13] For example, anthropologist Olga Nájera-Ramírez argues that the *charreada* is a form of cultural resistance against US domination: Olga Nájera-Ramírez, Haciendo Patria: La Charreada *and the Formation of a Mexican Transnational Identity, in* TRANSNATIONAL LATINA/O COMMUNITIES: POLITICS, PROCESSES, AND CULTURE 168, 170 (Carlos G. Vélez-Ibañez, Anna Sampaio, & Manolo González-Estay eds., 2002).

"Bad Newz Kennels." The police investigation showed that Vick had killed several of his dogs by drowning and hanging, and that he left many more neglected on his property.[14] When the press described these events, Vick became the victim of extreme racism. His acts were framed as the epitome of animal cruelty and his blackness was considered instrumental to his acts of cruelty, since "only black people" treat animals so horrendously. Some people went so far as to call for Vick's execution.[15] The Vick case underlines how easily animal law is appropriated to serve underlying motives of racism or other forms of oppression like sexism and ableism.[16]

Consider also the long-standing public debate in Australia on live exports of animals. Australia is one of the largest exporters of live animals, in particular to the Middle East and South East Asia. In March 2011, Animals Australia, an animal advocacy organization, released footage that showed how cows were subjected to "abuse through eye gouging, kicking, tail twisting and tail breaking"[17] before being slaughtered in Indonesian abattoirs. These events led to media coverage and protests across Australia on a scale unmatched by any other Australian animal welfare campaign.[18] The discourse centered around "our" "Australian" animals or cows—prefaces and adjectives that indicate an emotional connection and proximity wholly absent in debates about animal abuse in Australian facilities.[19] Where Indonesian practices of slaughter attracted shame and reprobation, Australian ways of killing animals were neither discussed nor criticized, though they are just as prevalent. To base extraterritorial animal laws on this racialized terrain suggests that there is a "tacit acceptance of the fact that animals do not require saving in general, they require saving from non-white others."[20]

Similarly, the 2002 Olympics in South Korea sparked massive protests in the country and around the world against dog meat production and trade. Protestors demanded dog slaughter be halted in South Korea, at least during the games.[21] If the International Olympic

---

[14] US District Court Judge Henry E. Hudson sentenced Vick to 23 months in prison, more than Vick's co-defendants and more than the 12 to 18 months prosecutors originally suggested as part of Vick's plea agreement: Juliet Macur, *Vick Receives 23 Months and a Lecture*, N.Y. TIMES, Dec. 11, 2007.

[15] *See* for a thoughtful analysis of these events: Melissa Harris-Perry, *Michael Vick, Racial History and Animal Rights*, THE NATION, Dec. 30, 2010.

[16] *See* for an intersectional analysis of race and speciesism: APH KO & SYL KO, APHRO-ISM: ESSAYS ON POP CULTURE, FEMINISM, AND BLACK VEGANISM FROM TWO SISTERS (2017). *See* for an intersectional analysis of ableism and speciesism: SUNAURA TAYLOR, BEASTS OF BURDEN: ANIMAL AND DISABILITY LIBERATION (2017). *See* for an intersectional analysis of patriarchy and speciesism: CAROL J. ADAMS & LORI GRUEN (EDS.), ECOFEMINISM: FEMINIST INTERSECTIONS WITH OTHER ANIMALS & THE EARTH (2015). *See further* on racism in the guise of animal welfare: VICKI HEARNE, BANDIT: DOSSIER OF A DANGEROUS DOG (2d ed. 2002).

[17] Animals Australia and RSPCA, Live Exports to Indonesia (2011), *available at* http://www.banliveexport.com/documents/FactSheet-cases.pdf (last visited Jan. 10, 2019).

[18] O'SULLIVAN (2011).

[19] Dalziell & Wadiwel, *Live Exports, Animal Advocacy, Race and "Animal Nationalism," in* MEAT CULTURE 77 (2017).

[20] *Id.* at 85.

[21] These protests continue until this day: Claire Czajkowski, *Dog Meat Trade in South Korea: A Report on the Current State of the Trade and Efforts to Eliminate It*, 21 ANIMAL L. 29, 61 (2015).

Committee (the NGO committee of the Olympic games, based in Lausanne, Switzerland) was obliged under Swiss law not to offer dog meat during any of its activities abroad, South Korea might protest on grounds of moral and legal imperialism. If protests to dog meat (which certainly do not have the force of extraterritorial laws) are already accused of feeding and fueling neocolonialist motives,[22] this is even more the case for extraterritorial jurisdiction.[23]

These cases and examples make apparent that, whether done on purpose or unintentionally, unchecked attempts to protect animals abroad may easily become a fig leaf for oppressing others. They point to structural problems that underlie the law of jurisdiction, in particular, clashes between majority and minority cultures, and raise the question of whether it is necessary, desirable, or even possible for the majority to accommodate "troubling" minority traditions.[24] In ethics, there is a broad consensus that there should be no "cultural defense" or "cultural exemption" for minority practices that contravene animal laws.[25] But this does not mean that we should condone selective enforcement that holds minorities accountable and exempts majority practices. We require a symmetry of moral scrutiny, as Kymlicka argues:

> If it is indeed true that all practices and traditions are morally accountable for their treatment of animals, then it seems possible, indeed likely, that very few of our practices are likely to pass a test of moral acceptability. Everyday majority practices of eating meat or visiting zoos stand in need of moral justification as much as minority practices of ritual slaughter. And virtually all philosophers who have attempted to evaluate these practices have concluded that they fail basic tests of moral acceptability, since they involve sacrificing the most basic interests of animals for trivial interests of humans.[26]

Until minority and majority practices are measured by the same yardstick, we must expect extraterritorial jurisdiction to reinscribe Eurocentric thinking and to impose laws on people

---

[22] Oh & Jackson 33 (2011). Koreans now feel more protective of these cultural rights than during the Olympic games in 1988 (*id.*). Interestingly, South Korea has decided to label dog meat as "non-livestock meat" (ostriches are also classified as such): Czajkowski 50 (2015).

[23] Though portrayed as an international conflict, the dog meat debate is as heated in affected states as it is between them. *See* Peter J. Li et al., *Dog "Meat" Consumption in China: A Survey of the Controversial Eating Habit in Two Cities*, 25 Soc. & Ani. 513, 530 (2017): "In China, the decline of dog 'meat' consumption is mostly a result of domestic opposition. A conflict over dog 'meat' consumption is in fact a Chinese 'civil war' between two Chinese groups. This is not a conflict between China and the outside world. With this in mind, international animal advocacy groups can confidently support the Chinese activists without worrying about being accused of imposing Western values on these countries. The bond between humans and companion animals is not Western. It is a trans-cultural phenomenon."

[24] Kim 8–9 (2015).

[25] *See especially* Luis Cordeiro-Rodrigues & Les Mitchell (eds.), Multiculturalism, Race and Animals: Contemporary Moral and Political Debates (2017). *See also* Will Kymlicka, *Afterword: Realigning Multiculturalism and Animal Rights*, *in* Multiculturalism, Race and Animals 295, 296 (2017): "All of us, majority or minority, are morally accountable for our treatment of animals, and merely saying that a practice is 'traditional' does not show that it meets standards of moral acceptability."

[26] Kymlicka, *Afterword: Realigning Multiculturalism and Animal Rights*, *in* Multiculturalism, Race and Animals 296 (2017).

who may never have had the opportunity to participate in any democratic form in the formation of that law.[27]

B. FORMS OF PROTEST

For the reasons mentioned above, states traditionally object to foreign jurisdiction through letters and statements, *amicus curiae* briefs, blocking and clawback statutes, or lawsuits. These tools have not yet been used in animal law, but it is easy to imagine how they could be. If the United States introduces an act to try its nationals for killing endangered animals abroad, South Africa could send a letter or statement to the US government to give its opinion on the right- or wrongfulness of the decision to assume jurisdiction over those animals.[28] States can in principle counter foreign extraterritorial animal laws in this abstract manner, but they are more likely to respond by intervening in a pending case court. South Africa might, for instance, choose to file an *amicus curiae* brief to the US court—a letter addressed to the court that offers information, expertise, insights, or simply an opinion about the issue at hand.[29] The court receiving the brief considers it at its sole discretion. If the brief goes unnoticed, South Africa can use diplomatic tactics, like protests, to oppose the reach of foreign laws.

When protests are ignored or there is a lot at stake, states tend to enact blocking statutes. Blocking statutes are intended to bar any extraterritorial effect of foreign (animal) laws by preventing foreign authorities from investigating and enforcing foreign judgments on domestic territory. Blocking statutes may also make it illegal for nationals or residents to abide by foreign laws, to cooperate with foreign authorities, or even to react to foreign laws. In antitrust law, which was heavily debated in the 1970s throughout the 1990s, states including Australia, Canada, the European Union, France, Germany, South Africa, and the United Kingdom have repeatedly enacted blocking statutes.[30] During the 1990s, the statutes gradually shifted from antitrust law to export control law.[31] A well-known and far-reaching blocking statute was enacted by the European Union in 1996, by which it sought to halt the

---

[27] States that adopt extraterritorial laws are not typically held accountable to those affected by their laws. In detail on this deficit: RYNGAERT, JURISDICTION 192 ff. (2015); RYNGAERT, UNILATERAL JURISDICTION AND GLOBAL VALUES 125 ff. (2015).

[28] ZERK, EXTRATERRITORIAL JURISDICTION 96 (2010). Although government officials usually do this, parliament members also actively involve themselves in disputes, like Senator Rockefeller who addressed the European Commission in *GE/Honeywell* in 2001: Allyson Lieberman, *Senator Slams EC—Rockefeller Threatens Retaliation on GE Deal*, N.Y. POST, June 21, 2001.

[29] *E.g.*, the Brief of the United Kingdom of Great Britain and Northern Ireland and the Kingdom of the Netherlands as Amici Curiae in Support of Petitioners, No. 03-724, Feb. 3, 2004, F. Hoffmann-La Roche v. Empagran, Ltd. 541 U.S. 155 (2004) (U.S.) expressed that the extraterritorial application of the FTAIA "is contrary to basic principles of international law regarding the allocation of jurisdiction between states."

[30] For the United Kingdom, *see* the Protection of Trading Interests Act 1980, c. 11 (U.K.). For Australia, Canada, the European Union, France, Germany, and other countries, *see* ZERK, EXTRATERRITORIAL JURISDICTION 96 (2010); Note, *Reassessment of International Application of Antitrust Laws: Blocking Statutes, Balancing Tests, and Treble Damages*, 50 L. & CONTEMP. PROBS. 197 (1987).

[31] *See* the adoption of the Cuban Liberty and Democratic Solidarity (Libertad) Act of 1996 by the U.S. [Helms-Burton Act], 22 U.S.C. § 6021 (U.S.) and Australia, Canada, and the United Kingdom's stance in *In Re Uranium Antitrust Legislation:* In Re Uranium Antitrust Legislation, 473 F. Supp. 382 (N.D. Ill 1979) (U.S.).

United States' aggressive embargoes against Cuba.[32] Council Regulation 2271/96 included a duty to inform the Commission if persons were indirectly or directly affected by the legislation (article 2). All authorities were told not to recognize or enforce judgments of foreign courts or tribunals and decisions of foreign administrative authorities (article 4). And private persons were not allowed to comply with any requirement or prohibition of foreign laws, either actively or by deliberate omission (article 5).

Blocking statutes are a popular countermeasure to extraterritorial jurisdiction in banking law, competition law, mergers and acquisitions, but they have also been used in fields of law dealing with social welfare, worker rights, and the like. In 1978, South Africa enacted the Protection of Business Act (PBA), which prohibited corporations and individuals from complying with US Ex-Im Bank laws on fair employment standards. The US Office of Southern African Affairs developed a fair labor standards questionnaire to assess if projects were eligible for funding. As a reaction to these inquiries, the PBA barred cooperation in all civil matters and stated that no person "shall in compliance with or in response to any order, direction, interrogatory, commission *rogatoire*, letters of request or any other request issued or emanating from outside the Republic in connection with any civil proceedings, furnish any information as to any business whether carried on in or outside the Republic."[33] South Africa could adopt the same or similar measures if the United States initiated proceedings against people for trophy hunting in South Africa. It might prohibit all persons from cooperating with US agencies and declare void all efforts of the United States to obtain evidence in South Africa. This is not unlikely because it seems that blocking statutes are at least partly driven by states' desire to counteract laws perceived as imperialist and not just to protect individuals from the effects of foreign laws.

In the labor law case mentioned above, a 2008 media statement from the South African Law Reform Commission indicated its change in opinion, 30 years after the laws were put in effect. The statement notes that the "principal aim of the Protection of Businesses Act 99 of 1978 was to protect South Africans from the draconian effects of certain foreign laws, in particular those allowing awards of penal or multiple damages," but that "[t]he Act frustrates what are, in the majority of cases, uncontentious requests for serving process, taking evidence or enforcing foreign judgments."[34] As South Africa's experience shows, we must find ways to begin a meaningful discussion about substantive standards that lay down the treatment of animals, rather than using extraterritorial animal laws in a "draconian" manner or blocking them off on the basis of these fears.

In addition to blocking statutes, states have provided for clawback statutes that grant addressees of foreign laws the right of recovery for all or for particular costs associated with the exercise of foreign extraterritorial jurisdiction.[35] Sometimes, blocking statutes directly provide for clawback clauses. Finally, states can always initiate proceedings at the ICJ,[36] the

---

[32] Council Regulation 2271/96 Protecting Against the Effects of the Extra-territorial Application of Legislation Adopted by a Third Country, and Actions Based Thereon or Resulting Therefrom, 1996 O.J. (L 309) 1.

[33] Protection of Businesses Act, No. 99 of 1978, art. 1(1)(b) (S. Afr.).

[34] Media Statement by the South African Law Reform Commission Convening its Investigation into Consolidated Legislation Pertaining to International Co-operation in Civil Matters (Project 121), Issued by the Secretary, Aug. 15, 2008.

[35] *E.g.*, Council Regulation 2271/96, 1996 O.J. (L 309) 1, 2, art. 6.

[36] ICJ Statute, art. 36.

WTO DSB (for trade matters),[37] or a special arbitral tribunal[38] to object to and invalidate extraterritorial animal laws.

§2 Conflicts of Animal Laws

A. ADDRESSING CULTURAL CLASHES

Before we begin to explore what must be observed legally, as a minimum, when states' animal laws conflict, we need to determine if using extraterritorial jurisdiction in animal law makes sense in the first place, considering the fact that it is likely to be used as a tool to oppress minorities. As we saw earlier, there is a great deal of intersectional oppression at play in animal law in general, and this risk is exacerbated in cases of extraterritorial jurisdiction, when the different ways in which humans use and exploit animals are highlighted.[39] It is easy to see how the danger of cultural imperialism and neocolonialism compels us to take a hands-off approach to extraterritorial jurisdiction. The chance this tool will be used to advance hidden agendas is so great that we may virtually end up entitling majority cultures to oppress minorities. The West would view itself as coming to the rescue of "uncivilized," "savage" nations and showing them how to "properly" use, kill, and eat animals. Instead of helping animals and advancing a just interspecies vision of society, we will find ourselves caught up in recurring spirals of discrimination and injustice.

We cannot solve this problem by making a shallow claim that many animal laws do not have hidden agendas and that, consequently, extraterritorial jurisdiction does not bear the danger of targeting minorities. Nor can we solve it by giving a free pass to cultural minorities when they violate the interests of animals.[40] This dilemma may seem insurmountable but it can be eased by using what Claire Jean Kim calls a "multi-optic vision." Kim has advocated for a multi-optic vision as a way of seeing that takes disparate justice claims seriously without presumptively privileging one over another.[41] Kim argues: "Animals suffer under minority practices just as they do under majority practices, and while the first type of suffering is no more important, morally speaking, than the second, it is no less important either."[42] Using the multi-optic vision, we should take a broader and less prejudiced view when we determine which practices result in harm for animals, while remaining sensitive to the unconscious appropriation of animal law to serve hidden discriminatory agendas. What the caveats of cultural imperialism and neocolonialism mandate, then, is not a hands-off approach to extraterritorial jurisdiction, but much more careful management of these laws.

So what would a thoughtful approach to these issues look like? Maneesha Deckha, drawing on a postcolonial and posthuman theory of cultural rights, argues that we need to base our legal efforts at the interface of animal law and multiculturalism on three pillars: (i) we must listen to other perspectives and be aware that colonialism taints Western ways of knowing; (ii) we must strive for consistency by criticizing mainstream practices and "conscientiously

---

[37] DSU, arts. 3 ff.

[38] *E.g.*, DSU, art. 25.

[39] *See* Chapter 10, §1 A.

[40] *Id.*

[41] Kim 19 (2015).

[42] *Id.* at 196.

and systematically avoiding the racialization of animal exploitation by selective practices;"[43] and (iii) we should make judgments only after good faith consultation and collaboration.[44] Ensuring that the law of jurisdiction rests stably on these pillars will be difficult, and we will have to fundamentally rethink and reverse many of our current practices. But this task is necessary, for otherwise, we would open the door to immense suffering, either by oppressing other humans or by letting free market principles govern the treatment of animals around the world. In the following, I foreground these principles in my inquiries, classifications, and proposals for resolution. I begin by disentangling the different types of legal conflicts that may emerge, and explore how they can be prevented, mitigated, and resolved.

B. EMERGENCE AND CLASSIFICATION OF JURISDICTIONAL CONFLICTS

A state may have strong and valid claims to extend its laws to animals in foreign countries, but its jurisdiction might still infringe on another state's personal, territorial, and organizational sovereignty, or it might simply prove less potent than another state's jurisdiction. In other words, the jurisdictional principles sketched by customary international law are only *prima facie* legal under international law.[45] We can see this as an advantage because multiple laws applied across the border create a strong jurisdictional net across the world that will help fill governance gaps. Some, however, may be dissatisfied with a solution they think will increase inter-state conflict and give rise to high legal and judicial costs. One way to reduce overlapping jurisdiction would be to give jurisdictional principles more than *prima facie* legality in international law by establishing a hierarchy of jurisdictional principles. For example, there are salient, but recurring claims that some (extraterritorial) jurisdictional principles are inferior to and must make way for territorial jurisdiction.[46] These claims may be a product of duties set up in special treaties or they may emerge from domestic law, but the law of jurisdiction as it exists under customary international law does not support this form of favoritism.[47] Chapter 2 has shown that the practice of states and international courts

[43] Deckha 220–3 (2007).

[44] *Id.* at 223.

[45] Bantekas, *Criminal Jurisdiction of States under International Law*, *in* MPEPIL 1 (2011); Bowett 15 (1982); OPPENHEIM'S INTERNATIONAL LAW 457 (1992). The final judgment on their legality under international law is determined by examining the claims of other states. *See* CRAWFORD 457 (2012): "[S]ufficiency of grounds for jurisdiction is normally considered relative to the rights of other states."

[46] Bowett bases this prerogative on the equality of states, the principle of nonintervention, and the principle of territorial integrity: Bowett 15–7 (1982). *See also* Mann 90–1 (1964).

[47] Dieter Anders, *Die Kollision von Strafgewalten in der Rechtspraxis*, *in* CONFLICTS OF JURISDICTION IN CROSS-BORDER CRIME SITUATIONS 109, 111 (2012); Bantekas, *Criminal Jurisdiction of States under International Law*, *in* MPEPIL 1 (2011); Cameron, *International Criminal Jurisdiction, Protective Principle*, *in* MPEPIL 6 (2007); Andreas V. Lowe, *Blocking Extraterritorial Jurisdiction: The British Protection of Trading Interests Act, 1980*, 75 AJIL 257, 267 (1981); O'Keefe 738 (2004); PETERS, VÖLKERRECHT 162 (2016); RYNGAERT, JURISDICTION 143, 144 (2015); SCHWARZE 30 (1994); Brigitte Stern, *Quelques observations sur les règles internationales relatives à l'application extraterritoriale du droit*, 32 ADFI 7, 43 (1986); JAN H.W. VERZIJL, INTERNATIONAL LAW IN HISTORICAL PERSPECTIVE vol. IV, 20 (1972). *See also* U.S. Restatement (Fourth) of the Foreign Relations Law, § 402, cmt. l.

supports neither the prevalence of territoriality nor a presumption against extraterritoriality in international law. In this respect, the ICTY noted in *Jankovic* :

> [A]ttempts among States to establish a hierarchy of criteria for determining the most appropriate jurisdiction for a criminal case, where there are concurrent jurisdictions on a horizontal level (i.e. among States), have failed thus far. Instead, States have agreed on various criteria and opted to give weight to certain criteria over others depending on the circumstances of a particular case.[48]

One reason why international law has not established a hierarchy of jurisdictional bases, is that they are shifting from field to field. In securities law, the place of conduct is considered decisive, but in anticompetition law, the place of effect is most important. And in export controls law, nationality indicates which state has jurisdiction.[49] Jurisdictional bases are thus sensitive to the substantive law at hand. States also dislike limiting their choice of jurisdictional principles. In practice, Kamminga explains, states simply pick and choose from the principles in order to justify the policies they want to adopt.[50] This, they claim, helps affected parties. Even if the absence of a clear hierarchy compromises predictability and legal certainty, a broad variety of jurisdictional principles is more likely to provide for justice in individual cases because it takes into account distinct features of each field of law.

Accepting many grounds of jurisdiction is bound to result in several (legitimate) claims of jurisdiction being made for the same state of facts. By and large, jurisdiction is therefore not exclusive, but concurrent, competing, or overlapping (these terms are used interchangeably). Concurrent jurisdiction points to a *positive competency conflict*: more than one state or regulatory entity purports to regulate the same state of facts. The opposite is a *negative competency conflict*, in which no state or regulatory entity claims jurisdiction and the matter remains essentially unregulated. In a perfect world, neither of these competency conflicts would arise. Regulatory authority would be properly allocated among states, generating neither overlapping jurisdiction nor legal loopholes. Although desirable in theory, aiming for this balance in the real world is pointless, considering our advanced levels of transborder interconnectedness. Faced with the choice between conflict-laden concurring jurisdiction and utopian allocation of jurisdiction that risks legal gaps, international law has chosen the lesser of the two evils. International law favors concurrent jurisdiction and, thus, legal pluralism, over legal loopholes.[51]

---

[48] Prosecutor v. Gojko Jankovic, Case No. IT-96-23/2-AR11*bis*2, Decision on Rule 11bis Referral ¶ 34 (Nov. 15, 2005).

[49] IBA Report Extraterritorial Jurisdiction 23 (2009).

[50] Menno T. Kamminga, *Extraterritoriality*, *in* MPEPIL 16 (Rüdiger Wolfrum ed., online ed. 2012).

[51] Inazumi 5 (2005); Robert Cover, *The Uses of Jurisdictional Redundancy: Interest, Ideology, and Innovation*, 22 Wm. & Mary L. Rev. 639 (1981). Concurring jurisdiction creates competition between substantive provisions, which brings about many benefits. Berman uses the example of universal jurisdiction to illustrate this claim, arguing that efforts by the Spanish judiciary to assert jurisdiction over former Argentine military members supported human rights efforts within Argentina. The Pinochet case initiated in Spain caused the Chilean Supreme Court to remove Pinochet's immunity and apply the Geneva Conventions without regard to limits like amnesties or statutory limitations. As a result, several hundred officers were convicted, many suspects indicted, and even more cases investigated: Berman, Global Legal Pluralism 237 (2012).

Now that the nature and desirability of positive competency conflicts are clearer, we can examine in more detail the potential for conflicts between states' laws. A state that exercises extraterritorial jurisdiction may prohibit acts done on animals, or require or permit certain acts be done with or on animals. It may also decide not to regulate such actions. Out of the four options (prohibiting, permitting, requiring actions or omissions, or not doing any of the three), 10 types of concurrent jurisdiction may emerge. If one state explicitly permits behavior another state is silent about, there is a *permissive-omissive conflict*. This is the case if state A expressly permits (but does not require) keeping dogs inside at all times, while state B's laws contain nothing about whether dogs must have opportunities to exercise (or, more generally, about whether dog owners have to ensure their dogs' well-being). If state A requires all dog owners to exercise dogs outside at least three hours a day, while state B remains silent on the point, a *requisite-omissive conflict* emerges. If state A prohibits keeping dogs inside at all times, while state B has still not enacted any laws on the matter, there is a *prohibitive-omissive conflict*. Though dog owners may not find themselves in a compliance conflict if they conform to state A's laws, state B might nevertheless claim that state A's laws are intrusive.[52]

If one state requires certain behavior that another state permits, this creates a *permissive-requisite conflict*. In this case, the laws of the state that calls for an action or omission are more intrusive than the laws of the other state. For example, state B allows owners of hens to debeak them, but state A obliges the owners to do so. If the owner of the CAFO abides by the laws of state A, the owner does not, in principle, violate the laws of state B. But if state B expressly permits what state A prohibits, this creates a *permissive-prohibitive* conflict, which is more delicate.[53] For example, state B still allows factory farmers to debeak hens, but state A has decided to prohibit debeaking because it inflicts immense and unnecessary suffering on animals. In this case, the factory owner does not violate state B's laws when conforming to state A's no-debeak policy.

The most precarious situation is created if one act prohibits what another requires (*prohibitive-requisite conflict*). This conflict emerges if state B introduces a law that makes it mandatory for factory farmers to debeak hens, but state A sticks to its policy of banning the mutilation of hens. The egg producer, if subject to the laws of both states, is now trapped in a compliance conflict. Abiding by state A's laws will cause the producer to violate state B's laws, and vice versa. States may also be caught in *omissive-omissive, permissive-permissive, requisite-requisite*, and *prohibitive-prohibitive* conflicts. In these cases, addressees of norms are not usually in conflict over compliance, but states may nevertheless claim that their jurisdiction should precede the others' or that the prescriptive jurisdiction of other states violates their rights under international law.

Sorting out the types of jurisdictional conflict can help us understand the severity of a given conflict, since the types indicate the extent to which a state will claim its sovereignty is

52 Omission to regulate conduct cannot be interpreted as being open to other state's extraterritorial laws, or as implicitly refusing them: SCHUSTER 592–3 (1996).

53 A famous example of this conflict is the *Microsoft* case, in which the European Union regarded Microsoft's position on the market as abuse, while the United States viewed it as a legitimate form of competition: Case T-201/04, Microsoft Corp. et al. v. Commission, 2007 E.C.R. II-3601.

violated, and the force with which it will protest the jurisdiction of another state. In the past, prohibitive-requisite conflicts were the most likely cause of international disputes locked in a stalemate.[54] These are the conflicts attracting the most attention. The United States, for example, considers only such prohibitive-requisite conflicts to be "direct conflicts of jurisdiction" that demand special attention from the government and its agencies.[55] Prohibitive-prohibitive conflicts can also give rise to conflicts in criminal law because there is a real danger an addressee of a norm will be prosecuted by two or more states for the same act.

C. PREVENTING AND MITIGATING JURISDICTIONAL CONFLICTS

I. The Rule of Law and the Prohibition of Double Jeopardy

Before serious conflicts arise, there are a number of unilateral measures states can take to prevent or mitigate conflicts of jurisdiction. In matters of criminal animal law, the rule of law and the rule of double jeopardy help states design and use extraterritorial norms with this goal in mind.

States that link criminal sanctions to their extraterritorial animal laws are called upon to pay attention to the principle of legality (also called the principle of the rule of law, *nulla poena nullum crimen sine lege*) and to the principle against the application of retroactive legislation (*nullum delictum, nulla poena sine praevia lege*). These are sometimes viewed as equivalent to or emanating from the principle of the rule of law, which mandates that criminal norms be formulated sufficiently clearly and precisely, that they be published, and that they not be retroactively applied.[56] The principle of the rule of law is recognized by the drafters of the UDHR,[57] the Geneva Conventions and Additional Protocols,[58] the International Covenant on Civil and Political Rights (ICCPR),[59] the African Charter on Human and Peoples' Rights,[60] the American Convention on Human Rights,[61] and the European Convention on Human Rights.[62]

If states did not abide by the rule of law, acts or omissions of persons could be criminalized *ex post facto*. Ensuring that addressees know the law before criminal behavior is manifested is not just a matter of fairness and justice. Lack of knowledge and foreseeability undermines the law's purpose and effectiveness. Knowledge about the law is a precondition for its observance,

---

[54] *E.g.*, Case T-210/01, General Electric Company v. Commission, 2005 E.C.R. II-5575. *See further* Eleanor M. Fox, GE/Honeywell: *The US Merger that Europe Stopped: A Story of Politics of Convergence*, *in* ANTI-TRUST STORIES 331 (Eleanor M. Fox & Daniel A. Crane eds., 2007).

[55] On direct conflict or foreign sovereign compulsion, *see* Chapter 11, §2 B.

[56] IBA REPORT EXTRATERRITORIAL JURISDICTION 194 (2009). *See also* CoE, *Extraterritorial Criminal Jurisdiction* 460 (1992).

[57] UDHR, art. 11 para. 2.

[58] Geneva Convention (III), art. 99; Protocol Additional to the Geneva Conventions (I), art. 2 lit. c.

[59] International Covenant on Civil and Political Rights, Dec. 16, 1966, 999 U.N.T.S. 171, art. 15 [ICCPR].

[60] African Charter on Human and Peoples' Rights, Oct. 21, 1986, 1520 U.N.T.S. 217, art. 7 para. 2 [Banjul Charter].

[61] Inter-American Convention on Human Rights, Nov. 22, 1969, 1144 U.N.T.S. 123, art. 9 [IACHR].

[62] Convention for the Protection of Human Rights and Fundamental Freedoms, Nov. 4, 1950, 213 U.N.T.S. 221, art. 7 [ECHR].

since, as Raz famously stated, "the law must be capable of being obeyed."[63] The same is true for extraterritorial laws, as underlined by the Council of Europe Report on Extraterritorial Criminal Law. The drafters of the report argue that, under the principle of the rule of law, the requirements of recognizability and predictability of law must apply to extraterritorial jurisdiction.[64] Once recognizable and predictable to its addressees, the law can legitimately be applied across borders (given the necessary jurisdictional basis). In this sense, the European Court of Human Rights determined in *Jorgic v. Germany* that Germany's crime of genocide extends to Jorgic's acts of ethnic cleansing in Bosnia and Herzegovina because the application of the law was foreseeable to the defendant at the time he committed the crime.[65]

It is fairly easy for a state to inform its citizens about the laws they must comply with, but how does it alert foreign addressees that its laws apply to them? As a first step, it is necessary for a state to publish the law, translate it into the most common languages (especially the languages of the countries where the law will apply), and make it freely and easily accessible. A state could notify its citizens residing abroad about changed regulations, it could warn people suspected of violating its law, it could announce its position in international fora, held by states or NGOs, or it could inform affected states. The duty to respect the rule of law applies preeminently to cases of direct extraterritorial jurisdiction (where there is an extraterritorial anchor point or extraterritorial content regulation). In contrast, indirect regulation (whose only extraterritorial facet is its ancillary repercussions) does not need to be foreseeable or known in order to be effective.[66]

States should also be mindful of the risks of double prosecution and punishment when they apply criminal animal law across the border. The rule of *ne bis in idem* (*nemo debet bis vexari pro una et eadam causa*), known as the prohibition of double jeopardy in common law, states that a person shall not be prosecuted more than once for the same conduct.[67] International treaties, like the ICCPR and the Rome Statute, establish protection against double jeopardy for a limited category of crimes, or they limit the rule of double conviction to a single state (so cross-border double jeopardy remains legal).[68] Because of its limited application, some scholars deny that *ne bis in idem* is a general principle or customary norm of international law.[69] However, numerous drafts

---

[63] Joseph Raz, *The Rule of Law and Its Virtue*, *in* THE AUTHORITY OF LAW 210, 213 (Joseph Raz ed., 2009). The rule of law is thus based on the logic that only if addressees of legal norms are aware of them, and only if the norms are sufficiently clear to them, can the law have a deterrent effect: Petrig 35 (2013). Seminal: WILFRIED KÜPER ED., PAUL JOHANN ANSELM FEUERBACH: REFLEXIONEN, MAXIMEN, ERFAHRUNGEN (1993).

[64] CoE, *Extraterritorial Criminal Jurisdiction* 460 ff. (1992).

[65] Jorgic v. Germany, 2007-IX Eur. Ct. H.R. 1 (2007), para. 113.

[66] UTA KOHL, JURISDICTION AND THE INTERNET: REGULATORY COMPETENCE OVER ONLINE ACTIVITY 153 (2007).

[67] *See* the Fifth Amendment to the U.S. Constitution: no person shall "be subject for the same offence to be twice put in jeopardy of life or limb."

[68] ICCPR, art. 14 para. 7; Rome Statute, art. 20 para. 3.

[69] Ireland-Piper 80 (2013). Conway explains this broad rejection: "Especially in the area of criminal liability, many states appear to have traditionally held to the view that they are best placed to protect their own interests through the application of the criminal law; in contrast, the effect of an international *ne bis in idem* principle would be to restrict the application of national criminal law." (Gerard Conway, Ne Bis in Idem *in International Law*, 3 INT'L CRIM. L. REV. 217, 218 (2003)).

and proposals for treaties suggest that the principle should be binding in international law.[70]

I propose a pragmatic solution to this problem. Even if the rule of law and the prohibition against double jeopardy might not be fully established in international law, states should observe them when they apply animal laws across the border to err on the safe side. Animal law has nothing to gain from punishing people twice for their behavior, but it has everything to lose if it becomes a tool used to undermine human rights guarantees. This being said, outside the criminal realm, addressees have no right to have their actions and omissions regulated by a single sovereign. Especially when people routinely act or do business on the territory of multiple states, they are seen as having waived such a claim. Multinational enterprises, for instance, are confronted on a daily basis by several states applying their norms to their actions. The real objection to concurring jurisdiction, Bowett argues, "lies in the quite different consideration that the jurisdiction assumed by State A may involve unwarranted interference in matters which have little or nothing to do with State A and are more properly the concern of State B and therefore more properly left to its jurisdiction."[71]

II. Principle of Reasonableness

Also under general international law, there are standards that help states prevent and mitigate conflicts of jurisdiction. These include the principle of reasonableness, the balance of interests test, and the principle of comity. There is little agreement on the application, scope, and content of these principles because they are uncodified, vary from state to state, and sometimes overlap. In the following, I will sketch them out and differentiate them as clearly as possible. I will argue that the principle of reasonableness is most helpful at a preconflict stage, and that the balance of interests test and the principle of comity should be applied after a jurisdictional dispute has emerged.

The purpose of the principle of reasonableness is to prevent conflicts of jurisdiction from arising. It refers to the process by which jurisdiction is unilaterally administered by states, by deciding whether, when, and how they ought to exercise jurisdiction. As codified in the US Restatement of Foreign Relations, the principle states that "[e]ven when one of the bases for jurisdiction [. . .] is present, a state may not exercise jurisdiction to prescribe law with respect to a person or activity having connections with another state when the exercise of such jurisdiction is unreasonable."[72] The principle mandates states employ a reasonableness test before they exercise jurisdiction, and that they refrain from exercising jurisdiction if extraterritorial jurisdiction is likely to produce unreasonable effects.[73]

---

[70] Harvard Research in International Law, *Jurisdiction with Respect to Crime* (1935), art. 13; *The Princeton Principles on Universal Jurisdiction* (2001), principle 9; IBA Report Extraterritorial Jurisdiction 192 (2009). Among the treaties in force, only the Schengen Convention endows the principle with *erga omnes* character, but limits it to instances of *res iudicata*: Convention Implementing the Schengen Agreement, June 14, 1985, 2000 O.J. (L 239) 13, art. 54 [CISA].

[71] Bowett 15 (1982).

[72] U.S. Restatement (Third) of the Foreign Relations Law, § 403 para. 1.

[73] CoE, *Extraterritorial Criminal Jurisdiction* 469 (1992); Zerk, Extraterritorial Jurisdiction 212 (2010). As the commentary to section 403 clarifies, the reasonableness test is not part of a reciprocal duty. It

The reasonableness test does not give guidance to states on when effects are unreasonable or which values must be prioritized. Most states have their own views and guidelines that specify the values that are most important to them, and determine how they should be weighted. In its Third Restatement, the United States took the view that the following factors must be considered:

(a) the link of the activity to the territory of the regulating state, i.e., the extent to which the activity takes place within the territory, or has substantial, direct, and foreseeable effect upon or in the territory;
(b) the connections, such as nationality, residence, or economic activity, between the regulating state and the person principally responsible for the activity to be regulated, or between that state and those whom the regulation is designed to protect;
(c) the character of the activity to be regulated, the importance of regulation to the regulating state, the extent to which other states regulate such activities, and the degree to which the desirability of such regulation is generally accepted;
(d) the existence of justified expectations that might be protected or hurt by the regulation;
(e) the importance of the regulation to the international political, legal, or economic system;
(f) the extent to which the regulation is consistent with the traditions of the international legal system;
(g) the extent to which another state may have an interest in regulating the activity; and
(h) the likelihood of conflict with regulation by another state.[74]

Factors (c) and (e) demand states take into account the importance of the matter, the desirability of its regulation, and universal values. The greater the need to protect animals abroad, the more justified the exercise of jurisdiction by a state. The more universally shared a certain treatment of animals is (consider the general principle of animal welfare), the more important it is to ensure its regulation. Overall, (c) and (e) allow considering the effects of jurisdiction on animals when making a decision about whether to exercise jurisdiction. But these considerations are only two of several factors that could be weighed differently.

Factors listed in (a) and (b) can be objectively determined; these links or connections are present, or they are not. But it seems harder to assess factors (c) to (h), the importance of regulation to the regulating state and the likelihood of conflict with regulation by another state. The more important a certain matter is to a state (for example, protecting animals), the easier it is for it to assume that another state's interests are negligible. To prevent subjective views from distorting their judgment, states would ideally use subfactors that consider the level of regulation and the issuer. For example, if Congress demands that an offense in animal law be

---

applies regardless of whether another state would exercise the same restraint or not: U.S. Restatement (Third) of the Foreign Relations Law, § 403, cmt. a.

[74] U.S. Restatement (Third) of the Foreign Relations Law, § 403 para. 2. This list is not exhaustive, *see id.* § 403, cmt. b. In the brand-new Fourth Restatement, these factors are not anymore listed: U.S. Restatement (Fourth) of the Foreign Relations Law, § 405.

investigated, this is more forceful than when a commission initiates an investigation.[75] States should further investigate the interests of other states by drawing on their public statements, legislation, case law, and participation in international fora on matters of animal law.

D. RESOLVING JURISDICTIONAL CONFLICTS

I. Unilateral Resolution

Once a state decides to exercise jurisdiction, as a consequence of which a jurisdictional conflict emerges, it can unilaterally resolve the conflict through the principle of reasonableness or the balance of interests test.[76] Both are designed to solve jurisdictional conflicts by examining and assessing the strength of a state's links to a state of facts and weighing them against those of other states.

The balance of interests test is a product of US-American jurisprudence and emerged from the *Timberlane* (1976) and *Mannington Mills* (1979) decisions.[77] Section 403 para. 3 of the Third US Restatement provides that if the laws of two (or more) states conflict, states should evaluate their own and the others' interest in regulation and defer to the state with the greatest interest. The balance of interests test *applies after a conflict has been ascertained*[78] but considers the same factors as the preconflict reasonableness test, including where an act was committed, where evidence is available, where the accused person has their domicile, the center of the wrong, the likelihood of adjudication, and interests of justice, among others. The stronger these factors are linked to a state, the more reasonable it is to let it have jurisdiction over the case. The balance of interests test is well-established in US jurisprudence and increasingly accepted by European courts.[79] Concern for animals are relevant for this test as

---

[75] U.S. Restatement (Third) of the Foreign Relations Law, § 403, cmts. b and c; U.S. Restatement (Fourth) of the Foreign Relations Law, § 405, reporters' note 4.

[76] Peters, for example, argues that the principles of reasonableness and comity allow finding a balance of interests: PETERS, VÖLKERRECHT 162 (2016). The IBA treats the principles as exchangeable: IBA REPORT EXTRATERRITORIAL JURISDICTION 168 (2009).

[77] Timberlane Lumber Co. v. Bank of America, N.T. & SA, 549 F.2d 597 (9th Cir. 1976) (U.S.) (application of the Sherman Act [15 U.S.C. § 1 (U.S.)] to foreign antitrust proceedings, including foreign government officials); Mannington Mills Inc. v. Congoleum Corporation, 595 F.2d 1287 (3d Cir. 1979) (U.S.) (violation of the Sherman Act by licensing practices).

[78] The development of reasonableness in this two-tiered fashion is not necessarily an international phenomenon. Though it may make sense for the United States to employ the test in this manner, other states may decline to do so. Applying a set of factors to determine if one will exercise jurisdiction and then applying the same set of factors in case of conflict to determine how to solve the conflict will probably have the same outcome, unless one shifts its priorities. Many states thus use one procedure to determine whether or not to exercise jurisdiction. But because the tests are so diffuse, it might well be that some legislators do an internal "exercise-jurisdiction-or-not" test and a "whose-jurisdiction-prevails" test.

[79] The principle of reasonableness is a general principle of EU law: Adelina Adinolfi, *The Principle of Reasonableness in European Union Law*, *in* REASONABLENESS AND LAW 383, 394 (Giorgio Bongiovanni et al. eds., 2009). An alternative argument is that the principle of reasonableness derives from the principle of proportionality. Ryngaert explains: "Proportionality may require that one State's jurisdictional assertion not encroach upon the interests of another State to an extent that is disproportionate to the object or aim of that assertion." (RYNGAERT, JURISDICTION 158 (2015)).

it is for the preconflict reasonableness test—based on the importance of regulation and the presence of shared values (section 403 para. 2(c) and (e) of the Restatement).

In the criminal domain, a similar balance of interests test was devised to deal with conflicts of jurisdiction. Principle 8 of the Princeton Principles, developed by the Princeton University Program in Law and Public Affairs, asks states to base their decision on an aggregate balance of the following criteria:

(a) multilateral or bilateral treaty obligations;
(b) the place of commission of the crime;
(c) the nationality connection of the alleged perpetrator to the requesting state;
(d) the nationality connection of the victim to the requesting state;
(e) any other connection between the requesting state and the alleged perpetrator, the crime, or the victim;
(f) the likelihood, good faith, and effectiveness of the prosecution in the requesting state;
(g) the fairness and impartiality of the proceedings in the requesting state;
(h) the convenience to the parties and witnesses, as well as the availability of evidence in the requesting state; and
(i) the interests of justice.[80]

These principles suggest that states with connections of territoriality and nationality are more likely to have stronger claims to jurisdiction. States with territorial jurisdiction often also satisfy other criteria, such as the likelihood of prosecution (f), conveniences to parties and witnesses, and availability of evidence (b). Indirect regulation via owners' nationality (c) and functional animal nationality (d) represent useful alternatives because they have a strong territorial connection but regulate content abroad. Resorting to interests of justice (h) may demand that we consider the interests of animals, since animals are sentient, conscious beings to whom the outcome of these legal disputes is of great importance.[81]

As previously mentioned, states each have established their own reasonableness and balance interests tests, which are unilaterally applied. The balance of interests test of section 403 para. 3 of the Third Restatement of the United States, for example, is performed by US authorities. The Canadian Supreme Court uses a "real and substantial connection test" in criminal matters that allows it to determine unilaterally whether and when to exercise jurisdiction.[82] And the European Union adopted a similar test as part of the European Arrest Warrant System.[83] Even if these tests consider foreign interests, they were unilaterally designed

---

[80] *The Princeton Principles on Universal Jurisdiction* (2001), principle 8. This list is not exhaustive: *id.* at 53.

[81] *See* Chapter 8, §1 on the role of animals in global justice.

[82] R v. Hape, [2007] 2 SCR 292, para. 62 (Can.): "Where two or more states have a legal claim to jurisdiction, comity dictates that a state ought to assume jurisdiction only if it has a real and substantial link to the event."

[83] Council Framework Decision on the European Arrest Warrant and the Surrender Procedures between Member States (2002/584/JHA), 2002 O.J. (L 190) 1. Art. 16 para. 1 demands that decisions on multiple requests must be taken "by the executing judicial authority," taking into account all circumstances, the place of the offenses, the dates of the European arrest warrants, and whether the warrant was issued for the purposes of prosecution or execution.

and are unilaterally applied without involving or consulting affected states. Consequently, these tests risk being used in an overly subjective manner and giving perfunctory consideration to other states, which may return inconsistent, unpredictable, and unjust results.[84] A better approach would be to determine, on a multilateral basis, the factors that bear on the test and their relative weight.[85] Under general international law, however, no treaty has yet been concluded that meets these goals.

Instead of claiming that the principle of reasonableness (in its preconflict "exercise-jurisdiction-or-not" application) or the combined balance of interests test and principle of reasonableness (in their acute conflict "whose-jurisdiction-prevails" application) objectively assess the interests of all involved parties, they should best be regarded as applications of the principle of comity.[86] Comity, whose acceptance and nature is disputed,[87] is based on the "reciprocal recognition of equality by the participants in international intercourse" and "a mutual respect for the integrity of each of the participants in international intercourse."[88] These mandate that states adopt an attitude of moderation and restraint in jurisdictional matters that affect other states. Based on comity, states interested in extending their laws to a state of facts abroad may decline to claim jurisdiction if another state has a greater interest (referred to as *negative comity*).[89] Under the principle of comity, states sometimes also incur soft duties to exchange information, mutually consult on a matter, or request adjudication (referred to as *positive comity*). Together, negative and positive comity form the heart of the principle of comity, which applies to all cases where states' laws conflict, in particular, but not only, to prohibitive-requisite conflicts.[90]

---

[84] Deborah Senz & Hilary Charlesworth, *Building Blocks: Australia's Response to Foreign Extraterritorial Litigation*, 2 MELB. J. INT'L L. 69 (2001). *See also* for a critique of the test: IBA REPORT EXTRATERRITORIAL JURISDICTION 24, 170 (2009); Note, *Predictability and Comity* 1322–3 (1985); RYNGAERT, UNILATERAL JURISDICTION AND GLOBAL VALUES 117 (2015); Laker v. Sabena, Belgian World Airlines, 731 F.2d 909 (D.C. Cir. 1984) (U.S.).

[85] Treaties on double taxation commonly include such factors: Mann 10 (1964); Oxman, *Jurisdiction of States, in* MPEPIL 54 (2007).

[86] This is also acknowledged in the Fourth Restatement, in which the balance of interests was dropped in favor of prescriptive comity and foreign state compulsion: U.S. Restatement (Fourth) of the Foreign Relations Law, § 405.

[87] There is little agreement on how widely the principle of comity is accepted. According to the Criminal Committee to the IBA Report, the scope of the principle in criminal law is unclear: IBA REPORT EXTRATERRITORIAL JURISDICTION 25 (2009). The US Supreme Court has used comity in deciding if there is a presumption against extraterritoriality in the FTAIA in F. Hoffmann-La Roche v. Empagran, 542 U.S. 155 (2004) (U.S.). In Europe, the comity principle is treated as discretionary: RYNGAERT, JURISDICTION 179 (2015).

[88] CoE, *Extraterritorial Criminal Jurisdiction* 459 (1992).

[89] Negative comity was used in *Empagran, see* F. Hoffmann-La Roche v. Empagran, 542 U.S. 155, 164–5 (2004) (U.S.): "This rule of statutory construction cautions courts to assume that legislators take account of the legitimate sovereign interests of other nations when they write American laws. It thereby helps the potentially conflicting laws of different nations work together in harmony—a harmony particularly needed in today's highly interdependent commercial world."

[90] The United States, in contrast, has limited the test of weighing state interests to prohibitive-requisite conflicts or what it terms "direct conflicts" or "foreign sovereign compulsion." These are conflicts in which a person is

II. Bilateral and Multilateral Resolution

The best option for states to resolve jurisdictional conflicts is to conclude bilateral or multilateral agreements that define conflicts of jurisdiction, describe how states can manage these conflicts unilaterally and independently on a daily basis, and determine how they should proceed if unilateral deference does not prevent conflict. Agreements that lay down rules on consultation and cooperation are among the most common treaties on jurisdiction in international law. In criminal law, cooperative agreements include mutual legal assistance treaties (MLATs),[91] the European Convention on Laundering of Search, Seizure and Confiscation of the Proceeds from Crime,[92] and the European Convention on Mutual Assistance in Criminal Matters.[93] In animal law, there is no agreement that obliges states to consult or cooperate on jurisdictional matters, but most of the 433 MLATs currently in force apply to criminal law in a generic manner and hence cover criminal animal law.[94]

Another area in which states have readily concluded agreements to consult and cooperate on jurisdictional matters is antitrust law. In 1991, after decades-long disputes about the reach of domestic antitrust policies, the United States and the European Union concluded an agreement that placed each country's competition authorities under a duty to cooperate and coordinate (*positive comity*, laid down in articles IV and V). Each state agreed to take into account important interests of the other when deciding "whether or not to initiate an investigation or proceeding, the scope of an investigation or proceeding, the nature of the remedies or penalties sought, and in other ways" (*negative comity*, laid down in article VI).[95] In 1998, the European Union and the United States concluded another agreement, as a partial revision of the initial agreement.[96] According to the new treaty, one party may request the other to investigate and remedy anticompetitive activities, "regardless of whether the

---

required (not only permitted) to commit or to refrain from committing an act by the laws of one state, which is at the same time prohibited by the laws of another state (U.S. Restatement (Third) of the Foreign Relations Law, § 403, cmt. e). In these cases, foreign sovereign compulsion operates as a defense, which is permissible under certain circumstances: DOJ, ANTITRUST ENFORCEMENT GUIDELINES, para. 3.32. The shortcomings of this approach are discussed by RYNGAERT, JURISDICTION 166 (2015).

[91] MLATs are agreements between governments that facilitate the exchange of information relevant to an investigation, hence, they are primarily criminal in nature. MLATs may be bilateral, multilateral, or regional. *See* Mutual Legal Assistance Treaties, MLAT Index, *available at* https://mlat.info/mlat-index (last visited Jan. 10, 2019).

[92] CoE, Convention on Laundering of Search Seizure and Confiscation of the Proceeds from Crime, Nov. 8, 1990, C.E.T.S. No. 141.

[93] CoE, European Convention on Mutual Assistance in Criminal Matters, Apr. 20, 1959 C.E.T.S. No. 30.

[94] Deciding whether administrative laws are covered by criminal assistance treaties will depend on the system of law, the characterization of administrative measures (e.g., seizure as a part of criminal or administrative law), and the specific scope of the assistance treaties.

[95] Agreement between the Government of the United States of America and the Commission of the European Communities Regarding the Application of their Competition Laws, Exchange of Interpretative Letters with the Government of the United States of America, Sept. 23, 1991, 1995 O.J. (L 95) 47.

[96] Agreement between the European Communities and the Government of the United States of America on the Application of Positive Comity Principles in the Enforcement of their Competition Laws, June 4, 1998 O.J. (L 173) 28.

activities also violate the Requesting Party's antitrust laws, and regardless of whether the competition authorities of the Requesting Party have commenced or contemplate taking enforcement activities under their own competition laws" (article III). Although requests to investigate do not lead to the extraterritorial application of a state's law, they help close legal loopholes abroad that would otherwise have reverse repercussions on domestic territory. But because states can, at their own discretion, decide whether to follow such a request, this rule is only a marginally useful alternative to extraterritorial jurisdiction.

The OECD also created guidelines for state cooperation in its 1995 Recommendation Concerning Cooperation Between Member Countries on Anticompetitive Practices Affecting International Trade.[97] And in 2007, with a view toward mitigating jurisdictional conflicts, the attorney-generals of the United Kingdom and the United States issued a joint paper titled "Domestic Guidance for Handling Criminal Cases with Concurrent Jurisdiction."[98] Both papers provide for early notification, coordination of proceedings, exchange of information, proper consultation, and requests for remedial action.

States may also conclude agreements aimed at mitigating and preventing conflicts of jurisdiction in a substantive sense, by specifying which state has jurisdiction in particular a case. Examples include the Hague conventions,[99] the Brussels Regulation,[100] and the Rome Regulations.[101] These treaties are considerably less common than treaties that focus on procedural aspects of jurisdiction, for several reasons. First, the likelihood of setting up a treaty that covers the entire field of extraterritorial jurisdiction is very low, because it is improbable that meaningful rules can be established where there are so many conflicting and differently aligned policy interests. Second, even if drafted only for a specific field (e.g., animal law), states can profoundly disagree on the optimal regulatory measures needed to address or resolve a specific problem. The difficulty of reaching a broad agreement is easily underestimated, and failure to reach an agreement is the rule, rather than the exception.[102]

---

[97] OECD, Revised Recommendation of the Council Concerning Cooperation between Member Countries on Anticompetitive Practices Affecting International Trade (OECD Publishing, Paris 1995).

[98] U.S.-U.K. Attorney General's Domestic Guidance for Handling Criminal Cases (2007). The Guidance is criticized for excluding third parties: IBA Report Extraterritorial Jurisdiction 56 (2009).

[99] *See, e.g.*, Convention of 19 October 1996 on Jurisdiction, Applicable Law, Recognition, Enforcement and Co-operation in Respect of Parental Responsibility and Measures for the Protection of Children, Jan. 1, 2002, 35 I.L.M. 1391.

[100] Council Regulation 1215/2012 on Jurisdiction and the Recognition and Enforcement of Judgments in Civil and Commercial Matters (Recast), 2012 O.J. (L 351) 1.

[101] Regulation 593/2008 of the European Parliament and of the Council on the Law Applicable to Contractual Obligations (Rome I), 2008 O.J. (L 177) 6; Regulation 864/2007 of the European Parliament and of the Council on the Law Applicable to Non-Contractual Obligations (Rome II), 2007 O.J. (L 199) 40.

[102] *See* the analysis in Chapter 2, §2. Attempts have even been made to codify general rules on extraterritorial jurisdiction. In 1992, The Hague Conference on Private International Law launched an international convention on jurisdiction and enforcement of judgments of municipal courts in civil and commercial matters, modeled after the Council Regulation 44/2001 on Jurisdiction and the Recognition and Enforcement of Judgments in Civil and Commercial Matters, 2000 O.J. (L 12) 1. The convention was never concluded due to "irreconcilable conflicts." The fact that treaties exist in matters of adjudicative and enforcement jurisdiction in civil and commercial matters, but not in matters of prescriptive jurisdiction and not in the fields of antitrust

But this is not necessarily bad, as Guzman claims. He points to what should be the core motivation of states to enter into agreements. Treaties, he argues, should be benchmarked at an optimal level of welfare that is determined from the perspective of the "global planner," whose goal it is to maximize the overall well-being of all global players.[103] *Mutatis mutandis*, we should use the metric of "maximum level of global animal welfare" to assess the benefits of an international agreement on jurisdiction in animal law.[104] If the agreement only benefits a few but does not address or even legitimates oppressing other humans and animals, finding agreement is not advisable. Conversely, if treaties on jurisdictional authority are diligently drafted and have a reasonable chance of creating net positive effects for a majority of animals and people, they are a useful complement to extraterritorial jurisdiction.

Economists have long recognized the benefits of cooperation in economic game theory. The prisoner's dilemma uses game-theoretic strategies to illustrate the advantages cooperation offers over aggregate but self-interested individual choices.[105] If a state pursues extraterritorial jurisdiction in its own interest and fails to coordinate with other governments, the result is likely damaging to all parties. But if governments cooperate over extraterritorial jurisdiction, jurisdictional gaps can be adequately filled, overlaps and international disputes prevented, and administrative costs reduced.

§3 International Legal Limits

Whether or not an attempt to protect animals abroad conflicts with the jurisdiction of another state, this may per se violate international law. Because state practice on extraterritorial animal law is not yet established and cases decided by international adjudicatory bodies on this matter are scarce,[106] determining when and how states overstep the limits of international law when they adopt extraterritorial animal law must be done on the basis of the law of jurisdiction in general.[107]

States that called an international court or tribunal to declare another state's extraterritorial laws void have typically argued that these laws violate the principle of sovereign equality, their right to territorial integrity, and the duty of noninterference. I next ask if and to what extent

law, securities law, export controls, and many others, shows that it is extremely hard to reach agreement on matters of extraterritorial jurisdiction. *See also* Oxman, *Jurisdiction of States, in* MPEPIL 55 (2007).

[103] Guzman defines the global welfare-maximizing policy as one that maximizes the sum of the consumer and producer surplus (Guzman 1510–1 (1998)), but his is not the only model.

[104] *See further* on this topic Chapter 2, and Guzman 1548 (1998).

[105] The prisoner's dilemma is often used to illustrate the race to the bottom and operates as its main rationale: Koenig-Archibugi, *Global Regulation, in* THE OXFORD HANDBOOK OF REGULATION 414 (2010). *See* for a philosophical inquiry: MARTIN PETERSON ED., THE PRISONER'S DILEMMA (2015).

[106] The situation is different for international bodies that have dealt with the matter in trade law. *See* Chapters 3 and 4.

[107] Because these cases are rare and because extraterritoriality plays a role in many fields of law, it is difficult to be certain about the legality of extraterritorial jurisdiction under general international law. As Zerk argues, media usually only pick up overt and offensive assertions of extraterritorial jurisdiction, so diversity in state practice has been obscured and academic debate has been oversimplified: ZERK, EXTRATERRITORIAL JURISDICTION 12 (2010).

extraterritorial jurisdiction in animal law threatens these principles. I begin with the principle of sovereign equality and then examine the right to territorial integrity, the principle of nonintervention, and the principle of self-determination of peoples.

A. PRINCIPLE OF SOVEREIGN EQUALITY

The principle of sovereign equality belongs to the fundamental rights of states and is a *Grundnorm* of the international legal order.[108] The ordering concept of international law as basically egalitarian and anti-hegemonial is central to an understanding of states' coexistence. As subjects of the international community, states are equal in the enjoyment of all rights and duties. As such, sovereign equality precludes a state from ascertaining its authority over another. States are subordinated to international law only; vis-à-vis one another, they are limited by the sovereignty of other states that are on an equal footing.[109] An integral part of the commitment to sovereign equality forms the recognition of states' juridical equality. Being recognized as equal before the law means that states hold the same position in the international legal order and have identical rights and duties.[110] This is not to say that international law ensures states are equal in power, wealth, territory, or the like. Instead, juridical equality recognizes and ensures states have equal rights and bear equal duties.[111]

If the principle of sovereign equality demands states be treated as equal bearers of jurisdictional authority, then it seems that extraterritorial jurisdiction, where one state purports to have a stronger interest in regulating a state of facts that properly seem to belong to another, violates or at least threatens this principle. These and similar arguments were advanced, for example, by the Congo in *Arrest Warrant*[112] and in *Certain Criminal Proceedings in France*.[113]

---

[108] The UN, since its establishment in 1945, was and continues to be based on the principle of sovereign equality (UN Charter, art. 2 para. 1). The principle is also laid down in the Charter of the Organization of American States (Apr. 30, 1948, 119 U.N.T.S. 3, art. 6), the Charter to the Organization of the African Unity (May 25, 1963, 479 U.N.T.S. 39, art. III.1), and the Charter of Economic Rights and Duties of States (G.A. Res. 3281 (XXIX), U.N. GAOR 29th Sess., U.N. Doc. A/RES/29/3281 (Dec. 12, 1974), art. 10). In light of its widespread codification, the principle of sovereign equality is recognized as fundamental and indispensable to the development of friendly relations among all nations: Nadine Susani, *Purposes and Principles of the United Nations*, *in* MPEPIL 11 (Rüdiger Wolfrum ed., online ed. 2009); Christian Tomuschat, *International Law: Ensuring the Survival of Mankind on the Eve of a New Century*, 281 RCADI 9, 171 (1999).

[109] Peters, *Humanity as the A and Ω of Sovereignty* 528 (2009); SCHWARZE 13 (1994).

[110] Sergio M. Carbone & Lorenzo Schiano di Pepe, *Fundamental Rights and Duties of States*, *in* MPEPIL 25 (Rüdiger Wolfrum ed., online ed. 2009).

[111] As famously stated by Vattel: "A dwarf is as much a man as a giant; a small republic is no less a sovereign state than the most powerful kingdom." (EMEL DE VATTEL, LE DROITS DES GENS, OU PRINCIPES DE LA LOI NATURELLE, vol. I, 47, préliminaires § 18 (1830)). Or, as Crawford puts it: "Obviously, the allocation of power and the capacity to project it in reality are different things, which suggests that while all states are equal, some are more equal than others." (CRAWFORD 449 (2012)). *See also* James Crawford, *Sovereignty as a Legal Value*, *in* THE CAMBRIDGE COMPANION TO INTERNATIONAL LAW 117, 119 (James Crawford & Martti Koskenniemi eds., 2012); Kokott, *Sovereign Equality of States*, *in* MPEPIL 2, 23 (2011).

[112] Arrest Warrant, 2002 I.C.J. 26 ¶ 62.

[113] Certain Criminal Proceedings in France (DRC v. France), Order, 2003 I.C.J. Rep. 102, 103 ¶ 1 (June 17) [Certain Criminal Proceedings in France, 2003 I.C.J.].

The guarantee of juridical equality demands, in essence, a condition of reciprocity among states under international law.[114] Reciprocity means that, in principle, one state cannot have rights another is denied, and one state cannot be exempted from duties another must incur. But extraterritorial jurisdiction is not a right or privilege given to one state and denied to another. Each state is equally entitled to use any principle of jurisdiction at any point in time. As long as this rule of reciprocity is guaranteed, we have no reason to believe the principle of sovereign equality has been violated.

Assume New Zealand uses functional animal nationality as a basis for protecting national animals from severe bodily and mental impairments on foreign territory. Some keas (the only alpine parrot in the world) born on New Zealand soil (which were declared nationals of New Zealand based on the *jus soli* rule) are shipped to Australia, where they will be used in invasive research. New Zealand asks the Australian research institutions to inform it about what they do to the animals. The information New Zealand receives is alarming, and it has reason to believe that the researchers are not meeting basic standards, so it orders the researchers to immediately cease experimentation. The Australian government quickly gets involved, raises objections, and files a complaint at the ICJ, arguing that New Zealand violated the principle of sovereign equality by attempting to regulate events on its soil. But sovereign equality, which includes the right to juridical equality, would only be violated if international law, while granting New Zealand extraterritorial jurisdiction, denied Australia the same right, namely, the right to extend its laws to New Zealand soil over national animals shipped to New Zealand. If international law treats all states equally, giving each the right to invoke the jurisdictional principles under the same conditions, then Australia's right to juridical equality is not violated. When the jurisdictional principles apply to all states equally, states do not, in principle, violate other states' juridical or sovereign equality by protecting animals across the border.

B. RIGHT TO TERRITORIAL INTEGRITY

That states have a right to territorial integrity is an established principle of international law.[115] Historically, territorial integrity served to protect state territory from military aggression and threat. Today, the principle more broadly protects a state's exclusive dominion within its territory and precludes other states from exercising authority on or over it.[116] Extraterritorial animal law could violate the principle of territorial integrity by challenging a state's exclusive dominion over its territory. For this to happen, jurisdiction must qualify as an authoritative state act capable of compromising dominion. Few scholars believe that territorial integrity can be threatened by all acts of another state, including extraterritorial prescriptive

---

[114] Bowett 16 (1982). The guarantee of juridical equality is therefore only violated if states are no longer regarded as equal before the law. *See* Reparations for Injuries Suffered in the Service of the United Nations, Advisory Opinion, 1949 I.C.J. Rep. 174, 177–8 (Apr. 11).

[115] Art. 2 para. 4 UN Charter prohibits the use of force against the territorial integrity and political independence of any state and art. 2 para. 7 UN Charter protects domestic jurisdiction by the prohibition of intervention. Together, they accord states a right to territorial integrity.

[116] Oliver Dörr, *Prohibition of Use of Force*, *in* MPEPIL 11 (Rüdiger Wolfrum ed., online ed. 2015); MENG 59 (1994); OPPENHEIM'S INTERNATIONAL LAW 563 (1992).

jurisdiction.[117] Most argue that the protection of states' territorial integrity from authoritative acts of foreign states primarily relates to a physical dimension.[118] Though the principle of territorial integrity has expanded from the use of force at war to other governmental actions, these must have a distinctly physical dimension. In their view, the essence of the right to territorial integrity is the right not to be subjected to force by other states.[119] The exercise of enforcement jurisdiction, which includes issuance of writs, service of documents, approaching or hearing witnesses, arrests of suspects, seizure of animals, entry into buildings, etc., has such a physical component and, as such, may endanger territorial integrity. But since prescriptive jurisdiction lacks this physical dimension, it cannot violate another state's territorial integrity.

This narrower interpretation was confirmed by the ICJ in *Certain Criminal Proceedings in France*, where the Court rejected the Congo's request to suspend French proceedings against several Congolese officials for grave human rights violations, holding that the Congo's territorial integrity had not been violated.[120] It is also supported by the ICJ ruling in *Corfu Channel*, where the Court declared that the United Kingdom's acts of minesweeping Albanian waters violated Albania's territorial sovereignty.[121] The ICJ thus considers it conceivable for territorial integrity to be violated if physical state acts are carried out on foreign territory, but not if states initiate proceedings without using physical force. In jurisdictional disputes involving acts of prescriptive jurisdiction, as in the case of extraterritorial animal law discussed herein, the principle of territorial integrity is of limited relevance because there is no use or threat of physical force.

C. *DOMAINE RÉSERVÉ* AND THE PRINCIPLE OF NONINTERVENTION

Another principle of international law that may be violated by extraterritorial animal law is that of nonintervention, the "core legal incident of external state sovereignty."[122] The 1970 Friendly Relations Declaration puts the principle in a nutshell:

> No State or group of States has the right to intervene, directly or indirectly, for any reason whatever, in the internal or external affairs of any other State. [. . .] No State may use or encourage the use of economic political or any other type of measures to

---

[117] Mann 129 ff. (1964); Albrecht Randelzhofer & Oliver Dörr, *Article 2 (4)*, *in* THE CHARTER OF THE UNITED NATIONS: A COMMENTARY, vol. I, 200, 208 (Bruno Simma et al. eds., 3d ed. 2012).

[118] Bowett 16 (1982); HENKIN 231 (1995); Andreas F. Lowenfeld, *U.S. Law Enforcement Abroad: The Constitution and International Law*, 83 AJIL 880 (1980), Continued, 84 AJIL 444 (1990); MENG 59–60 (1994); ORAKHELASHVILI 213–6 (2019); RATNER 105 (2015); Weil, *International Limitations on State Jurisdiction*, *in* EXTRA-TERRITORIAL APPLICATION OF LAWS AND RESPONSES THERETO 33 (1984).

[119] RATNER 105 (2015).

[120] This was decided because there was "no irreparable prejudice to the rights" of the accused persons: Certain Criminal Proceedings in France, 2003 I.C.J. 102, 110–1.

[121] Corfu Channel, 1949 I.C.J. 4.

[122] Peters, *Humanity as the A and Ω of Sovereignty* 528 (2009). The principle of nonintervention is based on art. 2 paras. 4 and 7 UN Charter, G.A. Res. 2625, U.N. GAOR 25th Sess., Declaration on Principles of International Law Concerning Friendly Relations and Cooperation among States in Accordance with the Charter of the United Nations, U.N. Doc. A/RES/25/2625 (Oct. 24, 1970) [Friendly Relations Declaration], the Declaration on the Inadmissibility of Intervention in the Domestic Affairs of States and the Protection of

> coerce another State in order to obtain from it the subordination of the exercise of its sovereign rights and to secure from it advantages of any kind. [. . .] Every State has an inalienable right to choose its political, economic, social and cultural systems, without interference in any form by another State.[123]

The core idea of the principle of nonintervention is that every state should be able to regulate its own affairs without outside interference by another state. Interference is not always impermissible, but it is illegal when it affects a state's *domaine réservé*. The reserved domain covers a state's jurisdiction over sovereign territory and the people, properties, and events on it, its choice of a political, economic, social, and cultural system, and the formulation of foreign policy.[124]

In relation to international law, strictly seen, this principle seems to create some obvious problems by declaring impermissible virtually every rule of international law. However, in its Advisory Opinion in *Nationality Decrees*, the PCIJ clarified that the reserved domain denotes matters where states remain the sole judges *and* which are not, in principle, governed by international law. Given the fast pace at which international norms emerge and evolve in response to global challenges, it might not always be easy to determine which matters are part of the *domaine réservé* of states. After all, "[t]he question whether a certain matter is or is not solely within the jurisdiction of a State is an essentially relative question; it depends upon the development of international relations."[125] The *domaine réservé* is a dynamic concept that develops relative to the state of international law, determined both by treaty obligations and customary international law.[126] In order to *remove* matters from the *domaine réservé*, international law does not have to be fully established in a certain matter.[127] And because international law has evolved from creating and preserving peace among nations to a highly developed legal system that today regulates a substantial portion of the domain previously reserved to states—including space exploration and use, the maritime sea and the continental sea shelf, the international monetary system, international environmental protection, rules on corruption and anti-bribery, the entire trade law system, international criminal responsibility, aspects of immigration, citizenship, and nationality, the guarantees of human rights, the conservation and preservation of natural resources (including animals), and much more—it leaves little room for issues that belong exclusively to the domestic affairs of states.[128]

Their Independence and Sovereignty (G.A. Res. 20/2131, U.N. GAOR 20th Sess., U.N. Doc. A/RES/20/2131 (Dec. 21, 1965)), and art. 3 ARSIWA.

[123] Friendly Relations Declaration.

[124] Corfu Channel, 1949 I.C.J. 35; Military and Paramilitary Activities in and Against Nicaragua, 1986 I.C.J. 108.

[125] Nationality Decrees, 1923 P.C.I.J. 24.

[126] Katja S. Ziegler, *Domaine Réservé*, *in* MPEPIL 2 (Rüdiger Wolfrum ed., online ed. 2013).

[127] Verzijl argues there are three ways to define the reserved domain. First, it may refer to the entire domain of matters not (yet) regulated by international law (negative definition). Second, it may denote matters a state does not yet want to regulate (positive definition). Third, it may denote matters that international law has not yet succeeded in regulating, but that require international regulation: VERZIJL, vol. I, 274–5 (1972).

[128] Nolte underlines that the domain reserved for states "has been increasingly eroded and emptied of substance." (Georg Nolte, *Article 2 (7)*, *in* THE CHARTER OF THE UNITED NATIONS: A COMMENTARY, vol. I, 280, 310 (2012)). *See also* Besson, *Sovereignty*, *in* MPEPIL 122 (2011); CRAWFORD 454 (2012); Ulrich K. Preuss, *Equality of States: Its Meaning in a Constitutionalized Global Order*, 8 CHI. J. INT'L L. 17 (2008).

If protecting animals is part of the exclusive competence of a state, the principle of non-intervention can be used as a means to block foreign extraterritorial jurisdiction. But if jurisdictional authority over animal welfare matters is not of exclusive concern to a state, the principle cannot be invoked. *Prima facie*, it is an important concern of legislators to determine the circumstances in which animals must be protected. These laws respond to societal demands and signal the public's opposition to violent, oppressive, and unethical behavior. Animal laws are conducive to the orderly structure of a state and are a manifestation of its organizational sovereignty. At the international level, no treaty or declaration yet safeguards states' interests in protecting animals. And the small body of customary international law that regulates human-animal relationship seems too weak to remove it from the exclusive jurisdiction of states.[129] Accordingly, animal protection matters seem to be, in principle, a matter of the reserved domain of states.

But the increasing entanglement and interdependence of states might weigh heavily against assuming the reserved domain has a large scope since "indisputable sovereign prerogatives of the territorial state have been subjected to a steady process of erosion."[130] Norms that protect animals across the border aim to establish obligations (e.g., duties to refrain from cruelty or duties to provide for care), or give rise to legal relations (e.g., functional animal nationality), but generally do not regulate the organization of foreign state institutions or policies. As such, the laws do not supplant domestic animal law and, therefore, they do not go to the core of jurisdictional authority.[131] In cases where legal relations and obligations are established across the border, jurisdiction must be exercised on the basis of a *valid and objectively demonstrable anchor to the prescribing state* (e.g., nationality, domicile, effects, constituent elements, special affectedness, or the issuance of funds). Because extraterritorial animal law neither threatens a state's organizational sovereignty nor assumes a state's animal laws apply to a state of facts unrelated to it, it is difficult to argue that these matters fall into another state's reserved domain. For example, if New Zealand demands its corporations that operate abroad adhere to the 3Rs in research, then it has a clear anchor to the subject matter, namely nationality jurisdiction. Australia, in whose territory New Zealand's 3Rs are applied, may claim to be threatened in its reserved domain because the way it regulates the use of animals in research on its territory is part of its organizational sovereignty. But since the 3Rs have limited application to New Zealand corporations, Australia's claim that its *domaine réservé* was violated is unjustified. Australia, in other words, does not have exclusive jurisdiction over foreign corporations operating on its territory.

Most cases in which extraterritorial law is prescribed are in fact about more than purely intraterritorial facts. Consider Norway's attitude toward whale and seal hunting. Its practice may

---

[129] *See* for an overview of international treaty and customary international norms in animal law, Charlotte E. Blattner, *The Potential and Potential Limits of International Law in Regulating Animal Matters*, 3 MID-ATLANTIC J.L. & POL. 10 (2015).

[130] Maier, *Jurisdictional Rules in Customary International Law, in* EXTRATERRITORIAL JURISDICTION IN THEORY AND PRACTICE, Comment by Andrea Bianchi 100 (1996).

[131] Jennings argues that the point at which a state interferes in another's foreign affairs is reached when extraterritorial laws supplant local laws: Jennings, *Extraterritorial Jurisdiction and the United States Antitrust Laws* 152–3 (1957).

be disparaged internationally,[132] but the question of whether this is legal and legitimate seems to be left to its discretion. In scenario A, where Norwegians hunt whales and seals and consume their kill, it is difficult to justify the claim that the international community or another state has a legitimate interest in the matter (unless they concluded a treaty on the matter). In scenario B, where Norway exports dead or live seal and whale bodies, the international community has more valid reasons to be concerned about this practice, since it has established anchors to the subject matter. This logic can be extended to other cases. Hunting becomes a concern of another state when animals cross state borders. Animal research is of interest to another state if research is outsourced to it. Animal slaughter is a concern of another state when animals are exported alive to that state. Farming becomes a cross-border issue where there is foreign investment, and so on. Only if there is no identifiable anchor to another state, the situation is different. In essence, the stronger the jurisdictional anchor to the prescribing state, the weaker the affected state's claim to exclusive jurisdiction over animal matters.

Even in the unlikely case that extraterritorial animal laws are regarded as interfering in another state's reserved domain, they are not necessarily illegal because not every form of interference constitutes an intervention. Only coercion renders an act of interference a prohibited intervention. Coercion, as the ICJ held, is "the very essence of the prohibition of intervention."[133] Historically, coercion was understood as military coercion but the contemporary understanding is that it encompasses all forms of political, economic, and other pressure.[134] The principle of nonintervention thus applies to a range of cases that exceed pure forms of military force, yet, intervention must still be forcible, dictatorial, or otherwise coercive for it to constitute an intervention.[135] The ICJ held that forced intervention took place where states indirectly supported subversive or terrorist activities in another state[136] and where they secured evidence in another state's territory.[137] Such coercive elements are also often found in cases of extraterritorial enforcement, where witnesses are approached, evidence is secured, people are tried, arrested, etc. But, as President Guillaume emphasized in his Separate Opinion in the *Arrest Warrant*, the claim that territorial integrity prohibits coercive action in principle leaves prescriptive jurisdiction unaffected.[138] Prescriptive extraterritorial jurisdiction that is not enforced in another state is not coercive and does therefore

[132] Anton Krag & Live Kleveland, *Challenges to Animal Protection in Scandinavia*, *in* The Global Guide to Animal Protection 28 (2013).

[133] Military and Paramilitary Activities in and Against Nicaragua, 1986 I.C.J. 108, ¶ 205.

[134] Peters, Völkerrecht 318 (2016).

[135] Kokott, *Sovereign Equality of States*, *in* MPEPIL 50 (2011); Lowe, International Law 109 (2007); Meng 67 (1994); Oppenheim's International Law 432 (1992); Peters, Völkerrecht 318 (2016); Ratner 127 (2015).

[136] Military and Paramilitary Activities in and Against Nicaragua, 1986 I.C.J. 108, ¶ 205.

[137] In 1949, the ICJ found the United Kingdom's "Operation Retail," which secured evidence in the territory of Albania for a future case the United Kingdom would bring before an international tribunal, was an unlawful form of self-help and constituted an intervention under international law: Corfu Channel, 1949 I.C.J. 35.

[138] Arrest Warrant, 2002 I.C.J. 35, 37 (Separate Opinion of President Guillaume). *See also* CoE, *Extraterritorial Criminal Jurisdiction* 459–60 (1992); Lowe, International Law (2007) 109; Meng 67 (1994); Oppenheim's International Law 432 (1992); Ratner 127 (2015).

not violate the principle of nonintervention. Purely and simply, interference and intervention are not the same.[139]

The international community has sometimes been accused of taking too narrow a view by limiting the principle of nonintervention to forcible, dictatorial, and other coercive measures. A wider interpretation suggests that the principle can be violated in extreme cases of extraterritorial prescriptive jurisdiction.[140] This is the case when one country calls for the laws of another country to be violated or when it prescribes laws extraterritorially that serve solely to undermine the jurisdiction of another state or to destroy its regime.[141] For example, India is frequently criticized for using its laws on cow protection to discriminate against minority religious groups, especially Muslims.[142] If India then extraterritorially employed only animal laws that protected cows, and only in Muslim countries like Bangladesh, and if there is evidence that India's ulterior motive is to subjugate Bangladeshi citizens or the country itself, these laws could violate the principle of nonintervention, even if India did not attempt to enforce them.

D. PRINCIPLE OF SELF-DETERMINATION OF PEOPLES

The principle of self-determination figures prominently in the UN as one of the central measures to strengthen and preserve universal peace.[143] The principle has an internal and an external dimension. In its external dimension, the principle of self-determination has been invoked to entitle non-self-governing territories, trust territories, and mandates to form independent states, as in the *Western Sahara* case and in the *Legal Consequences for States of the Continued Presence of South Africa in Namibia* case.[144] This external dimension has proved critical in fostering processes of decolonization and restorative justice. Later, the principle was centered for debate in cases where peoples claimed a right to self-determination

---

[139] CoE, *Extraterritorial Criminal Jurisdiction* 459–60 (1992): "Not every outside influence on the freedom of action of a state should be considered as inadmissible intervention under public international law. The point has already been made that acts of executive jurisdiction, which are performed within the territory of another state without its consent, may be assumed to be inadmissible. But this cannot in general be contended with respect to acts of legislative jurisdiction."

[140] Maier, *Jurisdictional Rules in Customary International Law, in* EXTRATERRITORIAL JURISDICTION IN THEORY AND PRACTICE, Comment by Andrea Bianchi 97 (1996); MENG 67 (1994); OPPENHEIM'S INTERNATIONAL LAW 430–1 (1992).

[141] Colombian-Peruvian Asylum Case (Colom. v. Peru), Judgment, 1950 I.C.J. Rep. 266, 286 (Nov. 20); LOWE, INTERNATIONAL LAW 109 (2007). Ratner argues that the principle applies to intelligence operations aimed at overthrowing a state's government, providing financial assistance to armed groups, and sabotaging computer networks with viruses: RATNER 128 (2015).

[142] *See* Chapter 9, §2 C.

[143] The principle builds on art. 1 para. 2 UN Charter as one of the purposeful means to the UN, and is further substantiated in arts. 55 and 73 of the UN Charter. It is enshrined in the ICCPR (art. 1) and in the International Covenant on Economic, Social and Cultural Rights (Dec. 16, 1966, 933 U.N.T.S. 3, art. 1 in conjunction with art 27 [ICESCR]).

[144] Western Sahara, Advisory Opinion, 1975 I.C.J. Rep. 12, 31–33 ¶¶ 54–59 (Oct. 16); Legal Consequences for States of the Continued Presence of South Africa in Namibia (South West Africa) notwithstanding Security Council Resolution 276 (1970), Advisory Opinion, 1971 I.C.J. Rep. 16, 31 ¶ 52 (June 21). *See also* G.A. Res. 1514, U.N. GAOR 15th Sess., Declaration on the Granting of Independence to Colonial Countries and Peoples, U.N. Doc. A/RES/1514(XV) (Dec. 14, 1960).

against their own state, i.e., concerning the internal dimension of the principle.[145] Outside these debates about decolonialization and secession, however, there is a remarkable degree of uncertainty about the principle. An obvious assumption is that in this sphere, self-determination encompasses the right of peoples to freely choose their own political system and to pursue their own economic, social, and cultural development.[146]

To violate this principle, extraterritorial animal law would have to deprive the people of another state of the ability to fully determine their political status and pursue their economic, social, and cultural development. In this context, is conceivable that, if the EU ban on seal products—which had indirect effects on (indigenous) peoples of Canada[147]—had been designed as an extraterritorial measure *stricto sensu,* it would violate the principle of self-determination, because it singled out in its effects a unified group of persons that constitute a people. But the measure would also have had to prevent or make it very difficult for these people to choose its political system or pursue its own economic, social, and cultural development. It is certainly possible that animal laws have a major impact on a people's economic, social, or cultural environment, particularly when power relations are as asymmetrical as that between the European Union and indigenous peoples of other countries. But these are exceptional cases. It is difficult to imagine that extraterritorial animal law typically hinders the full economic, social, and cultural development of the people of another state. International case law suggests that, for this to happen, there must be some form of gravity or even subjugation involved. For example, Israel built a wall that the ICJ held was "reducing and parceling out the territorial sphere over which the Palestinian people are entitled to exercise their right to self-determination."[148] The *Wall Opinion* might be a straightforward case in this respect, but this is far from suggesting that merely prescribing law that aims to protect animals abroad subjugates, parcels out, and severely affects the people of that state.

Apart from the claims of peoples, it seems that noncolonial, nonsecessional, and non-intrastate aspects of the principle of self-determination are already captured by the principle of nonintervention, which ensures the choice of a state for a political, economic, social, and cultural system.[149] In this area, as Thürer and Burri note, the principle of self-determination "essentially refers to the principle of sovereign equality of States and the prohibition of intervention which

---

[145] Daniel Thürer & Thomas Burri, *Self-Determination, in* MPEPIL 15 (Rüdiger Wolfrum ed., online ed. 2008). Judge Higgins highlighted that "[t]he Court has for the very first time, without any particular legal analysis, implicitly also adopted this second perspective [of the principle of self-determination]" (Wall Opinion, 2004 I.C.J. 207, 214 ¶ 30 (Separate Opinion by Judge Higgins) (July 9) [Wall Opinion, 2004 I.C.J.]).

[146] RATNER 144 (2015); Thürer & Burri, *Self-Determination, in* MPEPIL 17 (2008).

[147] The exceptions granted a *de facto* advantage to products from Greenland (more specifically its Inuit population), which was not immediately and unconditionally accorded to like products from Canada. *See Seals,* AB Report ¶ 5.95.

[148] Wall Opinion, 2004 I.C.J. 182 ¶ 115.

[149] Military and Paramilitary Activities in and Against Nicaragua, 1986 I.C.J. 108; Ziegler, *Domaine Réservé, in* MPEPIL 1 (2013). Vranes describes states' right to self-determination as the "mirror image" of the principle of nonintervention: VRANES 128 (2009). Despite these scholarly claims, nothing about the principle seems certain. As Brownlie explains, self-determination can mean different things in different contexts: BROWNLIE 646–7 (2008).

are already part of international law."[150] Accordingly, the limits established in this context are decisive.[151]

E. INFLUENCE OF THE EXTRATERRITORIALITY FRAMEWORK ON INTERNATIONAL LEGAL LIMITS

So far, we have examined the legality of extraterritorial animal law on the basis of relatively abstract principles, but any judgment will strongly depend on the manner and means by which jurisdiction is exercised, in particular how directly or indirectly it is exercised.[152] For example, norms that have ancillary repercussions abroad are less likely to violate established principles of international law because they do not regulate content abroad. Or, if regulation is based on intraterritorial anchor points to regulate content extraterritorially (type γ), this is often considered less intrusive than regulation that uses extraterritorial anchor points to regulate content extraterritorially (type α).[153] For example, it is less problematic to impose a duty to respect the rights of animals on a domestic parent corporation that manages foreign subsidiaries than to regulate the foreign subsidiary.

International case law reinforces the claim that the legality of jurisdiction is assessed by taking into account the anchor point, content regulation, and ancillary repercussions. In *Arrest Warrant*, the ICJ decided not to address the legality of the universality principle, where the jurisdictional assertion relied on extraterritorial anchor points (heinous crimes committed abroad) and regulated content extraterritorially (holding a foreign minister responsible for crimes committed abroad) (type α regulation). In *Lotus*, by contrast, the Court declared legal norms with intraterritorial anchor points (the crime consummated on domestic territory) that regulated content extraterritorially (holding a foreigner responsible for the crime) (type γ regulation). But this does not release states from the duty to take into account foreign interests, viewpoints, and reactions, since courts use the presence or absence of protests as evidence of *opinio juris*.[154] Overall, factors like the subject matter,

---

[150] Thürer & Burri, *Self-Determination, in* MPEPIL 17 (2008). *See also* Bowett 17 (1982).

[151] *See* Chapter 10, §3 C.

[152] *See especially* VRANES 129 ff. (2009). Verzijl argues that "[t]he way the state exercise jurisdiction may still constitute infringement" (VERZIJL, vol. IV, 21 (1972)). *See also* Maier, *Jurisdictional Rules in Customary International Law, in* EXTRATERRITORIAL JURISDICTION IN THEORY AND PRACTICE, Comment by Andrea Bianchi 79 (1996); ZERK, EXTRATERRITORIAL JURISDICTION 15 (2010).

[153] ZERK, EXTRATERRITORIAL JURISDICTION 5 (2010).

[154] *Cf.* Lotus, 1927 P.C.I.J. 29: "[T]he Court feels called upon to lay stress upon the fact that it does not appear that the States concerned have objected to criminal proceedings in respect of collision cases before the courts of a country other than that the flag of which was flown, or that they have made protests: their conduct does not appear to have differed appreciably from that observed by them in all case; of concurrent jurisdiction. This fact is directly opposed to the existence of a tacit consent on the part of States to the exclusive jurisdiction of the State whose flag is flown, such as the Agent for the French Government has thought it possible to deduce from the infrequency of questions of jurisdiction before criminal courts. It seems hardly probable, and it would not be in accordance with international practice, that the French Government in the *Ortigia-Oncle-Joseph* case and the German Government in the *Ekbatana-West-Hinder* case would have omitted to protest against the exercise of criminal jurisdiction by the Italian and Belgian Courts, if they had really thought that this was a violation of international law." (Emphasis in original).

degree of consensus and the degree of potential to generate conflicts, proportionality, expected and achieved effects, the degree to which foreign interests are taken into account, flexibility, levels of consultation and cooperation, and availability of procedures for resolution all strongly influence the outcome of a dispute.[155] Judging the legality or illegality of an extraterritorial norm under international law is thus not the result of an elaborate scientific process, but remains a matter of degree and is susceptible to political climate.

§4 Legal Consequences of Exorbitant Extraterritorial Animal Law

If extraterritorial animal laws of a state violate established principles of international law, it must be determined when and how the state will be held accountable. On the international level, the law of state responsibility determines "the legal consequences of the international wrongful act of a State, the obligations of the wrongdoer, on the one hand, and the rights and powers of any State affected by the wrongdoing, on the other."[156] According to article 1 of the International Law Commission's Draft Articles on Responsibility of States for Internationally Wrongful Acts (ARSIWA), "[e]very internationally wrongful act of a State entails the international responsibility of that State." [157] If a state addresses the Court to determine another state's international responsibility, it may demand cessation (if the law is still in effect) and nonrepetition (article 30 ARSIWA), and reparation (articles 31 and 34 *et seq.* ARSIWA) in the form of restitution (article 35 ARSIWA), compensation (article 36 ARSIWA), or satisfaction (article 37 ARSIWA). Any affected state may itself react to the breach with unilateral countermeasures, retorsion, or reprisal (articles 49 *et seq.* ARSIWA).

To date, no court or tribunal has yet determined the consequences of excessive prescriptive jurisdiction. In *Lotus*, the ICJ held that Turkey had not violated international law, and that "there is no occasion to give judgment on the question of the pecuniary reparation which might have been due to Lieutenant Demons if Turkey, *by prosecuting him* as above stated, had acted in a manner contrary to the principles of international law."[158] Accordingly, the prosecution of Lieutenant Demons (which forms part of enforcement jurisdiction), and not prescriptive jurisdiction, was considered critical to give rise to pecuniary reparation. In the *Corfu Channel* case, where the United Kingdom seized evidence in Albania, the Court determined that the United Kingdom violated Albania's sovereignty and stated that the declaration of the Court "constitutes in itself appropriate satisfaction."[159] In the *Arrest Warrant*, Belgium violated international law by issuing and circulating an arrest warrant against Mr. Adbulaye Yerodia Ndombasi, and was ordered to cancel it.[160] Attempting enforcement may therefore lead to the revocation of the enforcement order, not to the annulment of the law

---

[155] PETERS, VÖLKERRECHT 318 (2016); ZERK, EXTRATERRITORIAL JURISDICTION 12, 213–4 (2010).

[156] ANTONIO CASSESE, INTERNATIONAL LAW 261 (2d ed. 2005) (emphasis omitted).

[157] The ILC Draft Articles are not legally binding, but they reflect the current state of international law: PARRY ET AL. 577 (2009) "state responsibility." Or, at the very least, they are soft law, representing a mix of existing responsibilities and a desirable future development of international law: PETERS, VÖLKERRECHT 363 (2016).

[158] Lotus, 1927 P.C.I.J. 32 (emphasis added).

[159] Corfu Channel, 1949 I.C.J. 36.

[160] Arrest Warrant, 2002 I.C.J. 33.

that gave rise to the order. In sum, case law indicates that excessive *enforcement* jurisdiction may give rise to declaration of violation, cancellation of orders, or pecuniary reparation, but it provides no guidance on what legal consequences a state faces when its *prescriptive* jurisdiction violates international law.

Given the lack of guidance in international law, legal scholars have developed different answers to this question. Some believe that excessive laws will give rise to the law of international responsibility *in toto*. In this sense, the Inter-American Court of Human Rights, in its Advisory Opinion in *International Responsibility for the Promulgation and Enforcement of Laws in Violation of the Convention*, argued that "the promulgation of a law that manifestly violates the obligations assumed by a state upon ratifying or acceding to the Convention constitutes a violation of that treaty and, *if such violation affects the guaranteed rights and liberties of specific individuals*, gives rise to international responsibility for the state in question."[161] Accordingly, if extraterritorial animal law violates human rights guarantees of persons abroad, it will give rise to full international legal responsibility.[162] This seems to be a logical conclusion, since no state is reasonably interested in violating basic rights of individuals abroad. But the rule does not guide us in cases where extraterritorial laws do not affect human rights but still violate the rights of another state under international law.

In the context of extraterritorial naturalizations, Peters argues that excessive naturalization must be treated as an internationally illegal act and be tied to the usual consequences for illegality under the law of state responsibility. Alternatively, if the act cannot be declared illegal, it must be made inoperable under international law by entitling the affected state not to recognize the laws of another state that excessively reach into its territory. As a third option, the act could be treated as *prima facie* valid, but objectionable.[163] We thus have the choice of declaring the law strictly illegal, exorbitant, or legal but opposable.

The majority believes that excessive prescriptive jurisdiction may encroach on the reserved domain or territorial integrity of other states, but the mere adoption of laws is not illegal and does not, therefore, lead to full international legal responsibility.[164] Only when a state attempts to enforce or actually enforces these laws does it assume full responsibility for illegality in international law.[165] The scholarly consensus is supported by the judgments of *Lotus*, *Corfu Channel*, and the *Arrest Warrant*, where the ICJ could have, but decided not to declare illegal extraterritorial prescriptive jurisdiction.

---

[161] International Responsibility for the Promulgation and Enforcement of Laws in Violation of the Convention (Arts. 1 and 2 of the American Convention on Human Rights), Advisory Opinion OC-14/94, Inter-Am. Ct. H.R. (ser. A.) No. 14, ¶ 50 (Dec. 9, 1994) (emphasis added).

[162] This rule is limited to instances of extraterritorial content regulation and does not affect indirect extraterritorial jurisdiction, i.e., where extraterritorial effects are ancillary: MENG 88 (1994).

[163] Peters, *Extraterritorial Naturalizations* 709, 714 (2010).

[164] Akehurst 187 (1972–3); CoE, *Extraterritorial Criminal Jurisdiction* 455 (1992); Coughlan et al. 32 (2007); DIXON 150 (2013) (*a contrario*); Fox, *Jurisdiction and Immunity*, *in* FIFTY YEARS OF THE INTERNATIONAL COURT OF JUSTICE 213 (1996); Mann 14 (1964); O'Keefe 741, n. 22 (2004).

[165] RYNGAERT, JURISDICTION 154–5 (2015). Ryngaert argues that this does not mean that the principle of non-intervention does not restrict prescriptive jurisdiction. The principle, he argues, mandates a prudent balance of interests: *id.* at 155.

Does this, *a contrario*, mean that excessive extraterritorial animal law is legal? Traditionally, the law of state responsibility categorized acts as either legal or illegal, so this suggests that excessive extraterritorial animal law is legal. As Peters' examination of extraterritorial naturalizations shows, exorbitance is a third item that was added to the law of state responsibility (which categorizes acts as either legal or illegal) following the ILC Report on Nationality by Special Rapporteur Mikulka.[166] Peters acknowledges this development but cautions against it:

> Once it is acknowledged that international law has a negative role to play [. . .] by setting up limits, any disregard of these limits should render the act illegal. In the modern law of State responsibility, there is no room for an intermediate category of acts which are neither legal nor illegal but merely opposable.[167]

Nevertheless, the strange intermediate category of exorbitance has persisted in practice and scholarship, creating distinct legal consequences that are neither covered by legality nor by illegality.[168] In *Nottebohm*, Liechtenstein's grant of nationality to Nottebohm was considered excessive and treated as having no effect on the international level. The Court stated:

> Guatemala is under *no obligation to recognize* a nationality granted in such circumstances. Liechtenstein consequently is *not entitled to extend its protection* to Nottebohm vis-à-vis Guatemala and its claim must, for this reason, be held to be inadmissible.[169]

By the same token, the only legal consequences of excessive extraterritorial animal law are that (i) these laws will have no effect beyond the domestic territory of the state which enacted them,[170] and (ii) affected states are not obliged to recognize these laws or the jurisdiction on which they are founded.[171] This view is supported by state practice. When states consider

---

[166] International Law Commission, 47th Sess., First Report on State Succession and its Impact on the Nationality of Natural and Legal Persons (Special Rapporteur Vaclav Mikulka), U.N. Doc. A/CN.4/467 (Apr. 17, 1995): "States are therefore subject to two types of limitations in the area of nationality, the first type relating to the delimitation of competence between States (whose non-compliance with the rules results in the nonenforceability against third States of the nationality thus conferred) and the second, to the obligations associated with the protection of human rights (whose nonobservance entails international responsibility)."

[167] Peters, *Extraterritorial Naturalizations* 710 (2010).

[168] RYNGAERT, JURISDICTION 169 (2015).

[169] Nottebohm, 1955 I.C.J. 26 (emphasis added).

[170] Dixon argues that jurisdiction in violation of international law is only effective at the local level: DIXON 150 (2013). Mann pleads for declaring such jurisdiction null outside that state's territory. Excessive jurisdiction will simply be ignored and treated as void by other states' courts: Mann 12 (1964).

[171] Fox, *Jurisdiction and Immunity*, *in* FIFTY YEARS OF THE INTERNATIONAL COURT OF JUSTICE 213 (1996); Robert Y. Jennings, *Nullity and Effectiveness in International Law*, *in* CAMBRIDGE ESSAYS IN INTERNATIONAL LAW: ESSAYS IN HONOUR OF LORD MCNAIR 64, 82 (Robert Y. Jennings ed., 1965). In the context of excessive prescriptive jurisdiction, Geisser argues that jurisdiction that violates another state's sovereignty gives the affected state the right to deny recognition: GEISSER 250 (2013). In the context of excessive nationalization: Peters, *Extraterritorial Naturalizations* 712 (2010).

the laws of another state to be exorbitant, they sometimes resort to blocking statutes, which indicate that the laws of another state are *neither recognized, nor declared enforceable* on the territory of affected states.[172]

§5 Interim Conclusion

States tend to oppose extraterritorial animal law of another state by claiming that it interferes in their domestic affairs, violates the principle of sovereign equality, causes unnecessary costs and increases legal risks, constitutes inappropriate cherry-picking, and imposes ethical and cultural values of majority cultures on minorities. These concerns are expressed through states' public statements, diplomatic notes, intervention in court cases through *amicus curiae* briefs, adoption of blocking statutes and clawback clauses, and in legal proceedings at an international court or tribunal.

Conflicts arise because the principles of jurisdiction have only relative validity (they do not give guidance on which state has "the better claim to jurisdiction"[173]) and because states have not explicitly or implicitly agreed on a hierarchy of the principles. Consequently, states are confronted with different forms of concurrent and conflicting jurisdictions, which can be classified along lines that indicate the severity of a conflict (depending on whether laws prohibit, permit, require, or omit certain conduct). Where laws lead to foreign compulsion, there is a greater likelihood of conflict than when addressees of conflicting norms can decide which laws they will obey. To mitigate and prevent conflict, a state should observe the principle of the rule of law and the prohibition of double jeopardy when it prescribes criminal animal law extraterritorially. Another unilateral measure that helps avoid and resolve conflict is the principle of reasonableness, which prompts a state to inform the prospectively affected state before a conflict emerges, and to consider deferring to that state. Concerns for animals can play a role in this assessment if they are a high priority on the regulator's agenda or if they are a common concern of states.

Closely related to the principle of reasonableness are efforts of states to unilaterally resolve international disputes at a conflict stage. These include the balance of interests test and the principle of comity—tests that are flawed because they create the perception that other states' interests are fully internalized, while foreign states have no say in their design or application. Conflicts might be more effectively resolved by establishing balances of interests through bi- or multilateral negotiations. Optimally, states enter cooperative and collaborative agreements that lay down duties of mutual assistance. In contrast, concluding substantive jurisdictional agreements that determine which state is competent to prescribe animal law should only be pursued if it is clear that these treaties will increase the global level of animal welfare.

---

[172] *E.g.*, Council Regulation 2271/96, 1996 O.J. (L 309) 1, art. 4. Blocking statutes are thus a form of countermeasure to extraterritorial enforcement jurisdiction: CRAWFORD 478 (2012); Kamminga, *Extraterritoriality*, *in* MPEPIL 26 (2012).

[173] Bowett 14 (1982).

Whatever the extent of conflict, a state can always violate established principles of international law by adopting extraterritorial animal laws. The principles most discussed in this context are those of sovereign equality, territorial integrity, nonintervention, and self-determination of peoples. Sovereign equality can be violated where states' juridical equality is disregarded. Because jurisdictional principles apply equally to all states, states have the same rights under the law to realize their claims to protect animals abroad. Therefore, the principle of juridical equality is not violated by animal laws with extraterritorial reach as long as they are based on rules of customary international law that apply equally to all states.

There are two views on whether extraterritorial animal law violates territorial integrity. In the first, nonforcible prescriptive extraterritorial jurisdiction is thought to have the potential to violate a state's territorial integrity. In the second, only extraterritorial enforcement jurisdiction can violate the territorial integrity of another state because enforcement has a physical component. Purely prescriptive jurisdiction, however, does not encroach on the territorial integrity of another state.

Of all principles, a state is most likely to violate the principle of nonintervention when it adopts animal laws with extraterritorial reach. For this to happen, the regulated matter must be part of the *domaine réservé* of another state, which is likely because states have not concluded an international treaty in animal law. However, as animal law has become so entangled across borders, many states now have a vested interest in protecting animals abroad. So the stronger the jurisdictional anchor of a prescribing state to a subject matter, the less probable it is that the matter belongs to another state's reserved domain. But even if it does, the principle of nonintervention will only be violated if a state uses forcible, dictatorial, or otherwise coercive means when it interferes in the affairs of another state. Most scholars argue that noncoercive extraterritorial jurisdiction falls below this threshold and simply coexists with another state's jurisdiction. Some hold a stricter view and claim that the principle can be violated without physical coercion if a state engages in foreign sovereign compulsion, subjugation, or regime destruction. The principle of self-determination of the people may thus be violated where extraterritorial animal laws single out particular peoples and make it impossible for them to freely choose their political system or to pursue their own economic, social, and cultural development. This may be the case, for example, when extraterritorial animal laws fundamentally affect the lives and livelihoods of indigenous communities.

A decisive factor in assessing the legality of extraterritorial animal laws is the extent to which the prescribing state takes into account the interests of affected states and the means it uses to protect animals abroad. Laws that create only extraterritorial ancillary repercussions are unlikely to violate principles of international law because they do not regulate content abroad. ICJ case law further suggests that jurisdiction based on intraterritorial anchor points to regulate content abroad is less likely to be considered excessive than jurisdiction that uses extraterritorial anchor points and regulates content extraterritorially.

In summary, the legality of extraterritorial animal law depends on four key factors. First, extraterritorial jurisdiction must be based on a reasonable link. Only where a state relies on a recognized principle of jurisdiction, and operates within its limits, can it be seen as observing international law. Second, the legality of extraterritorial animal law depends on the specific subject matter and the extent of its regulation under international law. Third, jurisdiction must be exercised for legitimate purposes. Fourth, a state must pay attention to the manner and the means by which it exercises jurisdiction.

When the laws of a state violate a principle of international law, the law of state responsibility is used to determine the legal consequences. There are broadly two views on the legal consequences of excessive extraterritorial jurisdiction. Some claim that states bear full responsibility under international law, which includes claims to cessation (if the law is still in effect), nonrepetition (to prevent the state from doing the same wrong in the future), and reparation (for the damage suffered). An alternative view, supported by the sparse judgments in international law and majority scholarly opinion, is that excessive extraterritorial animal laws are exorbitant but not illegal and that they can therefore be countered by a declaration of nullity, and a right to nonrecognition by affected states.

The legal limits that states face under international law may help dispel concerns about extraterritorial jurisdiction but they still leave ample room for the imperialist exercise of extraterritorial animal law that targets ethnic and cultural minorities, their forms of government, and their ideologies. Postcolonial studies have long demonstrated the need and urgency to go beyond limited legal approaches and strive to avoid continued imperialism.[174] After all, majority cultures have suppressed minorities for centuries to impose on them their ways of using and abusing animals. To allow this to happen in extraterritorial jurisdiction would be to accept that the protection of animals is not an end itself but a means of oppressing others. Neither international law nor animal law can afford to take this risk. Ways to preclude this and ensure extraterritorial jurisdiction benefits both humans and animals include listening to other perspectives and being aware that colonialism taints Western ways of knowing, striving for consistency by criticizing mainstream practices and engaging in self-reflective inquiry, and making judgments only after good faith consultation and collaboration.[175]

---

[174] Dalziell & Wadiwel, *Live Exports, Animal Advocacy, Race and "Animal Nationalism," in* Meat Culture 85 (2017); Deckha 201 (2007).

[175] Deckha 223 (2007); Will Kymlicka & Sue Donaldson, *Animal Rights and Aboriginal Rights, in* CANADIAN PERSPECTIVES ON ANIMALS AND THE LAW 159, 177 (Peter Sankoff, Vaughan Black, & Katie Sykes eds., 2015).

11 Conclusion

TOWARD LEGAL PLURALISM, POSTCOLONIALISM, AND INTERSPECIES JUSTICE

I BEGAN THIS book by noting the structural limits of our ethical, social, and legal efforts to work toward a more just world for animals in an era of globalization. The vision of neoliberalization of the 1970s and 1980s has always been to create a highly mobile system of production and distribution with few or no regulatory burdens, but we have seen no reduction or leveling of these developments ever since trade liberalization began to dominate political agendas across the world. The industries that use animals—be it factory farms, slaughterhouse businesses, basic research and testing, or entertainment and sports industries—are characterized by high levels of cross-border investment, manufacture, transport, and trade. The animals used by these industries constitute the absolute majority of all domesticated animals on this planet and they are almost exclusively owned by multinational corporations.[1] Multinationals enjoy competitive advantages in goods markets since they can readily exchange information and assets, draw on superior management skills, profit from global patents and trade secrets, and access substantial capital.[2] These advantages make it easy for them to deploy resources to more business-friendly environments, which often goes hand in hand with a lack of laws designed to protect animals.

This ease of movement has intimidated most legislators, who expect and fear an exodus of industry through outsourcing, and the consequent loss of local jobs and tax revenues. Corporations are increasingly outsourcing, but this is only half the story. The states themselves have made considerable efforts to prevent the mounting instances of outsourcing

[1] Park & Singer 122 (2012).

[2] *Seminal*: KINDLEBERGER 14–27 (1969).

by adapting their regulatory environments to suit businesses. This book has touched on numerous cases where legislators decided not to enforce their own laws, abolished established protections, and ignored the will of their constituents who were firmly committed to protecting animals better and more consistently.

Since efforts to improve the legal situation of animals—be it through protections, rights, or duties of care—are manifestly and almost inextricably linked to economic considerations, animal law is bound to be a volatile and fragile field of law. The fact that protecting animals is "subject to an economic analysis" or "must be balanced against economic and social considerations,"[3] which is reiterated in so many laws, court decisions, and policy debates, has certainly not helped to counter this development. But is this what citizens expect from their states when they entrust them with drafting and enacting animal laws? The purpose of animal law, after all, is to shield animals from exploitation, regardless of whether it is profitable or not, just as human rights law is designed to protect humans from becoming victims of exploitation, however lucrative it may be. But unlike human rights law, animal law cannot claim that states have a uniform and international commitment to unequivocally protect animals even if exploiting them is exceedingly profitable.[4] Most states are afraid of losing taxpaying animal industries if they pass stricter animal laws and fear that their neighbor states will happily host these industries and pocket the cash.

The situation in animal law is akin to a prisoners' dilemma. States could reap great benefits if they cooperated on matters of animal law, but they fail to do so because they find it difficult or expensive, or because they are afraid of free-riders. For example, Swiss parliament members are reluctant to prohibit invasive animal experiments because they fear the industry will relocate. In Germany, male baby chicks continue to be shredded alive by the poultry and egg industry because authorities believe that a ban on the practice will shift production abroad. Other states are reluctant to abolish the intense confinement of animals in agriculture because they fear these animals will be moved abroad and confined anyway.[5]

It makes sense that each state should want to ensure its economic returns, but from a collective point of view, this strategy is irrational as it leads to convergence toward a lower common denominator, also known as competition in laxity or race to the bottom.[6] Even if legislators do not refer to economic calculi or flag fears of outsourcing, there is profound uncertainty across jurisdictions since states do not know the legal possibilities and limits of protecting animals whenever there is a cross-border relation involved. This leads to legislative inertia, or, as regulatory theorists call it, regulatory chill. Across the entire field of animal law, we are seeing impasses and retrenchments from commitments to protect animals, which stand in stark contrast to growing public demand that animals be granted a more stable and

---

[3] In this sense, *see, e.g.*, Council Directive 2008/120, 2009 O.J. (L 47) 5, at 12; Council Directive 2007/43/EC, 2007 O.J. (L 182) 19, at 20.

[4] This gap is also noted by: Cunniff & Kramer, *Developments in Animal Law*, *in* The Global Guide to Animal Protection 230 (2013); Favre, *An International Treaty for Animal Welfare*, *in* Animal Law and Welfare 92 (2016); Peters, *Global Animal Law* 13 (2016).

[5] *See* in detail Chapter 2, §3.

[6] *See* for a general description of the dilemma: Peter P. Swire, *The Race to Laxity and the Race to Undesirability: Explaining Failures in Competition Among Jurisdictions in Environmental Law*, 14 Yale L. & Pol'y Rev. 67, 89 (symposium issue 1996).

protected legal status. The fact that states do not take this mandate seriously is detrimental to democracy because it proves that, at least in animal law, corporations have succeeded at circumventing the will of the people.[7] But it is also alarming from the animals' perspective, who do not have a say in any of these matters and are in extreme forms of vulnerability, not because of who they are but because the law makes them so.

Of the scholars who specialize in this field, most recognize that economic entanglement and interdependence have made it difficult for states to protect animals effectively, and argue that we need global governance schemes that regulate our duties toward animals in a uniform and consistent manner across the globe.[8] This, they claim, eliminates the problem of free-riders and could be backed by international bodies that adjudicate these matters, which would bring about consistent enforcement. At the heart of these voices is an important recognition, namely, that the success of each state in protecting animals depends on its ability and willingness to engage in international coordination and cooperation. But they fail to recognize that it is unlikely states will be able to agree on an international treaty that establishes duties owed to animals or determines which state is competent to protect them.[9] Even if a formal consensus can be put in writing, the result will almost certainly be painfully lax,[10] and undesirable in the first place given the growing call for rooted cosmopolitanism.[11]

In this book, I considered the arguments for and implications of an alternative to international treaty-making that could help us narrow down, tackle, and potentially solve these issues: extraterritorial jurisdiction. I focused on extraterritorial jurisdiction as a state's act of prescribing law across the border to people, events, or properties situated thereon *in order to protect animals*. I embedded extraterritorial jurisdiction as a part and necessary consequence

---

[7] As the work of Grear, Hornborg, Malm, and Mayer shows, intra- and interspecies inequalities have contributed significantly to the greatest economic and technological successes of corporations. Today, corporations are not only a central feature of the global order; they represent the "contemporary apotheosis" of the *anthropos*. *See* Anna Grear, *Deconstructing* Anthropos: *A Critical Legal Reflection on "Anthropocentric" Law and Anthropocene "Humanity,"* 26(3) LAW & CRITIQUE 225, 237–40 (2016); Andreas Malm & Alf Hornborg, *The Geology of Mankind? A Critique of the Anthropocene Narrative*, 1(1) ANTHROPOCENE REV. 62, 64 (2014); Carl J. Mayer, *Personalising the Impersonal: Corporations and the Bill of Rights*, 41 HASTINGS L.J. 577, 589 (1990).

[8] Consider in this respect the Universal Declaration on Animal Welfare of 2003, proposed by the World Society for the Protection of Animals, or the International Convention for the Protection of Animals of 1988, proposed by the International Fund for Animal Welfare. *See* for a discussion of these treaties, Blattner, *The Potential and Potential Limits of International Law in Regulating Animal Matters* (2015). *Cf.* Peters, *Global Animal Law* 20 (2016), who calls for a legal approach that combines a host of different norms, such as national, international, regional, state, and private regulation.

[9] In a seminal article on antitrust law, Guzman used an economic analysis to determine the likelihood that states would enter into an international treaty on jurisdictional matters. He hypothesized that economic incentives are the main motivation for states to sign or reject a treaty, and argued that finding common ground for a treaty will be difficult, if not impossible, when consumers and producers are unevenly distributed among states: Guzman (1998). Guzman's probability analysis can be neatly extrapolated to animal law, because economic considerations play such an important role in its policymaking, and because a large portion of the world's animal products is produced in the majority world.

[10] *See further* Charlotte E. Blattner, *Can Extraterritorial Jurisdiction Help Overcome Regulatory Gaps of Animal Law? Insights from Trophy Hunting*, 111 AJIL UNBOUND 419, 420 (2017).

[11] *See further* on rooted cosmopolitanism as an alternative to internationalization: Kymlicka & Walker, *Rooted Cosmopolitanism*, *in* ROOTED COSMOPOLITANISM 3 (2012).

of broader developments like deterritorialization of state sovereignty, the acceptance of an entangled web of relationships that led to an approximation of state markets and policies, and the rise of a global consensus on the need to better protect animals. To prevent states from misusing terminological uncertainty about extraterritorial jurisdiction to advance their momentary interests, I established a definitional and conceptual framework of extraterritoriality. The framework helps to distinguish contentious claims to jurisdiction from legitimate ones and shows that the dichotomy between legal territorial and problematic extraterritorial jurisdiction is a false one.

Two tasks lay at the heart of this book. The first was to gain legal certainty about the many ways that states can use their laws to better protect animals *within their borders*. At its basis, the law of jurisdiction is intended to produce greater certainty about the breadth and limits of the prescriptive authority of states. This is urgently needed in animal law where legal insecurities about the power to protect animals in cases involving cross-border relations continue to prevent states from protecting animals. Eliminating these enables states to reliably determine when and how they can protect animals in cases that involve a wealth of cross-border relations. This empowers states to reclaim their compromised powers over animal issues and gives new impetus to animal rights and protection movements. But this is not the only benefit of the law of jurisdiction. The second task of this book was to explore reasonable ways to protect animals *across the border*. One of my central hypotheses was that the factual entanglement of people, property, and commerce cannot be sorted out if we rely on each state to meticulously apply its animal laws and enforce them on domestic territory. Factual entanglement calls for legal entanglement, i.e., extraterritorial jurisdiction. Tools of extraterritorial jurisdiction that states have available and readily use in criminal, human rights, commerce, banking, and antitrust law can also be used to protect animals across the border. These include indirect and direct forms of extraterritorial jurisdiction, bilateral or multilateral agreements, soft law, corporate social responsibility, reporting, impact assessments, and many more. In presenting these options, I made clear the urgency of moving beyond the presumption that animals are merely "regulated objects" in the law of jurisdiction. Animals are individual beings with their own lives to live, and as such deserve to be directly linked to a state's jurisdiction, for example through functional nationality, which offers advantages like material consistency and temporal continuity in the law of jurisdiction. I have also determined the substantive standards needed to ensure extraterritorial jurisdiction can do justice to animals, including the need to work toward better outcomes for animals when law is applied across the border, claims for consistency, presumptions in favor of animals, the state duty to protect, and the corporate duty to respect animals. In the last chapter, I explored the legal limits of extraterritorial animal law and the means available to prevent, mitigate, and resolve conflicts that may emerge from it.

In this concluding chapter, I do not want to review these findings beyond what I just mentioned. Instead, I want to return to the structural challenges and the question of whether extraterritorial jurisdiction can help overcome them, by taking a broader multidisciplinary perspective. In particular, I want to critically evaluate whether the law of jurisdiction truly has the potential to bolster domestic efforts to protect animals, what social and societal risks (as opposed to legal risks) we run with this strategy, and whether we have options to mitigate these. The social and political sciences highlight three concerns. First, it is not obvious that moving away from territorial jurisdiction could create legal certainty and help fill regulatory gaps. If anything, extraterritorial jurisdiction might increase insecurity about legal limits and confuse legislators, making it even more difficult for states to meaningfully protect animals. Second, animal law lacks the rich history and empirical experience necessary to apply it across the border with a good conscience. If we begin to apply animal laws across the border prematurely, we run the risk of exacerbating their problematic aspects and deficits, which are already surfacing at the domestic level. Third, many readers will be concerned that extraterritorial jurisdiction could awaken hidden notions of nationalism and promote the view that social, cultural, and legal values of one state can or should be imposed on the people of another, which would fuel fears of neocolonialism and Euro-American-centrism. Given the lack of state practice on the subject, I cannot counter these fears and concerns with empirical evidence that proves otherwise. I can offer an alternative viewpoint informed by the experience in many other areas of law where extraterritorial jurisdiction is fully established and plays an important role in regulating social life. I argue that extraterritorial jurisdiction, if properly set up and applied, creates a multitude of overlapping and concurring laws that reduce the likelihood of regulatory gaps in animal law. By forcing states to compare and reflect critically on their animal laws and practices, extraterritorial jurisdiction has the power to induce new ways of seeing and accepting cultural diversity, and can push states into a race to the top. In the remainder, I will elaborate on these claims.

Fear of outsourcing prompts states to roll back their regulatory achievements in animal law and adapt laws to the benefit of tax-paying and job-creating corporations. This is a cause for concern because these developments point to a more general failure of the law to regulate corporations, the most powerful of which make annual profits larger than the GDP of many countries.[12] In animal law, agricultural industries are largely exempt from the law, or they create their own codes of conduct.[13] In research, the industry itself sits on animal ethics committees to assess whether it complies with the law.[14] This perverts justice by making corporations their own private legislators or allowing them to do what they wish to animals. And since corporations own most domesticated animals, anything done to them usually falls through the cracks of law. The situation in animal law is particularly despicable, but it is not the only field of law that succumbs to corporate power. We can see similar developments, from tax and business law to environmental and human rights law.[15] These gaps have become a breeding ground for environmental pollution, human rights violations, accumulation

---

[12] The NGO "Global Justice Now" ranks the world's top 100 global economic entities based on their revenues but without regard to their form. The ranking reveals that 69 of the top 100 economic entities are corporations, not countries. Rank 10 is occupied by the first corporation, Walmart. Walmart, Apple, and Shell are all economically more powerful than Russia, Belgium, and Sweden: Global Justice, Corporations vs. Government Revenues, 2015 Data (2016), *available at* http://www.globaljustice.org.uk/sites/default/files/files/resources/corporations_vs_governments_final.pdf (last visited Jan. 10, 2019).

[13] *See* Sullivan & Wolfson (2007); Wolfson & Sullivan, *Foxes in the Hen House*, *in* ANIMAL RIGHTS: CURRENT DEBATES AND NEW DIRECTIONS 205 (2004).

[14] *See* Mara-Daria Cojocaru & Philipp van Gall, *Beyond Plausibility Checks: A Case for Moral Doubt in Review Processes of Animal Experimentation*, *in* ANIMAL EXPERIMENTATION: WORKING TOWARDS A PARADIGM CHANGE 289 (Kathrin Herrmann & Kimberley Jayne eds., 2019).

[15] For many, *see* Charlotte E. Blattner & Odile Ammann, *Animal Agriculture and Farmer Rights in Light of International Human Rights Law* (forthcoming 2019).

of corporate wealth at the expense of citizens, and, in animal law, cruelty done to animals on a massive institutional and systematic scale.[16] We cannot solve these problems simply by asserting that creating laws for animals and fully enforcing them will help counter this development. Even under the best circumstances, territorially bound laws manifestly fail to deliver the results needed to halt competition in laxity, precisely because these laws are not applied across the border. There is an urgent need to hold corporations accountable for their many actions that evade the law. The extralegal sphere in which they operate must be superseded by extraterritorial jurisdiction to ensure accountability and responsibility for what is done to animals.[17]

Closing these gaps with extraterritorial jurisdiction, rather than through an international treaty, ensures that we do not adopt the lowest acceptable standards for animals but build on respectable achievements in animal law and gradually improve on them. It is true that applying laws extraterritorially does not always make it clear which state is competent to regulate a case, but instead of seeing this as a failure, we should recognize that this is the safest option available. It is safe because it leads to positive competency conflicts that result in various forms of overlapping jurisdiction. This is the best bet for animals because it ensures that what is done to them is going to be governed by at least some laws. The alternative scenario we have today is a prevalence of negative competency conflicts where no state considers itself responsible for protecting animals caught in cross-border production, trade, movement, and other ties.

The legal pluralism created by positive competency conflicts offers states an excellent opportunity to engage in cross-border comparisons of their laws. Many states wrongly believe that they have some of the best laws to protect animals because they lack the knowledge, expertise, exposure, and sensitivity needed to suggest otherwise. Today, states can cross-compare their levels of animal protection to determine if their laws are "off standard" and can use this information to improve their laws or even lead by example. The World Animal Protection Index (API) is a convenient tool for states to check the ranking of their animal laws against other countries. The factors the API uses for its assessment are the formal recognition of animal sentience, support for the Universal Declaration on Animal Welfare, government accountability, engagement with the OIE, providing humane education, promoting communication and awareness, laws that prohibit animal suffering, and laws that protect animals in farming, captivity, companionship, draught and recreation, scientific research, or in the wild.[18] The Australian NGO Voiceless created another ranking system called the Voiceless Animal Cruelty Index (VACI), which focuses specifically on the welfare of land-farmed animals and ranks the harms states inflict on them. A country is ranked on the basis of three criteria: producing cruelty (the number of farmed animals they slaughter for

---

[16] In 2017, the number of land animals killed for food exceeded 69 billion, including 66 billion chickens, 1.5 billion pigs, 1 billion sheep and goats, and 300 million cows: FAOSTAT (search criteria "World"+"Meat total"+"Producing Animals/Slaughtered"+"2017," *available at* http://faostat.fao.org/ (last visited Jan. 10, 2019).

[17] Also in other fields of law "direct extraterritorial jurisdiction has been recognised as useful in closing regulatory and accountability gaps, and delivering justice." (ZERK, EXTRATERRITORIAL JURISDICTION 10 (2010)).

[18] World Animal Protection (WAP), Indicators (2019), *available at* https://api.worldanimalprotection.org/indicators (last visited Jan. 10, 2019).

food every year), consuming cruelty (the number of farmed animals they consume), and sanctioning cruelty (their regulatory framework that protects, or fails to protect, farmed animals).[19] If, under the extraterritoriality scheme, the laws of two or more states can claim to regulate the same matter, we could evaluate the strength of their interests in regulating the matter, the degree of factual entanglement, whether applying one or the other law would have adverse consequences, and which laws will help animals most, to decide which states' laws must take precedence. States would begin to compare their laws more openly, and API and VACI rankings would help them determine whether they need to raise their laws to the level of their competitors. This is one way we could promote extraterritorial jurisdiction, but it does not go far enough.

The comparative analyses in this book made it clear that even the best animal laws simply clean up around the edges while missing the heart of the matter. Most of these laws simply enshrine and make legal the routine and systematic exploitation of animals. For example, condemning "unnecessary suffering" of animals does in no significant sense benefit animals. It makes the *prima facie* claim that animals are available for our use if we wish them to be, even if that use causes them extreme suffering, deprives them of lives worth living, and, ultimately, leads to their death. Rather than protecting animals, which is the mandate of animal law, these laws protect our use of animals. It is thus fair to say that animal law has not yet achieved much and has worked against animals by making them available for human use and rendering them vulnerable and disposable.[20] The standard views and ranking systems of animal law are limited to this narrow thinking, and they tell us nothing about the broader shortcomings and the most urgent changes needed to live up to our commitment to protect animals as sentient and conscious co-inhabitants of this world.

If we were to set up a global ranking system that assesses countries based on factors that indicate where we want to go as a global multispecies society, the ranking system and the place occupied by countries would look radically different. Even those with the highest current level of animal law would find themselves occupying the lowest ranks, which would force them to realize that their levels of animal protection are much closer to each other than they thought, and much further away from what they should be. Although extraterritorial jurisdiction produces overlapping and concurring laws that facilitate cross-comparisons, these comparisons are no excuse for states to be complacent—not if we take seriously the claims animals have on us. These comparisons must instead prompt states to radically expand their current visions of animal law and engage seriously the growing call for interspecies justice.[21]

---

[19] Voiceless, The Voiceless Animal Protection Index (2019), *available at* https://vaci.voiceless.org.au/about-the-vaci/ (last visited Jan. 10, 2019). Also ALDF offers rankings of animal protection laws, focused on US states: Animal Legal Defense Fund, 2018 U.S. Animal Protection Laws State Rankings, *available at* https://aldf.org/project/2018-us-state-rankings/ (last visited Jan. 10, 2019).

[20] Lori Gruen, *Disposable Captives*, OUP Blog, Apr. 10, 2014: "Death is a natural part of life, and perhaps we would do well to have a less fearful, more accepting attitude about death. But those who purposefully bring about premature death run the risk of perpetuating the notion that some lives are disposable."

[21] *See* for recent work on interspecies justice: Alasdair Cochrane, Sentientist Politics: A Theory of Global Inter-Species Justice (2018); Donaldson & Kymlicka (2011); Garner & O'Sullivan eds. (2016); Marilyn Matevia, *Justice for All: Revisiting the Prospects for a Biocommunitarian Theory of Interspecies Justice*, 19(3) J. Int'l Wildlife L. & Pol'y 189 (2016); Heather McLeod-Kilmurray, *Commoditizing Nonhuman Animals and Their Consumers: Industrial Livestock Production, Animal Welfare, and Ecological*

The cross-comparisons that the law of extraterritoriality facilitates do not only unveil the biases and shortcomings of animal law in relation to animals but also in relation to humans. Many suspect extraterritorial jurisdiction will succumb to androcentric and Eurocentric power hierarchies. There is already a great deal of intersectional oppression in law, and cross-border governance exacerbates this danger by condemning only certain ways in which humans use and exploit animals while ignoring or even legitimating others. Chances that extraterritorial jurisdiction is used, consciously or not, to advance hidden agendas are so large that we might ultimately end up entitling majority cultures to oppress minorities. The West comes to the aid of the "uncivilized," "savage" nations and shows them how animals are "properly" used, killed, and eaten.[22] Instead of actually helping animals and guiding us toward a just interspecies society, extraterritorial animal law can keep us trapped in recurring cycles of discrimination and injustice.

But do the dangers of cultural imperialism and neocolonialism compel us to take a hands-off approach to extraterritorial jurisdiction? I believe we should not make the cursory assertion that extraterritorial jurisdiction never has a hidden racial or otherwise discriminatory agenda, nor should we jettison extraterritorial jurisdiction *in toto* and fully succumb to the law of the market. My claim, which may seem counterintuitive, is that by creating overlapping forms of jurisdiction, extraterritorial jurisdiction gives rise to legal pluralism that is conducive to multiculturalism and promotes the interests of animals. Deckha has pointed to the limited investigations at the interface of human and animal oppression, whose central question is: "Is multiculturalism bad for animals?"[23] These are questions that put non-Western communities on the defensive and fail to acknowledge the many forward-thinking legal developments of the majority world that transcend the Western discourse of animal protection.[24] Instead of generically declaring one culture superior to another, playing them off against each other, and holding on to an illusion of universal objectivity and neutrality, the global community would be better off embracing the dialogue that emerges when spheres of jurisdictions begin to intersect and overlap. Concurring forms of jurisdiction stimulate discourse that fosters multicultural sensibility, awareness of shared histories, and an understanding of the intersectional forms of oppression, including intersections of race and speciesism, of sexism and speciesism, and of ableism and speciesism.[25] As such, concurring jurisdiction can uniquely encourage us to work toward curtailing, preventing, and eradicating

---

Justice, 32(1) BULL. SCI., TECH. & SOC'Y 71 (2012); MARCEL WISSENBURG & DAVID SCHLOSBERG EDS., POLITICAL ANIMALS AND ANIMAL POLITICS (2014); ANDREW WOODHALL & GABRIEL GARMENDIA DA TRINDADE EDS., ETHICAL AND POLITICAL APPROACHES TO NONHUMAN ANIMAL ISSUES (2017); Rafi Youatt, *Interspecies Relations, International Relations: Rethinking Anthropocentric Politics*, 43(1) MILLENNIUM J. INT'L STUD. 207 (2014).

[22] *See* for some very careful and thoughtful analyses: Deckha 192–3 (2007); KIM (2015); Kim 234 (2007); Kymlicka & Donaldson 126 (2014); Oh & Jackson 31 (2011).

[23] *E.g.*, Paula Casal, *Is Multiculturalism Bad for Animals*, 1(1) J. POL. PHIL. 1 (2003).

[24] Deckha refers in particular to the legal developments in India: Maneesha Deckha, *Is Multiculturalism* Good *for Animals?*, *in* MULTICULTURALISM, RACE AND ANIMALS 61, 64, 70 ff. (2017). *See also* KIM (2015).

[25] *See* for an intersectional analysis of race and speciesism: KO & KO (2017). *See* for an intersectional analysis of ableism and speciesism: TAYLOR (2017). *See* for an intersectional analysis of patriarchy and speciesism: ADAMS & GRUEN EDS. (2015).

forms of oppression.[26] Contrary to the belief of many, extraterritorial jurisdiction is thus not the enemy of multiculturalism, but an important ally to begin materializing its demands through law. For extraterritorial jurisdiction to succeed in this task it must, like the law in general, commit itself to listening to the perspectives of affected parties and consulting with them, to fully investigate the rights and wrongs of its own approaches, and to develop a sense of duty to do better.[27] Only if this happens, can the legal pluralism that extraterritorial jurisdiction promises to spur become a unique opportunity for states to advance an agenda for respectful human-animal relationships.

Coming back to my initial claim that extraterritorial jurisdiction promises to change the dynamics of animal law for the better, both nationally and globally, I hope this book has shown exactly that. Extraterritorial jurisdiction is a promising new area of research, which has the potential to overcome the inertia and deregulation that characterize animal law to this day and to enable states to regain the regulatory capacity they need to fully protect animals at home and abroad. The international doctrine of jurisdiction has created an opportunity to abandon our archaic territorial conception of jurisdiction that binds individuals to it in an exclusive fashion and fences off other sovereigns. The territorial primacy a state might once have enjoyed over its regulatees left ample room for misuse by bereaving regulatees—who are at the mercy of this single regulator—of protection, welfare, and rights. The jurisdictional options presented herein offer a useful and meaningful alternative to these dystopian visions of animal law. They are particularly valuable to animals—more than to any other group that profits from extraterritorial jurisdiction—because animals, as the worldwide greatest number of regulatees, lack a voice in the formation of law and the opportunity to escape oppressive jurisdictional authority. Extraterritorial jurisdiction thus offers hope for the future of animal law.

But extraterritorial jurisdiction can only be as revolutionary as the substantive laws that apply across the border. If these are minimum standards, we merely skirt the edges of what is truly wrong with what we do to animals, and hence, extraterritorial jurisdiction risks not only losing its revolutionary potential but also becoming complicit in permanently subjugating the interests of animals to those of humans. Only if animals gain access to robust rights of protection, membership, and justice, will we have reason to believe that extraterritorial jurisdiction can succeed at creating a more just world for animals. And only if these laws simultaneously and fully respond to the caveats raised by postcolonial studies, can we ensure that human rights and animal rights are not played off against each other but work in tandem. These conditions may be delicate and the challenges they face difficult to overcome, but they demonstrate that there is a way forward, which should not be taken for granted. If carefully designed and implemented, with attention and the best intentions, extraterritorial jurisdiction can revolutionize domestic and international animal law the same way it has revolutionized human rights law.

---

[26] Deckha makes this argument about multiculturalism in general, not with regard to extraterritorial jurisdiction: Deckha, *Is Multiculturalism* Good *for Animals?*, *in* MULTICULTURALISM, RACE AND ANIMALS 61, 87 (2017).

[27] Deckha 223 (2007). *See also* Kymlicka & Donaldson, *Animal Rights and Aboriginal Rights*, *in* CANADIAN PERSPECTIVES ON ANIMALS AND THE LAW 177 (2015): "This requires conscious efforts at inclusion, dialogue, cross-cultural learning and listening, a commitment to consistency and self-reflective inquiry, epistemic humility, and the avoidance of tokenism, essentialism and exoticism. We are far from having these preconditions in place."

Bibliography, Newspaper Articles, and Press Releases

BIBLIOGRAPHY

ABATE, RANDALL S., Dawn of a New Era in the Extraterritorial Application of U.S. Environmental Statutes: A Proposal for an Integrated Judicial Standard Based on the Continuum of Context, 31 Colum. J. Envtl. L. 87 (2006).

ABBOTT, ALISON, Swiss Court Bans Work on Macaque Brains, 453 Nature 833 (2008).

ACEVEDO, ANTONIA, The EEC Dyestuffs Case: Territorial Jurisdiction, 36 Modern L. Rev. 317 (1973).

ACH, JOHANN S., Interesse, in Lexikon der Mensch-Tier Beziehungen 173–175 (Arianna Ferrari & Klaus Petrus eds., Transcript, Bielefeld 2015).

ADAMS, CAROL J. & GRUEN, LORI EDS., Ecofeminism: Feminist Intersections with Other Animals & the Earth (Bloomsbury, New York, London 2015).

ADDIS, ADENO, Community and Jurisdictional Authority, in Beyond Territoriality: Transnational Legal Authority in an Age of Globalization 13–34 (Gunther Handl & Joachim Zekoll eds., Martinus Nijhoff, Leiden 2012).

ADINOLFI, ADELINA, The Principle of Reasonableness in European Union Law, in Reasonableness and Law 383–404 (Giorgio Bongiovanni, Giovanni Sartor, & Chiara Valentini eds., Springer, Dordrecht et al. 2009).

AKEHURST, MICHAEL, Jurisdiction in International Law, 46 BYIL 145 (1972–1973).

AMERICAN LAW INSTITUTE, Restatement (Second) of Conflict of Laws of the United States (The American Law Institute, Philadelphia 1971).

AMERICAN LAW INSTITUTE, Restatement (Third) of the Foreign Relations Law of the United States (The American Law Institute, Philadelphia 1987).

Protecting Animals Within and Across Borders. Charlotte E. Blattner.

American Law Institute, Restatement (Fourth) of the Foreign Relations Law of the United States (The American Law Institute, Philadelphia 2018).

Anders, Dieter, Die Kollision von Strafgewalten in der Rechtspraxis, in Conflicts of Jurisdiction in Cross-Border Crime Situations 109–121 (Arndt Sinn ed., Universitätsverlag Osnabrück, Göttingen 2012).

Antunes, José Engrácia, The Liability of Polycorporate Enterprises, 13 Conn. J. Int'l L. 197 (1999).

Appleby, Michael C., Cussen, Victoria, Garcés, Leah, Lambert, Lesley A., & Turner, Jacky, Long Distance Transport and Welfare of Farm Animals (CABI, Oxfordshire, Cambridge 2008).

Archibald, Catherine Jean, Forbidden by the WTO? Discrimination Against a Product When Its Creation Causes Harm to the Environment or Animal Welfare, 48 Nat. Res. J. 15 (2008).

Argenti, Paul A., Corporate Social Responsibility (SAGE, Los Angeles 2016).

Arthurs, Harry W., Extraterritoriality by Other Means: How Labor Law Sneaks Across Borders, Conquers Minds, and Controls Workplaces Abroad, 21 Stan. L. & Pol. Rev. 527 (2010).

Arthurs, Harry, Reinventing Labor Law for the Global Economy: The Benjamin Aaron Lecture, 22 Berkeley J. Emp. & Lab. L. 271 (2001).

Augenhofer, Susanne, Rechtsvergleichung, in Grundlagen des Rechts 193–216 (Julian Krüper ed., Nomos, Baden-Baden, 2d ed. 2013).

Augenstein, Daniel, Study of the Legal Framework on Human Rights and the Environment Applicable to European Enterprises Operating Outside the European Union, Prepared by the University of Edinburgh for the European Commission (University of Edinburgh, Edinburgh 2010).

Baldwin, Robert, Regulation: After Command and Control, in The Human Face of Law 64–84 (Keith Hawkins ed., OUP, Oxford 1997).

Baldwin, Robert, Cave, Martin, & Lodge, Martin, Understanding Regulation: Theory, Strategy, and Practice (OUP, New York, 2d ed. 2013).

Bantekas, Ilias, Criminal Jurisdiction of States under International Law, in Max Planck Encyclopedia of Public International Law (Rüdiger Wolfrum ed., OUP, Oxford, online ed. 2011).

Bartels, Lorand, A Model Human Rights Clause for the EU's International Trade Agreements (German Institute for Human Rights, Berlin 2014).

Bartels, Lorand, Article XX of GATT and the Problem of Extraterritorial Jurisdiction: The Case of Trade Measures for the Protection of Human Rights, 36 J. World Trade 353 (2002).

Bassiouni, Cherif, Crimes Against Humanity: The Need for a Specialized Convention, 31 Colum. J. Transnat'l L. 457 (1994).

Behrens, Peter, Der Durchgriff über die Grenze, 46 RabelsZ 308 (1982).

Bekoff, Marjorie, Institutional Animal Care and Use Committees: Nonaffiliated Members, in Encyclopedia of Animal Rights and Animal Welfare 338 (Marc Bekoff & Carron A. Meaney eds., ABC-CLIO, Santa Barbara 2010).

Bendor, Ariel L. & Dancig-Rosenberg, Hadar, Animals Rights in the Shadow of the Constitution, 24 Animal L. 99 (2018).

Bentham, Jeremy, An Introduction to the Principles of Morals and Legislation (Clarendon, London 1781).

Bernstein, Steven & Hannah, Erin, Non-State Global Standard Setting and the WTO: Legitimacy and the Need for Regulatory Space, 11 J. Int'l Econ. Law. 575 (2008).

Bertele, Joachim, Souveränität und Verfahrensrecht: Eine Untersuchung der aus dem Völkerrecht ableitbaren Grenzen staatlicher extraterritorialer Jurisdiktion im Verfahrensrecht (Mohr Siebeck, Tübingen 1998).

Besson, Samantha, Sovereignty, in Max Planck Encyclopedia of Public International Law (Rüdiger Wolfrum ed., OUP, Oxford, online ed. 2011).

Bevan, Stephen, Isles, Nick, Emery, Peter, & Hoskins, Tony, Achieving High Performance: CSR at the Heart of Business (The Work Foundation, London 2004).

Beyerlin, Ulrich & Holzer, Vanessa, Conservation of Natural Resources, in Max Planck Encyclopedia of Public International Law (Rüdiger Wolfrum ed., OUP, Oxford, online ed. 2013).

Bhala, Raj, Gantz, David A., Keating, Shannon B., & Simões, Bruno Germain, WTO Case Review 2014, 32 Ariz. J. Int'l & Comp. L. 497 (2015).

Bianchi, Andrea, Human Rights and the Magic of *Jus Cogens*, 19 EJIL 491 (2008).

Biermann, Frank, The Rising Tide of Green Unilateralism in World Trade Law: Options for Reconciling the Emerging North-South Conflict, 35 J. World Trade 421 (2001).

Bilchitz, David, Does Transformative Constitutionalism Require the Recognition of Animal Rights?, in Is this Seat Taken? Conversations at the Bar, the Bench and the Academy about the South African Constitution 173–208 (Stu Woolman & David Bilchitz eds., Pretoria University Press, Pretoria 2012).

Blattner, Charlotte E., Animal Labour: Toward a Prohibition of Forced Labour and A Right to Freely Choose One's Work, in Animal Labour: A New Frontier of Interspecies Justice? (Charlotte E. Blattner, Kendra Coulter, & Will Kymlicka eds., OUP, Oxford forthcoming 2019).

Blattner, Charlotte E., Can Extraterritorial Jurisdiction Help Overcome Regulatory Gaps of Animal Law? Insights from Trophy Hunting, 111 AJIL Unbound 419 (2017).

Blattner, Charlotte E., Rethinking the 3Rs: From Whitewashing to Rights, in The Ethics of Animal Experimentation: Working Towards a Paradigm Change 168–193 (Kathrin Herrmann & Kimberley Jayne eds., Brill, Leiden 2019).

Blattner, Charlotte E., Tackling Concentrated Animal Agriculture in the Middle East through Standards of Investment, Export Credits, and Trade, 10(2) Middle East Law and Governance 141 (2018).

Blattner, Charlotte E., The Potential and Potential Limits of International Law in Regulating Animal Matters, 3 Mid-Atlantic J.L. & Pol. 10 (2015).

Blattner, Charlotte E., 3R for Farmed Animals: A Legal Argument for Consistency, 1 Global J. Animal L. 1 (2014).

Blattner, Charlotte E. & Ammann, Odile, Animal Agriculture and Farmer Rights in Light of International Human Rights Law (forthcoming 2019).

Blattner, Charlotte E., Coulter, Kendra, & Kymlicka, Will, Animal Labour: A New Frontier of Interspecies Justice? (OUP, Oxford forthcoming 2019).

Blumberg, Phillip, Accountability of Multinational Corporations: The Barriers Presented by Concepts of Corporate Juridical Entity, 24 Hastings Int'l & Comp. L. Rev. 297 (2001).

BLUMBERG, PHILLIP, The Multinational Challenge to Corporation Law: The Search for a New Corporate Personality (OUP, New York 1993).

BOLLIGER, GIERI, Europäisches Tierschutzrecht: Tierschutzbestimmungen des Europarats und der Europäischen Union (mit einer ergänzenden Darstellung des schweizerischen Rechts) (Schriften zum Europarecht, Schulthess, Zürich, Bern 2000).

BOLLIGER, GIERI, Tierquälerei, in Lexikon der Mensch-Tier Beziehungen 357–360 (Arianna Ferrari & Klaus Petrus eds., Transcript, Bielefeld 2015).

BOLLIGER, GIERI, RICHNER, MICHELLE, & RÜTTIMANN, ANDREAS, Schweizer Tierschutzstrafrecht in Theorie und Praxis (Schulthess, Zürich, Basel, Genf 2011).

BOLLIGER, GIERI & RÜTTIMANN, ANDREAS, Rechtlicher Schutz der Tierwürde: Status quo und Zukunftsperspektiven, in Würde der Kreatur: Ethische und rechtliche Beiträge zu einem umstrittenen Konzept 65–92 (Christoph Ammann, Birgit Chistensen, Lorenz Engi, & Margot Michel eds., Schulthess, Zürich, Basel, Genf 2015).

BOSCH, ULRICH, Extraterritorial Rules on Banking and Securities, in Extraterritorial Jurisdiction in Theory and Practice 200–212 (Karl M. Meessen ed., Kluwer Law International, London 1996).

BOUSFIELD, BARRY & BROWN, RICHARD, What Is Animal Welfare?, 1 Animal Welfare 1 (2010).

BOWETT, DEREK W., Jurisdiction: Changing Patterns of Authority over Activities and Resources, 53 BYIL 1 (1982).

BOWLES, DAVID, PASKIN, ROBERT, GUTIÉRREZ, MARIO, & KASTERINE, ALEXANDER, Animal Welfare and Developing Countries: Opportunities for Trade in High-Welfare Products from Developing Countries, 24 Rev. Sci. Tech. Off. Int. Epiz. 783 (2005).

BOWMAN, MICHAEL, DAVIES, PETER, & REDGWELL, CATHERINE, Lyster's International Wildlife Law (CUP, Cambridge, 2d ed. 2010).

BRATTON, WILLIAM W., MCCAHERY, JOSEPH, PICCIOTTO, SOL, & SCOTT, COLIN, Regulatory Competition and Institutional Evolution, in International Regulatory Competition and Coordination 1–55 (William W. Bratton, Joseph McCahery, Sol Picciotto, & Colin Scott eds., Clarendon Press, Oxford 1996).

BREE, AXEL, Harmonization of the Dispute Settlement Mechanisms of the Multilateral Environmental Agreements of the World Trade Agreements (Berichte des Umweltbundesamtes, Band 01/03, Berlin 2003).

BRELS, SABINE, Animal Welfare Protection: A Universal Concern to Properly Address in International Law, J. Animal Welfare L. 34 (2012).

BRILMAYER, LEA, The New Extraterritoriality: *Morrison v. National Australia Bank*, Legislative Supremacy, and the Presumption Against Extraterritorial Application of American Law, 40 Sw. L. Rev. 655 (2011).

BRODOWSKI, DOMINIK, ESPINOZA DE LOS MONTEORS DE LA PARRA, MANUEL, & TIEDEMANN, KLAUS, Regulating Corporate Criminal Liability: An Introduction, in Regulating Corporate Criminal Liability 1–11 (Dominik Brodowski, Manuel Espinoza de los Monteors de la Parra, Klaus Tiedemann, & Joachim Vogel eds., Springer, Cham et al. 2014).

BROOM, DAVID, International Animal Welfare Perspectives, Including Whaling and Inhumane Seal Killing as a W.T.O. Public Morality Issue, in Animal Law and Welfare: International Perspectives 45–62 (Deborah Cao & Steven White eds., Springer, Cham et al. 2016).

BROWNLIE, IAN, Principles of Public International Law (OUP, Oxford, 7th ed. 2008).

Bucchieri, Rebecca L., Bridging the Gap: The Connection between Violence Against Animals and Violence Against Humans, 11 J. Animal & Nat. Res. L. 115 (2015).

Burnett, Susan E., U.S. Judicial Imperialism post *Empagran v. F. Hoffmann-Laroche*? Conflicts of Jurisdiction and International Law in Extraterritorial Antitrust, 18 Emory Int'l L. Rev. 555 (2004).

Butler, A. Hays, The Growing Support for Universal Jurisdiction in National Legislation, in Universal Jurisdiction: National Courts and the Prosecution of Serious Crimes under International Law 67–76 (Stephen Macedo ed., University of Pennsylvania Press, Philadelphia 2004).

Buxbaum, Hannah L., Conflict of Economic Laws: From Sovereignty to Substance, 42 Va. J. Int'l L. 931 (2002).

Buxbaum, Hannah L., Territory, Territoriality and the Resolution of Jurisdictional Conflict, 57 AJCL 631 (2009).

Buxbaum, Hannah L., The Viability of Enterprise Jurisdiction: A Case Study of the Big Four Accounting Firms, 48 U.C. Davis L. Rev. 1769 (2015).

Calver, Michael C., Grayson, Jacky, Lilith, Maggie, & Dickman, Christopher R., Applying the Precautionary Principle to the Issue of Impacts by Pet Cats on Urban Wildlife, 144(6) Bio. Cons. 1895 (2011).

Cameron, Iain, International Criminal Jurisdiction, Protective Principle, in Max Planck Encyclopedia of Public International Law (Rüdiger Wolfrum ed., OUP, Oxford, online ed. 2007).

Cameron, Iain, The Protective Principle of International Criminal Jurisdiction (Ashgate, Aldershot 1994).

Cane, Peter, Responsibility in Law and Morality (Hart, Oxford, Portland 2002).

Caney, Simon, Justice Beyond Borders: A Global Political Theory (OUP, Oxford 2005).

Carbone, Sergio M. & Schiano di Pepe, Lorenzo, Fundamental Rights and Duties of States, in Max Planck Encyclopedia of Public International Law (Rüdiger Wolfrum ed., OUP, Oxford, online ed. 2009).

Carpanelli, Elena, General Principles of International Law: Struggling with a Slippery Concept, in General Principles of Law: The Role of the Judiciary 125–144 (Laura Pineschi ed., Springer, Cham et al. 2015).

Carpenter, Angus I., Rowcliffe, J. Marcus, & Watkinson, Andrew R., The Dynamics of Global Trade in Chameleons, 120 Biological Conservation 291 (2004).

Carruthers, Bruce G. & Lamoreaux, Naomi R., Regulatory Races: The Effects of Jurisdictional Competition on Regulatory Standards, Tobin Project Working Paper, 1–88 (Cambridge 2009).

Casal, Paula, Is Multiculturalism Bad For Animals, 1(1) J. Pol. Phil. 1 (2003).

Cassese, Antonio, International Law (OUP, Oxford, 2d ed. 2005).

Cassese, Antonio, Realizing Utopia: The Future of International Law (OUP, Oxford 2012).

Cassuto, David N., Bred Meat: The Cultural Foundation of Factory Farm, 70 L. & Contemp. Probs. 59 (2007).

Charnovitz, Steve, Green Roots, Bad Pruning: GATT Rules and Their Application to Environmental Trade Measures, 7 Tulane Envtl. L.J. 299 (1994).

Charnovitz, Steve, The Law of Environmental "PPMs" in the WTO: Debunking the Myth of Illegality, 27 Yale J. Int'l L. 59 (2002).

Charnovitz, Steve, The Moral Exception in Trade Policy, 38 Va. J. Int'l L. 689 (1998).
Chaudhri, Radhika, Animal Welfare and the WTO: The Legality and Implications of Live Export Restrictions under International Trade Law, 42 Fed. L. Rev. 279 (2014).
Chehtman, Alejandro, The Philosophical Foundations of Extraterritorial Punishment (OUP, Oxford 2010).
Chen, Johannes M., The Right to Nationality as a Human Right, 12 HRLJ 1 (1991).
Chen, Yifeng, ILO, Extraterritoriality and Labor Protection in Republican Shanghai, in Fundamental Labor Rights in China: Legal Implementation and Cultural Logic 83–116 (Ulla Liukkunen & Yifeng Chen eds., Springer, Cham et al. 2016).
Cheng, Thomas K., The Corporate Veil Doctrine Revisited: A Comparative Study of the English and the U.S. Corporate Veil Doctrines, 34 B.C. Int'l & Comp. L. Rev. 328 (2011).
Childress, James F., Moral Considerations: Bases and Limits of Public Health Interventions, in Essentials of Public Health Ethics 21–44 (Ruth Gaare Bernheim, James F. Childress, Richard J. Bonnie, & Alan L. Melnick eds., Jones & Bartlett Learning, Burlington 2015).
Choi, Stephen J. & Guzman, Andrew T., Portable Reciprocity: Rethinking the International Reach of Securities Regulation, 71 S. Cal. L. Rev. 903 (1997).
Clapham, Andrew, The Question of Jurisdiction under International Criminal Law over Legal Persons: Lessons from the Rome Conference on an International Criminal Court, in Liability of Multinational Corporations under International Law 139–196 (Menno T. Kamminga & Saman Zia-Zarifi eds., Kluwer Law International, The Hague, London, Boston 2000).
Cleveland, Sarah H., Human Rights Sanctions and the WTO, in Environment, Human Rights and International Trade 199–262 (Francesco Francioni ed., Hart, Oxford, Portland 2001).
Cochrane, Alasdair, Animal Rights without Liberation (Columbia University Press, New York 2012).
Cochrane, Alasdair, Labour Rights for Animals, in The Political Turn in Animal Ethics 15–32 (Robert Garner & Siobhan O'Sullivan eds., Rowman and Littlefield, London 2016).
Cochrane, Alasdair, Sentientist Politics: A Theory of Global Inter-Species Justice (OUP, Oxford 2018).
Coggins, George C. & Head, John W., Beyond *Defenders*: Future Problems of Extraterritoriality and Superterritoriality for the Endangered Species Act, 43 Wash. U. J. Urb. & Contemp. L. 59 (1993).
Cohen, Jean L., Globalization and Sovereignty: Rethinking Legality, Legitimacy, and Constitutionalism (CUP, Cambridge 2012).
Cohen, Mathilde, Regulating Milk: Women and Cows in France and the United States, 65 AJCL 469 (2017).
Cohen, Morris R., Property and Sovereignty, 13 Cornell L.Q. 8 (1927).
Cojocaru, Mara-Daria & van Gall, Philipp, Beyond Plausibility Checks: A Case for Moral Doubt in Review Processes of Animal Experimentation, in Animal Experimentation: Working Towards a Paradigm Change 289–304 (Kathrin Herrmann & Kimberley Jayne eds., Brill, Leiden 2019).
Conrad, Christiane R., Processes and Production Methods (PPMs) in WTO Law: Interfacing Trade and Social Goals (CUP, Cambridge 2011).
Conway, Gerard, *Ne Bis in Idem* in International Law, 3 Int'l Crim. L. Rev. 217 (2003).

Cook, Kate & Bowles, David, Growing Pains: The Developing Relationship of Animal Welfare Standards and the World Trade Rules, 19 Rev. Eur. Comm. & Int'l Envtl. L. 227 (2010).

Coomans, Fons & Künnemann, Rolf, Cases and Concepts on Extraterritorial Obligations in the Area of Economic, Social and Cultural Rights (Intersentia, Cambridge 2012).

Cordeiro-Rodrigues, Luis & Mitchell, Les eds., Multiculturalism, Race and Animals: Contemporary Moral and Political Debates (Basingstoke, Palgrave Macmillan 2017).

Corten, Olivier, Reasonableness in International Law, in Max Planck Encyclopedia of Public International Law (Rüdiger Wolfrum ed., OUP, Oxford, online ed. 2013).

Coughlan, Stephen, Currie, Robert J., Kindred, Hugh M., & Scassa, Teresa, Global Reach, Local Grasp: Constructing Extraterritorial Jurisdiction in the Age of Globalization, 6 Can. J.L. & Tech. 29 (2007).

Coulter, Kendra, Animals, Work, and the Promise of Interspecies Solidarity (Palgrave MacMillan, Basingstoke 2016).

Cornish, Amelia, Raubenheimer, David, & McGreevy, Paul, What We Know about the Public's Level of Concern for Farm Animal Welfare in Food Production in Developed Countries, 6(11) Animals 74 (2016).

Cover, Robert, The Uses of Jurisdictional Redundancy: Interest, Ideology, and Innovation, 22 Wm. & Mary L. Rev. 639 (1981).

Cowie, Helen, Exhibiting Animals: Zoos, Menageries and Circuses, in The Routledge Companion to Animal-Human History 298–321 (Hilda Kean & Philip Howell eds., Routledge, Oxon & New York 2018).

Craig, Katrina J., Beefing up the Standard: The Ramifications of Australia's Regulation of Live Export and Suggestions for Reform, 11 Macquarie L.J. 51 (2013).

Crawford, Emily, Proportionality, in Max Planck Encyclopedia of Public International Law (Rüdiger Wolfrum ed., OUP, Oxford, online ed. 2011).

Crawford, James, Brownlie's Principles of Public International Law (OUP, Oxford, 8th ed. 2012).

Crawford, James, Sovereignty as a Legal Value in The Cambridge Companion to International Law 117–134 (James Crawford & Martti Koskenniemi eds., CUP, Cambridge 2012).

Cresswell, Julia, The Oxford Dictionary of Word Origins (OUP, New York, 2d ed. 2010).

Cunniff, Peggy & Kramer, Marcia, Developments in Animal Law, in The Global Guide to Animal Protection 230–231 (Andrew Linzey ed., University of Illinois Press, Urbana, Chicago, Springfield 2013).

Cupp, Richard L., Human Responsibility, Not Legal Personhood, for Animals, 16 J. Federalist Soc. 34 (2015).

Curnutt, Jordan, Animals and the Law: Contemporary Legal Issues (ABC-CLIO, Santa Barbara 2001).

Czajkowski, Claire, Dog Meat Trade in South Korea: A Report on the Current State of the Trade and Efforts to Eliminate It, 21 Animal L. 29 (2015).

D'Agnone, Giulia, Determining the Nationality of Companies in ICSID Arbitration, in The Changing Role of Nationality in International Law 153–168 (Alessandra Annoni & Serena Forlati eds., Routledge, Oxon, New York 2013).

Da Costa, Karen, The Extraterritorial Application of Selected Human Rights Treaties (Martinus Nijhoff, Leiden 2013).

Dalziell, Jacqueline & Wadiwel, Dinesh J., Live Exports, Animal Advocacy, Race and "Animal Nationalism," in Meat Culture 73–89 (Annie Potts ed., Brill, Leiden, Boston 2017).

Daniels, Marc, Grundlagen und Begriff des Sachenrechts (Grin, Norderstedt 2015).

Darwin, Charles, On the Origin of Species by Means of Natural Selection, or the Preservation of Favoured Races in the Struggles for Like (John Murray, London 1859).

Darwin, Charles, The Descent of Man, and Selection in Relation to Sex (John Murray, London 1871).

Darwin, Charles, The Expression of the Emotions in Man and Animals (Republication University of Chicago Press, Chicago 1872).

Dawkins, Marian S., Evolution and Animal Welfare, 73(3) Q. Rev. Biol. 305 (1998).

Dawkins, Marian S., Using Behavior to Assess Animal Welfare, 13 Animal Welfare 3 (2004).

Day Wallace, Cynthia, The Multinational Enterprise and Legal Control: Host State Sovereignty in an Era of Economic Globalization (Kluwer Law International, The Hague 2002).

De Brouwer, Anne-Marie, GATT Article XX's Environmental Exceptions Explored: Is There Room for National Policies? Balancing Rights and Obligations of WTO Members under the WTO Regime, in The WTO and Concerns Regarding Animals and Nature 9–59 (Anton Vedder ed., Wolf Legal, Nijmengen 2003).

De Haan, Cornelis, van Veen, Tjaar, Shillhorn, Brandenburg, Brian, Gauthier, Jérôme, Le Gall, François, Mearns, Robin, & Siméon, Michel, Livestock Development, Implications for Rural Poverty, the Environment, and Global Food Security (The World Bank, Washington 2001).

De Mestral, Armand L.C., The Extraterritorial Extension of Laws: How Much Has Changed?, 31 Ariz. J. Int'l & Comp. L. 43 (2014).

De Mestral, Armand L.C. & Gruchalla-Wesierski, Tad, Extraterritorial Application of Export Control Legislation (Martinus Nijhoff, Dordrecht, Boston 1990).

De Schutter, Olivier, Extraterritorial Jurisdiction as a Tool for Improving the Human Rights Accountability of Transnational Corporations (Business and Human Rights Resource Center, London 2006).

De Vattel, Emel, Le Droits des gens, ou Principes de la Loi Naturelle (Auillaud, Paris 1830).

Deckha, Maneesha, Animal Justice, Cultural Justice: A Posthumanist Response to Cultural Rights in Animals, 2 J. Animal L. & Ethics 189–229 (2007).

Deckha, Maneesha, Critical Animal Studies and the Property Debate in Animal Law, in Animal Subjects 2.0 45–80 (Jodey Castricano & Lauren Corman eds., Wilfried Laurier University Press, Waterloo 2016).

Deckha, Maneesha, Is Multiculturalism Good for Animals?, in Multiculturalism, Race and Animals: Contemporary Moral and Political Debates 61–93 (Luis Cordeiro-Rodrigues & Les Mitchell eds., Palgrave Macmillan, Basingstoke 2017).

Dederer, Hans-Georg, "Responsibility to Protect" and "Functional Sovereignty," in Responsibility to Protect (R2P): A New Paradigm of International Law? 156–183 (Peter Hilpold ed., Brill, Leiden 2015).

DELGADO, CHRISTOPHER, ROSEGRANT, MARK, STEINFELD, HENNING, EHUI, SIMEON, & COURBOIS, CLAUDE, Livestock to 2020, The Next Food Revolution (International Food Policy Research Institute (IFPRI), Washington D.C. 1999).

DELLA CANANEA, GIACINTO, Reasonableness in Administrative Law, in Reasonableness and Law 295–311 (Giorgio Bongiovanni, Giovanni Sartor, & Chiara Valentini eds., Springer, Dordrecht et al. 2009).

DEMARET, PAUL, Environmental Policy and Commercial Policy: The Emergence of Trade-Related Environmental Measures (TREMS) in the External Relations of the European Community, in The European Community's Commercial Policy after 1992: The Legal Dimension 305–386 (Marc Maresceau ed., Martinus Nijhoff, Leiden 1993).

DIEBOLD, NICOLAS F., Non-Discrimination in International Trade in Services: "Likeness" in WTO/GATS (CUP, Cambridge 2010).

DIEM, ANDREAS, Freihandel und Umweltschutz in GATT und WTO (Dissertation University of Tübingen, Baden-Baden 1996).

DINGLE, HUGH, Migration: The Biology of Life on the Move (OUP, Oxford, 2d ed. 2014).

DISKANT, EDWARD B., Comparative Corporate Criminal Liability: Exploring the Uniquely American Doctrine through Comparative Criminal Procedure, 118 Yale L.J. 126 (2008).

DIXON, MARTIN, Textbook on International Law (OUP, Oxford, 7th ed. 2013).

DOLZER, RUDOLF & SCHREUER, CHRISTOPH, Principles of International Investment Law (OUP, Oxford, 2d ed. 2012).

DONALDSON, SUE & KYMLICKA, WILL, Rights, in Critical Terms for Animal Studies 320–336 (Lori Gruen ed., University of Chicago Press, Chicago, London 2018).

DONALDSON, SUE & KYMLICKA, WILL, Zoopolis: A Political Theory of Animal Rights (OUP, Oxford, New York 2011).

DÖRR, OLIVER, Nationality, in Max Planck Encyclopedia of Public International Law (Rüdiger Wolfrum ed., OUP, Oxford, online ed. 2006).

DÖRR, OLIVER, Prohibition of Use of Force, in Max Planck Encyclopedia of Public International Law (Rüdiger Wolfrum ed., OUP, Oxford, online ed. 2015).

DORSETT, SHAUNNAGH & MCVEIGH, SHAUN, Jurisdiction (Routledge, Oxon, New York 2012).

DU, MICHAEL MING, Domestic Regulatory Autonomy under the TBT Agreement: From Non-discrimination to Harmonization, 6 Chinese J. Int'l L. 269 (2007).

DU, MING, What Is a "Technical Regulation" in the TBT Agreement? 6 Eur. J. Risk Reg. 396 (2015).

DUNCAN, CHRISTOPHER J., The 1998 Foreign Corrupt Practices Act Amendments: Moral Empiricism or Moral Imperialism, 1 APLPJ I (2000).

DUNCAN, IAN J.H., The Changing Concept of Animal Sentience, 100 Appl. Animal Behav. Sci. 11 (2006).

EATON, DEREK J.F., BOURGEOIS, J., & ACHTERBOSCH, THOM J., Product Differentiation under the WTO, An Analysis of Labelling and Tariff or Tax Measures Concerning Farm Animal Welfare (Agricultural Economics Research Institute (LEI), The Hague 2005).

EDMUNDSON, WILLIAM A., Do Animals Need Rights?, 22 J. Pol. Phil. 1 (2014).

EIDENMÜLLER, HORST, The Transnational Law Market, Regulatory Competition, and Transnational Corporations, 18 Ind. J. Global Legal Stud. 707 (2011).

EINARSEN, TERJE, The Concept of Universal Crimes in International Law (Torkel Opsahl Academic EPublisher, Oslo 2012).

EISEN, JESSICA, Animals in the Constitutional State, 15(4) Int'l J. Const. L. 909 (2017).

EISEN, JESSICA, Beyond Rights and Welfare: Democracy, Dialogue, and the Animal Welfare Act, 51(3) U. Mich. J.L. Reform 469 (2018).

EISEN, JESSICA & STILT, KRISTEN, Protection and Status of Animals, in Max Planck Institute for Comparative Constitutional Law (Rainer Grote, Frauke Lachenmann, & Rüdiger Wolfrum, OUP, Oxford, online ed. 2017).

EISNITZ, GAIL, Slaughterhouse: The Shocking Greed, Neglect, and Inhumane Treatment inside the U.S. Meat Industry (Amherst Prometheus Books, New York 1997).

EL OUALI, ABDELHAMID, Territorial Integrity in a Globalizing World, International Law and States' Quest for Survival (Springer, Berlin et al. 2012).

ENGLE, ERIC, The History of the General Principle of Proportionality: An Overview, 10 Dartmouth L.J. 1 (2012).

EPSTEIN, RICHARD A., Animals as Objects, or Subjects, of Rights, in Animal Rights: Current Debates and New Directions 143–161 (Cass R. Sunstein & Martha C. Nussbaum eds., OUP, Oxford 2004).

EUROPEAN FOOD SAFETY AUTHORITY (EFSA), Animal Welfare Aspects of the Killing and Skinning of Seals, Scientific Opinion of the Panel on Animal Health and Welfare (AHAW), adopted Dec. 6, 2007, 610, EFSA J. 1 (2007).

EVANS, ERIN, Constitutional Inclusion of Animal Rights in Germany and Switzerland: How Did Animal Protection Become an Issue of National Importance?, 18 Soc. & Ani. 231 (2010).

FALLER, RICO, Staatsziel "Tierschutz": Vom parlamentarischen Gesetzgebungsstaat zum verfassungsgerichtlichen Jurisdiktionsstaat? (Duncker & Humblot, Berlin 2005).

FASEL, RAFFAEL, BLATTNER, CHARLOTTE, MANNINO, ADRIANO, & BAUMANN, TOBIAS, Grundrechte für Primaten, Positionspapier (Sentience Politics, Apr. 2016), *available at* https://sentience-politics.org/wp-content/uploads/2016/06/Grundrechte-fuer-Primaten.pdf (last visited Jan. 10, 2019).

FAVRE, DAVID, An International Treaty for Animal Welfare, in Animal Law and Welfare: International Perspectives 87–108 (Deborah Cao & Steven White eds., Springer, Cham et al. 2016).

FAVRE, DAVID, Living Property: A New Status for Animals within the Legal System, 93 Marq. L. Rev. 1021 (2010).

FAVRE, DAVID & TSANG, VIVIEN, The Development of Anti-Cruelty Laws during the 1800's, 1 Det. C. L. Rev. 1 (1993).

FEDDERSEN, CHRISTOPH T., Der *ordre public* in der WTO, Auslegung und Bedeutung des Art. XX lit. a) GATT im Rahmen der WTO-Streitbeilegung (Duncker & Humblot, Berlin 2002).

FEDDERSEN, CHRISTOPH T., Focusing on Substantive Law in International Economic Relations: The Public Morals of GATT's Article XX(a) and "Conventional" Rules of Interpretation, 7 Minn. J. Global Trade 75 (1998).

FELDMAN, MARK B., The Restructuring of National Security Controls under the 1985 Amendments to the Export Administration Act: Multilateral Diplomacy and the Extraterritorial Application of United States Law, 21 Stan. J. Int'l L. 235 (1985).

Ferrari, Arianna, Eigenwert, in Lexikon der Mensch-Tier Beziehungen 89–92 (Arianna Ferrari & Klaus Petrus eds., Transcript, Bielefeld 2015).

Ferrari, Arianna & Gerritsen, Vanessa, Güterabwägung, in Lexikon der Mensch-Tier Beziehungen 139–143 (Arianna Ferrari & Klaus Petrus eds., Transcript, Bielefeld 2015).

Fikuart, Karl, von Holleben, Karen, & Kuhn, Gerhard, Hygiene der Tiertransporte (G. Fischer, Jena, Stuttgart 1995).

Fitzgerald, Peter L., International Issues in Animal Law: The Impact of International Environmental and Economic Law upon Animal Interests and Advocacy (Carolina Academic Press, Durham 2012).

Fitzgerald, Peter L., "Morality" May Not Be Enough to Justify the EU Seals Products Ban: Animal Welfare Meets International Trade Law, 14 J. Int'l Wildlife L. & Pol. 85 (2011).

Fox, Eleanor M., Can We Solve the Antitrust Problems of Globalization by Extraterritoriality and Cooperation? Sufficiency and Legitimacy, 48 Antitrust Bull. 355 (2003).

Fox, Eleanor M., GE/Honeywell: The US Merger That Europe Stopped: A Story of Politics of Convergence, in Anti-trust Stories 331–360 (Eleanor M. Fox & Daniel A. Crane eds., Foundation Press, New York 2007).

Fox, Hazel, Jurisdiction and Immunity, in Fifty Years of the International Court of Justice: Essays in Honour of Sir Robert Jennings 210–236 (Vaughan Lowe & Malgosia Fitzmaurice eds., CUP, Cambridge 1996).

Fox, Michael Allen, Anthropocentrism, in Encyclopedia of Animal Rights and Animal Welfare 66–68 (Marc Bekoff & Carron A. Meaney eds., ABC-CLIO, Santa Barbara 2010).

Francione, Gary L., Abolitionismus, in Lexikon der Mensch-Tier-Beziehung 13–17 (Arianna Ferrari & Klaus Petrus eds., Transcript, Bielefeld 2015).

Francione, Gary L., Animals, Property, and the Law (Temple University Press, Philadelphia 1995 (Reprint 2007)).

Franzina, Pietro, The Evolving Role of Nationality in Private International Law, in The Changing Role of Nationality in International Law 193–209 (Alessandra Annoni & Serena Forlati eds., Routledge, Oxon, New York 2013).

Frasch, Pamela D., Hessler, Katherine M., & Waisman, Sonia S., Animal Law in a Nutshell (Thomson Reuters, St. Paul, 2d ed. 2016).

Fraser, David, Animal Ethics and Animal Welfare Science: Bridging Two Cultures, 65 Appl. Animal Behav. Sci. 171 (1999).

Friedrich, Jürgen, Codes of Conduct, in Max Planck Encyclopedia of Public International Law (Rüdiger Wolfrum ed., OUP, Oxford, online ed. 2010).

Frowein, Jochen A., Ius Cogens, in Max Planck Encyclopedia of Public International Law (Rüdiger Wolfrum ed., OUP, Oxford, online ed. 2013).

Gabor, Barbara, Regulatory Competition in the Internal Market: Comparing Models of Corporate Law, Securities Law and Competition Law (Edward Elgar, Cheltenham 2013).

García-Salmones Rovira, Mónica, The Project of Positivism in International Law (OUP, Oxford 2013).

Gardiner, Richard K., International Law (Pearson Education Limited, London 2003).

Garner, Robert & O'Sullivan, Siobhan, Introduction, in The Political Turn in Animal Ethics 1–14 (Robert Garner & Siobhan O'Sullivan eds., Rowman and Littlefield, London 2016).

Garriga, Elisabet & Melé, Domènec, Corporate Social Responsibility Theories: Mapping the Territory, 53 J. Bus. Ethics 51 (2004).

Garry, Franklyn B., Animal Well-Being in the U.S. Dairy Industry, in The Well-Being of Farm Animals: Challenges and Solutions 207–240 (G. John Benson & Bernard E. Rollin eds., Blackwell Publishing, Oxford 2004).

Gatto, Alexandra, Multinational Enterprises and Human Rights: Obligations under EU Law and International Law (Edward Elgar, Cheltenham 2011).

Gehrig, Tanja, Struktur und Instrumente des Tierschutzrechts (Schulthess, Zürich 1999).

Geisser, Greger, Ausservertragliche Haftung privat tätiger Unternehmen für "Menschenrechtsverletzungen" bei internationalen Sachverhalten (Schulthess, Zürich, Basel, Genf 2013).

Gerber, David J., Global Competition: Law, Markets, and Globalization (OUP, Oxford, New York 2010).

Gerick, Nicole, Recht, Mensch und Tier (Nomos, Baden-Baden 2005).

Gerritsen, Vanessa, Evaluation Process for Animal Experiment Applications in Switzerland, 4(1) ALTEX Proceedings 37 (2015).

Gerrodette, Tim, The Tuna-Dolphin Issue, in Encyclopedia of Marine Mammals 1192–1195 (William F. Perrin, Bernd Wursig, & J.G.M. Thewissen eds., Academic Press, San Diego, 2d ed. 2009).

Gibney, Mark, On Terminology: Extraterritorial Obligations, in Global Justice, State Duties: The Extraterritorial Scope of Economic, Social and Cultural Rights in International Law 32–47 (Malcolm Langford, Wouter Vandenhole, Martin Scheinin, & Willem van Genugten eds., CUP, Cambridge 2013).

Gibney, Mark & Skogly, Sigrun, Introduction, in Universal Human Rights and Extraterritorial Obligations 1–11 (Mark Gibney & Sigrun Skogly eds., University of Pennsylvania Press, Philadelphia 2010).

Glock, Jana, Das deutsche Tierschutzrecht und das Staatsziel "Tierschutz" im Lichte des Völkerrechts und des Europarechts (Nomos, Baden-Baden 2004).

Gobert, James & Punch, Maurice, Rethinking Corporate Crime (LexisNexis Buttersworth, London 2003).

Godt, Christine, The So-Called "Waiver Compromise" of Doha and Hong Kong: About Contested Concepts of the Nature of the International Intellectual Property System, in Intellectual Property, Public Policy, and International Trade 201–228 (Inge Govaere & Hanns Hullrich eds., P.I.E. Peter Lang, Brussels 2007).

Goldner, Colin, Lebenslänglich hinter Gittern: Die Wahrheit über Gorilla, Orang Utan & Co in deutschen Zoos (Alibri Verlag, Aschaffenburg 2014).

Gordon, Suzanne E., Changing Concepts of Sovereignty and Jurisdiction in the Global Economy: Is There a Territorial Connection? (The Canadian Centre for German and European Studies/Le Centre canadien d'études allemandes et européennes (CCGES/CCEAE), Working Paper Series Number 1, 2001).

Gray, Kevin R., Right to Food Principle vis à vis Rules Governing International Trade (British Institute of International and Comparative Law, London 2003).

Grear, Anna, Deconstructing *Anthropos*: A Critical Legal Reflection on "Anthropocentric" Law and Anthropocene "Humanity," 26(3) Law & Critique 225 (2016).

GREGER, MICHAEL, Bird Flu: A Virus of Our Own Hatching (Lantern Books, New York 2006).

GRETHE, HARALD, High Animal Welfare Standards in the EU and International Trade: How to Prevent Potential "Low Animal Welfare Havens"?, 3 Food Pol'y 315 (2006).

GRIFFIN, DONALD, The Question of Animal Awareness (Rockefeller, New York 1976).

GROPP, WALTER, Kollision nationaler Strafgewalten—*nulla prescutio transnationalis sine lege*, in Conflicts of Jurisdiction in Cross-Border Crime Situations 41–63 (Arndt Sinn ed., Universitätsverlag Osnabrück, Göttingen 2012).

GUZMAN, ANDREW T., Is International Antitrust Possible?, 73 N.Y.U. L. Rev. 1501 (1998).

HACKWORTH, GREEN HAYWOOD, Digest of International Law, vol. 2 (U.S. Government Printing Office, Washington D.C. 1940–1944).

HADARI, YITZHAK, The Structure of Private Multinational Enterprise, 71 Mich. L. Rev. 729 (1973).

HAFNER, CHRISTINE & HAVENSTEIN, JULIA, Animal Suffering Is Inherent in Long Distance Transports: Lisbon Treaty Necessitates Ban of Long Distance Transports (Animals' Angels, Frankfurt a.M. 2012).

HANDL, GUNTHER, Extra-territoriality and Transnational Legal Authority, in Beyond Territoriality: Transnational Legal Authority in an Age of Globalization 3–12 (Gunther Handl & Joachim Zekoll eds., Martinus Nijhoff, Leiden 2012).

HARRISON, RUTH, Animal Machines (Vincent Stuart, London 1964).

HARVARD RESEARCH IN INTERNATIONAL LAW, Jurisdiction with Respect to Crime, 29 AJIL 435 (Supp. 1935).

HARVARD RESEARCH IN INTERNATIONAL LAW, The Law of Nationality, 23 AJIL 11 (Supp. 1929).

HATHAWAY, OONA A., LEVITZ, PHILIP, NIELSEN, ELIZABETH, NOWLAN, AILEEN, PERDUE, WILLIAM, PURVIS, CHELSEA, SOLOW, SARA, & SPIEGEL, JULIA, Human Rights Abroad: When Do Human Rights Treaty Obligations Apply Extraterritorially?, 43 Ariz. St. L.J. 389 (2011).

HAYASHI, MIKA N., Objective Territorial Principle or Effects Doctrine? Jurisdiction and Cyberspace, in Le nouve fronitere del diritto internazionale 97–118 (Carlo Focarelli ed., Morlacchi, Perugia 2008).

HEARNE, VICKI, Bandit: Dossier of a Dangerous Dog (Akadine Press, New York, 2d ed. 2002).

HENKE, NICOLE CLAUDIA, Tierschutzstandards im wohlfahrtsökonomischen Kontext: Hühnereiproduktion in der EU und Brasilien (Akademiker, Saarbrücken 2011).

HENKIN, LOUIS, International Law: Politics and Values (Martinus Nijhoff, Dordrecht 1995).

HERLIN-KARNELL, ESTHER & KONSTADINIDES, THEODORE, The Rise and Expressions of Consistency in EU Law: Legal and Strategic Implications of European Integration, in The Cambridge Yearbook of European Legal Studies, vol. 15, 2012–2013 139–168 (Catherine Barnard, Albertina Albors Llorens, Marcus Gehring, & Robert Schütze eds., Hart, Oxford, Portland 2013).

HERTWICH, EDGAR & VAN DER VOET, ESTER, Assessing the Environmental Impacts of Consumption and Production: Priority Products and Materials (UNEP, International Panel for Sustainable Resource Management, Geneva 2010).

HESSLER, KATHY, TISCHLER, JOYCE, HART, PAMELA, & WAISMAN, SONIA, Animal Law: New Perspectives on Teaching Traditional Law (Carolina Academic Press, Durham 2017).

HIGGINS, ROSALYN, Problems and Process, International Law and How We Use It (Clarendon Press, Oxford 1995).

HIMELFARB, ALLISON J., The International Language of Convergence: Reviving Antitrust Dialogue between the United States and the European Union with a Uniform Understanding of "Extraterritoriality," 17 U. Pa. J. Int'l Econ. L. 909 (1996).

HOFSTETTER, KARL, Sachgerechte Haftung für multinationale Konzerne: Zur zivilrechtlichen Verantwortlichkeit von Muttergesellschaften im Kontext internationaler Märkte (Mohr Siebeck, Tübingen 1995).

HOHFELD, WESLEY NEWCOMB, Fundamental Legal Conceptions as Applied in Judicial Reasoning (Yale University Press, Yale 1919).

HOLDO, RICARDO M., HOLT, ROBERT D., SINCLAIR, ANTHONY R.E., GODLEY, BRENDAN J., & THIRGOOD, SIMON, Migration Impacts on Communities and Ecosystems: Empirical Evidence and Theoretical Insights, in Animal Migration: A Synthesis 131–143 (E.J. Milner-Gulland, John M. Fryxell, & Anthony R.E. Sinclair eds., OUP, Oxford, New York 2011).

HONORÉ, A.M., Ownership, in Oxford Essays in Jurisprudence: A Collaborative Work 107–147 (A.G. Guest ed., Oxford University Press, London, New York 1961).

HORTA, OSCAR, Expanding Global Justice: The Case for the International Protection of Animals, 4 Global Pol'y 371 (2013).

HORTA, OSCAR, RUDE, MATTHIAS, & CAFFO, LEONARDO, Speziesismus, in Lexikon der Mensch-Tier Beziehungen 318–323 (Arianna Ferrari & Klaus Petrus eds., Transcript, Bielefeld 2015).

HOWSE, ROBERT, Sovereignty, Lost and Found, in Redefining Sovereignty in International Economic Law 61–75 (Wenhua Shan, Penelope Simons, & Dalvinder Singh eds., Hart, Oxford, Portland 2008).

HOWSE, ROBERT & LANGILLE, JOANNA, Permitting Pluralism: The Seals Products Dispute and Why the WTO Should Accept Trade Restrictions Justified by Noninstrumental Moral Values, 37 Yale J. Int'l L. 367 (2012).

HOWSE, ROBERT & REGAN, DONALD, The Product/Process Distinction: An Illusory Basis for Disciplining "Unilateralism" in Trade Policy, 11 EJIL 249 (2000).

HOWSE, ROBERT, LANGILLE, JOANNA, & SYKES, KATIE, Pluralism in Practice: Moral Legislation and the Law of the WTO after Seal Products, 48 Geo. Wash. Int'l L. Rev. 81 (2015).

HUNER, JAN, The Multilateral Agreement on Investment and the Review of the OECD Guidelines for Multinational Enterprises, in Liability of Multinational Corporations under International Law 197–208 (Menno T. Kamminga & Saman Zia-Zarifi eds., Kluwer Law International, The Hague, London, Boston 2000).

IETTO-GILLIES, GRAZIA, Transnational Corporations and International Production: Concepts, Theories and Effects (Edward Elgar, Cheltenham, 2d ed. 2012).

INAZUMI, MITSUE, Universal Jurisdiction in Modern International Law: Expansion of National Jurisdiction for Prosecuting Serious Crimes under International Law (Intersentia, Antwerp, Oxford, Portland 2005).

INOCENCIO, FLAVIO G.I., Reconceptualizing Sovereignty in the Post-National State: Statehood Attributes in the International Order: The Federal Tradition (Authorhouse, Bloomington 2014).

IRELAND, PADDY, Corporate Social Responsibility (CSR), in The New Oxford Companion to Law (Peter Cane & Joanne Conaghan eds., OUP, Oxford, online ed. 2009).

IRELAND-PIPER, DANIELLE, Prosecutions of Extraterritorial Criminal Conduct and the Abuse of Rights Doctrine, 9 Utrecht L. Rev. 68 (2013).

JACKSON, JOHN H., Sovereignty: Outdated Concept or New Approaches, in Redefining Sovereignty in International Economic Law 3–26 (Wenhua Shan, Penelope Simons, & Dalvinder Singh eds., Hart, Oxford, Portland 2008).

JACOB, MARC, International Investment Agreements and Human Rights, INEF Research Paper Series on Human Rights, Corporate Responsibility and Sustainable Development (Institute for Development and Peace, University of Duisburg, Duisburg 2010).

JEDELHAUSER, RITA, Das Tier unter dem Schutz des Rechts: Die tierethischen Grundlagen eines rechtlichen Schutzmodells für das tierschutzrechtliche Verwaltungshandeln (Helbing Lichtenhahn, Basel 2011).

JEFFERS, AGATHA E., MENGYU, WEI, & SIDNEY, ASKEW, The Switch from US GAAP to IFRS, 7 Proceedings of the Northeast Business & Economics Association 48 (2010).

JENNINGS, ROBERT, General Course of Principles of International Law, 121 RCADI 323 (1967).

JENNINGS, ROBERT & WATTS, ARTHUR EDS., Oppenheim's International Law, vol. I (Longman Group UK Limited, Essex, 9th ed. 1992).

JENNINGS, ROBERT Y., Extraterritorial Jurisdiction and the United States Antitrust Laws, 33 BYIL 146 (1957).

JENNINGS, ROBERT Y., Nullity and Effectiveness in International Law, in Cambridge Essays in International Law: Essays in Honour of Lord McNair 64–87 (Robert Y. Jennings ed., Stevens & Sons, London 1965).

JOHNSTON, ANGUS & POWLES, EDWARD, The Kings of the World and Their Dukes' Dilemma: Globalisation, Jurisdiction and the Rule of Law, in Globalisation and Jurisdiction 13–54 (Piet Jan Slot & Mielle Bulterman eds., Kluwer Law International, Leiden 2004).

JONES, DENA M., Slaughter, in The Global Guide to Animal Protection 172–173 (Andrew Linzey ed., University of Illinois Press, Champaign 2013).

JOSEPH, SARAH, Taming the Leviathans: Multinational Enterprises and Human Rights, 46 Netherlands Int'l L. Rev. 171 (1999).

JOWETT, BENJAMIN, The Complete Works of Aristotle 2, in Politics (Jonathan Barnes ed., Princeton University Press, Princeton 1984).

JOY, MELANIE, Why We Love Dogs, Eat Pigs, and Wear Cows: An Introduction to Carnism (Conari Press, San Francisco 2011).

KAGAN, SHELLY, Kantianism for Consequentialists, in Immanuel Kant, Groundwork for Metaphysics of Morals 111–156 (Allen W. Wood ed., Yale University Press, New Haven, London 2002).

KAHN, SARAH & VARAS, MARIELA, OIE Animal Welfare Standards and the Multilateral Trade Policy Framework (OIE Publishing, Paris 2013).

KAMMERHOFER, JÖRG & D'ASPREMONT, JEAN EDS., International Legal Positivism in a Post-Modern World (CUP, Cambridge 2014).

KAMMINGA, MENNO T., Extraterritoriality, in Max Planck Encyclopedia of Public International Law (Rüdiger Wolfrum ed., OUP, Oxford, online ed. 2012).

KAMMINGA, MENNO T. & ZIA-ZARIFI, SAMAN, Introduction, in Liability of Multinational Corporations under International Law 1–15 (Menno T. Kamminga & Saman Zia-Zarifi eds., Kluwer Law International, The Hague 2000).

KAUFMANN, CHRISTINE, Globalisation and Labour Rights: The Conflict between Core Labour Rights and International Economic Law (Hart, Portland 2007).

KAUFMANN, CHRISTINE, Konzernverantwortungsinitiative: Grenzenlose Verantwortlichkeit?, 1 SZW/RSDA 45 (2016).

KELCH, THOMAS G., Globalization and Animal Law: Comparative Law, International Law and International Trade (Kluwer Law International, Alphen aan den Rijn 2011).

KELCH, THOMAS G., Towards Universal Principles for Global Animal Advocacy, 5 TEL 81 (2016).

KENNEDY, KEVIN C., Resolving International Sanitary and Phytosanitary Disputes in the WTO: Lessons and Future Direction, 55 Food & Drug L.J. 81 (2000).

KERR, JEFFREY S., BERNSTEIN, MARTINA, SCHWOERKE, AMANDA, STRUGAR, MATTHEW D., & GOODMAN, JARED S., A Slave by Any Other Name Is Still a Slave: The Tilikum Case and Application of the Thirteenth Amendment to Nonhuman Animals, 19 Animal L. 221 (2013).

KEYSAR, ELIZABETH, Procedural Integration in Support of Environmental Policy Objectives: Implementing Sustainability, 48 J. Envtl. Plan. & Mgmt. 549 (2005).

KHAN, DANIEL-ERASMUS, Territory and Boundaries, in The Oxford Handbook of the History of International Law 225–249 (Bardo Fassbender & Anne Peters eds., OUP, Oxford 2012).

KIM, CLAIRE JEAN, Dangerous Crossings: Race, Species, and Nature in a Multicultural Age (CUP, Cambridge 2015).

KIM, CLAIRE JEAN, Multiculturalism Goes Imperial: Immigrants, Animals and the Suppression of Moral Dialogue, 4(1) Dubois Rev. 233 (2007).

KINDLEBERGER, CHARLES P., American Business Abroad: Six Lectures on Direct Investment (Yale University Press, New Haven, London 1969).

KING, LEONARD WILLIAM trans., The Code of Hammurabi (CreateSpace Independent Publishing Platform 2014).

KINGSBURY, BENEDICT, Sovereignty and Inequality, 9 EJIL 599 (1998).

KIRBY, DAVID, Animal Factory (St. Martin's Press, New York 2010).

KIRSHNER, JODIE A., Why Is the U.S. Abdicating the Policing of Multinational Corporations to Europe? Extraterritoriality, Sovereignty, and the Alien Tort Statute, 30 Berkeley J. Int'l L. 259 (2012).

KITE, SARAH, The Trade in Primates for Research, in The Global Guide to Animal Protection 106–107 (Andrew Linzey ed., University of Illinois Press, Urbana, Chicago, Springfield 2013).

KLERMAN, DANIEL, Jurisdiction, Choice of Law and Property, in Law and Economics of Possession 266–290 (Yun-chien Chang ed., CUP, Cambridge 2015).

KLEY-STRULLER, ANDREAS, Die Staatszugehörigkeit juristischer Personen, 2 SZIER 163 (1991).

KNIGHT, ANDREW, Tierversuche, in Lexikon der Mensch-Tier Beziehungen 382–383 (Arianna Ferrari & Klaus Petrus eds., Transcript, Bielefeld 2015).

Knox, John H., Diagonal Environmental Rights, in Universal Human Rights and Extraterritorial Obligations 82–103 (Mark Gibney & Sigrun Skogly eds., University of Pennsylvania Press, Philadelphia 2010).

Ko, Aph & Ko, Syl, Aphro-ism: Essays on Pop Culture, Feminism, and Black Veganism from Two Sisters (Lantern Books, Brooklyn 2017).

Koch, Harald, Magnus, Ulrich, & Winkler von Mohrenfels, Peter, IPR und Rechtsvergleichung: Ein Studien- und Übungsbuch zum Internationalen Privat- und Zivilverfahrensrecht und zur Rechtsvergleichung (C.H. Beck, München 2010).

Koene, Paul, Welfare Indicators for Zoo and Wild Animals: Theories and Examples from Practice (Livestock Research and Wageningen Centre for Animal Welfare and Adaptation, Brussels 2013).

Koenig-Archibugi, Mathias, Global Regulation, in The Oxford Handbook of Regulation 407–437 (Robert Baldwin, Martin Cave, & Martin Lodge eds., OUP, New York 2010).

Kogan, Lawrence A., REACH Revisited: A Framework for Evaluating Whether a Non-Tariff Measure Has Matured into an Actionable Non-Tariff Barrier to Trade, 28 Am. U. Int'l L. Rev. 489 (2013).

Kohl, Uta, Jurisdiction and the Internet: Regulatory Competence over Online Activity (CUP, Cambridge 2007).

Kokott, Juliane, Sovereign Equality of States, in Max Planck Encyclopedia of Public International Law (Rüdiger Wolfrum ed., OUP, Oxford, online ed. 2011).

Koskenniemi, Martti, International Legal Theory and Doctrine, in Max Planck Encyclopedia of Public International Law (Rüdiger Wolfrum ed., OUP, Oxford, online ed. 2007).

Koskenniemi, Martti, The Politics of International Law (Hart, Oxford 2011).

Kotchach Bleustein, Irina, Jelleher, Lauren J., & Zeitz-Winston, Danielle, Corporate Criminal Liability, 52 Am. Crim. L. Rev. 851 (2015).

Kotzur, Markus, Article 13 TFEU, in European Union Treaties: A Commentary 225–226 (Rudolf Geiger, Daniel-Erasmus Khan, & Markus Kotzur eds., Verlag C.H. Beck München 2015).

Krag, Anton & Kleveland, Live, Challenges to Animal Protection in Scandinavia, in The Global Guide to Animal Protection 28–29 (Andrew Linzey ed., University of Illinois Press, Champaign 2013).

Krebs, Angelica, Ethics of Nature, Perspectives in Analytical Philosophy (de Gruyter, Berlin, New York 1999).

Krepper, Peter, Zur Würde der Kreatur in Gentechnik und Recht: Thesen zum gentechnischen Umgang mit Tieren in der Schweiz unter Berücksichtigung des internationalen Rechtsumfelds (Dissertation University of Bern, Bern 1998).

Kuckertz, Wera, Der Haftungsdurchgriff auf ausländische Unternehmen und Geschäftsleiter nach französischem Recht (Verlag Recht und Wirtschaft, Heidelberg 2002).

Kuhlau, Frida, Höglund, Anna T., Evers, Kathinka, & Eriksson, Stefan, A Precautionary Principle for Dual Use Research in the Life Sciences, 25 Bioethics 1 (2011).

Kunz, Peter V., Konzernhaftung in der Schweiz, 5 Der Gesellschafter 282 (2012).

Küper, Wilfried ed., Paul Johann Anselm Feuerbach: Reflexionen, Maximen, Erfahrungen (Manutius, Heidelberg 1993).

KURTYCZ, LAURA M., Choice and Control for Animals in Captivity, 28(11) The Psychologist 892 (2015).
KUYPER, PIETER J., European Community Law and Extraterritoriality: Some Trends and New Developments, 33 ICLQ 1013 (1984).
KWAKWA, EDWARD, Regulating the International Economy: What Role for the State?, in The Role of Law in International Politics: Essays in International Relations and International Law 227–246 (Michael Byers ed., OUP, Oxford 2000).
KYMLICKA, WILL, Afterword: Realigning Multiculturalism and Animal Rights, in Multiculturalism, Race and Animals: Contemporary Moral and Political Debates 295–304 (Luis Cordeiro-Rodrigues & Les Mitchell eds., Basingstoke, Palgrave Macmillan 2017).
KYMLICKA, WILL, Social Membership: Animal Law beyond the Property/Personhood Impasse, 40(1) Dalhousie L.J. 123 (2017).
KYMLICKA, WILL& DONALDSON, SUE, Animal Rights and Aboriginal Rights, in Canadian Perspectives on Animals and the Law 159–186 (Peter Sankoff, Vaughan Black, & Katie Sykes eds., Irwin Law, Toronto 2015).
KYMLICKA, WILL & DONALDSON, SUE, Animal Rights, Multiculturalism, and the Left, 45(1) J. Soc. Phil. 116 (2014).
KYMLICKA, WILL & WALKER, KATHRYN, Rooted Cosmopolitanism: Canada and the World, in Rooted Cosmopolitanism: Canada and the World 1–30 (Will Kymlicka & Kathryn Walker eds., UBC Press, Vancouver, Toronto 2012).
KYPRIANOU, MARKOS, Member of the European Commission Responsible for Health and Consumer Protection, Speech to the Animal Welfare Intergroup of the European Parliament (Animal Welfare Intergroup of the European Parliament, Brussels, June 8, 2005), *available at* http://www.fao.org/fileadmin/user_upload/animalwelfare/speech_05_335_en.pdf (last visited Jan. 10, 2019).
LA ÏDA, ZAKI, BRICS: Sovereignty Power and Weakness, 49 Int'l Pol. 614 (2012).
LAM, REBEKAH & CUNG, DANIEL, Animal Law: Rethinking Boundaries of Legal Personhood, 7 LSJ 90 (2015).
LANDERS, TIMOTHY F., COHEN, BEVIN, WITTUM, THOMAS E., & LARSON, ELAINE L., A Review of Antibiotic Use in Food Animals: Perspective, Policy, and Potential, 127 Public Health Rep. 4 (2012).
LANGFORD, MALCOLM, COOMANS, FONS, & GÓMEZ ISA, FELIPE, Extraterritorial Duties in International Law, in Global Justice, State Duties: The Extraterritorial Scope of Economic, Social and Cultural Rights in International Law 51–113 (Malcolm Langford, Wouter Vandenhole, Martin Scheinin, & Willem van Genugten eds., CUP, Cambridge 2013).
LANGFORD, MALCOLM, VANDENHOLE, WOUTER, SCHEININ, MARTIN, & VAN GENUGTEN, WILLEM EDS., Global Justice, State Duties: The Extraterritorial Scope of Economic, Social and Cultural Rights in International Law (CUP, Cambridge 2013).
LAUTERPACHT, ELIHU ED., International Law: Collected Papers of Hersch Lauterpacht, vol. I (CUP, Cambridge 1970).
LAZARUS, RICHARD, The National Environmental Policy Act in the U.S. Supreme Court: A Reappraisal and a Peek Behind the Curtains, 100 Geo. L.J. 1501 (2012).
LEE, JONG-HEE, A Comparative Analysis of Foreign Workers and Citizenship in Korea and Germany, in Citizenship and Migration in the Era of Globalization: The Flow of Migrants

and the Perception of Citizenship in Asia and Europe 71–87 (Markus Pohlmann, Jonghoe Yang, & Jong-Hee Lee eds., Springer, Heidelberg et al. 2013).

Lennkh, Sabine, Die Kodifikation des Tierschutzrechts: Modellvorstellungen (Nomos, Baden-Baden 2012).

Leondarakis, Konstantin, Menschenrecht "Tierschutz": Die Verletzung von Menschenrechten durch die Verletzung von Belangen an Tieren (Nomos, Baden-Baden 2006).

Levy, Philipp I. & Regan, Donald H., *EC—Seal Products* (TBT Aspects of the Panel and Appellate Body Reports): Seals and Sensibilities, Robert Schuman Centre for Advanced Studies Research Paper No. 2014/108, *available at* http://papers.ssrn.com/sol3/papers.cfm?abstract_id=2535213 (last visited Jan. 10, 2019).

Lezcano Navarro, José Maria, Piercing the Corporate Veil in Latin American Jurisprudence: A Comparison with the Anglo-American Method (Routledge, Oxon, New York 2016).

Li, Peter J., Sun, Jiang, & Yu, Dezhi, Dog "Meat" Consumption in China: A Survey of the Controversial Eating Habit in Two Cities, 25 Soc. & Ani. 513 (2017).

Lim, Alwyn & Tsutsui, Kiyoteru, The Social Regulation of the Economy in the Global Context, in Corporate Social Responsibility in a Globalizing World 1–24 (Kiyoteru Tsutsui & Alwyn Lim eds., CUP, Cambridge 2015).

Lin, Doris, Ag-gag Laws and Farming Crimes Against Animals, in The Routledge International Handbook of Crimes of the Powerful 466–478 (Gregg Barak ed., Routledge, New York, Oxon 2015).

Linzey, Andrew ed., The Link between Animal Abuse and Human Violence (Sussex Academic Press, Brighton, Portland 2009).

Linzey, Andrew, Sentientism, in Encyclopedia of Animal Rights and Animal Welfare 311 (Marc Bekoff & Carron A. Meaney eds., ABC-CLIO, Santa Barbara 1998).

Lorz, Albert & Metzger, Ernst, Tierschutzgesetz: Kommentar (C.H. Beck, München, 6th ed. 2008).

Lowe, Andreas V., Blocking Extraterritorial Jurisdiction: The British Protection of Trading Interests Act, 1980, 75 AJIL 257 (1981).

Lowe, Andreas V., Extraterritorial Jurisdiction: An Annotated Collection of Legal Materials (Grotius, Cambridge 1984).

Lowe, Vaughan, International Law (OUP, Oxford 2007).

Lowenfeld, Andreas F., International Economic Law (OUP, Oxford, 2d ed. 2008).

Lowenfeld, Andreas F., International Litigation and the Quest for Reasonableness, 245 RCADI 9 (1994).

Lowenfeld, Andreas F., U.S. Law Enforcement Abroad: The Constitution and International Law, 83 AJIL 880 (1980), Continued, 84 AJIL 444 (1990).

Lurié, Andrew & Kalinina, Maria, Protecting Animals in International Trade: A Study of the Recent Successes at the WTO and in Free Trade Agreements, 30 Am. U. Int'l L. Rev. 431 (2015).

Luy, Jörg, Schlachtung, in Lexikon der Mensch-Tier Beziehungen 310–312 (Arianna Ferrari & Klaus Petrus eds., Transcript, Bielefeld 2015).

Macey, Jonathan & Mitts, Joshua, Finding Order in the Morass: The Three Real Justifications for Piercing the Corporate Veil, 100 Cornell L. Rev. 99 (2014).

MacMillan, John & Linklater, Andrew eds., Boundaries in Question: New Directions in International Relations (Pinter Publishers, London, New York 1995).

Maier, Harold G., Jurisdictional Rules in Customary International Law, in Extraterritorial Jurisdiction in Theory and Practice 64–102 (Karl M. Meessen ed., Kluwer Law International, London 1996).

Main, David C.J., Mullan, Siobhan M., Atkinson, C., Cooper, M., Wrathall, J.H.M., & Blokhuis, H.J., Best Practice Framework for Animal Welfare Certification Schemes, 37 Trends in Food Sci. & Tech. 127 (2014).

Maljevic, Almir, Extraterritorial Jurisdiction: The Applicability of Domestic Criminal Law to Activities Committed Abroad in Bosnia and Herzegovina, in National Criminal Law in a Comparative Legal Context: General Limitations on the Application of Criminal Law 206–225 (Ulrich Sieber, Konstanze Jarvers, & Emily Silverman eds., Duncker & Humblot, Berlin 2011).

Malm, Andreas & Hornborg, Alf, The Geology of Mankind? A Critique of the Anthropocene Narrative, 1(1) The Anthropocene Rev. 62 (2014).

Mann, Frederick A., The Doctrine of International Jurisdiction Revisited after Twenty Years, 186 RCADI 9 (1984).

Mann, Frederick A., The Doctrine of Jurisdiction in International Law, 111 RCADI 1 (1964).

Manzini, Pietro, Environmental Exceptions of Article XX, in International Trade Law on the 50th Anniversary of the Multilateral Trade System 811–848 (Paolo Mengozzi ed., Dott. A. Guiffrè Editore, Milan 1999).

Marceau, Gabrielle, The Future of International Trade Law: How Best for Trade to Deal with (New) Non-trade Concerns?, in The Law of the Future and the Future of Law, vol. II, 279–296 (Sam Muller, Stavros Zouridis, Morly Frishman, & Laura Kistemaker eds., Torkel Opsahl Academic, The Hague 2012).

Marceau, Gabrielle & Trachtman, Joel P., GATT, TBT and SPS: A Map of the WTO Law of Domestic Regulation, in The WTO Dispute Settlement System 1995–2003 275–340 (Federico Ortino & Ernst-Ulrich Petersmann eds., Kluwer Law International, The Hague 2004).

Marceau, Gabrielle & Trachtman, Joel P., The Technical Barriers to Trade Agreement, the Sanitary and Phytosanitary Measures Agreement, and the General Agreement on Tariffs and Trade: A Map of the World Trade Organization Law of Domestic Regulation of Goods, 36 J. World Trade 811 (2002).

Marceau, Justin, Beyond Cages: Animal Law and Criminal Punishment (CUP, Cambridge 2019).

Martha, Rutsel Silvestre J., Extraterritorial Taxation in International Law, in Extraterritorial Jurisdiction in Theory and Practice 19–38 (Karl M. Meessen ed., Kluwer Law International, London 1996).

Martin, Michael J., Thottathil, Sapna E., & Newman, Thomas B., Antibiotics Overuse in Animal Agriculture: A Call to Action for Health Care Providers, 105(12) Am. J. Public Health 2409 (2015).

Martina, Elizabeth & Hine, Robert, A Dictionary of Biology (OUP, Oxford, 6th ed., online ed. 2014).

Mason, Jim & Singer, Peter, Animal Factories (Harmony Books, New York 1980 (Revised 1990)).

Mastronardi, Philippe, Kommentar zu Art. 7 BV, in Die schweizerische Bundesverfassung (Bernhard Ehrenzeller, Philippe Mastronardi, Rainer J. Schweizer, & Klaus A. Vallender eds., Dike, Zürich, St. Gallen, 3d ed. 2014).

Matevia, Marilyn, Justice for All: Revisiting the Prospects for a Biocommunitarian Theory of Interspecies Justice, 19(3) J. Int'l Wildlife L. & Pol'y 189 (2016).

Matheny, Gaverick & Leahy, Cheryl, Farm-Animal Welfare, Legislation and Trade, 70 L. & Contemp. Probs. 325 (2007).

Matheson, John H., Why Courts Pierce: An Empirical Study of Piercing the Corporate Veil, 7 Berkeley Bus. L.J. 1 (2010).

May, Larry, Crimes Against Humanity: A Normative Account (CUP, Cambridge 2005).

Mayer, Carl J., Personalising the Impersonal: Corporations and the Bill of Rights, 41 Hastings L.J. 577 (1990).

McCausland, Clare, The Five Freedoms of Animal Welfare Are Rights, 27 J. Agric. & Envtl. Ethics 649 (2014).

McCorquodale, Robert & Simons, Penelope, Responsibility beyond Borders: State Responsibility for Extraterritorial Violations by Corporations of International Human Rights Law, 70 Mod. L. Rev. 598 (2007).

McDorman, Ted L., The GATT Consistency of US Fish Import Embargoes to Stop Driftnet Fishing and Save Whales, Dolphins and Turtles, 24 Geo. Wash. J. Int'l L. & Econ. 477 (1991).

McGivern, Brendan, The WTO Seal Product Panel: The "Public Morals" Defense, 9 Global Trade & Customs J. 70 (2014).

McGuire, Chad J., Environmental Law and International Trade: Public Morality as a Tool for Advancing Animal Welfare, in What Can Animal Law Learn from Environmental Law? 293–310 (Randall S. Abate ed., Environmental Law Institute, Washington D.C. 2015).

McLeod-Kilmurray, Heather, Commoditizing Nonhuman Animals and Their Consumers: Industrial Livestock Production, Animal Welfare, and Ecological Justice, 32(1) Bull. Sci., Tech. & Soc'y 71 (2012).

Meessen, Karl M. ed., Extraterritorial Jurisdiction in Theory and Practice (Kluwer Law International, London 1996).

Meng, Werner, Extraterritoriale Jurisdiktion im öffentlichen Wirtschaftsrecht (Springer, Berlin et al. 1994).

Meyer, John W., Pope, Shawn M., & Isaacson, Andrew, Legitimating the Transnational Corporation in a Stateless World Society, in Corporate Social Responsibility in a Globalizing World 27–72 (Kiyoteru Tsutsui & Alwyn Lim eds., CUP, Cambridge 2015).

Michaels, Ralf, Global Legal Pluralism, 5 Ann. Rev. L. & Soc. Sci. 243 (2009).

Midkiff, Ken, The Meat You Eat: How Corporate Farming Has Endangered America's Food Supply (St. Martin's Press, New York 2004).

Milanovic, Marko, Extraterritorial Application of Human Rights Treaties: Law, Principles, and Policy (OUP, Oxford 2011).

Miller, Sandra K., Piercing the Corporate Veil Among Affiliated Companies in the European Community and in the U.S.: A Comparative Analysis of U.S., German, and U.K. Veil-Piercing Approaches, 36 Am. Bus. L.J. 73 (1998).

Mills, Alex, The Confluence of Public and Private International Law (CUP, Cambridge 2009).

MITCHELL, LORRAINE, Impact of Consumer Demand for Animal Welfare on Global Trade, in Changing Structure of Global Food Consumption and Trade 80–89 (Anita Regmi ed., Economic Research Service (ERS), USDA, Washington D.C. 2001).

MORRISH, LISA MARIE, The Elephant in the Room: Detrimental Effects of Animals' Property Status on Standing in Animal Protection Cases, 53(4) Santa Clara L. Rev. 1127 (2014).

MUCHLINSKI, PETER T., Corporations in International Law, in Max Planck Encyclopedia of Public International Law (Rüdiger Wolfrum ed., OUP, Oxford, online ed. 2014).

MUCHLINSKI, PETER T., Multinational Enterprises and the Law (OUP, Oxford, 2d ed. 2007).

MURPHY, DALE D., The Structure of Regulatory Competition: Corporations and Public Policies in a Global Economy (OUP, Oxford 2004).

NADAKAVUKAREN SCHEFER, KRISTA, Social Regulation in the WTO: Trade Policy and International Legal Development (Edward Elgar, Cheltenham 2010).

NÁJERA-RAMÍREZ, OLGA, Haciendo Patria: La Charreada and the Formation of a Mexican Transnational Identity, in Transnational Latina/o Communities: Politics, Processes, and Culture 168–180 (Carlos G. Vélez-Ibañez, Anna Sampaio, & Manolo González-Estay eds., Rowman and Littlefield, London 2002).

NARULA, SMITA, International Financial Institutions, Transnational Corporations and Duties of States, in Global Justice, State Duties: The Extraterritorial Scope of Economic, Social and Cultural Rights in International Law 114–153 (Malcolm Langford, Wouter Vandenhole, Martin Scheinin, & Willem van Genugten eds., CUP, Cambridge 2013).

NATTRASS, KATE M., "... Und die Tiere" Constitutional Protection for Germany's Animals, 10 Animal L. 283 (2004).

NEO, HARVEY & NGIAM, J.Z., Contesting Captive Cetaceans: (Il)Legal Spaces and the Nature of Dolphins in Urban Singapore, 15 Soc. & Cult. Geography 235 (2014).

NEUMANN, JAN, Die Koordination des WTO-Rechts mit anderen völkerrechtlichen Ordnungen: Konflikte des materiellen Rechts und Konkurrenzen der Streitbeilegung (Duncker & Humblot, Berlin 2002).

NÍ MHURCHÚ, AOILEANN, Citizenship beyond State Sovereignty, in Routledge Handbook of Global Citizenship Studies 119–127 (Engin F. Isin & Peter Nyers eds., Routledge, Oxon, New York 2014).

NIELSEN, LAURA, The WTO, Animals and PPMs (Martinus Nijhoff, Leiden 2007).

NIERENBERG, DANIELLE, Happier Meals, Rethinking the Global Meat Industry (Worldwatch Institute, Washington D.C. 2005).

NOLLKAEMPER, ANDRÉ, The Legality of Moral Crusades Disguised in Trade Laws: An Analysis of the EC "Ban" on Furs from Animals Taken by Leghold Traps, 8 J. Envtl. L. 237 (1996).

NOLTE, GEORG, Article 2 (7), in The Charter of the United Nations: A Commentary, vol. I, 280 (Bruno Simma, Daniel-Erasmus Khan, Georg Nolte, & Andreas Paulus eds., OUP, Oxford, 3d ed. 2012).

NOSKE, BARBARA, Beyond Boundaries: Humans and Animals (Black Rose Books, Montreal 1997).

NOTE, Alternative Methods of Piercing the Corporate Veil in Contract and Tort Cases, 48 B.U.L. Rev. 123 (1968).

NOTE, Developments in the Law of Extraterritoriality, 124 Harv. L. Rev. 1226 (2011).

NOTE, Predictability and Comity: Toward Common Principles of Extraterritorial Jurisdiction, 98 Harv. L. Rev. 1310 (1985).

NOTE, Reassessment of International Application of Antitrust Laws: Blocking Statutes, Balancing Tests, and Treble Damages, 50 L. & Contemp. Probs. 197 (1987).

NOTE, The Eighth Amendment, Proportionality and the Changing Meaning of Punishments, 122 Harv L. Rev. 960 (2009).

NUSSBAUM, MARTHA C., Beyond "Compassion and Humanity," in Animal Rights: Current Debates and New Directions 299–319 (Cass R. Sunstein & Martha C. Nussbaum eds., OUP, Oxford 2004).

NUSSBAUM, MARTHA C., Frontiers of Justice: Disability, Nationality, Species Membership (HUP, Cambridge 2006).

O'KEEFE, ROGER, Universal Jurisdiction: Clarifying the Basic Concept, 2 J. Int'l Crim. Just. 735 (2004).

O'NEAL TAYLOR, CHERIE, Impossible Cases: Lessons from the First Decade of WTO Dispute Settlement, 28 U. Pa. J. Int'l Econ. L. 309 (2007).

O'SULLIVAN, SIOBHAN, Animals, Equality and Democracy (Palgrave Macmillan, New York 2011).

OFFER, IYAN I.H. & WALTER, JAN, GATT Article XX(a) Permits Otherwise Trade-Restrictive Animal Welfare Measures, 12(4) Global Trade & Customs J. 158 (2017).

OH, MINJOO & JACKSON, JEFFREY, Animal Rights vs. Cultural Rights: Exploring the Dog Meat Debate in South Korea from a World Polity Perspective, 32 J. Intercultural Stud. 31 (2011).

ORAKHELASHVILI, ALEXANDER, Akehurst's Modern Introduction to International Law (Routledge, New York, 8th ed. 2019).

ORLANS, F. BARBARA, The Injustice of Excluding Laboratory Rats, Mice, and Birds from the Animal Welfare Act, 10 Kennedy Institute of Ethics J. 229 (2000).

OTTER, CALEY, O'SULLIVAN, SIOBHAN, & ROSS, SANDY, Laying the Foundations for an International Animal Protection Regime, 2 J. Animal Ethics 53 (2012).

OXMAN, BERNARD H., Jurisdiction of States, in Max Planck Encyclopedia of Public International Law (Rüdiger Wolfrum ed., OUP, Oxford, online ed. 2007).

PACHIRAT, TIMOTHY, Every Twelve Seconds: Industrialized Slaughter the Politics of Sight (Yale University Press, New Haven, London 2011).

PAINTER, RICHARD W., The Dodd-Frank Extraterritorial Jurisdiction Provision: What Is Effective, Needed or Sufficient?, 1 Harv. Bus. L. Rev. 195 (2011).

PALENZUELA-MAURI, ALEXANDER, The International Court of Justice and the Standing of Corporate Shareholders under International Law: *Elettronica Sicula v. Raytheon (U.S. v. Italy)*, 1 U. Miami Int'l & Comp. L. Rev. 292 (2015).

PALMER, CLARE & SANDØE, PETER, Welfare, in Critical Terms for Animal Studies 424–438 (Lori Gruen ed., University of Chicago Press, Chicago, London 2018).

PARK, MIYUN & SINGER, PETER, The Globalization of Animal Welfare: More Food Does Not Require More Suffering, 91 Foreign Aff. 122 (2012).

PARMAS, ANDRES & SOOTAK, JAAN, Länderbericht Estland in Conflicts of Jurisdiction in Cross-Border Crime Situations 279–290 (Arndt Sinn ed., Universitätsverlag Osnabrück, Göttingen 2012).

PARRY, CLIVE, GRANT, JOHN P., & BARKER, J. CRAIG, Encyclopaedic Dictionary of International Law (OUP, Oxford, 3d ed. 2009).
PAUER, NADA INA, The Single Economic Entity Doctrine and Corporate Group Responsibility in European Antitrust Law (Kluwer Law International, Aalphen aan den Rijn 2014).
PAUWELYN, JOOST, Conflict of Norms in International Law: How WTO Law Relates to Other Rules of International Law (CUP, Cambridge 2003).
PEARCE, DAVID, A Welfare State for Elephants? A Case Study of Compassionate Stewardship, 3(2) Relations 153 (2015).
PEDERSEN, HELENA, Knowledge Production in the "Animal Turn": Multiplying the Image of Thought, Empathy, and Justice, in Exploring the Animal Turn: Human-Animal Relations in Science, Society and Culture 13–19 (Erika Andersson Cederholm, Amelie Björck, Kristina Jennbert, & Ann-Sofie Lönngren eds., Pufendorfinstitutet, Lund 2014).
PELLET, ALAIN, Art. 38, in The Statute of the International Court of Justice 731–871 (Andreas Zimmermann, Karin Oellers-Frahm, Christian Tomuschat, & Christian J. Tams eds., OUP, Oxford, 2d ed. 2012).
PERISTERIDOU, CHRISTINA, The Principle of *Lex Certa* in National Law and European Perspectives, in Substantive Criminal Law of the European Union 69–96 (André Klip ed., Maklu, Antwerpen, Apeldoorn, Portland 2011).
PETERS, ANNE, Competition between Legal Orders, 3 Int'l L. Res. 45 (2014).
PETERS, ANNE, Extraterritorial Naturalizations: Between the Human Right to Nationality, State Sovereignty and Fair Principles of Jurisdiction, 53 GYIL 623 (2010).
PETERS, ANNE, Global Animal Law: What It Is and Why We Need It, 5 TEL 9 (2016).
PETERS, ANNE, Humanity as the A and Ω of Sovereignty, 20 EJIL 513 (2009).
PETERS, ANNE, Liberté, Égalité, Animalité: Human-Animal Comparisons in Law, 5 TEL 25 (2016).
PETERS, ANNE, Privatisierung, Globalisierung und die Resistenz des Verfassungsstaates, in Staats- und Verfassungstheorie im Spannungsfeld der Disziplinen 100–159 (Philippe Mastronardi & Denis Taubert eds., Franz Steiner Verlag, Stuttgart 2006).
PETERS, ANNE, Realizing Utopia as a Scholarly Endeavour, 24 EJIL 533 (2013).
PETERS, ANNE, Sind transnationale Unternehmen verpflichtet, (internationale) Menschenrechte zu respektieren zund zu fördern?, in Menschenrechte und Wirtschaft im Spannungsfeld zwischen State und Nonstate Actors 127–135 (Peter G. Kirchschläger, Thomas Kirchschläger, Andréa Belliger, & David J. Krieger eds., Stämpfli, Bern 2005).
PETERS, ANNE, The Growth of International Law between Globalization and Great Power, 8 Austrian Rev. Int'l & Eur. L. 109 (2003).
PETERS, ANNE, Völkerrecht Allgemeiner Teil (Schulthess, Zürich, Basel, Genf, 4th ed. 2016).
PETERSON, MARTIN ED., The Prisoner's Dilemma (CUP, Cambridge 2015).
PETRIG, ANNA, The Expansion of Swiss Criminal Jurisdiction in Light of International Law, 9 Utrecht L. Rev. 34 (2013).
PETRUS, KLAUS, Leben, in Lexikon der Mensch-Tier Beziehungen 217–218 (Arianna Ferrari & Klaus Petrus eds., Transcript, Bielefeld 2015).
PETRUS, KLAUS, Schaden, in Lexikon der Mensch-Tier Beziehungen 305–307 (Arianna Ferrari & Klaus Petrus eds., Transcript, Bielefeld 2015).
PETRUS, KLAUS, Würde, in Lexikon der Mensch-Tier Beziehungen 424–427 (Arianna Ferrari & Klaus Petrus eds., Transcript, Bielefeld 2015).

PICCIOTTO, SOL, The Regulatory Criss-Cross: Interaction between Jurisdictions and the Construction of Global Regulatory Networks, in International Regulatory Competition and Coordination 89–123 (William W. Bratton, Joseph McCahery, Sol Picciotto, & Colin Scott eds., Clarendon Press, Oxford 1996).

PIETH, MARK & IVORY, RADHA, Emergence and Convergence: Corporate Criminal Liability Principles in Overview, in Corporate Criminal Liability: Emergence, Convergence, and Risk 3–62 (Mark Pieth & Radha Ivory eds., Springer, Dordrecht et al. 2011).

POHLE, K. & CHENG, H.-W., Comparative Effects of Furnished and Battery Cages on Egg Production and Physiological Parameters in White Leghorn Hens, 88 Poultry Sci. 2042 (2009).

POHLMANN, MARKUS, The Migration of Elites in a Borderless World: Citizenship as an Incentive for Professionals and Managers?, in Citizenship and Migration in the Era of Globalization: The Flow of Migrants and the Perception of Citizenship in Asia and Europe 59–70 (Markus Pohlmann, Jonghoe Yang, & Jong-Hee Lee eds., Springer, Heidelberg et al. 2013).

POORE, J. & NEMECEK T., Reducing Food's Environmental Impact through Producers and Consumers, 360(6392) Science 987 (2018).

PORCHER, JOCELYNE, The Ethics of Animal Labor (Palgrave MacMillan, Basingstoke 2017).

PREUSS, ULRICH K., Equality of States: Its Meaning in a Constitutionalized Global Order, 8 Chi. J. Int'l L. 17 (2008).

PŘIBÁŇ, JIŘÍ, Sovereignty in a Post-Sovereignty Society: A Systems Theory of European Constitutionalism (Routledge, Oxon, New York 2015).

PUNCH, SAMANTHA, Exploring Children's Agency Across Majority and Minority World Contexts, in Reconceptualizing Agency and Childhood: New Perspectives in Childhood Studies 183–196 (Florian Esser, Meike S. Baader, Tanja Betz, & Beatrice Hungerland eds., Routledge, London, New York 2016).

PUTH, SEBASTIAN, WTO und Umwelt: Die Produkt-Prozess-Doktrin (Duncker & Humblot, Berlin 2003).

QURESHI, ASIF H., Extraterritorial Shrimps, NGOs and the WTO Appellate Body, 48 ICLQ 199 (1999).

QURESHI, ASIF H., International Trade and Human Rights from the Perspective of the WTO, in International Economic Law with a Human Face 159–173 (Friedl Weiss, Erik Denters, & Paul de Waart eds., Kluwer Law International, The Hague, Dordrecht, Boston 1998).

RADAELLI, CLAUDIO M. & DE FRANCESCO, FABRIZIO, Regulatory Impact Assessment, in The Oxford Handbook of Regulation 279–301 (Robert Baldwin, Martin Cave, & Martin Lodge eds., OUP, Oxford 2010).

RADFORD, MIKE, Animal Welfare Law in Britain: Regulation and Responsibility (OUP, Oxford 2001).

RAHMATULLAH, KHAN, Global Compact, in Max Planck Encyclopedia of Public International Law (Rüdiger Wolfrum ed., OUP, Oxford, online ed. 2011).

RANDALL, KENNETH C., Universal Jurisdiction under International Law, 66 Tex. L. Rev. 785 (1988).

RANDELZHOFER, ALBRECHT & DÖRR, OLIVER, Article 2 (4), in The Charter of the United Nations: A Commentary, vol. I, 200 (Bruno Simma, Daniel-Erasmus Khan, Georg Nolte, & Andreas Paulus eds., OUP, Oxford, 3d ed. 2012).

Raspé, Caroline, Die tierliche Person (Duncker & Humblot, Berlin 2013).

Ratner, Steven R., The Thin Justice of International Law: A Moral Reckoning of the Law of Nations (OUP, Oxford 2015).

Raustiala, Kal, Empire and Extraterritoriality in Twentieth Century America, 40 Sw. L. Rev. 604 (2011).

Raustiala, Kal, The Evolution of Territoriality: International Relations and American Law, in Territoriality and Conflict in an Age of Globalization 219–250 (Miles Kahler & Barbara Walter eds., CUP, Cambridge 2006).

Raz, Joseph, The Rule of Law and its Virtue, in The Authority of Law 201–232 (Joseph Raz ed., OUP, New York, 2d ed. 2009).

Regan, Tom, Empty Cages: Facing the Challenge of Animal Rights (Rowman and Littlefield, Oxford 2005).

Regan, Tom, The Case for Animal Rights (University of California Press, Berkeley, 3d ed. 2004).

Regan, Tom, The Radical Egalitarian Case for Animal Rights, in Environmental Ethics: Readings in Theory and Application 81–89 (Louis P. Pojman ed., Wadsworth, Boston, 6th ed. 2012).

Rege, Vinod, GATT Law and Environment-Related Issues Affecting the Trade of Developing Countries, 28 J. World Trade 95 (1994).

Reiterer, Michael, Internationaler Handel und Umwelt: Bilanz der GATT-Arbeitsgruppe über "Environmental Measures and International Trade" (EMIT) sowie der Uruguay-Runde, 49 Aussenwirtschaft IV 477 (1994).

Reps, Markus, Rechtswettbewerb und Debt Governance bei Anleihen (Mohr Siebeck, Tübingen 2014).

Richli, Paul & Ruf, Claudia, Wieviel Tierschutz erlaubt das GATT? (Hochschulverlag, Zürich 1995).

Risch, Thomas, Die Haftung aus Konzernvertrauen, Die Haftung des herrschenden Unternehmens aus Konzernvertrauen für konzernspezifische Handlungen und Erklärungen (Dissertation University of Bern, Balzers 2009).

Ritvo, Harriet, On the Animal Turn, 136 Daedalus 118 (2007).

Robertson, Ian A., Animals, Welfare and the Law: Fundamental Principles for Critical Assessment (Routledge, Oxon 2015).

Rollin, Bernard E., Animal Rights and Human Morality (Prometheus Books, Amherst, 3d ed. 2006).

Rousing, Tine, Bonde, Marianne, & Sørensen, Jan T., Indicators for the Assessment of Animal Welfare in a Dairy Cattle Herd with a Cubicle Housing System, in Improving Health and Welfare in Animal Production: Proceedings of Sessions of the EAAP Commission on Animal Management & Health, The Hague, Netherlands, 21–24 August 2000 37–44 (Harry J. Blokhuis, E. Dinand Ekkel, & Beat Wechsler eds., EAAP Publication No. 102, Wageningen Pers Publ., Wageningen 2000).

Rowlands, Mark, Can Animals Be Moral? (OUP, Oxford 2012).

Rudolf, Walter, Territoriale Grenzen der Staatlichen Rechtsetzung, in Referate und Diskussion der 12. Tagung der Deutschen Gesellschaft für Völkerrecht in Bad Godesberg vom 14. bis 16. Juni 1971 33 (Walther J. Habscheid & Walter Rudolf eds., Müller, Karlsruhe 1973).

Rudolf, Walter, Territoriale Grenzen der staatlichen Rechtsetzung, 11 BerDGVöR 7 (1973).

Ruggie, John G., Territoriality and Beyond: Problematizing Modernity in International Relations, 47 Int'l Org. 139 (1993).

Ruggie, John G., U.N. SRSG for Business & Human Rights Keynote Presentation at EU Presidency Conference on the "Protect, Respect and Remedy" Framework Stockholm, Nov. 10–11, 2009, *available at* http://www.reports-and-materials.org/sites/default/files/reports-and-materials/Ruggie-presentation-Stockholm-10-Nov-2009.pdf (last visited Jan. 10, 2019).

Ruggie, John Gerard & Nelson, Tamaryn, Human Rights and the OECD Guidelines for Multinational Enterprises: Normative Innovations and Implementation Challenges (Harvard University, Corporate Social Responsibility Initiative Working Paper No. 66 2015).

Russell, William M.S. & Burch, Rex, The Principles of Humane Experimental Technique (Methuen, London 1959).

Rüttimann, Andreas, Tierschutzbewegung, in Lexikon der Mensch-Tier Beziehungen 371–373 (Arianna Ferrari & Klaus Petrus eds., Transcript, Bielefeld 2015).

Rüttimann, Andreas, Tiertransport, in Lexikon der Mensch-Tier Beziehungen 379–381 (Arianna Ferrari & Klaus Petrus eds., Transcript, Bielefeld 2015).

Ryan, Oliver, Animal Welfare and Economic Development: A Financial Institution Perspective, in Animals, Ethics and Trade: The Challenge of Animal Sentience 238–247 (Jacky Turner & Joyce D'Silva eds., Earthscan, London 2006).

Ryder, Richard, Sentientism, in The Great Ape Project 220–222 (Paola Cavalieri & Peter Singer eds., St. Martin's Griffin, New York 1993).

Ryngaert, Cedric, Extraterritorial Export Controls (Secondary Boycotts), 7 Chinese J. Int'l L. 625 (2008).

Ryngaert, Cedric, Jurisdiction in International Law (OUP, Oxford, 2d ed. 2015).

Ryngaert, Cedric, Jurisdiction over Antitrust Violations in International Law (Intersentia, Antwerp, Oxford, Portland 2008).

Ryngaert, Cedric, Jurisdiction: Towards a Reasonableness Test, in Global Justice, State Duties: The Extraterritorial Scope of Economic, Social and Cultural Rights in International Law 192–211 (Malcolm Langford, Wouter Vandenhole, Martin Scheinin, & Willem van Genugten eds., CUP, Cambridge 2013).

Ryngaert, Cedric, Unilateral Jurisdiction and Global Values (Eleven International Publishing, The Hague 2015).

Sanders, Astrid, The Impact of the "Ruggie Framework" and the "United Nations Guiding Principles on Business and Human Rights" on Transnational Human Rights Litigation, in The Business and Human Rights Landscape: Moving Forward, Looking Back 288–315 (Jena Martin & Karen E. Bravo eds., CUP, Cambridge 2016).

Sandrock, Otto, Über Sinn und Methode der zivilistischen Rechtsvergleichung (Alfred Metzner, Frankfurt a.M., Berlin 1966).

Sands, Philippe, Turtles and Torturers: The Transformation of International Law, 33 N.Y.U. J. Int'l L. & Pol. 527 (2000).

Satz, Ani, Animals as Vulnerable Subjects: Beyond Interest-Convergence, Hierarchy, and Property, 16 Animal L. 65 (2009).

Saucier-Bouffard, Carl, The Legal Rights for Great Apes, in The Global Guide to Animal Protection 235–237 (Andrew Linzey ed., University of Illinois Press, Urbana, Chicago, Springfield 2013).

SCHACK, HAIMO, Der prozessuale Durchgriff im internationalen Konzern, in Gedenkschrift für Jürgen Sonnenschein 705–718 (Joachim Jickeli, Peter Kreutz, & Dieter Reuter eds., De Gruyter Recht, Berlin 2003).

SCHAFFNER, JOAN E., An Introduction to Animals and the Law (Palgrave Macmillan, Hampshire, New York 2011).

SCHIFF BERMAN, PAUL, Global Legal Pluralism: A Jurisprudence of Law Beyond Borders (CUP, Cambridge 2012).

SCHLOCHAUER, HANS-JÜRGEN, Die Extraterritoriale Wirkung von Hoheitsakten (Klostermann, Frankfurt 1962).

SCHMID, OTTO & KILCHSPERGER, RAHEL, Overview of Animal Welfare Standards and Initiatives in Selected EU and Third Countries: Final Report (EconWelfare, Socio-Economic Aspects of Farm Animal Welfare, Research Institute of Organic Agriculture (FiBL), Frick 2010).

SCHMIEDEKNECHT, MAUD H. & WIELAND, JOSEF, ISO 26000, 7 Grundsätze, 6 Kernthemen, in Corporate Social Responsibility: Verantwortungsvolle Unternehmensführung in Theorie und Praxis 299–311 (Andreas Schneider & René Peterschmid eds., Springer Gabler, Berlin, 2d ed. 2015).

SCHOBEL, THOMAS, Home Country or Recipient Country? Confining the Extraterritorial Reach of Domestic Banking Law, 41 Int'l Law. 75 (2007).

SCHOENBAUM, THOMAS J., Free International Trade and Protection of the Environment: Irreconcilable Conflict?, 86 AJIL 700 (1992).

SCHOFIELD, JOHN C., Analgesic Best Practice for the Use of Animals in Research and Teaching: An Interpretative International Literature Review (FAO, Wellington 2002).

SCHREUER, CHRISTOPH, International Protection of Investments, in Max Planck Encyclopedia of Public International Law (Rüdiger Wolfrum ed., OUP, Oxford, online ed. 2013).

SCHRÖDER, MEINHARD, Precautionary Approach/Principle, in Max Planck Encyclopedia of Public International Law (Rüdiger Wolfrum ed., OUP, Oxford, online ed. 2014).

SCHUSTER, ALINE, Trade and the Environment: The Legality of Unilateral Measures with Extraterritorial Effect to Protect the Environment under the WTO/GATT (Minor Dissertation University of Cape Town, Cape Town 2012).

SCHUSTER, GUNNAR, Die internationale Anwendung des Börsenrechts (Springer, Berlin et al. 1996).

SCHWARZE, JÜRGEN, Die Jurisdiktionsabgrenzung im Völkerrecht (Nomos, Baden-Baden 1994).

SCHWENZER, INGEBORG & HOSANG, ALAIN F., Menschenrechtsverletzungen: Schadenersatz vor Schweizer Gerichten, 21 SZIER 273 (2011).

SCOTT, JOANNE, Extraterritoriality and Territorial Extension in EU Law, 62 AIJL 87 (2014).

SEAMAN, KATE, UN-Tied Nations: The United Nations, Peacekeeping and Global Governance (Ashgate, Surrey, Burlington 2014).

SEBASTIAN, MARCEL, Deadly Efficiency: The Impact of Capitalist Production on the "Meat" Industry, Slaughterhouse Workers, and Nonhuman Animals, in Animal Oppression and Capitalism Vol. I, 167–183 (David Nibert ed., ABC-CLIO, Santa Barbara 2017).

SEJIAN, VEERASAMY, LAKRITZ, JEFFREY, EZEJJ, THADDEUS, & LAL, RATTAN, Assessment Methods and Indicators of Animal Welfare, 6 Asian J. An. & Vet. Advances 301 (2011).

SENZ, DEBORAH & CHARLESWORTH, HILARY, Building Blocks: Australia's Response to Foreign Extraterritorial Litigation, 2 Melb. J. Int'l L. 69 (2001).

SHAFFER, GREGORY C., The World Trade Organization under Challenge: Democracy and the Law and Politics of the WTO's Treatment of Trade and Environment Issues, 25 Harv. Envtl. L. Rev. 1 (2001).

SHAFFER, GREGORY & PABIAN, DAVID, The WTO EC-Seal Products Decision: Animal Welfare, Indigenous Communities and Trade, 109 AJIL 154 (2015).

SHAPIRO, PAUL, Moral Agency in Other Animals, 27 Theoretical Med., & Bioethics 357 (2006).

SHARPLESS, IKE, Farm Animal Welfare and WTO Law: Assessing the Legality of Policy Measures 1–73 (Master of Arts in Law and Diplomacy Thesis, The Fletcher School, Tufts University, Medford 2008).

SHELTON, DINAH, Human Rights and the Environment: Substantive Rights, in Research Handbook on International Environmental Law 264–284 (Malgosia Fitzmaurice, David M. Ong, & Panos Merkouris eds., Edward Elgar, Cheltenham, Northampton 2010).

SHELTON, JO-ANN, Killing Animals That Don't Fit In: Moral Dimensions of Habitat Restoration, 13(4) Between Species 1 (2004).

SIMMA, BRUNO & PULKOWSKI, DIRK, Of Planets and the Universe: Self-contained Regimes in International Law, 17 EJIL 483 (2006).

SINGER, PETER, Animal Liberation (New York Review, New York, 2d ed. 1990).

SINGER, PETER, Practical Ethics (CUP, Cambridge 1993).

SINN, ARNDT, Das Strafanwendungsrecht als Schlüssel zur Lösung von Jurisdiktionskonflikten? Rechtsvergleichende Beobachtungen, in Conflicts of Jurisdiction in Cross-Border Crime Situations 501–530 (Arndt Sinn ed., Universitätsverlag Osnabrück, Göttingen 2012).

SIRONI, ALICE, Nationality of Individuals in Public International Law: A Functional Approach, in The Changing Role of Nationality in International Law 54–75 (Alessandra Annoni & Serena Forlati eds., Routledge, Oxon, New York 2013).

SKORDAS, ACHILLES, Supranational Law, in Max Planck Encyclopedia of Public International Law (Rüdiger Wolfrum ed., OUP, Oxford, online ed. 2014).

SLAUGHTER, ANNE-MARIE, Defining the Limits: Universal Jurisdiction and National Courts, in Universal Jurisdiction: National Courts and the Prosecution of Serious Crimes under International Law 168–192 (Stephen Macedo ed., University of Pennsylvania Press, Philadelphia 2004).

SLAUGHTER, ANNE-MARIE, The Real New World Order, 76 Foreign Aff. 189 (1997).

SLOANE, ROBERT D., Breaking the Genuine Link: The Contemporary International Legal Regulation of Nationality, 50 Harv. Int'l L.J. 1 (2009).

SLOT, PIET JAN & BULTERMAN, MIELLE, Introduction, in Globalisation and Jurisdiction 1–11 (Piet Jan Slot & Mielle Bulterman eds., Kluwer Law International, Leiden 2004).

SMITH, ADAM, An Inquiry into the Nature and Causes of the Wealth of Nations (W. Strahan and T. Cadell, London 1776).

SNEDDON, LYNN U. & LEACH, MATTHEW C., Anthropomorphic Denial of Fish Pain, 3(28) Animal Sentience (2016).

SORNARAJAH, MUTHUCUMARASWAMY, Linking State Responsibility for Certain Harms Caused by Corporate Nationals Abroad to Civil Recourse in the Legal Systems of Home

States, in Torture as Tort: Comparative Perspectives on the Development of Transnational Human Rights Litigation 491–512 (Craig Scott ed., Hart, Oxford 2001).

STAKER, CHRISTOPHER, Jurisdiction, in International Law 289–315 (Malcolm D. Evans ed., OUP, Oxford, 5th ed. 2018).

STEINER, GARY, Anthropozentrismus, in Lexikon der Mensch-Tier Beziehungen 28–32 (Arianna Ferrari & Klaus Petrus eds., Transcript, Bielefeld 2015).

STERN, BRIGITTE, Quelques observations sur les règles internationales relatives à l'application extraterritoriale du droit, 32 ADFI 7 (1986).

STESSENS, GUY, Corporate Criminal Liability: A Comparative Perspective, 43 ICLQ 493 (1994).

STEVENS, SARAH, The Increased Aggression of the EC Commission in Extraterritorial Enforcement of the Merger Regulation and Its Impact on Transatlantic Cooperation in Antitrust, 29 Syracuse J. Int'l L. & Com. 263 (2002).

STEVENSON, PETER, The World Trade Organisation Rules: A Legal Analysis of Their Adverse Impact on Animal Welfare, 8 Animal L. 107 (2002).

STILT, KRISTEN, Constitutional Innovation and Animal Protection in Egypt, 42(3) Law & Soc. Inquiry (2017).

STILT, KRISTEN, Law, in Critical Terms for Animal Studies 197–210 (Lori Gruen ed., University of Chicago Press, Chicago, London 2018).

STILT, KRISTEN, Trading in Sacrifice, 111 AJIL Unbound 397 (2017).

STOHNER, NILS, Importrestriktionen aus Gründen des Tier- und Artenschutzes im Recht der WTO (Stämpfli, Bern 2006).

STOKES, WILLIAM S., Best Practices for the Use of Animals in Toxicological Research and Testing, 1245 Ann. N.Y. Acad. Sci. 17 (2011).

STONE SWEET, ALEC & MATHEWS, JUD, Proportionality Balancing and Global Constitutionalism, 47 Colum. J. Transnat'l L. 72 (2008).

STOPFORD, JOHN & STRANGE, SUSAN, Rival States, Rival Firms: Competition for World Market Shares (CUP, Cambridge 1991).

STRANGE, SUSAN, The Retreat of the State: The Diffusion of Power in the World Economy (CUP, Cambridge 1996).

STRIBBE, ARRAN, Animal Erased: Discourse, Ecology, and Reconnection with the Natural World (Wesleyan University Press, Middletown 2012).

SULLIVAN, LAUREN, The Epic Struggle for Dolphin-Safe Tuna: To Be Continued—A Case for Accommodating Nonprotectionist Eco-labels in the WTO, 47 Vand. J. Transnat'l L. 861 (2014).

SULLIVAN, MARIANN & WOLFSON, DAVID J., What's Good for the Goose . . . The Israeli Supreme Court, Foie Gras, and the Future of Farmed Animals in the United States, 70 L. & Contemp. Probs. 139 (2007).

SUMMERS, JAMES, The Internal and External Aspects of Self-Determination Reconsidered, in Statehood and Self-Determination 229–250 (Duncan French ed., CUP, Cambridge 2013).

SUNSTEIN, CASS R., Introduction: What Are Animal Rights?, in Animal Rights: Current Debates and New Directions 3–18 (Cass R. Sunstein & Martha C. Nussbaum eds., OUP, Oxford 2004).

SUSANI, NADINE, Purposes and Principles of the United Nations, in Max Planck Encyclopedia of Public International Law (Rüdiger Wolfrum ed., OUP, Oxford, online ed. 2009).

SWIRE, PETER P., The Race to Laxity and the Race to Undesirability: Explaining Failures in Competition Among Jurisdictions in Environmental Law, 14 Yale L. & Pol'y Rev. 67 (symposium issue 1996).

SYKES, CATHERINE, Beasts in the Jungle: Animal Welfare in International Law (Master Thesis, Dalhousie University, Halifax, Nova Scotia August 2011).

SYKES, KATIE, Sealing Animal Welfare into the GATT Exceptions, 13 World Trade Rev. 471 (2014).

TABLER, G. TOM & MENDENHALL, A.M., Broiler Nutrition, Feed Intake and Grower Economics, 5 Avian Advice 8 (2003).

TAO, BETSY, A Stitch in Time: Addressing the Environmental, Health, and Animal Welfare Effects of China's Expanding Meat Industry, 15 Geo. Int'l Envtl. L. Rev. 321 (2003).

TAYLOR, PAUL W., Respect for Nature: A Theory of Environmental Ethics (Princeton University Press, New Jersey 1986).

TAYLOR, SUNAURA, Beasts of Burden: Animal and Disability Liberation (New Press, New York 2017).

THIERMANN, ALEX B. & BABCOCK, SARAH L., Animal Welfare and International Trade, 24 Rev. Sci. Tech. Off. Int. Epiz. 747 (2005).

THOMAS, BARBARA S., Extraterritorial Application of the United States Securities Laws: The Need for a Balanced Policy, 7 J. Corp. L. 189 (1982).

THOMAS, EDWARD M., Playing Chicken at the WTO: Defending an Animal Welfare-Based Trade Restriction under GATT's Moral Exception, 34 B.C. Envtl. Aff. L. Rev. 605 (2007).

THÜRER, DANIEL & BURRI, THOMAS, Self-Determination, in Max Planck Encyclopedia of Public International Law (Rüdiger Wolfrum ed., OUP, Oxford, online ed. 2008).

TOMKA, PETER, *Elettronica Sicula* Case, in Max Planck Encyclopedia of Public International Law (Rüdiger Wolfrum ed., OUP, Oxford, online ed. 2007).

TOMUSCHAT, CHRISTIAN, International Law: Ensuring the Survival of Mankind on the Eve of a New Century, 281 RCADI 9 (1999).

TOOLEY, MICHAEL, Are Nonhuman Animals Persons?, in The Oxford Handbook of Animal Ethics 332–370 (Tom L. Beauchamp & R.G. Frey eds., OUP, Oxford 2011).

TRAJANO DE ALMEIDA SILVA, TAGORE, The Constitutional Defense of Animals in Brazil, Animal Law and Welfare: International Perspectives 181–194 (Deborah Cao & Steven White eds., Springer, Cham et al. 2016).

TRENT, NEIL, EDWARDS, STEPHANIE, FELT, JENNIFER, & O'MEARA, KELLY, International Animal Law, with a Concentration on Latin America, Asia, and Africa, in The State of the Animals III, 65–77 (Deborah J. Salem & Andrew N. Rowan eds., Humane Society Press, Washington 2005).

TREVISANUT, SELINE, Nationality Cases before International Courts and Tribunals, in Max Planck Encyclopedia of Public International Law (Rüdiger Wolfrum ed., OUP, Oxford, online ed. 2011).

TRIEBOLD, CLAUDIUS, Rechtliche Grundlagen des Umweltschutzes in GATT und WTO: Am Beispiel des international Warenverkehrs (Schulthess, Zürich 2000).

TRÜEB, HANS RUDOLF, Umweltrecht in der WTO: Staatliche Regulierungen im Kontext des internationalen Handelsrechts (Schulthess, Zürich 2001).

TULLY, STEVEN, The 2000 Review of the OECD Guidelines for Multinational Enterprises, 50 ICLQ 394 (2001).

Turner Johnson, James, Sovereignty: Moral and Historical Perspectives (Georgetown University Press, Washington D.C. 2014).

Uralde, Jimena, Congress' Failure to Enact Animal Welfare Legislation for the Rearing of Farm Animals: What Is Truly at Stake?, 9 U. Miami Bus. L. Rev. 193 (2001).

Vagts, Detlev F., Extraterritoriality and the Corporate Governance Law, 97 AJIL 289 (2003).

Van den Bossche, Peter & Zdouc, Werner, The Law and Policy of the World Trade Organization (CUP, Cambridge, 4th ed. 2017).

Van Lith, Hélène, International Jurisdiction and Commercial Litigation: Uniform Rules for Contract Disputes (CUP, Cambridge 2009).

Van Panhuys, Haro F., The Role of Nationality in International Law: An Outline (Sijthoff, Leiden 1959).

Van Waas, Laura, Nationality Matters: Statelessness under International Law (Intersentia, Antwerp, Oxford, Portland 2008).

Vandekerckhove, Karen, Piercing the Corporate Veil (Kluwer Law International, Alphen aan den Rijn 2007).

Veissier, Isabelle, Butterworth, Andrew, Bock, Bettina, & Roe, Emma, European Approaches to Ensure Good Animal Welfare, 113 Appl. Animal Behav. Sci. 279 (2008).

Vernon, Jan & Nwaogu, Tobe A., Comparative Study on Cosmetics Legislation in the EU and Other Principal Markets, With Special Attention to So-called Borderline Products, Final Report Contract No. FIF.20030624, Prepared for European Commission DG Enterprise (Norfolk 2004), *available at* http://rpaltd.co.uk/uploads/report_files/j457-final-report-cosmetics.pdf (last visited Jan. 10, 2019).

Verrinder, Joy M., McGrath, Nicki, & Phillips, Clive J.C., Science, Animal Ethics and the Law, in Animal Law and Welfare: International Perspectives 63–86 (Deborah Cao & Steven White eds., Springer, Cham et al. 2016).

Verzijl, Jan H.W., International Law in Historical Perspective (A.W. Sijthoff, Leiden 1972).

Verzijl, Jan H.W., The Controversy Regarding the So-Called Extraterritorial Effect of the American Antitrust Laws, 8 Nederlands Tijdschrift voor Internationaal Recht 3 (1961).

Villiger, Mark E., Commentary on the 1969 Vienna Convention on the Law of Treaties (Martinus Nijhoff, Leiden 2009).

Visser, Wayne, CSR 2.0: Transforming Corporate Sustainability and Responsibility (Springer, Heidelberg 2014).

Vogel, David, Trading Up: Consumer and Environmental Regulation in a Global Economy (HUP, Cambridge 1995).

Vogel, David & Kagan, Robert A. eds., Dynamics of Regulatory Change: How Globalization Affects National Regulatory Policies (University of California Press, Berkeley 2004).

Von der Crone, Hans Caspar & Roth, Katja, Der Sarbanes-Oxley Act und seine extraterritoriale Bedeutung, 2 AJP 131 (2003).

Von Keyserlingk, Marina A.G. & Hötzel, Maria José, The Ticking Clock: Addressing Farm Animal Welfare in Emerging Countries, 28 J. Agric. & Envtl. Ethics 179 (2015).

Von Lutterotti, Lukas, US Extraterritorial Economic Sanctions and the EU Blocking Statute (Dissertation, University of Vienna, Vienna 2003).

Vranes, Erich, Trade and the Environment: Fundamental Issues in International Law, WTO Law, and Legal Theory (OUP, Oxford 2009).

Wagman, Bruce A. & Liebman, Matthew, A Worldview of Animal Law (Carolina Academica Press, Durham 2011).

Wagner-von Papp, Florian, Competition Law, Extraterritoriality & Bilateral Agreements, in Research Handbook on International Competition Law 21–59 (Ariel Ezrachi ed., Edward Elgar, Cheltenham 2012).

Waldau, Paul, Animal Rights: What Everyone Needs to Know (OUP, Oxford 2011).

Waldau, Paul, Second Wave Animal Law and the Arrival of Animal Studies, in Animal Law and Welfare: International Perspectives 11–44 (Deborah Cao & Steven White eds., Springer, Cham et al. 2016).

Wautelet, Patrick, What Has International Private Law Achieved in Meeting the Challenges Posed by Globalisation?, in Globalisation and Jurisdiction 55–77 (Piet Jan Slot & Mielle Bulterman eds., Kluwer Law International, Leiden 2004).

Webster, John, Sentience and Animal Protection, in Encyclopedia of Animal Rights and Animal Welfare 507–511 (Marc Bekoff & Carron A. Meaney eds., ABC-CLIO, Santa Barbara 2010).

Weil, Prosper, International Limitations on State Jurisdiction, in Extra-territorial Application of Laws and Responses Thereto 32–42 (Cecil J. Olmstead ed., ESC Publishing Limited, Oxford 1984).

Weis, Paul, Nationality and Statelessness in International Law (Sijthoff and Noordhoff, Alphen, 2d ed. 1979).

Weis, Tony, The Global Food Economy: The Battle for the Future of Farming (Fernwood, Black Point 2007).

Weiss, Michael, Hybride Regulierungsinstrumente: Eine Analyse rechtlicher, faktischer und extraterritorialer Wirkungen nationaler Corporate-Governance Kodizes (Mohr Siebeck, Tübingen 2011).

Wells, Celia, Corporations and Criminal Responsibility (OUP, New York, 2d ed. 2001).

Welp, Dietrich, Internationale Zuständigkeit über auswärtige Gesellschaften mit Inlandstöchtern im US-amerikanischen Zivilprozess (Duncker & Humblot, Berlin 1982).

Welty, Jeff, Humane Slaughter Laws, 70 L. & Contemp. Probs. 175 (2007).

White, Steven, Regulation of Animal Welfare in Australia and the Emergent Commonwealth: Entrenching the Traditional Approach of the States and Territories or Laying the Ground for Reform?, 35 Fed. L. Rev. 347 (2007).

White, Steven & Cao, Deborah, Introduction: Animal Protection in an Interconnected World, in Animal Law and Welfare: International Perspectives 1–10 (Deborah Cao & Steven White eds., Springer, Cham et al. 2016).

Whitfort, Amanda, Evaluating China's Draft Animal Protection Law, 34 Sydney L. Rev. 347 (2012).

Wild, Markus, Bewusstsein, in Lexikon der Mensch-Tier Beziehungen 57–60 (Arianna Ferrari & Klaus Petrus eds., Transcript, Bielefeld 2015).

Wilde, Ralph, Compliance with Human Rights Norms Extraterritorially: "Human Rights Imperialism"?, in International Law and the Quest for Its Implementation, *Liber Amicorum* Vera Gowlland-Debbas 319–350 (Laurence Boisson de Chazournes & Marcelo Kohen eds., Martinus Nijhoff, Leiden 2010).

Wilkins, David B., Animal Welfare in Europe: European Legislation and Concerns (Kluwer Law International, The Hague 1997).

WILLIAMS, ERIN E., Factory Farms, in Encyclopedia of Animal Rights and Animal Welfare 245–250 (Marc Bekoff & Carron A. Meaney eds., ABC-CLIO, Santa Barbara 2010).

WISE, STEVEN M., An Argument for the Basic Legal Rights of Farmed Animals, 106 Mich. L. Rev. 133 (2008).

WISE, STEVEN M., Drawing the Line: Science and the Case for Animal Rights (Perseus Books, Cambridge 2013).

WISE, STEVEN M., Legal Personhood and the Nonhuman Rights Project, 17 Animal L. 1 (2010).

WISE, STEVEN M., Rattling the Cage: Toward Legal Rights for Animals (Perseus Publishing, New York 2000).

WISSENBURG, MARCEL & SCHLOSBERG, DAVID EDS., Political Animals and Animal Politics (Palgrave Macmillan, New York 2014).

WOLD, CHRIS, Empty Promises and Missed Opportunities: An Assessment of the Environmental Chapter of the Trans-Pacific Partnership (International Environmental Law Project (IELP), Lewis & Clark Law School, Portland 2016).

WOLFSON, DAVID J. & SULLIVAN, MARIANN, Foxes in the Hen House: Animals, Agribusiness, and the Law: A Modern American Fable, in Animal Rights: Current Debates and New Directions 205–233 (Cass R. Sunstein & Martha C. Nussbaum eds., OUP, Oxford 2004).

WOLFSON, YOSSI, Animal Protection under Israeli Law, in Animal Law and Welfare: International Perspectives 157–180 (Deborah Cao & Steven White eds., Springer, Cham et al. 2016).

WOODHALL, ANDREW & GARMENDIA DA TRINDADE, GABRIEL EDS., Ethical and Political Approaches to Nonhuman Animal Issues (Palgrave Macmillan, Cham 2017).

WÖRNER, LIANE & WÖRNER, MATTHIAS, Länderbericht Deutschland in Cross-Border Crime Situations 203–262 (Arndt Sinn ed., Universitätsverlag Osnabrück, Göttingen 2012).

WOUTERS, JAN & COPPENS, DOMINIC, An Overview of the Agreement on Subsidies and Countervailing Measures—Including a Discussion of the Agreement on Agriculture, Working Paper No. 104, 70 (Institute for International Law, K.U. Leuven, Leuven 2007), *available at* https://www.law.kuleuven.be/iir/nl/onderzoek/wp/WP104e.pdf (last visited Jan. 10, 2019).

WYCKOFF, JASON, Toward Justice for Animals, 45(4) J. Soc. Phil. 539 (2014).

YAVITZ, LAURA, The WTO and the Environment: The Shrimp Case That Created a New World Order, 16 J. Nat. Res. & Envtl. L. 203 (2002).

YOUATT, RAFI, Interspecies Relations, International Relations: Rethinking Anthropocentric Politics, 43(1) Millennium J. Int'l Stud. 207 (2014).

YOUNG, MARGARET A., Fragmentation, Regime Interaction and Sovereignty, in Sovereignty, Statehood and State Responsibility: Essays in Honour of James Crawford 71–89 (Christine Chinkin & Freya Baetens eds., CUP, Cambridge 2015).

ZERK, JENNIFER A., Extraterritorial Jurisdiction: Lessons for the Business and Human Rights Sphere from Six Regulatory Areas (Corporate Social Responsibility Initiative Working Paper No. 59, Harvard University, Cambridge 2010).

ZERK, JENNIFER A., Multinationals and Corporate Social Responsibility: Limitations and Opportunities in International Law (CUP, Cambridge 2006 (Reprint 2008)).

ZIEGLER, KATJA S., Domaine Réservé, in Max Planck Encyclopedia of Public International Law (Rüdiger Wolfrum ed., OUP, Oxford, online ed. 2013).

ZIMMERMAN, JAMES M., Extraterritorial Employment Standards of the United States: The Regulation of the Overseas Workplace (Quorum Books, New York 1992).

NEWSPAPERS AND PRESS RELEASES

2050: A Third More Mouths to Feed, FAO MEDIA CENTRE, Sept. 23, 2009.

Agriculture Ministry Orders Installation of Cameras in All Slaughterhouses, THE JERUSALEM POST, Dec. 28, 2015.

Allison, Simon, Stories of 2015: Man Who Identified Cecil the Lion's Killer Vows Death Will Not Be in Vain, THE GUARDIAN, Dec. 25, 2015.

Armstrong, Jeremy, Thirty Years Ago the Mirror's Kent Gavin Took a Horrific Picture That Shocked the World: This Week He Returned to the Killing Fields of Canada, But Had Anything Changed?, THE MIRROR, Apr. 4, 1998.

At Last! Denmark Bans Bestiality, PETAUK, Apr. 2015.

Barkham, Patrick, Sandra the "Nonhuman Person" Is Sadly Not the Face of a Welfare Revolution, THE GUARDIAN, Dec. 22, 2014.

Borkert, Stefan, Tierhalteverbot für Schafbauer, THURGAUER TAGBLATT, May 10, 2010.

Bundeskartellamt verhängt Bußgelder gegen Wursthersteller, BUNDESKARTELLAMT, July 15, 2014.

Capecchi, Christina & Rogers, Katie, Killer of Cecil the Lion Finds Out That He Is a Target Now, of Internet Vigilantism, N.Y. TIMES, July 29, 2015.

Carus, Felicity, UN Urges Global Move to Meat and Dairy-Free Diet, THE GUARDIAN, June 2, 2010.

Castellon, David, USDA Threatens Action on Cargill Slaughter Operation, THE BUSINESS JOURNAL, Nov. 28, 2018.

Chandrasekhar, Anand, Nestlé Pledges Humane Treatment of Farm Animals, SWISSINFO, Aug. 22, 2014.

Colombian President Signs Legislation Banning Animal Abuse into Law, LATINO FOXNEWS, Jan. 7, 2016.

Denmark Passes Law to Ban Bestiality, BBC NEWSBEAT, Apr. 22, 2015.

Domínguez, Iñigo, Animals to Stop Being "Objects" under Spanish Law, EL PAÍS, Dec. 14, 2017.

Drozdiak, Natalia, German Cartel Office Fines Wurst Makers: Authority Accused Meat Producers of Fixing Prices, WALL ST. J., July 15, 2014.

Dyer, John, Luxembourg Is Set to Become the Most Animal-Friendly Country in the World, VICE NEWS, May 13, 2016.

Ehlers, Jörn, Bruno der "Problembär": Chronik eines angekündigten Todes, WORLD WIDE FUND FOR NATURE, WWF 2009.

European Commission, The Common Agricultural Policy (CAP) and Agriculture in Europe, Press Release, Brussels, June 26, 2013.

Gerzabek, Barbara, Experten einig: Verbot der Ferkelschutzkästen verursacht Tierleid, 643.000 Ferkel würden jährlich "zu Tode geliebt", APA-OTS, May 17, 2011.

Globe Editorial, Hunting for Logic in the WTO's Seal-Hunt Ruling, THE GLOBE AND MAIL, Dec. 1, 2013.

Granville, Ken, The Trans-Pacific Partnership Trade Accord Explained, N.Y. TIMES, July 26, 2016.

Grossarth, Jan, Käfig-Eier aus der Ukraine, FRANKFURTER ALLGEMEINE, June 13, 2013.

Harris-Perry, Melissa, Michael Vick, Racial History and Animal Rights, THE NATION, Dec. 30, 2010.
Hickman, Martin, The End of Battery Farms in Britain—But Not in Europe, THE INDEPENDENT, Dec. 27, 2011.
Italien schützt seine Wölfe, Schweiz und Frankreich schießen sie ab, DER STANDARD, Nov. 13, 2006.
Italienischer Wolf streift durchs Puschlav, BLICK, May 16, 2013.
Khaled, Rana, Animal Rights Advocates in Egypt Call for Laws to Be Activated, DAILY NEWS EGYPT, July 25, 2016.
Kokoll, Emily, Spain Fines Danone, Nestle, Others $98M for Dairy Cartel, LAW360, Mar. 4, 2015.
Laster, Jill, Plan to Breed Lab Monkey Splits Puerto Rican Town, U.S. NEWS & WORLD REPORT, Nov. 30, 2009.
Lieberman, Allyson, Senator Slams EC—Rockefeller Threatens Retaliation on GE Deal, N.Y. POST, June 21, 2001.
Loki, Reynard, Helping Animals Through CSR: Exclusive Interview with Animal Legal Defense Fund, JUSTMEANS, Feb. 25, 2011.
Los Animales ya no Son Cosas en Portugal, PARTIDO ANIMALISTA PACMA, Dec. 22, 2016.
Macalister, Terry, Wildlife Group Sues Government Agency over Sakhalin-2, THE GUARDIAN, Aug. 16, 2007.
Macur, Juliet, Vick Receives 23 Months and a Lecture, N.Y. TIMES, Dec. 11, 2007.
Mason, Rowena, Government Planning to Repeal Animal Welfare Codes, THE GUARDIAN, Mar. 25, 2016.
Mason, Rowena, Ministers Abandon Plan to Scrap Farm Animal Welfare Codes, THE GUARDIAN, Apr. 7, 2016.
McKenna, Maryn, The Looming Threat of Avian Flu, N.Y. TIMES, Apr. 13, 2016.
MEP Call on Bulgarian PM to Ban Stray Dog Euthanasia, NOVINITE, May 20, 2012.
Mercer, Phil, Unease Grows over New Australian Dual Citizenship Rules, BBC NEWS, June 1, 2015.
Middleton, Kristie, Three Reasons Farm Animal Welfare Is an Important CSR Tenet for the Food Industry, TRIPLE PUNDIT, June 21, 2012.
Millward, David, Indian Border Guards Deployed to Stop Cattle Crossing into Bangladesh, THE TELEGRAPH, July 4, 2015.
Milman, Oliver & Evershed, Nick, Alive and Kicking: Australia's Animal Export Trade Booms Despite Persistent Claims of Cruelty, THE GUARDIAN, Aug. 3, 2015.
Nationalrat zementiert "Lex Conny Land," NZZ, May 29, 2012.
Mishra, Sudhir Kumar, Illegal Cattle Trade Headache for Cops, THE TELEGRAPH, June 16, 2018.
Neslen, Arthur, Europe Strengthens Ban on Seal Products after WTO Challenge, THE GUARDIAN, Sept. 8, 2015.
New Poll Reveals Majority of Americans Oppose Trophy Hunting Following Death of Cecil the Lion, HUMANE SOCIETY OF THE UNITED STATES (HSUS), Oct. 7, 2015.
Nolen, R. Scott, U.S. Horse Slaughter Exports to Mexico Increase 312%, AVMA NEWS, Jan. 15, 2008.
O'Dwyer, Gerard, Swedish Pig Farmers Call for State Support, GLOBAL MEAT NEWS, Mar. 3, 2014.
O'Sullivan, Siobhan, "Ag gag" Laws: The Battle for Animal Welfare Is a Battle over Information, THE GUARDIAN, May 5, 2014.

Onishi, Norimitsu, Outcry for Cecil the Lion Could Undercut Conservation Efforts, N.Y. Times, Aug. 10, 2015.

Osike, Felix, Uganda Losing Billions in Poultry Imports, New Vision (Daily Uganda), Mar. 10, 2012.

Outsourcing's Third Wave, The Economist, May 21, 2009.

Owens, Jared, Australia to Restart Live Sheep and Cattle Exports to Egypt, The Australian, Mar. 20, 2014.

Pickles, Kate, Killing a Cow Is Equal to Raping a Girl Claims Hindu Nationalist Organisation as 30,000 Indian Troops Are Told to Stop the Sacred Animals Being Smuggled Across the Border into Bangladesh to Be Eaten, Mail Online, July 2, 2015.

Pocha, Jehangir S., Outsourcing Animal Testing: US Firm Setting Up Drug-Trial Facilities in China: Where Scientists Are Plentiful but Activists Aren't, Boston Globe, Nov. 25, 2006.

Rabschnuk, Alison, Tyson Launches 100% Plant-Based Brand, The Good Food Institute, Feb. 26, 2018.

Rampant Animal Cruelty at California Slaughter Plant: Undercover Investigation Finds Abuses at Major Beef Supplier to America's School Lunch Program, Humane Society of the United States (HSUS), Jan. 30, 2008.

Ripley, Amanda, A Big Test of Police Body Cameras Defies Expectations, N.Y. Times, Oct. 20, 2017.

Saudi Arabia to Target Agro-Investments Abroad, Arab News, Nov. 11, 2013.

Siebert, Charles, EU Court: Animal Welfare Rules Apply to Animals Leaving EU, BBC News, Apr. 23, 2015.

Stewart, Will, The Animals Left to Starve to Death in Ukrainian Zoo as New Government of Debt-Ridden Country Divert Funds Elsewhere, MailOnline, Mar. 7, 2014.

Stop Using Antibiotics in Healthy Animals to Prevent the Spread of Antibiotic Resistance, WHO News Release, Nov. 7, 2017.

Storm, Stephanie, Tyson Foods, a Meat Leader, Invests in Protein Alternatives, N.Y. Times, Oct. 10, 2016.

Suddath, Claire, The Problem with Factory Farms, Time Magazine, Apr. 23, 2010.

Sullivan, Rory & Amos, Nicky, Farm Animal Welfare Consistently Ignored in Sustainability Reports, The Guardian, Nov. 5, 2015.

Tabuchi, Hiroko & Simons, Marlise, U.N. Court Orders Japan to Halt Whaling, N.Y. Times, Mar. 31, 2014.

Takada, Kazunori & Martina, Michael, China Fines Milk Powder Makers $110 for Price Fixing, Reuters, Aug. 7, 2013.

The Editorial Board, The Death of Cecil the Lion, N.Y. Times, July 31, 2015.

Victor, Daniel, Japan to Resume Commercial Whaling, Defying International Ban, N.Y. Times, Dec. 26, 2018.

Vince, Gaia, UK and India Call on China to Ban Tiger Farms, The Guardian, July 26, 2012.

Vincent, Christopher, Brussels Parliament Adopts Crucial Animal Rights Bill, The Brussels Times, Nov. 23, 2018.

Wellesley, Laura, Can Eating Less Meat Help Reduce Climate Change?, BBC News, Nov. 24, 2015.

WSPA and Partners Get Animal Welfare onto Earth Summit Agenda, World Animal Protection, Sept. 16, 2011.

WSPA Hails New ISO Standard as First to Promote Animal Welfare, U.N. FAO, Nov. 9, 2010.

Index

Page numbers followed by *f* indicate figures; page numbers followed by *t* indicate tables.